CHARITY U.S.A.

Also by Carl Bakal

The Right to Bear Arms

CHARITY U.S.A.

*An Investigation into the Hidden
World of the Multi-billion Dollar
Charity Industry*

Carl Bakal

Times
BOOKS

Acknowledgment is gratefully made to the following for their permission to reprint from copyright materials:

Time for the excerpt on the muscular dystrophy telethon from the issue of September 17, 1973. Copyright 1973 by Time Inc. *Medical Economics* for the excerpt from "It Pays to Give to Charity—With Strings Attached" by Dorothea Garber Cracas, November 6, 1972. Copyright 1972 by Litton Industries, Inc. Sapphire Songs for the lyrics from "Look At Us, We're Walking" by Nancy Reed. Copyright 1955 by Sapphire Songs. Random House, Inc. for the excerpt from *The American Jews* by James Yaffe. Copyright 1968 by James Yaffe. Fiddleback Music Publishing Co., Inc. for the lyrics of "Charity Ball." Words and music by Don Tucker. Copyright © 1973 by Fiddleback Music Publishing Co., Inc. All rights reserved. E. P. Dutton for the excerpt from *Ball: A Year in the Life of the April in Paris Extravaganza* by William Wright. Copyright 1972 by William Wright. *Fund Raising Management* for the excerpt from the article by Paul Franklin, September/October, 1971. Copyright 1971 by Hoke Communications Inc.

Published by TIMES BOOKS, a division of Quadrangle/The New York Times Book Co., Three Park Avenue, New York, N.Y. 10016

Published simultaneously in Canada by Fitzhenry & Whiteside, Ltd., Toronto

Copyright © 1979 by Carl Bakal

Library of Congress Cataloging in Publication Data

Bakal, Carl, date.
 Charity U.S.A.: an investigation into the
hidden world of the multi-billion dollar charity
industry.

 Bibliography: p. 460
 Includes index.
 1. Charities—United States. 2. Charitable
uses, trusts, and foundations—United States.
3. Fund raising. I. Title.
HV48.B34 1979   361.7'0973   78-20681
ISBN 0-8129-0815-5

Manufactured in the United States of America

Second printing, February 1980

In memory of
Esther Bakal
1890-1974
And for Shirley
with love

These Americans are the most peculiar people in the world. You'll not believe me when I tell you how they behave. In a local community in their country a citizen may conceive of some need which is not being met. What does he do? He goes across the street and discusses it with his neighbor. Then what happens? A committee comes into existence and the committee begins functioning in behalf of that need.

—Alexis de Tocqueville (1830)

Contents

PART VI: YOU AND CHARITY

PART VII: THE FUTURE OF CHARITY

Foreword

"Will it be an exposé?" people would invariably ask during the five years this book was in the making.

"No," I would reply, venturing to explain, however, that many (including my publisher) might regard the finished work as a sensational, muckraking exercise, designed to expose the more unseemly, unsavory aspects of charity.

For, as you will see, I have some serious criticisms to make about charity in general, as well as about particular charities, including some of America's most sacred cows.

Nor is this just another book about fund raising, as many have also surmised, although it does devote considerable space to the various, often ingenious, techniques charitable organizations use to raise money.

What I have attempted to do is to present an exposition—as opposed to an exposé—of American charity in all of its many aspects. My aim was also to examine closely—without prejudice or pretension—an institution (also a $100 billion industry) others have thought too pious to probe or question, at least in the depth this book attempts to. Finally, my purpose has been to offer, for reasons of enlightenment or entertainment, a candid, behind-the-scenes, inside view of charity in action, much as John Gunther's classic *Inside U.S.A.* offered a study of democracy in action in this country.

Among the questions I set out to answer were:

Who gives to charity—and why?

Is enough given and is it given where most needed?

Are the funds collected sensibly and efficiently?

And, perhaps more important, how well are they spent to carry out the ostensible purposes for which they are collected?

How can one distinguish the worthy charities from the unworthy?

And, most fundamentally, are charities really desirable or necessary in today's society? Or should their functions be the responsibility of government?

To arrive at the answers to these and other questions, I looked into the operations of literally hundreds of the hundreds of thousands of the groups the Internal Revenue Service classifies as charitable organizations. They ranged from such household names as the American Red Cross, Boy and Girl Scouts, Salvation Army, UNICEF, CARE, Father Flanagan Boys' Home, American Cancer Society, National Foundation-March of Dimes, and the sponsors of those ubiquitous Christmas and Easter Seals to the myriad of religious groups and churches (which collectively take in nearly one half of the U.S. charity dollar), hospitals, conservation groups, schools, libraries, museums, symphony orchestras, animal shelters, and "adopt-an-orphan" and other foreign-aid agencies that also make up the world of *Charity U.S.A.*

One of my most perplexing problems was deciding which charities to include. Some merited inclusion, I felt, because of their size, prominence, and importance, and others, though relatively small or unimportant, because of their familiarity that often stemmed from the pervasiveness and magnitude of their appeals. Still others were selected because of their exotic or illicit nature or in order to illustrate some points I wished to make. For obvious reasons I decided to omit, with few exceptions, purely local charities.

Once I had decided which charities to include (the book describes at length or gives passing mention to some 400), I sent them detailed questionnaires (calling for detailed answers to 24 questions) and asked for material—including an annual report, audit, and budget—to elicit information as to their histories, purposes, governing bodies, fund-raising practices, programs, and accomplishments, supplementing all of this with material gathered from other sources. During the course of my investigations, I crisscrossed the country several times (traveling a total of some 10,000 miles) to visit many of these organizations, interview their top officials, and talk to their volunteers and see them at work. In the pages that follow, the reader will observe a Planned Parenthood volunteer counseling pregnant teen-agers, listen to an American Cancer Society Research to Recovery volunteer advising a mastectomy victim, watch Seeing Eye dogs being trained and assigned to blind people, follow a professional fund raiser on his mission of raising $67 million for a university, sit in at United Way budget hearings (generally closed to the press or public), and accompany me to a charity ball.

Much of this book, as you will see, is based on other first-hand observations and personal experiences. To capture the flavor of what charity is all about, I've answered phones at a telethon, pedaled for palsy, danced for dystrophy, attended United Jewish Appeal and United Way fund-raising affairs, even gotten a job in an illegal boiler-room operation (to sell tickets to a charity circus)—all of which is also described in the pages that follow. I've spoken to beggars and millionaires (among the latter, philanthropists Laurance Rockefeller, W. Clement Stone, and Mary Lasker); evangelists and epileptics; Indians and the blind. (In Des Moines, I had the unique experience of being the guest of honor—and only sighted person—at a cocktail party attended by about one hundred blind people.)

Peopled in these pages, too, are others involved in charity in one way or another: historic figures like Andrew Carnegie and John D. Rockefeller; celebrated contemporaries like Jerry Lewis, Ethel Merman, Muhammad Ali, and Betty Friedan; givers, big and small; foundation officials, corporation executives, and other philanthropoids (as philanthropy's bigwigs are called); mail promoters and empire builders; tax experts and lawyers; phony priests, Santas, and other charity cheats.

And since charity touches on almost every aspect of human endeavor, the book also deals with and attempts to offer some helpful insights into the status and problems of religion, health and medical research, education, the arts, youth and juvenile delinquency, minorities and race relations, foreign aid, environment and conservation, civil rights and liberties—and thereby also presents a broad panorama of America today.

But enough by way of introduction. Let us now begin our journey inside Charity U.S.A.

New York City   — Carl Bakal
May 1979

PART I

PRESENT AND PAST

Chapter 1

The American Way of Giving

Outside New York's fashionable Saks Fifth Avenue, an old man in a faded green army fatigue jacket and black wool cap stands jangling a tin cup. Around his neck hangs a white sign with red lettering:

PLEASE HELP

I AM BLIND

THANK YOU   GOD BLESS YOU

At his feet sits a black German shepherd dog, a red-and-white striped tie draped around its neck. Together, the beggar, with his sightless, rheumy, red-flecked eyes, and the dog make a pathetic, poignant spectacle that few can resist, and the tin cup clinks with the cacophony of incoming coins.

*

In front of Tiffany, a few blocks north, at an eye-catching 6-foot-high green booth shaped like a television set, a middle-aged matron in a tweed suit and Hermès scarf accepts a fistful of nickels and dimes from a group of high school students on their way to Central Park. The booth is one of 85 scattered throughout the New York Metropolitan area and staffed by 2000 volunteer members of Friends of Channel 13 engaged in the public television station's annual spring fling for funds and new members. Some prankish passersby ask the ladies if they are selling kisses.

*

Across the street that same spring morning, a group of saffron-robed Hare Krishna kids, most of them in their teens or early twenties, the men's heads completely shaved except for odd, little topknots, are banging drums and clanging cymbals as they jump up and down ecstatically while singing their hypnotic chant over and over. Between chants they hand out invitations and solicit funds for their temple.

*

At a card table nearby, those harbingers of spring, green-clad members of a Girl Scout troop, are taking orders for those familiar cookies which, it should be

3

noted, account for 5 percent of the total sales of the entire U.S. cookie industry. "I must buy some," says one scurrying shopper, ordering three boxes of chocolate mints (the national favorite) and one box of shortbreads. "Why, refusing to buy Girl Scout cookies is like refusing to stand up while the national anthem is being played."

*

At another card table a block away, volunteers from the Women's Division of United Cerebral Palsy of New York are seated selling raffle tickets at 50 cents each, or three for a dollar. First prize is the spanking new tan Chevy Vega air-conditioned estate wagon parked at the curb behind them.

*

Up on the 56th floor of 30 Rockefeller Center, overlooking Fifth Avenue, Laurance Rockefeller, member of the illustrious clan that has given away hundreds, if not thousands, of millions of dollars, is preoccupied at the moment with the problem of *raising* money—a paltry million and a half or so—to translate into reality the concept of an LBJ Memorial Grove, a 15-acre park on the Potomac to honor the memory of our thirty-sixth president. For of the $2 million needed, only $500,000 has so far been pledged, $100,000 of this by Rockefeller himself who, because of his special interest in conservation, has agreed to head the fund-raising drive.

His brow wrinkled, Mr. Laurance, as he is called by everyone at Rockefeller headquarters, is composing a form letter to potential contributors. To whom shall the letter go? "We should write to everyone who's ever had a meal at the White House," he tells an aide. "I've also got the names of eight or ten possible big givers floating around in my head."

He leans forward intently. "Joseph Hirshhorn is one," he says, referring to the Croesus of art collectors who, thanks to Lyndon Johnson, has a museum named after him in the nation's capital. "I don't know him personally. But he surely ought to be one of our $100,000 prospects. Doug Dillon may give us ten or twenty-five. I've already talked to Averell [Harriman]. He's not a big giver, but he may also be good for twenty-five. Mary Lasker has already cut herself off at ten. If I handle it right, June Englehard might join with me in giving a second hundred. I'd also approach John Loeb, but he's already given two fifty to the Johnson Library. . . ."

In the lexicon of the super-rich, figures like these are, of course, understood to be in the thousands.

*

That same day, in a large, dingy loft room just around the corner from the fine Fifth Avenue store of Lord & Taylor, a crew of sweet-talking solicitors is busy on a battery of 30 telephones in cubicles lining the walls. Their "sucker list" is made up of names from the Manhattan telephone directory. Representing themselves as calling for the New York City Jaycees, the solicitors are selling tickets to a circus, ostensibly for the benefit of crippled and handicapped children. None of the gullible ticket purchasers know, however, that only 10 to 15 cents of every dollar they send in will go to the charity described in the "pitch." Most of the rest will go into the pockets of the "boiler-room" promoters or will be used to pay the commissions of the solicitors, the telephone bills, and the other expenses of this unscrupulous and illegal operation.

*

In the dignified wood-paneled Fifth Avenue offices of the fund-raising counseling firm of Marts & Lundy, a photo in the reception room is of E. Claiborne Robins, head of A. H. Robins, the pharmaceutical manufacturing company. A caption on the photo mentions the fact that Mr. Robins gave a gift of $50 million to the University of Richmond in 1969—"thought to be the largest individual gift to a private institution up to that time." The photo, as well as the dozens of others blanketing the walls, attests to the success of Marts & Lundy which, since its inception in 1926, has helped some 3600 clients, including the University of Richmond and others, largely in the educational field, raise the awesome total of over $2.6 billion. In the offices now, there is a meeting of the national campaign committee of Lehigh University which has embarked on a $67 million fundraising drive. Each of the 16 committee members, all top industrial leaders and, of course, all Lehigh alumni, reports on the calls he has made on prospects for big gifts (about 90 percent of the money will come from 10 percent of the contributors). Then Tozier Brown, head of the three-man Marts & Lundy team assigned to this drive, reports on the 40 area campaigns taking place in South Florida, Los Angeles, and elsewhere—wherever there are large concentrations of Lehigh graduates. All in all, things are going rather well. About $22 million has already been raised toward the $30 million goal of the first phase of the campaign.

*

Over on First Avenue and 56th Street is the world headquarters of Catholic Relief Services, the overseas relief agency of the Roman Catholic Church in the United States, which ships food, clothing, and medicine—valued at more than $225 million in 1978—to an estimated 18 million disaster-stricken and other needy persons in some 86 countries. "Wherever possible, we try to work with a government or private agency—it needn't necessarily be Catholic—in each country," explains CRS's assistant executive director, Monsignor Andrew P. Landi, a man of sixty or so with wispy gray hair and in black clerical garb. "As I like to put it, we're in the wholesale business, more or less jobbers. We let the local people be the retailers, as it were."

*

Farther uptown, in her duplex apartment in Manhattan's East Sixties just off Fifth Avenue, the very social Mrs. H. Donald Sills, a svelte, stylish lady in her fifties, sighs wearily as she checks the last-minute things she still has to do for a luncheon and fashion show she is chairing for the benefit of the New York Heart Association. The menu, which will feature quail eggs and game hens, has already been planned and pretasted. But with the event less than a week off, she still has to oversee the rehearsal, arrange for the Waldorf to have spotlights and tables and mirrors for the models, and meet with the commentator and fashion people at the house of Giorgio di Sant' Angelo. And, of course, work out the table arrangements to make sure that ex-lovers, mistresses, and enemies are seated far apart. But Ruth Sills, perhaps New York's busiest volunteer chairlady, is happy. Of the 400 expected guests, 250 will be friends of hers—what she calls "my people"—a tribute to her formidable following. "I sent out only 350 invitations, but most have already come back with checks. You know, it's just like turning on the hot water tap. It just comes."

*

In its sleek, modern quarters that occupy an entire floor of a skyscraper on the Avenue of the Americas, just a block west of Fifth Avenue, the United Jewish Appeal helps direct a nationwide campaign, involving more than 700 local drives, that has raised as much as $660 million a year for Israel and local Jewish causes. To raise this colossal sum, UJA's quintessential fund-raising techniques are an amalgam of procedures that borrow from the best in American business, technology, and the CIA. At UJA, a computer can produce the number of Jewish families in any American city and the amount that city raised in previous campaigns—going back to 1967. In the office of associate national campaign director Robert Pearlman, a young man with fashionably long hair and attired in a mod gray suit and a red-and-white striped shirt and red tie, is a file containing hundreds of folders, arranged geographically, each representing a giver of $10,000 or more annually. "We revise and upgrade these records periodically," says Pearlman. "Let's say we have someone rated as a $100,000 giver. Then we learn from a friend or business associate of his or from our local people in his community that he's had a banner year and probably made a minimum of a million dollars. On this basis, we figure he could now easily give $200,000 or $250,000."

To keep its fingers on the financial pulse of its Jewish constituency and to search for "paper millionaires" or other wealthy Jewish names not already on its prospect lists, UJA has a division whose researchers scan the financial pages, stock prospectuses, corporate reports, even the obituary notices, the latter for leads to wealthy widows. "One of our most successful techniques," Pearlman tells me, "is to have our volunteers pay a personal call on prospects. Let's say one of our wealthy New York contributors is making a business trip to Tulsa. We'll contact our field man in Tulsa and ask him which people haven't yet made pledges or which pledges are still outstanding or need upgrading. From the names we get, we compile a list of prospects for our volunteer to call on, preferably people in his own business. Naturally, if we can get him to exert some leverage because of their business relationship, so much the better.

"Fund raising requires not only personal contacts but also finesse. It often takes some tact to suggest to a new prospect just how much he should give. One common way we have of getting around to this is to say that it costs $75,000 to transport a Jewish family of four from the Soviet Union and settle them in Israel for the first year. Then we may say, 'We feel that you can save one or two such families.' Now, we may not always get the $75,000 or $150,000 or so it would take to do this. But you'd be surprised to know how many people are willing to give enough to save even half a Soviet Jewish family.''

*

On the opposite side of Manhattan, in a modern office building a few blocks east of Fifth Avenue, the executive staff of the American Cancer Society, largest of the health charities, is having its biweekly meeting. Seated in sleek red and black armchairs around the long walnut table in the board room are eighteen department heads—seven of them possessors of M.D.s or other doctorates, most of them men in their forties or fifties, conservatively dressed in somber suits (there is only an occasional striped shirt and loud tie). In general, the atmosphere is one we would associate with any multi-million dollar enterprise, which the ACS certainly is, with its budget of $149 million, paid staff of 2900 plus 2,500,000 volunteer workers divided among 58 regional divisions and 3000 local units. Presiding over the proceedings with an air of easy informality is the ACS's $75,000-a-year executive vice-president, Lane W. Adams, affable, genial, low key, handsome as a movie star but graying at the temples, a former banker. Little signs throughout the room ask all to refrain from smoking.

There is a good deal of banter as Adams goes around the room, soliciting reports with a ''What's happening in your department, Alan?'' ''What have you got to say, Irving?'' or ''What's on your mind, John?'' Public Information reports that the latest Annual Science Writers Seminar has drawn a bigger batch of clippings than any other previous meeting and that actor William Gargan (a victim of cancer of the larynx) will be presented with the Society's Courage Award at the White House. Medical Affairs & Research says that a sequence on self-examination of breasts is being planned for a forthcoming public television series on health education. There is discussion of a proposed New York ordinance that would segregate smokers and nonsmokers in restaurants. ''Funny, that restaurants would want this,'' someone says. ''That's because cigarette ashes won't get into the butter, which restaurants can use the next day,'' another pipes up. The major items on the agenda, however, concern the budget for the next fiscal year (which will, of course, be higher) and the Crusade which, the fund-raising director reports, is moving along very well.

Contributing to the success of the Crusade no doubt is the ingenuity and inventiveness of the society's fund-raising geniuses. In Atlanta, for example, the varied events used to raise money to fight the Big ''C'' range from a Bill Blass fashion show to a pie-throwing contest at which contributors bid for the opportunity to hurl custard pies at local politicians, television and radio personalities, athletes, and other celebrities.

*

But ingenuity is not just confined to the Cancer people. In Latrobe, Pennsylvania, 12 St. Vincent College students staged a *bed push* for the county March of

Dimes. The students not only raised $2000 but claimed the world bed-pushing record by completing 819 miles around the campus during an eight-day marathon, surpassing the previous record of 738 miles.

*

Meanwhile, more prosaically, in Stamford, Connecticut (and in San Diego, Chicago, St. Louis, everywhere), the Boy Scouts are having their day at the doorbell, raising money by selling peanut brittle, first aid kits, light bulbs, you name it! They carry their wares in a plastic shopping bag. Unlike the Girl Scouts, who usually take orders for delivery later, the Boy Scouts deliver on the spot. Generally, each Scout has his territory. But Greg Chuckas, a stocky, dark 11-year-old boy with a Prince Charlie haircut and glasses, of Stamford's Troop No. 38, is complaining. "A kid from Chestnut Hill Lane sold on my street. So now I'm going to sell wherever I can." However, the dog got into Greg's peanut brittle while it languished (along with the light bulbs and first aid kits) in his closet. "We made him pay for the package the dog ate," Mrs. Chuckas chuckles. "I said, 'You should have had it out of the house by now!'"

Still, three weeks later, although Greg had sold quite a bit of the peanut brittle at a dollar a box, he hadn't yet disposed of all his wares. His mother and father nagged him about this, although his mother was secretly sympathetic.

"When a kid rings the doorbell, I always buy something," she says. "If I had to do it, I'd just die!"

Mrs. Chuckas *did* in fact ring doorbells, the year before, for the United Way. But that's another story.

As these scenes suggest, just the fund-raising aspects of charity can take on an astonishing variety of forms. But whether personified by the blind beggar with his tin cup, by Lords and Ladies Bountiful of Big Business and High Society, by khaki-clad youngsters ringing doorbells, or by well-groomed executives in their sleek offices charity is essentially begging.

Of course, the dictionary gives us many other definitions, too. *Charity, Webster's Third New International Dictionary* tells us, is derived from the Latin *caritas,* or love, and, apart from its spiritual and social connotations, variously means "kindly and sympathetic disposition to aid the needy or suffering," the actual act of aiding the needy, as well as the recipient of such assistance. *Charity, Webster's* also tells us, is an organization, institution, or agency engaged in the "free assistance of the poor, the suffering, or the distressed" or, in the case of a hospital, library, or school, used by the public for any beneficial or salutary purpose.

What then about the word *philanthropy,* which is derived from the Greek roots for love and mankind? There is a subtle, semantic distinction between *charity* and *philanthropy,* although the latter carries with it more of the connotation of large-scale giving—and not necessarily to the poor and the suffering. (Giving a few dollars to a blind beggar or a destitute orphan may be characterized as charity; a large gift of money to an educational institution or a symphony orchestra is philanthropy.) The historian Lecky distinguished between *charity,* which "alleviates individual suffering," and *philanthropy,* which "deals with large masses and is more frequently employed in preventing than in allaying calamity.'' However, in this book we will use both terms more or less interchangeably.

The term "charitable" also has a generally accepted legal meaning (although the vaguer "philanthropic" does not). For the purposes of taxation, most organizations generally eligible to receive contributions that are deductible for federal income tax purposes are defined under Section 501(c)(3) of the Internal Revenue Code of 1954 as those

> organized and operated exclusively for religious, charitable, scientific, testing for public safety, literary, or educational purposes, or for the prevention of cruelty to children or animals, no part of the net earnings of which inures to the benefit of any private shareholder or individual, no substantial part of which is carrying on propaganda, or otherwise attempting to influence legislation, and which does not participate in, or intervene in (including the publishing or distributing of statements), any political campaign on behalf of any candidate for public office.

Given this definition, however, there is no sure way of knowing just how many charities there are in this country. Not even the Internal Revenue Service (IRS) has any reliable figures, although its 1978 Cumulative List of tax-exempt organizations contains 280,355 entries, most of them 501(c)(3) organizations. However, some single entries may embrace literally dozens or even hundreds of tax-exempt organizations. For example, the entry "Baptist Churches in the U.S. and the Institutions Thereof" includes all the congregations and other entities belonging to some 29 bodies of that general denomination, or a total of probably well over 100,000 additional units. Similarly, entries for many national organizations like the American National Red Cross or the American Cancer Society fail to take into account their thousands of chapters or other local units. On this basis, there may be as many as 800,000 individual tax-exempt U.S. organizations, large and small, that raise money in the name of charity, according to one IRS official estimate, and, according to other estimates, there may be as many as 6 million. But nobody really knows.

With regard to finances, too, there is a serious dearth of definitive data on charities. Although the government keeps statistics on everything from abrasives (amount produced) to zoology (degrees conferred), it has no figures of any consequence on charities, except for those in occasional reports by the Internal Revenue Service based on income tax returns and large charitable bequests. But on the basis of the information compiled annually by the American Association of Fund-Raising Counsel (AAFRC), our burden of beneficence is enormous, certainly unmatched by any other country in the world.

According to the latest available AAFRC data, Americans give money to charity at the rate of nearly *$110 million a day*—or an all-time record total of $39.6 billion in 1978. This works out to an average of about $180 for every man, woman, and child in the country—a figure not even approached by any other nation. (By contrast, Canadians give an average of only $35 per capita and the figure for the United Kingdom is about $20.) Our total giving amounts to about 7 percent of our national budget and is more than the *total* budgets of all but nine of the 160 nations listed in the *World Almanac*.

U.S. giving has also grown steadily over the years. The total contributions of

$39.6 billion in 1978 were more than double those of a decade earlier and about eight times as much as the $5 billion given in 1954. If one added up all of the estimated annual contributions since 1910, the total would come to well over $400 billion, a sum so astronomical as to be beyond the average person's comprehension. But to give you some idea: If one-dollar bills were stacked one on top of another, 400 billion of them would make a pile 27,147 miles high. The same number of dollar bills, if laid end to end, would stretch 38.8 million miles, enough to circle the earth 1560 times or reach the moon 163 times. Or, put another way, if you started spending money at the rate of $10,000 a minute from the moment you were born, you would be 76 years old before you spent $400 billion.

Who gives to charity? Contrary to popular opinion, big business is not the largest donor. Individuals account by far for the most contributions—83 percent (or $32.8 billion) of all that was given in 1978. Surprisingly, people in the lowest income brackets generally give a larger proportion of their take-home pay than most of those earning more. Bequests account for another 6.6 percent (or $2.6 billion) of total contributions, which means that individuals, living and dead, are responsible for nearly 90 percent of all charity giving. The rest comes from foundations (5.5 percent, or $2.2 billion), and corporations (5 percent, or $2 billion).

Where does the money go? Religious organizations and causes receive the largest slice of the philanthropic pie—46.5 percent, or $18.4 billion, in 1978. About 14 percent, or $5.5 billion, goes to education; 13.8 percent, or $5.4 billion, for health and hospitals; some 10 percent, or $4 billion, to social welfare agencies; 6.3 percent, or $2.5 billion, to arts and the humanities; 2.9 percent, or $1.1 billion, to civic, housing, and environmental causes; and the remaining 6.5 percent, or nearly $2.6 billion, to a miscellany of other causes, largely foreign aid.

These figures, it should be stressed, are merely estimates, which, though highly informed, are based on data which may or may not be correct. The estimated total given by individuals, for example, may be high if one considers the possibility that people are prone to overstate the charitable contributions on their income tax returns. On the other hand, the AAFRC estimates for bequest giving may be low since they are based on Internal Revenue Service figures covering only estates of $60,000 or more. On the recipient side, reliable figures are even more difficult to come by, particularly in the religious field, because few statistics are available from the Roman Catholic Church or from Jewish congregations. And the AAFRC frankly admits that it roughly estimates, with no pretense of any scientific accuracy, Protestant giving (for which statistics are also woefully incomplete and spotty) to be 40 or 50 percent of all religious giving. So it evidently must take some statistical abracadabra on the part of the AAFRC to have the totals given to and received by charity come out to the same pat, precise figure year after year. However, for better or for worse, its figures are the only ones we have to go by—even if they are off by a billion or two one way or the other.

Getting even an approximate measure of the total assets of our charities is virtually impossible. Some years ago, a team of economists attempted to estimate the financial strength of the U.S. nonprofit sector but concluded that it simply couldn't be done.

Some hard data are available. Published reports, for example, show the assets of the American Cancer Society, largest of the voluntary health agencies, to total $229 million, mainly in cash or securities, at the end of its 1978 fiscal year. (Most of this, however, would go for program expenditures during the coming year.) The nation's 1835 YMCAs own buildings and other assets valued at $1 billion but this figure is probably low as the buildings are listed at cost.

Yet these figures pale when set beside those of other institutions also supported largely by philanthropy. The endowment fund of Harvard University stands in excess of $1.4 *billion*, and the funds of 13 other universities at $200 million or more. A survey of just 1006 of our 2400 colleges, universities, professional schools, and junior colleges showed them to have endowments adding up to $14.4 billion in 1976. The same year our nation's 7000-odd hospitals reported assets of $64 billion. And what value can possibly be placed on all the treasures in our 1800 museums when a single item in just one museum—say, Rembrandt's "Aristotle Contemplating a Bust of Homer" in New York's Metropolitan Museum—may be valued at millions of dollars. Or, for that matter, on the buildings or on the land on which all of these institutions and others, particularly our 350,000 churches, stand? The tax-exempt real estate in the United States has been estimated to be worth at least $600 billion, with that of religious bodies alone coming to over $150 billion. Whether these figures fall short of or exceed what is actually the case, there can be no question that the collective wealth of U.S. charity in all its forms must run well into the hundreds of billions of dollars, perhaps even into the trillions and, according to one estimate, may account for 15 percent of all of the nation's private wealth.

Even all of these figures scarcely do justice to the pervasive role of philanthropy in American life, thanks to what John J. Schwartz, president of the AAFRC, has referred to as the "ripple effect" of our annual giving, a consequence of the partnership of philanthropy and government. A classic example of this partnership is the Hill-Burton Act which, from its inception in 1946 to 1972, just before steps were taken to phase out its grants program, provided $3.8 billion in federal funds for new hospital construction. However, this sum was amplified to more than $12 billion, of which nearly $4 billion came from philanthropy and the rest from local government sources. Similarly, the Educational Facilities Act provided $2 billion for new construction on 1500 college and university campuses over a four-year period. During this period, however, these same institutions raised over $7 billion from private sources to amplify the construction stimulated by the government. In the field of the arts, America's museums derive about 40 percent of their support from the government (municipal, county, state, and federal); the remaining 60 percent comes from private sources. Music and other of the performing arts and cultural activities also owe their existence to some combination of government and private giving. The matching provisions of the National Endowment for the Arts and the National Endowment for the Humanities may generate as much as $3 to $4 for each dollar the government provides. "This added support literally has meant the difference between survival and death for many cultural activities across the land," says Schwartz.

In attempting to measure the size and scope of the world of charity, one must therefore also take into account the considerable sums our various nonprofit institutions and agencies receive from government. One must also not overlook the large portion of their income that comes from the sale of goods and services, including patient charges, tuition, admission fees, and the like. In fact, such fees and charges plus government grants and contracts may often comprise the bulk of the income of many organizations. Of the total income of $135 million of the National Association for Retarded Citizens, for example, only $25 million comes from contributions, with most of the rest from government and the sale of goods and services; similarly, only $25 million of the total revenues of $105 million of Planned Parenthood comes from contributions.

Back in 1974, when the AAFRC estimated U.S. giving at $25.3 billion, a study estimated the total income of our nation's philanthropic institutions to be $80.6 billion; the difference was provided by government ($23.2 billion) and service fees and other types of income ($32.1 billion). Although no more recent figures of this sort are available, it is not unreasonable to assume, allowing for inflation, that the total today stands at well over $100 billion. (In the years since 1974, U.S. giving alone has increased to $39.6 billion, as we have just seen.)

If one accepted this $100 billion estimate and considered charity an industry, it would rank as the largest in the nation, well ahead of such giants as contract construction (with an income of $77.2 billion in 1977), health ($69.4 billion), agriculture ($44.6 billion), machinery (excluding electrical, $47.0 billion), electrical machinery ($34.8 billion), motor vehicles ($34.8 billion), and food ($32 billion). (Measured in terms of its income from contributions alone, charity would rank as the fifth largest industry.)

Using employment—the other major yardstick for measuring the size of an industry—charity would also rank as the largest in the nation: In 1974, according to another study, the nonprofit charitable sector employed 4.6 million persons, or 5.2 percent of the U.S. work force (and 16 percent of all professional workers), far more than the number then employed in health (4.2 million), agriculture (3.6 million), and contract construction (3.5 million).

No overview of U.S. charity would be complete without taking into account the time, talent, and labor that the nation's legion of volunteers—de Tocqueville's "peculiar Americans"—devote to a multitude of causes. One measure of the value of voluntarism can be found in a statement by Elliot L. Richardson who, when Secretary of Health, Education, and Welfare, said "to extend the present range of HEW services equitably to all in need would cost a *quarter of a trillion dollars* . . . [and] the addition of 20 million trained personnel." Back in 1963, Austin V. McClain, then president of the fund-raising firm of Marts & Lundy, placed the value of the time and talent donated annually to philanthropic causes by America's business and professional leaders alone at $5 billion. The estimate was based on the assumption that some ten million executives were devoting ten days each year, at the then and now very conservative average value of $50 a day, guiding education, hospitals, churches, and other philanthropies. More recently, in 1974, a Census Bureau study estimated the value of unpaid volunteer work to be around $34 billion a year.

But here again we have a profusion, if not confusion, of statistics, for actually no one knows exactly how many Americans are engaged in volunteer work. The number, however, must be considerable. A recent poll by the National Center for Voluntary Action indicated that from 45 to 55 million Americans do volunteer work, but this figure does not reflect our entire volunteer strength, excluding as it does most children: Certainly to be reckoned as a formidable element of our volunteer force should be our 3.4 million Boy Scouts, 2.6 million Girl Scouts, and 700,000 Junior Red Cross members, to say nothing of the countless teenagers who make up the membership of other organizations or who serve in hospitals. Some estimates have placed our total volunteer strength at anywhere from 60 to 100 million, although the latter figure probably does not take into account duplications; many volunteers of course serve more than one cause.

Adding everything together—numbers of organizations, assets, contributions, revenues from the government and other sources, and the people involved both as paid workers and volunteers—Charity U.S.A. is a formidable factor in the lives of all of us.

But all is not as well as it should be in the world of charity. Nor has it been for quite a number of years. Back in 1969, the year that marked our slide into a depression after 102 consecutive months of economic growth, a Commission on Foundations and Private Philanthropy (the so-called Peterson Commission) warned that "without important new sources of funding amounting to billions of dollars," the 1970s would see the full force of a "charitable crisis." This bleak prediction was predicated on the belief that giving would not continue to rise in proportion to the gross national product. As things turned out, it did not.

If anything, the charitable crisis is still in its early stages, and philanthropy today is in deepening trouble, beset with a host of problems that are likely to continue to plague it in the years to come: inflation, rising costs, disenchantment not only with giving but with volunteering, growing public criticism of the fund-raising and other practices of charities, and the increasingly ferocious competition for the charity dollar, which—marking a relatively new development— has led not only to open hostility but also to bitter law suits among various factions of the world of sweet charity. Questions are also being raised increasingly about the relevancy of charity. And looming up over all of these problems are the government's unfavorable tax policies and gradual pre-emption of traditional "charitable" functions—trends which, in the words of John W. Gardner, the founding chairman of Common Cause and a former Secretary of Health, Education, and Welfare, threaten the very "survival of the nonprofit sector."

Inflation is the most serious immediate problem. While the dollar amounts given annually to charity are reported to reach record highs year after year, the gains are largely illusory. The $39.6 billion given in 1978, for example, was not much more in real dollars, after adjusting for inflation, than the level of contributions a decade earlier. For the most recent three-year period for which figures are available, giving grew 32.5 percent; inflation, however, rose 33 percent during the same period.

No doubt responsible to some degree for the fact that giving has failed to keep pace with inflation have been the recent increases in the standard income tax deduction—six in the last nine years; as a result, the number of taxpayers itemizing their deductions has decreased from almost 50 percent in 1970 to less than 25 percent today. This trend has also had the effect of discouraging charitable giving, for contributions are not tax deductible if the standard deduction is used instead of itemized deductions. And with fewer taxpayers itemizing deductions (and thus having an added incentive to make charitable donations), the losses to charity have been considerable; in 1977 alone, they were estimated to amount to some $1.3 billion.

Corporate giving, on the other hand, has lagged even further behind inflation, and in recent years has been about 0.9 percent of pretax net income—not far from an all-time low—even though the federal government, as an incentive to business, permits corporations to deduct up to 5 percent of their pretax net income for charitable contributions. And giving by foundations in terms of real dollars has dropped drastically, too, during the past decade as a consequence of inflation, the 1969 Tax Reform Act's provision levying a 4 percent tax (recently reduced to 2 percent) on the investment income of foundations and, perhaps most importantly, because of the erratic behavior of the stock market, all of which, together with the high payout requirements under another provision of the 1969 act, have combined to deplete the assets of the nation's major foundations by about $500 million since 1972.

Inflation, with its impact on family budgets, has not only discouraged cash contributions to charity in general but has also cut down on donations of used clothing, furniture, and other household items to the thousands of nonprofit thrift shops run by the Salvation Army, Goodwill Industries, and independent local charities. "The garage sale is our biggest competitor," said the executive director of the St. Vincent de Paul Society, a Detroit group.

Inflation has taken its toll on the expense, as well as the income, side of the charity ledger, sharply driving up costs for labor, fuel, supplies, rent, and construction—costs that most nonprofit organizations, unlike businesses, cannot easily absorb or pass on in the form of higher prices. "There is no way we can economize," complained the manager of a symphony orchestra struggling for survival. "After all, we can't play a symphony with fewer musicians, or try to play a piece faster. And we've gone as far as we dare go in raising ticket prices." Although many nonprofit arts organizations as well as hospitals and schools have managed to survive through the infusion of government funds, charities in the social service and other fields have had to slash their budgets, cut back on their services, and reduce their staffs in order to stay afloat; at the same time, there is concern that the spread of Proposition 13 fever may cut the availability of government funds for social services, thus placing an extra burden on charities for these services. In the spring of 1979, a social worker in the Catholic Social Services office in Galesburg, Illinois, said that her caseload was running between 75 and 100, up from 50 the year before.

Compounding the problems of charities is the fact that philanthropy has always been a labor-intensive industry, vulnerable to the vagaries of volunteers and to any increases in the wages of workers in paid jobs. Even in good times, volunteers have not always been easy to come by, particularly those at the doorbell-ringing level. The National Foundation's famous door-to-door drive, known as the "Mothers' March," has been abandoned in many communities. And the story is the same for many other national organizations, such as the American Cancer Society, whose fund-raising director, John Ewing, says that the group's recent difficulty in getting volunteers stems from changing economic and social conditions, which has seen millions of housewives take paying jobs to boost the family income or for reasons of personal fulfillment. Another deterrent to volunteering, particularly in high-crime urban areas, is fear. "Many people who never would have thought anything of it in the past are afraid to walk down the street with money—even if it's a Sunday afternoon," says the executive vice-president of the Cancer Society's New Jersey division.

Problems have also arisen because the interests—and demands—of volunteers have changed in recent years. "There is no trouble in recruiting volunteers for issue-oriented programs, like lobbying for women's causes," says Stephen McCurley of the National Center for Voluntary Action. "But the pool of those who will do anything is getting smaller. The idea of carrying bedpans is resisted." Says Joan Hanlon of Houston's Volunteer Action Center: "We're seeing a lot of people volunteering, but not too many are turned on by the traditional volunteer duties, like clerical work, office filing, or working in a hospital gift shop—the kind of thing I teethed on. They want more meaningful, direct client contact."

As a result, the National Council of Jewish Women in Atlanta, for example, must now pay women to stuff envelopes and drive in car pools—routine jobs that were once performed by volunteers. Many other charity groups must even hire telephone operators to solicit fund raising volunteers. At times, however, even paid help is hard to come by. Says William Schafer, head of the American Rescue Workers, which raises funds through its thrift stores: "Our greatest obstacle in getting paid truck-drivers or people to sort clothes is welfare checks. They get more from those than we can pay them."

To fill the gap left by the vanishing volunteer and attract competent professionals, more and more charities are having to pay salaries competitive with industry and government and—in a recent development—are even finding they have to face up to such realities as strikes. In the mid-1970s, 120 staff members of New York's Association for the Help of Retarded Children walked out in a wage dispute and did not return to work until they had received $800 annual increases over their pay scales, which ranged from $5100 to $10,000. The salaries of philanthropoids—the higher-echelon people who run charities—are still not comparable with those of captains of industry. However, emoluments of $50,000 to $60,000 a year or even more are not uncommon for the top officials of fairly large agencies. Five officers of Disabled American Veterans are paid more than $49,000 and the top man takes home nearly $63,000.

Adding to the woes of charities is the increasing public criticism of them. Whereas it was once considered graceless and gauche to question those whose goals were, after all, noble, during the past decade or so, the media, legislators, and various self-appointed watchdogs have not hesitated to probe one of our few remaining sacred cows. Of the 32 charitable organizations *Changing Times* rated in its December, 1973, issue for honesty, efficiency, and certain other criteria, the magazine concluded that only seven met all standards. Exactly three years later, only 17 out of 53 charities were found by the magazine to meet virtually the same standards.

No more than 66 well-known charities—only 10 percent of those queried—even bothered to respond to requests for information from the Council of Better Business Bureaus. Of the 360 charities on the CBBB's quarterly rating list, about

210 meet the organization's standards; the rest do not. However, only 125 of the 365 charities rated monthly by the National Information Bureau meet all of its standards; 50 do not. (The rest are in the process of being evaluated, have not provided sufficient information by which they can be evaluated, or have prompted substantial questions that have made it difficult for the agency to state whether they do or do not meet standards.)

As we shall see in later pages, the charities given negative ratings by these two leading consumer watchdogs as well as by others include some of the oldest and most prestigious in the nation, the charges against them ranging from mismanagement and misrepresentation to outright fraud. As a result, there has been growing sentiment for legislators to put charitable organizations under rigid controls, which are now virtually nonexistent: There are now no federal laws regulating the operations of charities, and the few state and local laws, as we shall also see, are insignificant, ineffectual, or unenforceable.

No laws, however, no matter how stringent, could possibly deal adequately with charities that are well-intentioned but poorly-managed, or with those which, while well-managed, may have outlived their original purpose. In saying this, I do not mean to slight the many past and present benefits philanthropy has brought us. As Vice President Walter F. Mondale once stated, while serving in the Senate: "During our lifetime, American charity has accepted the challenge of some of our most terrible problems. It has helped to virtually eliminate tuberculosis and polio . . . to feed millions of hungry children . . . to aid the crippled and disenfranchised . . . and to offer new hope and new life to countless victims of our society."

On the other hand, because of these accomplishments, it would be equally wrong to close our eyes to the existence of any problems in philanthropy. "There are three things wrong with philanthropy," is the way an executive of one of the country's greatest philanthropic organizations saw things. "One, people don't give enough; two, they don't give wisely; three, much of what they give is spent wastefully."

This criticism leads in turn to a host of questions. Because of the large sums of money many organizations apparently spend on fund raising, it is pertinent to ask, for example, whether charities exist to raise funds or raise funds to exist. But in the fetish for evaluating a charity on the basis of the percentage of its income it spends on fund raising, one may overlook what is the perhaps even more important question of just what it does with the rest of its money and, perhaps still more important, the question of what these expenditures have accomplished.

In view of the hundreds of millions, if not billions, of dollars the health agencies have poured into "public information," "education," and "research" during the past quarter of a century, it may be pertinent to ask how much better informed the public is about disease today or how many diseases are any closer to conquest. (In spite of the 30-year existence of the Arthritis Foundation, the most common treatment for this crippling disease is still aspirin.)

That familiar word *relevancy* is bouncing around as questions are also being raised about the priorities of philanthropy.

In the health field, for example, contributions and consequently expenditures seemingly bear no relationship to relative needs. About one-third less is given annually to aid our nearly 32 million arthritis and rheumatism sufferers than is given for our 500,000 victims of multiple sclerosis. While mental ailments rank second (just after heart conditions) as a cause of illness, the Mental Health Association ranks twelfth among health agencies in the collection of funds. Just about as many donations go to assist cerebral palsy victims as go to help retarded children, although the latter outnumber the former eight to one.

At a 1971 conference of the National Council on Philanthropy, Vernon E. Jordan, Jr., then director of the United Negro College Fund, charged that "American philanthropy, like the nation itself, has been insensitive and unresponsive to the major domestic crisis in this country—race relations" and cited statistics to demonstrate that minority causes still got only a fraction of private donations, no more than 1.2 percent of the United Way funds collected in 97 cities that year. (The United Way now claims that 13 percent of its funds go to minority groups.)

In similar vein, critics of the United Way are asking if too much money is being funneled into primarily white, middle-class institutions such as the Boy Scouts, the American Red Cross, and the YMCA at the expense of more community-oriented organizations providing more help for blacks, other minorities, and low-income families. To resolve this question, various precedent-setting court actions have been instituted in recent years. Two, still unresolved at this writing, challenge the United Way domination of solicitations among private business and civil service employees. (For further details on these and other law suits, see Chapter 25.)

Still broader questions arise. Is the present concept of private charity outmoded as the government spreads its social welfare umbrella further and further each year? In 1929, government giving in the categories of health, education, and welfare amounted to 3.9 percent of the gross national product. By 1960, such expenditures had jumped to 10.6 percent, and by 1976 they had almost doubled to 20.6 percent, amounting to $331 billion, this constituting 73.1 percent of all public and private spending for "social welfare" purposes.

Could not *all* the functions of charity be better assumed by the government? Indeed, since these functions are largely to satisfy public needs, *shouldn't* they be assumed by the government? If education, medical care and research, museums, neighborhood youth programs, hospitals, planned parenthood agencies, training activities for the handicapped, symphony orchestras, and the like are important enough to be worthy of considerable government support, why should they not be supported *entirely* by government?

Needless to say, the mere suggestion of such a possibility sends shock tremors through the philanthropic establishment. "Can government afford to carry on the work of thousands of agencies, or to replace millions of hours of unpaid volunteer service with full pay, and fully fringe-benefited, government help?" rhetorically asked one fund raiser in an industry trade paper, *Fund Raising Management*. His own response was blunt and unequivocal: "Pray God that the answer will be, 'No!' Volunteerism and voluntary giving is an integral fiber in our social fabric. It has endured for 4,000 years—perhaps more—and it should be preserved. It should not be usurped as a function of city, county, state and federal governments to deprive the individual of the sacred privileges of free expression and freedom of choice."

However, this dire possibility as well as the growing criticism levied at philanthropy was of sufficient concern to prompt the formation of a Commission on Private Philanthropy and Public Needs, which was initiated in 1973 by the late John D. Rockefeller III (who had also inspired the Peterson Commission) with the blessings of the then House Ways & Means Chairman Wilbur Mills, the then Treasury Secretary George Shultz, and his then deputy (and later Secretary) William E. Simon. Headed by John H. Filer, chairman of Aetna Life & Casualty, the commission's 32 illustrious members included two former Cabinet officers, corporate and university presidents, foundation officials, and other philanthropic panjandrums.

Given the commission's auspices and membership, its principal focus, quite understandably and in the words of its executive director, was on "the impact of the tax system upon the private sector"—specifically, "whether, in what manner, or if at all, the existing tax system should be modified." Implicit in this rhetoric, of course, was the hope that any modifications in any future tax legislation would be more favorable to the private sector than the restrictive measures embodied in the 1969 Tax Reform Act.

In order to formulate its recommendations, however, the Commission addressed itself to a formidable series of key questions which had perhaps never before been faced by so august a group: Should American society continue to encourage the formation and support of private organizations and institutions as a major means of satisfying our public needs? Would the fabric of American society be altered if government were to assume the primary role of defining and providing for our public needs, replacing the private effort which has traditionally done this? Is the present system of private support for society's needs providing adequate resources to serve those needs? Or should we expect and encourage the current trend toward increased direct government involvement and support to continue and to expand?

But as long as private charities continue in some form or another and as long as they receive tax benefits (including $600 million of taxpayer money that is appropriated every year to make up for their lower postal rates) that all of us in effect pay for, whether or not we contribute to charity, it is also legitimate to ask: Do the accomplishments of charities justify these tax benefits? Should charities be subject to government regulation and, if so, what kind?

These are among the questions we shall seek to answer as we continue our journey through Charity U.S.A.

Chapter 2

4000 Years of Philanthropy

To set matters in perspective, it may help to step back into history and trace the pedigree of philanthropy. Surprisingly, the word *philanthropy* itself, though derived from two venerable Greek roots meaning "love of mankind," was not commonly used before the eighteenth century.* The word *charity,* whose etymological roots also carry with it connotations of love, is of much older vintage, probably dating back to the early Christian era. However, the acts referred to by both words, which we are here using interchangeably, are as old as society itself, although they have meant different things at different times.

Historically, philanthropy, or charity, grew out of the obligation in most primitive societies of a family, clan, tribe, or other close-knit group to take care of its members and see to it that each was adequately fed, clothed, and sheltered. For the sake of survival in a precarious, capricious environment, every man, in biblical terms, simply had to be his brother's keeper; one never knew when one might need help oneself. As society became more complex, the functions of what we would today call welfare—the material and even spiritual well-being of people—were assumed by the state and its wealthier citizens.

In the ancient Mesopotamian city-states, for example, where work was regarded as a universal obligation, there was also provision for a sort of social security for the less fortunate. The great Code of Hammurabi, inscribed on a seven-foot column about 2000 B.C., commanded Babylonians to see that "justice be done to widows, orphans, and the poor." The ancient Egyptians, too, had the rudiments of a social welfare system aimed at meeting the basic needs of the destitute and disabled.

To the early Greeks and Romans, on the other hand, philanthropy was directed primarily at enriching the life of the community as a whole. Cimon of Athens gave parks and gardens to his city; and Xenophon, in addition to building a temple to Artemis, provided for an annual festival and feast at which everyone, rich and poor alike, would receive "barley meal and loaves of bread, wine and sweetmeats, and a portion of the sacrificial victims from the sacred herd as well as the victims taken in the chase." Similarly, Pliny the Younger gave funds to support a school in his native town, and other rich Romans gave freely for municipal games as well as for schools and other institutions.

Beggars and vagrants (as distinguished from the working poor), who have persisted in all cultures from the earliest times, though tolerated, were regarded

*The first known use of *philanthropy* was in a sermon delivered in London in 1650 by Jeremy Taylor, an English preacher who also served as chaplain to King Charles I.

as nuisances, much as they are today. Plautus had a character in one of his plays utter this universal sentiment: "He does the beggar but a bad service who gives him meat and drink; for what he gives is lost, and the life of the poor is but prolonged to their own misery."

Generally, there was little sympathy for even those who were poor through no fault of their own. This is not to say that the poor were ignored completely everywhere. In the Greek community of Boeotia, for example, well-to-do farmers shared their produce and other resources with needy neighbors as well as strangers; and elsewhere in Greece brotherhoods developed that supported a kind of common relief fund. But the extravagant Roman "bread and circuses" staged for the poor and the handouts of grain or money given them were not so much demonstrations of charity or generosity as acts taken to curb the threat of revolt by a hungry populace. By the end of the first century A.D., institutions called *alimentationes* came into being to care for poor children, as did also *valetudinaria,* or hospitals for slaves and poor freemen. But there is reason to believe that they might have been inspired by the then emerging examples of early Christian charity.

Charity as we know it today also owes a great deal to the influence of the great religions, all of which encourage almsgiving. This probably evolved out of the pagan custom of offering sacrificial articles and animals (and, on occasion, even humans) to propitiate the gods. Later, anthropologists have suggested, the gods made it known that the gifts to them could be put to more practical use by the poor and needy. And so charity supposedly began. Apropos, perhaps the oldest record of giving is the Egyptian *Book of the Dead,* the collective title given to some 2000 papyrus rolls dating from at least 2600 B.C. They have been found in the tombs of the wealthy and prominent who, while still living, had purchased the rolls from priests as insurance policies, hopefully guaranteeing them a happy immortality after death. Since it was believed that good works would assist the soul in attaining salvation on judgment day, the entombed funerary literature bore not only its quota of magical prayers, formulas, and passwords but also such self-serving statements as: "I have given bread to the hungry, and water to him that was athirst, and apparel to the naked man."

Buddhism also stresses the importance of good works not only as one of man's duties but also as a hedge for the hereafter. A scriptural writing of Theravada Buddhism, the *Khuddaka Patha,* counsels: "By charity . . . man and woman alike can store up a well-hidden treasure. . . A wise man should do good—that is the treasure which will not leave him." The sentiment is reminiscent of that expressed centuries later when Jesus, in the Sermon on the Mount, prescribed charity as a means of salvation: "If thou wilt be perfect, go and sell what thou hast, and give to the poor, and thou shalt have treasure in heaven."

Just as benevolence was decreed by Buddha as one of the five ways a follower of the faith should "minister to his friends and familiars," so was charity later to become one of the five "pillars" or obligatory duties of Islam. As early as the seventh century A.D., the Prophet prescribed a special graduated yearly tax on property as well as income for the relief of the poor; in addition, the haves were also expected to give voluntarily to the have-nots. "Of their good take alms, so that you may thereby purify and sanctify them," reads one of the numerous passages in the Koran that encourages giving.

The Jews also stressed the importance of giving a tithe—literally, one-tenth—of their income, either in money or in kind (in biblical times, usually crops), to charity; indeed, this form of self-taxation was actually written into the basic Jewish law. Some say that the custom of tithing, at least for religious and charitable purposes, was originated by Moses about 1300 B.C.; however, it probably began somewhat earlier with Abraham's gifts to the priest-king Melchizedek.* The Mosaic code of laws also specified that a corner of one's field be unreaped and left for the poor to harvest. To Jews, giving was, and is, not even regarded as "charity"; rather, it is an obligation, one's duty to one's fellow man. For that matter, the Jews don't even have a word for charity; the Hebrew word used for it is *tsedaka*, which actually means justice or righteousness.

To Jews, some forms of giving are more praiseworthy than others. About 1180 A.D. the great Jewish theologian Maimonides set down eight distinct "degrees of charity," which he ranked in the following descending order of desirability:

1. To take hold of a Jew who has been crushed and to give him a gift or a loan, or to enter into partnership with him, or to find work for him, and thus to put him on his feet so that he will not be dependent on his fellowmen.
2. One who gives charity to the poor, but does not know to whom he gives it, nor does the poor man know from whom he receives it. [In other words, when the gift is completely anonymous from every point of view.]
3. When the giver knows to whom he gives, but the poor does not know from whom he receives.
4. When the poor knows from whom he receives but the giver does not know to whom he gives.
5. When one gives even before he is asked.
6. When one gives after he has been asked.
7. When one gives less than he should but graciously.
8. When one gives grudgingly.

Christianity, in later taking over from Judaism the virtue of charity, added to the concept of duty the attribute of love. The love of one's fellowman, as manifested by charity, was linked to God's love for man and man's reciprocal love for God. St. Augustine summed this up: "Charity is a virtue which, when our affections are perfectly ordered, united us to God for by it we love Him." Jesus entreated His followers to "Love thy neighbor as thyself," as giving was extended even to the despised, but good, Samaritan who had gone to the aid of a half-dead victim of thieves after a priest and a Levite had refused him help.

With the establishment of the church as the Roman state religion early in the fourth century, substantial sums for good works now began to flow into the coffers of the church. A landmark date in philanthropy is 321 A.D., when Emperor Constantine for the first time permitted citizens to will money or property to the church, which soon became the principal recipient and dispenser of philanthropic funds. The funds were used not only to support religious activities

*In modern times, relatively few Jews tithe in a formal sense and those who do generally give one-seventh of their income to charity, while Christians who tithe still give the traditional one-tenth. However, many Jews give much more than one-tenth of their income to all the causes in which they are interested.

but also the parish poor, aged, infirm, and widows, at first principally in their homes, then by building orphanages, almshouses, guest houses for travelers, and, gradually, schools and hospitals, many of them prototypes of the institutions which still exist today. What may have been the forerunner of the first hospital in the modern sense (earlier ones were actually places of hospitality for travelers) was the one established by St. Basil at Caesarea in 396 A.D.

Voluntary giving, however, was seldom adequate to support all these institutions and activities. For this reason, jousting tournaments were often staged, much like present-day charity balls or other special events, as benefits for medieval hospitals. To bolster revenues, the church also found it necessary to exhort and even compel its followers to emulate the Old Testament practice of tithing mandated under Jewish law but not enjoined on the early Christians. Councils of the church, starting with that of Tours in 567, first urged and then tried to enforce the payment of tithes, threatening excommunication to the delinquent, and Charlemagne in the late eighth century made such payments to the church a legal obligation; in the centuries that followed, obligatory tithing spread with the church all over Europe.

A crass commercial note was introduced into Christian charity when the church began to encourage further contributions by granting indulgences, or pardons of temporal punishment for certain sins, upon the payment of specified sums. No doubt much early Christian almsgiving was also encouraged by the desire of the giver to win salvation in the afterlife, as numerous Scriptural reminders promised. To lay up "treasure in heaven," as Jesus put it, no one could do better than free oneself from the encumbrance of riches by giving to the poor who, in Ben Whitaker's phrase, were seen as providing a fire escape to heaven for the rich. Indeed, in this sense, poverty was a theological necessity. Arguing that God had put the poor on earth to make charity—and hence, the purchase of grace—possible, St. John Chrysostom, an early church father, stated: "If there were no poor the greater part of your sins would not be removed." And it is difficult to disagree with the contention of some historians that St. Augustine's doctrine holding that "alms have power to extinguish and expiate sin" was a dominant factor in the rising riches of the church in the Middle Ages.

So vast were the funds accumulated by the church that by the twelfth century in England alone somewhere between one-third and one-half of the country's entire public wealth was under ecclesiastical control. Foreshadowing accusations leveled at some charities today, there were charges that revenues intended for the poor were being diverted either to purely religious purposes or private purses; there were complaints, for example, that monasteries were distributing less than 2.5 percent of their income in alms. The situation in England led to a prolonged struggle between the church and the state. This ended with the confiscation of church properties and the shifting of the responsibility for charity to secular control in the sixteenth century. A key factor in the government's growing interest in providing for the welfare of its citizens was the social and economic unrest associated with the transition from feudalism to capitalism. The transition created a growing class of mobile laborers who were often victims of the caprices of economic shifts and the agricultural seasons. As a result, poverty increased far beyond the ability or willingness of the church to cope with it. And the church's attitude that poverty did after all serve a religious end by enabling the prosperous to purchase their salvation through almsgiving served to sanctify and stimulate, rather than to discourage, begging, which had become a public nuisance.

As Roman Catholicism was challenged and supplanted by Protestantism not only in England but also elsewhere in Europe, there was a change in attitude toward charity. In the stern ideology of the Protestant "work ethic," poverty was not a virtue but rather the consequence of personal immorality or laziness. To Martin Luther, salvation could no longer be obtained simply by giving alms and he denounced the demands of beggars as blackmail. Begging, he said in 1523, should be outlawed and the poor, if able-bodied, should be forced to work, with aid provided only to the old, the weak, and those who had "honorably labored at their craft or in agriculture" but who could no longer find the means to support themselves.

The laws subsequently enacted in England reflected this Protestant or, more specifically, Calvinist point of view. Ordinances were passed either prohibiting begging or limiting it to those deemed incapable of self-support; those caught begging without proper authorization were subject to punishment, which included public whipping or imprisonment. Beginning in 1536 a series of statutes was passed providing for special compulsory taxes to be used for the relief of the poor and establishing the principle that the poor were a local responsibility; accordingly, charity overseers were appointed in each parish, the smallest local unit of government, to assess and levy taxes and to dole out donations to the destitute. To prevent the poor of one parish from moving to another, restrictive laws were passed which, though aimed primarily at vagrants, had the effect of interfering with the mobility of poor laborers sincerely seeking work. In 1601 all of these statutes were codified into the Elizabethan Poor Law, known officially as the Statute of Charitable Uses, which has become the cornerstone of Anglo-Saxon law on charity. Other provisions of this act called for work programs for the able-bodied poor, houses of correction for vagrants and others unwilling to work, the care of the helpless (the aged, the sick, the blind, and infants) either in their own homes or in almshouses, and the farming out of older children as apprentices.

In spite of the Reformation, however, the motivation for these relief laws and others that followed was political rather than religious or humanitarian. Like the "bread and circuses" of the old Roman days, they were largely inspired by the practical purpose of preventing civil disorder or even worse, the possibility of which was particularly great in the turbulent Tudor period. John Stuart Mill suggested the importance of his country's relief system in maintaining civil order in England when he wrote in 1863:

> The hatred of the poor for the rich is an evil that is almost inevitable where the law does not guarantee the poor against the extremity of want. The poor man in France, notwithstanding the charitable relief that he may get, has always before his eyes the possibility of death by starvation; whereas in England he knows that, in the last resort, he has a claim against private property up to the point of bare existence; that not even the lowest proletarian is absolutely disinherited from his place in the sun.

And the British historian Trevelyan went so far as to credit England's relief system to the fact that his country never had anything comparable to the French Revolution.

The 1601 Elizabethan Poor Law became the model for the colonial, and later the state, statutes on welfare in the New World. As in England, it was left to each town to levy the taxes that would provide for the relief of its own poor. Colonial towns even continued the old English custom of "warning out" strangers who looked like potential paupers, and also the practice of "passing on" poor newcomers—that is, sending or escorting them back to the town line. A 1775 North Carolina law even provided for the whipping of vagrants before they were "passed on." But even the resident poor eligible for relief did not generally have an easy time of it. In many of the colonies, they had to wear a stigmatic emblem, such as the letter "P" in Pennsylvania.

The Puritan variant of the Protestant "work ethic" continued to equate poverty with sin and even crime and to prescribe work as the antidote to poverty. A constant expounder of this view was that perhaps most famous of Puritan divines Cotton Mather (1663–1728) who wrote that it was "not lawful for a Christian ordinarily to Live without some Calling." At the same time, however, Mather, who was the chief exponent of do-goodism in colonial America, recognized the pragmatic values of charity by conceding, much as the Tudors did, its importance as an instrument of social control necessary to maintain public order.

Mather's views greatly influenced Benjamin Franklin who, in addition to everything else, was involved in an astonishing number of philanthropic activities. As early as 1727, when he had just turned 21, the industrious Franklin helped organize the Junto, an informal discussion and mutual improvement club made up of young Philadelphia go-getters, which was probably a forerunner of such present-day service clubs as Rotary. Junto's need for books and his own thirst for reading led him to establish America's first circulating library in 1731. He also formed Philadelphia's first volunteer fire department and played a leading role in founding the American Philosophical Society (1743), the first American institution dedicated to the promotion of research in the natural and social sciences, the Academy of Philadelphia (1749), which later became the University of Pennsylvania, and the Pennsylvania Hospital (1751), the first in America.

In establishing these eleemosynary enterprises, Franklin also lay claim to being America's champion pioneer fund raiser. For the Pennsylvania Hospital fund-raising campaign, he used the now common device of matching funds: When he saw that private contributions would come nowhere near the campaign's goal of 4000 pounds, he ingeniously arranged for the introduction in the Pennsylvania Assembly of a bill which provided that when contributions to the hospital project reached 2000 pounds, the Assembly would match this with a grant of 2000 pounds.

So formidable were Franklin's fund-raising skills that many of the other techniques he employed are the bases of successful campaigns today. When asked to help in raising funds for a new Presbyterian meeting house in Philadelphia, he for once begged off, offering the excuse that he was "unwilling to make myself disagreeable to my fellow citizens by too frequently soliciting their contributions." However, he offered the minister this classic advice:

In the first place, I advise you to apply to all those whom you know will give something; next, to those whom you are uncertain whether they will give anything or not, and show them the list of those whom have given; and lastly, do not neglect those who you are sure will give nothing, for in some of them you may be mistaken.

Probably the first noteworthy voluntary group formed here was the Scots' Charitable Society, founded in 1657 by 27 Scotsmen living in Boston for the purpose of aiding their poor and sick countrymen whose only other source of help were the already overburdened local government agencies. The oldest social agency still functioning in the United States, it became the prototype of the thousands of ethnic, religious, fraternal, and other voluntary groups that were to wax and wane in the centuries to follow.

So rapidly did such groups proliferate that the larger cities were actually blessed with an overabundance of benevolent organizations. In 1835 Alexis de Tocqueville, that perceptive French observer of the American scene, commented on the unique American disposition to organize and join voluntary associations:

Americans of all ages, all stations in life, and all types of disposition are forever forming associations. They are not only commercial and industrial associations in which all take part, but others of a thousand different types—religious, moral, serious, futile, very general and very limited, immensely large and very minute. Americans combine to give fetes, found seminaries, build churches, distribute books, and send missionaries to the antipodes. Hospitals, prisons, and schools take shape in that way. Finally, if they want to proclaim a truth or propagate some feeling by the encouragement of a great example, they form an association. In every case, at the head of any new undertaking, where in France you would find the government or in England some territorial magnate, in the United States you are sure to find an Association.

It was also about this time that young America, although still far from affluent, somehow found the wherewithal to begin its tradition of lending a helping hand to unfortunates in other parts of the world. Religious missionaries here had been active in this regard for a century or longer. But what was probably the first such secular effort took place in the late 1820s when volunteer committees arranged charity balls, fairs, auctions, debating contests, and theatrical benefits and used virtually every other technique of present-day charity drives to raise money for the Greeks in their war of independence. In the decades that followed, relief in the form of dollars and foodstuffs was also sent to the starving people of the Cape Verde Islands and Madeira (whose appreciative people filled the returning relief ships with casks of choice old Madeira) and to victims of the Irish Famine of 1847-1848, a calamity described by fund raisers in such heart-rending terms that they drew contributions from even the poor Choctaw Indians.

At home, however, during the first half of the nineteenth century, the poor were still not viewed with such benevolence. Many were incarcerated in almshouses or workhouses which in some communities were operated in conjunction with the local jail. "The growing number of poor immigrants, the periodic food riots, the crime obvious in some areas, and the strain on public assistance programs—all these factors combined to provide the social crucible within which attitudes toward the poor would become even more negative and inflexible," says Joe R. Feagin in his *Subordinating the Poor*. Since the view still persisted that poverty was the result of an array of un-Christian character flaws ranging from sloth to intemperance, this was a period when reformers set up societies to distribute Bibles and temperance tracts and otherwise work for the moral reform and redemption of sinners.*

The social and economic changes wrought by the Industrial Revolution and the enormous relief problems created by the Civil War saw the emergence of a new era of philanthropy marked by the acceleration of all sorts of relief programs necessary to cope with the rapidly altering character and needs of the country.** While the poor continued to be cared for largely in almshouses and would continue to be well into the twentieth century, increasing reliance was also placed on private charities that multiplied at an unprecedented rate after the Civil War. In Philadelphia alone, in 1878, there were some 800 voluntary charitable agencies, compared with just 33 in that city only 50 years before.

The first effort at federated fund raising took place in Philadelphia in 1829 when a local publisher, Mathew Cary, attempted to induce his fellow citizens to give a single donation on behalf of all of the city's then 33 agencies. The effort was a dismal failure: A total of $276.50 was collected from 137 subscribers during the course of a three-week campaign. Federated fund raising was next tried in Denver in 1888, again unsuccessfully; in 1895, Jewish charities in Boston and, a year later, their counterparts in Cincinnati established what was to grow into today's United Jewish Appeal. (A Community Chest campaign held in Cleveland in 1913 was the prototype of the nation's United Way drives which now raise more than a billion dollars annually in some 2300 communities.)

This was an era, too, when some of America's great fortunes, built during this country's transformation into an industrial society, contributed to the beginnings of large-scale philanthropy. Leading the way was Andrew Carnegie who was born in a Scottish weaver's cottage in 1835, came here as a poor immigrant boy, amassed a $30 million fortune in the steel industry, and, then, at age 54, declared that "the man who dies thus rich, dies disgraced." To save himself from such shame, Carnegie decided to spend the rest of his life giving away his wealth which by 1901 amounted to $492 million, the sum he received when he that year, sold his steel company to the United States Steel Corporation and retired from business to devote himself entirely to philanthropy.

In a celebrated essay, *The Gospel of Wealth*, published in 1889, Carnegie had set forth his philosophy of philanthropy, which differed radically from the traditional view that saw giving as largely a religious duty; this view was based on the so-called doctrine of stewardship which, as earlier enunciated by William Penn, held that since the rich were indebted to God for their wealth, they were also

---

*The same charitable attitude led to the establishment during this period of schools and institutions for the blind, deaf, and mentally ill who could not of course be held to account for their inability to work.

**As Ben Whitaker perceptively observed in *The Philanthropoids*: "It is significant how times of violent change—during Tudor England, the Industrial Revolution and the twentieth century—have always produced bursts of philanthropic activity." War, many others have also noted, has traditionally given philanthropy a greater impetus than periods of peace.

accountable to Him for what they did with it for they were, in effect, the temporary, temporal trustees of His wealth. Carnegie, on the other hand, was one of the first men to argue that philanthropy was not so much a religious duty as a social obligation. Echoing the theories of social Darwinism, he saw his riches— and trusteeship—as having devolved not from Providence but rather from nature which had selected him as one of the fittest in the struggle for survival to amass and redistribute in the public interest.

However, he inveighed against indiscriminate giving. "It were better for mankind that the millions of the rich were thrown into the sea than so spent as to encourage the slothful, the drunken, the unworthy," he warned. Possibly for this reason, he concentrated his charity efforts on the able and industrious, favoring gifts that would contribute to the sustenance of the spirit rather than of the body.

The first-chosen instruments for his philanthropy were free public libraries. Beginning with a donation of a library to his adopted home town of Allegheny, Pennsylvania, in 1890, he eventually spent $60 million for the building of 1946 libraries in towns and cities across the nation and another 816 in the United Kingdom and Canada. As a general rule, he would pay for building and equipping a library if the community would provide the site and maintenance.

At first, Carnegie opposed higher education on the ground that this would benefit only a select few; but later colleges and universities, as well as scientific institutions, also became beneficiaries of his benevolence. In 1900 he founded the Carnegie Institute of Technology in Pittsburgh and, two years later, the Carnegie Institution in Washington, D.C., continuing the tradition, begun more than two centuries before, which had seen private philanthropy as responsible for the creation of such institutions as Harvard (dating from 1636, the beneficiary of the first systematic fund-raising effort on this continent), Yale, Princeton, Columbia, Brown, Rutgers, Dartmouth, Cornell, and Johns Hopkins.

Unlike Carnegie, John Davidson Rockefeller I, his contemporary (1839–1937), adhered to the old-fashioned religious doctrine of stewardship. "God gave me my money," the legendary industrialist, perhaps the richest man of his era, used to say. His philosophy, paraphrased from a passage in a sermon by John Wesley on *The Use of Money,* was: "A man should make all he can and give away all he can."

Belying the frequent charges that his benefactions, like those of the other so-called millionaire "robber barons," were intended to serve as a shield against public censure, giving for Rockefeller was a lifetime habit, developed long before he became a man of wealth. As early as 1855, when he was still a teen-ager, he started the practice of giving away up to 10 percent of his earnings, first to his Sunday school and its religious missions; and his contributions increased steadily over the years. In 1857, his meticulously kept account books showed, he gave away $28.37 to several churches and the YMCA. By 1860 the amount had increased to $107.35; by 1864, to $675.85; and by 1869, when the oil business was starting to make him rich, to $5489.62. In 1888 his donations to various good works totaled $170,000; and in 1889, the year Carnegie's *Wealth* was published, Rockefeller gave $600,000 to help found the new University of Chicago, following this up with $1 million contributions in each of the next two years. During the course of his lifetime, Rockefeller gave away a total of $531 million, more than any other man in history.

In order to find a more efficient way of organizing and conducting what Rockefeller called "this business of benevolence," he and his capitalistic compeer Carnegie decided to funnel their mounting millions into that fiscal philanthropic device known as the foundation which, loosely defined, is a private, charitable grant-making fund. In the first two decades of the twentieth century, they established a series of foundations, notably the Carnegie Corporation, founded in 1911 (which soon was spending more on education than the federal government), and the Rockefeller Foundation, begun in 1913, which were the first of the huge, modern foundations we know today.

In 1889—the same year that Andrew Carnegie enunciated his gospel of wealth—Jane Addams founded Hull House in Chicago, the best known of our early settlement houses. (The first, the Neighborhood Guild in New York City, was started in 1886.) A product of the Industrial Revolution, this new type of welfare institution, which still exists today, was usually situated in lower-income city neighborhoods and conducted a variety of educational, health, recreational, and welfare activities for the people of the neighborhood with the aim of improving their quality of life. With the growing number of paid workers in the settlements and other welfare agencies, the term "social work" began to replace what up to the late nineteenth century had been called charity. About the same time, national labor unions, concerned with the health and welfare of their members, evolved from local and regional worker groups that were little more than professional guilds.

The late nineteenth century and early twentieth century also saw the development of other types of national organizations to deal not so much with the plight of the poor as with the pressing community, social, and spiritual problems that had become a part of America's new urban character. Many relied on dues and donations from the public at large as well as on contributions from wealthy private benefactors.

The YMCA movement, launched in London in 1844 by a group of salesmen "to improve the spiritual condition of young men in the drapery and other trades," was transplanted to these shores in Boston seven years later and grew rapidly, finding fertile soil here in the series of religious revivals that swept across the nation during the second half of the nineteenth century. But what really gave the movement its impetus was the support it received from the railroads which, in stretching across the continent, found they needed inexpensive housing for their employees. It is more than coincidence, therefore, that the decade of 1880–1890 not only marked the most rapid expansion of America's railroad lines but also the period of greatest growth of local YMCAs, which mushroomed across the country like the present-day Holiday Inns. By 1890 there were Ys at 89 railroad terminal points, many of them still known as "Railroad" YMCAs, all supported by one railroad company or another. The customary practice was for the railroad to bear 60 percent of a Y's operating costs, with the employees paying the balance. The railroads also contributed somewhat more than half of the construction costs of the buildings which had grown to 113 in number by 1913, when the railroad network was largely complete and the Ys began to turn to other sources of support.

The Salvation Army which, like the YMCA, had its roots in England, came to this country in 1880 to bring its own brand of religion and a variety of social services to people in spiritual and material need. The American Red Cross came into being as the American Association of the Red Cross in 1881 and was another foreign offshoot of sorts, being a branch of the international Red Cross movement that grew out of a conference in Geneva, Switzerland, in 1863.

Since it does not ordinarily take care of the needy, the sick, and the elderly except when providing disaster relief, the Red Cross has never been a charity in the conventional meaning of the term. Nor, in the strictest sense, have been the other special national organizations concerned with improving the social environment that began to develop between the turn of the century and the beginning of World War I, such as the National Association for the Advancement of Colored People (1909), the Boy Scouts (1910), Camp Fire Girls (1910), and Girl Scouts (1912), as well as those concerned with specific diseases, among them the National Tuberculosis Association (now the American Lung Association) in 1904 and the American Cancer Society in 1913.

The first two decades of the twentieth century also saw the beginning of those organizations of distinctively American origin—clubs of businessmen dedicated to community service. Rotary, the first, started as a single club in Chicago in 1905 and soon sponsored similar clubs in other U.S. communities as well as in many parts of the world; all came under the umbrella of Rotary International in 1912. The same pattern led to the organization of Kiwanis International and Lions International which date their origins, respectively, to 1915 and 1919. They, coincidentally, also grew out of clubs formed in Chicago. All three groups—there are, of course, many smaller, lesser-known ones—today have a total membership of about 2,300,000 in some 55,000 local clubs.

Up to the Great Depression of the 1930s, however, very little had been done to alter the patterns of care for the poor. Indeed, even in the early years of the Depression, there was still unshaken faith in the doctrine, virtually unchanged since colonial times, that the poor were a local rather than a federal government responsibility. If the poor needed more help than the local authorities could provide, this help should come from private charity efforts, said the exponents of rugged individualism. "Works of charity are the tests of spiritual development of men and women and communities," unctuously said President Herbert Hoover. Although he had made a reputation as a humanitarian feeding starving Belgians and Germans, Hoover in 1930 saw no anomaly in opposing an appropriation to feed starving American farmers while approving one to feed their livestock. Taunted at his lack of mercy, he suggested that if America meant anything it meant the principles of individual and local responsibility. "If we break down these principles," he said, "we have struck at the roots of self-government."

Under Franklin Delano Roosevelt's leadership, the government finally enacted legislation, including the landmark 1935 Social Security Act, which marked the beginnings of a federally supported welfare system to care for the aged, the handicapped, and dependent children and to protect workers against some of the hazards of age and unemployment. Again, cynics, not without justification, attributed the government's action not so much to humanitarianism as to expedience. What led government to proffer aid, suggested sociologists Frances Fox Piven and Richard A. Cloward, was the rising surge of political unrest that accompanied the economic catastrophe which saw upwards of 20 million people unemployed.

But whatever the motivation, the New Deal also saw the beginnings of increasing government support, particularly after World War II, of education, health, the fine arts, theater, music, and other areas which had traditionally been the primary responsibility of philanthropy. In 1929 government giving in the categories of health, education, and welfare amounted to 3.9 percent of our gross national product. By 1960 such expenditures had jumped to 10.6 percent and by 1976, the last year for which figures are available, had almost doubled to 20.6 percent, amounting to $331 billion, this constituting 73.1 percent of all public and private spending for "social welfare" purposes, as stated earlier.

Since even this government spending has been inadequate to assure all our citizens against want or satisfy our society's other needs, philanthropy has still continued to play an important role in American life over the years. Since 1929 contributions to philanthropy have increased from about $1 billion to more than $39 billion annually. What has also changed is that private charities no longer cater only to the poor and they are no longer supported only by the rich; indeed, in their concern for more than the basic wants of the past, and because of the fact that they use taxpayers' money, they have become the common concern of all citizens.

PART II

THE DONORS

Chapter 3

The People Who
Give—and Why

F. Emerson Andrews, who, with five decades of philanthropic work behind him, was the doyen of the field, liked to tell the story of a farm woman in the Great Smoky Mountains of Tennessee. During the Depression of the 1930s, when the government was making small allotments to impoverished farmers, a welfare agent approached the woman with the question: "If the government could allot you two hundred dollars, what would you do with it?" The woman thought a moment. Her cabin had no floor, its roof leaked, and light came through chinks in its walls. Her dress was tattered and she was thin and tired, for she worked from dawn to dusk to scratch survival from her two acres of land. Finally, she straightened up, leaned on her hoe, and said, "Reckon I'd give it to the poor."

More recently, Thomas Cannon, a 53-year-old, $16,000-a-year black postal worker in Richmond, Virginia, attracted nationwide headlines when it was revealed that he had somehow managed to give away $33,000 in five years. The money, usually in $1000 amounts, went to strangers whose misfortunes or good deeds Cannon had read about: a South American orphan who needed heart surgery; a couple who have been foster parents to 40 children; the widow of a policeman killed in a shootout; a former boxer who gives boxing lessons to street youngsters; a 14-year-old boy who was taunted by his schoolmates for returning $25 he found on a school bus. "The quest for money and acquisitions can be very self-destructive," explained Cannon who, in order to give away as much as he can, drives a battered 14-year-old Chevrolet and lives with his wife in a house with a leaky roof, dangerously obsolete wiring, and in desperate need of paint.

In America just about everyone, rich and poor, gives to charity, perhaps to a greater extent than any other people. With the announcement of a crisis, a cause, a tragedy, a person in need, Americans invariably tend to respond quickly, compassionately, generously. When world heavyweight champion Muhammad Ali heard that a New York day-care center for handicapped old people, most of them white, was about to be shut down for lack of funds, he pledged $100,000 to keep it going. When a 28-year-old New York carpenter was shot and killed while trying to subdue an armed robber who had wounded a police officer in a local hospital, people started a fund for the victim's six orphaned children (they had lost their mother in an auto accident a year earlier); less than two weeks after the shooting, gifts to the fund exceeded $100,000 and a year later they amounted to $435,000.

A Ronkonkoma, Long Island, church started a "Save a Home Fund" to help inflation-trapped parishioners who faced foreclosure on their mortgages. In Chicago a local organization raised more than $4600 to bring a 5-year-old girl from Greece and help pay for her open-heart surgery. People from all over the United States mailed money to pay for the dream Hawaii vacation of a 14-year-old dying cancer victim from Belleville, Illinois, and shortly after her return, to pay for her funeral. A Florida group calling itself the Broward County Marijuana Dealers Association contributed $2000 in $100, $50, and $20 bills to a fund to pay for the heart operation of a 6-year-old boy.

Contrary to what many may think, it is people, rather than foundations or big business, who account for the vast bulk of dollars that go to charitable causes. Of the $39.6 billion given to charity in 1978, $32.8 billion or 83 percent—more than four out of every five dollars—came from living individuals. Bequests were responsible for another $2.6 billion, or 6.6 percent of the charity dollar. This means that the contributions of people, living and dead, amounted to $35.4 billion, or nearly 90 percent of all U.S. giving.

Patterns of Giving

Who gives how much to whom and why? As one might expect, patterns of giving vary according to the giver's income and wealth, education, age, marital status, and other factors.

Not surprisingly, the rich give more than the poor. According to the latest available figures from the Internal Revenue Service, people give—or claim they give—an average of nearly 3 percent of their adjusted gross income, or an average of $685 annually. However, those in the $100,000-and-over income bracket give 5.5 percent of their adjusted earnings, or an average of $9901. Difficult as it may be to believe, the biggest category of givers, proportionately, according to the IRS, are families with incomes of $5000 to $6000, with average charitable contributions estimated at $428 annually, or 6.3 percent of income—an estimate that seems extraordinarily high for those well below the government's official poverty level. (For the average giving figures for other income brackets, see Chapter 27.)

However, since there are relatively few people in the upper-income brackets (only 2.6 percent of America's 57 million families have incomes of $50,000 or more), most of the total dollars given come from low- and middle-income earners: Those making between $10,000 and $50,000 contribute nearly three-quarters (72 percent) of the total, and under-$10,000-income families account for another 8 percent (according to IRS figures).

The amounts given, a study by the Commission on Private Philanthropy and Public Needs also showed, tend to increase with the education level of the giver: A college graduate, for example, gives six times as much as someone with an elementary school education. Even when allowing for such factors as the higher income that normally accompanies a higher education, the giving of college graduates is still three times that of those who have no more than an elementary school education. According to the study, the old give more than the young, not because older persons are necessarily more altruistic, but probably because they have fewer economic responsibilities and greater assets. Other findings showed married people to give more than single, small-town residents to give more than city dwellers, and religious people to give more than the nonreligious.

Although no extensive studies have ever been made of giving by occupational group, doctors are supposed to be notoriously poor givers, ostensibly—or so doctors rationalize—because they make up for their penuriousness by the free time they give to hospitals and voluntary health agencies. A possibly apocryphal story tells of a large, well-attended United Jewish Appeal fund-raising dinner at which a guest was stricken with a heart attack. The dinner chairman got up and asked if there was a doctor in the house. No one responded. However, a United Way of America survey once concluded that "physicians are not the worst" compared with other professions. The survey showed that while physicians give far less annually on a per capita basis ($62 on the average) to their local United Way than corporation executives ($88), they are still somewhat ahead of lawyers ($58) and dentists ($33). (But, the income of doctors is much higher, too.)

Athletes and entertainers are probably more generous than other professional people. In addition to that $100,000 contribution mentioned earlier, Muhammad Ali is also said to give better than 50 percent of his earnings to his Muslim church. Golfers Jack Nicklaus and Gary Player have contributed $25,000 winning purses to charity, and Minnesota Vikings quarterback Fran Tarkenton once made a gift of his Super Bowl share of $7500 to programs to assist retarded children and drug addicts. Singer Paul Anka, on opening a ten-performance engagement at New York's Palace Theater, announced that he would turn over his fee for each performance to a different charity. And he and other stars donate literally millions of dollars of their services every year appearing at benefits for various causes. (Comedian Alan King estimates he receives between 55 and 60 requests a year to appear at charity functions.) Songwriter Irving Berlin has turned over all of the royalties from "God Bless America"—since 1940, $675,000—and several other patriotic songs to the Boy Scouts and Girl Scouts.

There are also certain patterns in terms of where the money goes. Lower-income people tend to concentrate their charitable giving on their church and other religious groups as well as on community drives of one sort or another, whereas the wealthy are more apt to give to hospitals, colleges, and cultural institutions such as museums, symphony orchestras, opera groups, and ballet companies. However, with the expansion of symphony audiences and museum programs in recent years, the small, less affluent donor has been playing an increasingly larger role in the support of the arts.

The Big Givers

Although John D. Rockefeller (1839–1937) is largely remembered as the wrinkled, bony nonagenarian who handed out dimes to strangers (he started with nickels but found them too heavy), he, as mentioned earlier, gave away a total of $531 million ($750 million according to the *Guinness Book of World Records*) during the course of his lifetime—more than any other man in history. In his era, he was rivaled as a big giver only by his son John D. Rockefeller, Jr., whose total lifetime giving came to $473 million and by Andrew Carnegie who gave away a fortune estimated at $351 million. While such grandiose giving by individuals is now a thing of the past, particularly since foundations have become a funnel for the funds of the rich, large-scale personal philanthropy still exists. Who are the big givers of today? The Rockefellers still are. When he was awaiting confirmation as vice-president in 1974, Nelson Rockefeller, a son of John D., Jr., disclosed that he had personally given $24.7 million to charity over the preceding 17-year period, this apart from the multimillions dispensed to philanthropic causes by the half a dozen or so Rockefeller family foundations. The late Nelson's brothers (the late John D. III, David, and Laurance) also contributed millions of their own money to an array of charitable causes ranging from cancer research and population control to conservation and art; and the gifts of all the Rockefellers, personally and through their charitable trusts, to New York's Lincoln Center alone have so far totaled over $30 million.

In recent times the Rockefellers have probably been rivaled only by the Mellons as big givers. Andrew Mellon (1855–1937), whose financial expertise made him one of the richest men in America in the early 1920s, was also one of the nation's foremost art collectors. In 1937 he gave his fabled collection (valued at $25 million), including 23 Rembrandts, six Vermeers, and a Raphael, to the U.S. government; he also donated $15 million to build the National Gallery of Art in Washington, D.C., in which to house the collection. His son Paul, now 72 and reputedly one of the five richest Americans, has continued the family's interest in philanthropy and the fine arts. (With no taste for finance, he prefers to list himself in Who's Who as an "art gallery executive.") Between 1966 and 1968 he laid out $18 million to build, equip, and maintain the Yale Center for British Art and paid for everything in it—a collection of paintings, drawings, and other works of art now valued at well over $100 million. Most of the $95 million cost of the National Gallery's spectacular new East Building was furnished by Mellon, his late sister, and the Mellon Foundation. Since World War II he, members of his family, and their foundations have contributed a total of at least $800 million to universities, art museums, historical societies, wildlife sanctuaries, and mental health programs.

In 1973 mining magnate Joseph H. Hirshhorn donated to the Smithsonian Institution his $100 million collection of sculpture and paintings (now housed in the Hirshhorn Museum in the nation's capital). This, with the possible exception of Paul Mellon's Yale gift, is perhaps the largest single gift ever made by a living American. However, the $50 million given to the University of Richmond in 1969 by pharmaceutical manufacturer E. Claiborne Robins is believed to be, as mentioned earlier, the largest cash gift ever given to a *private* institution by a person during his lifetime.

Other present-day big givers include H. Ross Perot, the Texas computer magnate, who made the nation's front pages in the early 1970s by offering $100 million for the release of American prisoners of war in Vietnam (his less-publicized benefactions have been for schools and scouting activities in ghetto areas); Ray A. Kroc, founder of the McDonald's hamburger chain, who marked his seventieth birthday in 1972 by donating a total of $7.5 million to St. Jude's Research Hospital and other health charities; Mary Lasker, who has given untold millions to advance the cause of medical research and, even more important, has prodded the federal government into appropriating billions more; and W. Clement Stone, the conservative Chicago insurance tycoon, who, although perhaps best known as the biggest single contributor to Richard Nixon's 1972 reelection campaign, has given more than $25 million to a mind-boggling array of causes ranging from youth groups, music camps, and street gangs (one, after receiving a Stone handout, changed its name from the Vice Lords to the Conservative Vice Lords) to health and religious organizations and rehabilitation programs for drug addicts and prisoners.

Stone is also an inventive fund raiser. A fellow Chicagoan recalls a luncheon Stone organized to raise funds for the rehabilitation of prisoners. "It was held in a prison cell with ten businessmen at each table. Halfway through the meal, Stone got up and dramatically announced that some of the 'businessmen' at each table were prisoners. For a while, there was quite a hush. But after some nervous laughter, the real businessmen coughed up quite a bit of money."

Then there is the young bachelor who lists himself in the Manhattan phone book as "Stewart R. Mott, philanthropist." The heir to a great General Motors fortune—his father, Charles Stewart Mott, who died in his nineties in 1973, was for years the company's largest stockholder—Mott is the most celebrated of the liberal angels. He contributed $350,000, more than anyone else, to George McGovern's 1972 presidential campaign and gave hundreds of thousands of dollars more to dozens of other candidates of liberal persuasion. (Ironically, his father was a conservative Republican.) During a recent ten-year period, he also donated $4.3 million to such causes as abortion law reform, arms control, research into human sexual response, renaissance music, America's exodus from Vietnam, extrasensory perception, "hippie-oriented urban service," and the impeachment of Richard Nixon. His donations of all kinds are now said to amount to nearly $1 million annually.

William Black, who founded the Chock Full o' Nuts restaurant chain, has by his own estimate given somewhere between $10 million and $12 million to Columbia's medical center, Lenox Hill Hospital, and Mount Sinai Hospital in New York. These, however, represent only a few of his philanthropies. Even a bigger giver is Walter H. Annenberg, the wealthy publisher (*TV Guide, Seventeen Magazine, Morning Telegraph, Racing Form,* and assorted radio and television properties) who served as Nixon's ambassador to the Court of St. James. Recent benefactions of Annenberg and his family include $12 million toward the cost of the $117 million Annenberg Building of New York's Mount Sinai Medical Center (1974), $3 million for a University of Pennsylvania art center (1971), and $8 million to the University of California.*

Although they are by no means familiar philanthropic names in the sense that the Rockefellers, Mellons, and Carnegies are, other big givers, according to the annual compilations of the American Association of Fund-Raising Counsel, are: Mrs. DeWitt Wallace, cofounder of *Reader's Digest,* whose charitable contributions include $5 million to the Juilliard School of Music; Conrad Hilton, the late hotel magnate, who gave $10 million to the Mayo Foundation; R. Brinkley Smithers, a former alcoholic, who provided $10 million to support the Smithers

*Although Annenberg usually receives personal credit for his gifts, many are made through the family's Annenberg Foundation. The gifts of other big givers are also made through their foundations, for reasons we'll go into in the following chapter.

Alcoholism Center and Rehabilitation Center of New York's Roosevelt Hospital; and Mrs. Charles S. Payson, whose recent benefactions have included a $5 million donation to New York's Metropolitan Museum of Art.

In a class by themselves are the big Jewish givers. At a United Jewish Appeal-Federation dinner some years ago I heard the industrialist Meshulam Riklis pledge $5 million almost as casually as if he were placing a $10 bet in Las Vegas; his annual contributions to the organization have for years reputedly run into seven figures. Samuel Bronfman, founder of the Seagram liquor empire, who died in 1971, also gave a minimum of $1 million a year, largely to Jewish causes. The Pritzkers, a Chicago family whose diverse concerns include *McCall's* magazine, the Hyatt Hotel chain, and scores of other enterprises engaged in manufacturing, steel, lumber, and real estate, give heavily to numerous Jewish and civic causes. In 1968 they gave $12 million to the University of Chicago, whose medical school now bears the Pritzker name. Other leading Jewish givers (to mention only a few) include Max Fisher, a prominent Detroit industrialist, William Rosenwald of the Sears Roebuck family, and the already-mentioned Annenbergs.

Bequests

Harry Golden once pointed out that one of the chief differences between Jewish and Gentile giving is that the Jew will give while he lives whereas the Gentile gives when he dies. Among Jews this distinction is summed up in the expression, "It's nice to smell the flowers when you're living." That giving during one's lifetime is more praiseworthy than posthumous giving is also set forth in the Old Testament: "In the hour of man's departure, neither silver nor gold nor precious stones nor pearls accompany him, but only Torah and good deeds." Not that this is a uniquely Jewish concept. Francis Bacon also declared that one should "defer not charities till death for certainly, if a man weigh it rightly, he that doth so is rather liberal of another man's than his own." And a beautiful seventeenth-century Quaker prayer makes a similar point: "I expect to pass through this world but once. Any good therefore I can do, or any kindness I can do to my fellow creatures, let me do it now. Let me not defer or neglect it, for I shall not pass this way again."

Nonetheless, posthumous gifts, or bequests, play an important part in America's philanthropic picture. While, as already mentioned, they account for only 6.6 percent of total giving, they represent a significant source of income for health agencies, museums, colleges, universities, and other educational, scientific, and cultural institutions. Arnaud C. Marts, one of America's great fund raisers, once estimated that 90 percent of the endowments of all our philanthropic institutions have come through bequests. Recent examples of big bequests include: $50 million from the estate of Mrs. Helen Bonfils to the Denver Center of Performing Arts; $85 million from Mrs. Geraldine Rockefeller Dodge to the foundation bearing her name plus another $2.85 million from her estate to St. Hubert's Giralda, an animal shelter; $67 million from Henry R. Luce to a miscellany of charities; $22 million from Joseph C. Wilson to the University of Rochester; and $20 million from Mrs. John D. Rockefeller, Jr., to New York's Lincoln Center for the Performing Arts, Metropolitan Museum of Art, and the Martha B. Rockefeller Fund for Music. Probably the biggest single bequest in the history of philanthropy was the approximately $1 billion worth of Johnson & Johnson stock bequeathed to the Robert Wood Johnson Foundation by the estate of Robert Wood Johnson in 1971.

Not all bequests are necessarily by big philanthropic names such as those just mentioned. In 1974 Raymond A. Schulein, a reclusive Chicago insurance agent who lived frugally all his life, left $4 million in stocks to 14 charities; he had acquired his small fortune through careful investments. Nor are all bequests reported in the newspapers extraordinarily large ones. Typical of the newspaper accounts one is likely to see from time to time is that of Andrew John Peldich, a Yugoslavia-born pump repairman at the Aluminum Company of America's East St. Louis plant, who, in 1974, bequeathed his estate of $50,000 to the Alcoa Foundation. In 1976 Maria Catherine Douglas, a slave's daughter who had worked as a domestic in Boston until she was 90, willed her entire life savings of $10,000 to the United Negro College Fund.

Why People Give

Why do people give to charity? Why do they give to certain charities and not to others? What do their giving habits tell about them? How do people really *feel* about giving?

Much has been written and endless studies have been made in the pursuit of answers to such questions, often with dubious conclusions. Several years ago, for instance, Save the Children Federation, wanting to know if it was using the right "media and message strategy" in soliciting contributions and "sponsors" for the waifs under its wing, hired the market research company of Daniel Yankelovich to conduct a survey. Among other things, the survey found that there are three basic reasons people give—or, at least, say they give—to charity. The great majority—about 60 percent—of the people polled said they give out of a sense of moral obligation; slightly more than a third (35 percent) said their motivation is the personal satisfaction of helping others; and a handful (2 percent) said they give to assuage the guilt they would have if they didn't give.

While professing a preference for charities which are not "chauvinistic"—that is, those that aid children all over the world—the survey's respondents, upon further questioning, stated by an overwhelming majority that their first loyalty was to America's needy children, Indians and Appalachians in that order. Only one out of every ten or so (12 percent) said they would prefer to help foreign children.

Should one take such findings seriously? Apparently the Save the Children Federation did not. For its favorite and presumably most successful advertising solicitations continued to be blatant appeals to guilt. A frequently run series featured a large photo of a wretched foreign (*not* American) child looking at us with inexpressibly sad eyes and the slogan: "You Can Help Save [name of child] for $15 [now $16] A Month. Or You Can Turn The Page." Moral obligation? Personal satisfaction? Hardly likely. It indeed takes a staunch soul not to feel a pang of guilt after turning the page.* Charity's mail-order mendicants, who send out unordered "gifts," know that many people will feel guilty if they keep the

*Christian Children's Fund, another of the many "sponsor-a-child" organizations, also knows the pulling power of an appeal to guilt. A recent ad featured the bold headline "READ THIS AND CRY" over the photos of two foreign children and copy devoted to tearful tales of woe about them.

items without sending a donation when, in fact, they don't have to acknowledge, return, or pay for such gifts.

"What makes you like to give?" asked the compilers of another survey, this one directed at Jewish givers. Again, most people said they gave because of an obligation to help the needy. However, when asked why *others* gave, they said the main motivating factors were the desire for social status, prestige, respect, and acclaim, and the pressures of all kinds which made it difficult to refuse to give.

Ask the psychologists and psychoanalysts why people give and you get still other answers. "When we give, we play God," says Dr. Ernest Dichter, Madison Avenue's Viennese-born dean of motivational psychologists. (His research findings inspired Esso's "Put A Tiger In Your Tank" campaign and the ads in which autos were sold as sex symbols.) Giving, he maintains, not only proves one's ability to make and therefore give money but it also is proof "of one's prowess, one's virility, one's capacity as a mighty hunter." At least this is what Dichter once told the United Way's fund-raising experts. On other occasions, however, Dichter, a bouncy, balding, ebullient man in his early seventies, is given to spouting different, equally dogmatic aphorisms like, "We give in order to be loved." In still another vein, Dichter will say that giving (or not giving) is somehow a product of our toilet-training habits: Good training habits are likely to give rise to a generous person, while habits developed through stresses and strains—through strict and punitive procedures, for example—are apt to produce an adult who is miserly, thrifty, parsimonious, and meticulous about money.

"Simplistic bullshit!" exploded one eminent psychiatrist when asked to comment on the views of Dichter who, like other popularizers with a talent for turning dogmas into dollars, does not have the approbation of most of his Freudian fellows. "I am appalled by Dichter's simplistic values for giving and not giving. The motive of playing God, for example, may apply to a certain percentage of people under certain circumstances, but other factors must come into play."

It is likely that no person ever gives for just one reason. An attitudinal survey by Robert H. Lewis, executive director emeritus of the Fresh Air Fund of New York, turned up no less than 110 different reasons for giving. Ranked by descending order of recorded frequency of mention, they ranged, in a so-called "subjective" category, from sense of responsibility, compassion, personal identification, and self-interest down to religious influence, guilt feelings, the need to be needed, and the substitution of giving for active participation in good works. Grouped in an "objective" category were various external factors actually triggering the act of giving: the mission and performance of the charitable organization, one's personal relationship to it, the organization's approach to prospective donors (its use of pressure, for example), and—mentioned, usually apologetically, by a fraction of the respondents—the tax benefits to be derived from the donation. The motivations that may apply to one person may not apply to another, or even to the same person at different times. And as Lewis acknowledged, "People themselves are often unsure about their own motivation for some of the things they do."

Giving, for one thing, reflects patterns of family life. One study, for example, showed that children of the poor tend to be less selfish than children of the rich,

also that children from larger families, which necessarily experience more sharing, are likely to be more generous than those from smaller families. Two-thirds
of those once surveyed for United Jewish Appeal also agreed that cultural and
family traditions are an important factor in giving. "I give because I was brought
up that way," says Harry Cantor, the proprietor of a prospering Long Island floor
covering and window supply firm. "I was told that if you have a nickel you share
it. Even during the Depression when we had almost nothing, if my father learned
of someone in need, he would bring him to our house, feed and clothe him, even
give him a bed, and then go around to our neighbors to collect a dollar or two
here and there so that he could give the person maybe $25 when he was ready to
go on his way." And philanthropist Laurance Rockefeller, the grandson of John
D., told me: "We were all brought up to give. My grandfather started it, my
father continued it, and we did it, too. As children, we all gave a certain
percentage of our allowance to what we called 'Benevolence,' which was one of
the headings in the account books we kept."

Since religion is an integral part of family life, it inevitably also plays a key
role in the development of attitudes toward giving, as noted in the previous
chapter. John D. Rockefeller, you may recall, felt that he was only giving away
money God had placed in his trust (he even called his fortune "God's gold"), in
keeping with the long Judeo-Christian tradition of loving one's neighbor as
oneself and belief that money belongs to God and must be shared with His
children. "The Christian," said Martin Luther, "gives not out of duty or guilt,
but out of love and gratitude to God for what He has done for him, in Creation
and in Jesus Christ." Jews, however, supposedly give principally out of a sense
of duty, a moral and religious obligation to act justly and generously to help
one's fellowman. In my growing-up years, every Jewish child was told and
taught early in life that it was a duty to give to the needy; and every Jewish home
contained *pushkes*—little metal containers, each provided by a particular charity,
into which coins were dropped, usually every Friday night before the Sabbath
candles were lit. Leo Rosten, in *The Joys of Yiddish,* recalls that those set out on
a shelf in his family's kitchen bore labels that read like a catalog of human
misery—and benevolence: For Orphans; For Widows; For Victims of Persecu-
tion; For the Blind; For the Lame; For Men Maimed While Returning From
Religious Services; For Meetings to Protest Pogroms in the Ukraine; For the
Hebrew Home for the Aged; For the Jewish Chicken Raisers in Kankakee Recently Bankrupted by the Ravages of Red Tick Among Rhode Island Roosters.
And so on.

Some Christians, as well as a handful of Jews, even continue to practice the
ancient custom of tithing—giving a certain percentage of their income to charity.
However, as also noted in the previous chapter, other than purely spiritual or
humanitarian considerations may be involved in this and other forms of religious
giving. No doubt, there are many who give to their church as a means of paving
the way for future favors from the Almighty, making premium payments on good
"hereafter" insurance. After Andrew Mellon had contributed a large sum to his
congregation toward the cost of building a new church, some cynics referred to
the edifice as "Andy Mellon's fire escape." During the ten-day period before
Yom Kippur, the most sacred day on the Jewish calendar, when the Book of
Judgment is sealed fixing the destinies of every human being for the coming

year, Jews may avert any evil decree by practicing three things: prayer, penitence, and charity.

Are the prayerful, the penitent, and the charitable perhaps more concerned with saving their own skins and souls? Or does the impulse to give have psychological roots that reach deep into all sorts of dark, Delphian dungeons of the subconscious? On the one hand, we have Richard Titmuss saying in his book, *The Gift Relationship,* that there is a "biological need to help . . . giving life, or prolonging life, or enriching life for anonymous others." But self-interest, if not self-love, has been suggested as the motivating force of giving by a long string of other philosophers. The Dutch Bernard Mandeville once wrote, "Charity is that Virtue by which part of that sincere love we have for ourselves is transferr'd pure and unmixed to other" and he maintained that at the bottom of every virtue is some form of selfishness.

Herbert Spencer analyzed altruism as nine parts self-interest gilt over with one part of philanthropy. Others have wondered if altruism really exists at all. Anna Freud once stated: "It remains an open question whether there is such a thing as a genuinely altruistic reaction to one's fellow-man, in which the gratification of one's own instinct plays no part at all, even in some displaced and sublimated form." Even our friend Dichter defines altruism as "a form of self-appreciation." "When you give, you're really saying, 'Am I not a wonderful person?'" he told an NBC-TV interviewer.

Of course, equating altruism with egoism (that eminent student of behavior Hans Selye even spoke of "egocentric altruism") leads us to a sort of *reductio ad absurdum*: By this process of logic, a person would risk his life saving someone from drowning in order to feel good about himself or, perhaps, to avoid guilt feelings. Yet we have the testimony of Will Kellogg, the "King of Cornflakes," who protested that the millions he gave away involved no sacrifice: "I love to do things for children because I get a kick out of it. Therefore, I am a selfish person and no philanthropist." Similarly, there is also Harry Cantor, mentioned earlier, whose generosity is so ingrained as part of his identity that he actually gets upset when he hears of a local charity to which he hadn't been asked to contribute. "I call up and say, 'How come you missed me? I'm insulted that you didn't ask me for a donation.'" Dropping a dime in a blind beggar's cup involves some kind of *quid pro quo* according to economist Kenneth E. Boulding. We give in this case, says Boulding, because the blind man gives us something. "We feel a certain glow of emotional virtue, and it is that we receive for our dime. Looked at from the point of view of the recipient, we might suppose that the blind man gives out a commodity or service which consists in being pitiable." Or as a manual on the techniques of fund raising crassly puts it: "A donation can be viewed as a transaction between donor and charity which takes place because each party feels he is receiving more than he gives up."

If we accept the theory that people give because they get something in return, it is easy to understand how giving can be sparked by gratitude—for example, to repay a debt people feel they owe to their alma mater, a hospital, or other institution. Pharmaceutical manufacturer Elmer H. Bobst, in explaining his $11 million gift that made possible New York University's new library, recalled his youthful studies with books borrowed from local libraries and said, "I am paying off a lifelong debt to libraries." The great rabbi Stephen Wise liked to tell the story of the time an ailing member of his well-known Free Synagogue was about to undergo an operation. When the rabbi visited his congregant in the hospital, the sick man pleaded, "Rabbi, pray for me and if I come out of this alive I'll give $25,000 to the synagogue." Several months later Rabbi Wise phoned the man, now fully recovered, and reminded him of his promise. "I pledged $25,000 to the synagogue?" said the congregant. "I remember no such thing." "Yes, you did," persisted the rabbi. "If I pledged $25,000 to the synagogue," said the congregant, "I must have been very sick."

Some psychologists would also interpret altruism as a way of assuaging guilt feelings, something exploited by fund raisers who know that the best time to solicit memorial or other gifts from people is as soon as possible after the loss of their loved ones. This is also seen in the case of the pastor who praised a young woman of his congregation for what seemed to be a very generous gift. "It is so insignificant," she responded. "You see, I have so many sins to pay for." More than ironic coincidence prompted Swedish munitions merchant Alfred Nobel (1833–1896) to provide in his will for the establishment of the Peace Prize and other international awards bearing his name. Evidently, they were his way of atoning to society for the destruction caused by his invention and sale of dynamite and smokeless gunpowder; on a more personal level, he apparently was also deeply troubled by the fact that shortly after he began the production of his explosives his factory blew up, killing his youngest brother. (His father also suffered a stroke as a result.)

Status, snob appeal, the desire for self-esteem, and social prestige also play a part in giving, as in most other human activities, this explaining the popularity of charity balls, fashion shows, and other public fund-raising functions. Our values, beliefs, interests, hopes, fears, and other feelings and habits not only motivate us to give but also determine to which causes we give. Professional fund raisers know, for example, that people who are energetic or aggressive by nature are likely to make donations expressing anger, which finds an outlet in causes ranging from the John Birch Society to the various Ralph Nader groups. Fear, on the other hand, is at the basis of much of the giving to the health charities and many other organizations. We give to cancer or heart research to buy possible protection for ourselves and our loved ones against these dread diseases, just as we give to our local volunteer fire department or ambulance corps to make sure that its services will be available to us in time of need. (Of course, gratitude for services rendered is another motivating factor in such giving.) As San Francisco's Institute for Fund-Raising suggests, many of the evangelistic religious organizations know they can loosen the purse strings of people, particularly the poor and less educated, by fanning fears of "hellfire and damnation," while the population control groups (Planned Parenthood, Zero Population Growth) appeal to the more sophisticated who fear overpopulation. During periods of ghetto rioting, fear, as much as compassion, accounts for much of the giving to groups dedicated to improving the lot of the blacks and other minority groups. (In recent years, it has also been considered chic to give to radical causes.) A similar motive lies behind the giving to many of the conservative political and quasi-political causes which seek to maintain the status quo.

As one would expect, the need to express love finds an outlet in Save the Children Federation and similar organizations, which draw their principal support from lonely, elderly persons who live alone, childless couples, and those afflicted with the "empty nest syndrome"—parents whose children have grown and left home. Not surprisingly, the SCF survey showed most of its current sponsors and contributors to be fifty and over; only 21 percent were found to be under thirty. Many, according to Ruth Malone in an article on the "Buy-a-Baby Market," are often widows, with some independent income, who want once again to feed, clothe, and bathe a helpless child, but with "hygienic freedom," that is, with only the inconvenience of sending a few dollars to some distant land.

Which brings us to the question of why Americans, reluctant though they may be to admit it, are more likely to reach across the oceans to help "save" children with names like Doan Thi Yen, Serita Remini, and Maria Almanazar (to cull a few from the Save the Children Federation appeals) rather than children from our own Appalachia, Indian country, or ghettos. As we shall see in Chapter 7, America's Jews are also more generous in their giving to Jews in Israel, Russia, and elsewhere abroad than they are to their many impoverished Jewish countrymen here—America's "invisible Jews" as they are called with good reason. How account for this?

Dr. Alfred Siegman, a prominent New York psychiatrist, suggests that the answer may lie in the fact that we Americans feel uncomfortable about the disadvantaged in our midst. "We want to deny that such things exist in our idealized society," he says. "So not giving is one way of denying these things." The readiness of Americans to "Save Venice," which for years has been slowly sinking inexorably into the sea, or to contribute to a multitude of other foreign cultural causes (as I write this, I am reading of a drive for contributions by Americans to save England's decaying Canterbury Cathedral) while turning their backs on other worthy cultural causes here at home suggests there is a certain cachet, or snob appeal, attached to identifying with foreign causes, just as there is in buying foreign fashions, wines, cars, and so on. By the same token, people are reticent about identifying with certain causes—venereal disease, unwed mothers, mental illness, and epilepsy, for example. Contributing to or working with such causes is not likely to build one's esteem.

Of course, all sorts of other subtle psychological factors may lead people to discriminate among charities. Why, for instance, are people more receptive to helping the blind than the deaf, although the latter are far more numerous? Perhaps because all of us are more fearful of being blind—something that may have deep oedipal roots—whereas deafness is often thought of as a minor aberration that could be overcome if the afflicted only tried a little harder. ("Are you deaf?" we are prone to ask irritably when we feel people aren't listening.) "Mental illness, apart from its stigma, is a disease that most people think of as incurable, at least for the foreseeable future," says Dr. Alfred Siegman. "People like to donate to causes, such as cancer research, which hold out hopes for a cure."

In terms of self-interest, there can be no question that tax considerations are also a factor in giving, although except for the very rich they may not have the overriding importance some people believe. Obviously, no matter what his tax savings, a person would still have more money in pocket if he gave nothing at all. "I don't know of anybody who has made a gift just to get a tax deduction," says Hayden W. Smith, an official of the Council for Financial Aid to Education, "because it almost always ends up costing them something." "Say what you will about the motives or morals of an Andrew Carnegie or John D. Rockefeller," says a university development officer, "but they were making enormous gifts at a time when all the money was coming out of their own pockets." (Tax deductions were not allowed for charitable gifts until 1917.)

If taxes have any impact, it is not so much on the decision of whether to give or not to give but rather on the amount people decide to give. A 1969 study showed that only 4 percent of a group of big givers (with a median annual income averaging $375,000 over a five-year period) said they would continue to give the same amount if there were no tax benefits. After all, most of what wealthy donors give does not come out of their own pockets. For instance, a person in the 70 percent bracket who gives $100 sacrifices just 30 percent of his own money; the remaining 70 percent would otherwise go to the government.

Whatever the inner motives that prompt people to give, it is unlikely that they would give so readily, at least to the extent they do, if they were not subjected to external pressures of one sort or another—the passing of a collection plate in a church or theater; the personal appeal of a friend, neighbor, or business associate; buttonholing by a street solicitor; or whatever. At an annual meeting of the National Conference of Philanthropy, Leo Brennan, vice-chairman of the Ford Motor Company's contributions committee, told the delicious story of the time John D. Rockefeller and his wife were touring Ireland. A priest approached Mrs. Rockefeller and induced her to persuade her husband to give $5000 to the Saint Thomas Asylum for Wayward Boys of which he, the priest, was the superintendent. The next day, Rockefeller, on opening his newspaper, was amazed to see the glaring headline, "Rockefeller Gives $50,000 to Saint Thomas Home." Livid with rage, Rockefeller summoned the priest and gave him a tongue-lashing the likes of which he had never had before. However, Rockefeller saw that it would be awkward for him to recant the gift for which he was now being commended in headlines and editorials throughout the world. He therefore decided to strike a deal with the priest to whom he said: "All right, I will give you the extra $45,000 if you let me do just one thing. When your new building is completed, I want you to let me write the inscription that will go above its entrance." The priest agreed, sighing with relief that he had been let off so easily. Time passed. At the building's dedication ceremonies, everyone's curiosity was at a fever pitch as the time approached for the removal of the drape covering the inscription. When Rockefeller finally stepped forward and pulled the string for the unveiling, the inscription was seen to read: "I was hungry and you fed me. I was naked and you clothed me. I came as a stranger and you took me."

However, perhaps we should not look too closely into why people give; perhaps instead we should applaud the fact that they give at all, whatever their reasons. As George Kirstein has noted, "History demonstrates that people frequently perform good deeds for the most contemptible reasons, while others with the noblest impulses create misery." And to those who view all giving with cynicism, we should point out that Dr. Karl Menninger, the dean of American psychiatrists, says unequivocally that to be able to give is indicative of mental health. "Generous people are rarely mentally ill people," he says, also offering the opinion that stinginess is a sign of neurosis.

Memorials: Posterity for a Price

Whatever the main motive, giving reaches an apotheosis of sorts in the long-established custom of memorialization—the attaching of names of big givers to things which, depending on the generosity of the giver, can range from an entire college, medical center, and cultural complex down to the component parts thereof; these, in turn, can range from a building down to a room, laboratory, hospital bed, stained glass window, pew, tree, each appropriately labeled or adorned with a plaque to commemorate the name of the donor or of a family member or friend.

The application of private philanthropy to memorialization is believed to have originated in England. For example, Oxford's Pembroke College, which dates from 1347, owes its origin to Mary de Saint Paul, who is celebrated in English history as "maid, wife and widow in a single day" because her husband, the Earl of Pembroke, was felled in a tournament only a few hours after their nuptials. However, memorialization has now become largely an American phenomenon. Perhaps the best-known early example of its occurrence here is in connection with a college of the Massachusetts Bay Colony—the first in the New World—which, after leading a brief, precarious existence as New Towne and then Cambridge, was in 1638 bequeathed half the estate and the 320-volume library of one John Harvard, and promptly renamed in honor of its benefactor.

According to a tally once made by Arnaud C. Marts, a leading fund raiser and former college president, no fewer than 165 American colleges and 450 of our hospitals bear the names of people whose generosity either helped found them or made their continued existence possible. In addition to Harvard, the colleges include: Yale, named after Elihu Yale (hence, the nickname, Elis, applied to the school's athletes); Brown, which was Rhode Island College until 1805, when Nicholas Brown bestowed upon it a gift of $5000; Duke, originally Trinity College, a struggling, little North Carolina Methodist school which also changed its name as a condition of the support rendered it by James Buchanan Duke of the tobacco family; Smith, the result of a $300,000 donation by Sophia Smith for the founding of a woman's college; Johns Hopkins, a memorial to a Baltimore gentleman of that name; and Bucknell, known as the University of Lewisburg until the generosity of William Bucknell led to its name change. Others named after benefactors are: (Paul) Tulane; (Matthew) Vassar; (Cornelius) Vanderbilt; (Leland) Stanford; (Ezra) Cornell.

Some audacious academies of learning have even changed their names to that of a prospective rich angel in anticipation of a possible benefaction, one example being the Nassau branch of Long Island University which in 1955 tranformed itself into the C. W. Post College after purchasing the estate of the late owner of Post Toasties. Mr. Post's daughter, Mrs. Marjorie Merriweather Post, was impressed enough to bestow gifts upon the college totaling nearly $2 million during the next decade.* In 1967 Colorado Women's College in Denver changed its name to Temple Buell College when a wealthy real estate developer of that name

---

*Mrs. Post, who until her death in 1973 at 86 reigned as the *grande dame* of American high society, was legendary for her many other philanthropies. During World War I she built and supported a 2000-bed field hospital in France. During the Depression she put her jewels (later given to the Smithsonian) into a vault, canceled their insurance, and used the money saved to finance a New

said he would leave the school $25 million in his will with the understanding that he be buried on its campus. The problem was that Mr. Buell continued to remain in the very best of health and other contributions dwindled to nothing because people mistakenly believed that the school was already receiving all the money it needed from Buell or, confused by its new name, thought of it as a religious institution. As a result of this confusion, the school in 1973 resumed its former name, whereupon Buell, then a vigorous septuagenarian, withdrew his bequest.

Hospitals across the land that bear the names of benefactors include the Payne Whitney Clinic at the New York Hospital-Cornell Medical Center, the new $117 million Annenberg Building of New York's Mount Sinai Medical Center—the largest structure in the country combining hospital and medical school facilities, Lankenau Hospital in Philadelphia, Barnes Hospital in St. Louis, the Baker Memorial Hospital and Collis P. Huntington Hospital in Boston, and the Scripps Memorial Hospital in La Jolla, California, to mention only a few. Some 4000 of the nation's libraries are named for donors, nearly 3000 of them for one man, Andrew Carnegie.

Also serving as individual or family memorials are literally thousands of other types of philanthropic institutions, such as the J. Paul Getty Museum of Art in Malibu, California, the Hirshhorn Museum in Washington, D.C., the Dorothy Chandler Pavilion at the Los Angeles Music Center, the Elmer Holmes Bobst Library at New York University, and the Hershey Industrial Institution in Hershey, Pennsylvania, which owes its origin to a gift of $60 million in money and property from the Hershey chocolate family. When Avery Fisher, the pioneer hi-fi manufacturer donated close to $10 million in the early 1970s to the deficit-ridden New York Philharmonic, the name of its home was changed from Philharmonic Hall to Avery Fisher Hall, which became the fourth Lincoln Center building to be named for a benefactor (Alice Tully Hall and the Vivian Beaumont and Mitzi E. Newhouse Theaters are the others). However, the greatest benefactor of all has preferred virtual anonymity: Only a bronze plaque honors John D. Rockefeller III, whose $20 million seed money turned the Lincoln Center idea into reality.

The names of the buildings at Harvard University alone read like a Who's Who in Philanthropy: Widener Library, Houghton Library, Loeb Theater, Harkness Commons, Kresge Hall, Lamont Library, Lehman Hall, Mellon Hall, Morgan Hall, Straus Hall. But, the cost of having one's name affixed to a building, let alone a whole college or other complex, comes rather high. In a booklet prepared several years ago by the New York University Medical Center for prospective donors, among the "naming gift opportunities" listed was a still anonymous medical science building which called for a contribution of $5 million. In a similar fund-raising Lehigh University booklet, the price tag on an unnamed classroom building was a more modest $1 million (payable in three annual installments). Ordinarily, the donor is expected to put up at least half the cost of a building for the privilege of naming it; otherwise, the general rule is that the

---

York Salvation Army kitchen that fed 1000 people daily. She donated the cost of the Boy Scouts of America headquarters in Washington, gave well over $1 million to the Washington National Symphony Orchestra, and gave $100,000 to the cultural center in Washington that was later to blossom into the John F. Kennedy Center for the Performing Arts.

largest contributor gets his name on the building if his donation is fairly substantial. Even though Homer C. Holland, a New York investment counselor and banker, put up only $465,000 of the $2,500,000 necessary for the construction of a student union building at Dickinson College (the federal government contributed most of the rest), the college named the building for him. Similarly, the Annenberg family contributed only about $12 million toward the cost of the $117 million Annenberg Building of New York's Mount Sinai Medical Center.

However, posterity at a price is also available to less affluent donors. The New York University Medical Center brochure also offered varying degrees of immortality through such bargains as laboratories, treatment rooms, and even a study carrel in the $50,000 to $5000 range; and Lehigh's "opportunities" ranged from department chairs ($750,000), distinguished professorships ($100,000), indoor track and playing fields ($200,000) and auditoriums ($150,000 to $75,000) down to classrooms ($65,000 to $30,000), locker rooms ($25,000), staff lounges ($15,000), stadium ticket windows ($10,000), and chromatography rooms ($5000). At some colleges, I've been facetiously told, posterity is possible even in the john, with lavatories or the bathroom fittings honoring the name of someone or other; for all I know this may be true.

However, for various reasons, some big givers prefer to keep their names off many of their benefactions. There are, as just mentioned, the Rockefellers, whose name adorns no building in Lincoln Center in spite of their huge gifts to the cultural complex. And the only clue to the donor responsible for the establishment of the University of Chicago are the words on its seal: "Founded by John D. Rockefeller." Although Andrew Mellon paid the entire cost of building the National Gallery of Art and bequeathed his superb collection of old masters to it, he declined to have his name attached to it, and only a small plaque commemorates his benefaction. By way of explanation, Tom Buckley said in *The New York Times*: "Aside from his natural modesty, Mr. Mellon was of the opinion, probably a correct one, that other men would be disinclined to leave their works of art to a museum that bore his name."

Yet such modesty is relatively rare. In fact, so great is the fetish for memorialization that during the past 50 years New York City has received—and turned down—innumerable offers to finance the installation in its Central Park of such embellishments as an exposition building, a stadium, an underground garage, a recreation center for the elderly, a restaurant, even a statue of Mary Poppins. "Not a year goes by that a rich man or a rich woman does not die and wish a suitable memorial in New York's front yard," said a Park Department official. "But the park is not a giant mausoleum." On the other hand, some years ago, the city of Omaha, Nebraska, in order to tap new sources of revenue, considered the possibility of holding a $1-a-ticket lottery, with the grand prize winner being guaranteed an immortality of sorts by receiving the privilege of having a public building named for himself or anyone he or she designated.

And donors' names are perpetuated on at least 90 percent of all foundations, to which we shall now turn in the following chapter.

Chapter 4

Foundations: Are They
an Endangered Species?

Henry Ford, who made billions when his Tin Lizzie ushered in the automobile age, hated charity and everything it stood for. "Give the average man something, and you make an enemy of him," was one of his favorite maxims. He was once heard to say that the only man on whom he ever bestowed charity—the munificent sum of $17—was ruined by it. "Why should there be any necessity for almsgiving in a civilized society?" he used to ask rhetorically, and his answer came in the form of such statements as "Endowment is an opiate of the imagination, a drug to the initiative" and "One of the great curses of the country today is the practice of endowing this and endowing that. . . ."

S. S. Kresge, who made more than $200 million from his dimestore chain, was also parsimonious beyond belief. The first two of his three wives divorced him, citing his stinginess as a major complaint. Kresge would wear shoes until they literally fell apart, boasted that he never spent more than 30 cents a day for lunch, and gave up golf because he could not bear the thought of losing the balls that went into the rough. Russell Sage, who amassed a $100 million fortune as a financier, was "the embodiment of the Yankee skinflint," to quote one of his contemporaries. Even at age 86 (he died in 1906 at the age of 90), Sage rode a trolley to work and ate a nickel sandwich for lunch; when an office boy once brought him a 15-cent sandwich by mistake, Sage deducted a dime from the boy's pay.

Yet, ironically, the names of Ford, Kresge, and Sage are perpetuated today on three of the nation's largest foundations, the devices through which many rich people channel their charitable gifts and perhaps the strangest, most improbable, and, as we shall soon see, most controversial animals in the bestiary of benevolence. "Like the giraffe, they could not possibly exist, but they do," says former Ford Foundation official Waldemar Nielsen. "Private foundations are virtually a denial of basic premises: aristocratic institutions living on the privileges and indulgences of an egalitarian society; aggregations of private wealth which, contrary to the proclaimed instincts of Economic Man, have been conveyed to public purposes."

Because they are so numerous and are identified with the names of some of our most celebrated tycoons—Rockefeller, Mellon, Duke, Kellogg, Sloan, Carnegie, Hartford, apart from those already mentioned—the popular misconception has arisen that most foundations have tremendous assets and are able to make

almost unlimited expenditures. The fact, however, is that the nation's 26,000 or
so foundations account for only 5.5 percent—a shade over $2 billion—of all
U.S. giving, and have assets recently estimated at about $32 billion. The fact,
too, is that most of these assets are concentrated in relatively few foundations.
The Ford Foundation, the giant of them all, alone has about $2 billion in assets, or
nearly 7 percent of the total of all foundations, and the 25 foundations shown in
the accompanying table, each with assets in excess of $100 million, to-
gether account for more than one-third of all foundation assets. Of the 26,000
foundations, only 2800 have assets exceeding $1 million or make annual grants
totaling $100,000 or more, these accounting for around 90 percent of all founda-
tion assets and more than 80 percent of all foundation giving. The remaining
23,000 or so foundations are relatively small operations, most of them no more
than family conduits for contributions to charity, without staffs and headquartered in a desk drawer in a lawyer's office; more than half have assets of less than
$50,000 (one Chicago fund listed assets of only $8) and the majority pay out
grants totaling no more than $2000 to $3000 a year.

Apart from size, foundations are also extraordinarily diverse in purpose.
Many, like Ford and Carnegie, pour most of their money into education, which
recently took 26 percent of all foundation grants of $5000 or more reported to the
Foundation Center. Other foundations, such as Robert Wood Johnson, Kellogg,
and Hartford, concentrate a good deal of their giving in the medical and health
field, which received 22 percent of all foundation money, with the rest being
divided as follows: sciences and technology, 17 percent; welfare, 13; international activities, 11; humanities, 9; and religion, 2. The work of many of the
major foundations straddles several areas: The Rockefeller Foundation has given
away more than $1 billion in the 60-odd years of its existence to support medical
education and research, public health, and projects concerned with overpopulation, hunger, and agriculture in many countries of the world; Kellogg, along with
health, is interested in the welfare of children; and Ford, in addition to education,
has been identified with a whole array of other concerns ranging from public
television, voter registration drives, and national and international affairs to
humanities and the arts and community action programs for minority groups—
the latter to such an extent that Ford is probably the most controversial of the
large foundations. Lilly funds education and religious programs and community and youth projects in Indiana; and Duke makes grants, principally in the
Carolinas, to hospitals, schools, orphanages, and rural Methodist churches.

Other foundations, however, channel their appropriations into certain
specialized areas. The Juilliard Musical Foundation, for example, helps educate
talented music students; the Solomon R. Guggenheim Foundation, dedicated to
advancing knowledge of modern art, operates New York's Guggenheim
Museum; and the John Simon Guggenheim Memorial Foundation is well known
for the fellowships it awards to creative people in all of the fine arts. Not as
widely known, however, is the Wilhelm Lowenstein Memorial Fund, established
by a wealthy bachelor New York fur dealer to furnish breakfasts for derelicts.
Foundation oddities would also include the Kansas-based Emma A. Robinson
Horses' Christmas Dinner Trust Fund, established to provide a meal of oats or
corn for 200 horses every Christmas, and the Share Your Birthday Foundation,

The 25 Largest U.S. Private Foundations
Ranked According to Assets

Name (and Year Established)	Assets (Millions of Dollars)*	Grants (Millions of Dollars)*
1. Ford Foundation (1936)	$2,159	$136.8
2. W. K. Kellogg Foundation (1930)	926	38.1
3. Robert Wood Johnson Foundation (1936)	916	29.2
4. Andrew W. Mellon Foundation (1940)	777	40.7
5. Rockefeller Foundation (1913)	744	44.9
6. Pew Memorial Trust (1948)	641	28.8
7. Kresge Foundation (1924)	607	30.0
8. Lilly Endowment (1937)	524	31.7
9. Duke Endowment (1924)	423	24.8
10. Charles Stewart Mott Foundation (1926)	419	22.0
11. Carnegie Corporation of New York (1911)	272	13.4
12. Alfred P. Sloan Foundation (1934)	253	14.0
13. Richard King Mellon Foundation (1947)	248	7.7
14. Houston Endowment (1937)	240	12.6
15. Bush Foundation (1953)	195	9.9
16. Rockefeller Brothers Fund (1940)	182	17.0
17. Moody Foundation (1942)	180	3.9
18. Edna McConnell Clark Foundation (1950)	171	9.2
19. Henry J. Kaiser Foundation (1948)	170	4.1
20. Frank E. Gannett Newspaper Foundation (1935)	168	5.7
21. Max C. Fleischmann Foundation (1952)	162	7.3
22. Commonwealth Fund (1918)	134	5.4
23. John A. Hartford Foundation (1942)	126	3.4
24. Robert A. Welch Foundation (1954)	122	6.7
25. Northwest Area Foundation (1934)	109	5.5

*Figures are the latest available as of 1977. Excluded from this table, but discussed later in this chapter, are "community" and "corporate" (company-sponsored) foundations, several of which have assets in excess of $100 million.

set up to encourage children to give up a birthday present to someone born on the same day. There is even a Benefit Shoe Foundation to provide for people with one foot.

Although the philanthropic foundation as we know it today is predominantly a twentieth-century American phenomenon, its roots go back thousands of years to ancient Egypt, Greece, and Rome. In our country, foundations date back at least to 1800 when the Magdalen Society was formed in Philadelphia to benefit "that class of females who have been unhappily seduced from the path of innocence and virtue and who at times seem desirous of a return thereto."

Generally regarded as the immediate predecessor of the modern foundation was the Peabody Fund, established in 1867 by investment banker George Peabody to promote education in the South. By 1900 there were some 26 American foundations and, in the first decade of the twentieth century, 16 more were established, among them the Russell Sage Foundation and the first of the great foundations set up by Andrew Carnegie, proponent of the view that "the man who dies rich, dies disgraced." From 1910 to 1920, foundations were being created at the rate of seven or eight a year; their number included such giants as the Carnegie Corporation of New York, the Rockefeller Foundation, and the Commonwealth Fund. However, by 1930 there were still no more than 270 foundations (fewer than 200, according to some counts); and between 1930 and 1940 an average of only 33 foundations a year were being set up. Coincidentally, the year 1936 marked the birth of what are now two of the nation's largest foundations—the Ford Foundation, originally the modest benefactor of a few local Michigan charities, and the Robert Wood Johnson Foundation, which remained a small philanthropic venture devoted to supporting charitable programs in New Brunswick, New Jersey, until 1971 when a bequest of a billion dollars worth of common stock in Johnson & Johnson, the surgical dressings manufacturer, from the estate of General Johnson, catapulted it that year into the No. 2 position behind Ford.* From the 1940s on, however, their rate of increase accelerated spectacularly—in fact, literally thousands were set up in some years—due to the high income, excess profits, inheritance and gift taxes that came as a result of World War II and the Korean War. Of the 26,000 foundations now in existence, over 90 percent were established since 1940.

For the rich and near-rich, foundations, at least until recently, were devices that offered significant financial advantages over direct giving. In many cases, they enabled a wealthy person to have his financial cake and eat it, too—that is, give his money or stock away and receive a tax deduction for his gift, which he could then borrow back at a modest rate of interest, also tax deductible. Foundations also provided a neat way of avoiding inheritance taxes and keeping control of a family business—the primary reasons behind the creation of the Ford Foundation.

By setting up the foundation and bequeathing 90 percent of their Ford Motor Company stock to it, the noncharitable Henry Ford and his son, Edsel, enabled their heirs to avoid an inheritance tax bill that would have come to $321 million. If the stock had passed directly from Henry and Edsel to their heirs, most of it would have had to be sold to pay that hefty tax. In parting with their holdings, the heirs would also have lost control of the company, but to forestall this possibility, all the stock given to the foundation was nonvoting. The 10 percent retained by the family had total voting power, maintaining the family's domination of the company. Moreover, the voting stock passed to the family tax-free, saving another $42 million, because the wills of Henry and Edsel provided that the taxes on this bequest be paid by the foundation.

This is not to say that all foundations—as one of their detractors put it—were "conceived in nothing more than deathbed greed" or for other avaricious reasons. It is easy to forget that some of the biggest foundations, such as those conceived by Carnegie and Rockefeller, were established when there were no tax laws. And so one must look elsewhere for the motives of their founders. "A clear majority of the big American foundations were created by rich men who had the good sense, late in their careers, to realize that they were but one short step of either outraged public opinion, their own uneasy consciences, or the tax collec-

*The Ford Foundation itself spun off three others: the Fund for Adult Education (1951), the Fund for the Advancement of Education (1951), and the Fund for the Republic (1952).

tor," says Joseph Goulden, noting piety and piracy to be well-documented characteristics of the American industrialist.

Some foundations were no doubt prompted by piety, others by guilt, and still others by the desire for a favorable public image or social prestige, the hope for immortality (about 90 percent of all foundations bear the names of their creators), the wish to keep money from ungrateful or bumbling heirs, the absence of any heirs (many founders like Peabody, Nobel, Sloan, and Vincent Astor had no children), the promotion of a favorite cause or whim, or any combination of these motives.

Posterity, the preservation of a business, and self-interest were among the motives behind the creation of the Duke Endowment, which was financed by James Buchanan Duke's tobacco and hydroelectric power empires. In explaining the rationale behind the endowment's health programs, Duke once frankly admitted: "People ought to be healthy. If they ain't healthy, they can't work, and if they can't work there ain't no profit in them." Sheer spite may have been the motive of Russell Sage's widow, who took posthumous revenge on her miserly mate by creating the Russell Sage Foundation with the funds from his estate; one of the foundation's first projects, under its mandate to improve social and living conditions in the United States, was an intensive investigation of moneylenders and usurers, a study which led the New York legislature to outlaw many of the practices through which Sage himself had become rich. Undoubtedly, some founders have even been impelled by feelings of simple kindness or humanitarianism (in themselves, as we've already seen, amalgams of many mixed motives). The late William Danforth, whose Purina became a household word, and Edwin Land, the founder of Polaroid, established their foundations because they seemed to have a genuine joy in doing things for people.

Whatever the motives of their founders, there can be no questioning the accomplishments of foundations. Foundations, for example, helped to eradicate hookworm and yellow fever and were instrumental in developing insulin, the polio vaccine (financing part of Jonas Salk's early research), the birth control pill, and the intrauterine device. In the field of medicine and education, they sponsored the investigation (by Abraham Flexner) that shook up and led to the reform of American medical education early in this century and, more recently—in the 1950s and 1960s—funded similar grants to James B. Conant and others, whose findings brought about changes in the nation's high schools, better salaries for college teachers, and introduced innovative reforms—teaching by television, electronic teaching machines, revolutionary new curricula, redesigned classrooms—throughout the U.S. school system. Foundation money built libraries and furnished fellowships, scholarships, and research grants that produced works ranging from Stephen Vincent Benet's *John Brown's Body,* perhaps America's greatest narrative poem, to Gunnar Myrdal's classic study of race relations, *The American Dilemma*, and scientific discoveries that won at least a dozen Nobel Prizes. To name only a few more of their frequently cited achievements, foundations were also responsible for the so-called "green revolution" that brought improved crops (such as hybrid corn) to the world's hungry; financed Dr. Robert H. Goddard's pioneering research in rocketry that ultimately led to man's exploration of space; contributed to the construction of the Mount Palomar Telescope and the National Gallery of Art as well as to the restoration of Colonial Williamsburg and to the production of such TV shows as "Sesame Street" and "Omnibus"; and virtually singlehandedly subsidized the development of public television. Because of such pioneering ventures, foundations, with good reason, have often been called the "venture capital" of philanthropy.

However, in spite of their laudable work, foundations have been the subject of severe criticism almost as long as they have been in existence. To many, they are nothing more than glorified tax shelters which, though using money that would otherwise have been paid to the government in taxes, have been remarkably free from public scrutiny and accountability in conducting activities that should be subject to government regulation or perhaps even be the province of government. Many have felt, too, that some foundations have frequently gone too far in promoting controversial social policies and even political viewpoints with what is essentially taxpayer money.

In the 1960s, when foundations were growing at a phenomenal rate and, hence, were increasingly in the public spotlight, they suddenly found themselves under unprecedented attack from diverse quarters because of a series of spectacular revelations that made front-page headlines. One was the disclosure that at least 39 foundations had been operating as conduits for Central Intelligence Agency funds destined for covert operations overseas. Another involved a $20,000 annual "research and writing" fee Supreme Court Justice Abe Fortas was receiving from a foundation set up by Louis E. Wolfson, the notorious corporation raider who at the time was under federal indictment and subsequently went to jail for stock manipulation. On the heels of Fortas' resignation from the court because of this disclosure came the revelation that another member of the court, Justice William O. Douglas, was on the payroll, at $21,000 a year, of the Parvin Foundation, whose donor, Albert Parvin, had extensive Las Vegas gambling holdings. (Coincidentally, Parvin and Wolfson had once been named coconspirators in a stock manipulation case.)

Other foundation grants, although also relatively small, were enough to provide critics with further ammunition in their arsenal of arguments to the effect that foundations were overstepping their bounds. One that attracted widespread attention was a Ford Foundation grant of $38,750 to the Congress of Racial Equality (CORE), which used the funds to finance a voter registration drive in the Cleveland black ghetto during a mayoral campaign in which a black candidate defeated his white opponent. In New York City, Ford, probably the most venturesome of the big foundations, financed a school decentralization program that exacerbated black-Jewish tensions in the city and resulted in a crippling 35-day teachers' strike that nearly cost John Lindsay his second term as mayor. Also having political overtones were Ford grants totaling $131,000 to eight former aides of the slain Senator Robert Kennedy to ease their transition from public to private life by providing them with "up to a year of leisure and freedom from immediate financial concern."*

Business and tax abuses involving foundations were also aired in the press as well as in the eight years of congressional hearings chaired by Rep. Wright

*In 1977, Henry Ford II resigned as a trustee of the Ford Foundation, accusing the foundation of spreading itself too thin and of having an antibusiness bias—or, at least, one that often failed to appreciate the capitalistic system that provided the money the foundation gave away.

Patman who, in his continuing vendetta against foundations, was concerned primarily with their economic implications rather than with their political and social biases. The thorny Texan Democratic populist passionately believed that many foundations were created to escape the payment of taxes. This, he argued, not only favored the rich at the expense of the poor, but also had resulted in the loss of almost $7 billion in federal taxes during the 1950s. Typical of the abuses uncovered was one involving a donor who gave $65,000 to his foundation, which then immediately lent the money (for which an income tax deduction had been taken) back to the donor's business. Other foundations were found to be trading in mortgages and securities or putting their research facilities to the donor's own private or commercial use. Not all foundations resorted to methods as crude as the one which paid its benefactor's company a large sum for the uranium rights to its parking lot. Quite common, however, was the practice of a company selling a property to a foundation and then leasing it back at a relatively low figure (possible because the property was now tax-free) or of a foundation making donations to the favorite causes of the donor's business clients in return for favors to the donor. Whatever the technique, businessmen resorting to such shenanigans were in effect using taxpayer dollars to gain a competitive advantage over organizations that were not exempt from taxes.

Not a few ingenious entrepreneurs, free from commercial ambitions, formed foundations for no other reason than to pay for the support of a relative or friend—an elderly millionaire admitted that his foundation had done nothing more than provide for a pair of sisters "through several years of parties and gay living," ostensibly on the ground that he needed their companionship—or to pay for their own travel or living expenses. The late James H. Rand, Jr., a former president of the Remington-Rand Corporation (now Sperry Rand), after selling his home to his foundation for $231,462, ostensibly for use as a research center, continued to live in it, with the foundation paying all the household expenses and servants' salaries; then he spent nearly $160,000 of the foundation's money on a so-called "research" garden to grow hydroponic vegetables for the Rand larder.

All this couldn't have happened at a worse time for foundations, for the 1960s was a period when there was a wave of public resentment at the burdens and inequities of our tax laws, especially their loopholes for wealthy people, oil companies, real estate and banking interests, and other privileged groups. Congress, while knowing it had to do something to appease the demand for tax reform, did not want to risk the ire of the powerful groups on whom it counted heavily for campaign contributions and other forms of support. So, big politics took over and foundations, which represented a far smaller and weaker constituency than the oil, real estate, and banking industries, became a convenient scapegoat.

The Tax Reform Act of 1969 was therefore somewhat of a misnomer in that it cracked down primarily on foundations. The act, among other things, imposed a 4 percent tax (recently reduced to 2 percent) on the net investment income of foundations and required them to pay out annually all of their net income or a percentage of their assets (fixed at 5 percent by the Tax Reform Act of 1976), whichever was greater. Significantly, the act banned anything that smacked of self-interest. For example, donors could no longer borrow money from their foundations, receive compensation from them, or use them as conduits for stock deals; and foundations were prohibited from owning more than 20 percent of a company's stock.* Also prohibited were any partisan activities that could be construed as attempting to influence legislation or the political process.

One possible consequence of this was all too clear. If a foundation's required payout exceeded its income or it wished to continue its traditional level of giving, it would either have to depend on capital gains or dip into its assets.

As if they weren't having enough trouble, foundation assets took a tremendous tumble during the severe stock market decline of 1974. The Ford Foundation's portfolio shrank from $3 billion in 1973 to $2 billion a year later (in 1966 the foundation's assets had stood at $4 billion); as a result, Ford was forced to lay off half of its 600 employees and reduce its disbursements by more than $100 million a year. During the same period, the Rockefeller Foundation's assets dropped from $980 million to $610 million, and Edwin Land's Rowland Foundation saw its assets dwindle from $108 million to less than $16 million. In recent years, Rockefeller's and Rowland's assets have risen somewhat—the former's to $744 million and the latter's to $34 million; but the collective assets of the nation's major foundations have declined $3 billion during the two latest years of record, largely because of the continuing vagaries of the securities market combined with inflation. "Our dividend and interest income has been going up, but not fast enough to keep up with inflation," says Jon L. Hagler, vice president and treasurer of the Ford Foundation.

What about the future of foundations? For one thing, with the removal of many of the financial incentives for their creation, they are declining in number. In 1968, according to a 12-state study by the Foundation Center, 1228 new foundations were established while 71 gave up the ghost; in 1972 only 128 new foundations were formed compared to 605 which died. They may be declining in importance, too, as government, during the past four or five decades, has been expanding its activities in almost every area except religion, so assuming many of the traditional functions of foundations. In 1977, for example, the government (federal, state, and local) spent nearly $57 *billion* on health—or 340 times as much as the $167 million foundations reported spending on their various health programs. Just federal funds allocated for education alone, the principal area of interest of foundations, were 20 times as much as all the foundations spent on everything. Today, foundations, apart from being a relatively small factor in philanthropy, play an insignificant role in the national scheme. Annual foundation grants now amount to less than half of one percent of the federal budget or, in other terms, to one-fourth of what Americans spend on toiletries and cosmetics, one-seventh of what they spend on tobacco, and one-twelfth of what they spend on alcoholic beverages. Foundation assets, the Foundation Center also tells us, are now only slightly more than one percent of all tangible U.S. wealth, and are less than the market value of the largest American corporation—AT&T.

Yet, in spite of their waning size and influence, foundations are still eyed with deep suspicion by many people, and critics continue to flail away at them from both right and left. On the one hand, former Alabama Governor George C. Wallace, for instance, sneers that they are nothing more than lackeys of the hated

*The percentage of Ford Motor Company stock held by the Ford Foundation dropped from 25 percent in 1969 to 7 percent in 1973. The following year the foundation disposed of all of its shares in the company.

Eastern Establishment, and conservative columnist Jeffrey Hart calls them a "shadow government" trying to force on the country "what they euphemistically call 'social change.'" On the other hand, Waldemar Nielsen, the former Ford Foundation official, questions their present willingness and ability to bring about social change. Characterizing the big foundations now as "far from the dynamic, creative, reformist institutions that some of their most eloquent defenders have claimed," Nielsen says, "Not one-tenth, probably not one-twentieth, of their grants have any measurable impact upon the major social problems confronting the nation at the present time."

Even foundation people still active in the field are inclined to agree. At an annual meeting of the prestigious Council on Foundations, David R. Hunter, executive director of the Ottinger Foundation and the Stern Family Fund, which have bankrolled community action and civil rights groups, said that foundations "have failed to address themselves in a fundamental enough way to critical issues," and called upon foundations "to be more yeasty, to make more ferment, produce more action for social change, not be so far above the battle, get into the fray more than they do."

What sort of critical issues? Among those ticked off by Hunter were: racism; war and peace; the question of the ascendancy of military institutions, attitudes, and budgets in our national life; the complex phenomena represented by Watergate, such as the purchase of government policy with private money, the abuse of power, illegal spying, the labeling of enemies of state, bureaucratic secrecy, and the vitiation of the criminal justice system; a tax system that hits little people harder than big people; and the reckless exploitation of natural resources.

Nonetheless, in response to the feeling that not enough foundations are concerned with basic social issues—something perhaps indicated by the fact that less than one percent of all the grants given annually have gone to the fields of economics, politics, and government—a growing number of activist foundations have been started in recent years. Called "alternative" or "radical" or "social change" foundations, many, ironically, have been set up by the radical offspring of wealthy people to fund community-based groups and projects considered too controversial, too risky, or too small for funding from traditional foundations.

In a suite of rooms in a shabby building in Cambridge, Massachusetts, is the Haymarket Foundation started in 1974 by George Pillsbury, Jr., 29-year-old heir to much of the Pillsbury baking fortune, and a group of friends. Explaining the foundation's origin, Pillsbury once told an interviewer: "When I turned 21, I and a number of friends inherited some money which we didn't feel comfortable about. We didn't understand it, we didn't feel that it was our money to have, and I think we all wanted to do something about it. I think we wanted our money to go, not into endowments, but immediately out into the community, to help groups gain power and gain some control in their lives."

A similar dilemma led young Obie Benz, who at age 21 inherited part of the Sunbeam food-processing fortune, and a group of his friends (heirs to money from such bastions of radicalism as J. C. Penney, Levi Strauss, Union Carbide, Sears Roebuck, Syntex, and Matson Shipping) to start the first of these foundations—the Vanguard Foundation, based in San Francisco. To Benz, now also 29, who works out of an office decorated with posters that proclaim some of his past and present concerns—the Vietnam war, the environment, feminism—the argument that foundations cannot fund social change projects because of the provisions of the 1969 Tax Reform Act or because of the Internal Revenue Service's expenditure responsibility requirement* is a lot of "bull." "I think that the argument is just a way to shunt off responsibility," says Benz who, by way of proof, points to the fact that Vanguard grants have gone to a group giving legal services to prostitutes, a prisoners' union, a shelter for battered women, counterculture radio stations, and an information center providing bilingual counseling to the Spanish-speaking community.

Roughly half of the $300,000 in grants now dispensed annually by Vanguard are decided on by a donor board, and the other half by a community board representing local activist groups. At Haymarket, however, whose annual distributions are about the same as Vanguard's, donors have no say as to where their money goes, the decisions on funding being left entirely to eight panels of community activists in the various New England areas in which it operates. This is a manifestation of George Pillsbury's belief that "revolutions have not been acts of the ruling classes but struggles of the poor and oppressed against those who hold power"—meaning that a "donor's control ends with his contribution."

Although there is still only a handful of these activist foundations and they are relatively small, Pillsbury likes to think of them as an alternative United Way; and now that his Haymarket has spread throughout New England, his dream is a network of community-oriented activist funding sources across the country. Whether or not this dream materializes and whatever the long-term effects or future of these groups, it is generally conceded, as one observer told *The Grantsmanship Center News*, that they have undertaken a "terribly worthwhile" experiment with the process by which foundations distribute money.

To serve the needs of communities or, in some cases, entire states, in a more orthodox way, there are also the older, broader-based "community" foundations which, although relatively unknown, make up the fastest growing and perhaps most significant movement in the philanthropic field. Since 1960 the number of these foundations (some are also called "trusts" or "funds") has increased from 80 to about 220, and their aggregate assets have more than tripled from $417 million to $1.4 billion; and, according to veteran foundation official John May, their number may double to 500 and their assets may at least triple to $5 billion by the mid-1980s. Other experts feel that by then community foundations may account for as much as one-fourth of all private foundation wealth, compared to the 4 percent they do today; and New York Congressman Barber Conable regards them as "the wave of the future." "They are what United Ways would like to be, but can't," said a staff member of an upstate New York community foundation.

On the other hand, there are many who regard these claims as overexuberant. Although an enthusiastic advocate of community foundations and perhaps the nation's leading authority on them, Eugene C. Struckhoff, president of the Council on Foundations, does not see their number increasing at the rate of more

---

*In essence, the requirement that foundation board members can be held personally responsible for the way the groups they fund use the money given to them.

than eight to ten a year. "For one thing, they would be suitable for only communities of a certain size," he says. "This is not to say that the community foundations—both the present ones and any new ones established—could not experience a tremendous growth in assets." However, he does not foresee these as increasing at the rate of more than $100 million a year.

Struckhoff also points out the essential differences between the community foundations and the United Ways. Unlike the nation's local United Way organizations which raise money annually, largely from the public or from business, solely to contribute to the operating expenses of their roster of member agencies, the community foundations, explains Struckhoff, dole out income from various trust funds over the years mainly for capital gifts that may go to any deserving local cause. The grants cover an astonishing variety of community needs. Boston's Committee of the Permanent Charity Fund, the fifth largest community foundation (about $70 million in assets), once appropriated $25,000 to help convert the city's civic auditorium into an opera house; and the Cleveland Foundation, the oldest and for many years the largest (with assets of $209 million, it now ranks second only to the New York Community Trust) gave $12,500 for new classrooms and fire escape equipment to a school for exceptional children.

However, grants are by no means limited to such brick and mortar projects. The New York Community Trust (assets, $216 million), which holds funds created in the names of such distinguished people as opera star Kirsten Flagstad, sportswriter Grantland Rice, and Henry Kissinger (he established a fund for scholarships with the $53,000 Nobel Peace Prize awarded him in 1973), has given grants to agencies involved in such diverse efforts as bringing meals to the housebound aged, supporting an arts program for young people in a Brooklyn ghetto, providing radiation treatment for indigent cancer patients, and establishing a research library in Harlem. The San Francisco Foundation donated $1000 to support a writer while he completed a novel, and the Chicago Community Trust gave a local horticultural society $10,000 to encourage school children to take up gardening on the rationale that it would not only make a good long-range hobby, but also curb vandalism. (As these examples indicate, community foundations are concerned more with cultural activities and are not as change-oriented as the alternative foundations.)

Donors of unrestricted gifts give community foundations the option of using these funds in any way they choose; other donors specify a particular organization or cause their money is to go to. However, if the original purpose becomes outmoded because of changed community circumstances—the classic example cited is the bequest of a tobacconist who stipulated that after his death his rents should be used to purchase snuff for the old women of his neighborhood—the foundations, through a legal doctrine (called *cy pres*, literally meaning "as near as") uniquely applicable only to community foundations, usually have the right to put the money to some other use. Community foundations also differ from other foundations in that at least 10 percent of their support is required to come from the public or the government, and in that their governing bodies are supposed to consist of "representative" members of the community, such as public officials, educators, clergymen, and others having special knowledge or expertise in the particular fields with which the foundations may be concerned.

Because of these "public" attributes, community foundations have a favored status that exempts them from the 2 percent excise tax on income, pay-out requirements, and other restrictions imposed on private foundations by the 1969 Tax Reform Act and other subsequent acts. The tax laws also give certain advantages to wealthy would-be givers to charity. A person wishing to set up his own private foundation may receive a deduction only on that part of his contribution to it amounting to no more than 20 percent of his adjusted gross income, with no carry-over allowed for any excess contributed; on the other hand, a donor to a community foundation is allowed a deduction on up to 50 percent of his adjusted gross income, with the privilege of deducting any excess over the next five years.

Actually, community foundations are not altogether new. The Cleveland Foundation dates back to 1914, only a few years after the creation of the private Carnegie and Rockefeller Foundations, and was not so much an innovation in philanthropy as an innovation in banking. Starting with the Cleveland Foundation, virtually all have been set up by banks; and built into the structure of community foundations is what has been called "the bank connection"—the trust departments of banks often go so far as to provide the foundations with their staff and office space. The bank connection, along with their favored tax status as "public" nonprofit organizations, has contributed in good part to the community foundations' recent rapid growth. Many of the small, and usually unstaffed, private foundations, having neither the inclination nor the expertise to cope with the restrictions of the 1969 Tax Reform Act, have chosen to transfer their assets to community foundations and become separate funds within them; in doing so, they may retain their nominal identity and purpose and yet avoid the costs and constraints they would be subject to as private foundations. Thus, the San Francisco Foundation, which recently absorbed the $17 million private Oakes Foundation, saw its assets jump from $6.7 million in 1965 to $50 million in 1977; and 15 of the 59 largest community foundations doubled, or more than doubled, their asset size during just the four-year period following the passage of the 1969 act.

Whether or not community foundations do become the wave of the future, the national headquarters of the United Way, at least, is not entirely happy with their spectacular growth. This may seem surprising for most of the local United Ways (and their predecessors, the Community Chests) have traditionally maintained close and friendly relationships with community foundations; in fact, many of the latter allow local United Ways to appoint one or more members to their grants distribution committees and in some cities the two organizations even share offices. However, what concerns the national United Way is the effect of the community foundations on its revenues, which come primarily from membership dues paid by the local United Ways, which turn over to national as much as one percent of the more than $1 billion annually now raised in their 2300 local campaigns.

As *The Grantmanship Center News* once explained the implications of this: "A woman in Dayton, for example, may choose to set up a $1 million fund for health service agencies in that city. Whether she gives the fund to the community foundation or the endowment fund of the local United Way, the city of Dayton has $1 million for health services. But if she chooses the community foundation, the national office of United Way of America is out $10,000."

Finally, we come to the comparatively new 1500 "corporate" or company-sponsored foundations, of which the 462 listed in the 1977 *Foundation Directory* had assets of $1.2 billion and made grants totaling nearly $244 million. However, since the giving practices of these foundations are the same as those of companies that do not have foundations, we shall consider them further in the chapter that follows.

With the continuing worry of inflation and the fear of further federal encroachment on their turf, it is easy to understand why foundations as a whole view the future with foreboding. Many foundations, however, still feel that they will continue to have a vital role because of their ability to pioneer in areas barred to public agencies.

"The private sector has unique advantages," said John D. Rockefeller III. "It can move swiftly, it can be patient in waiting for results, it can venture into new or sensitive areas and try out new ideas without being afraid of occasional failures."

Nonetheless, at the hearings preceding the passage of the 1969 tax reform bill, Rep. John Byrnes of Wisconsin asked Rockefeller whether it was proper for the government, through its tax laws, to permit "a segment of our society to set up a government of its own to render philanthropic services," particularly since the nonrich must pay extra taxes to finance them. At one of the congressional hearings that have been held periodically since then, public-interest lawyer Patricia S. Senger made much the same point when she stated, ". . . so much of the money foundations use is a federal subsidy . . . but the average taxpayer has no voice in the use or amount of that money, no voice in choosing the projects it supports, and no voice in deciding whether or not charity should be so heavily supported in the first place."

Chapter 5

The Myth of Corporate Largesse

Although it may distress an occasional stockholder, American Telephone & Telegraph Company, besides serving the nation's communications needs, shows concern for the less fortunate. Together with the 23 phone companies that make up the Bell System, Ma Bell now doles out more than $24 million a year, or 0.31 percent of its pretax net income (PTNI), to hospitals, educational institutions, the Red Cross, and other local and national charitable causes, either directly or through such federated drives as the United Way.

The Aluminum Company of America, another corporate giant, dispenses via its Alcoa Foundation $6.1 million a year, a sum amounting to 2.1 percent of its PTNI*, not only to similar worthy causes but also to an array of organizations ranging from the American Horticultural Society and Accion International (which helps small businessmen in South and Central America) to the Pennsylvania Program for Women and Girl Offenders and the World Council of Pittsburgh.

Even though some 200 corporations are larger in terms of revenues, the Minneapolis-based Dayton Hudson Corporation ranks as one of the nation's top 15 corporate philanthropists, spending $6.3 million a year, or 5 percent of its PTNI, on good works of various sorts, ranging from the arts (the Minnesota Orchestra, a southwestern Indian art preservation program) to welfare projects (a T-shirt printing enterprise providing training for disadvantaged students) in the 19 states in which it operates department stores and specialty shops, including the B. Dalton bookstores.

Some years ago, McDonald's, the hamburger chain, donated 5 cents from the sale of every soft drink for an entire week in order to help raise funds for the mentally retarded. As I write this, a newspaper ad proclaims that the evening telecasts of the Boston Symphony and *Madame Bovary* are being sponsored, respectively, by Manufacturers Hanover and Mobil.

All told, American business now gives about $2 billion a year to charity, more than twice its outlay in the mid-1960s and about seven times that in the mid-1940s. However, the current contributions of all the nation's corporations, numbering in the millions, actually come to slightly less than the amount given by our 26,000 philanthropic foundations and account for only 5 percent of all charitable

*Actually, the $6.1 million comes not from the company but from the earnings on the investments of the foundation, which was funded in 1952 with a one-time grant of $16.8 million from the company. The company, like most others, does not make public the amount of its annual contributions to charity.

giving. Moreover, although companies can receive tax deductions for contributions amounting up to 5 percent of their net income, their charitable gifts, on the average, have hovered at just below the one percent mark for the past few decades. In relation to the GNP, corporate giving, if anything, has gone down. It stood at an all-time high of 0.136 percent in 1953; the latest figures place it at 0.083. And in terms of real dollars, as measured by the consumer price index, business gives no more today than it gave a decade ago. Even the probusiness Rockefeller-financed Filer Commission on Private Philanthropy and Public Needs concluded that "the record of corporate giving is an unimpressively and inadequate one." *Forbes* has also called corporate contributions "scandalously low."

Many, however, argue that business already gives too much and, in fact, should give nothing at all. "Give money to charity?" sputtered one company president to F. Emerson Andrews. "Why, that's nonsense. Any money we would give must be taken from profits, which belong to stockholders, or from wages of employees, or show up in higher prices to our customers. We have no right to do any of these three things." A leading academic proponent of this view is the redoubtable Milton Friedman, the University of Chicago's noted Nobel prize-winning economics professor, who is famous for his dictum that the one and *only* responsibility of business is to increase profits.

On the other hand, taking the opposite point of view, in a controversy that has raged with particular fervor since the riot-ridden days of the mid-1960s, are the social responsibility advocates who argue that profit maximization isn't enough, that business has both a moral obligation and a compelling need to deal with social problems. In a formal debate with Friedman on the issue of corporate social responsibility in 1973, the late Eli Goldston, then president of Eastern Gas & Fuel Associates, suggested, "The great danger of this harping on maximization is that it lets the cheapest louse in every operation say what's good for the country." Paul Samuelson, also a Nobel laureate, put it bluntly: "A large corporation these days not only may engage in social responsibility: it had damn well better try to do so."

The raging debate over corporate social responsibility may, however, be somewhat specious. For, as *Fortune* once noted, critics of the concept don't really object to giving as long as it yields some return—direct or indirect—to a company, and social responsibility advocates aren't necessarily pushing pure altruism. The fact is that "social responsibility" or such euphemisms as "corporate citizenship" can mean different things to different people and so cloak a multitude of reasons for corporate giving. For example, the specter of Big Government no doubt prompted Henry Ford II, on the occasion of the establishment of the Ford Motor Company Fund in 1949, to say: "Traditional sources of financial support of [private] institutions are tending to disappear. We do not like the consequences of private institutions turning to government for financial aid. This situation places an increasing responsibility upon American businessmen in their role of industrial citizens." A president of Standard Oil of New Jersey (now Exxon) once echoed the same view.

As a recent study by University of Delaware sociologist David Ermann pointed out, it is more than coincidence that the oil companies, members of one of the least socially responsible industries and hence one with the most public relations problems, are the largest contributors to the Public Broadcasting System (PBS), a fact that has caused some wags to dub it the Petroleum Broadcasting System. Ermann says that the oil companies give to PBS because it reaches precisely the audience they wish to influence—a national educated elite. He quotes a Mobil executive who told *Fortune* that "the purpose of all this effort to win credibility, and to associate our company's name with quality is to provide access to, and rapport with, key groups and special publics—legislators and regulators, the press, intellectuals and academics." Another Mobil official said that "these programs, we think, build enough acceptance to allow us to get tough on substantive issues." Significantly, Ermann also found that the average tax rate of oil companies contributing to PBS was much lower than that of oil company noncontributors (9.9 percent as opposed to 14.8 percent).

But the two main reasons for corporate giving—sheer self-interest and an altruistic desire to be responsible to society—are not necessarily mutually exclusive. Said one of some 400 executives surveyed by the Conference Board: "It takes a healthy society for corporations to operate; they should contribute to that health."

The relationship between corporate well-being and that of society was graphically demonstrated some time ago when Sears Roebuck, looking into reasons for declining sales in a five-county area of Kentucky, found that the area was economically depressed because of the depletion of its coal mines. When a Sears study also found the area's land and climate were ideally suited for growing strawberries, the company began to distribute seeds to 4-H club members. Before long, strawberry-growing in the area was a million-dollar business and a strawberry ice cream plant was set up. With the extra cash these enterprises put into the pocketbooks of the people of the area, Sears' sales were soon back to their former levels.

Self-interest, rather than altruism, was responsible for the first major example of corporate giving about a century ago when, as previously mentioned, the need of our railroads for inexpensive transient housing for their train crews led them to contribute to the construction and operating costs of the early YMCA buildings.

Otherwise, there was no substantial corporate giving until World War I, when business, carried away by the surge of patriotic sentiment of that era, contributed nearly $18 million to the Red Cross War Fund. However, at that time, any philanthropic gifts not yielding a "direct benefit" to the corporate giver were deemed to be of dubious legality, this juridical yardstick stemming from an 1883 decision of the English jurist, Lord Justice Bowen, that "charity has no business to sit at the board of directors." Recognizing that Bowen's pregnant phrase might offer dissident stockholders a weapon for attacking a philanthropic-minded management, the Red Cross was able to collect the funds it did through the ingenious device of urging companies to declare a "Red Cross Dividend"—in effect, an extra dividend—which stockholders could, if they wished, sign over to the Red Cross War Fund.

After the war corporate giving continued on a more modest scale. Then, in 1935, it was encouraged with the passage of federal legislation permitting corporations to receive tax deductions for charitable contributions in amounts up to 5 percent of their net income. The prime mover in securing this legislation was the Community Chests and Councils of America (now the United Way), which stood to benefit heavily from any increased corporate largesse. However, although the new law established the tax deductibility of such gifts, it still left unsettled the question as to whether stockholder money could be given away unless there was a "direct benefit" to the corporation or its employees. To resolve this question, New York, Illinois, Texas, and four other states, had in 1935 enacted legislation authorizing corporations to donate to charity, and by 1948 the number of states with similar specific permissive legislation had increased to fifteen.

But any lingering doubts about the need for corporate contributions to meet the "direct benefit" standard were finally laid to rest in the landmark 1953 case of *A. P. Smith Manufacturing Co.* v. *Barlow*. This case, sometimes referred to as the Magna Charta of the corporate giving movement, involved the validity of a $1500 contribution to Princeton University by A. P. Smith, a small New Jersey manufacturer of fireplugs. Actually, the case originated when the top officials of U.S. Steel, General Motors, General Electric, Standard Oil of New Jersey, and several other corporate goliaths interested in contributing to private colleges induced the Smith company to allow itself to be used as a stalking horse to test the legality of an educational grant for which no direct benefit would be claimed. By prearrangement, a South Orange, New Jersey, housewife named Ruth F. Barlow filed a stockholder complaint over the unrestricted $1500 Smith donated to Princeton. Following the planned scenario, Smith then asked for a declaratory judgment authorizing the contribution. The New Jersey Supreme Court came through as expected, ruling that such a gift was "essential to public welfare, and therefore, of necessity, to corporate welfare." Suggesting that even public relations gains would be an adequate benefit, the court also said that corporations could make donations that they felt would "conduce to the betterment of social and economic conditions, thereby permitting such corporations . . . to discharge their obligation to society while . . . reaping the benefits which essentially accrue to them through public recognition of their existence." The New Jersey Supreme Court also said in part: ". . . the contribution here in question is towards a cause which is intimately tied into the preservation of American business and the American way of life. Such giving may be an incidental power, but when it is considered in its essential character, it may well be regarded as a major, though unwritten corporate power. It is even more than that. In the court's view, it amounts to a solemn duty."

Today, most states have laws on the books validating this concept of corporate rights; and the overwhelming majority of stockholders favor or, at least, do not oppose it, although occasional dissidents like the unabashable Evelyn Davis regularly give company chairmen a hard time at annual meetings by presenting resolutions to limit charitable contributions and by her diatribes from the floor on the subject. "Don't make any charitable contributions, Mel," she once advised Melvin W. Alldredge, chairman of the Great Atlantic & Pacific Tea Co. "Give us higher cash dividends so *we* can make more contributions to whomever we want."

Surprisingly, in spite of the recent climate of permissiveness, all the talk about social responsibility, and the tax incentives for giving, only 20 percent of the 1.7 million corporate taxpayers in 1970 reported any charitable contributions and only 6 percent made contributions of over $500. These findings, based on a special Treasury tabulation, are startling and seem highly improbable; but one possible explanation may be that some corporations treat donations to certain charities, the underwriting of public television programs, and the sponsorship of community projects as business expenses rather than as charitable contributions. One would expect the largest corporations to be the most generous; but another unexpected revelation of the Treasury tabulation was that they actually give the least, as a percentage of their pretax net income. The corporations giving 5 percent or even more of their net income were for the most part "smaller" or "medium-sized" firms, that is, those with incomes of around $120,000; this may be because small firms are usually closer to their customers and suppliers and presumably are, therefore, more subject to pressures to give. For similar reasons, local companies are more generous than national companies.

Among industry groups, according to the latest annual survey by the Conference Board, the most generous givers of all are merchandising firms, which give 1.53 percent of their domestic pretax net income; they are followed by business services (1.42), banking (1.39), mining (1.21), and the primary metals industries (1.19). The least generous are the telecommunications companies (0.32) and utilities (0.33)—presumably because of the restrictions placed on these businesses by government regulatory bodies.

Although mechanisms for giving vary widely, in many firms today they are generally haphazard ad hoc affairs, not much different from the way they were in 1952 when F. Emerson Andrews observed that "corporation giving is not at present a carefully considered, integrated program in most companies. . . . The 'program', if it may be called that, is usually last year's contributions plus a few new items based on spot decisions of the president or another chief officer made in the short time he is able to borrow from his ordinary and urgent duties."

This is still particularly true of small companies, where requests for contributions go directly to a single top executive, usually the president himself. In larger companies, the requests are received and reviewed by the already overburdened executives heading such departments as public relations, public affairs, personnel, community relations, finance, or urban affairs. In really large companies, probably the most common mechanism for screening donations and administering the giving program is a contributions committee made up of representatives of the aforementioned departments and perhaps the chief executive. Three out of four of the 457 major corporations responding to a Conference Board survey sent to all the firms on the *Fortune* 1300 list were found to have contributions committees.

Some committees have the authority to act on their own; others function in merely an advisory capacity, with the final decisions left to the chief executive and/or board of directors. Chicago's CNA Financial Corp. is one of the few companies to have a social responsibility committee on its board. All this does not necessarily mean that each and every request for a donation must be reviewed at the top. For example, although IBM's board of directors' executive committee makes most of the decisions on gifts, the company's Fund for Community Service also allows employees to obtain funds for local organizations in which they are active, simply upon approval of the employee's immediate manager and one senior executive.

Many companies, usually the large ones, have found it to their advantage to do some or all of their giving through their own foundations for tax and other reasons. The reasons include: ability to build and maintain a reservoir of funds and therefore sustain giving, even over a long-term period, in spite of any year-to-year fluctuations in company earnings; greater administrative efficiency and at lower cost; better ability to respond to disasters and crises; and more independent review of requests for funds through insulation of company officers from customer and other pressures. Fifty-three percent of the 457 major corporations in the survey mentioned above reported having company-sponsored foundations (in many instances, in addition to contributions committees or other corporate giving mechanisms). However, since the passage of the 1969 Tax Reform Act, the role of company-sponsored foundations has diminished, although they still remain a significant factor in corporate giving.*

The modern era of corporate giving has seen the development of a new species of corporate executive whose job it is to direct the contributions of corporations so that they not only serve corporate interests but, equally important, also have the most effective impact in meeting society's needs. The man generally conceded to be the paterfamilias of this new and rare breed of executive, who of course can be found in only the largest companies, is W. Homer Turner, whose flock of a dozen degrees, a number befitting the many disciplines called for by his work, includes earned doctorates in law and philosophy and a master's in engineering. In his 31 years of service with U.S. Steel, 17 as executive director of its foundation until his retirement in 1970, Turner, a tall, jaunty, professorial-looking man in his seventies addicted to wearing polka-dot bow ties, dispensed about a quarter of a billion dollars, beyond question more than any other corporate giver in history.

How do U.S. Steel and other companies decide on whom to bestow their largesse? This is an awesome task, considering the number of requests for donations many companies receive. During his tenure with U.S. Steel, Dr. Turner estimates he and his staff of eight fielded 60,000 requests, an average of 2000 a year, of which about one-third were approved. Citibank of New York receives about 1000 requests annually, Exxon as many as 5000, and Ford about 4000, of which it approves 150 or so, or one out of every 25. Companies with fairly large budgets usually spell out their criteria for giving in policy statements or manuals, which are also explicit in describing the areas for which donations are invariably denied. U.S. Steel and Ford, like most companies, automatically turn down all requests from religious institutions (other than church-affiliated hospitals, schools, and welfare agencies such as the Catholic Bishop's Relief Fund), political parties and candidates, veterans organizations, labor unions, fraternal orders, and ethnic groups. General Motors, however, once contributed $100,000 toward a new home for the Xavier Mission Sisters in Warren, Michigan, a suburb of Detroit, General Motors' headquarters city.

Generally, the corporate apple doesn't fall far from the corporate tree. Ninety percent of the contributions of General Motors go to local organizations; most other companies also dispense the greater part of their donations to organizations in the communities where they have their headquarters, sales or branch offices,

*The ten largest, in terms of giving, are the Ford Motor Company Fund, Alcoa Foundation, U.S. Steel Foundation, Xerox Fund, Gulf Oil Foundation of Delaware, Exxon Education Foundation, Eastman Kodak Charitable Trust, Amoco Foundation, General Electric Foundation, and Mobil Foundation.

plants, and distribution facilities. Listed as "qualified" for contributions by most companies are such traditional establishment groups or causes as the Boy Scouts and Girl Scouts, YMCA, YWCA, Red Cross, Salvation Army, Cancer Fund and Heart Fund drives, hospitals, schools and colleges, museums, symphony orchestras and other cultural institutions, and the United Way. In fact, business funnels about half of all the funds it gives to local causes through United Way campaigns.

On the other hand, many companies also give to causes which are remote, geographically as well as economically, from their own apparent interests. During one year, for example, contributions by the Ford Motor Company Fund (which Ford executives are careful to distinguish from the completely independent Ford Foundation) included $25,000 to the American Red Cross to help build Iranian cities damaged by an earthquake, $10,000 for the victims of a Chilean earthquake, $80,000 to the Detroit Etruscan Foundation to help repair the damages wrought by a flood in Florence, and $50,000 to CARE for relief to the poor in the Philippines. That same year, the Ford Fund also gave $2.8 million to schools, colleges, and universities; and it also often doubles its employees' gift to educational institutions whereas many other firms merely match them. (About 700 corporations now have some sort of matching gifts program.)

If any one generalization can be made, it is that corporate givers have been shifting their emphasis over the years from health and welfare, traditionally the chief beneficiaries of business, to education which more and more companies have come to regard as an investment both in the nation's and their own future. "If a college like Lehigh is receiving contributions," said a leading fund raiser, "one reason is that corporate donors are looking to the school as a future source for engineers."

According to the Conference Board, the biggest slice—38 percent—of the corporate philanthropic dollar still goes to health and welfare, most of it through federated drives such as the United Way; but this represents quite a decline from the 66 percent registered for this category in 1947. On the other hand, education now receives nearly 36 percent of the corporate dollar, compared with only 14 percent three decades ago. Civic and cultural causes claim the next biggest share, 20 percent, about seven times that of two decades ago. (Earlier comparative figures are not available.) Corporate giving to the arts alone has multiplied four times in just the past decade.

Another noticeable trend has been the movement in recent years toward more innovative giving as opposed to responsive giving, that is, in response to appeals made upon the company by outsiders. The Cummins Engine Company, for example, sets aside funds in its budget for meeting architectural fees for the design of schools and other public buildings in its headquarters city of Columbus, Indiana. For many years Sears Roebuck funded a program to help small doctorless communities to build medical facilities and thereby attract physicians. (The program was eventually phased out because of the company foundation's increasing emphasis on urban programs.) The Bulova Watch Company, one of the relatively few companies that gives a full 5 percent of its net income to charity, supports a free watchmaking school for the disabled, and to avoid any appearance of self-interest does not itself hire any of the trained men, who graduate to well-paid jobs, usually in retail jewelry stores. And in spite of image building as a strong factor in the interest of the oil companies in the arts, their innovative support of public television, museums, music, and the like has been to the public good.

But, as Marion Fremont-Smith writes in her study, *Philanthropy and the Business Corporation*, "The few enlightened programs of corporation philanthropy must not be used to blur the fact that they are rare indeed, and that despite the efforts of dedicated, informed members of the academic, the philanthropic, and the business community, they have not been widely copied."

The fact is that most corporate gifts do consistently go to the same "safe" traditional establishment causes year after year—the United Way, local hospitals, the Boy Scouts, the Red Cross, the local symphony orchestra and museum, and others already mentioned. Ninety-one percent of the companies sampled in one survey were found to give at least half of their contributions to the same annually recurring drives; 18 percent of the companies gave all of their contributions to them. This is not surprising since corporate contributions officers often meet regularly with their counterparts in other companies and many company policy manuals read as if they were written by the same person.

Pressure from within and without is also as prevalent in corporate as in other forms of giving. James V. Lavin, a Boston fund-raising expert, once offered this blunt, succinct formula for what motivates many companies to give: "It can be summed up in three factors: (1) Who puts the bite on whom. (2) Which of the top officers is particularly interested in this cause. (3) You scratch my back, I'll scratch yours."

Nonetheless, corporate gifts, however they are dispensed and whatever the motivations behind them, furnish funds to many worthy causes that might otherwise wither. Yet the criticisms persist. Political scientist Andrew Hacker, for example, argues that the giving is aimed primarily at perpetuating established philanthropies and, moreover, preserves the illusion that needy causes are being taken care of. Jack Shakely of the Grantsmanship Center offers the thought that some corporations "hide behind a philanthropic wall, passing out pennies to charity like a Punch and Judy show passes out candy to children, while behind the wall it practices cost overruns, senseless pollution, even government coups that would make Jay Gould blanch." Economist John Kenneth Galbraith blanketly condemns all corporate giving on the ground that it gives business too much power to shape society to its own particular selfish needs.

Following this line of reasoning, a Ralph Nader study group, while recognizing the positive impact of corporate giving, views some of DuPont's donations in Delaware, the company's fiefdom, as detrimental. The company, according to the Nader group, has aggravated the inequality of educational opportunity between the DuPont-run and supported predominantly white University of Delaware and the predominantly black Delaware State College, which operates on a shoestring budget. Even DuPont's support of a community-initiated effort to encourage minority business enterprise wins no praise from Nader who sees the program as a scheme to keep the federal government out of Delaware. And the company's willingness to permit employees to pursue charitable and political activities on company time is also regarded by Nader as part of a scheme to run the state.

The value of the time (to say nothing of the talent) given by company employees to fund-raising drives and other volunteer work, often on company time, is considerable. No precise recent estimate of the dollar value of this time is available but, as already mentioned, back in 1963 the services that just our business and professional leaders donated annually to philanthropic causes was estimated to be $5 billion. This figure would probably be many times higher today.

Of the 457 major corporations responding to that oft-mentioned Conference Board survey, 73 percent loaned employees to voluntary organizations on a part-time basis while continuing to pay their salaries, and 41 percent loaned employees on a full-time basis. A small but growing number of companies are even giving employees paid extended leaves for periods up to a year so they can do charitable work of their choice. Under Xerox's renowned Social Service Leave Program, for example, company employees have worked on projects ranging from providing vocational training for juvenile delinquents, rehabilitating alcoholics, and recording for the blind, to setting up a "marriage enrichment" counseling clinic, running programs for handicapped boys, and giving legal aid to the poor and aged.

Other contributions under the banner of "corporate social responsibility" should also include the value of any donated or loaned products or equipment, the cost of job training for the disadvantaged and physically handicapped, and investments in such areas as urban renewal and environmental preservation. If a price tag were put on such activities and the value of the time donated by employees and executives, the figure of $2 billion for corporate giving would be at least doubled, according to an estimate by the Conference Board.

But even this is hardly enough in terms of what corporations could give. Nor is corporate giving likely to increase significantly, if at all, in the foreseeable future in spite of the Filer Commission's rosy recommendation that corporations increase their giving to a minimum of 2 percent of their pretax net income by 1980. Even companies convinced that giving is good are unlikely, unless mandated by congressional fiat, to give much more than they now do. This is indicated by the fact that perhaps no more than 50,000 of the nation's 2 million corporate taxpayers now give at the 5 percent legal limit, although if all did, it would result in as much as $10 billion in corporate contributions annually instead of the current $2 billion.

In making its recommendation, the Filer Commission said: "It is ironic at least that the business community, which has so often expressed its wariness of Washington and the growing size of government, should fall so far short of legal limits in helping select and support publicly beneficial programs outside of government, through nonprofit charitable organizations. Former President Johnson recognized this irony in 1971 when he chided a group of business leaders about not contributing more to charity. 'In spite of the fact that your federal government has seen fit to allow a charitable deduction of 5 percent of your profits,' he said, 'the record is quite clear that you business leaders still feel that the federal government can spend this money more wisely than you can.'"

Chapter 6

The Volunteer: Saint or Scab?

It's a serious, stern, responsible deed,
To help an unfortunate soul in need,
And your own reward, when you quiet his plaint,
Is to feel like an opulent, careworn saint.

—Clarence Day

The American view of charity—and the volunteer—has altered considerably since the kindly Mr. Day wrote *Life With Father* in 1935. To many, his notion, as *Time* once commented, "seems old-fashioned, more closely allied with the times of the original good Samaritan than with the thrust of contemporary society."

Some suggest that the change began to take place with the coming of Franklin D. Roosevelt's welfare state which, providing as it did for many of the needs of the poor, the sick, the disabled, and the old, lessened their dependence on charity—dispensed through the largesse of the prosperous or at least better off, and through the services of the volunteer. In recent years the entire concept of volunteering, one of our most venerable institutions, has been buffeted as a consequence of a confluence of various currents in American life: the need or desire of many women, who traditionally have comprised the bulk of the volunteer force, to find paying jobs; the feeling, championed by feminist groups, that women who work for free are being exploited; and growing complaints by labor unions that volunteers, both male and female, are taking paying jobs away from their members.

Yet, surprisingly, volunteers still seem to be a very important part of the American charity scene. No one really knows just how many Americans are currently involved in volunteer work but a recent National Center for Voluntary Action survey put the number at anywhere from 45 to 55 million—at least one out of every four Americans over the age of 13—and other estimates have ranged up to as much as 100 million, although undoubtedly with some duplication. Whatever the exact number of volunteers, one must also take into account the value of their unpaid labors, which probably *exceeds* the amount of money given to charity. As mentioned earlier, the Census Bureau estimated the value of volunteer work to be around $34 billion back in 1974—a year when the Ameri-

71

can Association of Fund-Raising Counsel (AAFRC) reckoned donations of money to total $25 billion. (Incidentally, surveys have found that the giving of time, in the form of volunteer work, generally correlates closely with the giving of money—that is, those who give one are likely to give the other.)

However, there are indications that voluntarism (or, as it is also called, volunteerism) has been on the decline in recent years and that, as the AAFRC says, "America may be heading for the day not enough volunteers volunteer." This is difficult to document with reliable statistics but various nonprofit organizations have reported drops in their volunteer forces and have also griped about the growing competition for volunteers. The annual AAFRC studies of 20 leading national charities have shown their combined volunteer strength declining from 22,677,000 in 1975 to 20,092,000 in 1977.*

In any event, volunteers still seem to be in evidence everywhere. Singer Ethel Merman puts in one day a week at Manhattan's Roosevelt Hospital gift shop (proceeds to the hospital) where startled patrons invariably ask, "Do you know, you look just like Ethel Merman?" Ann Landers does volunteer public relations for the American Cancer Society, and Joanne Woodward works with autistic children. Volunteers, a survey showed, work an average of nine hours a week, one-third of them on fund raising. About 60 percent of them are women; the typical volunteer is a married, white woman between 25 and 44, holds a college degree, and is of the upper middle class.

There are, however, others far from typical who exemplify the good old American tradition of do-goodism. Here are several examples:

Certainly, the one-man crusade against alcoholism and cancer of Arch Avary, a silver-haired retired Georgia banker, is one of the legendary stories of contemporary charity. Something of a phenomenon in banking circles, Avary at 21 was president of the Central Florida Institute of Banking, and while still in his thirties, he was marked for the presidency of the largest financial institution in the Southeast. But then he was suddenly fired for excessive drinking. His wife filed for divorce, he lost his friends and, in quick descending order, he went from one lesser job to another until finally, broke and rejected, he committed himself voluntarily to a state institution for alcoholics where, as he says, "everyone except myself had either a jail sentence or a tattoo." There the former wealthy banker was assigned to such chores as washing dishes and raking leaves. One day, a hobo with whom Avary had struck up a friendship looked him squarely in the eye and said, "Avary, I've never gone to church, but you did. You were on the board of a big Methodist church and taught Sunday school. Well, I have no religion and don't want any. But I've been wondering what sort of religion you had that would let you wind up here with a bunch of bums and tramps like us."

Shaken by the hobo's words, Avary walked out of the institution with the

*The more recent breakdown: UNICEF, 3.5 million; American Cancer Society, 2.5 million; American Heart Association, 2 million; Muscular Dystrophy Association, 1.8 million; United Cerebral Palsy, 1.6 million; American National Red Cross, 1.4 million; Boy Scouts, 1.2 million; American Lung Association, 1 million; Multiple Sclerosis, 900,000; Easter Seal Society, 900,000; YMCA, 689,000; Girl Scouts, 557,000; Salvation Army, 376,000; Boys' Clubs, 375,000; Arthritis Foundation, 335,000; National Association for Retarded Citizens, 265,000; National Foundation-March of Dimes, 250,000; YWCA, 159,000; Camp Fire Girls, 144,000; USO, 40,000. In addition, there are about 20 million United Way volunteers.

resolve to give up drinking and make a new life for himself. In 1957, at the age of 50, he began working his way back up the ladder. Two years later, he became executive vice-president of the Trust Company of Georgia, one of the state's major banking firms. In his spare time, he devoted his energies to a wealth of health and civic activities. Among other things, he inveighed against the evils of alcoholism in countless public appearances, and picked up the cudgel against cancer on behalf of the Georgia Cancer Society of which he eventually became president.

And then an ironic blow struck: He discovered that he himself had cancer—of the colon. Friends feared that he would again reach for the bottle—he used to drink a fifth a day—to sustain himself against the shock. But fortunately he did not and he was operated on successfully, although it took him some time to get used to what he calls "the hole in my side" and with the hour-and-a-half irrigation his colostomy still requires every day. Because he credits his cure to the early detection of his condition, Avary, since his operation, has dedicated himself almost full-time (although he retired, technically, in 1972, he still serves the bank as a consultant) to encouraging others to have adequate checkups, appearing as many as 300 times a year before civic groups and other organizations. (One day he gave seven talks, starting at a professional women's club breakfast and winding up at a Lions Club dinner. "When I got through," he says, "I felt like a bar of soap after a week's washing.")

In his spellbinding talks, Avary, who has the rapid speech of a man who wants to make the most of time, comes on like a combination evangelist and tobacco auctioneer, using what he calls a bold, new dramatic approach aimed at motivating people to protect themselves. Brandishing a coffin handle in one hand and a proctoscope (used by physicians to inspect the lower colon and rectum for cancer) in the other, he says that if not for the proctoscopic examination he'd probably be wearing the coffin handle today. Then, as an inducement to get people past the "fear barrier" of being examined, he offers an array of prizes, ranging from men's suits and towel sets to transistor radios and cases of Coca-Cola, to those who agree to go for checkups and to students who persuade their parents to do so. Avary, who coaxes business and manufacturers into donating the prizes, says, "If trading stamps can motivate people, then I believe gifts for the examination to fight cancer can also motivate people."

The success of his crusade can be measured in practical terms. One spring he spoke to 37 school and other groups during a 45-day period. As a result, 371 persons reported for examinations, more than 80 percent for the first time in their lives. Cancer was detected in 38 of these persons.

To CARE, the overseas relief agency, the "ultimate volunteer" and a shining example of good works is personified in Mrs. Louise Morse, a gutsy, humorous grandmother in her seventies. For many years, this former Newbury, Massachusetts, teacher has crisscrossed the globe for six weeks to two months at a time, visiting CARE projects in Africa, Asia, Latin America, and the Middle East. Her journeys have seen her astride a donkey crossing a frail rope-bridge over a gorge in the Andes, in a jeep passing through barricades in Cyprus, and chatting with Lesotho women in the remote regions of Africa. Back in this country, she recounts her travel adventures at women's clubs and church groups, the proceeds of her talks raising huge sums of money to finance CARE-sponsored clinics, schools, roads, disease-free pure water systems, and other projects.

If any do-gooder deserves to be called a saint, it is Detroit's Mrs. Charleszetta Waddles, a smiling black woman with a startling resemblance to Aunt Jemima. In her "Perpetual Mission" open 24 hours a day in the city's black ghetto, Mother Waddles, as she is affectionately known, and a faithful band of volunteers tend to the needs of the have-nots who descend on the mission in droves. Some come for food to feed their hungry children. One man needed someone to stake him to union dues. A woman needed a Greyhound ticket to the South in order to bury her mother. A young lady needed a prescription filled but had no money to pay. Somehow or other, Mother Waddles, who is in her sixties, finds the wherewithal to take care of every need, although she is always at least $100,000 in debt, even with the occasional fund drives on her behalf and the donations she scrounges; she even once pumped gas at a service station to earn money for the mission. In spite of the fact that it operates on the skimpiest of budgets, the mission manages every year to feed some 100,000 indigents, distribute 1400 Christmas baskets, serve 400 hot Christmas dinners, provide college scholarships for 100 high school graduates, and dispense bus tickets, canned goods, and used clothing as well as good cheer and refuge, aiding an average of 75 families a day.

An ordained nondenominational minister, Mother Waddles, who is assisted by her ten children from three marriages, goes about her good works with a Christian devotion tempered by shrewd ghetto sensibilities. "I don't preach," she explains, "but if people ask for a message, I've got something for them." She likes to ask: "Did you do something for someone today? Did you knock on a neighbor's door and ask how she is? Did you say you'd watch her children so she could go downtown? Did you just let her know you'd help if she needed help? And have you prayed, so that the hungry may be fed, the naked may be clothed, those folks outside can be taken in?"

But even Avary, Morse, and Waddles do not reflect the changes taking place in volunteering and volunteers—changes that have seen the emergence of a new breed of volunteer. A far cry from the upper-middle-class Lady Bountiful stereotypes and the familiar den mother-church worker or doorbell ringer, volunteers today are as likely to be college kids teaching illiterates to read and write, grandparents spending time with children at day-care centers, or minority women organizing tenant groups against slum landlords.

These changes, which had their roots in the 1960s, can be attributed to a variety of factors: shorter workweeks; earlier retirement (the number of early retirees joining the ranks of volunteers increased by 50 percent during a recent ten-year period, according to one study); and the growing number of young people who aren't forced—or aren't able—to find pay jobs; plus the need for personal involvement that many of them have.

The discovery of poverty in the 1960s also served to stimulate the new volunteer spirit which the federal government harnessed when, in a five-year burst of activity, it established in rapid succession the Peace Corps overseas; its domestic counterpart VISTA (Volunteers in Service to America); the Foster Grandparents

Program, under which elderly poor persons care for emotionally, mentally, and physically handicapped children, usually in institutions; RSVP (Retired Senior Volunteer Program), which allows senior citizens to put their skills to use on various community projects; and SCORE (Service Corps of Retired Executives) and ACE (Active Corps of Executives), created to make available the expertise of retired and active businessmen to struggling small businesses and minority-owned enterprises.

Oddly enough, a good deal of the credit for the new voluntarism must also go to that selfless soul, Richard M. Nixon. In a 1968 campaign address, one month prior to his election, Nixon called for "voluntary action by people who care," and in his inaugural address, he elevated his campaign idea into official policy. "We are approaching the limits of what government alone can do," he said. "Our greatest need is to reach beyond government, to enlist the legions of the concerned and committed. What has to be done has to be done by government and people together, or it will not be done at all." In 1971 he merged the Peace Corps, VISTA, and the other federal volunteer programs into a new umbrella agency called ACTION as "the first step toward a system of voluntary service which uses to full advantage the power of *all* the American people to serve . . . the nation." A year earlier, established with his encouragement was the National Center for Voluntary Action (NCVA), a privately funded, nongovernmental agency with the purpose of mobilizing volunteer resources outside of ACTION. (Cynics, suspicious of Nixon's motives even before Watergate, made the point that at the same time he was promoting voluntarism as a cure-all for our social ills, he was cutting down federal spending for social welfare by impounding funds and vetoing legislation for health, child care, education, and housing—all of which would have meant higher taxes for his businessmen cronies.)

Under the aegis of NCVA, a spate of local Voluntary Action Centers (VACs) or Volunteer Bureaus have sprung up in some 300 communities across the country. Operating much like employment agencies, each keeps tabs on which organizations and institutions need what jobs done and recruits volunteers with the time and talents to fill them. Many also serve as catalysts for community projects they feel need implementation. At the VAC office in Chicago, which now places over 2500 volunteers annually with over 450 agencies, would-be volunteers go through a half-hour interview in order to ascertain their special skills, interests, and time availability. The agencies listed with the office range from hospitals, youth clubs, museums, Ys, Planned Parenthood, and the local Cancer Society to such lesser-known groups as Educational Tape Recording for the Blind (which needs volunteers to tape-record textbooks), Altrusa Language Bank (needs translators and interpreters), and Star-Fish (an emergency help service). One bank employee was placed in a volunteer job playing the guitar for the elderly; a lawyer volunteered to serve evenings as a guidance counselor to children. The VAC in Holland, Michigan, arranged for a volunteer pilot to fly an invalid from Chicago to see his dying father.

Here are other ways in which the new breed of volunteer is putting his or her time and talent to use to meet a tremendous variety of community and social needs:

In Minneapolis, Minnesota, a retired member of the Minnesota Orchestra gives violin lessons to children at a cultural arts center, a physical therapist operates a Saturday evening recreational program for deaf teen-agers, and a formerly obese real estate secretary runs a "Fat Children's Anonymous" club at an elementary school.

In El Paso, Texas, a volunteer instructor from a modeling school teaches senior citizens the proper way to walk and apply makeup so they can participate in fashion shows displaying the clothes they have made.

In Topeka, Kansas, volunteers, with the cooperation of the local library, conduct story hours in the city's parks during the summer and at day-care centers during the winter.

In Chicago, Metro-Help, a telephone crisis service, is manned by volunteers around the clock to handle calls from people needing help for problems ranging from drugs to suicidal impulses.

In Atlanta, a convicted felon serving a life sentence for shooting a man to death during a robbery is working to keep others out of prison by working three times a week as an advisor and confidant to youngsters at a juvenile detention center.

Singled out for the "activist" awards the NCVA gave recently was a Dallas citizens' group that helped peacefully integrate the city's school system, and a doctor in Kensington, Maryland, who set up four "mobile medical care" clinics to bring free or low-cost health care to the poor in his county.

Even in the hospital field, volunteering has taken on a new look, although many of the nation's 1,500,000 hospital volunteers still work at such traditional chores as manning the information desk and gift shop, maintaining records, delivering and arranging flowers, transporting patients to and fro, and assisting the nurses and nurses' aides. But at the University of California Hospital in Los Angeles, a retired department store executive selects and shows movies to the hospitalized children. In a Detroit hospital clinic for drug addicts, volunteers obtain patient specimens, dispense methadone, and refer patients to specialty clinics. In New York's Greenwich Village, a Wall Street executive does ambulance duty on weekends. In Oklahoma City, volunteers assist in a program of screening children for visual and hearing problems. At San Diego's Mesa Vista Hospital, specially trained volunteers take turns keeping a 24-hour watch on potentially suicidal patients. And in many hospitals across the country, cured cancer victims visit cancer patients to prove that a return to an active life is possible.

Perhaps symbolizing the new look is the fact that whereas female volunteers formerly wore only pink, they now also blossom out in uniforms of yellow, blue, and other colors. (The Red Cross Gray Ladies now work largely in military and veterans hospitals.) Although teen-age girls still wear candy stripes, the American Hospital Association is now discouraging the use of the term "candy-striper." Why? "Because of its female connotation," laughed the AHA's director of volunteer services, "and because we're trying to get more boys into our programs. Right now, they number only about 7 or 8 percent."

In a recent 10-year period, the number of college student volunteers rose from 5000 on 30 campuses to more than 400,000 in 80 percent of the nation's colleges and universities. At Furman University in Greenville, South Carolina, more than half of the student body of 2000 is involved in 55 volunteer projects; in one, students are teaching janitors and maintenance men how to read and write. At Franklin High School in Livonia, Michigan, 300 students, compared to only 18 five years ago, now participate in projects which range from the presentation of antidrug seminars to the tutoring of elementary school pupils.

Hundreds of schools even give academic credit for volunteer work. Under a government-sponsored program, University Year for Action, more than 1500 students at about 40 colleges and universities are getting a year's credit plus an average of $200 a month for living expenses for serving in poor communities, where their duties range from teaching school to providing legal advice. Whether they receive credit or not, students often find their volunteer work a valuable career learning experience.

At the opposite end of the age spectrum, some 4,500,000 older Americans, according to a recent Louis Harris poll, are now engaged in volunteer activities, and there are another 2,000,000 who say they'd like to be volunteers. Possibly the oldest U.S. volunteer is a black New Orleans woman, Mrs. Rose Richardson, who at age 102 works at home making pillows for Charity Hospital and, in addition, finds time to tend to the needs of her 107-year-old bedridden husband, keep their six-room house clean, wash their clothes on a scrub board, and tend the garden. In Dallas a spry 88-year-old spends 200 hours a year reading to elementary school children; in Boston another school volunteer is 92. And everybody knows by now that President Carter's remarkable mother, Miz Lillian, packed up and went to India as a Peace Corps volunteer in a hospital at the age of 68.

Why do people volunteer? Apart from the reasons already given, a majority (60 percent) of those asked in the 1974 Census Bureau study said they volunteered because of a desire to help people, and a substantial number (38 percent) said they did so out of a sense of duty. Many said they enjoyed volunteer work; others said they volunteered because they had a child in the program, could not refuse when asked, had nothing else to do, or hoped their work would lead to a better-paying job. But motivations, as we already know from our consideration of why people give money, are much more complex than the Census study would seem to indicate. Altruism, of course, plays its role. But as one executive explained, "Aside from the altruism, you know, you get involved for selfish reasons. Sometimes I wake up early in the morning and wonder what I'm really here for. If it isn't to make a contribution, I don't know what it is." Volunteer after volunteer frankly admitted to me that their work probably fulfilled their own needs more than those of the people they helped. "It's a very selfish secret," is the way one cheerful 80-year-old volunteer with the Los Angeles Lung Association put it. "I try to live so that somebody will miss me when I'm gone."

But not all people feel this way. . . .

Returning to New York one November evening after attending a United Way "victory" celebration in Stamford, Connecticut, I boarded the commuter train at midnight. At that hour, there was only one other person in the car I entered—the feminist leader Betty Friedan, an old friend. She was coming from New Haven, she explained, where she had just delivered a lecture to 200 students at the Yale Political Union. What did you tell them? I asked. "That I wasn't the witch of Salem out to seduce the happy housewife," she said in her deep voice. "But that there were still too many women who were dissatisfied and believed something was wrong with them—that they were freaks because they didn't have an orgasm waxing the kitchen floor.'' Our conversation then turned to the United Way meeting I had attended, and from this to a discussion of volunteers for the Red Cross, March of Dimes, and other organizations. What do you think of volunteers—like the Marching Mothers, for example? I asked. ''Oh, f--- the Marching Mothers!'' Betty said in her characteristic, earthy manner. Less than a year later, she was sworn in as a member of—would you believe it?—the national Girl Scout board.

Because so much of traditional voluntarism still persists, so has controversy over its goals, its character, and, indeed, its basic purposes.

Among feminists, as Patricia L. Lucas, an editor of *The Volunteer Leader*, pungently put it, ''voluntarism has become one of the stormiest issues since Susan B. Anthony was arrested for voting in 1872.'' Some elements of the women's movement, like the National Organization for Women (NOW), of which Betty Friedan was the founder and first president, argue that volunteerism is ''a powerful reinforcement of the feminine mystique,'' downgrading women's abilities, and, by increasing their economic dependence on men, jeopardizing their chances for ''equal pay for equal work.'' However, a NOW resolution distinguishes between volunteer activities that contribute toward social or political change (such as those for the League of Women Voters, certain civil rights and conservation groups, school boards, and, of course, NOW), of which it approves, and volunteer labor for social services, which it regards as little more than an extension of demeaning, unpaid housework.

When her children were in school, Mrs. Lorraine J. Fromm, a Glen Cove, New York, housewife, offered her services to the community hospital. ''The 'fulfilling' job I was given was doing dishes in the coffee shop and working behind the counter,'' she says. ''At age 36, I have decided to forget this whole idea of volunteering as it has been most unfulfilling and degrading, and I have gone back to college for some selfish fulfillment and find I am now looked up to and respected, rather than being asked, 'Oh, do you have too much time on your hands? Well, we'll find something to keep you busy.'''

''I wish all women would quit volunteering,'' says Mrs. Connie Siegel of Bedford, New York, who kicked the habit after 12 years to go into public relations. ''Now, I realize all the wonderful, marvelous bedpan things Gray Ladies do, but volunteer work has got women running around doing dirty work. The idea is when a woman finished cleaning the toilet at home, well, let her go do a little striped-lady work at the hospital.''

Women, and not necessarily women's libbers, also complain that many charities, apart from perpetuating the image of women as servants, support other sexist traditions. In their division of work and power, they say, there is little, if any, room for women at the top, and their activities are usually confined to a so-called ''women's division.'' *Lilith*, a Jewish women's quarterly, has pointed out that the United Jewish Appeal's National Young Leadership Cabinet, for example, the grooming ground for future UJA leaders, is restricted by policy to Jewish *men* between the ages of 25 and 40. (Emphasis added.) One of the main reasons lamely offered for excluding women is the fear that their attendance at the cabinet's traditional retreats would lead to extramarital affairs! A cabinet member, however, was more blunt when he joked: "I think women should have equal opportunity, equal rights at every level—so long as they know their place."

On the other hand, the Junior League, that elite organization of predominantly wealthy and socially prominent young women, which was organized in 1901 to promote voluntarism, believes that, contrary to keeping women subordinated to men, volunteer work has allowed women "to achieve management positions that were denied them elsewhere." While conceding that the status of a volunteer is often degrading, Mrs. Ellen Straus, founder and head of "Call for Action," a nationwide volunteer-staffed consumer complaint radio program, defends volunteers as the vigilantes necessary to the well-being of our society. To upgrade the status of the volunteer, Mrs. Straus is a leading proponent of the concept of what she calls the "volunteer professional." "The volunteer professional," she explains, "would be hired and fired, trained, supervised and promoted exactly like any paid worker, and be given written job references if she cared to go from the voluntary professional world to the paid professional world."

There is also a growing movement favoring the idea of permitting volunteers to take tax deductions or tax credits for the time they contribute (based on the federal minimum wage), reimbursing them for certain out-of-pocket expenses, such as meals and baby-sitting (the Internal Revenue Service now only allows deductions for uniforms, transportation to and from the place of service, and meals and lodging away from home under certain circumstances), and giving them insurance coverage. Unlike paid workers, who are covered by Workers' Compensation, a volunteer injured on the job or sued in connection with his or her duties is generally personally liable. In recent years the National Center for Voluntary Action has made available to agencies a special volunteer insurance plan at the cost of $1.50 a year for each volunteer's policy. The suggestion has also been made that tax incentives be given to companies that allow their employees to participate in volunteer activities during working hours.

Since many of the chores performed by volunteers are identical to positions found in the salaried work world, involved in the controversy, too, are labor unions, which view volunteering as an insidious threat to their members. Says Thomas Hobart, president of the 200,000-member New York State Teachers Union, which has taken a strong position against volunteers in the schools: "We're not opposed to volunteers per se, but what we have in New York is a situation where there are 50,000 unemployed certified teachers and an attempt is being made to substitute volunteers for those performing professional services." Hospital volunteering is also seen as taking jobs away from people, particularly low-paid employees who, moreover, find their leverage for higher pay demands weakened by the availability of competing free labor. The fact that volunteers have occasionally crossed picket lines—in hospitals, schools, nursing homes, and other institutions—has also prompted union officials as well as feminists to raise the question, "Saint or scab?"

Even the government has been drawn into the controversy with National Center for Voluntary Action Chairman George Romney attacking the $200 million-a-year agency ACTION's policy of paying stipends to many of its volunteers, and going so far as to say that the federal government "will be the biggest sweatshop operation in America if ACTION continues to pay its workers."*

Those inclined to agree with Romney assert that unpaid volunteers have a special dedication and freedom of action that is lost if they lean on government money and supervision—what they charge has happened to some social workers. ACTION officials, on the other hand, argue that the stipends increase professionalism and effectiveness by allowing full-time devotion to the task.

But underlying these donnybrooks are some serious fundamental questions. Should our society depend on volunteers in the first place? If they serve needs that are important, if not crucial, to the nation's well-being, should not the government have the obligation to assume these needs? Or, is voluntarism merely an attempt to mask the inadequacies in our social order?

NOW, in addition to arguing that voluntarism is a depressant to women's status, also rests its case on the broader issue of responsibility and calls for government to assume those of its obligations that are now being palmed off on volunteers. "So many of the services that women provide should be picked up by the government and the private sector," says Mrs. Pat McCormick of NOW. "Rather than have a woman teach a child to read on a one-to-one basis, we would like to see a woman devote her efforts to changing the system that failed to teach the child to read. As long as women don't continue to challenge that national priorities be reordered, they are propping up a system that would fail without them. These women are rushing in with Band-Aids for a system that is in need of massive reorganization."

Not all women and women's groups agree; in fact, the great majority probably does not. Dorothy I. Height, president of the National Council of Negro Women, an umbrella organization of 26 national groups, concedes that volunteerism might sometimes seem like a Band-Aid. "But," she also points out, "the funny thing is that at times all you need is a Band-Aid, and if you don't have it, it could be crucial and grow into something worse. Most black women's organizations wouldn't be here at all if it weren't for volunteers. You have to work in both directions, social service and change. While you work to open the doors, you have to salvage the talents, interests and spirits of people so they will be ready to walk through those doors."

Says Ellen Straus in agreement: "Anyone who believes social change only comes about in certain forms of volunteering or only through paid employment is plain wrong. Talk about social changes—how can paid employees make changes or even complain about what they see when their jobs are at stake? Volunteer workers are the only ones not afraid to speak out, who blow the whistle on conditions in schools, nursing homes, mental institutions, homes for the elderly. Besides, no one can tell me that working on a one-to-one basis with a child in school, someone in a prison or a mental patient is degrading."

Jacqueline K. Levine, cochairperson of the American Jewish Congress, makes

---

*Peace Corps volunteers receive from $275 to $325 a month (depending on the country in which they serve) plus a "readjustment" allowance of $125 a month; VISTA volunteers receive from $300 to $400 a month plus a "readjustment allowance of $75 a month; Foster Grandparents average $35 for a twenty-hour week.

a similar point: "Without the pressure and the concern of the volunteers, American institutions would be even more conformist, controlled and stratified than they are." Recalling the time she tutored a black student in Newark, she adds: "Let's be honest. We're in a period of a constricting economy. If money isn't there for all the other absolute necessities, it certainly isn't there for the jobs that volunteers do. I'm not willing to say, 'OK, all you kids in Newark, you'll never learn to read because we're waiting for government funds.'"

And here is the late Margaret Mead in defense of volunteers: "We live in a society that always has depended on volunteers of different kinds—some who can give money, others who give time and a great many who freely give their special skills, full time or part time. If you look closely, you will see that almost anything that really matters to us, anything that embodies our deepest commitment to the way human life should be lived and cared for, depends on some form—more often, many forms—of voluntarism."

However, no less a distinguished student of our history than Henry Steele Commager takes a more cynical view. Referring to President Nixon's promotion of voluntarism, Commager wrote in *The New York Times* of March 4, 1973:

> The object of President Nixon's "new federalism" (which is neither new nor federalism) is to balance the budget, dismantle ineffective social services, and to provide more money for the military. It is submitted to the people not in this bold fashion, however, but as a reduction in Big Government and a return to localism and voluntarism. . . . The notion that voluntarism and local authorities can deal effectively with the national and global problems which crowd us is without support in logic or history and is dangerous to the well-being of the Republic.

What would happen if the people of American could or would no longer volunteer? Where would the billions and billions of dollars come from to pay for the services they now render? NOW's answer is that where high priorities are given, the "work which otherwise would not get done gets done, and it gets done by paid employees in a planned coordinated manner." Pointing out that voluntarism has not been suggested in such high-priority areas as the development of space technology or in military or national defense, NOW asks: "How much would have been accomplished in the field of space if the government had asked of its citizens that they volunteer their services, in their free time and at no pay, to get a rocket to the moon? Are our social problems any less complex or important than a journey to the moon?"

PART III

THE DONEES

Chapter 7

In the Name of Religion: Giving in Good Faith

In Miami not too long ago, an electrical worker named Hugh McNatt, a Baptist, sued his church for the return of his tithes. His pastor, McNatt said, had promised that "blessings, benefits, and rewards" would come to those who tithed—that is, gave the church one-tenth of their income. McNatt claimed that after three years of tithing he had received neither blessings, benefits, nor rewards.

The incident is unusual in that many religious givers do not expect tangible benefits from tithing—a custom that goes back to biblical times. In fact, nowadays relatively few givers tithe, although many Christian churches still preach the value of such giving, often invoking the words of God from the book of Malachi, chapter 3, verse 10: "Bring ye all the tithes in the storehouse and prove me now if I will not open you the windows of heaven and pour out a blessing."

Nonetheless, even without such pastoral prompting, nearly half—or, by far, the largest share—of the U.S. charity dollar goes to the nation's churches, synagogues, and similar religious institutions. In 1978 such contributions amounted to $18.4 billion, or 47 percent of the total of $39.6 billion given to all charitable causes, according to the latest estimate by the American Association of Fund-Raising Counsel (AAFRC). However, the estimate, admittedly no more than a well-informed guess, is probably on the conservative side.* For example, in 1972, when the AAFRC estimated religious giving to total $9.7 billion, the Commission on Private Philanthropy and Public Needs (the so-called Filer Commission) came up with the somewhat higher figure of $12.5 billion.

Even these estimates, however, fail to give a complete picture of how much our religious institutions actually receive. The figures, for example, include only fragmentary data on such other major segments of church and synagogue income as endowment earnings and other earned income, interest from investments, and bequests. They also fail to include the large sums given to the so-called "church-related" institutions and agencies—such as schools, hospitals, homes for the aged, child-care centers, and other welfare organizations—whose annual receipts the Filer Commission estimated at an additional $7.5 billion.

*The AAFRC estimate is based on projections of samplings of data on donations provided by the major Protestant denominations to the National Council of Churches as well as on extrapolations of sparse data available on Catholic and Jewish giving. The NCC readily admits to the probable inaccuracy of the figures it compiles annually.

What makes it virtually impossible to get any precise figures on religious giving is that they are known only to God. As a dubious extension of the "separation of church and state" clause of the Constitution, religious institutions, unlike other nonprofit groups, are exempt from filing or making public their financial figures; and most of the 235 established church bodies* in the United States, with the exception of some 45 Protestant denominations, prefer to regard their finances as a confidential matter. (That such confidentiality can lead to abuse or even outright fraud is something we'll get into later.)

The Church of Christ, Scientist, even forbids the release of figures as to the number of its members. Otherwise, generally accepted estimates place total church membership at 132 million, or 61 percent of the U.S. population. Of these religiously affiliated Americans, approximately 71.5 million are classified as Protestants (a classification embracing our 2 million Latter-Day Saints, or Mormons, although they do not consider themselves as Protestants), 49.3 million as Roman Catholics, and about 6 million as Jewish. Another 3.7 million are Eastern Orthodox, 846,000 are members of the Polish National Catholic and Armenian Churches, 60,000 are Buddhists, and the rest are members of a miscellany of other Christian and non-Christian sects—Spiritualists, Ethical Culture, Hare Krishna, as well as such groups as the Rev. Sun Myung Moon's controversial Unification Church and Guru Maharaj Ji's Divine Light Mission.

How does giving compare from one religious group to another? Annual per capita giving among Protestants averages $159 but obviously is much higher in denominations that practice tithing. Topping the list of the major denominations tallied by the National Council of Churches is the Seventh-Day Adventist Church, whose 522,000 members contribute an average of $602; lowest on the list is the African Methodist Episcopal Zion Church, whose 1.8 million members contribute an average of $44. The largest Protestant denomination, the 13 million members of the Southern Baptist Convention, gives at the rate of $137 per capita. No comparable data are available on Catholic and Jewish giving but it is probably at least as high as the Protestant average, perhaps even higher.

Collection procedures differ somewhat in each of the three major faith groups. The collection or offering plate is a traditional fixture at the Sunday services of Protestant and Catholic congregations. To facilitate collections and stimulate regular giving, all Catholic parishes, as well as many Protestant churches, now also use the envelope system of soliciting money: Once a year every adult parishioner is given a package of envelopes, each predated for all the Sundays and holy days of the year ahead.

To supplement the Sunday cash and envelope collection, a handful of Protestant churches, in what may presage the fund-raising procedures of the future, have been participating in a National Council of Churches fledgling program called ACTS (for Authorized Contribution Transfer Services), which allows parishioners to charge contributions automatically at monthly or quarterly intervals, against their bank accounts. Because the more observant Jews can't handle money on Saturday, their day of worship, the bulk of synagogue income is from annual membership dues. In response to the occasional appeals conducted during

---

*Actually, our nation is blessed with 1275 distinct "primary" religious groups, according to the National Council of Churches, but these groups include UFO cults, practitioners of witchcraft, and other exotic sects.

the course of the year, synagogue members generally pay by putting a check in the mail, sometimes after filling out a pledge card. (During Jewish High Holy Days, when observant Jews also aren't allowed to write, some synagogues distribute imprinted pledge cards, which contributors can notch to indicate the amount pledged.) Some synagogue and church income also comes from the proceeds of bazaars, bingo, raffles, theatre parties, cake sales, and other fund-raising events.

An estimated three-quarters of the receipts of all three major faith groups goes for sacramental, or strictly religious, purposes—that is, for the maintenance of the houses of worship and conducting services and related activities. The remainder is to support various nonsacramental activities both inside and outside the congregation—educational and youth programs, health and community activities, welfare work, as well as an array of cultural, environmental, and even civil rights activities as more and more churches have become involved in social action in recent years.

Typical of some nonsacramental activities and also reflecting the recent ecumenical movement that sees more and more congregations of different denominations working (and on occasion, even worshiping) together is a community effort in Atlanta where 12 churches are sponsoring a center that operates free clinics, sells old clothes, and donates food to nearly 200 needy families a year. In similar vein, 11 churches in the Houston area are jointly sponsoring a day-care center and counseling programs for troubled families and drug abusers.

However, the great bulk of nonsacramental activities are conducted not by the churches themselves but rather by church-related institutions and agencies, which, it should be noted, receive about two-thirds of their support from service fees and government grants. But the sources of support vary from one faith group to another: Jewish organizations, for example, rely heavily on gifts from individuals, whereas Catholic ones depend on grants from the parishes, dioceses, and other religious bodies, while Protestant institutions and agencies receive more United Way funds than the other faith groups.

How the money is spent also varies considerably from group to group. Nearly three-quarters of Jewish expenditures are concentrated on hospitals and health agencies, with most of the rest channeled into social welfare and relatively little allocated to education. Catholic expenditures are almost equally divided between education and health; far less goes to social welfare proportionately than that characteristic of Jewish agencies. On the other hand, Protestants focus most of their expenditures on social welfare, with large proportions also going to education and health activities. Jewish agencies also send far more overseas (largely to Israel)—perhaps twice as much—than Catholic and Protestant agencies combined.

But perhaps the best way of examining and evaluating religious giving is by taking a close look at each of the major faith groups in turn, starting with the oldest.

Jewish Giving

At the Lincoln Square Synagogue, a handsome, marble, modern Orthodox house of worship on Amsterdam Avenue in midtown Manhattan. It is the Monday evening of October 8, 1973, scarcely 48 hours after the surprise Arab attack on Israel on Yom Kippur, the holiest day on the Hebrew calendar. An emotional meeting, hastily convened, is in progress. Although little more than a *minyan,* the ten male Jews required for religious services, is usually present in a synagogue on a weekday, 300 people are in attendance this Monday evening.

To open the meeting, the cantor chants the psalm, *Shir Hamaloth* ("Out of the depths I cry to Thee, O, Lord"), as the congregation repeats each verse after him. "There is nothing casual about someone who loses his life," says Rabbi Steven Riskin, his voice quivering with emotion. "Yet it is my sad task to tell you that the casualties at this moment are greater than they were during the Six Day War. The great majority of them are young men between the ages of 18 and 21." He reads a prayer in memory of the Jewish martyrs, *Eil Molei Rohamin,* and concludes: "In their hallowed memory those in this congregation offer charity. . . ."

A representative of the United Jewish Appeal then takes over. "Thirty years ago there was an all-out assault to destroy the Jewish people in Europe," he begins. "At that time various statements were made as to how much a life was worth. For example, there was an offer to trade 10,000 trucks for a million Jews. This involved only a truck for every 100 Jews, but the people concerned decided that the Jews weren't worth that much—or that little—and so they weren't saved. We must now raise money, big money. You can either give through the UJA or you can buy Israel bonds. And for those who didn't bring their checkbooks, we have blank checks here."

He then reads the names of those who have already given or pledged contributions: "The Albert family is donating $5000. Jerome and Jane Stern, $5000. William and Fanny Kaplan, $1000. Anonymous, $1000. . . ." Each of the names read is greeted by applause. A member of the assemblage marches to the podium. "I want it understood I don't want any applause, please, and I want it to remain anonymous," he says. "But Mrs. Goldberg and I pledge $10,000. . . ."

Across town at the Park East Synagogue, 500 of the congregation's affluent Orthodox worshipers contributed $2.5 million, and Beth-El synagogue in the suburban Long Island community of Great Neck raised nearly $2 million. The United Jewish Appeal of Greater New York reported that its switchboard was "absolutely swamped" with calls pledging aid to Israel and that more than 7500 people had come to its offices personally—some of them, youngsters with piggy banks—to make contributions from 50 cents to $25,000 during the first four days since the outbreak of the war. One New Yorker who had given $5000 the year before contributed $250,000. "The response is fantastic," said the UJA's campaign director who smilingly added: "I even believe the Orthodox are talking to the Reform."

Across the country, there was a similar outpouring of sentiment and funds. On that Monday evening following the surprise attack, no less than a million Jews—one out of every six in the nation—were gathered at the hastily summoned meetings in 1000 synagogues. At a Memphis synagogue $1 million was raised for Israel and at synagogues in Cincinnati and Columbus, Ohio, another $1.4 million. In Chicago a woman came to her synagogue with a check for $2000 and deposited her jewelry in a handkerchief. In the same city doctors at Mount Sinai Hospital pledged over $28,000 and several, along with 22 nurses, volunteered to serve in Israel. Jews took out loans, sold stock, and mortgaged their homes in order to contribute or to buy Israel bonds. A Milwaukee bank offered loans to Jewish contributors at 8 percent, several points lower than the commercial rate. Some banks, like the Trust Company of Georgia, headquartered in Atlanta, purchased more than $200,000 in Israel bonds during the week following the attack. A waggish apocryphal story, inspired by the Jewish penchant for pledges, had it that robbers of a Miami bank made off with $20,000 in cash and $2 million in pledges.

All in all, donations ran way ahead of the record sum of $175 million contributed during the month following the Six Day War of 1967. In the first week alone of the Yom Kippur War, what the Jews themselves call "checkbook Judaism" produced nearly $250 million for their beleaguered spiritual homeland, $145 million through the sale of Israel bonds (which pay only 4 percent interest) and more than $100 million in outright contributions to the UJA. Certainly, both catastrophes, that of 1967 and 1973, demonstrated the remarkable willingness of America's Jews to give.

Even under ordinary circumstances the record of Jewish giving is spectacular. America's 6 million or so Jews make up less than 3 percent of the population and are divided on many fronts—religious, cultural, political, among others—with rivalries that are frequently more venomous than friendly. (As a saying goes, in a group of three Jews you'll find four opinions.) Yet virtually all share one common ground—giving, particularly where Israel is concerned. The nation's Jews give nearly half as much to the annual United Jewish Appeal-Federation of Jewish Philanthropies Campaign (about $460 million in 1977) as 37 million Americans of all faiths, including Jews, give annually to the nonsectarian United Way (a shade over $1 billion in 1977). The "gross national product" of Jewish philanthropy—that is, the aggregate cost of the various communal services it provides—has been estimated to be close to $3 billion a year; the figure, in addition to donations, includes service fees and government payments to Jewish hospitals and other institutions but excludes such things as the endowment income of the federations and local agencies, local capital fund campaigns, and synagogue operating expenses.

What accounts for such phenomenal giving to Jewish causes? The religious tradition of *tzedaka*—the closest Hebrew equivalent to "charity"—no doubt has something to do with it. But Jews, in spite of their sectarian bickering, make up a social and cultural community as well as a religious one. A common heritage has forged in Jews a feeling of kinship to the point where a Manhattan Jew can identify more closely with a Moroccan Jew than he may with his next-door neighbors. And perhaps more important, centuries of oppression, in the ghettos of Eastern Europe and the *shtetls* of the tsars, taught the Jews that if they were to survive they would have to depend on themselves—for everything from education and medical care to the barest necessities of life. Jewish philanthropy is also spectacularly successful because of the unique, ingenious techniques used to induce Jewish people to give, but this we'll go into at length in a later chapter.

In contrast to the nearly $3 billion that goes to Jewish communal causes every year, only about $300 million goes to the nation's 3100 synagogues, which fall into three major groupings: Orthodox or traditional congregations, Conservative, and Reform, the most liberal. About two-thirds of this comes from annual membership dues, the sale of seats to the High Holiday services, plus extra donations by members, and the proceeds of bazaars, theater parties, and other special events and from occasional assessments for projects of one kind or another. The remaining one-third, roughly $100 million, comes from tuition fees for schools which have an estimated enrollment of 400,000—125,000 in Sunday schools, 200,000 in week-day afternoon classes, and 75,000 in all-day schools.

On what do the synagogues spend their money? Since not all the costs of operating their schools—about $150 million a year—are met by tuition fees, $45 million of the total synagogue receipts of $300 million goes for education, with most of the rest used for strictly religious purposes. A small amount of synagogue income is also allocated for club programs, public lecture series on contemporary issues and problems, volunteer work on behalf of the needy and disabled, and participation in the work of community organizations ranging from Red Cross to Scout Councils. Some synagogues even sponsor hot meal programs for elderly shut-ins.

Outside the synagogues, Jewish activities are supported by funds collected through annual federated drives in approximately 235 communities.* The local Jewish federations, which in some communities are called "welfare funds" or "community councils," are joined in a national coordinating body, the Council of Jewish Federation and Welfare Funds, founded in 1932 and headquartered in Manhattan. The United Jewish Appeal conducts more than 700 local campaigns, which are combined with those in the 235 federated communities wherever they exist; elsewhere, usually in the smaller communities, they are independent campaigns.

Of the funds raised in the UJA-Federation joint campigns, an average of 35 to 40 percent goes to local charities—hospitals, day schools, homes for the aged, YMHAs and YWHAs, and so on. The largest of the campaigns is in Greater New York, which, with a Jewish population of 2 million to call upon, now raises about $85 million a year. On a per capita basis, however, the premier campaign in the country is in Cleveland which, though with only 80,000 Jews, raises $16.5 million a year. Detroit, with about as many Jews as Cleveland, raises just a shade less. Comparing relatively unfavorably is Los Angeles, whose 450,000 Jews— more than five times the number of those in either Cleveland or Detroit— contribute $27 million annually—less than all the Jews in both of the smaller cities.

The remaining 60 to 65 percent of campaign money goes to the United Jewish Appeal, which is probably the most successful money-raising machine in the history of philanthropy. Beginning with collections of $15 million in 1939, the year it was founded from several existing organizations, the amounts raised have grown spectacularly year after year, reaching a total of $240 million in the year of the Six Day War and a peak of $510 million in 1974 (the year following the Yom Kippur War), when combined UJA-Federation campaign receipts were a

*The federated drive, one of the contributions of Jewish fund raising to American philanthropy and the forerunner of the nonsectarian United Way, was first done successfully by a number of Jewish charities in Boston in 1895, and a year later in Cincinnati before spreading to other Jewish communities.

record $660 million. From 1939 through 1977 the combined campaign total exceeded $7 billion, of which $4.5 billion was allocated to the UJA. (About 10 percent of the UJA's receipts come from its local independent campaigns.)

The national UJA does not of course solicit contributions in communities where combined campaigns are conducted, although it will provide a local federation with everything from speakers to publicity materials. Under a complicated mathematical formula, the UJA in turn parcels out its receipts to its member agencies. The bulk—86 percent in a typical year—is allocated to the United Israel Appeal which finances programs to transport and resettle needy immigrants in Israel, providing them with everything from housing and health care to job training; 11 percent goes to the American Jewish Joint Distribution Committee—widely known as The Joint—which provides a wide range of health, social welfare, and educational services to about 400,000 needy Jews in some 30 foreign countries, including Israel, and which through ORT (Organization for Rehabilitation and Training) offers vocational training courses to hundreds of thousands of Jews around the world. The rest of the receipts goes to NYANA (New York Association for New Americans), except for a small grant to HIAS (Hebrew Immigrant Aid Society), another agency concerned with the resettlement of Jewish refugees.

Not to be confused with charitable contributions, although a formidable factor in Jewish overseas aid, are purchases of State of Israel bonds. Since 1950 total bond sales in the United States have exceeded $3 billion, with the proceeds channeled into agriculture, industry, power and fuel, housing and schools, transportation, communications, and other sectors of the Israeli community.

As if things aren't complicated enough, there are also at least 300 Jewish national and countless local organizations which, for one reason or another, prefer to remain outside the Federation-UJA umbrella—outside the pale, one might say—and conduct their own independent campaigns.

Among the bigger or better-known ones with overseas programs are Hadassah, the women's Zionist group, whose 360,000 members practice benevolence and sociability by raising $30 million a year to maintain a network of medical, educational, youth, and other social welfare programs in Israel; the National Committee for Labor Israel, which raises $3.5 million a year to support the welfare activities of Histradut, Israel's labor federation; Israel's Hebrew University, Technion, and Weizman Institute, whose fund drives bring in a total of $35 million a year; and the America-Israel Cultural Foundation, which raises about $2 million annually to support and promote Israeli cultural activities involving musicians, painters, dancers, and others engaged in the creative arts. To show you that there is no limit to what America's Jews are asked to do for their spiritual homeland, there is even an organization soliciting funds here to build homes for Israel's newlyweds.

For the benefit of Jews on these shores, there is even a greater plethora of independent groups. B'nai B'rith (Sons of the Covenant), founded in New York City in 1843 to unite "Israelites in the work of promoting their highest interests and those of humanity," today has 500,000 members, including women and young people, in chapters and lodges all over the world. The oldest service organization in America, its $25 million budget is used for various cultural, recreational, and social activities and programs: The Anti-Defamation League, a separate arm of B'nai B'rith, fights anti-Semitism through a continual monitoring and publicizing of evidence suggesting such sentiment as well as through legal action; the Hillel Foundations, operating on some two hundred campuses, are roughly equivalent to the Catholic Newman societies and the Methodist Wesleyan clubs. Other B'nai B'rith activities include adult study programs, career guidance and job counseling, and volunteer work for Jewish welfare campaigns here and abroad.

The elitist American Jewish Committee, with a membership of about 40,000 and an annual budget of $9 million, also works to combat bigotry and to protect the civil and religious rights of Jews here and abroad; it also conducts educational programs on anti-Semitism, Israel, civil rights, interfaith problems, and other subjects of interest to Jews, and publishes the lively intellectual and influential journal *Commentary*. The more middle-brow American Jewish Congress, with 50,000 members and a budget of nearly $4 million, has somewhat similar purposes but operates at a more international level. The 100,000 members of the National Council of Jewish Women, sometimes characterized as the domestic, upper-class equivalent of Hadassah, works with the handicapped, the disadvantaged, and the sick, and pioneered in the formation of the Golden Age Clubs for the elderly. The organization operates on an annual budget of $2 million.

Among the better-known institutions conducting independent campaigns are Brandeis University, which raises about $18 million a year, and Yeshiva University and its Albert Einstein Medical School which raise $5 million. The City of Hope Hospital in Los Angeles and the National Jewish Hospital in Denver both raise a total of $19 million with only nominal support from local federations. No accurate estimate exists as to how much is raised through all these and other independent campaigns but some authorities put the total at about $200 million a year.

Compared to other charities, the operating costs of Jewish philanthropy are relatively low. During the Federation-UJA combined campaigns of recent years, fund raising and overhead costs have ranged between 9 and 11 percent of the amounts collected and pledged; equally small ratios of expenses to proceeds are characteristic of many of the independent Jewish charities. One reason for this is the extensive use of volunteers, many of whom pick up the expenses involved in their fund-raising efforts. Another lies in the heavy reliance on big gifts. Gifts of $1000 or more account for 80 percent of all federated campaign receipts, and it obviously costs less to raise a few sums this size than it does to bring in lots of relatively smaller ones. The UJA's seemingly low fund raising expenses do not take into account the fact that many of these expenses are assumed by the Federation in the communities where combined campaigns are conducted. And so Jewish charities in general are rarely ever criticized for their fund-raising costs.

However, critics of the Jewish charity establishment do question whether the funds are being spent to fit the changing needs of today's Jews, and, in fact, wonder to what extent so-called Jewish charity is really Jewish. They deplore, for example, the use of funds to support so-called Jewish-sponsored hospitals which, though originally established to serve patients who observed the Jewish dietary laws and to provide training and job opportunities for Jewish doctors, are now nonsectarian as far as patients and doctors are concerned (in some, fewer than a third of the patients are now Jewish) and, moreover, are largely supported by service fees and government, Blue Cross, and other "third party" money. New York's Beth Israel Hospital, for example, now gets only about $400,000 a year—less than one-half of one percent of its total operating revenues of $88 million—from the local Jewish Federation.

For similar reasons, also criticized is Federation support of "Jewish" homes for the aged and the various agencies serving the handicapped, the retarded, the blind, the deaf, the orphaned, and the troubled, as well as the nation's 100 country camps and 300 or so YMHAs and YWHAs, and other Jewish community centers, many of which are patronized by Gentiles as well as Jews. In Boston a survey by the local federation found that only 9 percent of Jewish people troubled with personal problems sought help at a Jewish agency, compared to 21 percent who chose to unburden themselves at a non-Jewish agency. At New York's Louise Wise Services, established in 1916 to help Jewish unwed mothers and place their offspring for adoption, virtually the entire residential, child care, and adoption caseload is now black and Puerto Rican, and otherwise non-Jewish.

The critics' attacks are also directed against the so-called "defense" agencies, such as the Anti-Defamation League, whose work combatting anti-Semitism is today scornfully regarded as irrelevant. That the real danger to the American Jewish community is not anti-Semitism, but attrition, is how James Yaffe sums up the sentiments of those who feel that in order to keep Jews in the fold, Jewish money should more properly go to institutions and agencies—notably schools, generally regarded as the stepchildren of organized Jewish philanthropy—that help perpetuate Jewish traditions and learning, particularly at a time when interfaith marriages and sociocultural influences are causing many Jews to stray from the faith. (According to one study, the proportion of Jews intermarrying rose from fewer than 10 percent in the first six decades of this century to more than 30 percent in recent years.)

Without denigrating the needs of Jews in Israel and elsewhere overseas, the young Turks of the Jewish movement also feel that much more attention should be paid to the needs of the relatively unpublicized Jewish poor here at home. In New York City alone there are from 250,000 to 300,000 Jews now living near or below the poverty level and there may be as many as 800,000 in the nation as a whole, according to one survey.

In responding to such criticisms, the UJA's executive vice-chairman Irving Bernstein says that the Jewish needy are the same whether they are in the Soviet Union, Israel, Morocco, or the United States. Federation officials, in answer to the charges that they have been slighting schools, say that over the years they have increased their allotments to education; and in fact the federations now provide $19 million a year for education, more than triple the allocation of the mid-1960s. However, even the increased figure still represents only about 18 percent of the total local allocations by federations. Moreover, the federation grants go largely for teacher training or communal schools, open to all the Jewish children of the community, rather than to synagogue schools, usually open only to children of members (although some will also accept nonmembers' children at a higher tuition charge).

All of which raises a host of other problems reflecting the power struggle also going on between the secular and religious elements of the Jewish establishment.

Federation and other lay leaders look at the various types of synagogue-sponsored schools (Orthodox, Conservative, and Reform) as too narrowly parochial, each so sectarian as to threaten the hoped-for ideal of Jewish unity. The rabbis, on the other hand, are not wildly enthusiastic about the communal schools, ostensibly on the ground that they are somehow less Jewish than their own but more probably because they regard them as competition. (After all, some people join synagogues, paying fairly hefty dues, primarily to be able to send their children to their schools.) For similar reasons, synagogues have even made plain their opposition to Federation-supported Jewish community centers. As one rabbi complained bitterly, "Why should their centers get support? We have our own centers! The competition is hurting us!" Similar feelings are vented about giving to hospitals. "Let's face it; hospitals can't save Jews for Judaism," is the way another rabbi put it. In the struggle, the secular element would seem to have the upper hand, for the federations do, after all, raise and control most of the money. At the same time, no federation campaign would get off the ground if the rabbis refused to give it their blessing or, even worse, denounced it from the pulpit.

This leaves Jewish philanthropy on the horns of a delicate dilemma. If the rabbis, by in effect equating Judaism with the synagogue, succeed in their efforts to pry more money out of the federations, many contributors who are not particularly religious could be lost to Jewish philanthropy. (Only about half—perhaps only a third—of all Jews are actually synagogue members, while only 16 percent attend services regularly.) They might well reduce their Jewish giving or cut it out entirely and perhaps channel their charitable donations into the avowedly nonsectarian causes. On the other hand, if the federations continue to raise money for secular causes, their Jewish following could be lost to them as more and more Jews cease to feel they are Jews and, by attrition and intermarriage, are lost to the synagogue.

Just how the dilemma is resolved can affect the future course of Jewish philanthropy for better or for worse. But as we shall see, similar dilemmas are also present in the Catholic and Protestant worlds of giving.

Roman Catholic Giving

Unlike Jewish giving, which has no central religious hierarchy to coordinate it, virtually all Roman Catholic giving, even for nonsacramental purposes, is under the control of the church, whose temporal universe in the United States is divided into 18,572 parishes which are grouped into 32 archdioceses and 130 dioceses, each an autonomous unit presided over by a bishop who reports his diocese's full financial figures only to Rome. However, since the Vatican is as reticent about revealing anything about its fiscal state as the dioceses, no official figures are available on just how much is given by the nation's 49.3 million Catholics.*

All we can therefore do is to work with the figures we have. Of the $2.8 billion estimated by the Filer Commission as the annual income of Catholic churches

---

*In reaction to strong lay criticism, some dioceses have moved in recent years to develop uniform accounting procedures and make public at least some of their figures. However, these generally fail to include what the dioceses receive from the local parishes, which represent a sizable portion of their income.

(other estimates range from $4 to $14 billion), nearly $9 out of every $10 (87.3 percent) comes from individuals, either through the Sunday and holy day plate collections or as extra gifts during the year. Another 1.3 percent comes in the form of bequests. (Approximating the findings for the other major faith groups, 45 percent of these contributions come from the top 20 percent of givers; the Jewish and Protestant top givers contribute, respectively, 50 and 52 percent.) Another 8 percent of parish income comes from the proceeds of bingo, bazaars, cake sales, and other special events; nearly 1 percent represents endowment earnings; and a minuscule amount—0.4 percent—comes as grants from the diocese and archdiocese. The remaining 2 percent is from various miscellaneous categories.

Where does the money go? Roughly 9 percent of church receipts is sent to the diocese as an assessment (the so-called *cathedraticum*) to help support its operations and institutions and agencies; also funneled to the diocese are the funds from the special collections—the Peter's Pence collection (the annual offering to Rome), the Bishop's Relief Fund (for overseas relief), and the Campaign for Human Development (poverty), among others. Most of the rest, as much as 70 to 80 percent, of the money collected by a church goes to cover its own expenses— salaries, maintenance, repairs, outlays for food, sacramental wines, vestments, and the other necessities of religious services.* Relatively little church income—about 11 percent, or $310 million of the $2.8 billion collected, according to the Filer Commission—goes for nonsacramental purposes, most of this concentrated on activities which see the parish priest in the role of social worker and community do-gooder.

These nonsacramental expenditures, which do not include the value of the donated services of priests, sisters, and other volunteers, account for but a mere fraction of all Catholic charitable activities. The Filer Commission estimated that $5.6 billion a year also goes to Catholic schools, hospitals, and other "church-related" institutions and agencies. To be sure, nearly two-thirds (63.9 percent) of this represents "service fees" (tuition, hospital charges, and other fees for services) and another 7 percent comes from government payments (largely to hospitals); only 12 percent comes from the church itself and 6.7 percent from individual gifts and bequests.

Just how is this $5.6 billion spent? About half of it—$2.6 billion—goes for education. No religious group supports education to the extent of the Catholics, who have a system that extends from the lowest primary grades to the highest level of university training. In a recent year, 3,268,291 students attended 9976 Catholic elementary and high schools, and 442,770 young men and women were enrolled in 241 Catholic colleges and universities, accounting for about 4 percent of the total enrollment of private institutions of higher education. Whereas the colleges and universities are financed primarily through fees and tuition and receive virtually no church support, the high schools and elementary schools depend heavily on diocesan, parish, and some private subsidies to supplement their tuition fees. Government subsidies to parochial schools are of course unconstitutional and whether or not they should be is a subject of passionate debate

---

*For those interested in delving more deeply into the financial details of the Catholic Church, a comprehensive, lively study is the book *Worldly Goods* by James Gollin (Random House, New York, 1971).

in not only the Catholic but also the Jewish community, with the Orthodox Jews generally aligned with most Catholics in favoring some sort of public aid to alleviate their schools' perpetual financial crisis.

In keeping with the church's age-old tradition of ministering to the sick, another big chunk of the church-related funds—44 percent or $2.3 billion—goes to hospitals and other health-care institutions. In a recent year, the church maintained 730 hospitals, with 170,145 beds, which treated 31.4 million patients; the same year, 19,967 student nurses were enrolled in 131 Catholic training schools. Although the hospitals to a large extent are staffed by members of religious orders, whether or not they can properly be called charitable institutions is open to question. A respectable portion of their receipts—about $200 million a year—do represent philanthropic contributions. But by far the largest part of their income—about $2 billion—is from patient fees and insurance payments, with another $230 million coming from federal government funds.

As counterparts of the Jewish federations, there are Catholic Charities corporations in most U.S. dioceses; their annual fund drives are on behalf of an array of causes which range from homes for the aged and Catholic Youth Organization athletic programs to "heroin baby" clinics and family and marriage counseling agencies. Although the services provided are, of course, aimed primarily at Catholic communicants, the diocesan-run corporations issue ecumenical disclaimers to the effect that they are available to all comers, regardless of religion or race. True, a sick old Jewish lady might prefer to drop dead before availing herself of the visiting nurse service of the Little Sisters of the Assumption, and a pubescent Protestant might hesitate before joining a Catholic Boy Scout troop. But the fact that this is at least theoretically possible enables Catholic Charities member agencies to tap government and other nonsectarian sources of funding. "There is much closer cooperation with government nowadays," said an official of New York's Catholic Charities. "In the welfare field, there is no separation of church and state."

According to the National Conference of Catholic Charities, of the estimated $332 million-plus a year raised by its member agencies in 1977, 46 percent came from the government, 11 percent from local United Ways, 17 percent from service fees, 6 percent from the annual Catholic Charities parish fund appeal, 4 percent from diocesan grants, 1 percent from foundation and other grants, and 15 percent from special gifts, endowment income, and a miscellany of other sources.

In Chicago, seat of the largest archdiocese, Catholic Charities, with a budget of approximately $40 million for its 122 member agencies, claims to spend less than 2 percent of its budget on fund-raising and administrative expenses. The claim is believable in view of the donated services and volunteer time Catholic Charities can muster for these activities.

Yet, echoing the complaints of the critics of Jewish philanthropy, some bishops feel that the church should concentrate on its education worries and leave *conventional* forms of welfare work to nonsectarian agencies or to the government. In some dioceses, Catholic Charities, reflecting the disinterest of the bishop, is a lackluster operation. During the renowned Fulton J. Sheen's tenure as Bishop of Rochester, where Catholics comprise nearly 30 percent of the city's population, the Catholic Charities corporation there didn't even conduct any

fund-raising drives; instead, Bishop Sheen asked Rochester's Catholics to contribute to the city's Community Chest (now United Way) and he himself, a
dedicated social activist, got the diocese deeply involved in work in the inner-city
and ghetto areas.

The church's concern about poverty can also be seen in its Thanksgiving
collection for the National Conference of Catholic Bishops' Campaign for
Human Development which got under way in 1970. Marking a new direction in
the course of Catholic benevolence, the Campaign mustered the resources of the
church nationally for the first time in order to attack the poverty problem.* The
total of nearly $60 million raised in the first eight annual campaigns was used to
fund more than 1300 self-help projects "administered by and for the poor."
They ranged from a Chicago program geared to train blacks and other minority
group members for jobs in trucking and a program in Tucson, Arizona, to train
Yaqui Indians in construction skills in order to provide low-cost housing for
Indian families to a project establishing a Hayti, Missouri, credit union to provide loans and financial counseling to the poor.

For the overseas needy, most church aid is channeled through Catholic Relief
Services, created in 1943, which, as mentioned earlier, now ships food, clothing,
medicines, and other necessities—valued at $225 million in 1978—to an esti-
mated 18 million persons in some 86 countries. Most of the foodstuffs are
donated by the U.S. government which, along with some of the recipient countries, also defrays shipping costs; some of the goods, such as clothing, blankets,
and bedding, are contributed through annual Thanksgiving Clothing Collections
at most Catholic parishes throughout the country. However, the basic church
support to CRS comes from the annual Laetere Sunday collection, generally
about the fourth Sunday in Lent, which in 1978 brought in about $9 million, of
which $8.3 million went to CRS, much of the rest going for migration and
refugee services.

In his midtown New York office, CRS's assistant executive director, Monsignor Andrew P. Landi, explains the agency's operations, which requires a domestic and overseas staff of about 900. "In general, we work through a local
government agency or private agency which need not necessarily be a Catholic
agency, for our work is nonsectarian. I would say that probably more than half of
the 18 million we assist during the course of a year are non-Catholic and probably
non-Christian. The reason I say this is because in Morocco, for example, we help
about 600,000 people, and practically all of them are Moslems."

Why does CRS, rather than the governments involved or the United Nations,
furnish such aid? "The significant contribution of the religious sponsored
agency," says a CRS brochure, "is that its assistance is social and spiritual as
well as economic. It is personal; it touches the whole man in a way governmental
or inter-governmental aid cannot."

There are also various international welfare programs run by many Catholic
missionary groups of one sort or another, such as the Catholic Medical Mission
Board (CMMB), a 50-year-old Jesuit agency that sends medicines, instruments

*This Thanksgiving campaign should not be confused with the annual Thanksgiving Hunger Fund
campaign, launched in 1978 on behalf of the world's hungry by an ecumenical coalition of agencies
representing the nation's three major religious faiths—Catholic Relief Services, American Jewish
Joint Distribution Committee, and Church World Service.

and other medical supplies to Catholic mission hospitals, clinics, and dispensaries overseas. In 1977 CMMB's shipments to 1594 missions in 46 countries had a wholesale market value of $8.7 million; although most of what it ships is donated by U.S. pharmaceutical companies, CMMB also purchases a "goodly amount" besides with the cash donations it receives, some in response to four mail appeals it sends out every year.

Whether or not one should respond to the appeals of such missionary and other religious groups will be discussed in the following chapter.

Protestant Giving

No other faith group is as large or diverse as the Protestant, whose 71.5 million adherents, about a third of the nation's population, hold membership in about 185 different denominations. In doctrine, Protestant churches range from those that subscribe to a strict and literal interpretation of the Bible (Seventh-Day Adventists, Baptists) to those that look upon it as no more than a library of inspired books (Lutherans, Methodists); in style of worship, they range from those that conduct quiet, conservative services to the evangelical sects which encourage a free flow of emotion; in organization, from denominations with hierarchical, episcopal forms of government to those with completely autonomous organizations; in size, from Michigan's Church of Daniel's Band with 4 congregations and 200 members to the coast-to-coast Southern Baptist Convention with 35,000 congregations and 13 million members. The diversity is further demonstrated by the fact that there are at least 29 different Baptist church bodies and 13 different Lutheran denominations. As one would expect, these and other differences are reflected in denominational giving habits.

As mentioned earlier, per capita giving varies considerably from denomination to denomination, being highest in the smallest sects and those that practice tithing. Different denominations may also hold varying views as to what should be regarded as sacramental and nonsacramental activities. In most denominations a certain portion of the funds collected by the local congregations are forwarded to their regional or national church bodies; some of these funds may flow back to underwrite special local projects of one kind or another. However, in some sects, such as the Assemblies of God, Church of God, and various Baptist groups, the local congregations assume the right to decide just how and where their funds will be used.

Of the $9.5 billion collected annually by Protestant churches, according to the Filer Commission's estimates, 90 percent comes from individuals, nearly 3 percent from endowment and investment earnings, about 5 percent from regional and national units of the denomination, and the remaining 2 percent from a miscellany of other sources. Most of the funds received—76.7 percent—are used for sacramental purposes, 7.7 percent goes to the churches' regional and national units, and 15.6 percent, or about $1.8 billion, is used for a wide variety of nonsacramental activities—much the same as those supported by Jewish and Catholic congregations, although with perhaps a greater emphasis on those involving social action.

This by no means accounts for all Protestant nonsacramental expenditures. Many regional denominational bodies, for example, contribute to the support of church-related institutions: hospitals, schools, homes for children and the aged, domiciles for unwed mothers, neighborhood or community houses, and welfare agencies of many types. There are also many interdenominational bodies concerned with social welfare and social action—state and local church councils, national groups like the National Council of Churches, and the thousands of YMCAs and YWCAs. But as financial data on all of these church-related institutions and agencies are not readily available, it is impossible to come up with a total for Protestant nonsacramental expenditures, although they would probably exceed the $7.5 billion estimated annually for comparable Catholic and Jewish organizations.

Many of the Protestant church-related institutions and agencies, like the Catholic and Jewish ones, have become increasingly secular. Almost all of the nation's 445 Protestant colleges, though under denominational auspices, admit students of all faiths*; Protestant hospitals, too, are generally nonsectarian and today receive less than one percent of their operating expenses from religious sources, although some may still have a certain religious character and, like other Protestant institutions and agencies, may have key churchmen on their boards.

The same situation holds true for the federations of Protestant welfare agencies, which, although not as numerous as their Jewish and Catholic counterparts, may be found in some large cities. The New York Federation, for example, although originated in 1922 under Protestant auspices, is no longer church-controlled and is nonsectarian in character; in fact, it now solicits funds from the general public, and its 300 member agencies annually serve 1.5 million persons of varying or no church affiliation. However, many of the member agencies, in name or spirit, still have a distinctly Protestant flavor—the Federation roster, for example, lists a Presbyterian Home for Aged Women, a House of St. Giles the Cripple, the Salvation Army, and a good many YMCAs and YWCAs (but no YMHAs or YWHAs).

Operating with a budget of about $2 million a year, about 20 percent of which is spent on fund-raising and other administrative costs, the Federation does not provide financial support to the extent that the Jewish Federations or Catholic Charities do; rather, it devotes most of its efforts to the role of coordinator and consultant for its member agencies, which are concerned with providing services to the aged, children, and the infirm, plus a variety of the traditional family welfare, youth, and community services. Since the beginning of the decade, however, the federation began shifting its attention to what it called "the very

*Most of our best-known colleges and universities were established under religious auspices. The Congregationalists founded Harvard, Yale, Dartmouth, Amherst, Williams, Western Reserve, Oberlin, among many others. The Presbyterians created Princeton, the University of Pittsburgh, and New York University, to name only a few. Born of Baptist initiative were Brown, Colgate, Bucknell, and Vassar; and the Methodists were responsible for Northwestern, Duke, Wesleyan, and Boston. Quaker contributions include Swarthmore and Earlham; and the Episcopalians can claim credit for William and Mary, Columbia, and Trinity. Indeed, of the 180 colleges and universities in existence in 1860, 150 were started by religious denominations. Of course, most of these institutions as well as others that came into being later now have only the most tenuous religious ties, if any at all; many, in addition to cutting their original denominational ties, have turned control over to lay boards, eliminated chapel services and mandatory religious services, and have otherwise sought to play down their religious identity. Among those approving this secular trend was George Bernard Shaw who once said that a church-related college was a contradiction in terms, feeling as he did that religious commitment and academic freedom are incompatible.

special problems of the Seventies,'' and it now devotes 40 percent of its resources and staff time to devising, implementing, and, on occasion, providing seed money for neighborhood self-help projects, which in recent years have included a storefront school organized by a former teacher to help neighborhood children with learning problems, a self-help day-care center, and a 27-foot community mobile health unit used to test for tuberculosis, venereal diseases, sickle cell anemia, lead poisoning, diabetes, and hearing and vision defects.

Within the Protestant churches themselves there has been a continuing controversy as to the role they should play in social problems. During the 1960s mainline Protestant churches were often in the vanguard of social and political activism. Clergymen marched at Selma for civil rights and in Washington against the war; the churches set up nationwide programs to fight poverty, build housing, and promote education. Protestant church leaders even went so far as to vote payment of some $5 million in ''reparations'' to blacks and other minorities; the United Presbyterian Church alone contributed $10,000 to the defense fund for black militant Angela Davis after her indictment for murder and conspiracy and gave another $25,000 for the bail and defense of a Black Panther accused of plotting public bombings. In recent years, however, something of a reaction has set in. There has been a growing feeling among many—parishioners as well as preachers—that the church should stick to religion and keep its nose out of race relations, politics, poverty, and all of society's other tender areas.

These views were articulated in January, 1975, when a group of 18 prominent conservative churchmen, after meeting in Hartford, Connecticut, issued a widely publicized white paper—a 13-page manifesto which came to be known as the Hartford ''appeal.'' The appeal urged Christians to reject the ''false and debilitating'' ideas the group charged had crept into the church, attacked the church's ''surrender to secularism,'' and urged that social action had no biblical justification. Feeling that the Hartford ''appeal'' strengthened a dangerous, escapist trend in religious thought, a group of 21 liberal Boston theologians, including the Harvard Divinity School's famed Harvey Cox, counterattacked a year later with a dramatic document that attracted front-page headlines across the nation. Titled the ''Boston Affirmations,'' it called on Christians to recognize God's concern for the world and insisted that Christians have a responsibility to help the poor and the oppressed and to combat other social ills.

There has been another element to the controversy. Many local activist congregations seriously committed to good works have been resentful of their national leaders or of such interdenominational groups as the National Council of Churches for committing them to programs over which they have had little say.

Whatever the cause of the resentment it sparked a growing ''pocketbook revolt'' for several years among the laity and adversely affected contributions to the national headquarters of many Protestant churches. Annual contributions to the traditionally activist United Church of Christ offices alone dropped by more than $1 million between 1968 and 1972, no doubt reflecting the results of a UCC survey which showed their church members to want more time and money devoted to the individual's ''faith crisis'' and to programs that would strengthen the local congregation. After the 1970 feud-ridden Episcopal church general convention, where the big bone of contention was the blacks' demand for ''reparations,'' 50 of the 92 Episcopal dioceses failed for a number of years to fulfill their quotas for contributions to the national church; a poll of the dioceses showed that parishioners wanted the church to give them more Christian education, more evangelism, and more programs for young people—"the church's own, rather than the alienated sector alone." Although other factors may have played a role in the drop in contributions, other denominations faced similar imperatives as a North American Interchurch Study survey found that whereas a heavy preponderance of lay people and clergy felt that the church's paramount duty was to "win others to Christ," 76 percent of the laity and 61 percent of the clergy disagreed or tended to disagree with denominations giving money to minority groups "with no strings attached."

Although church social action programs have consequently diminished somewhat in recent years, the controversy over social action has also embroiled Church World Service, the overseas relief arm of the National Council of Churches. Set up in 1947 in response to the needs of the areas devastated during World War II, CWS has since broadened its program to offer help wherever it is called for. In 1977 it shipped to 61 countries all over the world, as well as to several disaster-struck areas in the United States, a total of 51.3 million pounds of clothing, blankets, textiles, medicines, vitamins, food, tools, and other goods valued at $12.5 million. Expenditures of $15.2 million for various program services brought total CWS aid for the year to over $27 million. The services included the resettlement of 2200 refugees (bringing the number assisted to a total of more than 200,000 since World War II) as well as disaster relief, agricultural development, family planning, nutrition, and educational job training.

None of these activities, one would think, would arouse any opposition. Yet for its humanitarian efforts, CWS has at one time or another been castigated by critics as red, fascist, liberal, reactionary, pro-American, anti-American, colonialist, imperialist, pro-Arab, pro-Israeli, pro-black, anti-black, an "agent of international Communism," "lackey of the State Department," and "traitor to American foreign policy," to cite only a few of the items in the catalog of calumny sardonically quoted by *A.D.*, a Presbyterian magazine, in a highly laudatory article on the much-maligned organization.

What has brought on these pejoratives has been the traditional penchant of CWS for helping people of all political persuasions. As *A.D.* pointed out, it did not suit American foreign policy at first for Church World Service to feed Biafran village children during the Nigerian civil war. Rightists were unhappy when CWS aided the political victims of the 1973 military coup in Chile, and leftists were unhappy when CWS helped fugitives from the oppressive Marxist regimes in Poland, East Germany, and China. In 1978 some federal officials were angered when CWS shipped grain worth $2 million to Vietnam, although the U.S. government had readily granted the export licenses for the shipment.

Should church funds be used simply to help people—feed them, resettle them, and otherwise provide relief—or should they also be an instrument for change, by, say, attacking the root causes of poverty and, if necessary, helping poor people acquire power and change the systems that created their poverty? The question has long been the subject of acrimonious debate in church circles and has reflected serious policy differences in the higher echelons of the National Council of Churches.

The differences burst into public view in the mid-1970s, when James McCracken, after nine years as the highly regarded executive director of Church World Service, was suddenly removed from his post by his superior, the Rev. Eugene Stockwell, head of the NCC's overseas division. "In order to perform our function, we have to work with people wherever and whoever they are," said McCracken, an intense, bespectacled man in his fifties. "Now if this means serving under a tough regime in Brazil or Biafra, this is more important than not being there at all. You have to work with all sorts of governments and accept them for what they are, or you don't operate. There are many things about the Brazilian government we may not approve, but there would be no way of serving people in need there if we were declared persona non grata."

McCracken also told *The New York Times* that Stockwell, on the other hand, believed that a top priority of the church was to educate people about "the vital need for systematic change from some of the more horrendous political regimes in the world." In favoring the addition of political emphasis to traditional relief work. Stockwell, according to those in the know, wanted to involve CWS in direct political and intelligence work overseas, including support for armed revolutionaries, if necessary. Stockwell, of course, denied all this, and a CWS statement stated emphatically that the agency was not "in the business of promoting violent change." The Associated Press also quoted him as saying that he did not want CWS to withdraw from work in any area. But, at the same time, he stated that he had been "raising clearly the questions about ways we may, even unintentionally, give undue support to repressive governments when we want to avoid such a thing."

Religious giving is so personal and subjective that it would seem almost presumptuous to question it, to apply to it the same standards that one does to other forms of giving. You give to your church or synagogue because, by heritage or by choice, you are a member of it and therefore, religious motivations aside, you have an obligation to support it, with the expectation of no more than certain spiritual satisfactions in return, unlike the disgruntled tither mentioned at the beginning of this chapter. If your house of worship does not choose to report its income and expenses or, if it does, spends its funds on activities not entirely to your liking, you are free to leave the fold.

But when any church, religious group, or church-related institution or agency reaches outside of its membership and solicits contributions from the public at large, that is quite a different matter. Many such organizations—Church World Service, the Salvation Army, the Jewish and Protestant federated agencies, even Catholic Charities, as well as most schools and hospitals—make available fairly detailed financial reports to guide prospective givers. However, other organizations do not, and the abuses, even chicanery, this can lead to is described in the pages that follow.

Chapter 8

Christian Charity— and Gullibility

Help these children with your contributions. They are but a sample of children in the Pallottine Missions who are either starving, sick or naked. Very few smile because malnutrition, disease and lack of clothes is no fun. . . . The Pallottine Missionaries will convert your contributions into food, vitamins, medicines and clothes.

From time to time over the years I used to receive heart-rending appeals like this from the Pallottine Fathers of Baltimore, a venerable Roman Catholic missionary order with 2200 priests and brothers in 23 countries. You probably did, too, for in just the 18-month period ending December, 1975, the Pallottines mailed no less than 150 million appeals, some of them including free offerings of ball-point pens, calendars, and prayer cards and, for those entering the "Free Pallottine Sweepstakes," the chance to win automobiles, sailboats, color TVs, stereos, cameras, pool tables, or cash prizes.

As a result of these appeals, the Pallottines raked in an estimated $20 million in contributions during the 18-month period (and a total of $56 million from 1970 through 1975). The problem was that only a pittance of these proceeds—less than 3 percent—ever reached the missions and their "starving, sick or naked." Where did the rest go? The bulk went to pay the costs of the mailings, including postage which alone came to as much as $2 million annually (ranking the order as the second largest bulk-mailer in Baltimore). But it was what happened to much of the remainder that aroused the curiosity of the state attorney general and the Baltimore *Sun*, whose revelations attracted national attention and led to the indictment and conviction in 1978 of the Pallottine's fund-raising director, the Very Rev. Guido John Carcich.

Millions were sunk into speculative motel and real estate deals in Florida and five other states and invested in various business ventures, one of them a portable classroom manufacturing company that figured in an investigation that resulted in the indictment of Maryland's school construction chief. One curious chunk—$54,000—found its way into a loan that helped pay for Maryland Governor Marvin Mandel's 1974 divorce. (And the Catholics don't even recognize di-

vorce!) Father Carcich, after previously professing his innocence, finally pleaded
guilty to diverting $2.2 million of the charitable contributions into 28 secret bank
accounts and squandering part of the money on fellow Pallottines, friends, and
relatives; the sum of $52,000, for example, went for the purchase of a house in
New Jersey for his niece. Under the plea-bargaining arrangement (which permitted him to plead guilty to only one count of the original 61-count indictment),
Carcich, for all his fiscal sins, was placed on probation for 18 months and
ordered to work for one year "ministering to the needs of prisoners" in the
Maryland penal system. Through all these revelations, the inquiries of the Maryland attorney general, as well as those from several other states, were repeatedly
rebuffed by the Pallottines, who claimed absolute exemption from financial
disclosure because of their status as a religious group.

True, as an aftermath of the revelations, senior officials of the Catholic Church
stripped the order of its fiscal autonomy and imposed a moratorium on future
Pallottine investments, loans, and mailings pending a "comprehensive study and
review of existing fund-raising methods, practices and philosophy." But who
knows how many other toilers in the vineyards of the Lord, providential enough
to avoid discovery, continue to hide similar abuses, if not out-and-out charla-
tanry, behind the shroud of secrecy erected by the church itself?

For example, as far as I know, the church has never been impelled to "review" the fund-raising practices of another of its legion of mail-order mendicants, St. John's Missions, although in some years not a dime of the dollars raised
by the Jesuit group to support its educational endeavors in Belize (formerly
British Honduras) ever got out of the United States. Curiously, the donors solicited through mail appeals were asked to send their contributions to a purported
St. John's "headquarters" in Jennings, Missouri, a suburb of St. Louis. Why
Jennings, Missouri?

When this question was posed to St. John's, its director, Father James Short,
writing from the mission's actual headquarters in Belize, said that the reason for
the Jennings address was to simplify the handling of responses "which would be
more difficult to handle here in Belize." The mission's New York-based attorney, Bernard Perlman, responding to a similar query from the Better Business
Bureau of Greater St. Louis, went even further, justifying Jennings on the ground
that "some of the people interested who can handle the work on a voluntary basis
are located there." He further explained that the work was being "supervised by
a member of the Jesuit order."

However, neither of Perlman's assertions were "entirely accurate," according
to a later letter to the BBB by the mission director himself, then a Father Leo
Weber, who said that there were neither volunteers nor Jesuits at Jennings. Instead, Father Weber explained, the contributions pouring into Jennings were
being processed by a local enterprise called Handi-Shop, which handles fund
appeal returns for a number of charities. Handi-Shop, in spite of its nonprofit
status, has consistently refused to furnish the BBB with any data about its
operations. It had been recommended to St. John's by the firm that prepared and
mailed its appeals, Gratian J. Mayer Associates, a Hyattsville, Maryland, direct
mail house now known as Creative Mailing Consultants of America (CMCA)

and, incidentally, also a Perlman client. For its services to St. John's, Handi-Shop received about $1800 a month, a figure that Father Weber confessed seemed to him "very high," according to his letter to the BBB. Father Weber also said that he was not entirely happy with some "loose ends" of the Handi-Shop operation. "For instance," he wrote, "I have no record of the number of envelopes opened by Handi-Shop. Then there is the question of all the returns getting to the bank. Checks, I presume, are safe. Cash could be a problem."

In any event, no one would say how much money was being funneled through this elaborate fund-raising apparatus. When I asked St. John's, it politely referred me to attorney Perlman. Perlman, a suave soul whom we shall meet again later in these pages, said he had no financial figures and referred me back to St. John's. The reason for this reticence is easy to understand for, as Father Weber (now head of the Missouri Jesuit Province) later reluctantly admitted to the *Washington Post*, 100 percent of the proceeds during the first two years of the appeal was earmarked for building a contributors list, that is, was spent to get new contributors. And what happened to the donations of the new contributors? Even in the third year of the campaign, only 20 percent of every dollar contributed, St. John's said, went to support its work in Belize (the rest presumably going to CMCA, Handi-Shop, and the U.S. post office). In 1974, the mission said, half of the money received was going to pay for its acts of benevolence in Belize. But who really knows?

Nor has the Catholic Church manifested any curiosity about the activities of the Southwest Indian Foundation of Gallup, New Mexico, which every year sends out 7 to 10 million letters appealing for funds to help the Navajo Indians of the area "bridge the gap between poverty and prosperity," as one solicitation put it. The appeals, which often contain such trinkets as "Indian-style" key chains (actually produced in places like Japan, Taiwan, and Hong Kong), cookie cutters, packets of marigold seeds, and greeting cards, promise that the donations will be put to use to improve the Navajos' humble homes ("$3 will pay for the fixtures in a bathroom"), provide water and electricity, build roads and bridges, and assist in the funding of similar projects.

Of course, there is no way for the recipients of the appeals to know that the foundation has any religious ties, let alone a Catholic connection. True, the appeals letters are signed by a "Reverend Dunstan Schmidlin" but they give no indication that he is a Catholic priest nor that the foundation is other than a secular operation. The fact, however, is that Father Schmidlin, a Franciscan and the nominal head of the foundation, is also chancellor to the bishop of the Roman Catholic diocese of Gallup, and the foundation itself is a benevolent arm of the diocese. Such a church affiliation, as we know by now, is enough to win an organization exemption from any nosy public disclosure laws and, as a by-product of this, the permission to raise money in New York, California, Pennsylvania, Massachusetts, Illinois, and many of the other states that ban solicitations with known high fund-raising costs.

When I also learned that Creative Mailing Consultants of America, from its Hyattsville, Maryland, base, turned out the Indian givers' engaging appeals, just as it did those for St. John's Mission, and that none other than Bernard Perlman of New York also served as the foundation's attorney, I decided to go to Gallup.

Before doing so, however, I sought to learn whatever else I could about the foundation.

The National Information Bureau, which monitors national charities, told me it had written repeatedly to the organization since 1969 "requesting information generally made readily available by sound agencies" but had received nary a reply; a bureau official said, however, that because the foundation mailed out unordered merchandise, generally an extremely expensive method of fund raising, it would automatically fail to meet the bureau's basic standards. Counselor Perlman was his usual evasive self: "They're part of the Church—that's all I can tell you. I don't have any information on their financial figures, either, and frankly, it doesn't matter. What they want to do in terms of making information available to the public is up to them." The nation's Better Business Bureaus had also drawn a similar blank in spite of innumerable inquiries about the foundation; the Los Angeles bureau alone showed me a file of 75 inquiries. In Hyattsville, CMCA president Raymond La Placa expansively told me, "The Indians are an extremely attractive cause today because there's an awful lot of guilt feeling resulting from what we white people did to the Indians." Then, in an unguarded moment, he said that $3 million was not an unreasonable estimate of the proceeds produced by the foundation's mailings during the course of a year. But what portion of the proceeds actually went to the Navajos and was this being put to any good use?

The Navajo Tribal Council wrote me that funds from the foundation were indeed being put "to good use." But then, in response to a follow-up letter, it confessed it did not know just how the money was being spent since it was not being channeled through the tribal office. Also in the dark was the government's Bureau of Indian Affairs which, moreover, challenged the foundation's appeals for implying that the organization was the only resource available to the Navajos: "This implication is not true." Nor could the Gallup-McKinley County Chamber of Commerce shed any light on the foundation's operations; the chamber referred me to the McKinley County manager who, while having some words of praise for the foundation's work in the county, said, "I am not aware of and have some doubts about how they raise their money, however."

Strangely enough, even the bishop of Gallup himself, the Most Rev. Jerome Hastrich, seemed somewhat embarrassed when asked about the foundation. "I have no knowledge of their income, their reserves, or anything else," he said. When it was pointed out to him that the foundation claimed to be part of his diocese, he replied, "Father Schmidlin emphasizes the diocesan connection when it's convenient for him."

The bishop's profession of ignorance may have been genuine. For, during the course of my visit to Gallup, William Grotefend, the lay person directing the foundation's day-to-day operations, told me: "Though we're affiliated with the Catholic Church, no money goes to the Church and no money comes from the Church for our operation."

"Then why the church connection?" I asked. "Why is the church involved at all?"

"That's because of our direct mail program," he said with a straight face. "In order to get the benefit of the lower postal rates to which religious organizations are entitled, we're attached to the church." I was incredulous. As even fledgling fund raisers know, religious organizations do not enjoy any lower rate than other nonprofit organizations. And Grotefend had cut his teeth on the direct mail campaigns of the Disabled American Veterans (see Chapters 14 and 17) and was for three years CMCA's planning and creative director, originating the Southwest Indian Foundation's mailing pieces, before foresaking Hyattsville for New Mexico.

Grotefend, a pleasant, affable man of about forty, would not tell me how much the foundation spent on the various projects it funded or even show me a list of the projects, but he did agree to take me to one. In his Chevrolet Blazer camper, we headed south of Gallup on a dusty, bumpy dirt road. "There's roughly 2000 miles of road in this area, but only 350 miles of it is paved," said Grotefend. "Now the way we work is that we try to fill gaps wherever they may exist—for bridges, culverts, water, housing, electricity, things like that. But we don't sponsor or do anything 100 per cent; we work only in cooperation with existing agencies." As we drove, dust seeped through the floorboards of the camper. "Now, let's take the bridge we're coming to." We pulled up to a small steel bridge over a gully. "Before this bridge was built, the road washed out whenever it rained. This prevented men from getting to work and kids from getting to school. Now they can in any kind of weather. We put up $1000 toward the building of the bridge, and the Bureau of Indian Affairs and the state highway department each put up another $1000. Other agencies donated equipment and manpower to the point where the total value of the bridge is about $25,000."

Could I see the vouchers to support the foundation's $1000 contribution? I asked. Grotefend said they would be difficult to dig up. He also said that only Father Schmidlin could answer the other questions I had. When we finally caught up with Father Schmidlin, he was, to Grotefend's dismay, on his way to the First State Bank of Gallup to check on the daily receipts from the mailings. Both men had no choice but to allow me to accompany them. In the bank, they proceeded to a locked basement room in front of which stood an armed guard. Inside the room, I saw 14 people, most of them women, doing nothing but sorting and opening huge piles of envelopes, extracting money from them and tallying the amounts on large sheets.

"Would it be unreasonable to ask what your contributions amount to in any given year?" I asked the priest, a tall, athletic-looking man, who seemed to be in his mid-forties.

"It wouldn't be unreasonable to ask but it would be unreasonable for me to answer," he said.

"Why? As a contributor to your organization, don't I have a right to know how much money you take in and how you spend it?"

"I don't see any reason why I shouldn't give you this information, but at the same time I don't see why I should."

"But if you filed a Form 990 [the detailed report of income and expenditure most charitable organizations are required to file with the IRS], this information would be a matter of public record."

"But, as a religious organization, we don't have to file a 990."

I tried a number of other approaches as the priest chafed under his collar. "You can try all day, but you won't get me to change my mind. You could even crucify me. . . ."

But if one accepts CMCA's estimate of $3 million as the foundation's annual income and Grotefend's statement to me that the foundation's fund-raising costs run from 45 to 47 percent of income, this would leave from $1.35 million to $1.41 million to be doled out to the Indians. Should one accept these figures in view of the fact that I was also told that the Indian givers were involved in only about 30 projects a year and that $1000 was a fairly large allocation for a project? There can be no question, however, that major beneficiaries of the foundation must include CMCA and the manufacturers of the merchandise that accompany the mailings.

To again appreciate the importance of a church connection, let us now move across the country to Lancaster, Kentucky, the heart of Appalachia and the base of operations of the Christian Appalachian Project (CAP), founded in 1964 as a self-help, nonsectarian, nonprofit organization to create jobs for and so improve the living conditions of the people of eastern Kentucky. As in the case of the Southwest Indian Foundation, CAP's appeal letters are signed by a man of the cloth, this time by the "Rev. Ralph W. Beiting," but again with no indication that project director Beiting is a Catholic priest, which he in fact is, holding down as he also does the post of pastor of Lancaster's St. William Roman Catholic Church. In the latter capacity, incidentally, Monsignor Beiting refers to himself and signs his chatty church newsletters and other communiqués as *"Father* Ralph W. Beiting," never as *"Reverend* Beiting," a ministerial honorific common in Protestant circles, but less prevalent among Catholics. Needless to say, there is also not a word in CAP's appeal letters to indicate that it has any connection with St. William.

This tactic, however, serves a number of purposes. Because explicitly Catholic causes have only parochial appeal, CAP's nonsectarian face is aimed at a wide range of prospective donors; its sub rosa Catholic face, on the other hand, frees the organization from the obligation of obeying the same regulations that nonreligious charities must, and enables it to solicit in the states which impose certain ceilings on fund-raising costs.

All this is not meant to denigrate Father Beiting's devotion to the destitute among whom he has worked selflessly ever since he came to the region, perhaps the most poverty-stricken in all of the United States, as a young priest in 1950. When first taken to meet him several years ago, I found him chopping some logs for firewood at Camp Nelson, a once-thriving community, not far from Lancaster, which CAP is now in the process of revitalizing. Father Beiting, a chunky, white-haired man in his early fifties with the build of a football linebacker, put down his ax, greeted me, and muttered: "We would have saved money if we'd burned the whole damn log pile. But we have the responsibility to conserve our resources and there are some people who can use the wood."

He said that during his early years in Appalachia he faced suspicion and mistrust from the region's mountain people, most of them fundamentalist in belief, who look like something right out of the movie *Deliverance*. "As a Catholic, I was about as welcome as a porcupine at a balloon party," he said. "A petition had even been gotten up to throw me out of town."

He began to win the people over, however, when he scrounged food, fuel, clothing, and shelter for them and, using part of his salary, purchased a piece of property and started a summer camp for their children. Then the old folks, earning an average of $1000 a year from primitive tobacco farming, asked what he could do for them. ''I found that giving them food and the other essentials of life didn't really change anything,'' said Father Beiting. ''Jobs seemed to me the only way to do that.'' He begged and borrowed money to buy land for farms the people could work cooperatively, then started a woodworking factory plus a number of stores and other industrial and retail enterprises in his four-county parish, eventually incorporating all of these activities under the name Christian Appalachian Project.

Raising money was, of course, a problem for the fledgling antipoverty organization. When Father Beiting got permission from his local bishop to start it, it was with the understanding that it would be completely independent of the church and would not count on the church for any support. CAP's articles of incorporation also said nothing about its having any ties to the church. To raise money, Father Beiting, though a complete neophyte in the use of direct mail, hit on the idea of getting up an appeal letter and sending it to cities with heavy concentrations of Catholics. ''We looked in the phone books for all the Irish, Polish, Italian, and Spanish names.'' From such appeals, CAP wasn't able to clear more than $5000 or so a year and remained a relatively small shoestring operation, although Father Beiting started to pick up awards almost annually for his humanitarian endeavors: In 1969, for example, he was designated Kentucky's Outstanding Citizen.

CAP's fortunes took a dramatic change for the better, however, in 1970 when it somehow came to the attention of those ubiquitous direct mail specialists—yes, none other than the firm now known as Creative Mailing Consultants of America in faraway Hyattsville, Maryland. Father Beiting agreed to let CMCA organize a national mail appeal for CAP, and by 1973 some 8 to 9 million letters a year, prepared with CMCA's customary panache and often accompanied by such items as address labels, plastic bottle caps, and soap holders, were drawing annual contributions of over $2 million and netting CAP about $650,000; the remaining two-thirds of the gross receipts went, of course, to pay for the cost of the mailings.

An amount so high would be bound to raise the hackles of those states, like New York, which limit fund-raising costs to no more than 50 percent of gross receipts from any direct mail campaigns including unordered merchandise, exempting from this regulation only religious groups. As familiar with these laws as anyone is New York attorney Bernard Perlman who, as an official of the New York State Department of Welfare in the late 1950s, did in fact help write the law that he now helps his charity clients outwit. That is why he almost hit the roof in 1974 when, in his new role as CMCA's legal counsel, he saw for the first time a CMCA-prepared CAP brochure stating that the project was not associated with any church, although the statement was technically true at the time.

''This [statement] should be removed immediately,'' Perlman wrote to CMCA's officials. ''We are informing all government agencies, the groups such as the BBB [Better Business Bureaus], etc., that CAP is associated with a church and as a result is exempt from the provisions of various statutes. To set forth in the brochure that it is not a church-related organization is going to cause waves and cause CAP to undergo a whole series of problems which may curtail its operations.''

Soon after, Perlman and CMCA president Raymond La Placa flew to Kentucky and attended a meeting at which the CAP board amended its corporate charter to include an assertion formally linking CAP to the Catholic church. But prospective donors are still not made aware of this. Nor are they aware that the prospering CAP empire now sprawls over 800 acres of land; has assets of at least $1.6 million, plus possibly another $2 million if one includes the value of its donors mailing list; has expanded its activities to include such enterprises as a motel, marina, restaurant, service station, printing plant, and Dairy Queen franchise. Father Beiting also proudly told me that CAP's annual payroll for its some 150 local and full-time and about 100 part-time employees amounted to about $500,000; and cheerfully confided that the gross income from CAP's business operations came to nearly $500,000 a year, leaving it with a net profit of about $136,000. He did not choose to mention, however, that this was only a fraction of the $1.5 million that flowed 600 miles away to Hyattsville, Maryland, headquarters of CMCA.

To what extent the figures Father Beiting gave me are true I have no way of knowing for he has failed to document them with audited financial reports in spite of my repeated requests in all the years since I've seen him. Apparently, CAP likes to send out mail but doesn't like to answer it. Nor have many other Catholic missionary groups bothered to respond to my inquiries for financial information, even though I have written to them several times.

Though the foregoing and other revelations may be embarrassing to Catholics, playing fast and loose with the moneys of religion is not a uniquely Catholic proclivity, as we shall now see.

At a Holiday Inn in the Detroit suburb of Southfield, Michigan, 250 people are assembled in a walnut-paneled meeting room. There are auto workers and doctors, ministers and merchants, business executives and salesmen, most of them with their wives. All are very white and very middle class; most appear to be in their fifties or sixties. On this cold wintry night, some had driven 150 miles just to attend this "Chicken Supper Rally" (at $6 per head) and hear the Rev. Billy James Hargis, the fiery evangelist preacher and leader of the Tulsa-based Christian Crusade, inveigh against communism and other social evils.

At 7:30 sharp, Hargis strides in unceremoniously, nodding to and greeting the people seated at tables of 12, many of them already dedicated Hargis followers. One of them, a worker at the Oldsmobile plant, is wearing a yellow lapel button bearing the initials *P.T.L.* When Hargis spots the button, he slaps the man on the back and says, "Praise the Lord, Brother." He stops to pose for a picture with his arm around one young woman. As he bends down to give an older woman a kiss on the cheek, he draws laughter from those nearby. When a young man identifies himself as a reporter from a local newspaper, Hargis also slaps him on the back and roars, "We won't hold that against you." More laughter. He has a friendly smile for everyone. There can be no denying that Hargis has a certain charm.

Like his followers, Hargis is dressed conservatively: a light blue suit, a blue patterned tie, and a white shirt. His only concession to style is a pair of dark blue patent leather shoes and a matching belt. Physically he is an unlikely crusader. He has a round boyish face with porcine features, reminiscent of the silent screen comedian Fatty Arbuckle. He has a tall, rotund, massive body; Hargis weighs about 235 pounds (down from his customary 270 pounds), the result, he likes to say, of too many nights on the road eating too many hamburgers. Since he gave up a comfortable Sapulpa, Oklahoma, pastorate in 1948 at the age of 23 to establish his Christian Crusade to promote his far-right political ideology and to fight religious apostasy, Hargis has traveled the road in one-night stands, like this one, exhorting and preaching 200 times a year in churches, auditoriums, and meeting halls. Last night, it was Minneapolis, and tomorrow night it will be Philadelphia, and then Lancaster and Indianapolis. The following week he begins a two-week tour of the Orient—Honolulu, Japan, Korea, Hong Kong, Thailand, and Taiwan. Then, after a week of rest at home, he is off on a speaking tour of Europe. It is hard work but the Message must be heard. And, equally important, money is needed to support his daily radio broadcasts (then heard on 140 stations), his Sunday television programs (112 stations), his weekly newspaper, his new American Christian College, his David Livingstone Missionary Foundation, his publishing operation, and the many other enterprises of his Christian Echoes Ministry, Inc. (the legal name of the Christian Crusade), which at the time had a multimillion-dollar budget (estimated at $3 million or more) and a staff of 200 people.

As the supper dishes are being cleared away, Hargis steps up to the podium to begin his presentation. "Speak up if any of you can't see me, although I can't imagine such a possibility," he says. Hargis has an engaging self-deprecating manner and, in his public appearances, is fond of poking fun at his imposing girth and his lack of formal education ("I'm president of a college and I've only had a year and a half of Bible school under my belt. Did you ever hear of anything more ridiculous?")*

He starts slowly with some announcements about his tour, his radio and TV programs, and a pilgrimage he will lead to the Holy Land, something he does three or four times a year, although the Crusade runs such group tours weekly. Over the years Hargis himself has conducted over 130 of these Holy Land tours, which are a major source of Crusade income, and he now invites members of the audience to sign up for the latest one at the "unbelievable" rate of $697, with Rome thrown in. Then comes a prayer, after which Hargis tells how Crusade, from its modest nondenominational origins, has grown into the massive, global entity it now is, with, he says, 1000 missionaries, 12 schools, 3 hospitals, 36 orphanages, and 3 leper villages in 17 countries.

Sprinkling his remarks with apt quotations from the Scriptures, Hargis, his voice rising, lashes out at what he calls the current rash of false Messiahs, citing as examples the Korean Rev. Sun Myung Moon and the then teen-age guru Maharaj Ji. "This guru is not even 16, as he claims," says Hargis. "He's 27 years of age—he's been 16 for 11 years." The members of the audience laugh

---

*Although Hargis holds a handful of baccalaureates and doctorates, most, if not all, of them were bestowed on him by diploma mills; moreover, the head of one of them, Belin Memorial University of Chillicothe, Missouri, was later sentenced to a one-year term in prison for using the mails to defraud.

appreciatively. Hargis stands squarely behind the podium, constantly shifting from side to side. Gradually he works into a discussion of current events, ranging over such topics as the energy crisis, environmentalism, national defense, foreign aid, the "giveaway" sale of wheat to Russia, the Middle East crisis, the decline of morals, and the prevalence of sexual sin in an increasingly lax society. In each case, the culprit or "the vehicle of the devil," as he puts it, is communism, aided and abetted by Congress, Big Government, the Eastern press, college radicals, the National Council of Churches, and other "liberal international schemers that want to bring our affluence down while raising the affluence of the Soviet Union." If Hargis has his devils, he also has his heroes, and he draws heavy applause when he announces that a Gallup poll has shown then Governor George Wallace to be the sixth most popular man in the world.

One pet Hargis theory is that the shooting of Lee Harvey Oswald, President Kennedy's alleged assassin, was carried out in collusion with the incongruous partnership of the Reds and the Black Hand, or Mafia. While accusing Israel of being militaristic because of its "constant forays into foreign territory," he is also critical of the Arabs because of "their alliance with the atheistic conspiracy headquartered in Moscow" and suggests we seriously consider landing the marines on the shores of Kuwait and Saudi Arabia if the Arabs cut us off from our oil supplies and investments in the Middle East. "I'd guarantee they'd change their minds right quick," cries Hargis, his body shaking with anger.

One is particularly aware of his Okie accent when he launches into a 20-minute brief for the oil producers of his home town of Tulsa. Thanks to Congress "acting more and more as representatives of socialism," he charges, "we don't have any new drilling activity any more, because there's no incentive for the investor who takes this tremendous risk." To support his view, he reads from a sheaf of statistics in his left hand, while he gestures with the glasses in his other hand. America can be saved, he says, if people reject the siren calls of sin and socialism, and have faith in God, country, and free enterprise.

With this upbeat peroration out of the way, now comes the Hargis pitch for money. He tells what wonderful things his organization is doing in this age of decadence and perversion and how these things require money. In dire need, he says, is his American Christian College, which he describes as "conservative, pro-American, anti-Communist, fundamental in Bible-believing and with strict moral standards" and, according to him, it is now fully accredited even though it first opened its doors only four years earlier. "Any one of our students can even—God forbid!—transfer to Harvard if they want to," he says.* Then he points to the plight of his radio and television programs which, he says, suffered

---

*In October, 1974, ten months after this meeting, Hargis suddenly resigned as president of the college, ostensibly because of failing health. The real reason, however, did not become apparent until February, 1976, when *Time* magazine reported that five students—four of them men—had admitted having sexual relations with Hargis. Confronted with the students' accounts, Hargis was quietly forced from his post. When the *Time* story appeared, Hargis declined to give a specific reply to the charges; through a lawyer, however, he stated: "I have made more than my share of mistakes. I'm not proud of them. Even the Apostle Paul said, 'Christ died to save sinners, of whom I am chief.' " Otherwise, Hargis has continued his other evangelistic activities, though on a somewhat more reduced scale. The college closed its doors in 1978.

a severe financial loss the month before. "To keep our network going around the country, we had to borrow $310,000 on a 30-day note, and I'm now trying to raise enough to pay off that note."

Hargis is a master pitchman. He is humble. "I need your help. I have no help but yours." He pleads. "I need some gifts—big gifts of $100, $500, $1,000. I need them *bad*—the pressure's on me," he says, reminding his followers that his name, not theirs, appears on the bank note. He invokes God. "I know that God will bless the people that help." He even begs. "Brethren, I beg of you to give all you can. I beg you to take that envelope on your table and give even $10 or $5 or only a few dollars if that's all you can."

It is a hard sell. But members of the audience begin to respond. Some give cash. Others fill out personal checks and still others fill out the blank checks thoughtfully provided in each envelope. Some offer monthly pledges. At the end of the collection, his followers flock around him and congratulate him on an inspiring talk. They ask his opinions on various topics. A very old man tells Hargis he will pray for him and says he will save the world. Hargis responds with his characteristic "God Bless" and wanders, very tired, out of the room. He has a plane to catch. Tomorrow he will be in Philadelphia, and the day after that somewhere else.

Hargis' success in raising money is remarkable in that the Internal Revenue Service revoked the Christian Crusade's tax exemption in 1966 because of its "substantial and continuous" political and lobbying activities; these included rallies featuring such notables as Governor George Wallace and General Edwin "Pro Blue" Walker, who first came to national attention when he distributed John Birch Society literature to his troops in Europe. To soften the impact of this ruling on his claimed 250,000 followers, who, like most people, prefer to be able to get a tax deduction for their contributions, Hargis has managed to incorporate at least several of his enterprises as separate nonprofit organizations which qualify for exemptions.

I met Hargis when I went to Tulsa to look into the operations of one of these organizations—the David Livingstone Missionary Foundation. The foundation was formed in 1970 to help orphans, lepers, disaster victims, and other unfortunates in various parts of the world. What I wanted to know is how much of the $2 million or more that the foundation then collected every year, mostly through mail solicitations, actually went to the unfortunates. The question was pertinent because in 1972 the foundation was denied a license to solicit in North Carolina because of the state's finding that a disproportionate amount of the contributions to the organization went for fund-raising and administrative expenses—83 percent, in fact. "Therefore, far too little of the amount contributed went to program services," ruled the state. (For a similar reason, the foundation was banned from soliciting in Michigan, among other states.)

But was even the money earmarked for the foundation's program services actually being used for this purpose? In his large paneled office filled with religious art, Hargis greeted me warmly—he is an extremely likable person—and said he would tell me anything I wanted to know about the foundation's finances; then he handed me an unaudited report for the ten-month period ended January 31, 1973, which showed cash receipts of $1,794,000 and expenditures abroad of $702,000 on mission work. (A promised audited report for the full fiscal year was never sent me in spite of my repeated requests.*) Hargis also gave me a sheet of paper with a breakdown of expenditures in each country: $243,000 in India, $217,000 in Korea, $130,000 in the Philippines, and so on.

But just how was the money spent in each country? Hargis and the foundation's president, Jess Pedigo (who had been hired away from faith healer T. L. Osborn's organization), gave me only vague data, none of it substantiated by any records, and some of it contradicting the few facts and figures previously given me. For example, Pedigo told me that the foundation gave $1500 a month to the world-famous Mother Teresa and her Missionaries of Charity in Calcutta. However, Mother Teresa herself said that all she got from the foundation was 1500 *rupees*—or about $200—a month. Pedigo also told me that foundation funds were being used to complete an orphanage in Nasik, 130 miles south of Bombay. The foundation's representative in Nasik at first said he knew nothing about the orphanage; later, he said there were plans for a home for "poor boys." A feature by Pedigo in the monthly *David Livingstone Bulletin* on the foundation's field hospital in Ramgati, one of the most depressed areas of Bangladesh, described how hundreds of "suffering men, women and children" were swarming to the facility every day for desperately needed care, food, and medicine. So enormous were the crowds, wrote Pedigo, that the facility was now inadequate and funds were needed to replace it with a new hospital. When the hospital was visited on two occasions, it was found completely deserted both times.

A check for $7000 that Pedigo told me had gone to Hong Kong to be used to "establish a church" actually went for a down payment on an apartment for the foundation's Hong Kong representative who, I also learned, said there were no present plans to establish a church. When I published this revelation in a magazine article, the foundation conceded that the money had gone to its representative for an apartment. At the same time, Hargis also insisted that "we do indeed have a church" in Hong Kong and—mirabile dictu!—pictures of the church even began to materialize in the foundation's *Bulletin*. The fact, however, is that the church, far from being newly established, was founded in *1954*—long before the existence of the foundation—and was being subsidized by various organizations before the foundation became one of its sponsors, too, coincidentally just about the time my article was published. In the Philippines, the foundation's representative was skeptical about Pedigo's claim that the missionary group had spent $130,000 in that country. Nor did he know anything about the ten $600 power boats and a $20,000 75-foot vessel for boat-riding evangelists to reach people in the more remote regions. Pedigo told me that he himself had ordered construction on these boats to begin.

All this, despite Hargis' promise of the truth and Pedigo's assurance that "from the first file in our office, through all our account books, and down to the last child in the most obscure corner of the earth, all our work can endure the most careful scrutiny and come out with flying colors."

---

*However, a report (unaudited) I later obtained from other sources showed total receipts of $2,923,302 and expenditures abroad of $832,471. In 1977 the foundation's annual income was $6,270,000 according to an audited financial statement filed with the state of North Carolina. However, the statement was not prepared in accordance with general accounting principles and the foundation was still denied permission to solicit in that state because its costs were more than 50 percent of contributions, far above the state's limit of 35 percent.

And what is one to make of the other men of God—evangelists, faith healers, tent prophets, bawl-and-stomp radio Gantrys, superpatriots, semimystics, spiritualists, satanists, and the dispensers of an assortment of various Eastern gospels? Although it would seem difficult to take them seriously, these pietistic pied pipers, making unfounded promises, manage to extract millions of dollars a year from their gullible followers, through the use of everything from modern computerized mailing techniques to Bible Belt revival methods.

The fund-raising gimmicks and claims of these "schlockministers," as the more outlandish are informally known to law enforcement authorities, are simply beyond belief. A Californian who proclaimed himself the King of Yahweh and specialized in the dissemination of "reincarnation revelations" advertised by mail that for a mere $25 he would tell people who they used to be; he built a thriving business on this psychic power before being indicted and convicted on 17 counts of mail fraud. The late radio evangelist Asa Alonzo Allen, a self-proclaimed miracle worker, maintained he could raise the dead, a claim that gave him problems when believers began shipping corpses to him. And then there are the more prosaic preachers who claim the ability to cure every disease from cancer to psoriasis or bring to their followers earthly prosperity as well as a place in Heaven.

A popular item in the faith healer's stock-in-trade is the "prayer cloth," a swatch of cheap material invested with curative powers or good-luck propensities. In extolling its potency, one minister gushed: "It would be wonderful if I could go to every home and hospital and personally lay my hands upon each one and pray for him, but because I am only one person, I cannot. Therefore, I am giving out Blessed Cloths—and the reports are coming in from far and near of how many kinds of sicknesses are being healed; the lame are made to walk, even those on their deathbeds are raised."

Another favorite—shades of Osiris!—is prayer insurance which schlockministers peddle to their flocks under such names as "God's Health and Happiness Plan" or "Pact of Plenty." Under these schemes, purchasers of the plans mail in a monthly contribution together with a page from their plan booklet, much as they would in making time payments on merchandise; in return, their spiritual leader agrees to pray for them that month with the promise, direct or implied, that the prayer will bring blessings in some form.

A classic example of one of the more successful purveyors of these gimmicks was the nondenominational fundamentalist Church of Compassion which, until its surprising demise several years ago, operated out of an elaborately-furnished movie theater building in Los Angeles. From this headquarters, the church sent out as many as 1.5 million folksy form letters a month, each computer-personalized with the typed-in name of the addressee and each "signed" by the Rev. Gene Ewing, the church's proprietor. To help pay the cost of refurbishing its offices and 2000-seat theater, one church appeal asked the "brothers" and "sisters" on the mailing lists to "mail in $5 to help upholster one chair for Jesus." Other fund-raising letters offered such items as a glow-in-the-dark light switch cover with an inscribed prayer. Recipients of the church's green anointed prayer cloth were instructed to sleep on it for four nights and then mail it back immediately to Reverend Ewing so that he could sleep on it, too. "Then you will get your Holy surprise blessing," said Reverend Ewing's letter, which also requested a contribution. Asked by a skeptic if the preacher did indeed sleep with tens of thousands of prayer cloths under his pillow every night, a church spokesman said that the preacher probably placed them under his bed.

However, a more serious logistical difficulty seemed to present itself in the case of the church's prayer insurance, which was offered in two versions: a $4-a-month "God's Gold Book Plan" and a $12 "Pillar of Gold Plan." With some 60,000 plan members said to be sending in their contributions every month, one wondered how Reverend Ewing could possibly find the time to offer the prayers promised in each individual's name. Rattling off a prayer and name at the rate of even one every five seconds would have consumed about 85 hours a month, an arduous task for even a man of God endowed with superhuman powers.

Nonetheless, Ewing's monthly magazine teemed with testimonials from those who, after joining one plan or the other, were in turn blessed with new homes, cars (invariably Lincolns or Cadillacs), businesses, jobs, mates, unexpected windfalls of money, even miracle cures. Exulted one member, identified only by initials, "I have been blessed with a Lincoln Mark III Continental and a savings account totalling $6,509. . . . Please continue to pray." Another: "I've been blessed with a restaurant business of my own, a new truck and a Lincoln Continental." Still another said two growths in his stomach had disappeared since he had become a Gold Book member.

Apparently, the blessing plans worked for Reverend Ewing, too. For the Texas-born preacher's mail-order cathedral took in over $3 million a year, enough to pay its head, the son of a sharecropper, a salary of $76,000. But, apparently, this was not enough to indulge Ewing's expensive tastes, which included a rented home in Beverly Hills across from singer Pat Boone, and a customized Stutz Bearcat, a Rolls Royce, and three Cadillacs—part of a fleet of nearly a dozen luxury limousines owned by him or the church. When Ewing and his Church of Compassion filed for bankruptcy in 1977, their fall from grace was attributed to rising printing costs, dwindling contributions, and judgments resulting from several of 50 lawsuits of an unspecified nature.

Another still-active purveyor of blessing plans is New York's Rev. Dr. Frederick H. Eikerenkoetter II (better known as "Reverend Ike"), a flamboyant mod-dressing black who preaches Green Power: "I have seen the power of money—it can do everything except raise the dead." Reverend Ike's United Church, also headquartered in a former movie palace, claims 2.5 million followers who pour into its coffers $6.5 million a year. Although the salary of His Divine Eminence, as he refers to himself, is a relatively modest $40,000, this is augmented by an almost unlimited expense account that enables him to purchase jewelry and clothing at the rate of $1000 a week, by his own reckoning, and to enjoy such emoluments as residences in both Beverly Hills and New York and three Rolls-Royces, two Mercedes, and a Bentley.

That the love of God can be combined with Mammon is also evident from the experience of various other promoters of spiritual, if not material, fulfillment.

Though the Korean Rev. Sun Myung Moon, regarded by many of his followers as the second Messiah, first brought his message—a blend of Christianity, Eastern philosophy, and anti-communism—to this country as recently as 1972, his controversial Unification Church's U.S. annual income was last estimated at $20 million. Most of this comes from the street and door-to-door peddling of peanuts, flowers, tea, candy, and candles by the cult's 30,000 American members who exist on a shoestring (7000 of them in 120 spartan Moon communes), while Moon himself, who also heads a $15 million Korean industrial conglomerate, lives in lordly fashion in an elegant 25-room mansion on an $8 million 47-acre estate in New York's Westchester County. The group also owns 300 nearby acres, a California ranch, and numerous other parcels of property across the country.

Guru Maharaj Ji, the 20-year-old Indian religious leader whose Denver-based Divine Light Mission expanded to this country in 1971, now claims 30,000 to 50,000 American followers, the most devout of whom turn over all their earnings to the group, sleep on straw pallets, and practice celibacy, vegetarianism, and abstinence from alcohol and other of life's customary worldly pleasures. Such ascetism, however, is in marked contrast to the lifestyle of their guru who, thanks to the group's $3 million annual income, has at his disposal plush homes in Denver, Los Angeles, New York, and London and a fleet of chauffered Mercedes and Rolls Royces.

A disenchanted former financial analyst of the Mission once testified in court that "approximately 60 percent of the gross receipts are directed to maintain the lifestyle of the Maharaj Ji and those close to him. So far as I could see, the whole function of the organization was to provide an opulent existence for the Maharaj Ji."

The chanting, dancing, drum-beating, saffron-gowned young devotees of Hare Krishna (formerly, the International Society for Krishna Consciousness)—they now number about 7000 in 80 cities—also have an aura of austerity and poverty. Few people solicited on the street for donations, however, are aware of the sect's rather sizable financial assets, which include a $2 million-a-year incense company, said to be the largest in the nation, and a profitable publishing company. So well-fixed is the group that several years ago it was able to bid, though unsuccessfully, slightly less than $1 million for a Manhattan building considered as a possible new international headquarters and New York center.

Should one give to groups such as those described in this chapter? Except where blatant fraud is involved, nothing they do or promise is really illegal (after all, one has the right to believe or hope what one wants to), although inasmuch as public disclosure is considered infra dig among God's spokesmen on earth, it is extremely difficult to establish in court the difference between a crook and a churchman, between the fraudulent and the holy. Adding to the difficulty is the reluctance of law enforcement officials to tangle with even self-proclaimed surrogates of God, sheathed as they are in their shenanigans by the protective raiments of the First Amendment of our Bill of Rights.

The real reason, however, for the reticence of most religious organizations to bare their financial souls has nothing whatever to do with the First Amendment. It was perhaps best summed up by George M. Wilson, executive vice-president of the Minneapolis-based Billy Graham Evangelistic Association (BGEA) which several years ago ran afoul of Minnesota's charities division in connection with its charitable gift annuity program. The state is the only one in the nation requiring organizations, religious or otherwise, offering such programs to file detailed financial reports, and the BGEA, faced with the threat of losing its program, had no choice but to comply, although it had previously held—in the words of one of its fund-raising pamphlets—that it was only ''accountable to God.'' Wilson explained that BGEA's financial position was not made public because ''many of the people who have been sending in checks might cut off their contributions if they knew how rich the organization is.'' (It collected $38.4 million in 1977.)

Shouldn't all churches and church-related bodies be subject to the same disclosure requirements as other nonprofit organizations? But even if this were the case, there would probably be no words of caution one could offer those innocents who simply want to believe. Except perhaps these words of admonition by Jesus: ''Behold, I send you forth as sheep in the midst of wolves; by ye therefore wise as serpents. . . .''

Chapter 9

The Tin Cup Approach
to Disease

Americans, as perhaps no other people, believe that money will conquer the misery of disease and bring about better health. Accordingly, they give ever-increasing amounts to health causes—$4.8 billion in 1977 and $5.4 billion in 1978, according to the annual tallies of the American Association of Fund-Raising Counsel (AAFRC), ranking health only behind religion and almost on a par with education as the largest recipient of philanthropic funds.

Few people, however, realize that the money they give for health, enormous as this may seem, represents only a tiny fraction—3 percent, on the basis of the AAFRC figures—of what is spent on medical care in this country. And according to government figures, the fraction is even smaller, philanthropy accounting for only $1.8 billion—or about 1 percent—of the nation's total public and private expenditures of $163 billion for health in 1977.*

Whichever estimate is correct (and both are probably wrong, as government statisticians admitted to me), there can be no doubt that philanthropy has been playing a declining role in our nation's health affairs over the years. In 1929, when our health care costs came to about $3.2 billion, philanthropic expenditures nearly equalled those of the federal government; in 1977 the $4.8 billion—or $1.8 billion—given to health causes was dwarfed by the $40 billion spent by the federal government plus the $17 billion more spent by state and local governments on health.

As part of this trend, the nation's 7000 or so hospitals have also long stopped depending on charity for much of their operating costs, particularly since the phenomenal growth of Blue Cross and other insurance coverage in the 1950s and 1960s and the increased government subsidies of health care that came with the introduction of Medicare and Medicaid in 1966.

Even in 1950 more than 62 percent of all hospital operating expenditures were already financed by private insurance (16 percent) and government funds (46 percent); another 34 percent came from patients who paid their bills directly while less than 4 percent was contributed by philanthropy and industry together. By 1977 more than 90 percent of these costs were paid for by private insurance (37 percent) and government (55 percent), with patient direct payments accounting for only 6 percent, and philanthropy and industry making up the minuscule remainder of a shade more than 2 percent. If this trend continues, hospitals will

*The preliminary estimate for 1978 is $182.2 billion.

119

eventually no longer be dependent on any gratuitous contributions for the care they provide.

Even hospital construction has come to depend less and less on private giving in recent years, as the cost of this is being borne increasingly by federal funds, tax-exempt bonds, and other financing sources. Recent studies have shown that philanthropy now accounts for as little as 11 percent of the outlays for hospital construction, compared to 24 percent in 1968.

How then account for the $4.8 billion the AAFRC says was given to health causes in 1977? No breakdown was given, but extrapolating the figures from a breakdown furnished the previous year, the largest portion of the $4.8 billion in donations—$1.3 billion—went for personal health care services, inappropriate as this may seem at a time when most Americans have some form of health insurance or are covered by government programs. Another $990 million was spent to endow hospital and other health institutions, and $770 million went to construct and equip health facilities of one kind or another. The sum of $242 million, according to the AAFRC, found its way into medical research, and $300 million was funneled into health-related activities through United Way agencies. Another $77 million went to the Red Cross for similar purposes. Finally, $1.1 billion went to those most visible and vocal elements of the charity scene—the so-called voluntary health agencies.*

No one knows just how many such agencies there are. Estimates have placed their number at anywhere from 20,000 to 100,000, with all but a few of them local and regional organizations. However, the 20 largest national health agencies alone accounted for exactly half—about $560,000—of all the donations to health agencies on the basis of the figures in the accompanying table.

Perhaps the most striking fact about the health agencies is that there often seems to be little correlation between the contributions they receive and the apparent seriousness of the diseases with which they are concerned. For example, the American Cancer Society raises about 70 percent more money than the American Heart Association, the second largest agency, although two-and-a-half times more people die from heart disease, which is also ten times as prevalent as cancer, yet the American Diabetes Association (No. 15 among our health agen-leading killer (after heart disease and cancer) and is twice as widespread as cancer, yet the American Diabetes Association (No. 15 among our health agencies) receives only one-seventeenth the income of the American Cancer Society. Although mental illness is said to afflict as many as 32 million Americans and is regarded by the U.S. Public Health Service as the nation's No. 1 health problem, the Mental Health Association ranks only twelfth among health agencies in contributions; and the public gives four times as much money to help our 200,000 victims of muscular dystrophy.

Let us look at a few more anomalies. Alcoholism afflicts thirteen times as many Americans as cerebral palsy. Yet the National Council on Alcoholism receives only one-tenth the contributions of the United Cerebral Palsy Associa-

---

*A horrible term, "voluntary," but nothing better has come along to replace it. Generally, it is applied to any nongovernmental agency that offers services to the public and is supported largely by voluntary contributions; such an agency also often uses volunteer or unpaid workers in addition to paid employees.

The 20 Largest National Health Agencies
Ranked According to Contributions*

1977

Name	Contributions* (Thousands of Dollars)	Total Income* (Thousands of Dollars)
1. American Cancer Society	$114,726	$126,767
2. American Heart Association	67,694	77,631
3. National Foundation-March of Dimes	57,695	60,874
4. Muscular Dystrophy Association	57,636	59,216
5. National Easter Seal Society for Crippled Children and Adults	43,843	90,374
6. American Lung Association	43,655	49,986
7. United Cerebral Palsy Associations	30,014	50,476
8. National Association for Retarded Citizens	25,759	135,527
9. Planned Parenthood Federation	25,657	105,265
10. National Multiple Sclerosis Society	22,443	23,049
11. Arthritis Foundation	15,605	17,590
12. Mental Health Association	13,882	20,878
13. Leukemia Society of America	9,761	9,804
14. Cystic Fibrosis Foundation	7,845**	9.230**
15. American Diabetes Association	6,750	10,496
16. National Kidney Foundation	5,872	6,919
17. Epilepsy Foundation of America	4,657	7,905
18. National Hemophilia Foundation	3,547	4,458
19. National Society to Prevent Blindness	3,522**	3,871**
20. American Foundation for the Blind	3,076**	6,451**

*Contributions refer to any donations or support received from the public, directly or indirectly, including legacies and bequests, receipts from special events, building-fund contributions, and allocations from United Way and other federated fund-raising organizations. Total income includes contributions plus all other revenues, such as fees and grants from government agencies, program service fees, investment income, sales to the public, and membership dues.

**Figures are also available for fiscal 1978: Cystic Fibrosis Foundation, $10,672 and $11,317; National Society to Prevent Blindness, $3,826 and $4,327; American Foundation for the Blind, $3,886 and $8,569. (Figures are again in thousands of dollars.)

tions. Approximately as many donations go to assist cerebral palsy victims as go to help our retarded citizens, although the latter outnumber the former eight to one. And one-third fewer dollars is given to aid our nearly 32 million arthritis sufferers as is given for our 500,000 victims of multiple sclerosis and related diseases.

Of course, death rate and incidence do not necessarily provide the only measures of the magnitude of a disease problem. In fact, the incidence of an ailment can be relatively inconsequential in this regard. The common cold, for example, in sneezes-per-capita, probably affects more people and interferes more with daily living—resulting in job absenteeism, for example—than any other ailment;

nutritional disturbances also affect large numbers of people. But these ailments have relatively little emotional impact on people. (A short-lived Common Cold Foundation was a resounding flop back in the 1950s and never managed to raise more than $75,000 a year.) The American Speech and Hearing Association can muster statistics to show that one of the most widespread maladies in the United States is loss of hearing, afflicting more than 14.5 million Americans, but few of the rest of us are likely to be greatly moved by this. All of which indicates that it is difficult to rate the relative seriousness of disease on the basis of just incidence or even death rate.

For this reason, government scientists, to guide themselves in their research priorities, also consider other factors: bed disability days (in which category influenza and pneumonia rank first, followed by upper respiratory conditions and heart disease); limitation of one's usual activities (heart disease, arthritis, impairments of back and spine); hospital days (heart disease, fractures and dislocations, mental disorders); and hospital discharges (heart disease, upper respiratory conditions, fractures and dislocations). On the basis of these factors, arthritis, although rarely, if ever, a cause of death, is nonetheless a serious problem, ranking as it does second in terms of "limitation of activity" and fourth in days of bed disability; heart disease is without question our most serious problem. The economic cost of an illness is another important factor. Cancer costs the economy an estimated $30 billion a year and cardiovascular disease $28 billion, much of this in lost work time, earnings, and, hence, purchasing power, while the annual economic costs of mental illness, alcoholism, and drug abuse (all closely related) have been estimated at $21 billion, $32 billion, and $10 billion, respectively, although there may be some overlap in these figures. Priorities would, of course, also depend on the complexity of the disease and the progress that has already been made in combating it.

Psychological factors are certainly also involved. People tend to respond to requests for help to fight diseases that have robbed them of a loved one or that they fear the most. Even though heart disease is more prevalent, cancer raises more money because it is feared more. On the other hand, people are reluctant to give to causes like epilepsy and mental illness because they can't—or don't want to—identify with these ailments, which still bear a social stigma, as does venereal disease. As already mentioned, people are not likely to be moved by an emotional appeal for the common cold. Who would respond to a poster child with a running nose?

In this vein, a report for the National Health Council once pointed out: "The picture of the suffering child takes priority over any appeal concerning adults. . . . Men at a luncheon club are stirred into giving by the sight of a crippled child. What may be a more serious handicap, the loss of hearing, evokes little sympathy and no generous outpouring. A brace is more dramatic than a hearing aid, canes for the blind more dramatic than spectacles for poor eyes."

There can be no question that the skills of the fund raisers in playing on these hopes and fears can be a crucial element in inducing people to give. ("On the one hand, you have to scare people to death, but, on the other, you have to hold out some hope so that people see some point in giving, have something to look forward to," is the way one expert put it.) A classic example of a "scare" campaign was the one conducted on behalf of polio, or infantile paralysis, from the mid-1930s through the early 1950s. In some years as many as 35 million polio leaflets of the most frightening nature were distributed to school children. As a child of that era, I recall wearing a chunk of camphor around my neck to ward off the evils of that dread disease. One Minnesota public health officer said that whenever polio struck a community he had two epidemics to deal with—"one of polio, the other of hysteria."

Yet polio was never a really serious disease. Even in 1952, the year of the nation's worst polio epidemic, the disease killed only 3145 people, of whom 1560 were children. This represented only 8 percent of the 40,000 or so afflicted, half of whom recovered fully; only 12 percent had serious, crippling aftereffects. That same year, however, heart and other cardiovascular diseases killed 796,871 people, 2392 of them children; and cancer claimed 223,277 lives, 3614 those of children. Yet, thanks to the ingenious, intensive efforts of what was then known as the National Foundation for Infantile Paralysis, people were made to believe that polio was a major killer and crippler and, accordingly, that year they gave $41.4 million to combat polio—more than six times the amount they gave to conquer heart disease, then and now our No. 1 killer, and more than double what they gave to fight cancer, the prime killer of children.

Returning to the present, what is one to make of the fact that the charisma of a comedian and the carnival atmosphere of a telethon are largely responsible for the public's giving four times as much money for muscular dystrophy as for mental illness? Should a slowly dying or crippled boy or girl—glorified by the honorific "poster child"—be displayed on television or be rushed around the country to raise money for *any* disease? If a disease (or, for that matter, any problem) is something of widespread community concern, is the way to fight it by waving tin cups in the breeze and asking for dimes and quarters—what one would call the tin cup approach to disease? Paraphrasing a thought by Hank Bloomgarden in *Before We Sleep*, a brief for increased federal expenditures for health research, one would not think of using tin cups and telethons to finance our excursions into space or to raise funds to fight an overseas enemy; yet this approach is used to fight our no less deadly enemies here at home—killing and crippling disease.

Considering the large sums already spent by the government on health, is there really any need for the voluntary health agencies at all? If so, how can we be sure that we are giving wisely, that our money is going where it is most needed? Just how does one go about evaluating a health agency (or, for that matter, any charity) in order to decide whether or not to contribute to it?

Evaluating a Charity:
By Its Fund-Raising and Administrative Costs

One customary way to evaluate a charity is by its fund-raising and administrative overhead (also referred to as "management and general") costs—collectively called its "supporting services." (Both must be considered because where fund-raising costs are low, the other costs may be high, and vice versa.) The amounts are often expressed as a percentage of a charity's total income (rather than total expenses, which could differ greatly from what the charity takes in). Applying this yardstick, the supporting services ratio of most of the member agencies of the National Health Council recently ranged from 10.6 percent (National Society for Autistic Children) to 33.5 percent (Epilepsy Foundation), with an average of 20.8 percent. (The fund-raising ratios alone ranged from 1.7 percent to 18.4 percent—the same agencies were again at the extremes—with an average of 10.9 percent.)

Here are the ratios, both overall and for fund raising alone (the latter shown in parentheses) for some of the bigger, better-known health agencies: American Cancer Society, 22.0 (12.1); American Lung Association, 31.2 (24.4); National Easter Seal Society, 22.4 (10.9); National Foundation-March of Dimes, 23.8 (17.2); United Cerebral Palsy Associations, 18.8 (6.9); Arthritis Foundation, 23.7 (12.3); and National Multiple Sclerosis Society, 21.8 (13.1).

These figures seem to be in line with the overall average of 26 percent for 127 Illinois charities tallied in a recent study. Another study of 2977 tax-exempt organizations registered in New York State showed 90 percent reporting fund-raising and administrative costs of 25 percent or less, 7 percent with costs ranging up to 50 percent, and 3 percent with costs over 50 percent.

With such a wide range of ratios, it is difficult to tell which are outlandish and which are reasonable. How much *should* a charity spend on fund-raising and administrative overhead? Although the question is raised time and time again, there is no easy answer to it. One popular rule of thumb holds that in a well-run charity, fund-raising and administrative expenditures should not exceed 25 percent of total income. No one knows just how this figure was arrived at, but it has been adopted as a yardstick by the U.S. Civil Service Commission to help it determine which charities may participate in the annual Combined Federal Campaign that solicits contributions from government employees.

The fact, however, is that there is no single yardstick that can be applied to all charities generally (or, for that matter, be used to compare one with another) because of all the variables involved. For example, a new charity, with special start-up expenses and needing time to make its name known and to build up a constituency, might have costs far in excess of 25 percent, perhaps as high as 50 percent in its first few years. This is also particularly likely in the case of even established charities espousing unpopular or undramatic causes (epilepsy, mental illness, ecology), handicapped as such charities are by a paucity of both volunteers and contributors. "You've got to realize the influence that stigma has on fund raising," said an official of the Epilepsy Foundation of America. "People avoid our cause just as they try to avoid people who have epilepsy and so it takes more effort to reach people—more appeals, more staff, more costs."

For such reasons, Arthur J. Grimes, who was for 14 years an official of the National Health Council, is of the opinion that even 50 percent fund-raising and administrative costs for a new agency or one with an unpopular cause could be reasonable for a period of time; some feel that as much as 50 percent could also be acceptable for any agency, under certain circumstances. Other professionals are leery when costs remain above 35 percent.

The particular fund-raising methods used also influence costs. Door-to-door solicitations by volunteers, widely used by the American Cancer Society and the American Heart Association, is the cheapest method but it is not appropriate for every organization.

"Can you imagine the problem of getting volunteers to go door-to-door to raise funds for research on the problems of alcoholism or epilepsy or venereal disease?" asks Malvern J. Gross, a partner with Price, Waterhouse and an expert on the accounting practices of philanthropic groups. "It just wouldn't work."

Consequently, such organizations have to resort to the more costly technique of mail solicitations, which is invariably associated with charities having the highest fund-raising costs (Epilepsy, American Lung Association, National Foundation).

The source of an organization's support also has a lot to do with its cost of raising money. Although the National Easter Seal Society, for example, uses the mail as its chief fund-raising tool, it also receives a large chunk—about a quarter of its income—from government grants. Including these in a charity's income when they are generally unrelated to any fund-raising efforts, naturally has the effect of reducing overall fund-raising costs. The same is true of organizations which derive relatively large portions of their income from patient and other fees (Cerebral Palsy, Retarded Citizens, Hemophilia).

For such reasons, many charity experts feel that it is more valid to measure fund-raising (and administrative) costs against public contributions only, excluding government grants, patient fees, investment income, sales of materials, membership dues, and other revenues not directly related to the fund-raising effort. This, too, presents problems because charities like the Red Cross, which rely on the United Way or other federated drives for much of their contributions, generally have lower fund-raising ratios than charities that do not.

Going even further, the National Information Bureau, in its periodic *Wise Giving Bulletins,* excludes from its definition of contributions such sources of funds as legacies or bequests, endowment gifts, and special events on the ground that they, because of their unusual or unpredictable nature, may not fairly reflect the efforts of a particular fund-raising campaign. Legacies, for example, may have been prompted by a previous campaign many years before or perhaps by no campaign at all; furthermore, certain charities may rely heavily on legacies for a good portion of their contributions (Cancer, Heart, Arthritis), whereas others do not. Naturally, the receipt of even a few large gifts could dramatically lower a charity's fund-raising ratio for a given year.

"A general rule of thumb is about 30 percent of contributions, excluding such things as legacies or bequests and endowment gifts," says the NIB's Jane Pendergast. "If fund raising costs exceed that level, then we would look at an organization very carefully and probably conclude that the costs were excessive." On the other hand, the Council of Better Business Bureaus' Nancy de Marco starts to become concerned when less than 50 percent of everything taken in—in other words, the charity's total income—is left for program services or expenses to carry out the primary mission of the charity.

Not that fund-raising costs per se, whether high or low, are necessarily always a sign of efficiency or innocence. Stated fund-raising costs can be misleading or deceptive, sometimes deliberately so, by being masked under such euphemisms as "public information," "education," or "community services." For example, several years ago, the Muscular Dystrophy Association allocated more than $1 million of its telethon expenses to "clinical, diagnostic and community services," thereby reducing its overall fund-raising expenses.

Even with the new uniform accounting procedures now recommended for health and welfare agencies,* shenanigans are still possible, particularly with salaries, which are the major items in the budgets of most charities. Since many agency employees divide their time among several activities, including fund raising, not too farfetched is this hypothetical conversation, reported in Harvey Katz's *Give!*, between an agency employee and comptroller who, at year's end, is desperately trying to bring the fund-raising figures down to some reasonable level. Says the comptroller:

"We don't want to question your judgment, but we were wondering about that Dallas trip you listed under fund raising. Is that all you did down there?"

"Well, no, I visited the chapter office to say hello."

"Ahhh. Community Services."

A friend who worked in the public relations department of one of the leading agencies told me that at the end of every week he had to fill out a time sheet allocating his time by hours to such various non-PR categories as "professional relations," "health education," "chapter organization," and "community services" even though he had never worked in those areas.

In a national organization, fund-raising and operating costs may vary considerably from chapter to chapter. Actually, you do not generally contribute to, say, the American Cancer Society or to the National Easter Seal Society, but rather to their local chapters which, depending on the organization, retain anywhere from 40 to 90 percent of all contributions, and forward the rest to national headquarters. Consequently, you should get financial data on your local chapter as well as the national organization. Some years ago, the New Orleans chapter of the Easter Seal Society was refused a city solicitation permit because its fund-raising costs were considered excessive, far higher than those for the society as a whole. Similarly, one year the Cleveland Mental Health Association, an affiliate of the Mental Health Association, was found to have spent 94 cents of each dollar it took in on fund raising and overhead, leaving little for the local services for which contributions were solicited.

Evaluating a Charity: How Much Does It Spend on Its Programs?

While fund raising provides some guide as to organizational efficiency, it is not a reliable measure of a charity's worth. One must look at what a charity does with the rest of the money it takes in. Most national health agencies allocate their funds in varying degrees to one or more of three basic functions: research and education, both usually directed from national headquarters; and some sort of

*These are spelled out in *Standards of Accounting and Financial Reporting for Voluntary Health and Welfare Organizations,* a 135-page book published in 1974 by the National Health Council, National Assembly of National Voluntary Health and Welfare Organizations, and the United Way of America. The same year, the American Institute of Certified Public Accountants (AICPA), adopting the major principles of *Standards,* which defines the common categories of income and expenditures and specifies how each is to be labeled in financial reports, published its *Audits of Voluntary Health and Welfore Organizations,* an audit guide for CPAs conducting audits. (Similar audit guides for use with hospitals, colleges, and universities are now also available.) Starting with the 1975 fiscal year, charities unwilling to conform with the principles of the audit guide and *Standards* (known as the "black book" in charity circles) have not been given a "clean" (unqualified) audit statement by any CPA.

service to patients, their families, and the community, done at the local level. The emphasis different agencies place on these so-called "program services" varies widely.

The Juvenile Diabetes Foundation, for example, spends 65 percent of its budget on research, and the Deafness Research Foundation, another small agency, 69 percent. At the American Cancer Society, about 32 percent of total expenditures now go for research; at American Heart Association, 28 percent. Also heavily research-oriented are Muscular Dystrophy (30), Arthritis (21), Myasthenia Gravis (57), and the Committee to Combat Huntington's Disease (45).

Yet—and here is another surprising, little-known fact about the health agencies—these expenditures represent only a small fraction of all the dollars spent on research in this country; most, of course, now comes from the government, usually for programs to battle the same ailments as the health agencies. Of the total of $5.6 billion spent on medical research in 1977, $3.6 billion or 64 percent came from the government, $1.6 billion or 28.5 percent came from private industry, notably pharmaceutical companies, and $186 million came from foundations and hospitals; only $103 million or less than 2 percent came from the health agencies and a good share of this—$36.5 million—came from just a single agency, the American Cancer Society, whose research expenditures were dwarfed by Congress' appropriation to the National Cancer Institute of $800 million, a substantial portion of which was spent for research. Similarly, the $20 million the American Heart Association and the American Lung Association together allocated for research was vastly exceeded by the appropriation to the National Heart, Lung, and Blood Institute of $350 million, largely for research work in the same fields. And the health agencies' role in research has been declining over the years: Back in 1960, their contribution to total research expenditures was 4 percent, still nothing substantial, but more than twice what it is today.

Nonetheless, some health agencies tend to emphasize research in their fundraising appeals because this come-on has been found to attract the most money, although many actually devote larger portions of their budgets to other activities. The National Easter Seal Society, for example, allocates about 70 percent of its total expenditures to "community" services, a larger percentage than any other major health agency; most of this outlay is used to treat patients at a network of rehabilitation centers. Services and facilities offered by other agencies encompass free outpatient clinics, transportation of patients to clinics or hospitals, the provision of wheelchairs, crutches, special beds, and other equipment for home use, counseling to both patients and their families, physical therapy, vocational programs, and employment information. The American Lung Association supports antismoking clinics, and Operation Stork, a joint venture of the National Foundation and B'nai B'rith, the Jewish service organization, assigns volunteers to prenatal care clinics and provides layettes to the expectant mothers there. The American Diabetes Association distributes a cookbook for diabetics and furnishes them with ID cards to prevent mistaken diagnoses should they be stricken with insulin shock when away from home. In what may be the most unusual service of all, several Mental Health Association chapters, as we shall later point out, sponsor courses that train bartenders, beauticians, barbers, and taxi drivers not only to lend a sympathetic ear to garrulous customers but also to spot the troubled and direct them to the appropriate sources of help.

Other agencies placing their primary emphasis on patient and community services include United Cerebral Palsy (which devotes 67 percent of its budget to this activity), Muscular Dystrophy (44), Multiple Sclerosis (35), Epilepsy (43), Hemophilia (63), American Diabetes (34), National Kidney (33), and the National Association for Retarded Citizens (86). Some agencies, such as the latter, concentrate on *obtaining* services; others, like Cerebral Palsy (which helps victims and their families), concentrate on *providing* them; and many, like the Easter Seal Society and Epilepsy, are involved in both activities.

Many agencies also carry on extensive programs of public and professional education to alert people to the symptoms of cancer, heart disease, glaucoma, diabetes, and other ailments for which prompt diagnosis and treatment is vital, to warn them of such health hazards as smoking, and to help keep physicians, nurses, and other health professionals up to date on the latest findings in their field.

Educational efforts are also directed at dispelling traditional misconceptions about many diseases—cerebral palsy, blindness, epilepsy, and mental illness, for example—and changing public attitudes toward them. The Epilepsy Foundation sees as one of its prime objectives the winning of greater understanding for the nation's estimated 2 million epileptics and removing the stigma that has prevented many from getting jobs and leading normal lives; it cites with satisfaction Gallup polls showing that whereas in 1949 only 45 percent of the people believed that epileptics should be employed, by 1969 the proportion had increased to 76 percent. During the same interval, according to the same polls, the proportion of people objecting to their children associating with epileptics had declined from 24 to 9 percent. The National Council on Alcoholism, which has worked to achieve recognition of alcoholism as a *health* problem, cites polls which show that well over half of all Americans now consider excessive drinking as a disease, contrasted with one in five in 1950.

The big question, however, is what good do all these programs really do? What about the educational efforts of the agencies, for example? Just what has been the effect of those billions of brochures distributed in the name of public education? Have the antismoking campaigns promoted by Cancer, Lung, and others really lowered the incidence of smoking? Have those ubiquitous leaflets graphically describing the "Seven Warning Signals of Cancer" really made people more aware of this disease? Who knows?

Interestingly, a Louis Harris survey conducted in the early 1970s for the Blue Cross Association found that only 13 percent of the population could identify four or more of the seven warning signals; 17 percent could identify only one of the signals; 30 percent could not identify any at all. Similarly, only one half of those polled were able to identify more than one of the 15-odd symptoms of a heart attack or heart condition; 27 percent—more than one out of four—were unable to identify a single symptom.

Moreover, creating awareness of a condition or a problem does not necessarily motivate people to do something about it, as evidenced by the many doctors who smoke. "Simply to repeat endlessly the facts about emphysema so that everybody in the country knows what emphysema is is not going to cure emphysema,'' says the National Information Bureau's Melvin Van de Workeen. "The American Lung Association has also had a tremendous campaign against smoking, but more people are smoking than ever before.''

"But wouldn't even more people be smoking, if not for the campaign?" he is asked.

"Probably. But how do you measure this? How do you therefore know whether to pump more money into the campaign or perhaps decide on another course of action?"

And if changes have really been wrought in knowledge, action, or attitudes, to what extent can the health agencies themselves claim a credit for them? The Epilepsy Foundation, though citing changes in attitudes toward epilepsy from 1949 to 1969, was founded only in 1968, albeit from the merger of several other organizations, and a foundation official was frank to admit that he didn't quite know what had brought about the changes in attitude. And any number of organizations, such as the American Medical Association and the American Psychiatric Association, can quite properly claim as much credit as the National Council on Alcoholism for the changes in attitude toward alcoholism.

What about those patient services? The extent of the aid available to patients through the voluntary agencies is sometimes exaggerated in the heat of fund-raising campaigns. All too frequently, the offer of help to medically indigent patients is nothing more than a referral to community agencies (which, in turn, are often unable to help). As we shall also see, where care actually is provided, it may duplicate that already available from other resources in the community or be of questionable quality.

And how meaningful are the research programs funded by the health agencies? At the Arthritis Foundation, officials mustered an impressive array of charts and reports to show me how some $40 million of foundation money had been spent over the past 30 years to support research aimed at finding a cure for arthritis. "But are we any closer to a cure now than we were then?" I asked. "My wife had some trouble with her hands recently and all the rheumatologist could do was to advise her to take aspirin. Thirty years ago, he would have told her the same thing.''

A statement made a quarter of a century ago about research grants by Dr. Isaac Starr of the University of Pennsylvania School of Medicine still has a good deal of validity today:

> Some agencies have more money than they know what to do with. Such groups, having raised their money by advertising their need, naturally feel it must be spent or next year's campaign would be conducted at a disadvantage. So they raise the ante and attract talent and personnel to their field without regard to the opportunities for advancing it. Good investigators leave promising problems to work in fallow fields simply because money can be so easily picked up. . . . Another temptation in a research investigator's path is to publish results prematurely or make exaggerated claims to insure next year's grant by producing what is desired this year.

I was reminded of this statement when a former health agency official told me that when the end of the agency's fiscal year approached and research funds were found to be unspent the agency would go into a near panic. "Our medical director would call up researchers frantically and beg them to accept grants, no matter how tenuous their projects," he said.

However, one should not assume that none of the research projects funded by the health agencies are without merit. But except for the Salk vaccine against polio, for which the then National Foundation for Infantile Paralysis (now the National Foundation) can validly claim credit, no research breakthrough of any major significance—or, at least, of comparable significance—has ever been funded by any voluntary health agency.

There are many other nagging doubts about the worth of the health agencies—the multiplicity of their appeals, their duplication of effort, and their never-ending competition for the charity dollar with little regard for the relative needs of the various diseases and disabilities. Cleveland has had two competing muscular dystrophy organizations since 1961 when a split occurred between the original local chapter and its national association. Since the early 1970s, rival lung disease groups, some of them disaffiliated by the American Lung Association, have been competing in about a dozen states for Christmas Seal sales. In Chatham County, Georgia, a tally once found 19 organizations passing the hat for the blind. Reflecting the long-standing differences between the United Way and such organizations as the American Cancer Society and the American Heart Association, which generally forbid their local chapters to participate in United Way fund drives, there are also rival cancer and heart groups in many cities.

Critics also point to what they regard as the duplication of efforts of the American Cancer Society, the Leukemia Society, and the Damon Runyon-Walter Winchell Cancer Fund and, in the field of child health, of such organizations as the National Foundation, the National Easter Seal Society, and the Cystic Fibrosis Foundation, to say nothing of the various organizations concerned with muscle disease.

Such criticisms date almost from the time the voluntary health agencies began to appear just around the turn of the century. As far back as 1913 Dr. Frederick Green of the American Medical Association called a conference of agency executives to discuss "mutual cooperation and the proper division of the field with a view to eliminating unnecessary organizations and the coordination of activities." Thirty-nine agencies attended the conference and appointed a committee which, after two years of labor, issued a report that was completely ignored by the very agencies that had sponsored it.

Shortly after World War I, Dr. George E. Vincent, president of the Rockefeller Foundation, again challenged the existence of "57 varieties" of societies interested in public health. "The health of a community is, after all, not a group of special interests," he said in an address before the American Public Health Association. "It is essentially a single interest with different aspects. To exalt one of them, to get it out of focus, and to urge it at the expense of other essential factors, is unscientific, wasteful and misleading. Only as the essential unity of the task is recognized and as those who represent different phases work together in constant conference and in accordance with a comprehensive program can the best results be secured."

It was this challenge that led the major agencies in 1921 to form the National Health Council, hailed by some as "one of the most important steps taken in the field of public health" but viewed by one critic as "the classic defense of beleaguered bureaucracy." For twenty years, the council functioned as little more than a trade association, unable to muster much support from its member agencies, each concerned with its own interests. Finally, the Council, with a grant from the Rockefeller Foundation, sponsored a three-year study conducted by two experienced health leaders, Selskar M. Gunn and Philip S. Platt. The Gunn-Platt report, issued in 1945, presented—according to one summary of it—"a devastating and carefully documented picture of useless activities, of failure to take up new problems and serve developing needs, of waste of contributors' money and failure to achieve health-protection goals that should long since have been reached and passed." Since the report also called for the National Health Council and its member agencies to mend their ways by, for example, pooling "the present separate, competitive and confusing appeals into a unified, nationwide campaign," nothing was ever done to implement its recommendations and it was quietly forgotten.

Fifteen years later, in 1960, in what seemed to be part of a recurring pattern, there came still another survey of the situation, this time by an ad hoc committee of private citizens, and again financed by the Rockefeller Foundation. One of the committee's major recommendations, calling for the adoption of uniform accounting procedures, was eventually implemented—a decade and a half later! The second major recommendation, urging the creation of a national commission to regulate and control the voluntary health and welfare agencies, has yet to be acted upon.

However, it would also be unfair to ignore the many good points of the health agencies—the fact, for example, that they have made many important contributions in the areas of public health, patient care, and public and professional education, particularly during their early years when they, together with the private foundations, were the only major factors in the health field. In recent years, they have continued to demonstrate a freedom, flexibility, and independence sometimes difficult for government to exercise. Planned Parenthood, for example, can press for birth control measures whereas a timorous government has to sidestep the issue so as not to tread on too many political and religious toes. Similarly, the American Cancer Society and the American Heart Association can be less concerned about the tobacco and dairy interests in their advocacy, respectively, of antismoking measures and the wider use of low-cholesterol (nondairy) foods.

While the health agencies do not need the massive funds for research they might have made a case for at one time, they have been a useful goad in prodding government to spend as much as it now does on research; and the American Cancer Society, the American Heart Association, the American Lung Association, the Arthritis Foundation, the American Diabetes Association, the National Kidney Foundation, and the Cystic Fibrosis Foundation, among others, have played an acknowledged role in creating the climate and lobbying for financial support for research on the diseases with which they are concerned. A Gallup poll showed a majority of our citizens favor voluntary health agencies continuing to work along these lines.

Yet in answer to other questions of who should do what for whom in our society, the public, responding to the same poll, offered some interesting answers. Who should handle medical research? Sixty-three percent of the public felt it should be handled by government and another 26 percent by professional societies or individual doctors; only 4 percent felt that research should be a responsibility of voluntary agencies. As for public health education, 76 percent of those responding felt this should be handled by government and only 7 percent by voluntary agencies.

The question therefore remains: Should government assume all the functions of the health agencies or are such agencies still needed? If so, which ones are the most deserving of support? Perhaps the answers may emerge after we look somewhat more closely at the various health agencies in the pages that follow.

Chapter 10

Are the Big Health Charities Outmoded?

> Over the years as they become institutionalized those who work for the agencies become more concerned with the institution than the purpose. . . . Since a health agency is set up with the highest of motives, those who direct its affairs may easily develop the feeling that the institution must live on at any cost. . . . The directors have a genuine, if mistaken, conviction that no other group is sufficiently competent to carry on the functions of the agency. The agency must therefore continue, even if it has outlived its usefulness.
>
> — Selskar M. Gunn and Philip S. Platt,
> *Voluntary Health Agencies* (1945)

Long known as the "Big Five" of the voluntary health agencies are the American Cancer Society, the American Heart Association, the National Foundation (March of Dimes), the National Easter Seal Society for Crippled Children and Adults, and the American Lung Association, ranked according to the support they receive from the public.* Together, their annual contributions now come to about $330 million and their income from all sources to more than $400 million, which is nearly one-half of the collective income of the 20 leading voluntary national health agencies listed in the previous chapter, and about one-third of the estimated $1.1 billion collected by all of the perhaps 100,000 voluntary health agencies in the nation. Yet two of the "Big Five," the American Lung Association and the National Foundation, were established to fight diseases for which cures have been found and which, consequently, have all but vanished from our midst—tuberculosis and polio.

But unlike aged generals, our health agencies never die; nor do they fade away. They may change their name or even their purpose; but not a one, if it can

---

*Actually, in terms of contributions, the Muscular Dystrophy Association today holds the No. 4 spot, ahead of the Easter Seal Society and the American Lung Association. But the other agencies, apart from being older, are still better known—in fact, virtually household words, particularly because of their ubiquitous Easter and Christmas Seals. In terms of total income, including government grants and service fees, the National Association for Retarded Citizens and Planned Parenthood now rank among the top five.

help it, ever disappears. With this in mind, let us now see what purpose the five leading health agencies ostensibly now fulfill and how well they seem to fulfill it.

TB or not TB: The Battle of the Christmas Seals

In 1882 Robert Koch, the German physician and bacteriologist, discovered the bacillus that caused tuberculosis. American medicine then, however, was not quick to embrace this epochal discovery, even though tuberculosis, at the turn of the century, was our leading cause of death, killing 200 out of every 100,000 Americans, far more than heart disease (132) and cancer (63). And so it was not until 1904 that a concerned group of physicians and laymen got around to forming an organization aimed at bridging the gap between Koch's discovery and its application. The organization, called the National Society for the Study and Prevention of Tuberculosis, and today known after a series of name changes as the American Lung Association, was the first national voluntary health association in the United States entirely devoted to the conquest of a single disease.*

In spite of the hostility of most physicians who clung to the fatalistic notion that tuberculosis was a hopeless, hereditary disease, the new organization and its affiliates (which grew from 23 to 431 within six years) first concentrated on informing the public that consumption, as the disease was also known, was communicable, preventable, and curable. As there were then no pills and potions to ward off tuberculosis and no medical cure for the disease, the society also preached the gospel of cleanliness and good health habits. The society worked for and stimulated public pressure for more and better hospitals, sanatoriums, and clinics for the tubercular, for the cooperation of health departments and other government agencies in fighting the disease, and for the enactment of appropriate laws (by the early 1920s all states required physicians to report every case of the disease to health authorities) and firm sanitary codes. The tuberculosis associations even took the leadership in a vigorous nationwide campaign against spiting. In Kansas and many other places, "Don't Spit" bricks were cemented into sidewalks; in Cincinnati, 700 volunteers stayed up all night to paint the city's streets with "Don't Spit" notices.

All of this cost money, which brings us to the story of the Christmas Seal, probably the most ingenious, effective fund-raising gimmick in the history of philanthropy. The story goes back to 1907 when an energetic social worker named Emily Bissell was casting about for ways to raise $300 to keep open the doors of a foundering eight-bed tuberculosis hospital housed in a small open shack on the banks of the Brandywine River in Delaware. The hospital's doctors, one of them her cousin, had told her that unless the $300 was raised, the patients would have to be sent home to die. By happenstance, Emily had recently read a magazine article by the Danish-American writer and social reformer, Jacob Riis, who well knew the tragedy of tuberculosis: Six of his brothers had died of the disease. Riis's article told the tale of a Danish postmaster named Einar Holboell

*Nearly two dozen local and state tuberculosis societies predated the national association; probably the first, in Pennsylvania, was formed in 1892 by Dr. Lawrence F. Flick, who was also the principal force behind the establishment of the National Society. The American Red Cross, which dates from 1881, was only incidentally concerned with health. As far back as the early 1890s, France, Denmark, and Austria also had national voluntary organizations which worked for health reform; however, none were ever to achieve the scope and zeal of ours.

who, several years before, had been inspired with the idea of having people buy a special Christmas stamp, with the proceeds of the sale to go to help sick and needy children. With the royal blessings of the King of Denmark himself, the warmhearted Danes bought enough stamps to build a children's tuberculosis hospital.

If far-away Denmark could fight tuberculosis with a Christmas stamp, why not the United States? thought Emily. She drew the design for our first Christmas Seal—a holly wreath and the greeting "Merry Christmas" against a bright red background—and borrowed $40 from friends to have 50,000 of the seals printed. Envelopes containing the seals bore this legend:

> Put this stamp with message bright
> On every Christmas letter;
> Help the tuberculosis fight,
> And make the New Year better.

When the U.S. Christmas Seal campaign of 1907 was over, Emily had raised, not the $300 she had hoped for, but $3000, and the Brandywine hospital was saved. For the next two years, the American Red Cross, regarding tuberculosis as a sort of disaster that could fall within its historic mandate, took over the campaign, and in 1910 the tuberculosis association became a partner in the venture. In 1920, the Red Cross, involved as it was in other activities and having other sources of funds, turned over the entire program to what was by then known as the National Tuberculosis Association which, as a gesture of independence, replaced the Red Cross emblem on the seal with the now-familiar double-barred cross.

From receipts of $3000 in 1907 the seals brought in $3.5 million in 1920; and by 1977, receipts had increased to over $38 million, accounting for close to 90 percent of the $44 million total contributions of the association and its affiliates; that year, the total of 93 million sheets of seals printed—the largest four-color printing of stamps in the world—was mailed to 60 million homes and businesses across the country. Only one out of every three mailings to previous donors draws a response, with an average contribution of $3.90; on the other hand, only one out of every 25 mailings to "prospect" lists results in a donation.

Yet, to most people, the arrival of the colorful seals, which over the years have featured the work of such well-known artists as Norman Rockwell, Howard Pyle, and Steven Dohanos, is an accepted and welcome Christmas tradition, no more to be questioned than Christmas itself. So closely identified are the seals with the association and its fight against lung disease that to discontinue their use would be unthinkable; indeed, to do so would no doubt result in a drastic drop in the association's revenues. But there can be no questioning the fact that the seals are an extremely expensive means of raising money. For every dollar collected from the public, the association and its affiliates pay out an average of 28 cents in fund-raising costs; the addition of 7 cents more for overhead brings the costs up to 35 cents. In other terms, these costs represent nearly 33 cents out of every dollar the association and its affiliates spend, leaving only 67 cents to be spent on all the other things the organization does to help fight lung disease.

How well has the organization done this? Certainly, it deserves some commendation for the efforts mentioned earlier which, according to an association history, "led—15 years after the founding of the National Association—*to a drop in the country's tuberculosis mortality rate of 33 percent.*" However, it does not deserve as much credit as this statement claims. As Richard Carter points out in *The Gentle Legions*, and as every epidemiologist knows, "The tuberculosis death rate had been declining for years before the establishment of the National Association in 1904. The additional reduction—from 188 [in 1904] to 125 deaths [in 1919] per 100,000 population—during the first 15 years of the association's existence was therefore not entirely attributable to its efforts. A rising standard of living, better diet, wholesome recreation, and other features of an improving national existence would have reduced the death rate even if there had been no association."

This is not to say that the pioneering efforts of the association had no impact whatever. Yet, at the same time, many of its actions have been characterized by inertia and complacency. For example, as long ago as 1939, the association's own director of health education, Dr. H. E. Kleinschmidt, questioned the usefulness of the so-called "tuberculosis preventoria"—many of them summer camps for children—maintained by association funds. "There is little evidence," said Dr. Kleinschmidt, "to show that they prevent or retard the developing tuberculosis once infection has taken place." However, he did concede their usefulness in stimulating Christmas Seal sales. Perhaps for this reason, 24 preventoria were still in operation three years later. (The last one was finally phased out as recently as 1968.)

Curiously, although the association has long tried to create the impression that it places special emphasis on research (one recent press release was headed: "LUNG DISEASE RESEARCH SPURRED BY CHRISTMAS SEALS"), the group spends less on research than virtually any other major voluntary health agency—in a recent year, only 2 cents out of every dollar of its total budget.* Indeed, some would even read a sinister motive into the association's attitude toward research. "It's a scandal!" says one of the most distinguished figures in the voluntary health movement. "But the TB people never did anything to help people who tried to do something about TB. For a good many years they completely disregarded the discovery of streptomycin by Selman Waksman and his colleagues in 1944. They also paid little attention at first to PAS [para-aminosalicylic acid] and isoniazid, the two other important antituberculosis drugs that came along a few years later. Why? Because they were afraid these drugs would put them out of business. If TB were licked, what would there be left for them to do?"

To such charges, the association, while expressing some chagrin that it did not fund the research on these landmark drugs, has a ready answer. "We were delighted when these drugs came along and demonstrated their usefulness," said Dr. Robert Anderson, a beefy, affable man who was the association's managing director up to 1974. "At the same time, our previous experience—and disillusionment—with other reported TB cures led our doctors to be conservative about accepting the reports of any new drugs before they were tested on large groups of individuals."

---

*Where does the rest go? Thirty cents goes for community services (case detection, work with government and other health agencies, etc.), 33 cents for public health and professional education and training, 2 cents for patient services, and, as already mentioned, 33 cents for fund raising and overhead. All this adds up to slightly less than one dollar, because I have rounded off the figures.

With the drugs now available, the continued improvement in socioeconomic conditions, and the public health measures the antituberculosis movement helped pioneer, the disease can no longer be considered a serious health problem. The once-dreaded "white plague" now ranks only eighteenth (behind even peptic ulcers, hernias, chronic bronchitis, and kidney infections) as a cause of U.S. death, claiming fewer than 3000 lives a year, or 1.4 per 100,000 population; and only 29,000 cases of tuberculosis were reported in 1978.

In recent years the association has therefore broadened its program to include other lung diseases such as emphysema (characterized by difficulty in breathing), chronic bronchitis, and asthma; it has also begun to campaign against cigarette smoking and air pollution, as in the past it battled spitting. Reflecting these broadened areas of interest, the National Tuberculosis Association changed its name to the National Tuberculosis and Respiratory Disease Association in 1968 and became the American Lung Association in 1973. The association, recognizing that tuberculosis was no longer a problem in many areas, implemented a major reorganization by consolidating its nearly 2000 state and local affiliates of a decade ago into its present-day total of around 200. "The larger number reflected the organizational pattern to battle tuberculosis," said an association official. "For the needs of the modern battle against lung diseases in general, the smaller number is more efficient and economical, and enables us to hire more highly-skilled people."

Critics point out, however, that many of the lung diseases now receiving the association's attention, though serious and prevalent, cause significantly fewer deaths than several other diseases being fought with inadequate funds. Emphysema and chronic bronchitis rank, respectively, eleventh and sixteenth on the list of causes of death, and asthma ranks twentieth.* Some critics also question the programs against these diseases. "Simply to repeat endlessly the facts about emphysema so that everybody in the country knows what emphysema is, is not going to cure emphysema," says the National Information Bureau's Melvin Van de Workeen. "If it were, why is emphysema now causing nearly twice as many deaths as it did a decade ago?" For similar reasons, also questioned are the association's antismoking and antipollution programs which, moreover, duplicate those of many other organizations. (Americans now smoke 620 billion cigarettes annually, an all-time high.)

Critics note, too, the way the assets of the association and its local affiliates keep piling up year after year to the point where they now exceed $69 million, mainly in cash and securities, compared to only $617,000 in 1945. Nearly 90 percent of these funds are in the hands of the locals. To be fair, however, since all of the association's chapters close their fiscal year on March 31, or shortly after the annual Christmas Seal receipts come in, most of the assets represent working funds for the year ahead; and a portion has to be put aside as a reserve against the uncertainties of the future, in accordance with the practice of most voluntary organizations. (Association policy recommends the retention of between 25 percent and 75 percent of the average of the previous three years' expenditures as a reserve against future contingencies.)

*In 1976 emphysema, associated with heavy smokers, killed an estimated 17,550, and is believed to affect 1.3 million people; chronic bronchitis killed 4490 of the nation's 6.5 million people afflicted with it; asthma, said to affect 6 million, killed 1800 persons.

Still, the question remains whether the locals (some with reserves in excess of 75 percent) are spending their funds to the best advantage, not only because of the reservations expressed about their programs but also because of others. Quite a few affiliates, recognizing the Christmas Seal promotion as a gold mine when tied to tuberculosis, still persist in battling that venerable foe, although some have opposing ideas as to how to do it. For this reason, the past few years has seen rival groups (many continuing to retain "tuberculosis" in their names) competing for Christmas Seal sales (with *different* Christmas Seals) in a growing number of areas in a dozen states, including Michigan, New York, Pennsylvania, Ohio, West Virginia, and California. Some groups have even disaffiliated themselves from the American Lung Association because the national organization objects to their use of tuberculin testing to detect cases of tuberculosis.

"The national organization is removing itself from all programs that provide direct service to individuals," says Ralph Childs, executive director of the disaffiliated Tuberculosis, Health and Emphysema Society of Kent County in Grand Rapids, Michigan. "We have a deep feeling that if you raise funds for special things, you should use them to help people with those specific problems."

Echoing this view is Ronald J. Clair, executive director of another disaffiliated Michigan group, the Oakland County Tuberculosis Association, founded in 1914. "National's big philosophy under its present reorganization is to centralize everything, stop all direct service programs, and turn everything into one big program run from New York."

However, the disagreement between the disaffiliated and the national organization runs much deeper than this, having its roots in a long-standing feud between the locals and the leadership in New York over the control of programs and policies. Contributing to the feud was the 1973 reorganization which, in addition to reducing the number of chapters (and, therefore, jobs), placed the remaining ones under more stringent review. What used to irk Ralph Childs was the fact that the state lung organization got a markup on everything he ordered—from Christmas Seals to pamphlets—from national headquarters, even though these materials were often drop-shipped to him. "If the money is raised locally, it should be spent locally," says Childs.

For its part, the American Lung Association, with its growing emphasis on educational programs, concedes that it has been discouraging patient services and urging that such services be turned over to private physicians and to health departments and other government agencies so that it can concentrate on developing other innovative programs, including demonstration projects proving the feasibility and value of patient services. In other words, the association now feels that services wherever possible should be rendered in ongoing medical facilities already existent in the community, rather than by its local affiliates.

"The influence and resources of national, constituent and affiliate associations," says an ALA policy statement, "are most effectively used to encourage the inclusion within the established health care systems of medical, nursing and rehabilitation services to persons with lung diseases. Program planning that is imaginative and innovative precludes an association from accepting long-term obligations in providing services."

If this attitude persists, what started as an antituberculosis movement may yet put itself out of business.

A President, Polio, and the March of Dimes

Polio, to even a greater extent than tuberculosis, has all but vanished from the American scene: In 1977 it caused only 17 deaths in all of the United States and only 20 new cases of it were reported. Not that polio was ever a really serious disease in terms of numbers. Yet it gave rise to an organization, the National Foundation for Infantile Paralysis—known today as the National Foundation-March of Dimes—which has raised well over $1 billion dollars in the some four decades of its existence and whose story is one of the wonders of American philanthropy. But what other charity can list as its "founder" and claim as its patron saint an adored president, Franklin D. Roosevelt who, as everyone knows, was a victim of polio?*

The story begins with the Georgia Warm Springs Foundation, established by Roosevelt in 1927 to support a small polio rehabilitation center in Warm Springs which the future president, then a private citizen, had first visited several years before. Initially, the Georgia foundation was financed largely by Roosevelt himself and a few wealthy friends. But the Depression made it increasingly difficult for them to continue their large gifts, and donations declined from a peak of $368,991 in 1929 to $30,331 in 1932.

The decision was made to embark upon a mass nationwide fund-raising campaign, one soliciting many small donations rather than just a few large gifts. With the election of Roosevelt to the presidency, the idea was also concocted of holding a series of annual dances to celebrate the president's birthday and at the same time raise money for Warm Springs. The first President's Birthday Ball, launched on January 30, 1934, was successful beyond the wildest expectations of its sponsors: $1,049,557 was collected from 4376 communities that held almost 6000 separate celebrations—occasions for people to "dance so that others may walk."

Crucial to the success of the celebrations and, later, an important factor in the growth of the National Foundation as a grass-roots social movement, was an idea proposed by Keith L. Morgan, a Warm Springs trustee and Roosevelt friend. It was to delegate Postmaster General James A. Farley to appoint the postmasters in each of the thousands of communities as chairmen of the local balls. It was an offer they couldn't very well refuse. "They just got jobs after ten Republican years," said Morgan. "They ought to be glad to do something for the boss."

To give the fledgling antipolio movement a more nonpartisan character and to broaden its purposes to include not only the relief and treatment of polio victims but also research into means of preventing the disease, the National Foundation for Infantile Paralysis was established four years later. Named as its nonsalaried president was Basil O'Connor, a close friend and former law partner of Roosevelt, treasurer of the Warm Springs Foundation, for some years president of the American National Red Cross, and one of the most colorful, cantankerous, and controversial characters in the annals of American philanthropy. A man of

---

*Known more formally as poliomyelitis (*polio* meaning *gray* and *myel*, *marrow*), it is an acute infectious virus disease marked by an inflammation of the spinal cord and brain. When the nerve cells in the gray marrow of the spinal cord are damaged or destroyed, the muscles controlled by the cells are unable to move and, hence, eventually wither. The disease is also called infantile paralysis because it often strikes in early childhood.

driving ambition, a genius at organization, and one whose imagination knew no bounds, O'Connor probably did more to change the nature of American charity than any other one person, pioneering mass fund-raising techniques later imitated by other health agencies.

While continuing the President's Birthday Balls, O'Connor, during the foundation's first month of existence, selected a week for an intensive fund-raising campaign dubbed the March of Dimes by comedian Eddie Cantor; that January week in 1938, an array of celebrities ranging from Cantor, Jack Benny, and Bing Crosby to Jascha Heifetz, Kate Smith, and the Lone Ranger went on radio with tear-jerking appeals for dimes to be sent to the White House. As a result of the appeals, a deluge of 2,680,000 dimes, some of them baked into cakes and pies, descended on the White House, disrupting the mail room there for months.

The early 1950s saw the introduction of another great fund-raising gimmick called the "Mothers' March," still responsible for about 13 percent of all National Foundation contributions. In this campaign activity, platoons of marching mothers, organized along military lines (the leaders, in many places, often have such titles as colonel, captain, and lieutenant), sweep through an entire community, stopping at the homes of people who turn on their porch lights at a designated hour as a signal they are willing to give a contribution. (Because of the rise of multiple-family dwellings, the character of this collection has changed in recent years.) *Harper's* once interviewed an early foundation supervisor of this gigantic mobilization of womanpower. "With the nostalgia of an old football star recalling a ninety-yard run, he described one of the first marches in Phoenix, Arizona—the advance publicity via press and radio, the lights shining, as directed, on the porches of willing donors, the fanfare of fire and police sirens as the triumphant mothers reaped an unprecedented harvest of $47,000 in a single hour."

As some 2600 chapters, many of them headed by local postmasters, were set up, the foundation's annual receipts zoomed from $1.8 million in 1938 to a peak of $67.4 million in 1954, by far more than that of any other health agency.* Yet, as already mentioned, although polio was never really a great menace in this nation, people gave the polio cause more than six times the amount they gave to conquer heart disease, then and now our No. 1 killer, and more than double what they gave to fight cancer, the prime killer of children.

If the end justifies the means, however, there can also be no question that the foundation was an unqualified success; indeed, it remains unique among voluntary health agencies in that it accomplished what it set out to do. O'Connor had committed the foundation to the conquest of polio, and the foundation deserves full credit for bringing this about. For the funds that poured into the foundation financed a large part of the research culminating in 1955 with the introduction of the Salk vaccine that resulted in the virtual eradication of polio. Some foundation critics say that it could have spent more on research than it did: Of the $550 million it spent from 1938 to 1958, a total of $34 million went for research—only 7 cents of every dollar contributed. The inference is that with more money allocated to research, the vaccine would have been discovered earlier. But who is

*Of the $1.8 million raised in the first campaign, 42 percent went for fund-raising and overhead expenses; similar high costs in many of the following years have brought the foundation continuing criticism down to the present.

to say this would have happened? To criticisms of this sort, O'Connor would respond: "What most people don't realize is that you can't spend an unlimited amount on research. There just aren't that many qualified researchers."

Moreover, as most of the $550 million—in some years, more than half of all foundation expenditures—went to pay for costly medical and hospital care and for equipment for polio patients, the foundation also deserves thanks for fulfilling another of its original mandates. True, it could afford to pay the huge sums it did because of the relatively low incidence of polio. Yet one cannot help but wonder how many more millions of dollars it would have been necessary to spend on patient care if not for that $34 million investment in research. (Foundation statisticians once estimated that if the 1951–1954 polio attack rate had prevailed two decades later, the cost for the approximately 31,000 cases that would have occurred would have cost the American public $312 million for treatment and rehabilitation services.)

But with polio no longer a threat by the late 1950s, the question arose: What would happen to the National Foundation for Infantile Paralysis? What *should* happen to it? To those who suggested that the foundation now fold its tent, O'Connor had a ready answer: "If we went out of business, the other agencies wouldn't benefit a nickel unless they went out for it. You have to go out and sell yourself to the American people."

He also said: "We had three choices: to pack up and go home; to confine ourselves to a single disease; or to expand. The foundation had built up experience and an army of volunteers, something belonging to the American people. We decided to go into something where our aptitudes could be put to good use."

But what would it go into? The foundation had been considering various options as early as 1952 when there were indications that Salk's efforts would soon result in a successful vaccine. After surveying the nation's major health problems, casting about for another disease, it quickly ruled out heart disease, cancer, and tuberculosis because it did not wish to tread on the toes of the giant agencies already involved with these ailments. In 1958 the foundation finally came to a decision, announcing with considerable fanfare that it was shortening its name to the National Foundation and widening its activities to include arthritis and birth defects.

Arthritis and the related ailment of rheumatism had been selected, O'Connor said, because they afflicted at least 11 million Americans and cost the nation over $1.5 billion annually in lost wages and medical costs. This field was already being plowed by what was then known at the Arthritis and Rheumatism Foundation (today, simply the Arthritis Foundation) but it was a relatively small agency, raising only about $3.5 million a year. Basil O'Connor held merger discussions with the arthritis group's lay chairman, Floyd B. Odlum. But the negotiations blew up when the latter's local chapters voted down the merger and told the conquerors of polio to get out of the arthritis field. "You're not going to steal our disease," one rheumatologist supposedly said. O'Connor angrily retorted that "individual diseases are not the personal property of individual organizations." Nonetheless, the National Foundation decided not to continue with arthritis and instead began to concentrate primarily on birth defects.

A stroke of genius worthy of O'Connor! With polio, the foundation had been concerned with no more than 30,000 to 40,000 cases a year. But birth defects were quite a different matter. One in every 16 babies—or about 250,000 American babies a year—are born with a birth defect, which the foundation defines as "an abnormality of structure or function, whether genetically determined or the result of environmental interference during embryonic or fetal life." Furthermore, according to the foundation, some 15 million Americans, young and old, have birth defects of one sort or another; and 1.2 million people are hospitalized each year because of them. What a potential constituency—and source of funds—this new cause represented for the foundation!

Nor could any one agency now accuse the foundation of appropriating its disease. For with birth defects, the foundation was now dealing with an entire supermarket of diseases, ranging from relatively minor disorders—color blindness and baldness—and deformities—clubfoot and cleft palate—to a whole array of diseases and deficiencies—sickle cell anemia, Tay-Sachs, Huntington's chorea, cystic fibrosis, hemophilia, mental retardation, diabetes, congenital heart, bone and muscle disease, hearing impairments, and errors of metabolism, as well as an endless variety of ailments caused by so-called environmental factors, such as a disease in the mother—German measles or venereal disease—or other conditions affecting the fetus.

Of course, much of this terrain, too, was already well populated by various individual agencies. As we shall see in the next chapter, there is even a Tay-Sachs and a Huntington's and a Sickle Cell Anemia Foundation. Moreover, like the Arthritis Foundation, none of these agencies intended to disappear. But the National Foundation was probably bigger than most of them put together. Even so, to keep the peace, it would aim to supplement, rather than supersede, the work of the others by directing much of its research efforts at the basic processes of life as opposed to "categorical" projects, as it had in seeking a specific vaccine for polio.

Of the foundation's current expenditures of about $57 million a year, 16 percent, or some $9 million, now goes for research; $1 million of this is allocated to the Salk Institute, a unique complex of laboratories set up with foundation help in La Jolla, California, in the 1960s to concentrate on "the molecular approach to cellular genetics, reproductive biology, autoallergic diseases, virology, the growth of normal and cancerous cells, and the very origins of life." Another 40 percent, or $22 million, goes for public and professional health education and related community services. About 17 percent, or $10 million, is spent on medical services, which include genetic counseling, prenatal care, and direct patient aid at some 230 centers across the nation in hospitals and medical centers which receive foundation support. The prenatal care (PNC) programs, many done in collaboration with organizations ranging from B'nai B'rith Women and Zeta Phi Beta (a predominantly black national sorority), bear such names as Stork's Nests and Operation Stork; they collect and distribute layettes and baby furniture as an incentive to women to keep their PNC appointments. As a hangover from its polio days, the foundation still spends around half a million dollars a year to supply and maintain respirators for the aging polio patients who still rely on the foundation for help.

All of which leaves about 27 percent, or over $15 million, of the foundations budget for fund-raising costs and overhead, which some foundation critics feel to be too high and perhaps even understated. The National Information

Bureau, for example, a respected nonprofit agency that uses certain financial yardsticks and other standards to evaluate charities, feels that the expenses for "chapter organization and development" the foundation charges off to "community services" should more properly be allocated to "management and general" or overhead. Almost from the beginning of the foundation's history, the NIB refused to give it a clean bill of health because it consistently spent less on research than on fund raising which, the NIB also felt, was based on misleading or incomplete data. For example, the foundation's 1957 annual report depicted a dime (of course) cut into percentage pieces to show how the March of Dimes money had been spent. Although all the pieces added up to 100 percent, missing was a piece to represent the outlay that year of more than $6 million, or 14.4 percent, of the budget for fund raising.

Locally, the NIB has from time to time also found some foundation chapters to be less than candid, reporting in 1967 that more than 40 cents of every dollar raised by the Fort Worth, Texas, chapter was being eaten up by fund-raising expenses, although the chapter's officials claimed that these costs were below the 20 percent limit allowed by the city's ordinance. But the city council, according to a *Wall Street Journal* story, challenged this claim and banned that year's Mothers' March, charging that the chapter had unfairly excluded its director's expenses and all but one month's rent and phone bill from its fund-raising expenses. More recently, in 1977, chapters in Florida's Santa Rosa and Jackson counties were found to be listing salaries under "printing and supplies" in their annual financial reports. County officials also questioned the chapters' mass mailing programs there, charging that expenses ran as high as 50 and 80 percent of total collections.

The NIB also once took umbrage at the fact that Basil O'Connor's status as the foundation's "unpaid volunteer" president continued to be widely proclaimed even after he began quietly drawing a salary in 1959. (When this was finally revealed in 1965, O'Connor was getting $48,000 a year plus an annual expense allowance of $20,000; at the time of his death in 1972, his part-time salary alone was the equivalent of $100,000.) Surprisingly, only three of the foundation's 28 trustees were aware that O'Connor was being paid, a situation that gave the bureau still another reason for disapproving the foundation since the bureau's minimum standards also call for "an active and responsible governing body." Even before he went on the foundation payroll, O'Connor aroused the ire of critics because of his free and easy ways with money and for what some regarded as a flexible ethical sense. A dapper man who always wore a fresh carnation in his lapel, he maintained a suite in the Waldorf-Astoria and in a single year would often rack up as much as $70,000 in expenses. Although no one questioned his dedication to the polio cause, he once spent $14.5 million of foundation funds to buy up every drop of gamma globulin in the country even after discovering it provided only limited and temporary protection against polio. He saw no conflict of interest in retaining his own law firm to do the foundation's legal work or in allowing himself to serve as president of both the National Foundation and the Warm Springs Foundation, although the latter over a 20-year period received from the National Foundation over $15 million in grants—a staggering sum for a regional, relatively small facility.

Although O'Connor felt that the National Information Bureau, in airing such matters, was conducting a personal vendetta against him and meddling in the management of the foundation's affairs, he was also regarded as a renegade by others in the philanthropic field. Thus, he took the foundation out of the National Health Council in 1963 when it voted 25 to 1, with his the lone dissenting vote, in favor of a Rockefeller Foundation committee report recommending the adoption of uniform accounting procedures and the creation of a national commission to regulate the voluntary health and welfare agencies. (See Chapter 9.) In O'Connor's view, such actions would threaten the independence of the agencies and destroy "one of the most cherished privileges of democracy by inflicting on volunteers a government by vigilante." For ostensibly similar reasons, charity's celebrated lone wolf successfully kept the foundation's chapters out of federated fund drives, threatening those tempted to participate with certain expulsion. (For more on this, see Chapter 25.)

With the death of the foundation's O'Connor in 1972 and his NIB nemesis, Paul Reed, almost exactly a year later, the two organizations have achieved a certain rapprochement to the point where the NIB in 1976 finally approved the foundation as meeting its standards. Recently, the National Health Council welcomed the foundation back into its fold. Since the early 1970s, however, the foundation's birth defects program has embroiled it in another sort of controversy. Right-to-life and other antiabortion groups have been claiming that the foundation has been encouraging abortion through its support of amniocentesis—a diagnostic technique used to determine the presence of abnormalities in an unborn child by analyzing the fetal cells in the amniotic sac, or bag of waters, of a pregnant woman. Incited by inflammatory editorials bearing such titles as "March of Death?", the prolife forces, including some Catholic groups, even began to boycott March of Dimes campaigns across the country. As a result, in one recent year, the Mothers' March in Visalia, California, collected only $600 compared to its usual $4600; the Greater Cincinnati chapter estimated its campaign loss at $100,000. The directors of some chapters were the subject of harassing phone calls that asked, "How do you like killing babies?" An unfortunately titled March of Dimes pamphlet "A Time To Be Born Or A Time To Die" did not help matters much. Although it merely spelled out the difference MOD-supported research, education, and medical services could make between the life and death of children, the antiabortionists seized on it to reinforce their allegations that the foundation favored abortion. Even though the allegations had no basis in fact, the foundation was forced to issue a statement repudiating any identification with proabortion (or antiabortion) policies; the statement also made clear that patients receiving diagnostic services, such as amniocentesis, in foundation-supported programs should not be required to give prior consent to an abortion. After widespread reports that the foundation was bowing to pressure and phasing out its genetic programs, the foundation called a press conference in 1978 to announce that it was continuing to support such programs at the level of $2.5 million a year.

What about the future of the foundation? "The number one thing we'll continue to be concerned with is the prevention of birth defects," says Charles L. Massey, the current foundation president, speaking with the remnants of a southern accent. To those who say that this goal is impossible to achieve because the task is too great, a foundation brochure responds: "Nonsense. When the original

National Foundation for Infantile Paralysis was founded by Franklin D. Roosevelt in 1938, it was 'impossible' to prevent polio.''

But with the multitude of diseases with which it is now involved, there is little risk of the foundation's again nearly becoming a victim of its own success—at least as long as Congress continues to equivocate about committing itself to federal funding of genetic health services and genetic education for laymen. In 1975 Congress approved the National Genetic Diseases Act, which authorized three years of support for these two activities. But, as the August 19, 1978, *New Republic* points out, Congress failed to fund the program for its first two years, and it was not until 1978 that $8 million was finally appropriated—''a drop in the bucket,'' according to one genetic services administrator.

More Seals—"To Help the Crippled"

Were the National Foundation ever to realize its utopian goal of preventing birth defects, one wonders if the National Easter Seal Society for Crippled Children and Adults would then have much reason for existence. Theoretically, it would, of course. For accidents and illnesses also cripple people after birth. We are reminded of these victims, as well as of those born with birth defects, every spring when the society mails out 38 million packets of those familiar Easter Seals and sponsors such advertisements and radio and TV announcements as these:

IF YOU DON'T HAVE A CRIPPLED CHILD,
WILL YOU HELP ONE OF OURS?

GIVE KIDS A CHANCE TO WALK.
GIVE TO EASTER SEALS.

The messages, as well as the seals themselves, invariably show a wistful child on crutches or wearing leg braces or perhaps bravely smiling at us from a wheelchair. Presumably, the dollars we are asked to donate will enable such children as these to recover the use of their limbs. That the appeal is successful is indicated by the fact that the society now receives $44 million in contributions annually, an amount exceeded by only four other health agencies.

Few people, however, are aware that relatively little of the money given to the society actually goes to help "crippled" children. Of the children served on an individual basis by the society, only 14 percent, by the society's own reckoning, have "orthopedic disabilities." More than twice as many—31 percent—suffer from "communications disorders" or, in plain language, have speech, hearing, or related disabilities. In fairness, another 24 percent of the children served individually by the society have "neurological-neuromuscular" disorders—conditions that may also call for (albeit not necessarily always) the use of leg braces, crutches, and other such aids. However, these children together with those with orthopedic disabilities account for only 38 percent—or little more than one-third—of the society's juvenile caseload. But obviously a picture of a deaf or dumb child would not have quite the same heart-rending fund-raising appeal as one of a child with a more visible disability. Nor would most people know by looking at the society's appeals that more than half of its entire annual caseload of 330,000 disabled are adults who, for fund-raising purposes, do not present quite the same image of pity as children. Hence, the plenitude of Easter Seal "poster" children, but never, never adults. (The same use of hyperbole extends, of course, to other health agencies.)

Most voluntary health agencies owe their origins to people who were personally affected by some specific disease or health problem. The father of the antituberculosis movement, Dr. Lawrence F. Flick, was a former consumptive and, as we have also seen, the National Foundation came about because of the deep involvement and sponsorship of a president with polio. The present-day Easter Seal Society grew out of the Ohio Society for Crippled Children, founded in Elyria, Ohio, in 1919 by Edgar F. Allen, who became concerned about the plight of the crippled during the fatal illness of his own son who had been seriously injured and died for lack of adequate medical care. Two years later, the Ohio society, with the encouragement of groups such as Rotary, became the National Society for Crippled Children; and in 1944 it added "Adults" to its name. The society changed its name to its present one to reflect growing public awareness of Easter Seals, which had been adopted as a fund-raising device in 1934.

Seal solicitations, as we have already mentioned in our account of Christmas Seals, are a relatively expensive form of fund raising. A sheet of Easter Seals costs a penny and to put it in the mail, with all the other enclosures, costs an average of 6.5 cents. When you multiply this by the 38 million Easter Seal letters mailed annually (a quantity exceeded only by the 60 million Christmas Seal mailings), the cost is considerable, especially since only one out of every ten Easter Seal recipients responds with a contribution. For every 1000 packages mailed, at a cost of $65, the society gets back $160 from its donor lists, clearing $95; on the other hand, the mailings to prospect lists draw only $35 above the $65 cost. This means that anywhere from 40 cents to 65 cents of every dollar donated goes to pay the cost of these mailings (and we are not even figuring the cost of overhead).

For this reason, the society over the years has been turning increasingly to other forms of fund raising: door-to-door solicitations, campaigns for memorials and bequests, coin containers, United Way and other federated drives, and all manner of special events ranging from movie benefits and horse shows to walkathons and "coffee days" (when restaurants offer a free cup of coffee with the purchase of an Easter Seal button). Probably the society's best-known special event is its annual telethon, a 20-hour entertainment extravaganza shown around Easter, most recently on some 114 stations.

However, even with this diversity, the fund raising and overhead costs of the society and its 2000 local affiliates run rather high, coming to about 23 percent of total income; but it would be double that—46 percent—if figured as a percentage of only public contributions, which account for about half of all the income of the society. A good chunk of the remainder—roughly a quarter of total income— comes from government fees and grants and another 15 percent comes from patient fees, paid for largely by insurance companies.

The figures, however, vary widely from chapter to chapter, which retain 90 percent of all contributions. (The 50 state and territorial affiliates, including the District of Columbia and Puerto Rico, but excluding Wyoming and Minnesota, receive 6.6 percent of all receipts, with the remaining 3.4 percent going to national headquarters.) In Minnesota, at one time, fund-raising costs were as high as 68.5 cents out of each dollar contributed. To offset local criticism, the society's national headquarters absorbed these costs entirely and also allocated about $110,000 raised in other states to the Minnesota chapter to reduce its apparent fund-raising costs. This and other difficulties in maintaining camping standards led to the disaffiliation over a year ago of the Minnesota as well as Wyoming groups. In the early 1970s the national organization also had to bail out its Louisiana chapter which, because of the high cost of some of its fund-raising activities, had been refused a solicitation permit by the city of New Orleans. The Louisiana chapter had signed a contract with a professional promoter to stage a country-western benefit. The contract called for the chapter and the promoter to split the proceeds of the benefit 50-50 *after* the promoter deducted his expenses for what was essentially a boiler-room operation. (See Chapter 17.) With an arrangement of this sort, the local Easter Seal group could have been left with virtually nothing.

The difficulty the society has controlling its chapters is not atypical of many national federations with separate affiliates, each of which thinks of itself as an independent duchy. "Basic to the problem is that we don't raise any money on our own," said an official of the society at its headquarters in Chicago. "You might regard us as a trade association. We issue a franchise much like McDonald's or anyone else. We give people a piece of territory, and this gives people the exclusive right to raise money in that territory. We sell them all the fund-raising supplies and other materials they need, although they can use their own if they don't like ours. We lay down certain policies, but as long as they give us a percentage of everything they raise, they're pretty much on their own, which can create trouble."

Another of the more troublesome affiliates has been the one in New York State. Founded in 1922, it has often had difficulty in managing to raise enough money to meet the society's quotas, which are based on a formula taking into account an area's population and economic status. (Affiliates are expected to raise 2 cents for every $1000 of their area's "effective buying income," or, roughly, income after taxes.) Moreover, of the $825,000 the affiliate raised in 1972, about 55 percent went for fund raising and overhead (a ratio that has reportedly come down to 25 percent in the years since). "That year came the moment of truth with the affiliate nearly thrown out of the lodge," says Peter Meek, who was the society's New York regional representative for five years before going on to serve a stint as president of the National Health Council. "If that were to happen, I don't know that anyone would suffer. Already the state health department provides much the same services. All the locals do here is supplement things or buy camperships for children and send them off to other people's camps."

On what does the Easter Seal organization as a whole spend its money? Of the organization's collective nearly $80 million budget, 70 percent goes for various patient services and recreational activities, about 5 percent for professional and public health education, and a minuscule 0.4 percent—$300,000 in a recent year—for research, although some chapters have unconscionably stressed research as a major Easter Seal activity in their public service announcements. To perform these services, the society and its affiliates operate some 2000 facilities and programs, including 258 rehabilitation and treatment centers, 30 sheltered workshops, 309 speech and hearing programs, 98 residential and day camps, 92 special education programs, and 179 information and referral centers.

Of course, not all of these facilities and programs are available everywhere. In some states, there are virtually no Easter Seal orthopedic services for children— services so widely proclaimed in the society's promotional material. The New York State society's annual report makes no mention of these services, although it lists a variety of other services provided by its eight affiliates—primarily speech and hearing therapy programs, camping activities, and the free use of wheel- chairs for handicapped shoppers at shopping centers.

I would like to think that many of the services provided are necessary and helpful. An elderly Georgian, Ben A. Hinson, who was advised by his doctors that he would never recover from his stroke, told the Atlanta *Journal* how he was helped to walk again at the Atlanta Easter Seal Rehabilitation Center:

> The first day I was there, I got on my feet. I went in there in a wheelchair. I had braces from the ground all the way up to my neck—those long, heavy steel braces. A little therapist, bless her heart, asked if I could get out of the braces by myself. I said I could, but it was easier with two working on it. I started at one end and she started at the other, and we got them off. She gave me a cane with four prongs and asked if I could walk with it. I said I would like to try and I got up and took my first step. I was so elated I felt like crying. I was a new man. It was the first time I had walked in over a year.

Stories like this seem to materialize mainly in the 30 days before Easter Sunday, which is Easter Seal fund-raising time. But I was impressed by a visit to the Easter Seal Rehabilitation Center in Stamford, Connecticut. Here again, contrary to the impression created by the center's fund-raising appeals, which typically show a kid on crutches, two-thirds of the center's annual caseload of 2000 are adults, and only half are orthopedic patients. It was also heartwarming to hear a rehab center staff member say that no patient referred to the center is ever turned away. "If a patient says he can't pay," she said, "the staff social worker tries to help round up outside money—Blue Cross, Medicare, Veterans Administration, Welfare—whatever applies. If there's no one else, the center will pay. But we encourage the patient to pay something, even if it's only two dollars a week."

Actually, Easter Seal money accounts for only 4 percent of the center's $1.5 million annual budget, although it is staffed by Easter Seal volunteers. Other private agencies, such as the United Way, Cerebral Palsy, and the Greenwich Health Association, provide another 20 percent, while 10 percent more comes from patient fees, including insurance. But the lion's share—45 percent—comes from government sources: Medicare, Medicaid, the Veteran's Administration, Welfare, and the federal-state Vocational Rehabilitation Program, to mention the major ones.

Which again brings us to the question: Why not have the government assume the entire burden of caring for the nation's 41 million handicapped,* a monstrous number compared to the Easter Seal caseload of 330,000? To a large extent, it

---

*The estimate is by the Department of Health, Education, and Welfare and is based on its definition of the term "handicapped." Other estimates range anywhere from 18 to 35 million, even

does so anyway. Every state already has its own services for crippled children, sometimes for adults as well; and many cities, like New York, also have centers that provide physical and occupational therapy, medical supervision, and educational and other programs for handicapped children. Appropriations for the federal-state Vocational Rehabilitation Program alone now come to a total of $1.6 billion a year and the budget for services just to crippled children under a Public Health Service program comes to another $100 million annually. This does not take into account other programs administered by the Office of Education, Department of Labor, Department of Defense, and other government agencies. And, of course, the disabled as well as the aged are covered under Medicare, Medicaid, and by the Veterans Administration.

How meaningful is the Easter Seal annual budget of nearly $80 million compared to these government billions—and the needs of the nation's handicapped? The question is particularly pertinent because so much of the money given to the society goes down the drain in overhead and fund raising, often utilizing, as we have seen, less than candid appeals on behalf of the "crippled." When I put the question to the society's long-time executive director, the late Jayne Shover, she waved the American flag.

"Part of being American is helping others," she said. "The beauty of the Easter Seal campaign and getting millions to contribute to it is that it fosters the idea of helping others. That's the very essence of America and I hope we never lose it."

The Timid Heart

> We are principally an organization of physicians and scientists who are attempting to learn something about cardiovascular disease—one of the great problems of our civilization—and are asking the general public to help us. We are not running a friendship club for the idle nor are we trying to solve social problems other than cardiovascular disease.
>
> — Leader of a state Heart Association as quoted in Richard Carter's *The Gentle Legions* (1961)

The statement, which to some extent still reflects the views of much of the leadership of the American Heart Association even today, provides an important clue as to why the association, ranked according to contributions, is only our second biggest health agency rather than the biggest, to match the health problem with which it deals.

After all, as the Heart Association tirelessly reminds us, cardiovascular disease is collectively the nation's No. 1 killer, claiming one million American lives a year—more than all other causes of death combined. In addition, nearly 30

---

as high as 67.9 million. The latter is based on the following breakdown: 6.2 million (noninstitutional) using orthopedic aids—wheelchairs, braces, crutches, etc.; 7.6 million suffering from heart conditions; 1.7 million blind or severely visually handicapped; 1.8 million deaf; 18.3 million hard of hearing; 14.5 million respiratory ailments; 18.3 million arthritics. Some persons, of course, fall into more than one of the categories. Other estimates include the 6.8 million developmentally disabled (retarded, severely emotionally disturbed, brain damaged, severe learning disabilities), and the 1.7 million homebound (due to chronic health disorders or such degenerative diseases as multiple sclerosis).

million Americans are afflicted by one form of cardiovascular disease or another: hypertension (high blood pressure), coronary heart disease, stroke, rheumatic heart disease, and those resulting from congenital defects. Moreover, the diseases represent an economic drain on our society of more than $28 billion annually in lost wages and productivity as well as the cost of medical care.

In view of all this, why is the Heart Association the Avis of the health agencies, a perennial and distant runner-up to the American Cancer Society, particularly when cardiovascular disease is ten times as prevalent as cancer and claims two and a half times as many lives? One explanation, of course, stems from the differing natures of the two categories of disease and in people's reactions to them. Cancer, for one thing, is a much more dreaded disease. But a more likely reason lies in the differing nature of the two organizations. The Heart Association, some observers feel, has been a sluggish body for much of its life.

To see why this is so, let us look into its history. Founded in 1924, the American Heart Association was originally a professional society of physicians and scientists, most of them card-carrying cardiologists. As in many professional societies, its members spoke largely to themselves, and the fledgling association, apart from stimulating the formation of some cardiac clinics, seemed to have no clearly defined purpose of any consequence. At first its office was a room generously donated by what was then known as the National Tuberculosis Association, and Dr. H. M. (Jack) Marvin, a cardiologist, who doubled as the heart group's unsalaried one-day-a-week executive secretary, had to type his own mail.

It was not until after World War II that the association reluctantly came to the realization that it could not expand its activities without public support, and in 1948 the professional society was formally converted into a voluntary health agency, with nonmedical people permitted to become members of the association and of its governing bodies. Seed money to launch the new agency came fortuitously from a contest conducted on "Truth or Consequences," a well-known radio program of that era. For week after week the program's millions of listeners were asked to guess the identity of a "Walking Man" through clues furnished by Ralph Edwards, the show's exuberant master of ceremonies. To enter the contest, listeners had to mail in their guesses together with donations and 25-words-or-less letters on why the public should support the Heart Association. At the conclusion of the contest, the "Walking Man" was revealed to be Jack Benny and the Heart Association found itself with a windfall of $1.7 million. This, together with an additional million dollars taken in by the association's 18 state affiliates, gave the organization an income of $2.7 million in 1948.

Since then, the number of affiliates has increased to 55 (one for each state plus others in our larger cities) with about 1200 local subdivisions, and the association's total annual income has increased to around $77 million, $67 million of this from contributions. The association's membership roster has also swollen from a mere handful to include 89,000 lay persons as well as 39,000 physicians and scientists. However, the association continues to remain unique among major health agencies, in that it is still under the firm control of doctors. Of the association's 100-member board of directors, its highest governing body, about 60—or comfortably more than half—are physicians, related scientists, and other health professionals, enough to preserve its original medical orientation; consequently, although the association likes to refer to itself as "a partnership of physicians, scientists, and laymen," the lay members of the partnership are somewhat less equal than the others, with little or no voice in policy. Or, as a former medical director of the association once put it, "The American Heart Association is democratically organized with the voice of its professional membership more than equal to that of its lay membership. Since our program is basically medical and scientific, the association leans most heavily upon its physician and professional membership for guidance."

As for the association's 89,000 lay "members" and 2 million volunteers, they have been delegated largely such responsibilities as money raising, public relations, management and clerical services, speech making, and, to a lesser extent, work in the association's various community service activities. There can be no question that most are dedicated in the performance of these labors. However, it can also be understood why these circumscribed roles may not make for the commitment characteristic of the volunteers in other organizations which give their lay people a meaningful role in the formulation and implementation of policy.

As war is too important to be left to the generals, so perhaps is the battle against heart disease. Still and all, for whatever reason, the association, even after its reorganization, has not yet been entirely able to shake off the shackles of its pre-1948 years.

It was the leaders of the association—acting, however, as individuals rather than as association spokesmen—who played a major role, along with that peerless philanthropist Mary Lasker, in bringing about the formation of the federal research agency, the National Heart Institute (recently renamed the National Heart, Lung, and Blood Institute) which, since its establishment in 1948, has received appropriations totaling more than $4 billion (in fiscal 1978 alone, $394 million). The association itself can claim credit for eventually mustering the support that resulted in much of these appropriations, although it did not fight for them too strenuously during its early years.

With some justice, the association and its affiliates can also take pride in having channeled more than $300 million of their own funds into research over the years, these expenditures now accounting for about 28 percent of their collective budget. In a recent year, $20.5 million in grants was allocated to about 1600 scientific investigators; of the total allocated, 47 percent came from national headquarters and the remaining 53 percent from local affiliates.

What has come out of the more than 25,000 research projects the association has funded during the past three decades? The association does not claim sole credit for any major scientific breakthroughs like heart-lung machines, artificial pacemakers, plastic heart valves, open heart surgery, and heart transplants, although it does say that "AHA-supported research" contributed to the knowledge that made possible these and a laundry list of other advances: improved diagnostic and surgical techniques, drugs for controlling high blood pressures, anticoagulant drugs, new methods of treating and rehabilitating stroke patients, the development of coronary care units, and so on.

Nonetheless, as far as I have been able to determine, no Heart Fund dollars at all were involved in the pioneering work of Drs. John H. Gibbon, Jr., and C. Walter Lillehei on heart-lung machines. However, as a specific example of an advance for which it says it was largely responsible, the association cites the now commonly accepted first aid technique of cardiopulmonary resuscitation (CPR)—a combination of external heart massage and mouth-to-mouth breathing used for the emergency treatment of victims of cardiac arrest. (Of the 650,000 U.S. deaths from heart attacks every year, more than 350,000 occur within the first two hours of an attack, most often outside a hospital; speedy treatment is also of the essence because irreparable brain damage results if the heart stops for more than four to six minutes.)

In its community service programs, the association conducts training courses in CPR for not only medical and hospital personnel but also for mining employees, firemen, students, and everyday citizens. A recent association annual report tells of a 13-year-old New Jersey girl who, thanks to the CPR training she received from her school nurse, saved her father's life: After he had suffered a massive heart attack, she was able to maintain his breathing and heart beat for ten minutes until medical help arrived. A recent notable saved by CPR was Judge John Sirica of Watergate fame.

Other community service programs, which account for nearly 20 percent of the AHA's expenditures, include smoking withdrawal clinics, nutrition and diet instruction, rehabilitation guidance for heart and stroke patients, high blood pressure screening, rheumatic fever control, screening children for hidden heart disorders, programs for management and labor groups to reduce the risk of heart attacks and strokes, and referral services for patients and their families.

The association's public and professional education programs, accounting for 28 percent of its expenditures, use every technique of mass communication—pamphlets, films, exhibits, audio-visual aids, canned speeches, and the mass media—aimed at helping people reduce the risk of heart attack and stroke by emphasizing the dangers of smoking and improper diet (foods rich in cholesterol and saturated fat) and the need for exercise and periodic health checkups. For physicians and scientists the association publishes specialized technical journals and manuals and conducts or sponsors an endless number of meetings, teaching institutes, conferences, symposia, and seminars.

Impressive as all these activities may seem, they still fail to quell critics of the association. A well-known philanthropist, once prominent in the association's affairs, says, "There is a lot more they could do if they followed the advice of laymen. In spite of the token laymen on their board, they're still basically an association of doctors who are really quite phlegmatic, quite willing to let well enough alone. In fact, instead of exercising bold, vigorous leadership, they often seem to resist change."

For example, even though the connection between coronaries and cholesterol as well as foods rich in saturated fats (butter, cheese, and fatty meats), which tend to raise the blood's cholesterol level, had been fairly well established by the early 1950s, it was not until 1960 that the association finally got around to endorsing "the reasonable substitution of polyunsaturated for saturated fats . . . as a possible means of preventing atherosclerosis and decreasing the risk of heart attacks and strokes." Yet, even here the association did some pussyfooting, for the endorsement suggested that the diet change be carried out under "medical supervision." Imagine seeing a doctor for permission to switch from butter to margarine! Similarly, the association was unduly laggard in coming out against smoking, something it did not do until 1960.

Some association apologists attribute its slowness to act to professional conservatism. However, in a special twentieth anniversary presentation at the association's annual meeting in 1968, Dr. Louis N. Katz, a revered AHA past president who had headed the committee that had finally found tobacco suspect, confided: "When I came in as chairman of the committee . . . there were subtle pressures—don't hit the TV and the Fourth Estate [which relied heavily on tobacco advertising], don't hit the tobacco industry, they're where we're going to get our money. . . . I'm not going to go into the amusing correspondence that's in my files on the subtle pressures applied to me and other members of the committee—don't do that, these are the big industries that will support the Heart Association."

"Yes, we've had some unhappy tobacco people and we've had some unhappy state Heart Associations in the tobacco country," says John T. Connolly, the national association's deputy executive vice-president for operations, who readily admits that his organization was somewhat reticent in making more positive stands on smoking as well as on diet. "We were guilty of pussyfooting in a number of areas like this," says Connolly, a bulky, affable, relaxed man in his middle fifties who acknowledges that even today the tobacco states of Kentucky, North Carolina, and Virginia and the big dairy states are not the most rabid supporters of the Heart Fund drives in their areas.

As for the future, Connolly, who has a master's degree in public health, says, "The direction of the association will be much more in causing things to happen rather than in reacting to them. For example, I think you're going to see more active work on our part in trying to develop legislative postures on drugs—for example, the antihypertensive drugs. The biggest problem we've got in all of cardiovascular disease is high blood pressure. And yet we know that there are a number of drugs that have been tested and retested but for one reason or another are still not on the market. We have to continue working on government agencies like the Food and Drug Administration to release some of these drugs. In the whole area of research and research training, the Heart Association is also going to get more vigorous and try to encourage even more spending, both by our own heart associations and by government.

"I think you're also going to see much more of an expanded information and education thrust on things like high blood pressure and other of the factors which cause a person to be a bad health risk—poor diet, smoking, obesity, lack of exercise. And as information begins to be developed, a much more vigorous and combined approach will be used for this kind of information program, combined meaning combined with government and with the drug houses, if they want to put their money into it."

Complicating the association's future was the shift of its headquarters from New York to Dallas in 1975, a move dictated, according to Connolly, by the difficulty of getting "promising people, especially those with families, to work in New York because of the city's high living costs and deteriorating quality of its schools." However, during the course of the move, which is rumored to have cost as much as $5 million, the association lost a number of its top paid staff people, including its medical director, Dr. Campbell Moses, one of the most esteemed names in cardiology.

Volunteers also remain a perennial problem. "The problem in attracting nonmedical volunteers is still before us," says Connolly. "We find that we're still not really doing a satisfactory job of getting enough volunteers to the degree we should have them."

"How would you sum up what's wrong with philanthropy today?" he is asked finally.

"A general attitude of timidity on the part of organizations in outlining and implementing programs that are meaningful to the public," he responds.

To what extent the association itself will shed its own timidity is something that only time will tell.

The Politics of Cancer

In the pre-Watergate year of 1971, President Richard M. Nixon officially declared war on cancer, with the signing of the National Cancer Act. "The time has come in America," said the president in his State of the Union message in January of that year, "when the same kind of concentrated effort that split the atom and took man to the moon should be turned toward conquering this dread disease." When the legislation mandating this effort became the law of the land on December 23, 1971, a White House aide proclaimed it the president's "Christmas present to the nation."

However, political considerations played perhaps even a larger part than humanitarian ones in the president's interest in the conquest of cancer, even though the disease was then killing 330,000 Americans a year (by 1979 the annual toll would increase to 395,000) and, according to repeated polls, was feared even more than cardiovascular disease, the nation's No. 1 killer. Sen. Edward M. Kennedy of Massachusetts, continuing the long series of efforts first initiated in Congress in the 1920s by Sen. Matthew Neely of West Virginia, had introduced a Conquest of Cancer bill in 1971; and President Nixon, not wishing to be upstaged by a Kennedy, possibly his leading contender for the presidency during the forthcoming election, had decided to have his administration introduce a competing bill. In fact, in his zeal to be thought of as even more anticancer than his rival, the president publicly vowed "to put our money where our hopes are" in the quest of a cancer cure, at one time promising the proposed program virtually unlimited funds. (Soon after the election, his enthusiasm apparently diminished, his administration impounding $50 million of the $426 million Congress had appropriated for the fight against cancer in the 1973 fiscal year.)

Largely responsible, however, for laying the groundwork and mobilizing congressional and public support for the law which finally made cancer control a national goal was the American Cancer Society, which for decades has lobbied relentlessly for more funds for cancer. And the prime mover behind the passage of the 1971 National Cancer Act was the Cancer Society's long-time honorary chairman, Mrs. Mary Lasker, a woman of great wealth, charm, and compassion, who, since the 1940s, has probably had a greater influence on health planning and spending in this country than any other one person.

No mere Lady Bountiful, she and her husband, Albert D. Lasker, the legendary advertising magnate, were philanthropists of a special kind. Their good works went far beyond the casual writing of checks; they were "doers," passionately involved in the causes which concerned them, which ranged from mental health, birth control, and blindness to heart disease, cerebral palsy, and cancer research.

The Laskers are generally credited with being the catalytic agents behind the transformation of the National Institutes of Health (NIH) from a moribund organization with a budget of $2.4 million in 1945 to its present eminence as the world's greatest biomedical research institution with a collective budget of about $3 *billion* in fiscal 1979.

Cancer had become a special interest of theirs when their cook was stricken with the disease and was consigned to a "Home for Incurables" where she eventually died. "It angered me very much that so little could be done for her, that so little zeal was being applied to the problem of cancer," said Mrs. Lasker, a smartly dressed, strikingly handsome woman with flashing blue eyes, who, though in her seventies, looks and acts twenty years younger.

In the sunny, dazzling-white flower-filled living room of her apartment overlooking New York's East River, Mrs. Lasker, seated under Renoir's "La Barque du Drapeau," one of the many painting in her fabled collection of French masters, told me of the role she and her husband (who died of cancer in 1952) played in the revitalization of what is today known as the American Cancer Society, which was founded in 1913 as the American Society for the Control of Cancer.* Like the American Heart Association, it was organized and run primarily by physicians and it remained relatively small as long as it was under medical domination. "When we became interested in the Cancer Society in 1944, it was a horse-and-buggy operation, a club of doctors largely devoted to the collection and dissemination of knowledge about cancer," recalled Mrs. Lasker. "The society had an income of only $350,000, not a penny of which—we were appalled to learn—was going for research."

The Laskers contributed $55,000 to start a research fund and agreed to pay the cost of retaining a professional fund-raising firm with the stipulation that 25 percent of all future funds raised would go into research. "It was a completely startling idea," Mrs. Lasker explained, as she sipped a sherry. "But since the money we expected to raise was mythical, this point was agreed to easily." The money, however, soon became a reality to an extent hardly anticipated. Three short *Reader's Digest* articles on cancer, inspired by Mary Lasker, brought the society $120,000 in small contributions, and the 1945 campaign as a whole, the first to be fully planned, organized, and carried out by the society under its new name and leadership, brought in a total of $4,292,000, a quarter of which, as the Laskers had insisted, was promptly earmarked for research. Flushed with success, the Laskers now insisted that the society board be expanded to include lay persons and, after much maneuvering and threats of mass resignation, a compromise was reached whereby the board positions were divided equally between physicians and laymen. In the 1946 campaign directed by its strong lay board the society raised $10.3 million and by 1959 it reached its present position as the leading voluntary health agency in terms of contributions, these exceeding $114 million in 1977. (Total income was nearly $127 million.)

Meanwhile, the society and Mary Lasker also labored to increase the government allocations for cancer, too. So successful were their efforts that the National Cancer Institute (NCI), oldest of the government agencies that make up the

*It is ironic that the Lasker largesse stemmed from the advertising fortune Lasker had built up, largely by promoting Lucky Strike cigarettes—albeit somewhat before the time the link between cigarette smoking and cancer came to be recognized.

National Institutes of Health, year after year received the biggest slice of federal research funds, its share zooming from a minuscule $559,000 in fiscal 1945 to an astounding $232 million in 1971—just before the actual implementation of the 1971 National Cancer Act.

Typical of Mary Lasker's methods of operations were those that led to the passage of the act. It was in 1969 she decided that the time had come for an all-out massive assault on cancer. Through the American Cancer Society's chief lobbyist in Washington, she arranged to have the Senate appoint a special panel of consultants to study the possibility of making the cure of cancer a "national goal" and recommending to the Congress the means of achieving it. All of the panel's illustrious, carefully screened 26 members, half of them scientists and half laymen, were of course friends or associates of Mrs. Lasker; most of them were past or present board members of the American Cancer Society and many were drawn from her so-called "stable" of doctor allies, among them Boston's famed cancer researcher, Dr. Sidney Farber, and Memorial Sloan-Kettering Cancer Center's vice-president, Dr. Joseph Burchenal. Not surprisingly, all of the panel members who testified at the hearings I attended were unanimously in favor of the proposed legislation, drafted by the Cancer Society's lobbyist, which also received unprecedented public support; a crucial element of this support was the million letters that descended on Congress in response to an emotional column written by Ann Landers, incidentally also a Cancer Society board member.

As finally passed, the compromise legislation finally agreed on called for a stepped-up appropriation of $400 million for cancer research in 1972, this to increase by increments of $100 million for each year thereafter to bring the total commitment to at least $800 million annually by 1976. Equally important, the NCI, though technically still under the NIH, was to have its budget subject to review only by the president; the NIH and the Department of Health, Education, and Welfare could comment on the budget but were not authorized to change it. (The original panel recommendation was that the NCI be replaced by a separate, new superagency completely independent and outside the framework of the NIH.)

From its very beginnings, however, what became known as the National Cancer Program and, popularly, as the "War Against Cancer" was, in spite of its eminent auspices, viewed with serious reservations and even frank disapproval by virtually the nation's entire scientific community. At the original hearings on the bill, it was opposed by all of President Nixon's scientific advisers, including Dr. Roger O. Egeberg, his then assistant HEW Secretary for health and scientific affairs, and the director of the NIH. Egeberg's successor, Dr. Charles C. Edwards, was also critical of the program, declaring upon his resignation in 1975 that it was politically motivated and based on "the politically attractive but scientifically dubious premises that a dread and enigmatic disease can, like the surface of the moon, be conquered if we will simply spend enough money to get the job done." Many scientists pointed to the irrefutable fact that the two challenges were hardly comparable, for whereas the technology necessary to get man to the moon was known long before the moon shot, hardly anything, by contrast, was known about even the cause of cancer, let alone a possible cure for it.

The government officials were also concerned that separating the cancer program from the rest of the NIH might have a destructive unbalancing effect on the programs of all the institutes and could eventually even result in the dismantling of the NIH. The few defenders of the program, however, attributed these criticisms to the normal petulance of those threatened with the loss or weakening of their bureaucratic powers.

But also opposed to the cancer program were such organizations as the Association of American Medical Colleges, the American Medical Association, and the FASEB (Federated American Societies of Experimental Biology), the latter representing all of the nation's most prominent research biologists. Nobel prize laureate biologist Dr. James Watson, though a future beneficiary of the program—his Cold Spring Harbor Laboratory would receive $1,685,000 from it in 1974 compared to $436,000 in NCI funds in the preprogram days of 1970—went so far as to publicly call it a "sham" and privately, in more earthy terms, described it as "a bunch of shit," his principal concern seeming to be the quality of research supported under the program. While challenging this concern, Benno C. Schmidt, chairman of the president's citizen panel set up to oversee the program, unhappily admitted, "I suspect that if we took a vote, most scientists would be happier if there were no special program."

In the years that followed, other critics said that the program would reduce efforts in much-needed basic or untargeted research, that it would take funds away from research on other diseases, that it had brought more optimistic political promises than scientists could fulfill (one exuberant congressman had even declared that cancer should be cured by 1976 as "an appropriate commemoration of the 200th anniversary of our country"), and that it had not produced any improvement in cancer survival rates.*

In a position paper, the Cancer Society said that much of this criticism was unjustified. At no time, it said, did the scientists and physicians who supported the National Cancer Act promise any immediate "breakthrough." Nor was it true that the cancer program would curtail expenditures on basic, untargeted research, said the society, citing figures to show that expenditures for that type of research by the NCI had increased three-fold, from $100 million to $300 million, in the five years after 1970. The society also gave figures to show that, contrary to expectations, the new emphasis on cancer research was not at the expense of research in other fields: In the 1975 fiscal year, there were increased appropriations for every institute of the NIH, along with the increases for cancer research.

As for the survival rates, the society noted that the comparisons made were based largely on statistics for 1969—before the actual implementation of the national cancer program in 1972—much too recently to yield definitive results. The society also pointed out that survival rates, though not necessarily the only criteria for evaluating research, had indeed increased since the 1960s and even during recent years for many major types of cancer—for example, breast and cervical cancer, leukemia, Hodgkin's disease, and, particularly, for almost all types of childhood cancers that had been fatal ten years before and for which survival rates of 50 percent or better were already being achieved. The society is also fond of saying that there are as many as 2 million Americans living today, who have been "cured" of cancer.

*Survival rates are determined by the proportion of cancer patients who are "cured"—that is, show no evidence of the disease at least five years after diagnosis and treatment.

To what extent the society's own research efforts may account for all of this is difficult to say. During the past three decades, the society itself has spent nearly $500 million of its own money to support research projects—a huge sum, to be sure, but one dwarfed by the $6.1 billion expended by the NCI during the same period. In 1977 the society's research expenditures amounted to $36.5 million, or nearly 30 percent of its budget, most of it for 676 grants to over 150 institutions and scientists both here and abroad. With the nearly $800 million appropriated for the NCI and perhaps another $100 million or so contributed to cancer research from private or other sources, cancer, by any reckoning, must be considered big business. In her illuminating book, *The Siege of Cancer*, June Goodfield repeats the dictum, "More people are now living off cancer than ever died of it," citing the startling statistic, supplied by the NCI, that an estimated 670,000 Americans are working on cancer—27.4 percent of them scientists, 14.1 percent research assistants, 14.9 percent technicians, 10.5 percent clerical staffers, with clinicians and others making up the rest.

What of the society's other functions? The society also conducts a myriad of vital activities in the areas of education, patient care, and community services. On the assumption that one out of two cancer victims could now be cured if the onset of the disease were detected and treated early enough, the society spends nearly as much—26 percent of its total expenditures—on public and professional education as it does on research. Scarcely an American alive has not been exposed to cancer's "Seven Warning Signals"* (shades of Beelzebub's seven danger signals!) nor to the barrage of other messages—disseminated through leaflets, pamphlets, films, radio and television spots and programs, advertisements, newspaper and magazine stories, meetings, and person-to-person contacts, usually in connection with fund raising—warning of the hazards of cigarette smoking, overexposure to sunlight and other known causes of cancer, and extolling the virtues of regular medical checkups, breast self-examination, and Pap tests.

Of course, as the society has come to realize, telling people what to do and getting them to do it are two quite different things, and Gallup studies commissioned by the society have confirmed the fact that behavioral changes in the American people have lagged far behind the dissemination of information to them. Back in 1968—14 years after the society was instrumental in establishing the link between cigarette smoking and lung cancer—I was invited to attend the annual dinner of the society at New York's Waldorf-Astoria. It was a sumptuous affair at which celebrities spoke and entertained, tributes were paid, awards were given out, and, of course, the horrors of cancer were described. I was seated at a table for twelve made up of physician-volunteers and officials of various cancer chapters. Virtually all of them were smoking!

*1. Change in bowel or bladder habits
 2. A sore that does not heal
 3. Unusual bleeding or discharge
 4. Thickening or lump in breast or elsewhere
 5. Indigestion or difficulty in swallowing
 6. Obvious change in wart or mole
 7. Nagging cough or hoarseness.

To help you remember them, note that the initial letter of each forms the acronym, CAUTION.

That is why the society in recent years has expanded its educational efforts by focusing on action-oriented programs, often for employee or club groups, which motivate people to discuss the facts about cancer and may include such activities as free instruction in breast self-examination, Pap testing, and "Helping Smokers Quit" clinics. The society, incidentally, is largely responsible for the current wide use of the Pap test—85 percent of all American women have had at least one—long believed to be 95 percent accurate in detecting cervical cancer in its early stages; although Dr. George N. Papanicalaou devised this simple vaginal-smear procedure as long ago as 1926, it won only limited acceptance among physicians until the society promoted its use by the medical profession and created the public demand for it.*

Similarly, the society has made its battle against the tobacco habit a major activity to the detriment of its fund-raising appeals in the Marlboro country. In addition to its "Helping Smokers Quit" clinics, several thousand of which are conducted every year, and annual Great American Smokeout (a day of abstention from smoking), the society, together with NCI, has been the sponsor of a series of World Conferences on Smoking and Health, one of which brought together 512 delegates from 53 countries. (And no more smoke-filled rooms: "No Smoking" signs now adorn the tables at all ACS meetings.) Nonetheless, so ingrained is the tobacco habit that the general trend of smoking, after experiencing a sharp decline from 1965 through 1971, is again continuing upwards, particularly among women and teen-agers, with the result that the female lung cancer death rate, once only one-sixth that of men, has doubled in the past ten years; and lung cancer is still the leading cause of all cancer deaths, killing 98,000 Americans a year. However, there is no way of knowing how much higher the death rate would be if it were not for the society's antismoking campaign; estimates are that 30 million Americans have given up smoking and, although there are still some 50 million smokers, the average intake of tars and nicotine is now half of what it was in the early 1950s, when the first major report on smoking hazards was released.

With breast cancer the leading cause of cancer deaths in women, striking down 35,000 annually, the stunning coincidence of First Lady Betty Ford and Happy Rockefeller undergoing surgery for breast cancer during a three-week period in the fall of 1974 provided a more powerful inducement than any educational programs could have in getting women to look at their breasts with renewed interest. Tens of thousands of women also phoned ACS offices all over the country for information as to where they could be tested, and poured into clinics, hospitals, and the 27 breast cancer diagnostic centers—a mass-screening project jointly funded by the ACS and NCI—which in late 1973 began giving free mammography (X-ray) examinations regularly to about 280,000 women 35 and over, the "high-risk" age group for breast cancer; the detection centers alone reported a 700 percent increase in calls during the three-week period.

The program, which was to run for five years, became controversial when critics charged that the exposure of younger women to X rays could result in

*However, in recent years a growing number of respected researchers have questioned the accuracy and efficacy of the test. As a result, two years ago the American Cancer Society subtly changed its recommendation that the test be performed annually; it now advises "periodic" or "regular" testing. *(Time,* November 13, 1978).

more cancers being caused than detected. Furthermore, there was a difference of opinion among experts as to the significance of the extremely small tumors the examinations had been discovering as well as in deciding which tumors were cancerous and which were benign. To resolve the controversy, NCI in late 1977 issued new guidelines recommending that routine mammography be used only for women over the age of 50 or for younger women in high-risk groups—those who had already had breast cancer or with mothers or sisters who had had it.

In the area of patient and community services, which account for about 22 percent of ACS annual expenditures, the society also supports other programs in cancer detection as well as in rehabilitation and provides referral and other information, counseling, the loan of sickroom equipment, transportation, and, depending on local resources, free dressings and medication and nursing and homemaker services. On call to carry out the society's programs is an army of two and one-half million volunteers whose activities may range from fund raising, taking medical histories, and manning the Quit Clinics to chauffering patients to and from treatment centers and assisting in the rehabilitation programs designed to help patients recovering from those physically and often emotionally disabling breast cancer, colostomy, laryngectomy, and other operations.

Reach to Recovery, the ACS's most unusual rehabilitation program, is made up exclusively of volunteer mastectomees who assist in the physical and psychological recovery of women who've just gone through the trauma of a breast removal, an operation that women understandably fear more than any other. The program, founded by Terese Lasser, the widow of tax expert J. K. Lasser, a year after she had had a mastectomy in 1952, has been sponsored by the ACS since 1969, and now has about 11,000 volunteers who make 52,500 visits a year, all in response to the requests of the patients and their physicians.

In a San Diego hospital, a Reach to Recovery volunteer, Pat Heim, a gracious former school teacher in her mid-forties, is visiting a 46-year-old woman who has just had a radical mastectomy.* She is married and the mother of three children. Running through the woman's mind as she awaits Pat's visit are some of the usual questions that nag a person who has undergone this operation: Will I die? Did they get it all? Am I now any less a woman? Am I a physical freak? But she is immediately reassured by the sight of Pat wearing frilly, feminine clothes and with no sign of any deformity and by Pat's telling her that it is six and one-half years since her operation.

Now Pat opens the gift kit she has brought with her and describes each item: a rubber ball on a string for use in exercises (after breast surgery, it is at first almost impossible for a woman to lift her arm as she used to); a temporary prosthesis, or breast form, made of washable Orlon; a list of stores that sell prosthetic devices; and a booklet describing suggested exercises and answering the many questions mastectomees customarily have. But after Pat has demonstrated some of the "reaching" exercises which will help the weaker arm to recover its full strength,

*In this operation not only is the breast removed, as in a simple mastectomy, but also the underlying chest muscles and the lymph glands extending back under the armpit, areas where the cancerous cells may have spread. Recent studies have revived the question of whether radical surgery is the most effective treatment for breast cancer. The conclusion of the Massachusetts Institute of Technology's Dr. Maurice S. Fox is that such surgery is "no more effective than more conservative, less mutilating treatment," according to *The New York Times*, January 29, 1979.

the woman is bubbling with questions: "Will I get the complete use of my arm again?" she asks, explaining that she is a medical stenographer. Pat says that she probably will in another month or so but suggests that she should try to get back to typing gradually.

"What about clothes?" the woman asks. "What won't I be able to wear?" Pat laughs and suggests that the only problem would be with spaghetti straps and some types of bikinis. For bathing suits, she recommends a plastic prosthesis that can be filled with fluid; she also describes some of the many other types which come in a variety of materials ranging from foam to silicone. "There is even a soft-filled prosthesis to fill a pretty nightgown."

Now come the more difficult questions, reflecting the concerns of most women about their husbands' reactions to the surgery, the fears as to how it may affect their relationship. There are tears in the woman's eyes as she asks about how her husband will feel. She says that although he has seemed concerned, she can't tell how he really feels. "How do I undress before him the first night I come home?" she asks. It is the question Pat is most frequently asked by the 35 women she visits, on the average, every year.

"Do exactly what you did before you went to the hospital," Pat advises. "If you've always undressed before your husband, don't hide in a separate room now, for he might think you are shutting him out. Realize that you are together in this and more now than ever before do you need each other." And she further reassures the woman by pointing to the fact that her own experience resulted in an even closer relationship. "A woman's womanhood is not in her breasts," she says.

"Can I get it again?" This is perhaps the hardest of the questions to answer but Pat is by now used to having it asked. And she tells this woman what she has told others: "I can't answer that. It's a fear we all have to live with. But I can tell you that your chances are no greater than anyone else's, anyone who hasn't had it before, of getting it again. Meanwhile, by what you've been through, you'll find, as I have, a greater awareness of how dear and precious life can be."

Pat's words have been a great comfort but—and what is more important—by acting normally, she has demonstrated that even those touched by cancer can return to a rich, rewarding, and useful life.

What about the future of the American Cancer Society? "The Cancer Society is a temporary agency," I was told by Lane W. Adams, the urbane former banker who has been the society's executive vice-president, or top salaried official, since 1959. "As soon as a cure is found for cancer, we will go out of business."

Fat chance of this happening, though, at least in the foreseeable future. For one thing, since cancer is not a single disease but rather a whole family of diseases, perhaps more than 100, ranging from carcinomas to the various forms of leukemia, they most likely have many causes, according to most experts, although Memorial Sloan-Kettering's famed president, Dr. Lewis Thomas, is inclined to the minority view that all cancers, exhibiting as they do certain common symptoms, are the result of a single mechanism. Cautioning that there is little prospect of any sudden conquest of all forms of the disease, Dr. Frank J. Rauscher, Jr., a former director of the NCI, and since 1976 the ACS's senior vice-president for research, says that it may be years before research is likely "to produce a single, dramatic means to prevent or cure all of the 100 or more forms of cancer.'' Octogenarian Dr. Alton Ochsner, one of medicine's Grand Old Men and internationally renowned founder of New Orleans' Ochsner Clinic and Hospital, places the time interval for controlling all forms of cancer at anywhere between ten and fifty years.

Yet, in spite of the fetish for finding a cure or cures through research, enough is known even today to cut down considerably on the present number of cancer deaths. Although the specific causes of only a few forms of cancer, like lung cancer, are known, there is general agreement today that between 75 percent and 90 percent of all cancers are caused by various environmental factors including—in addition to smoking—air pollution, drugs, chemicals, food additives, and others prevalent in an industrialized society. The male cancer death rate in the United States is twice that of neighboring Mexico, nearly four times higher than the Philippines' or Egypt's, and six times that of Thailand; and in the United States itself, the highest death rates from lung, liver, and bladder cancer are in those areas of the country that also happen to have chemical plants—and chemical pollution.

At least 100,000 American cancer deaths a year—30 to 40 percent of the annual toll—could be prevented by changes in smoking, drinking, and eating habits, according to NCI scientist Dr. Marvin Schneiderman; and the feeling of others is that as many as 60 percent of all cancers could be prevented if changes were also made in our industrial operations. However, it may be asking too much to get people to change their living habits or to have our government adopt stricter measures that would protect the public against exposure to industry's chemical carcinogens.

"Studying the history of medical progress," says Dr. Sidney M. Wolfe of the Ralph Nader Public Citizen Health Research Group, "it is clear that the major improvements in the status of health of people come not through drugs to treat disease but through political and public health measures to prevent disease. The solution to the cancer problem will be cleaning up the work places, cleaning up the environment, keeping cancer-causing chemicals out of food supplies. . . ." And so we now have the anomaly of our government spending $23 million a year for National Cancer Institute research on the hazardous substances in tobacco and cigarette smoking and passing measures to restrict cigarette advertising and, in absurd contradiction, also spending $80 million a year of taxpayer money to subsidize the growing and sale of tobacco, which, our government has already determined, is dangerous to the health of the public.

As long as this situation prevails, it may be a long time, as some fear, before the massive movement of government into the "War on Cancer" might make the role of the American Cancer Society unnecessary. It may also be a long time before a future president of the United States, in a vision foreseen by Lane W. Adams, will be able to say to the president of the American Cancer Society: "We have been able to achieve the conquest of cancer because the dedicated men and women of the American Cancer Society moved with their customary courage and vigor to take up the new responsibilities which fell to them in the new era of the fight against cancer.''

Chapter 11

The Disease-of-the-Month Club

In the pages of a national magazine not long ago appeared a "public service" ad by something called the TF Foundation of America. The headline over a large photo of a shattered toilet bowl read

SOMETIMES SILENT—ALWAYS DEADLY

and proclaimed TF to be "the nation's Number One killer." Among TF's 140 "warning signs," the ad further read, were localized cloud formations, peeling wallpaper, lack of friends and acquaintances, defoliated trees and shrubs, scorched mattresses, and unaccountable pet deaths. "TF—it's not to be sniffed at," concluded the ad.

What is TF? A TF Foundation fund-raising letter, also reproduced in the magazine, described the disease as follows:

> TF is Terminal Flatulence, also known as Crepitation Terminalus and Ubu's Disorder. It is a member of the "aerosol" family of lower digestive diseases, and though its causes are as yet unknown, its effects are all too familiar—stabbing pains in the lower colon, involuntary contractions of the facial muscles, falling plaster, spasms of the retentor/eliminator muscle system, wilted house plants, depletion of the ozone layer, quarantine, weight loss, and lingering, painful death.

"Too many people think of TF as a passing disorder," also said the letter. "It is not. It is a killer, sometimes silent, always deadly. Of TF it can truly be said, 'It embarrasses people to death.'"

Although there of course is no organization soliciting funds for TF—the ad was a spoof by *National Lampoon*—no disease or disorder is too obscure or too trivial to justify an appeal on its behalf. Listed by the National Information Bureau are no less than 60 appeals revolving around the human body, including 16 by organizations passing the hat for the blind, nine for victims of various neuromuscular diseases, six for the crippled, six for cancer, four for mental illness, two each for kidney disease, diabetes, and deafness, and one apiece for other diseases ranging from arthritis and cystic fibrosis to hemophilia and VD. Of course, these 60 appeals represent but a fraction of the hundreds, perhaps even thousands, of national and local appeals conducted in this country, some on behalf of such relatively little-known ailments as myasthenia gravis, which is somewhat similar to muscular dystrophy, and systemic lupus erythematosus, a

163

rheumatic ailment which, if undiagnosed, kills 80 percent of its victims in five years (with care, only 20 percent die) and is most common among women in the early child-bearing years. In terms of victims, there are even organizations for ethnic diseases, such as Tay-Sachs and sickle cell anemia, which afflict largely Jewish people and blacks, respectively.

With all of these organizations carving up the calendar—for fund raising purposes—into an impossible number of monthly and even smaller segments, it would not be out of order to refer to them collectively as "The Disease-of-the-Month Club." Obviously, it would take a volume the size of an encyclopedia to describe all of its members in any detail. What follows, therefore, are capsule critiques of a representative sampling of the larger, more important or otherwise noteworthy agencies concerned with the more common diseases and disorders.

The Neuromuscular Diseases

Disturbances of the brain and central nervous system have historically been among the most tragic, disabling, and intractable scourges of mankind. Not only do these disorders claim lives but they also sentence many to a lifetime of total or partial disability and they sap medical and financial resources far out of proportion to the numbers afflicted. For instance, amyotrophic lateral sclerosis (ALS), also known as "Lou Gehrig's disease" for the star baseball player struck down in his prime, afflicts only about 10,000 Americans and claims 1400 lives a year, yet the cost of caring for its victims is estimated at over $300 million annually.

All in all, however, about 4 million Americans suffer from one or another of the 200 to 300 neurological disorders tallied by the National Institute of Neurological and Communicative Disorders and Stroke. Space limitations will permit us to deal only with the more prevalent: cerebral palsy, muscular dystrophy, multiple sclerosis, epilepsy, and, very briefly, with Parkinsonism and just a few others.

Cerebral Palsy

Actually, cerebral palsy is not a specific disease but rather the general term applied to a group of conditions affecting muscle control that is caused by damage or injury to the brain, usually during pregnancy or at birth. There are about 750,000 persons in the United States affected by various forms of the disorder and an estimated 10,000 more are born every year.* Concerned with the plight of these unfortunates are the United Cerebral Palsy Associations (UCPA), launched in 1949 when a group of distressed parents met in a New York living room to discuss the needs of their cerebral palsied children. One of the parents,

---

*About half of the victims are spastic, the most familiar type, marked by their stiff movements and gutteral voice. Most of the rest are athetoid, characterized by the constant, slow, uncontrolled writhing movements of their arms and legs. Less common are the ataxic victims who, because of their poor balance, uncertain, weaving walk, and frequent falls, are often mistaken for drunks. Most—from half to three-quarters—of the afflicted are also mentally retarded to some extent and many have speech, hearing, and visual defects as well. Because of these multiple difficulties, many of the cerebral palsied have limited employment possibilities and, in fact, are so helpless that they must rely on the assistance of others, often for a lifetime, for such everyday functions as dressing, feeding, and toileting. Perhaps only one out of every five can be trained to be independent enough to hold down a competitive job.

Leonard Goldenson, has long doubled as chairman of the American Broadcasting Company and UCPA which, over the years, has grown into a federation of 264 state and local affiliates and about 1.7 million volunteers. Thanks in good part to the educational efforts of UCPA, public understanding about the palsied has spread to the point where they are no longer hidden away in upstairs bedrooms as "closet children," blights on the good family name.

Since the parents of the afflicted are quite understandably more concerned with the pragmatic realities of today than the research promises of tomorrow, the emphasis of UCPA is on patient services, which now account for about two-thirds of its annual expenses. The services include programs of rehabilitation, special education, vocational training, and psychological counseling. Many of the programs involve parents, whose support is crucial in the care and treatment and development of the child. Parents need support, too, often through psychological counseling, to help them cope with the guilt and trauma that usually go with the bearing and rearing of a less-than-perfect child, as well as with the emotional burden of worrying about what will happen to their child after they die. Thanks to the improvement in care, the victims surviving childhood now have normal life expectancies. With new developments in drug therapy and surgery, which have been helpful in controlling certain symptoms, some victims have been able to lead near-normal lives. The most dramatic recent development is a brain pacemaker which is implanted under the scalps of patients to control the tremors in some types of palsy. However, there is as yet no cure for the disorder because brain tissues, once damaged, cannot be replaced.

And so the present emphasis is on preventing future cases—through genetic counseling and prenatal care, for example. UCPA's research emphasis, conducted at the national level, is also on prevention. The organization's annual research expenditures of nearly $1 million represent only a minuscule portion—less than 2 percent—of its $50 million-a-year total expenditures and a fraction of the recent federal annual research expenditures of $18 million on cerebral palsy. Nonetheless, UCPA claims to have contributed to the research resulting in the development of the rubella vaccine. While this may be true, the National Foundation-March of Dimes and other organizations make similar claims. There can be no question, however, that UCPA has played a role in stimulating research by government and others into the means of preventing cerebral palsy and improving the treatment and management of its victims.

Because of the visual appeal of these victims, it is not surprising that UCPA should resort to the telethon as its principal fund-raising device. Indeed, it is interesting to note that UCPA, together with the Muscular Dystrophy Association and the National Easter Seal Society—all three concerned with crippled children—are the leading practitioners of the telethon. (All three also rank among the ten leading health agencies in terms of contribution income.) Whether or not this is an ethical or even desirable means of raising money is something we will go into in Chapter 20. But the telethon can lend itself to abuses, particularly in the case of an organization like UCPA whose affiliates operate like independent duchies, retaining 70 percent of all the funds raised locally. In the mid-1970s, for example, the Nashville affiliate reported raising $277,000 through the segment of the telethon carried in its area. Of this, only $166,000 was ever collected and about $80,000 eventually wound up for the benefit of cerebral palsy. Part of the rest was frittered away on lavish gifts and expense accounts. Of course, this is but an isolated example, although it again makes the point that the local affiliates of national organizations should be studied by would-be contributors.

Nonetheless, no one can dispute the fact that the cause of cerebral palsy has gained recognition in the past two or three decades. Indeed, the organization's executive director, Earl Cunerd, confessed to me that he had never even heard of the disorder when he was recruited for the board of his local affiliate back in the late 1950s.

Muscular Dystrophy

Only two or three decades ago, muscular dystrophy was also all but unknown and the few people outside the families of patients who had ever heard of it often confused it with other neuromuscular diseases. Today, muscular dystrophy is virtually a household word thanks to comedian Jerry Lewis' annual Labor Day telethons on behalf of the Muscular Dystrophy Association. Like the United Cerebral Palsy Associations, the association was founded—in 1950—by a small group of parents, in this case, of victims of muscular dystrophy, which is the name given to an entire family of chronic diseases, all of which progressively destroy voluntary or skeletal muscles (as opposed to internal muscles such as the diaphragm).* With the conviction that there is no "incurable" disease, the aim of parents was to support the research studies of Dr. Ade T. Milhorat, who at the time was the only physician giving major attention to muscular dystrophy.

However, no cure has as yet been found for the affliction and, unlike cerebral palsy, it invariably leads to an early death. Of its estimated 200,000 victims in the United States, nearly two-thirds are children between the ages of 3 and 13; of these, almost all will die before adulthood, usually not from the disease itself but from complications such as bronchitis or pneumonia (due to the weakening of the muscles affecting lung or heart action). Even a trifling cold can be a serious threat to an MD patient, whose wasted muscles may leave him unable to raise mucus, creating the danger of suffocation.

No one knows exactly how many fatalities are attributable to muscular dystrophy, either directly or indirectly, even though Jerry Lewis, as we say in Chapter 20, is wont to proclaim on his telethons that "in the next 20 hours, 80 of my kids will die." (When I challenged this claim, the MDA arranged a conference call between me and a number of its top experts, including none other than Dr. Milhorat; none could substantiate Jerry Lewis' figures or offer any of their own.)

Nonetheless, the grim prognosis for muscular dystrophy creates fund-raising problems for the MDA: People don't like to contribute to a seemingly hopeless cause. And so the association, while pointing to the horrors of dystrophy on the one hand, takes a sanguine stance on the other, a typical appeal for contributions

---

Dystrophy means imperfect nutrition and, although its exact cause is as yet unknown, is believed to result from a metabolic abnormality, probably the lack of some specific enzyme or enzyme system essential for the conversion of foods into tissue and energy. However, it has been fairly well established that heredity is a factor in most dystrophies. Symptoms in children are a peculiar side-to-side waddling gait, frequent falling, difficulty in rising or climbing stairs, and apparent *increases* in the size of the weakened affected muscles (because of fat replacing the muscle fibers). In older persons, the first symptoms may be weak facial muscles which produce a "flat smile" and leave the person unable to whistle or drink through a straw.

promising "help today and hope for tomorrow to thousands of adults and children afflicted with neuromuscular diseases."

That such appeals have been successful is evidenced by the fact that MDA has grown over the years to become the fourth largest health agency (just beind the National Foundation) in terms of public support, with 230 affiliates and with recent annual contributions of around $57 million, roughly half of which is produced by the telethon. Over $20 million (nearly 45 percent of the association's annual expenditures) is used for patient and community services, largely at MDA's nationwide network of some 190 hospital-affiliated clinics where victims of muscular dystrophy and related muscle disorders* receive diagnosis, follow-up medical care, therapy, counseling, and orthopedic appliances—incidentally, all free of charge. There is also a summer camping program in 35 states and Puerto Rico for dystrophic youngsters, each of whom is provided with his own volunteer counselor. None of these, however, while easing the lives of the patients and their families, has had any significant lasting effect on the course of the diseases being treated.

What then about MDA's research into a cure, to which the association now allocates about $14 million a year, around 30 percent of its annual expenditures? This currently goes to support more than 500 individual research projects around the world and ten university-based research and clinical centers, where neuromuscular diseases are being studied, in the United States and Great Britain. One, of course, would like to believe that this is money well spent and that, as MDA's promotional material promises, it is bringing us closer to a cure. But there is nothing to indicate that this is not still a long way off. Of the remainder of MDA's expenditures, 7.5 percent goes for public and professional education and training, 13.7 percent for fund raising (in terms of contributions, 11.2 percent), and 3.3 percent for overhead.

The National Information Bureau is not entirely happy with MDA's financial reporting—for example, its allocation of a portion of its telethon expenses to "clinical, diagnostic and community services" instead of to fund raising. The charity-monitoring agency also wonders if MDA may be taking in more money than it can spend. In 1976, MDA chapters returned to national headquarters about $1.7 million which had been allocated to patient services in prior years and had not been spent. The following year MDA went on to raise $57.6 million more from the public, but spent only $47.1 million, leaving it with a net surplus of nearly $11 million. Some physicians have also questioned the quality of care in at least some of MDA's clinics.

Nonetheless, the NIB concedes that MDA performs a number of useful services and recognizes its role as a rallying point for those concerned with muscular dystrophy and other related diseases. Certainly this role will continue to be important as long as our government sees fit to allot less—about $10.5 million in a recent year—for research into these diseases than does MDA, whose Jerry Lewis has raised more than $150 million for muscular dystrophy since 1966 through his telethons.

At the same time, it is somewhat discomfiting to think that the future course of

*Among them: myositis, characterized by inflammation of the skeletal muscles; myasthenia gravis; and the various muscular atrophies, a group of diseases, including amyotrophic lateral sclerosis, involving degeneration of the motor nerve cells in the spinal cord.

the fight against this baffling, tragic disease should depend so much on the dedication of an entertainment personality or, for that matter, any one person.

Multiple Sclerosis

On May 1, 1945, the following two-line classified ad appeared in *The New York Times*:

> MULTIPLE SCLEROSIS—will anyone recovered from it please communicate with patient. T272 Times.

The ad was placed by a 30-year-old New Yorker, Sylvia Lawry, whose brother had just been diagnosed as having this little-known neurological disorder. The responses that poured in and the exchange of information back and forth led to the foundation a year later of the National Multiple Sclerosis Society with Miss Lawry as its guiding spirit. Today, the society, still headed by Miss Lawry, serving what is probably the longest tenure of its kind in the charity world, has about 160 chapters across the country and an annual total income of around $23 million, virtually all of it from contributions.

The society has brought about a greater understanding of multiple sclerosis, even though it is often confused with muscular dystrophy. Moreover, the disease does not present as bleak a picture for its victims as it did three decades ago when medical journals advised physicians not to tell patients that they had MS. For many of the some 500,000 Americans afflicted with it, its course is almost always downhill, producing blurred vision, slurred speech, difficulties in walking, tremors, numbness, loss of coordination, impaired bladder control, paralysis, and, in some cases, premature death.* On the other hand, many victims are affected to only a limited extent and are indistinguishable from other people, have normal life spans, and can even continue working; one study showed two out of three MS patients following a prescribed regimen of diet, exercise, and rest to be gainfully employed 20 years after the onset of the disease in spite of the prejudice against employing people with MS. One female Chicago suburban realtor, who had been selling more than 1 million dollars worth of real estate a year, was fired when her employer learned about her condition; in San Diego, a stricken former Navy pilot was turned down for 150 jobs, including some with the Veterans Administration.

Although MS was first identified as a distinct disease more than a century ago, no really effective treatment has ever been developed for it, and a preventive or cure has so far eluded all research efforts. Nor is there even any clear-cut test that will diagnose the disease in its early stages which seem to come between the ages of 20 and 40—ironically, the prime years of life—with women three out of every five victims. (A recent celebrated victim: the beautiful, young cellist, Jacqueline du Pré.) Scientists have suspected for many years that MS might be caused by a virus, possibly as a long-delayed aftereffect of a childhood disease, such as measles. Some link this cause to a malfunctioning of the body's protective immunological system, which normally serves as a defense against invading

---

*Sylvia Lawry's brother, Bernard Friedman, died in 1975 at the age of 56.

viruses or germs. The fact that the disease is far more prevalent in cool climates than in hot ones suggests that environmental factors may also play a role.*

Whatever the cause, the disease attacks the fatty myelin insulating sheath that protects the nerve fibers of the brain and spinal cord. As the attacks recur, sometimes at intervals of months or even years, more and more of the myelin is eaten away in irregular patches at different locations (hence the term "multiple"), thus short-circuiting the nerve impulses controlling the bodily functions, and producing the symptoms described.

Although the big hope in MS lies in research, the disease has long been a fiscal stepchild at the National Institute of Neurological and Communicative Disorders and Stroke, which the society was instrumental in establishing. Of the $178 million appropriated for the institute in a recent year, less than $13 million was allocated to MS, an amount criticized as "unconscionably small" by a National Advisory Commission on Multiple Sclerosis established by federal law in 1972, again with the prodding of the society. To supplement the federal agency's expenditures, the society spends around $3 million, or about 20 percent of its total annual expenditures, on research. With another 15 percent spent on fund raising and 10 percent on overhead, most of the rest goes to provide therapy, counseling, and other services to patients and their families in the some 78 chapter-supported clinics, clinical programs, and centers around the country and on public and professional education and training aimed at finding the answers Miss Lawry sought in her newspaper ad of more than three decades ago.

Epilepsy

Before looking into the operations of the Epilepsy Foundation of America, I agreed with some foreboding to accept an invitation to spend an evening with an epileptic in what was to be a novel experience for me. Since childhood, I had had the notion, shared by many, that every epileptic was a strangely deranged soul, given to suddenly throwing wild fits, writhing on the floor, and foaming at the mouth like a person possessed, although I no longer clung to the ancient belief, not yet entirely dispelled, that held this behavior to be the work of evil spirits. My apprehensions were enhanced by reading Michael Crichton's best seller, *The Terminal Man*, which suggested that certain epileptics were violent, desperate, and potentially murderous.**

To my relief, the epileptic who greeted me in his elegant high-rise apartment on Chicago's Gold Coast did not seem to fit any of these stereotypes—feared and shunned since ancient times. He was Tom Ramsier, a successful commercial artist and designer. In manner, appearance, and speech, Ramsier, a handsome, debonair, immaculately dressed bachelor in his forties, gave no indication of being an epileptic, one of the estimated 2 million in the United States. The exact number is not known and could be as high as 4 million or even 10 million, according to Ramsier, since many epileptics take pains to conceal their condition, fearing job and social discrimination. Among the celebrated contemporaries afflicted with the disorder, he mentioned the late opera star Maria Callas, a famous American symphony conductor, and several internationally known indus-

*Its prevalence rate is only 1.6 per 100,000 in Mexico City as compared to at least 60 per 100,000 in Minnesota.

**Crichton, who as a physician should have known better, later publicly apologized.

trialists, as well as such historical figures as Socrates, Julius Caesar, Alexander the Great, Dante, Byron, Tchaikovsky, and Dostoevski, belying another popular notion that epileptics are of inferior intelligence. He also said that, among our presidents, Theodore Roosevelt and Calvin Coolidge had had seizures (the term epileptics prefer to "fits").

Although epilepsy usually strikes in childhood, Ramsier, after pouring some drinks, traced his own first attack to the time a Navy ship on which he was serving in World War II was hit off Guam. "Being a young brat—I was then only 16—I was scared to death and the fright and shock probably brought it on," he recalled. Also linked to epilepsy, he said, are brain and head injuries—"auto and motorcycle accidents have resulted in quite a few cases in recent years"—abnormal pregnancies and certain infectious illnesses, such as measles, meningitis, encephalitis, and whooping cough, that can affect the brain tissues; however, in three out of four cases, no specific cause can be identified. Contrary to another popular belief, he also pointed out, epilepsy is no longer attributed to heredity, masturbation, worms, or VD. And like cerebral palsy, epilepsy is not a specific disease but rather the general term applied to the convulsive seizures that occur when excessive discharges of electricity—they have been compared to an "electrical storm"—in the brain send unprogrammed messages to various parts of the body; it is these that cause the erratic behavior associated with epilepsy.

There are four main types of seizures. Ramsier said his were of the "grand mal" ("great sickness") type, the most dramatic and most frequently associated with epilepsy; they typically last two to five minutes. The far less noticeable "petit mal" ("little sickness") seizures, he said, occur mainly in children and are marked by "blank" or staring spells, lasting from 10 to 30 seconds, that are often mistaken for daydreaming. Psychomotor seizures are characterized by odd physical activities, such as picking at clothing, and focal seizures by a sudden jerking of one area of the body, such as the arms and legs or by sensations such as numbness or tingling.

Thanks to new drugs and improvements in diagnostic techniques, seizures can now be eliminated completely or greatly reduced in incidence in about 80 percent of all epilepsy patients. Ramsier, who used to have two or three—and, during some periods, as many as ten or eleven—seizures in one day, said he hadn't had any in the past ten years.

But with the fears, misconceptions, and superstitions of centuries still surrounding the word, epilepsy, even today, continues as much a social as a medical problem. "Epilepsy is probably the only common disorder," declared Ramsier, "where the sufferer is more handicapped by the attitudes of society than by his disability."* He pointed out that although most laws discriminating against

*Why, in this medically and otherwise enlightened age, is epilepsy still so feared? Why, for example, is there not the same prejudice against diabetics whose seizures are not too dissimilar from those of epileptics? The answer, suggests Ramsier, stems from the special feelings people have about the brain and goes back to the early days of witchcraft. "Even if the idea of 'demonic possession' no longer has many adherents," ventures Dr. David A. Kahn, a Pennsylvania psychiatrist, "epilepsy retains something of that atmosphere. To the uninformed observer, a seizure is still an extremely mysterious event. After all, something is 'going on' within the brain, something over which the individual has no control. Finally, that loss of control, occurring unpredictably and for reasons that are ill-understood, touches a deep dread. We fear loss of control in anyone, in any form, whether temporary or permanent. Most of all, we fear the possibility within ourselves—and each reminder in others renews that fear."

epileptics have been repealed (the last of the many state laws forbidding epileptics to marry was repealed in 1967; however, five states still have sterilization
laws applying to epileptics), public attitudes still make it difficult for epileptics to
marry, have children, and hold jobs. "To get a job, an epileptic has to lie," said
Ramsier. "If you're candid with employers and tell them about your condition,
95 out of 100 won't hire you but they'll never give you the real reason. On the
other hand, if you lie about your condition and later have seizures at work, you'll
be fired for lying." Epileptics who have not had seizures for anywhere from six
months to two years can now generally get driving licenses. But they find it
difficult to get insurance, which in effect prevents them from driving. Before his
seizures were brought under control, Ramsier experienced his share of marital,
job, and social rebuffs. Indelibly engraved in his memory is the time he was
invited for a weekend in the country by a couple he had just met. When he
arrived at their home, laden with gifts for their children, he discovered that his
hostess had sent them away to her mother's because of the fear that he might
frighten them. Ramsier says it will take a massive educational effort—on the part
of the epileptic, his family, society, and government—before the disorder will be
taken as matter of factly as diabetes or heart disease.

Working to bring this about is the Epilepsy Foundation of America, headquartered in Washington, D.C. Formed in 1968 through the merger of two smaller
epilepsy groups (in 1978 it also absorbed the Chicago-based National Epilepsy
League which Ramsier ran for several years), EFA operates on an annual budget
of about $7.5 million. "The single most important task we have is the correct and
truthful education of a public which seems to remain largely ignorant of the
problem," said EFA's executive director, Jack McAllister; accordingly, his
organization devotes a good part of its expenditures to the spread of such en-
lightenment. This hasn't been an easy task because of the organization's intrinsic
handicap in attracting both volunteers and donations for the reasons already gone
into.

Prejudices against epilepsy have no doubt contributed to EFA's traditionally
high fund-raising costs which, however, have declined from 47 percent of donations in 1970 to about 30 percent in recent years. Some have also attributed these
costs to EFA's inclusion of a penny in its mail solicitations. In response to
criticisms, this fund-raising practice was discontinued in early 1978, although
McAllister is not too sanguine about what effect this may have in lowering costs.
"Our tests have consistently produced from 12 to 16 percent higher returns with
the penny mailing than with just plain letters," he said.

Nonetheless, in the past few years, the organization has been making sincere
efforts not only to diversify its funding base and lower its costs but also to
develop and implement new programs for persons with epilepsy. More than 40
percent of its annual expenditures now go for community and patient services
such as counseling and job assistance. "We're also much more of an advocacy
organization now," said McAllister, citing as an example EFA's stormy press
conference and other activities that in 1978 forced the Food and Drug Administration to discontinue delaying approval of the antiepileptic drug sodium
valproate.

Although it is difficult to measure to what extent the gradual changes in public
attitudes toward epilepsy are due to the efforts of EFA, there can be no question
that more and more epileptics are beginning to bring their disorder out of hiding

and demanding to be treated like anyone else with a simple physical disability. Slowly epilepsy is emerging from years of dark superstition to be illuminated by openness and understanding, as I myself discovered during the course of my evening with Tom Ramsier. ''The subject has become my soapbox,'' he said as we parted. ''Maybe one day everyone will understand and no one will have to fear epilepsy again. And conversations like ours will be unnecessary.''

Parkinsonism, etc.

No account of the neuromuscular diseases would be complete without some mention of Parkinsonism, the term collectively applied to the group of paralytic disorders (the most common of which is Parkinson's disease), which is believed to affect 1.5 million Americans and claim 50,000 new victims annually, mostly over age 50. Victims may be recognized by their stooped posture, shuffling walk with arms held rigidly at the side but with the hands trembling, and expressionless face. Although there is no known cause or cure for the disease,* many of its symptoms can be relieved in three out of four victims by the relatively new drug called L-Dopa. (In this sense, Parkinson's ranks with epilepsy as a medical success story.) The federal government now spends about $7 million a year for research into the disease. Possibly because the disease is under control and affects largely older persons, the various voluntary agencies in this field have not been able to attract much public support. The largest, the Parkinson's Disease Foundation, last reported an income of less than $280,000 ($153,000 from contributions) and, like the other Parkinson's groups, does not meet the National Information Bureau's standards because it provides only sketchy details about its financial operations and holds infrequent board meetings.

As one would expect, the agencies concerned with such relative rarities as amyotrophic lateral sclerosis (ALS), myasthenia gravis, and Huntington's disease, are also fairly small. The two agencies concerned with ALS—the ALS Society of America and the National ALS Foundation—together take in less than $500,000 a year. The Myasthenia Gravis (its name means grave muscular weakness) Foundation, concerned with a disease that afflicts an estimated 240,000 Americans, has a total annual income of about $350,000. Huntington's disease, a hereditary incurable degeneration of the brain cells, which killed folk singer Woody Guthrie, probably does not affect more than 15,000 Americans at any one time. To fight it, the singer's widow, Marjorie, founded the Committee to Combat Huntington's Disease, which has a total income of less than $200,000 a year. Some have suggested that all of these organizations, involved as they are with related diseases, could be more effective if they merged into one of the larger neuromuscular disease groups. However, it is understandable that the parents and relatives, who largely comprise the supporters of the smaller organizations, should want to have them as rallying points, which can often be influential. Partly as a result of the work of Marjorie Guthrie's committee, for example, Congress created a Commission for the Control of Huntington's Disease in 1976 to develop plans for combating and coping with this baffling brain disorder.

---

*Some feel the disorder to be caused by the viruses of influenza or encephalitis; others believe that genetic factors or hardening of the arteries may contribute to it. Although the disease is seldom fatal, it can totally disable a victim if untreated and can hasten death from other causes. One of its more famous victims was *Life* photographer Margaret Bourke-White.

Arthritis

At its 1978 annual meeting, the Arthritis Foundation released new figures from the National Center for Health Statistics indicating arthritis (which literally means inflammation of the joints and is the umbrella term applied to the more than 100 forms of rheumatic disease) to be our most widespread chronic disorder—with the possible exception of heart disease. Counting people with related diseases such as bursitis, low-back and shoulder pain, juvenile arthritis, lupus erythematosus, and scleroderma, a total of 31.6 million Americans now suffer from arthritis severely enough to require medical care.* Of this total, about 7.3 million are disabled at any one time, the disability causing 26.6 million days of lost work and 525 million days of restricted activities annually. About 15 percent of Social Security disability payments go to people with arthritis-related conditions and the disease is believed to cost the nation an estimated $13.5 billion annually, mostly in lost wages and taxes, medical bills, and government expenditures for disability and arthritis care programs.

That is nearly nine hundred times the $15.6 million a year in donations now raised by the Arthritis Foundation which came into being in 1948 as the Arthritis and Rheumatism Foundation to cope with this major health problem; coincidentally, this was around the time the artificial hormone, cortisone, was first used and hailed as the "final" cure for arthritis. (As we've since learned, the drug and its derivatives, although effective, have proven to be a mixed blessing, often producing side effects, at times worse than the disease itself.)

How effective the Arthritis Foundation has been in carrying out its mandate is a matter of conjecture. Certainly, there is still no cure for arthritis; nor, over the years, has there been a major breakthrough in arthritis research comparable in caliber to the use of cortisone. Although the foundation has spent some $40 million on research during the three decades of its existence, and in recent years has allocated over 20 percent of its annual expenditures for this purpose, today, as in the precortisone era, good old aspirin remains the white knight of drugs— the "drug of choice"—for combating arthritic pain and inflammation. There have been some recent advances in surgical techniques, notably the use of artificial hip and other joint implants, but the foundation does not claim any direct credit for these in the rundown it gives of its major accomplishments.

What the foundation with its 73 chapters does best, devoting nearly 20 percent of its budget to this activity, is educate people about arthritis and the treatment available to them, limited as this may be: There are only 2000 rheumatologists treating patients in the entire country, one for every 7000 victims. Through its two professional sections, the American Rheumatism Association and the Allied Health Professional Section, physicians in various specialties, therapists, nurses, and other paraprofessionals are kept abreast of the latest developments in the field, this activity accounting for 15 percent of the foundation's budget. As one

*It is not known just what causes most types. Some are believed to be of genetic origin and others the result of an infection. Other possible causes are thought to be fatigue, shock, and allergy. However, people who work outdoors in active jobs appear to be hit harder than those in sedentary occupations. Twice as many women as men get rheumatoid arthritis, the most devastating and crippling form. On the other hand, most of the victims of gout, which affects the big toe and other joints of the foot, are men.

result, three-quarters of all U.S. medical schools now offer substantial training in rheumatology (compared to less than 10 percent 30 years ago).

Another 20 percent or so of the foundation's money is used by the chapters to encourage or support such community services as clinics, home care programs, rehabilitation and transportation services, loan closets for wheelchairs and other self-help aids, vocational guidance, patient information and referral, even social clubs. (After all, everyone likes to talk about his troubles.) However, one criticism of the foundation I have heard is that it does not apply strict enough standards to its review of the clinics. Of the remainder of the foundation's annual expenditures, about 13 and 12 percent, respectively, go for fund raising and overhead.

Like other voluntary health agencies, the foundation has constantly pressed for more government support; it has, however, had only moderate success, possibly because arthritis itself rarely kills people. For all the misery and money it costs, the federal budget for research to fight arthritis in the mid-1970s was only about $33 million a year—less than $1.5 per arthritis patient at the disease's then prevalence rate. (By contrast, the federal research budget was $122 for every cancer patient and $74 for every heart and blood-vessel disease patient.) In the early 1970s, a National Advisory Committee on the Future of Arthritis Research had forecast that a breakthrough "seemed imminent" if Congress would triple or quadruple the funds available for the disease. This seemed likely when the foundation's efforts finally led to the passage of the National Arthritis Act, which was signed by President Ford on January 4, 1975. The first arthritis legislation in 25 years, it authorized an additional $50 million for arthritis, part of this to go for the development and operation of a nationwide network of "arthritis centers" to bring together people involved in the research, education, and treatment aspects of the disease, and the rest for community demonstration projects and a national data system.

Three years later, however, less than $10 million of the authorized funds had been appropriated. And federal funds for research amounted to only $40 million—less in real dollars than in the mid-1970s despite the rising prevalence of arthritis.

Diabetes

What can happen, however, when Congress is seriously interested in providing funding for a disease can be seen in the case of diabetes. Although long ranked as the nation's fifth leading cause of death (after heart disease, cancer, accidents, and pneumonia and influenza), claiming 38,000 lives a year, many Americans have never viewed the disease as a major health problem. When a recent Gallup Poll asked Americans which disease they feared most, diabetes did not even make the Top Ten. (The leaders were cancer, blindness, and heart disorders.) Probably the main reason is that most diabetics, thanks to the use of insulin, work at almost every type of job and can appear as healthy as normal people. Another related reason stems from the popular misconception that insulin is a "cure" for the disease; all the hormone does is control it but it does not prevent the complications that may result from it.*

*Diabetes is a disorder characterized by the failure of the pancreas to produce or release enougn insulin to utilize the body's intake of sugars, starches, and other carbohydrates (which during

Until recently, the American Diabetes Association, which was formed in 1940 as a professional society of physicians and scientists, did little to impress upon the public consciousness the seriousness of diabetes as a health problem. Consequently, even half a century after the discovery of insulin in 1921, there was no ground swell demanding that our government attack diabetes with the same vigor that it was fighting heart disease, cancer, and the communicable diseases. A turning point in this situation came in 1970 when the ADA opened its membership to lay people (who now comprise half of the association's board), initiated an annual fund-raising campaign, and, with its growing grassroots support, began to beat at the doors of Congress. A key contact was Sen. Richard S. Schweiker of Pennsylvania, who was to become the ranking Republican on the Senate Health Subcommittee. In 1972 the Pennsylvania affiliate of the ADA had three people from the senator's home state call on him. One of them was going blind from diabetes, another had a daughter threatened with the same fate, and the third had a child who was also seriously ill with the disease.

Schweiker took a personal interest in their plight and decided to hold hearings. Others enlisted the support of Sen. Gale McGee of Wyoming, one of the nation's 6 million diabetics; others are actress Mary Tyler Moore, hockey player Bobby Clark, baseball player Ron Santo, and tennis players Ham Richardson and Billy Talbert.

All these efforts led to the passage in 1974 of the National Diabetes Mellitus Research and Education Act, which established a National Commission on Diabetes consisting of 17 members, seven of them ADA board members. Nine months later, the commission reported that there was strong evidence that diabetes and its complications were responsible for as many as 300,000 deaths a year (many from heart or kidney failure, for example, could be attributed to diabetes), thereby making the disease the nation's *third* ranking cause of death. The commission also said that half of the nation's diabetics were unaware that they had the disease, the incidence of which was increasing at the rate of 6 percent a year. Among the commission's other startling findings: The disease was the leading cause of new cases of blindness; and people with the disease were 17 times more prone to kidney disease, over five times more prone to gangrene (often leading to amputation), and twice as prone to heart disease and stroke.

To cope with the disease and its estimated $5.5 billion economic drain on the nation, the commission called for vastly increased federal spending on diabetes research, education, and control programs. An awed Congress responded to the point where federal appropriations for diabetes have grown from $11.9 million to $123 million since the passage of the 1974 act.

---

digestion are normally converted into a form of sugar called glucose), both for immediate energy needs and for storage for future needs. As a result, a surplus of glucose accumulates in the blood and spills over into the urine. The kidneys have to work overtime to get rid of some of this surplus and in the process take water and salt from the body. At the same time, the body must draw on fats and proteins instead of glucose for the energy it needs. All this results in a disruption of total body metabolism that can lead to a host of serious complications. Moreover, there is some evidence that the high blood sugar levels alone may directly cause damage to the eyes, kidneys, and nerves. Although the cause of the disease is not known, it seems to run in families and is 50 percent more likely to develop in women than in men. Obesity and age also seem to play significant roles: The chance of developing the disease doubles with every 20 percent of a person's extra weight and doubles again with each decade of advancing age. Four out of five diabetics are 40 or over. Infections and other hormonal disturbances may be other contributing factors. There are also indications that heredity plays a role.

In spite of this heroic accomplishment, the American Diabetes Association remains one of the smallest and least known of the major health agencies, with 54 affiliates, 700 chapters, about 50,000 volunteers (mostly diabetics and their relatives), and an annual income of $10.5 million, $6.7 million of this from donations. Of its annual expenditures of $9.5 million, about $1.7 million or 18 percent is plowed into research to supplement the government's much more monumental research efforts. Probably of much greater value, however, are the association's activities to maintain the government's interest in research, and its educational efforts to make the public better aware of the seriousness of the disease. It also works to locate the millions of as yet unknown diabetics through an annual "Diabetes Detection Drive." Fund-raising costs run to about 14 percent of all contributions.

Also involved importantly in the lobbying efforts that resulted in the National Diabetes Act was the even smaller Juvenile Diabetes Foundation which, as the name implies, is concerned with the 10 percent or so of all diabetes cases that appear in childhood or adolescence. In this so-called "juvenile-onset" and more severe type of diabetes, the pancreas usually fails to secrete any insulin at all, in contrast to the more common "maturity-onset" form where insulin is produced but not in sufficient usable quantities. Formed in 1970 in Pennsylvania (significantly, the home state of Senator Schweiker) by parents of diabetics and other lay people impatient with the efforts then being made by the ADA, the foundation recently reported annual expenditures of about $2 million. Of this, 65 percent was allocated for research, 18 percent for public education and counseling, 6 percent for overhead, and 10.6 percent for fund raising. (Fund-raising expenses also amounted to 11.8 percent of contributions.) The ADA has long favored merging with the foundation, but the latter, actually formed as an ADA splinter group, is interested in keeping its autonomy.

Kidney Disease

As recently as a decade ago, says the National Kidney Foundation, as many as 6000 Americans a year died of kidney failure simply because they could not afford the cost of artificial kidney treatments—known as dialysis—or of a kidney transplant. Kidney failure was the one major disease where money, and money alone, could mean the difference between life and death for its victims. Then, in 1972, Congress passed a historic measure that, through an amendment to the Social Security Act, authorized Medicare to pay 80 percent of most dialysis and transplant expenses, marking the first move to extend Medicare payments to persons under 65 and to provide assistance for a specific disease.

What has since become known as the End Stage Renal Disease Program (ESRD) was a dream come true for the little National Kidney Foundation (total income about $7 million a year) which was largely responsible for the program's becoming a reality. The foundation, formed in 1950 as the National Nephrosis Foundation, exerted strenuous efforts to win the public to its cause and mustered a battery of persuasive witnesses to testify before Congress. (During one hearing before the House Ways and Means Committee a patient with end stage renal disease was actually dialyzed in the committee room.)

But now there are fears that the dream, in one sense, is turning out to be a nightmare. "Have we fathered a monstrosity?" wonders a recent NKF president, Dr. James C. Hunt, the Mayo Clinic's famed chairman of medicine. For the program, which began in 1973 by serving about 11,000 persons at a cost of $250 million in its first year, served at least three times that many in 1978 at a cost of $900 million and it is projected to cost $2.3 billion by 1982, when the program is expected to help 56,000.

The main reason for the rise, apart from the growing numbers being treated as more and more are kept alive, is the ever-increasing high cost of the treatment itself. Thanks to inflation, dialysis, which removes waste materials from the blood, now costs $8000 to $12,000 a year if done by the patient himself at home and from $15,000 to $30,000 if done in a hospital or dialysis center, where costs include enormous institutional overhead salaries.* The only alternative, a kidney transplant, can cost from $20,000 to $30,000 and is often of dubious value: In transplants from well-matched living donors, 80 to 95 percent of the kidneys function for at least two years; however, the success rate with cadaver kidneys is only from 40 to 60 percent.

Although it would, of course, be too late to pull the plug on the kidney patients, there are many who wonder if an inordinately large share of our tax dollar isn't going to them. Of the 13 million Americans who have some form of kidney disease, about 54,000 die each year because of it. Currently another 36,000 are being kept alive by dialysis. By contrast, 395,000 persons die of cancer each year and about 1 million die of heart disease and circulatory ailments. Yet neither cancer nor heart disease nor any other single health problem receives federal funding to the extent the kidney program does.

This leads to more fundamental questions such as how much is life worth and which segments of our population should be favored? "We're seeing a resurgence of certain dangerous diseases because children are not getting their shots," says Dr. Robert Grossman, acting director of the dialysis program at the Hospital of the University of Pennsylvania. "Wouldn't we be better off spending the dialysis money on basic health care to keep the general population healthy?"

Most kidney specialists, however, feel that the ultimate solution lies in putting more money into research into the causes and prevention of kidney disease so that the need for dialysis or transplants is eventually eliminated. Some go so far as to say that part of the money spent on the Medicare program could be better spent on research.

"We need basic research badly to solve the problems," says Dr. Benjamin T. Burton, chief of the artificial kidney program of the National Institute of Arthritis, Metabolism, and Digestive Diseases (NIAMDD). "Otherwise we will wind up with expensive treatments. We would have had to keep thousands of people in iron lungs if polio vaccines hadn't been found."

Yet only about 10 percent or $27 million of NIAMDD's annual budget now goes for renal research and, ironically, this allotment has been going down year after year since the ESRD Program got under way. Counting the funding from other NIH agencies, the military, and the Veterans Administration a total of $65

---

*To encourage the less expensive home dialysis procedure and so help reduce the cost of the government program, Congress passed legislation in 1978 authorizing Medicare to pay the full cost, instead of 80 percent, of a home kidney machine as well as the cost of supplies and backup help from dialysis centers.

million is now spent annually on research into all of the kidney and related disorders—still a relatively small sum considering the magnitude of present and projected expenditures for the care of kidney patients, both inside and outside the government program. For this reason, the National Kidney Foundation and its 55 affiliates continue to regard the support for research as their most important single goal and, in their quest into the causes of kidney disease, not only push for more government funding but also allot about $1 million or 15 percent of their expenditures for research projects of their own. Apart from another 22 percent that goes for fund raising and overhead (the ratio of fund raising to contributions is 12 percent), the rest goes for public and professional education and for such patient and community services as "early warning" detection and screening programs, the operation of drug banks providing medication at reduced prices, counseling and referral programs for patients and their families, and the promotion of an organ donor program, covering kidneys as well as other organs.*

One of the foundation's problems is that it is often confused with the American Kidney Fund, which acquired an unsavory reputation soon after it was established in 1971 "to provide direct financial help to people with chronic kidney disease." In its first year of operation, the fund raised nearly $800,000 but spent only $39,000—less than 5 cents on the dollar—on its stated purpose. The remaining 95 percent was spent on administration and fund raising, including $640,000 on a nationwide direct-mail campaign, part of which was handled by a mailing house founded by the president of the fund. Prodded by investigations by the Postal Service and several states, the fund replaced its president and many of its board members and took steps to improve its operations which, after the government's ESRD Program went into effect, were directed primarily at paying supplementary expenses for transportation, medication, special diet, and other health-related items. Although fund-raising expenses have come down in recent years to 35 percent of contributions, they are still too high to enable the fund to meet the standards of both the Council of Better Business Bureaus and the National Information Bureau.

Cystic Fibrosis

Although cystic fibrosis is not an uncommon disease—one out of every 1500 babies in the United States is born with it, adding to the 50,000 already afflicted, and as many as 10 million Americans are believed to be carriers—its name has not registered on the public consciousness in spite of the publicity efforts of the Cystic Fibrosis Foundation.

Dr. John Herndon, a former medical-scientific director of the foundation, likes to tell the story of the time his secretary made reservations for him at the Palmer House in Chicago. When he showed up at the reception desk, he was asked, "Where's the nun?" Dr. Herndon looked puzzled. "A reservation was made for you and a nun," said the clerk. "I don't know what you're talking about," said

---

*The program, however, has been a tremendous flop. Since the beginning of the decade, the foundation and its affiliates have distributed more than 20 million "uniform donor cards," which allow a person to sign up to donate his organs upon death. But the foundation admits that very few donations have actually come about as a result of the card. "We know that many people who request a card don't even fill it out," said a foundation official. "It's obvious that people are interested in the subject, but it's difficult for them to confront their feelings about their own mortality."

Dr. Herndon. "There must be some mistake." The clerk handed him the reservation form, which read, "Dr. Herndon with Sister Fibrosis."

Soon after the foundation was formed by a group of parents in 1955, Sen. Abraham Ribicoff, then governor of Connecticut, agreed to speak at a CF banquet. Upon his arrival there, he went up to Doris Tulchin, a recent foundation president and mother of a CF child, and asked, "Doris, what *is* it?" The question was quite valid for at the time few doctors were aware of the disease and those who were found it completely baffling. For this reason, it for the most part either went undiagnosed and untreated or was misdiagnosed as asthma, whooping cough, or other ailments.

Cystic fibrosis (known more technically as "mucoviscidosis") is a genetic disorder that produces a thick, sticky mucus which clogs the bronchial tubes of the lungs, interfering with breathing. It also plugs up the ducts of the pancreas, preventing the flow of digestive enzymes to the intestine, thus impeding proper digestion of food. In addition to causing progressive damage to the lungs and overworking the heart, CF also leaves its victims susceptible to bronchitis, pneumonia, and other lung infections. Two decades ago, diagnosis of CF was literally a death sentence; only a handful of afflicted children survived beyond their preschool years.

Nowadays, thanks to the foundation's beating the drums for improved diagnosis and medical care, as well as expanded research, 50 percent of those born with the disease live past 18 and the upper limits of survival are not known. More than ever before, survivors can even look forward to reasonably normal lives, although at considerable cost in terms of money and convenience. Many CF patients must take 40 or more pills a day (at a cost of upwards of $5000 annually) and, in order to clear the lungs of mucus, must follow a rigorous routine of inhalation treatment and physical therapy as often as two or three times a day. Many must also sleep in mist tents and endure hospitalization several times a year, usually in connection with infections.

The foundation established and helps support a nationwide network of some 125 medical centers, usually associated with large medical schools and teaching hospitals. The centers, which have the triple function of care, research, and teaching, have an annual patient load of 10,000 CF victims plus 16,000 more children who suffer from other lung-damaging conditions, such as bronchitis, asthma, and emphysema, which have also been part of the foundation's program for the past decade.

In accordance with its primary goal of conquering these diseases through research, the foundation with its 300 local chapters allocates about 36 percent of its $10.4 million annual expenditures for clinical grants, fellowships, and research activities and 15 percent for other medical programs. Another 25 percent goes for public and professional information and education and about 10 percent for patient and community services. Fund-raising expenses amount to about 14 percent of contributions from the public.

Until a cure for the disease itself comes along, a major emphasis of the foundation is on prevention through genetic counseling and research. There is hope that the next decade will bring a test for pregnant women that will establish the presence of CF in the fetus, as well as a test for detecting CF genes in the carriers. All that genetic counselors know now is that a CF birth can occur only when both parents carry the gene and, even so, there is only a one-in-four chance of such a birth occurring. This will take place only if the child receives a CF gene from each parent. On the basis of the law of averages, there are two chances in four that the child will receive the gene from only one parent; in these cases, the child will not have the disease but be a carrier. Finally, there is another one-in-four chance that the child will not receive any of the CF genes. However, since the averages seldom work out so neatly, as every dice player knows, some parents do wind up with two or three CF children in a row.

Meanwhile, parents of CF children hope that each year will bring some progress that will at least enable their children to live a little longer—until that cure finally comes along.

Mental Illness

Dominating the modern reception room of the Mental Health Association (MHA) in Arlington, Virginia, is a large bronze bell cast from the chains and shackles once used to bind mental patients. The bell, which also appears on all of the association's letterheads, publications, and campaign materials, is symbolic of the changes that have taken place in the care of the mentally ill since MHA was founded. The association dates its origin back to 1908 when the philosopher William James (who was also a physician) and the psychiatrist Adolph Meyer helped start a National Committee on Mental Hygiene after a popular book, *The Mind That Found Itself*, an autobiographical account by Clifford Beers of his confinement in a mental institution, stirred public sympathy. In 1950 the committee merged with two other organizations into the National Association for Mental Health, which in 1976 became the Mental Health Association, to form a united front to fight mental illness.

MHA's task is a formidable one for, as a President's Commission on Mental Health recently reported, about 32 million Americans or 15 percent of the population need some form of mental health care. An estimated 7 million actually seek professional help every year, and nearly 2 million are sick enough to be hospitalized, occupying on any given day one out of three of the nation's hospital beds. (Not too long ago, they occupied every other bed.) About 160,000 are incarcerated in state mental institutions, an improvement over the situation two decades ago when the population in such institutions averaged 570,000. The downward trend is attributable to a number of factors: the increasing belief that institutionalization is harmful to mental patients; the development of powerful tranquilizers like Thorazine, which make outpatient treatment more feasible; and the increased availability of outpatient care facilities, which today handle most of the people seeking treatment for mental illness. These facilities include not only the offices of psychiatrists, psychologists, and other specialists and public and private clinics of various kinds but also the some 650 largely federally funded community mental health centers that have sprung up across the country during the past 15 years. (Even with all this, only about one out of every seven persons afflicted with mental illness receives any kind of care at all.)

Yet this trend has not been without drastic consequences. For the fact is that many of the patients discharged from hospitals are ill-equipped to cope with the outside world; in fact, half of the patients discharged from state hospitals are readmitted, at least temporarily, within a year of their release. Because of the inadequacy of present facilities, others, put on drugs and left to waste away in communities ill-prepared to receive them, simply vanish into miniature snake pits—decaying welfare hotels and shabby rooming houses—that have mushroomed across the country as havens for the mentally ill.

The cost of mental illness to the nation is conservatively estimated to be $21 billion a year, a figure that includes lost wages and productivity, loss in purchasing power, and the cost of treatment and research. It does not include the estimated costs of $32 billion resulting from alcoholism and upwards of $10 billion due to drug abuse, both of which are closely linked to mental and emotional problems. To deal with these problems, the government now spends nearly $1 billion a year through its Alcohol, Drug Abuse, and Mental Health Administration; about half of this is for mental health.

Whether because of the stigma attached to mental illness or because of a lack of aggressive leadership, it seems unlikely that MHA can make much of a dent in a problem of this magnitude. Its revenues have always been small; in a recent year, its total income was a minuscule $21 million, of which only $14 million came from the public. Its expenditures, in its own words, are for activities to "support research, engage in social action and legislative activity to stimulate provision of adequate services for mentally ill persons in every community, provide services to patients and their families, and educate and inform the public and special groups about mental illness and the mentally ill."

Most of these activities are carried out by the association's 800 local chapters which, among other things, distribute to the public and schools such leaflets as "How to Deal With Your Tensions" and "How to Deal With Mental Problems," provide mental health information to TV, radio, and newspapers, conduct speakers' bureaus, and present films to clubs, organizations, and employee groups. Some chapters, working with local community agencies, have helped organize mental health centers, social and halfway clubs to help former patients readjust to society, suicide prevention centers, and rehabilitation programs.

In what may be the most unusual program offered by any health agency, chapters in North Dakota (a state with only about 20 psychiatrists), Wisconsin, Pennsylvania, and some other states sponsor courses that train bartenders, barbers, beauticians, and taxi drivers (the nation's unpaid psychiatrists) not only to lend an ear to garrulous, troubled customers but also to direct them to appropriate sources of help. Although I was inclined to smile when I first learned of this program, it has won praise from the American Psychiatric Association and the Department of Health, Education, and Welfare and the results, though spotty, have been gratifying. In Milwaukee, where the program has trained 75 bartenders, a depressed customer walked into a tavern and confessed he had just found out his wife was having an affair. The owner kept him talking until 2 A.M and the next morning the customer returned to thank her. "You kept me from killing my wife," he said. In Pittsburgh, an indoctrinated taxi driver prevented a suicide by driving a female fare, who was threatening to kill herself with a butcher knife, to a community health center.

MHA's national office maintains liaison with and conducts conferences for psychiatrists, psychologists, social workers, nurses, and other specialists, supports some scientific research, pushes for greater federal appropriations and presses for more community mental health centers; the 650 now in existence (out of a projected 1400 or 1500) can serve only 40 percent of the population.

How effective the association's activities have been is difficult to measure. "There wouldn't be one community mental health center today if not for the association," Mrs. Geridee Wheeler, a past president of the organization, told me. How true this is there is no easy way of knowing, although there can be no question that the MHA has played a useful "watchdog" role in getting the government to do more than it otherwise might in the cause of mental health. No doubt the association has also contributed to the improved care and treatment in state hospitals and other psychiatric facilities, the lessening of the stigma of mental illness, and the creation of a climate conducive to the other changes that have taken place in all the years since it was founded.

The outlook, however, is not sanguine in spite of this utterance by the President's Commission on Mental Health: "The time has come for mental health care to become part of a broader effort to deal with human needs." Formed with great fanfare, with Rosalynn Carter as its honorary chairman, the commission issued 14 recommendations for expanding mental health care services and learning more about the causes of mental illness. However, it suggested an increase of only about $150 million a year in spending for these purposes in federally funded *research*—the equivalent of less than $5 a year more per patient. No wonder that skeptics like Catholic University of America's Alvin L. Schorr feel that the commission's work seems fated to travel the road taken by an earlier commission about which the new commission tersely observed, "Many of its recommendations were acted upon."

Mental Retardation

My friends, Sid and Sally Stutz of San Diego, parents of a mongoloid boy, arranged for me to spend an evening with them and a mental retardate, who turned out to be a 26-year-old woman named Sonia Kozko.* To the casual observer, Sonia, a stocky, dark-haired, bubbly person, not at all unattractive, would not appear to be retarded. At dinner, she chatted pleasantly about herself and her family. Born in Philadelphia of Czech-Russian parentage, she had spent her early years in Guam, Okinawa, and Japan with her father, a Navy man, mother, and four sisters. Now, with her father based at the moment in Turkey, her mother living in Tennessee, and her sisters—all normal—in the Los Angeles area, she lives alone in San Diego. She talked about her job as a file clerk at the Arrow Center, a local sheltered workshop and recreational facility for retarded adults and, like most people, she complained of the difficulty of keeping on a tight budget. In her spare time, Sonia said, she loved to dance and watch television and she apparently understood enough of the news programs she watched and the simple newspaper stories she could read to talk fairly knowledgeably of the world around her. Her conversation was usually fluent, sometimes even sprinkled with humor, and she had a way of punctuating her enthusiasm with the expression, "Wow!" Her life included a steady boyfriend—a neighbor of hers at Eucalyptus Gardens, the name given to the unique, low-cost 28-unit housing project entirely occupied by retarded young people and operated by the Salvation Army with the cooperative efforts of a dozen of the area's social service and governmental agencies. Later, Sonia proudly showed us through her one-

*The name has been changed to protect the privacy of the individual.

bedroom apartment unit (rent: $31.50 a month). It was tastefully furnished and as neat as a pin. On a table in the living room was a stack of *Reader's Digest* magazines which, she said, provided some of her favorite reading matter.

Sonia is one of the estimated 6 million persons in the United States, nearly 3 percent of our population, who are classified as mentally retarded. About 125,000 of the babies born every year—one every five minutes—will be added to this group for reasons that are not entirely known, but could involve anything that hinders or interferes with the development of the brain before or during birth or in the early childhood years. Although more than 100 causes have been identified, these account for only 25 percent of the cases of mental retardation.* The condition, resulting in the failure of the brain to reach full normal development, limiting the ability of the victim to learn, and, in general, to cope with everyday living, is often wrongly confused with mental illness, which may occur at almost any age in previously normal people; however, mentally retarded persons can also be mentally ill and vice versa.

Another popular misconception is that very little can be done for the retarded, who are often regarded as perpetual children—helpless and hopeless—who should be tucked away somewhere and forgotten. As a matter of fact, about 160,000 are confined to public institutions—incidentally, at considerable expense to the taxpayer: The cost of such lifetime institutional care for a person from age six can range from $300,000 to $800,000. Yet the great majority of retardates are considered to be educable.** Experts believe that as many as 75 to 85 percent are capable, like Sonia Kozko, of holding a job, becoming self-supporting and living on their own with proper education and training.

Some retardates are capable of discussing fairly complex ideas and many, I was surprised to learn, are even quite literate. Sonia is a member of the California Youth Council (CYC), a group made up entirely of retarded people, who meet periodically to discuss their mutual problems, often in carefully planned workshops, as well as means of better communicating their needs to society as a

---

*Among the specific identified causes are German measles (rubella) in the mother during the first three months of pregnancy; childhood diseases like meningitis, whooping cough, and chicken pox; extraordinary prolonged labor, hemorrhages, or other birth conditions that may injure the infant brain; toxoplasmosis; Rh-factor incompatibility between mother and infant; lead poisoning in the young child; and chromosomal abnormalities. Among the most common and best known of the latter is Down's syndrome (mongoloidism) which occurs in one out of every 2500 babies born to mothers below the age of 40 but in one out of every 40 born to mothers over 40. Mental retardation is also linked to poverty; three-fourths of the nation's mentally retarded are to be found in impoverished rural and urban areas. The probable reason is the lack of prenatal care among poor women who are also less likely to have adequate food than the more affluent.

**Although people with an I.Q. in the region of 70 or below are classified as retarded (an I.Q. of 100 is regarded as average), there is wide variation in their degree of retardation, which is usually divided into four levels. About 89 percent are "mild" (or "educable") cases, with I.Q.s in the 53–72 range and frequently scarcely distinguishable from the "dull normal" members of our population; although limited in their potentials for academic achievement, most can be made self-sufficient through special education techniques. About 6 percent are labeled "moderate," with I.Q.s between 36 and 52 (the upper limit is equivalent to the intelligence of the average normal six-year-old); many in this category can learn to take care of their personal needs, travel in their neighborhood, and perform useful tasks at home or in a sheltered working situation. The remaining 5 percent are in the still lower "severe" (20 to 35) and "profound" (below 20) categories; the former rarely achieve even limited economic usefulness but can learn self-care, while the latter generally require constant care. However, there are only about 90,000 in this lowest range.

whole. Several years ago, at an annual convention of the California Association for the Retarded (CAR), whose membership consists largely of parents and friends of the retarded, CYC delegates passed out mimeographed sheets of resolutions which they themselves had drafted without any outside help whatever! So that you can be as amazed as I was, I am setting down the resolutions verbatim:

The CYC delegates composed of us exceptional adults have met today and the following are proposals by us that we urge CAR to consider when planning for the future.

1. We urge that CAR and all of its members who call us exceptional consider changing the name of CAR to the California Association for Exceptional People.

2. We propose that CAR devise a ways and means committee to promote funding for the CYC group so we can "speak out."

3. We propose that CYC join CAR in preparing legislation designed to benefit all exceptional people.

4. We propose that CYC and CAR join together and we have a convention as a body of oneness.

5. We propose that CAR consider these problems we have and help to seek solutions:

    a. Helping exceptional people to get together after work for leisure activities;

    b. Helping us exceptional people integrate with normal people so we can speak out.

6. We propose that the CAR Residential Care Committee investigate the potential of expanding the concept of the San Diego Community Living Project statewide.

7. We propose that the CAR and CYC work together in seeking more productive programs for exceptional people both in sheltered and non-sheltered settings.

8. We propose to CAR to look into ways to promote public transportation.

9. We propose that exceptional people like ourselves be involved with the board of directors of CAR and its local units.

The California Association for the Retarded is one of some 1800 state and local units affiliated with the National Association for Retarded Citizens (NARC). Organized in 1950 as the National Association of Parents and Friends of Mentally Retarded Children, a name that still reflects the character of most of its membership of 250,000, it is the only major national organization devoted to promoting the welfare of the retarded, whose needs are considerable even after NARC's nearly three decades of effort. Despite changing concepts of educating retarded children and the growing belief that as many as 50 percent might be reclassified as "normal" with the benefit of *early* training, programs for retarded babies, from birth to age three, are relatively rare, numbering less than 100 across the country. NARC also estimates that only half of the nation's retarded youngsters of school age receive any educational services and that some states educate fewer than 15 percent of their retarded children, even though recent state and federal court decisions have ruled that the retarded have the right to be educated in public schools. Many of the institutions in which the retarded are confined are inadequate and obsolete; a President's Committee on Mental Retardation once reported the average age of the buildings to be 44 years, with some over 100 years old.

There can be no question that this situation would be even more grim if not for NARC, which, however, can claim as its perhaps most outstanding accomplishment of recent years its success in getting jobs for the retarded. Through its federally funded job training project, NARC has trained and placed 20,000 retarded in jobs during the past decade, and placements are now running at the rate of 4000 a year. Most of the jobs are at minimum wages and menial—dishwashers, janitors, maids, and cafeteria workers are among the most commonly filled categories. But others call for more skilled, if repetitive, tasks. American Motors Corp. has more than 100 retarded employees on its regular work force earning $6.25 an hour assembling auto parts; and other companies have retarded workers in jobs ranging from baker and key punch operator to welder, telephone operator, and machine repairman. In addition, half of the 450,000 handicapped working in the 3000 sheltered workshops around the country are retarded; they do such work as assembling ball point pens, boxing perfume, and stuffing envelopes.

Since retardation costs the nation at least $5 billion a year in just lost productivity, the $2 billion a year now spent by the federal government on mental retardation programs, including income maintenance, seems relatively small, although it dwarfs the $135 million revenues of NARC and its affiliates. (These revenues, incidentally, make NARC the largest of the voluntary health agencies in terms of total income.) Of these revenues, less than 15 percent comes from donations from the public. Over 50 percent is from government grants and fees, with most of the remainder received from service fees charged at NARC's facilities for the retarded and from sales to the public of sheltered workshop products, books, manuals, and other educational materials. The great bulk of NARC's expenditures goes to obtain or support community services ranging from special classes and nursery groups to sheltered workshops and recreational facilities like those combined in Sonia Kozko's Arrow Center.

Much more could be done for the retarded. Meanwhile, it is a commentary on our sense of values to note that no more than 4 percent of the nation's 1 million to 2 million gifted children are fully getting the special educational services they require and that only $6.5 million in federal money is being spent annually on the gifted (who, ironically, are under the wing of the Bureau of Education for the Handicapped), while $600 million is allotted for the education of the truly handicapped and $2 billion for the education of the economically disadvantaged.

What the Planned Parenthood People Are Up To

At Planned Parenthood's office in Chicago's Loop, Phyllis Gordon, a volunteer counselor, is talking to a 16-year-old pregnant girl who has come in for advice. With the girl (I will call her Millie) is her 20-year-old married sister. The family drama unfolds. The sister explains that she, too, had been pregnant before her marriage. "When my mother learned about it, she hit the roof. But it was easier because I was 18 at the time, older than Millie is now; and besides I was planning to get married soon anyway. Millie isn't and so the news would kill our mother.''

Millie, a young Liv Ullmann type, says she has definitely decided on an abortion but that money is the big hang-up since she, of course, doesn't want to ask her mother for it. The sister says that her husband can probably borrow the money from his boss. Millie says that her boyfriend is also working at a job after school to help out. Since Millie has indicated that she is about four and one-half months pregnant, Mrs. Gordon explains the saline procedure, the most generally used type for late abortions (those done in the third through sixth month). She also says it would be faster and cheaper to have it done in New York, even after allowing for the air fare. Mrs. Gordon then outlines the procedure for having a New York abortion. Basically, Millie has to make her own appointment with the hospital there, as well as her own airline reservations. Mrs. Gordon, of course, tells her exactly whom to call for an appointment, and also suggests that she take the early 8 A.M. flight so that she can arrive at La Guardia Airport before noon. A hostess in a pink smock will meet her there and escort her to a Planned Parenthood shuttle bus that will take her directly to the hospital.*

Toward the end of the interview session, however, a problem comes to light. Women under 18 must usually have parental consent for a New York abortion.** Millie and her sister ponder this very briefly and finally decide that they will have to tell their mother after all. It seems that this might even solve the financial problem for Mrs. Gordon mentions that the mother's health insurance might cover the cost of the abortion.

For Phyllis Gordon, a chic, petite woman in her late forties with a degree in sociology, this was fairly typical of the interviews she conducts during the 12 hours or so a week she averages as a Planned Parenthood volunteer. Among the more unusual situations she recalls is that of a woman who had gotten pregnant while her husband was in jail, and wanted an abortion when she learned he was about to be released. Then there was the mother who wanted advice when she learned that her ex-husband had made her daughter pregnant.

Abortion advice is only one of the many services offered by the Planned Parenthood Federation of America today through its family of 190 affiliates with more than 700 clinics across the country, which collectively make up the nation's largest private network dealing with the many aspects—and often, consequences—of copulation. At one location or another, more than 1 million Americans a year now also avail themselves of Planned Parenthood's contraceptive services, physical examinations, and medical tests (for pregnancy, venereal disease, blood pressure, breast and uterine cancer, and sickle cell and other anemias), problem pregnancy counseling, sex education, vasectomies, and fertility tests. Because unwanted teen-age pregnancies have reached what Planned Parenthood called the "epidemic" stage—more than 1 million adolescent girls (one in every ten) now get pregnant and 600,000 of them give birth every

---

*Since this interview took place, changing conditions have made it possible for Chicago Planned Parenthood to refer most of its pregnancy cases to such nearby states as Indiana, Michigan and Wisconsin instead of New York. Consequently, the Planned Parenthood shuttle bus is no longer used in New York.

**Although New York law does not require parental consent, some local clinics and most hospitals won't give abortions to minors, particularly those under 16, unless they've gotten parental consent.

year—more than a score of affiliates have set up special teen clinics where boys and girls can participate in rap sessions and receive individual counseling and medical care, including contraceptives. Paradoxically, although Planned Parenthood has built its reputation largely on preventing unwanted pregnancies, it is also the nation's leading promoter of medical treatment for infertility, a condition found in about 15 percent of our married couples.

All this is in accordance with the federation's credo that "each new infant be a wanted child born by choice and not by chance to responsible parents." Extending this mandate geographically, the federation has also made it its goal to alert the American people to the gravity of the world population crisis and to the need for expanded public and private programs to cope with it.

All this has also not been without its share of controversy both at home and abroad. "Our major problem around the world has been the unwillingness of the governments of the less developed countries to recognize that there is a crisis and to convince them that our program isn't a plot by the developed countries to impose 'population control' on them," a federation official told me. Well known, too, is the fact that Planned Parenthood has long been at odds with the Roman Catholic Church, many of whose members play key roles in the militant Right to Life movement which, in its unwavering opposition to abortion, has been waging a relentless war to revoke the Supreme Court's famous 1973 decision affirming every woman's right to have an abortion.

But Planned Parenthood has known controversy from its very beginnings, which date from the time a spirited young public health nurse, Margaret Sanger, defied the laws of her day to open the nation's first birth control clinic in Brooklyn in 1916, an action for which she was arrested and served 30 days in jail. The same year she founded the National Birth Control League which, after a series of name changes and mergers, became the Planned Parenthood Federation of America (PPFA) in 1942. She was the organization's first president and later its honorary chairwoman until her death in 1966. In 1961 PPFA merged with the World Population Emergency Campaign, the combined organization using the name Planned Parenthood-World Population, although its official corporate title continues to be Planned Parenthood Federation of America.

Commenting on the changes that have taken place in the field over the years, one of the doyennes of the movement, Edna McKinnon, an octogenarian who headed Planned Parenthood's Chicago affiliate for 12 years in the 1940s and 1950s, recalls the time when the words "birth control," "pregnancy," and especially "abortion" couldn't even be whispered on a radio program.

A tiny woman with a birdlike face, she explained that at first the greatest obstacles to the movement were ignorance, apathy, and the Roman Catholic Church. In some countries, she explained, it was "imperative" to convince leaders that she was not pushing population control but rather was working for the improved health of mothers and children. (Some blacks in this country have criticized the movement on the same grounds.) It is mainly apathy now, she said, with the greatest "foe" being the lack of an adequate government-sponsored program.

Federal spending for family planning services and research into population control now amounts to only about $400 million a year, and funding from state and local governments comes to about $35 million more. From an economic point of view, these penurious allotments make little sense for it has been shown that federally supported family planning programs actually yield more in short-term savings to the public treasury than they cost simply by preventing unwanted births. For every dollar spent on such programs, a Planned Parenthood study once showed, the government could save between $1.80 and $2.50 in the following year alone. Four-fifths of the estimated savings, the study showed, would result from avoiding the costs of medical care in pregnancy. However, the study understated by far the potential savings in government expenditures. The Department of Health, Education, and Welfare itself estimated the cost of an abortion in the first three months of pregnancy to be $150, compared to the $2200 first-year cost of supporting an unwanted child. If we take the child beyond the first year to the brink of adulthood and add the cost to the government of lost earnings to women who have to give up their jobs during pregnancy and the early child-rearing period *plus* the government assistance needed for the families who might have to go on welfare because of an unwanted birth, the total costs become astronomical!* Of the $9.4 billion disbursed to welfare families in 1975, about half went to households with women who had their first child while in their teens. Yet 40 percent of low-income women still cannot obtain medically supervised birth control services, with unwanted children the inevitable result.

In view of all this, how can one account for the apparent reluctance of the government to do more to prevent unwanted births? Bureaucratic inertia may be one reason, the Catholic influence another. A Planned Parenthood official also wryly offered this reason: "The government would be more likely to act if men, who make up the bulk of our legislators, did the child bearing."

Meanwhile, Planned Parenthood continues to face up to the challenges that confront it in its seventh decade with annual revenues now totaling $105 million. Of this total, only about $26 million comes from public contributions, with $35 million coming from clinic fees and sales (though no one is turned away because of the inability to pay), and $38 million from government grants, mostly to help support the clinics and to train nurses and other aides. About 70 percent of expenditures go to support the federation's medical, educational, and other community programs here and overseas. Fund-raising expenses are about 10 percent of contributions from the public and 2.6 percent of total income.

Venereal Disease

In much the same way that Planned Parenthood is really a genteel synonym for sex, the 67-year-old American Social Health Association's euphemistic name primly blankets its primary concern with such social evils as commercialized prostitution and, particularly, venereal disease. To help stamp out the latter, it has labored valiantly for most of its life, dispensing information about the signs, symptoms, and preventive means needed to eradicate this age-old scourge, enlisting in its crusade women's clubs, parent-teacher groups, churches, schools, and an array of other community organizations and government agencies. All seemingly to no avail for year after year new cases of gonorrhea and syphilis reach record highs and are now believed to total 3 million annually—roughly one

*Admittedly, this is an oversimplification that may lead to an unwarranted conclusion. For who knows how many of the unwanted births could result in future productive, tax-paying members of society, perhaps even geniuses?

every ten seconds. They even occur among the best of people, according to those public service VD messages quoted later in Chapter 18.

Lack of money, of course, is one of the biggest obstacles to combating the VD epidemic. The American Social Health Association has to do what it does—public education, research, and the organization of citizen action programs—on an income of little more than half a million dollars a year and, considering the nature of its cause, it is unlikely to raise much more. As our preeminent sex scholar, Dr. David Reuben, once asked: "Can you imagine a little girl ringing the doorbell imploring you to give a dime to fight syphilis? What aspiring beauty queen looks forward to being crowned Miss Gonorrhea? Would anyone buy a couple of tickets to the Annual Venereal Disease Ball? Who would respond to a television appeal picturing a sweating, red-faced truck driver as a victim of VD?"

Nor is our government particularly responsive. The federal Venereal Disease Control Division of the National Center for Disease Control now has only $32 million a year to battle the disease, and our state agencies spend perhaps $60 or $70 million a year more. Yet U.S. taxpayers lay out over $60 million a year to support the thousands of syphilitics in our mental hospitals and a total of $750 million to $1 billion annually to pay for all of the consequences of VD.

Miscellaneous Maladies

As already suggested, there are also countless other organizations, each with varying claims to uniqueness, based on either the vaunted prevalence of the ailment of its concern or, going to the other extreme, its exotic nature. But most have as their common denominator the fact that they are relatively small, reflecting their limited public interest, which of course does not necessarily diminish their importance, if only to their coterie of supporters.

For example, organizations like the Deafness Research Foundation and the American Speech and Hearing Association can muster statistics to show that the most widespread malady in the United States today is loss of hearing, afflicting more than 14.5 million Americans. But, rightly or wrongly, few of the rest of us are likely to be as moved by this as we are by blindness, which is the subject of our next chapter. Although 35 million or more Americans—one in six—suffer from one or more major allergies, the Asthma and Allergy Foundation of America receives only about $200,000 in contributions. Considering the fact that about 10 million Americans are problem drinkers, the National Council on Alcoholism deserves at least a passing mention, although its annual contributions amount to less than $3 million.

Because of the ubiquitousness of its mail appeals and the prominence of its founder, entertainer Danny Thomas, also deserving some comment is American Lebanese Syrian Associated Charities (ALSAC), organized in 1957 to raise funds for St. Jude Research Hospital in Memphis, which conducts research and provides care to children suffering from leukemia and other catastrophic diseases. No one can question the noble purpose of this undertaking for which ALSAC raised about $14 million in donations in 1977. However, the National Information Bureau questions the exaggerated nature and high cost of ALSAC's appeals, which often include "sweepstakes" tickets. Fund raising and overhead costs in 1977 amounted to 42 percent of contributions and, in one state, Washington, the cost of solicitations was 48 percent of donations. Moreover, a recent appeal stated that the donations were needed to pay for "massive research plus free care to 3370 stricken children" treated by the hospital during the course of a year. No mention was made of the fact that St. Jude received $4.6 million in research grants, apparently primarily from the government, and health insurance payments of $1.8 million for its patients in 1977. Only 1100 of the annual caseload of 3370 are actually treated on an inpatient basis; this averages out to 15 or 16 patients a day—far below the hospital's 48-bed capacity. This 36 percent occupancy rate, one of the lowest in the entire country, also contributes to the fact that the charity's operating costs are much higher than they should be.

In the field of leukemia, another relatively large organization is the Leukemia Society of America, with a recent annual income of nearly $10 million (virtually all from contributions) which, after fund-raising and overhead expenses (about 35 percent), is allocated largely in almost equal amounts to research, patient aid, and education. Because the war against leukemia is also being waged by the American Cancer Society, some feel that the two organizations should merge. Concerned with other types of blood diseases are the National Hemophilia Foundation and Cooley's Anemia Blood and Research Foundation, the latter involved with a type of anemia prevalent in children of Mediterranean origin.

There is also a National Society for Autistic Children, a National Sudden Infant Death Syndrome Foundation, an American Trauma Society, an American Leprosy Foundation, and a group called Anorexia Nervosa and Associated Disorders. There is even something called the Human Lactation Center which is dedicated to worldwide education and research—on breastfeeding!

Chapter 12

The Battle of the Blind

"Blind people are normal," the blind man told me, stoutly insisting that blindness per se is not a handicap. "Blindness is only a characteristic—a normal characteristic, of no more importance than hundreds of others with which each of us must deal."

The proponent of this view is Kenneth L. Jernigan, president of the National Federation of the Blind (NFB), an organization of blind people dedicated to improving their social and economic well-being. I was having breakfast with him several years ago at his home in Des Moines where the NFB was then headquartered. At the time, Jernigan was also director of the Iowa Commission for the Blind, a state agency responsible for providing rehabilitation and other services to the approximately 6000 blind Iowans. His sighted wife Anna poured coffee as Jernigan, using a small piece of bread in his left hand, pushed some of the scrambled eggs on his plate onto the fork in his right hand.

"This is not to deny that blindness is a limitation," Jernigan went on. A lean, nattily dressed man of fifty or so, with angular features, he spoke in a somewhat oratorical manner, as if addressing a large audience. "But *every* characteristic— those we regard as strengths as well as those we regard as weaknesses—is a limitation. Poverty, ignorance, and old age are among the most obvious examples of limitations. But take the very opposite of old age—youth. This would be a limitation for certain jobs. Or let us take another unlikely handicap—not that of ignorance but its exact opposite. Can it be said that *education* is ever a handicap? The answer is definitely yes. I would not hire Albert Einstein under any circumstances for a job in my agency if he were today alive and available. He would be bored to madness by the routine of most of our jobs—his intelligence would be a severe limitation."

"But consider what *you* might have done if you had been sighted and still had all the other qualities you now possess," I then said.

"Why single out my lack of sight?" he answered. "If we are going down that track, why not ask me what I might have done if I had been born with Rockefeller's money, the brains of Einstein, and the physique of the young Joe Louis?"

Jernigan, who has been blind from birth, has an obsession about blind people being considered anything but normal. When he told me he had an older brother, I caught myself asking, "And is he . . . ?"

"You were going to say, 'normal,' weren't you?" said Jernigan, laughing wryly. "You know damn well you were going to say 'normal.' This proves that you, like most other sighted people, have quite a bit to learn."

Nor does he consider it at all a compliment to be told that he does things so

well that one is apt to forget that he is blind. Nonetheless, his achievements have
been remarkable. A native of Tennessee, upon graduation from high school he
ran a furniture shop, selling tables, lamps, smoke stands, and other items that he
himself had designed and made. "I sawed and planed, drilled and measured,
fitted and sanded, and did every single operation except the final finish work, the
staining, and varnishing, although I could have done that, too." Then after
earning a bachelor's degree in social science at Tennessee Technological University and a master's in English from Peabody College in Nashville, he taught
English for four years and sold insurance on the side. This was followed by a
five-year stint with a state agency for the blind in California. In 1958 he became
director of the Iowa Commission for the Blind, a post which paid him $29,000 a
year when he suddenly relinquished it in April, 1978, in the midst of a controversy over his activities at the commission, which he allegedly ran with an
iron hand, seldom consulting his legal superiors, the commissioners, on major
decisions. An ad hoc committee appointed by the governor, while conceding that
the commission under Jernigan's direction had grown from a small underfunded,
slipshod agency to one of the best of its kind in the nation, found some improprieties and made 25 recommendations for corrective action.

Most of the controversy, however, which was fanned by a year-long series of
almost daily articles in the Des Moines *Register*, centered on the possible conflicts of interest between Jernigan's dual role as a director of a public agency for
the blind and as an official of various private organizations and enterprises
concerned with the blind. For example, Jernigan was an organizer and president
of the now-defunct National Eye Care Association, a profit-making company
which, operating through participating optometrists, sold insurance against total
accidental blindness and provided other eye-care services.* During much of his
twenty-year tenure with the Iowa Commission, he was also president of Fedco, a
profit-making fund-raising arm of the National Federation of the Blind, which he
first joined in 1952 and has served as president (an unsalaried post) from 1968 to
the present, except for one year starting July, 1977, when he resigned, citing
health reasons. However, others suggest as more likely reasons the financial
problems of the federation, as well as the problems caused him by the *Register*
articles, which were no doubt instrumental in the departure of both Jernigan and
the federation from Iowa in 1978 for the more hospitable home base of
Baltimore.

Aside from his recent difficulties, Jernigan, one of the most controversial
figures in the world of charity, regards himself as a much misunderstood person.
He also regards all of the blind as a much misunderstood, much mistreated
minority, one in about the same plight as the blacks of a generation ago, both
groups being the victims of stereotypes that impose arbitrary limits on the aspirations of their members. "The black was seen as a shuffling, bowing Uncle Tom
or a shiftless Stepin Fetchit who, when he worked, was usually a laborer, porter,
janitor, or servant," said Jernigan. "Similarly, the blind person has been depicted as a crippled and helpless Tiny Tim fit for employment only as a chair
caner, broom maker, basket weaver, or piano tuner."

---

*The business, which ceased operation in late 1978 after failing to win a hoped-for endorsement
from the American Optometric Association, was a potentially lucrative venture because total accidental blindness is extremely rare, afflicting less than one out of every million persons per year.

Drawing on another analogy, Jernigan is also fond of saying that his federation, with its claimed membership of 50,000, is to the blind what the NAACP is to the blacks, although, as a leader, he himself fits more the mold of a Malcolm X than of a Roy Wilkins. Tough, tireless, egotistic, and articulate, he is a supremely confident person, with a constant sense of outrage that infects his followers. His militant tirades, rattled off in a messianic, mesmeric manner (he can read a braille text as fast as most people can read print) bear such titles as ''To Man the Barricades,'' ''Blindness—The Triple Revolution,'' ''Blindness—Milestones and Millstones,'' and ''Blindness—Discrimination, Hostility, and Progress.'' Laced with a caustic wit and humor and peppered with quotations from Abraham Lincoln and Will Rogers to Shakespeare, Sophocles, and the Scriptures, they inveigh against the discrimination the blind encounter in travel, housing, insurance, and, particularly, in job opportunities.

For instance, something that gets Jernigan's dander up is a 1938 federal law that allows the blind (and other handicapped) working in so-called sheltered workshops to be paid as little as one-fourth the statutory minimum wage. (By contrast, administrators of the workshops often receive salaries in the $50,000 range, plus luxury cars and other substantial benefits.) So strongly does Jernigan feel that the blind should be treated like everybody else that he has even opposed legislation that would enable a blind person to travel by air together with a sighted guide for only a single fare.

He is also irate about some of the things blind people have to put up with when traveling. At an NFB convention in New York several years ago, he recalled that one of the delegates could not get a drink in a bar because he was blind. ''To refuse to serve him was illegal, of course, because the city's law says that you can't serve liquor only to someone who is drunk,'' Jernigan said angrily. ''But the bartender's rationale was that someone there had to be responsible for the blind person.'' In some states, he also pointed out, blind people still cannot stay alone in hotels. ''The excuse here is that a blind person might not be able to get out in case of a fire. At one such hotel, I told the manager that I could get out better in the dark than most of the sighted guests.''

What the blind are capable of doing may seem incredible to most people who find it difficult enough coping with two eyes and ten fingers. There are blind lawyers, teachers, engineers, machinists, tool-and-die makers, lathe operators, farmers, switchboard operators, income tax consultants, journalists, film splicers—the list is endless. A list once published of 7000 different jobs held by blind men and women also included the following occupations: social worker, insurance agent, private detective, musician, mathematician, florist, dictaphone typist, piano tuner, clergyman, college student, computer programmer, salesman, psychologist, secretary, and masseur. Many of the tapes of the interviews used in the research for this book were transcribed by a blind woman, Marcia Stein; indeed, her typewritten transcripts were far more accurate than those of most of the sighted transcribers I also used.

Mrs. Stein, a big, apple-cheeked, roly-poly woman around 50, is a remarkable person. Born blind (as was also a brother who earned a Ph.D. in mathematics and now teaches at the University of Detroit), she somehow managed to hold down a full-time job as a typist with various New York City government agencies and raise two children, both sighted, with some help from her sighted parents. (Her husband is also blind.) Yet she herself mixed the baby formulas, cooked (using a braille cookbook), shopped, washed dishes, and cleaned the house—chores she still performs today. She is one of the jolliest persons I know. Getting around with a guide dog, she sings regularly with a chorus, is a member of an acting group, bowls, plays bingo (with her own braille board), and poker and rummy (with a braille deck of cards). When she visits me, she often carries a little portable TV set for blind people; it is, of course, screenless, receiving only the audio portion of telecasts as well as AM and FM radio stations.

Like most productive blind people, she is resentful of blind beggars. "I shudder and cringe every time I pass one; it takes all my willpower not to punch him in the nose," she laughs. "If they wanted to, they could get work. It's a very demeaning thing for me as a blind person myself who has made my way in the world and gotten a job and really tried to make a life for myself with family and children to know that people associate me with them."

She also resents the blind having what she calls second-class citizenship. "Here's a case in point. A couple of weeks ago, I got a letter to serve on a jury. Now because of the fact that I'm blind, I'm unable to serve on a jury. And I think this is really wrong because although there may be cases like murder where you have to see track marks and ballistic studies and things like that, there are many civil cases which don't require any sight whatever. Just a good head and the ability to listen. That's why I joined the National Federation of the Blind, and I think Jernigan's doing a good job to make blind people independent and end the discrimination against them."

To impress me with the caliber and capabilities of the blind, Jernigan arranged for me to meet about one hundred of them at a reception he gave for me in Des Moines. It was a weird experience finding myself the only sighted person in a roomful of blind people. In turn I was introduced to a lawyer, a nutritionist, an engineer, a high school math teacher, a college student, and a data processing equipment designer.

All agreed that far more difficult than learning or working at their jobs were the barriers they faced in *getting* their jobs. Attitudes, they said, that held the blind to be helpless, completely dependent persons must be constantly dealt with. The teacher cited as the most discouraging aspect of her blindness the frequent treatment of her as a nonperson. "A real put-down is to have a waitress turn to a sighted companion to ask for my order. Now, I may not be able to read the menu but I'm capable of making a decision. And I'm not deaf and dumb."

Another mentioned his recent difficulty in buying a train ticket to Chicago. "Now I'd ridden that train probably 100 times but this time they wouldn't sell me a ticket and insisted I must travel with a companion. They wouldn't tell me exactly why. Maybe they thought I couldn't go to the bathroom alone."

To lighten the mood, the student cracked, "Every date I have is a blind date and I check them all out by the braille system. That's why I may forget a voice but never a body."

"We do not hear, smell, nor feel any better than you do," said the engineer, dispelling one of the common myths about the blind. "There is no mysterious sixth sense that the blind develop. But when the sense of sight is lost, we gradually learn to make sharper use of the other senses."

Then some of the guests, after fingering their braille watches, began to leave, most guiding their way out with the use of canes.

Back in his office, Jernigan had some harsh words for many of the government and private agencies established to assist the blind. "More often than not, their policies and programs serve as stumbling blocks to keep us down and out," he said. "Far from advancing the welfare and well-being of the blind, they set our cause back and do us harm." For such views and because of his generally abrasive manner, he is regarded as a maverick in the field of the blind.

One of his bêtes noires is the American Foundation for the Blind (AFB), long identified with Helen Keller, which Jernigan regards as an establishment organization comparable to General Motors in contrast to his own National Federation of the Blind which he also sees as the equivalent of the United Auto Workers. He takes pains, too, to point out the subtle significance of the "of" and the "for" in the names of the two organizations, noting that his group is made up largely of blind people, whereas most of the AFB's hierarchy, staffers, and supporters are sighted.

While conceding that the AFB does provide some useful services, Jernigan is incensed by what he feels to be its generally patronizing attitude toward the blind, an attitude that, in his view, perpetuates the popular notion of the blind as inferiors. As an example, he likes to cite a 240-page AFB publication entitled *A Step-by-Step Guide to Personal Management for Blind Persons* which offers by-the-numbers instructions in such everyday rituals as how to bathe, dress, wash, diaper a baby, cook, set a table, dial a telephone, light a cigarette, shake hands, even applaud.

"The first step listed in the 16-step procedure in the bathing exercise," says Jernigan—who now pauses briefly for dramatic effect—"is 'Disrobe'! Now, let us get the significance of this bit of instruction," he explodes. "What does it tell us about the intelligence—the *presumed* intelligence—of the blind person? It tells us that he doesn't have the sense to take off his clothes before he takes a bath. He is presumed to be either a mental case or a recent immigrant from the jungle who has never taken a bath before."

Jernigan is perturbed that the blind do not have a greater voice on the policy-making boards of the AFB and the National Accreditation Council for Agencies Serving the Blind and Visually Handicapped (NAC), another organization with which he has been feuding for years. He served two turbulent terms on the NAC board before resigning in a huff in the early 1970s to protest the lack of influence he felt the blind, and NFB representatives in particular, had in deciding which agencies serving the blind should be accredited.

Although Jernigan says that he doesn't "try to look for an enemy under every bed," he makes no secret of his feeling that there is a gigantic conspiracy on the part of the other blind organizations against him. In fact, an unsigned article in the May, 1978, *Braille Monitor,* the NFB house organ, charged that NAC and the AFB had conspired to destroy the NFB and its president, using the Des Moines *Register* as the "vehicle" for the assault. Going even further, the National Eye Care Association (NECA), in 1977 and 1978, filed two $10 million damage suits, one each against NAC and the AFB, alleging a conspiracy on the part of the organizations to harm the company's business. (Though Jernigan recently claimed he was then no longer associated with NECA, in which he had invested $18,000, he gave sworn depositions in the law suits.)

"Our tax status was once questioned by some enemies who sicced the Internal Revenue Service people on us," he also confided, while wondering out loud if I hadn't been sent by the AFB and NAC to spy on him. He even went so far as to say, very dramatically, "There are people in this country who would be glad to assassinate me."

It is therefore easy to believe the sworn allegations of former employees of the Iowa Commission for the Blind that Jernigan, during his tenure there, assembled an arsenal of automatic rifles and ammunition and fortified the commission headquarters by bricking up its main floor windows and installing bulletproof doors—all this, ostensibly as a self-defense measure against possible urban riots and antiwar demonstrations. One employee also said that he had instructed the blind Jernigan—who denied all the allegations—in shooting techniques and built a silencer for a small handgun Jernigan is said to have kept in his desk drawer.

In no other field of charity is there such a profusion and confusion of agencies—and such competition among them—as in those serving the blind. NAC accredits no less than 75 agencies and the National Information Bureau finds at least 16 large enough to merit its attention.* According to NAC, there are over 400 separate organizations and agencies—national, state, and local—assisting the blind in one way or another. Virtually all, however, deal with specialized constituencies among the blind or with specialized problems within the field. Nine agencies alone supply guide dogs for the blind. At least 28 agencies publish, sell, or provide without charge books, magazines, and educational materials in braille, large print, records and tapes—many of them catering to special interests; there are, for example, a Christian Record Braille Foundation, a Jewish Braille Institute, a John Milton Society for the Blind, a Xavier (Catholic) Society for the Blind, and even a Louis Braille Foundation for Blind Musicians which, in addition to transcribing music into braille, supports paid engagements for qualified blind musicians. There are, of course, countless schools, rehabilitation centers, workshops, and homes for the blind; and there is at least one national agency that sends blind children to camp (and allows you to charge your donation to credit cards). Other agencies have been set up to supply corneas for transplants (there are some 60 eye banks in the country), to supply services to the blind, to fight specific diseases like retinitis pigmentosa (an inherited disease said to affect nearly 100,000 people), and to conduct research into the prevention and cure of all eye diseases.

Because of the fragmented nature of the field and the frequently bitter competition for contributions, often for overlapping activities, none of the blind agencies are really large when compared to others in the health field. The three biggest and best-known groups concerned solely with visual impairments or eye disease—the National Society to Prevent Blindness, Research to Prevent Blindness, and the National Council to Combat Blindness (whose fund-raising arm is called Fight for Sight)—have a combined annual income of about $6 million, or not much more than that now raised every year by the one agency concerned with

*However, only one recently met all NIB standards—Recording for the Blind.

hemophilia, a far less prevalent affliction. Within the blind field itself, there is also a certain anomaly in the fact that the specialized Seeing Eye organization, oldest and second largest of the nine guide dog agencies, has an annual income that is about the same (recently around $4 million) as that of the National Society to Prevent Blindness, dedicated to eliminating the causes that lead to the need for the dogs.

From the National Society to Prevent Blindness, which was founded in 1908 (to combat ophthalmia neonatorum or gonorrheal blindness in the newborn), we learn that 1.7 million Americans have "severe visual impairments," ranging from total blindness to the inability to read ordinary newspaper print even with strong glasses. However, only about 500,000, or roughly one in 400 of the population, are classified as "legally blind" (and therefore eligible for Social Security and other benefits and services). A legally blind person is one with a visual acuity of 20/200 or less in the better eye with the best correcting lenses—that is, one who can see no more at a distance of 20 feet than a person with normal sight can see at 200 feet—or one whose field of vision is limited to an angle of 20 degrees or less, or a field comparable to that obtained by looking through a drinking straw. About half of the legally blind are 65 or over; another 10 percent are under 20. A substantial number of the legally blind, however, can read print in large-size type or with a low vision aid, or even watch TV; perhaps fewer than 40 percent, or not more than 200,000 persons, are totally blind or have no useful vision.

To tend to the varied needs of the blind and visually handicapped, there is no central national broad-spectrum organization comparable to, say, the American Cancer Society or American Heart Association. The organization that comes closest to assuming such a broad national leadership role is the American Foundation for the Blind, with a recent income of about $8.5 million; slightly less than half of this is derived from contributions and bequests, and most of the rest from the sale of "talking books" (recorded versions of books and magazines) to the Library of Congress and other organizations and the sale of about 400 special sensory aids and appliances to the blind. The latter, which though sold at cost are felt to be overpriced by some blind, include such items as braille watches, clocks, and thermometers; syringes that allow a blind diabetic to administer his own insulin; all sorts of kitchen equipment; an electronic carpenter's level; an audible directional compass for blind scouts; braille playing cards and brailled versions of such games as Scrabble, bingo, and Chinese checkers; even basketballs and soccer balls that emit beeping sounds.

Founded in 1921, the AFB does not otherwise provide any services directly to the blind. It does, however, administer the one-fare travel concession permitting a blind person and a sighted companion to travel together on most railroad and bus lines at a reduced rate; about 18,000 I.D. cards have been issued to those of the blind wishing to avail themselves of this privilege. The greater part of the foundation's activities are devoted to collecting and disseminating information about blindness and, through its specialists and consultants in education, rehabilitation, and social services, to counseling the hundreds of agencies and schools for the blind. It also conducts seminars, training institutes, and workshops for professional workers and puts out a raft of publications for their use; serves as a consultant and lobbyist on legislation relating to the blind; and spends a modest amount (about \$750,000 a year) on research, largely of a psychosocial or technological nature rather than that dealing with the medical aspects of blindness. (Although the AFB has an outstanding program that provides an array of useful services, the National Information Bureau questions its accumulation of assets, which over the past decade have increased an average of \$720,000 per year, which the NIB feels to be beyond the amount required for the following year's budget of the organization.)

Supervising the staff of now nearly 200, most of them at AFB headquarters in downtown New York, for 25 years was M. Robert Barnett who retired as the organization's second executive director at the end of 1974. The director's office is the same large wood-paneled room in which Helen Keller* used to work whenever she was in New York, and Barnett was seated at her desk, its most striking feature a railing around three of its sides. "That was to keep her piles of papers from falling off," explained Barnett, a tall, hearty man in his sixties. "Since she used a braille typewriter to prepare her manuscripts and then copied them on a regular typewriter, she had paper stacked up on all sides."

"Some people think she was one of our founders but technically she was not," Barnett went on. "She joined the foundation staff in 1924, three years after we got started, and remained with us until her death in 1968. She raised a great deal of money for us through her talks at churches, synagogues, and town halls across the country. But her job was more than just fund raising. Wherever she traveled, she worked tirelessly to improve the living and working conditions of the blind and brought about a tremendous change in attitudes toward the blind. It was she who persuaded the Lions Clubs to undertake their work in providing services and various aids, like guide dogs and white canes, to the blind. As you may know, it was the Lions who successfully lobbied for the first white-cane law that gave the right of way at intersections to blind people carrying a white cane. She was also no slouch as a lobbyist herself. Whenever we wanted to get action on some legislation affecting the blind, we would call upon her and she would handle things in her inimitable style and with what we would call her Kellerisms. You see that slogan over her bust over there?"

It read: "While they were saying it cannot be done, it was done."

"I still think she stole that from Rudyard Kipling," Barnett said, laughing uproariously but without a trace of malice.

Born in Jacksonville, Florida, in 1916 with normal vision, Barnett was blinded in a freak accident at the age of 15. "Two other boys and I climbed the fence of an orange grove as a Halloween prank. We had our shirts filled with oranges when the hired hands shot at us. One of the pellets went through my left eye and severed the optic nerve in my right eye. I was left totally blind."

Nonetheless, he enrolled at Stetson University in Deland, Florida, became editor of both the college magazine and weekly newspaper, and graduated with straight As. "Unlike the other students, I did my exams on a typewriter," he says. "I got straight As because my exam papers were the only ones the professors could read."

Continuing his interest in journalism after graduation, he—astonishingly!—

---

*Struck deaf, blind, and mute by an illness at the age of 19 months, the remarkable Miss Keller later did learn to speak after a fashion. She also learned to lip read by placing her fingers on the lips and throat of the speaker, the words being simultaneously spelled out for her.

became a reporter for several Florida newspapers and the Associated Press, getting around with a guide dog, taking notes on a braille pocket slate, and either phoning in his stories or returning to the office to bang them out on a typewriter. During the early 1940s he was also a volunteer worker for the newly created Florida Council for the Blind, a state agency comparable to the one Jernigan managed in Iowa; he abandoned journalism to become the council's executive director in 1945. He remained in that post for four years before joining the American Foundation for the Blind.

Barnett told me that at least $500 million a year was then being spent in this country on support, services, and devices for the blind.* Despite this enormous expenditure, he felt that much still remained to be done. "We know for certain," he said, echoing a foundation report, "that tens of thousands of visually hand-icapped persons are not yet receiving the types of assistance and the sensory aids that best meet their needs. We are also moving from the emphasis on total blindness toward people with low vision. Only about 12 percent of the severely visually handicapped—about 200,000 persons—are in the U.S. labor force. This percentage must be improved. The elderly blind and handicapped children must also come in for more study. . . ."

I interrupted him to say, "It's the contention of one of your colleagues that blindness is not a handicap, that a blind person is no different from any other person."

"Oh," he laughed, "you've probably been speaking to Ken Jernigan. Well, ask Mr. Jernigan if he can drive a car, fly an airplane, or thoroughly enjoy a Broadway play or a movie. There might even be some vicarious visual pleasure in being able to watch a symphony orchestra. Now you're making me take the extreme other side of this situation. I think what all of us are trying to get across is that a person who is blind is no different in the things he *wants* out of life, and this certainly is true. But I wonder just how much good is done by constantly harping on the theme that makes blindness sound like nothing worse than a bad cold or a bald head."

"So you do agree then that the inability to see is quite a serious handicap?"

"If it isn't," he said, in an effort to lighten the conversation, "then there are an awful lot of agencies for the blind that had better go out of business."

He became serious again. "I say in my speeches that there is almost no job which some blind person can't do. But that doesn't mean he isn't handicapped. Obviously, a blind person can't be an airplane pilot or a brain surgeon. I don't think he can even be a bookkeeper."

"What about Jernigan's contention," I asked, "that you put down the blind by the patronizing tone of some of your publications like the one on personal management?"

"Oh, so he went into that, too? And I suppose he told you how unhappy he was about the section on taking a bath. Well, we found that there were lots of blind kids from poor families who did not literally know how to do these things. And so we had to appeal to the lowest common denominator."

Barnett made light of the long-standing feud between him and Jernigan, mak-

*In 1979 federal expenditures for these purposes were estimated at from $700 to $750 million, and state expenditures at an additional $150 million for a total of from $850 to $900 million, according to the Department of Health, Education, and Welfare's Bureau for the Blind and Visually Handicapped.

ing it seem like nothing more than a good-natured rivalry. Still, he managed to get in an occasional dig at Jernigan, too. "When Ken talks about the blind leading the blind, he is quoting the Scriptures incorrectly. If you read the *whole* passage from St. Matthew, it says, "They be blind leaders of the blind. And if the blind lead the blind, both shall fall into the ditch." Barnett also wryly questioned if the NFB wasn't being hypocritical in preaching self-help to its heavily blind membership, while relying for the most part on contributions from the nonblind.

As a matter of fact, the NFB's fund-raising operations have been widely criticized on somewhat more serious grounds. These stem from the NFB's long-time practice of soliciting funds by the mass mailings of unordered merchandise, usually neckties and Christmas cards—a method of fund raising that the Council of Better Business Bureaus and the National Information Bureau, among others, frown on because it is extremely costly: A fairly high percentage of the funds contributed must go to pay for the merchandise and mailings since relatively few people bother to send contributions or return the merchandise. (They are not legally required to.)

Just how costly the merchandise mailings were for the NFB before it discontinued them in 1977 was difficult to ascertain from Jernigan. In fact, when pressed, he made the astonishing claim that the NFB had virtually no fund-raising costs at all. This contention was based on a rather ingenious gimmick of which few, if any, NFB contributors were aware. Although NFB appeals made no mention of the fact, the contributions solicited did not go directly to the NFB itself; instead, they were funneled through a wholly owned NFB subsidiary called Fedco, a St. Louis mail-order vendor of neckties and greeting cards, and the firm actually responsible for the solicitations. Fedco, after deducting the costs of its fund-raising operation, then turned over what were presumably all of its net profits to the NFB.

What did these profits amount to? Jernigan was no longer friendly when asked this question and refused to answer it. However, most tax-exempt organizations, with the exception of church-affiliated charities, are required to file annual returns, known as Form 990s, itemizing their income and expenditures; and these returns may be inspected upon request at offices of the Internal Revenue Service. The NFB's latest available return, that for 1973, listed as a "contribution" from Fedco the sum of $833,000, this accounting for almost all of NFB's total income of $867,000 that year.

But what did it cost to raise the $833,000? What expenses were involved in paying for the neckties and promotional materials as well as the cost of mailing them? These costs did not appear on the NFB's Form 990 because, technically, they had been paid by Fedco. And Fedco, as a private, profit-making enterprise, filed a separate tax return which, like that of any other business or individual, was not a matter of public record. Jernigan, who was then also the nominal head of Fedco (a fact he does not choose to include in his detailed biographical data), refused to give me any details of its financial operations. Equally close-mouthed was the mystery man in the whole scheme, a Bernard Gerchen who, while receiving $15,000 a year to manage Fedco's operations, also ran a flock of other busy family-owned mailing services from the same St. Louis address, one of them with an average checking balance reportedly in the high five figures.

Curiously, it was from none other than Gerchen that the NFB purchased Fedco for $500,000 back in 1967.

In view of their reticence, a number of other intriguing questions naturally came to mind. Just what was Fedco's gross income—or, in effect, the sum total of the contributions intended for the NFB—and what portion of this income did the $833,000 in "profits" represent? How much of the difference actually went to pay not only for the neckties and mailings but also for overhead, salaries (Fedco, I learned, has as many as 80 employees during its peak periods), and perhaps even outside mailing services? What, if any, other perquisites was Gerchen receiving in addition to that $15,000, a seemingly paltry stipend for a man running a business showing a profit of nearly $1 million a year? Could it be that Fedco's actual profits were really higher than those represented by what it doled out to NFB? Apparently the operation was profitable enough to enable Fedco to shell out $450,000 to buy a plastics company that, incidentally, came to a sad end several years after its purchase.

Was this a valid use to which to put the money of contributors who, as far as they knew, were giving to help the blind? Would they have given so readily if they had known that only a fraction of their contributions—perhaps as little as 10 cents of every dollar—would wind up with the blind? When I put the latter question to Jernigan, he responded: "When I go to a clothing store and buy a $100 suit, I don't hesitate to pay the $100 even though the merchant may be realizing only a $10 profit, with the rest going into the pockets of wholesalers, manufacturers, landlords, and so on."

I protested that the analogy was not quite valid. "When you deal with a profit-making enterprise, you *know* that someone is making a profit and there is no obligation on anyone's part to tell you how big or how little the profit. In the case of a nonprofit organization such as yours, however, the contributor has the right to know just how money is being spent. In fact, all taxpayers do because Uncle Sam's money is also being used to support the organization."

However, an explanation for Jernigan's reticence as well as some inkling as to the profitability of his fund-raising operation came when I did some more digging into the background of the NFB. In the late 1950s the NFB and an outfit called Federated Industries of St. Louis were named in a Post Office Department fraud complaint following a mailing on the NFB's behalf of several million boxes of Christmas cards, each box accompanied by a request for contributions. The investigation showed that of the $1.7 million grossed by Federated Industries, not more than $200,000, or less than 12 percent of the gross, went to the NFB. As a result of the complaint, both organizations promised to make clear in future solicitations the proportion of the contributions each was getting. A partner in Federated Industries, which discontinued business in 1960, at least under that name, was—Bernard Gerchen.

What led the NFB in 1976 to dissolve Fedco—its fund-raising successor to Federated Industries—and then cease its mailings of unordered merchandise were similar difficulties, this time with the growing number of state charitable regulatory bodies—most recently in Ohio and Pennsylvania where the NFB settled lawsuits by agreeing not to solicit in those states until it complied with state registration and reporting requirements. But there can be no doubt that the NFB's fund-raising costs ran high. Audited financial statements show that in

1976 it raised $3.4 million by its direct mail solicitations. Of this sum, nearly $3 million, or 86 cents out of every dollar, went for fund raising. How well the NFB will fare with its latest solicitations, which feature the slogan "Down With Neckties! Up With Positive Attitudes!" and include an appeal by Pat Boone, only time will tell.

How does one evaluate agencies for the blind? As with any charitable agencies, one can apply the criteria used by monitoring organizations like the National Information Bureau and Council of Better Business Bureaus or refer to the reports of these organizations. But the agencies of the blind also have their own monitoring organization—that already mentioned bête noire of Jernigan's known as NAC, short for National Accreditation Council for Agencies Serving the Blind and Visually Handicapped. NAC was set up in 1967, largely with funds from the American Foundation for the Blind and the Department of Health, Education, and Welfare (the former still accounts for slightly more than half of NAC's $360,000-a-year income) to accredit agencies on the basis of certain standards developed by an ad hoc Commission on Standards and Accreditation of Services for the Blind (COMSTAC) after a three-year study.

Eligible for accreditation are only agencies, local as well as national, that provide *direct* services to the blind: rehabilitation centers, clinics, residences, schools, sheltered workshops, libraries, publishing facilities, and guide dog schools. This rules out agencies like NFB and even AFB which may devote only a portion of their efforts, if any at all, to such services. Although some 75 agencies have so far won accreditation (and hence the right to use the NAC symbol on their letterheads and promotional materials), the fact that an agency is not accredited is not necessarily a black mark against it; many well-known, reputable agencies have not—at least, as yet—applied for accreditation for a variety of reasons. Some regard themselves sufficiently preeminent; others simply do not want to go to the bother of subjecting themselves to the required searching self-study and filling out of forms, procedures that may take a year or more, and the customary three-day on-site examination that an application for accreditation entails.

On the other hand, the credentials of some NAC-accredited agencies could probably be questioned. For example, whereas the celebrated Seeing Eye guide dog school, generally regarded as the leader in its field, is not accredited (by its own choice, although Seeing Eye played an active role in developing NAC's standards), a rival school, Guiding Eyes for the Blind, is accredited although its fund-raising methods have been criticized (specifically, its practice of including in its appeals a postage stamp, which is considered unordered merchandise). NAC's standards for fund raising, however, are not very precise: Although they do call for "truthful, dignified and ethical" fund-raising methods, they do not specify any desired percentages of fund-raising costs; but they do single out as undesirable the use of telephone solicitations, canisters and coin boxes, and the mailing of unordered merchandise. NAC's standards, however, also range over about a dozen other subject areas, such as physical facilities, administration, finances, accounting, and program services.

One of NAC's first presidents as well as one of the most respected figures in the blind movement—in fact, its Grand Old Man—is Peter J. Salmon, who has also been associated with Brooklyn's Industrial Home for the Blind since 1917, first as business manager and later as executive director. Since his "retirement" in 1966, he has held the title of administrative vice-president and otherwise been as busy as ever. Now 84, Salmon is a short, stocky, vigorous man with white hair, a pink Irish complexion, and very blue eyes. Actually, he is not completely blind but, due to a congenital defect, he is extremely nearsighted and needs enormously thick glasses to barely make out print two or three times the size of the type on this page; he gets around with the help of a chauffeur. As a boy, he attended the famous Perkins School for the Blind in Watertown, Massachusetts, another of whose graduates was Helen Keller's teacher, Anne Sullivan. A leading authority on the problems of the deaf-blind, he has received every major award offered in the field of services to the blind. He was responsible for the establishment of many new services for the blind, including the first vocational placement service for them in 1929; he also played a key role in the passage of much significant legislation, such as the 1938 Wagner-O'Day Act which stimulated employment of the blind by favoring workshops for the blind with government contracts, now amounting to about $70 million a year. Indeed, his life has spanned the whole modern era of the blind movement.

"When the Industrial Home for the Blind was founded in 1893, just two years before I was born," he recalls, "the idea of a blind person being employed was almost unknown. Blind people were considered objects of charity and benevolence, and the idea that they could be employed was revolutionary; some people even thought it was cruel to have them work. And so we've had a very uphill battle to fight. It's only within the past few years that we've gotten to the point where blind people who were trained and received their college degrees and teaching certificates would be accepted by school systems. Agencies like the Industrial Home for the Blind, which were the first to start workshops, have also helped in the matter of employment."

Justifying the lower wage scales permitted by law in sheltered workshops, Salmon, like Barnett, opposes the views of Jernigan. "You have to understand," says Salmon, "that many workshops are not profit-making organizations; technically, they are therapeutic institutions that make it possible for the handicapped to derive some pleasure and feel productive by being able to earn at least a little money. In the case of workshops that operate more like a regular business and have to sell their products at a competitive price, I don't see why a blind person should be paid as much as a sighted person who is able to turn out more work. If the law were amended to permit this, as Jernigan wishes, I would predict that at least half of the workshops would be forced out of business within six months. Now, how would this help the cause of the blind? But even with things the way they are now, many of the blind, working on a piece rate basis, are actually making more than the government minimum because they're capable of doing it. The reason, however, why we feel that people in workshops should be paid on their ability to work and produce is because of our feeling that it is not the province of the private agency to provide income maintenance for people. Back in the 1930s, the United States made the decision that if someone's earnings were below the poverty level his income would be supplemented by government programs, such as welfare and social security, rather than by private agencies."

With regard to Jernigan's desire to have more blind people, including those accountable to NFB, represented on the NAC board, Salmon says that this, for one thing, could be a violation of the New York State corporation law governing the accountability of board members. Actually, nearly half of NAC's 35 board members are blind. Not that Salmon feels that this proportion should necessarily hold. "It is no more reasonable to expect that NAC board members themselves be blind than it is to expect that the board of the American Cancer Society be made up only of cancer victims."

A favorite story of George Werntz, long-time executive vice-president of The Seeing Eye, Inc., is about a beggar—and, of course, a dog.*

"I was down in New Orleans for a conference," began Werntz, who, incidentally, is sighted, "when I saw a fellow walking along with a tin cup and a sign that read: 'Please Help Me Buy A Seeing Eye Dog.' 'That's an interesting sign you have,' I said. I asked him what it cost to get one of those dogs and he told me it cost $500. 'Who told you that?' I then asked. He said the outfit in New Jersey that supplied the dogs had told him that. 'Well,' I said, 'I happen to be connected with that organization and I can tell you it doesn't cost $500; it costs $150 and if you try to raise the money this way you won't get a dog.' 'Now, why do you suppose those people up in New Jersey told me it would cost $500?' he said, innocently. Well, we continued to talk some more and I could see that he was beginning to get a little annoyed with my questions. Finally, he said, 'If you don't like this sign, brother, how about this one?' And he turned his sign over. Its other side read, 'Help Me Get an Eye Transplant.'"

Contrary to popular belief, not all guide dogs for the blind are Seeing Eye dogs, which take their name after the oldest and one of the largest schools that train and provide dogs for the blind. Situated on a handsome 50-acre spread in Morristown, New Jersey, 30 miles west of New York City, the school, with its Georgian-type brick headquarters building and lovely winding paths and walks, has somewhat the atmosphere of a country club or college campus.

Although dogs have been companions and aides to the blind for centuries, the formal training of them for this purpose did not begin until 1923. This was when the Germans, because of their success in training dogs to carry messages and perform other specialized tasks during World War I, decided to open a center in Potsdam to train dogs—German shepherds, of course—to assist blinded veterans. Dorothy Eustis, an American dog breeder living abroad, was so impressed by what she saw at the center that upon returning to the United States she founded what she called The Seeing Eye. In 1929, its first year, it trained and provided 17 dogs to the blind and since then it has turned out—"produced" is the trade term—over 7000, currently at the rate of about 215 a year.

In his book-lined office, Werntz, a tweedy, professorial, pipe-smoking man in his middle sixties told me that Seeing Eye is one of nine guide dog schools in the United States, their combined "output" being between 900 and 1000 dogs a year. Seeing Eye now ranks second to Leader Dogs for the Blind of Rochester, Michigan, which was founded in 1939, is largely supported by the Lions Clubs, and produces about 250 dogs a year. In third place is Guide Dogs for the Blind in San Rafael, California, with an output of 175 dogs, followed by Guiding Eyes for the Blind in Yorktown Heights, New York, with an output of 130. The dogs

*Werntz, after 25 years with Seeing Eye, retired on July 1, 1975.

and training methods of all the schools are more or less the same, although some schools are wont to disparage the dogs of the others as inferior.

Although it costs as much as $4000 to $5000 to turn out a guide dog and train it with its master, the fee for a first dog at Seeing Eye is a nominal $150 ($50 for subsequent dogs); this also covers the dog's equipment (the special leather harness and stiff U-shaped handle), the student's room and board while at the school for the required month's training period, and round-trip transportation to Morristown from anywhere in the United States or Canada. "We feel that even the nominal fee is important for psychological reasons: It gives the blind person the feeling that the dog is truly his own and that he isn't getting something for nothing, even if this means paying it to us at the rate of $1 a month over a period of many years," said Werntz. "However, even the nominal fee is waived for those who don't have any funds. And so there is no excuse for anyone begging to raise money for a dog. In fact, many of the other schools, as a matter of policy, don't charge anything for their dogs."

Even so, there are actually more dogs than people to give them to and the schools are seldom filled to capacity. Although Seeing Eye, for example, can accommodate 216 students annually, it graduated an average of only 198 annually during a recent five-year period. For the fact is that most blind people either don't want guide dogs or aren't qualified to use them. A 1958 study sponsored by Seeing Eye and completed by Columbia University's New School of Social Work indicated that somewhat less than one percent of America's blind population use guide dogs and that not more than another one percent (at the time, 3268) of the blind is qualified to use them; most of the latter, however, had no immediate plans, if any at all, to get a guide dog.

Dogs are generally given only to persons between the ages of 16 and 55 who are in good health: Younger persons, it is felt, do not have the maturity or sense of responsibility needed to care for the dog; those over 55, it has been found, often do not have the physical strength to handle one. Also considered unqualified are persons with faulty hearing, low intelligence, marked emotional instability, or insufficient motivation. "Like other reputable schools, we will not accept beggars and will take our dogs away from anyone caught begging," said Werntz. "We would like the person in some sort of job, running a household, attending school, or doing something else constructive with his life. Because if the person is just going to sit around or use the dog just to go down to the corner pub, the dog is going to become a bum, too."*

There are any number of reasons, Werntz also told me, why people who, although otherwise qualified, may not want a dog: They may not want the trouble and bother of caring for it, lack the space for it, face the opposition of family, employers, or fellow workers, have dog phobias or simply not like dogs, or prefer to get around with a cane or the help of a sighted person. Some may wish to avoid the occasional discrimination faced by blind persons accompanied by guide dogs.

Actually such discrimination is now relatively rare and guide dogs may now freely accompany their masters virtually anywhere. Virtually all states now have laws forbidding discrimination in hotels, restaurants, trains, planes, and other public conveyances and places; such laws even supersede local health codes

*Stories crop up from time to time about schools that train dogs for blind beggars sub rosa.

which forbid animals in places where food is prepared. Still, some restaurateurs are either unaware of these laws or choose to ignore them. "Chinese restaurants still seem to be a great stumbling block," Werntz wryly commented. "I'm not quite sure why, unless it's because in the Chinese culture the dog is usually eaten."

Before joining Seeing Eye in 1950, Werntz taught English at a private boys' school in Tarrytown, New York, and later was an associate dean at Colgate University, his alma mater, where he was a protégé of Henry A. Colgate, a university trustee who was also volunteer board chairman of Seeing Eye. Knowing that Werntz was frustrated in his university job, Colgate tapped him to succeed the paid staff head at Seeing Eye who was planning to retire. "I had never even had a dog in my life," recalled Werntz with a laugh. "And I knew next to nothing about accounting, budgeting, or fund raising. But they said they would teach me all this and they did. Until I was named executive vice-president in 1954, I even worked as an apprentice trainer and cleaned out the dog runs. You might say I learned the business from the bottom up."

Werntz said that Seeing Eye breeds most of its dogs, although it also obtains some through purchases and donations. Although all of the dogs bred and most of those used are German shepherds, also used are boxers, collies, golden retrievers, and yellow and black Labradors; about 80 percent are spayed females; males, when used, are altered. The dogs are bred for stable temperament and size (all must be about 24 inches in height at maturity) and must otherwise meet certain rigid physical specifications (a common cause for rejection is hip displacia) and pass a series of aptitude and intelligence tests; the uncanny abilities of some guide dogs is attested to by the experience of one who led police to a man who had mugged his master.

As pups the dogs are placed in the homes of nearby 4-H youngsters for "socialized" rearing in a family setting. At the age of about 14 months they are taken back to the school to begin their three-month training period. The dog first learns basic obedience and then such specialized skills as how to judge heights so as to be able to lead its master away from branches, awnings, and other low-hanging obstacles. The dog is also taught to stop at every street corner so that the blind person can orient himself before going on. In spite of what most people believe, dogs are color blind and therefore unable to read traffic lights; the blind person, after gauging the flow of traffic by ear, decides when it is safe to command his dog, "Forward," and proceed to cross the street. Finally, the dog is taught what is called "intelligent disobedience," that is, to disregard a command if it would lead to danger, for instance from a passing car. To determine if the dog has mastered its instructions and is ready to be assigned to a blind person, its trainer is blindfolded and led across Morristown's busiest intersections, a supervisor following closely behind to observe how the dog meets each challenge.

When trained to perfection, the dogs are ready to be paired with the blind. From 16 to 24 persons at a time come to the Seeing Eye school for their four weeks of team training with the dogs assigned to them. Of the 17 in training when I visited there, 12 were adventitious, as opposed to congenital, blind persons, that is, they had suddenly or gradually lost their sight as the result of an accident or illness; 7 of the 17 were women. The group included a computer programmer, a housewife active in volunteer work, a farmer, an engineer, a dictaphone typist, a vending stand operator, an electronics technician, a salesman, a printer, and a former Peace Corps volunteer now with the Department of Labor. Some had returned for their second or third dog: The average life span of a guide dog is about 9 years, although some have lived and worked to the age of 12 or 13 or even longer.

To see a blind person being introduced to a creature on whom his life may depend for perhaps the next decade is a poignant experience. Dogs are not merely assigned at random. Great care is taken to see that the personalities, temperaments, and physiques of both the student and the dog are matched as closely as possible. "A small woman, for instance, needs a smaller dog than a man with a longer stride," said Werntz. "A vigorous young person probably will adapt better to an active dog than will an older person." There is a period of awkwardness when the dog meets his new master for the first time, for the dog is still emotionally attached to his trainer. But after the blind person feeds the dog several times and pets and praises it while they are undergoing their training and sharing quarters together, the strained feeling vanishes. A sense of camaraderie also develops among all the class members as they pass the daily tests required of them and their dogs.

"How did you do today?" you hear the farmer ask the engineer as the latter enters the school lounge after his instruction session on the streets of Morristown.

"Knocked 'em dead!" the engineer replies confidentially. "I soloed into the department store and had no trouble with the elevator."

"Well, if you can do it," the farmer says jokingly, "then I can do it."

Those who use guide dogs are invariably enthusiastic about them. Nonetheless, representatives of many of the schools have to spend a good deal of time crisscrossing the country looking for people to give their dogs to, in much the same way that corporate recruiters visit college campuses to court promising graduates. So frenetic is their pace that they are often hot at each other's heels and at times they literally bump into each other. In a recent year, Seeing Eye's field representative traveled 62,000 miles in 33 states and Canada to confer with 41 applicants and to solicit additional leads at 78 agencies for the blind, 10 schools for the blind, 15 professional and medical nursing groups, and 27 specialized conferences and meetings.

Aware that a day would come when there would be more dogs than people to give them to, the Seeing Eye people were perspicacious enough to note as far back as 1944: "Realizing the generosity of the American people, The Seeing Eye foresees a grave danger of building up within this and other organizations large sums of money earmarked for a purpose for which they may never be used in their entirety."

Still, the organizations continued to solicit funds, and the unknowing public, its imagination captured by the deeds of the dogs, celebrated in countless popular magazine and newspaper articles, deluged the schools with millions of dollars in contributions, far in excess of their need. By 1957 the annual income of Seeing Eye alone was $1 million more than its expenditures and the organization had accumulated assets that included a securities portfolio with a market value of $10 million. When the National Information Bureau published this revelation, Seeing Eye, in an action probably unprecedented in the philanthropic field, discontinued future solicitations and told contributors it no longer needed their donations.

However, it did continue to mail its quarterly newsletter to some 30,000 "members." The newsletter is largely devoted to the inspiring accomplishments of Seeing Eye graduates: a computer designer, a hospital social worker, a chemist, a painter who uses an ingenious system of tactile markers to keep colors apart, a darkroom technician, an attorney who achieved the noteworthy distinction of being probably the first blind person to be admitted to the Supreme Court bar, and a physician (blinded after he started to practice) who achieved what could have been another "first" by traveling around the world accompanied only by Binty, his German shepherd dog.

Not surprisingly, contributions continued to flow in, largely in the form of legacies; and by 1976 Seeing Eye had piled up assets to the point where its securities portfolio alone had a market value of $25,600,000. The organization's income from its investments, capital gains, trusts, and unsolicited legacies and other contributions still exceeded its expenditures. Nonetheless, late that year Seeing Eye suddenly announced that it would resume the solicitation of contributions, citing the present and projected effects of inflation and "the need to improve, expand and upgrade the quality of services" it offered.

What about all those accumulating assets that now amounted to about *nine* times the organization's budgetary needs? Said a Seeing Eye statement: "Our decision to resume fund raising was based on an historical analysis of the trends of the past ten years and a projection of future need for our services and how they could be maintained *without spending the principal we now have invested.*" (Emphasis added.) In other words, one reason Seeing Eye was resuming its fund raising was in order to maintain or increase its so-called "investment fund."

What about the future of Seeing Eye? "We will, of course, continue to carry out our original function of training guide dogs and providing them to people who can use them," Werntz told me. However, perceiving the limited demand when he commissioned the 1958 New School for Social Work study, he was also farsighted enough even then to use a small special fund in order to initiate a grants program to support research into the prevention of blindness and the rehabilitation of blind persons. In 1965 the organization formally broadened its charter to permit the increased support of these activities under a director of grants and it now spends about $135,000 a year, or 7 percent of its budget, for this purpose.

Seeing Eye put up some of the original money that led to the development of the Optacon, a revolutionary portable reading device, about the size and weight of the average portable cassette tape recorder, that enables people without sight to "read" most printed materials through tactile impressions. The Optacon's miniature camera scans the printed page, picks up the optical images of the letters, one at a time, and transmits the shapes of the letters to the reader's fingers by means of vibrating wires. Seeing Eye has also established a low-interest loan fund to enable people to buy the Optacon, which costs about $3000. It is also supporting the development of a speaking Optacon.

Yet Werntz feels there should be a greater emphasis on prevention. "There is still too great a disparity between funds available for research into the prevention of blindness compared to that given so freely for the alleviation of those already blinded, which is like putting the cart before the horse," he said. "It's unfortu-

nate that helping the blind has stronger emotional appeal than preventing blindness in the first place.''

But with $900 million or so, as already mentioned, now given every year
simply to support, serve, or otherwise help the blind, compared to the relatively
meager $85 million now allotted annually in federal funds plus the few millions
more from private sources to prevent blindness or even restore sight, Werntz's is
a point to ponder, particularly in view of the fact that half of the 34,000 new
cases of blindness every year, mostly among older people, are now considered to
be preventable.

Chapter 13

The Red Cross: Disasters, Blood, and Money

I could not have chosen a worse—or, from another point of view, better—time for my first visit to the "Marble Palace," as Red Cross staffers good-naturedly refer to the many-pillared, opulent, gleaming Grecian structure, a former Civil War memorial that, together with two other only slightly less imposing white marble buildings, now houses their national headquarters in Washington, D.C., only a stone's throw from the White House.

On that April day in 1974, it was scarcely a week since nearly 100 twisters, the most devastating salvo of tornadoes to hit the United States in half a century, had roared out of the sky over an 11-state area in the South and Midwest, leaving over 300 persons dead, thousands injured, and destroying or damaging homes and other property worth about $400 million.

The aftermath of the disaster was still being felt in Red Cross headquarters, with many of the staff away directing rescue operations that were providing emergency help for the homeless, hungry, and injured. In Xenia, Ohio, for example, where one-half of this city of 25,000 had suffered severe damage or destruction, the Red Cross was operating six shelters housing and feeding 2400 people and was combing the city giving tetanus shots and administering other first aid to disaster victims.

As Pete Upton, the organization's husky, red-faced then public relations director, explained to me, most of his staff was also in the field to publicize the Red Cross role in the rescue efforts; he himself had only just returned to supervise a barrage of press releases and other publicity material summing up these efforts and, not incidentally, mentioning that local Red Cross chapters across the country were accepting "special disaster fund contributions" to help finance their good works.

The contributions were sorely needed because the year before the Red Cross had been confronted with the greatest number of disasters in its history. During the course of that year, it had assisted more than 731,000 victims of no less than 25,273 "disaster situations"—floods, hurricanes, tornadoes, fires, and other major and minor catastrophes, including the devastation caused by Hurricane Agnes and the record flooding of the Mississippi River basin—at a cost of $37.7 million, this expenditure reducing the agency's disaster reserve fund, once as high as $20 million, to absolute zero. (Because of the popular misconception that the organization was entirely broke, country singer Tex Ritter assigned the royalties of his new recording of "America, the Beautiful" to the Red Cross.)

Although disaster relief is the most publicized of all Red Cross activities, it is by no means the major concern of one of our oldest and largest charitable organizations, with an annual total income of about $350 million. The Red Cross provides about one-half of the nation's blood supply through its well-known blood program, to which it devotes the biggest chunk of its budget—about 50 percent, compared to less than 10 percent allocated for disaster relief. The Red Cross also provides instruction in water safety, lifesaving, first aid, home nursing, mother and baby care, and other health subjects. Its 1.4 million volunteers are familiar figures in hospitals and are involved in a great variety of other community projects aimed at enabling the Red Cross to fulfill its self-proclaimed role as "The Good Neighbor." Probably less well known, however, are its various activities on behalf of the military, which include serving as a liaison between servicemen and their families, counseling them on their personal problems, arranging for emergency furloughs, bringing a touch of home to their camps and hospitals, giving them any needed financial assistance, providing the recently discharged with guidance as to their benefits and vocational opportunities, and in wartime maintaining contact with and looking out for the interests of those unfortunate enough to be taken prisoner. Although such military services now represent the second biggest item in the Red Cross budget, accounting for about 15 percent of it, the agency does not emphasize, or even omits, them in its fund-raising appeals, for, as its own surveys have shown, people, since the days of Vietnam, would not knowingly give as readily to the Red Cross to finance services for the military as they would for, say, disaster relief.

The American Red Cross even reaches out worldwide, allocating a portion of its budget to help victims of earthquakes, avalanches, famines, and floods, to help reunite families separated by wars and other upheavals, to give shelter and food to refugees, and to bring technical assistance and health and safety education to people on every continent. So ubiquitous is the Red Cross presence, particularly in connection with fund raising, that it is easy to believe the probably apocryphal story of the mountaineers stranded for days on some Alp who, upon seeing a Red Cross-armbanded rescue party approach, instinctively waved it away, shouting, "We gave!"

Surprisingly, however, this entire welter of activities has nothing whatever to do with the original purpose of the Red Cross movement whose beginnings go back more than a century to a young Swiss banker named Henri Dunant. During the course of a visit to a battlefield in northern Italy in 1859, Dunant was deeply affected by the fact that the wounded, after the custom of the times, were left behind to die. The horror of the scene never left him and, in 1863, Dunant arranged for a conference to be held in Geneva, attended by representatives of 16 nations, out of which grew what has come to be known as the Geneva Conventions or international humanitarian treaties. Dunant's idea, accepted at the conference, was that volunteer aid societies be formed in each country to care for the wounded in wartime; moreover, a treaty, signed by all the countries, would guarantee the neutrality of the civilian volunteers so that they could go about their humanitarian work freely in the battle areas without being shot at. As a tribute to Dunant (who in 1901 was awarded the first Nobel Peace Prize), a red cross on a white background—the Swiss flag with colors reversed—was adopted as an easily recognizable symbol of neutrality (to be worn by the volunteers) as well as of the movement itself, and the national organizations formed were called Red Cross societies.*

The United States, however, fearful of entangling foreign alliances, did not get around to ratifying the Geneva (or Red Cross) Convention until 1882, a year after the founding of the American National Association of the Red Cross, as it was first called. Today it is one of 123 national societies, each an independent, self-governing organization with its own program, although all belong to a mutual help international association, the League of Red Cross Societies, head-quartered in Geneva. (Also located there is the completely separate International Committee of the Red Cross, an all-Swiss organization founded by Dunant, which today functions as a neutral intermediary and whose special interest is the welfare of prisoners of war. It is also concerned with the promotion of humanitarian law, primarily through the Geneva Conventions.)

Largely responsible for the U.S. ratification of the Red Cross Convention and the guiding spirit behind the founding of the American group was Clara Barton, an indomitable, remarkable woman whose service as a volunteer Civil War field nurse caring for the soldiers of both the Union and the Confederacy anticipated the duties proposed by Dunant and earned her the name "Angel of the Battlefield." She was sixty in 1881 when she founded the society and, with wars then a less frequent occurrence than they are today, she soon broadened its program to include disaster relief, which was the organization's major activity until World War I. It was also through her efforts that the society, having demonstrated that its activities had a certain value to the nation, won an official standing of sorts by receiving a congressional charter in 1900.

The charter, as revised in 1905 and amended in 1947, now requires the Red Cross to furnish volunteer aid to the sick and wounded in time of war, to serve as a "medium of communication" between our troops and the folks at home in both war and peace, and to provide a system of relief "mitigating the sufferings caused by pestilence, famine, fire, floods, and other great national calamities."

Under the terms of its charter, the Red Cross honorary chairman is none other than the president of the United States and its honorary counselor and treasurer are, respectively, the attorney general and secretary of the treasury. The president appoints the chairman of the 50-member board of governors and—usually from his cabinet—seven other members. The chairman in turn designates, subject to board approval, the Red Cross president, its paid staff head. The charter also provides that the Red Cross financial statements and accounts be audited not only by independent public accountants but by the Department of Defense. Across the nation, its 3100 chapters are usually headed by the most illustrious members of the community.

No other charity can match the prestige of its leadership or the dedication and size of its following and its organizational strength: In addition to its 1.4 million volunteers, it has a paid staff of about 16,000 employees, and its work is supported by approximately 3.8 million volunteer blood donors, by over 6 million

---

*In some countries, however, other names and symbols are used: a red crescent in Turkey, Egypt, and some of the Soviet Republics; a red lion and sun in Iran; and a red Star of David in Israel where the society is known as the Magen David Adom.

students participating in Red Cross programs in schools, and by 33 million members signed up at the annual March membership drives (a contribution of $1 or more makes one a Red Cross member).

All in all, there has never been a charitable institution quite like the Red Cross, one so awesome in its auspices, size, resources, and ubiquitousness, nor one so revered by so many Americans. Even the British political scientist Harold J. Laski—not the gentlest observer of the American scene—was once moved to call the American Red Cross "the outstanding example of international generosity in the whole world." Yet the agency has been embroiled in controversy and been the subject of often bitter criticism, from within and without, since its earliest years.

Although there is no questioning the selflessness of Clara Barton, the "Florence Nightingale of America," as she was also called, she was cast in the same despotic mold of most great humanitarians. She delegated little authority and was an inept administrator who kept poor records and was often wont to confuse Red Cross funds with her own; once she was accused of diverting $12,000 in contributions to the purchase of a farm. The resentment she aroused finally resulted in a bitter power struggle with a faction led by Mabel Boardman, another strong-willed person of intense ambition, and in 1904 Miss Barton felt she had no choice but to resign her lifetime presidency. "Seldom in organization history has the bitterness of an almost unaccountable hatred so overshadowed an otherwise noble program," says a Red Cross history, which notes that the Red Cross founder was even threatened by a congressional investigation if she had chosen to remain in office. So bitter was the Barton-Boardman rivalry that years later, when Miss Barton was a candidate for canonization in the Hall of Fame of Great Americans, her successor, Miss Boardman, lobbied actively against her; significantly, no memorial to Clara Barton has ever been erected at Red Cross headquarters, although two large marble torchères there honor the memory of Mabel Boardman.

Both women, however, must unwittingly share the blame for giving the organization an imprint that was to have even more harmful effects than the temporary schism created by the struggle between them. To attract the money and prestige they felt their young organization needed in order to grow, they began to people it with leaders and volunteers whose chief credentials were wealth and social position, thereby endowing the Red Cross with the image, one that still persists today, of an elitist group of upper-class do-gooders in starched white uniforms.

The dominant role played by the social elite and businessmen in the Red Cross also used to arouse the continuing suspicion and criticism of organized labor, and the flames of this feud were fanned in the 1920s and 1930s when the Red Cross repeatedly refused to give aid to the families of strikers and the otherwise unemployed, maintaining that economic strife or distress were not natural calamities calling for the emergency relief it traditionally furnished.

Over the years, there have also been complaints that the Red Cross has been slow in responding to disasters, particularly in black and Indian areas. Victims of a tremendous flood in Rapid City, South Dakota, in 1972, echoing complaints in other areas, told the *National Observer* that the head of the nearest Red Cross chapter did not reach Rapid City from his home 50 miles away until the day after the calamity. Although some 800 Red Cross volunteers ultimately fed, clothed, and housed thousands there at a cost of nearly $1.2 million, according to the *National Observer*, people of the ravaged region also grumbled that the Red Cross "dispensed aid capriciously, failed to bring them expected food and water . . . and exploited the town's suffering by using it as an excuse for a national fund drive that requested 'much more money than needed for local relief.'" Also bobbing up invariably during disaster relief operations are those perennial stories of the Red Cross selling what it is supposed to give away. A black victim of the famous tornado that hit Mississippi in 1970 told me that the Red Cross was selling blankets and even water. There is no way of verifying the truth of such recurrent rumors: When rewards were offered for proof of them after one flood, there were no takers. However, Red Cross president George Elsey has acknowledged that his organization did not respond as well as it should have to the needs of the black victims of the Mississippi tornado, and Cynthia Wedel, the Red Cross director of volunteers, admitted to me with equal candor that in Rapid City "the local chapter was unfortunately tied up with the White Power structure of the community and was, in fact, anti-Indian." As a result, she went on, "a lot of Red Cross aid was misused and misdirected at the people who needed it least and not given to the Indians, who needed it most." Rapid City Sheriff Glenn Best, like people elsewhere, said he felt organizations like the Salvation Army were doing a better job helping disaster victims, and a survey once taken after a Michigan tornado showed 27 percent of the residents of a town to evaluate the help of the Red Cross negatively. Similarly, a detailed study of an Alaska earthquake by the prestigious National Academy of Sciences (NAS), reported the Red Cross as being late in bringing aid to one town and as finding no emergency in another, though it had sunk three and one-half feet and was being inundated with water. It was left to Salvation Army workers, the NAS study said, to provide money for the disaster victims and help to "raise water-front houses above the reach of flood tides."*

On the other hand, and to balance the views of the critics, here is a typical expression of gratitude from a Pennsylvania coal miner watching Red Cross disaster relief workers in his area: "Thank God for 'em. Thank God for the Red Cross. They couldn't do more than what they're doing." There can also be no doubt that agencies like the Red Cross, which attempt to do the most or of which the most is expected, are the most visible during a disaster and therefore are the ones most likely to be criticized for their sins of omission and commission, particularly by people seeking a target for their frustrations. And decades of Red Cross image-building, a by-product of the organization's ceaseless quest for donations, has undoubtedly led people to expect more of "America's Good Neighbor" than it may be able to always deliver.

In spite of its record of good works, much of the ill will against the institution is often due to other misunderstandings and misconceptions, and even myths, which are often grounded in enough realities to make them credible. For example,

---

*To dispel a growing public view that the two organizations are in competition with each other, the national leaders of the American Red Cross and the Salvation Army signed an agreement in August, 1975, aimed at preventing the duplication of services in emergency situations. "We've had cases of people getting clothing from one organization and then getting the same thing from another," said a Red Cross spokesman. Other agencies involved in disaster relief include the Volunteers of America, Goodwill Industries, Catholic Charities, the Lutherans, and other church groups.

although the Red Cross has never had any avowed Jim Crow policies, it has often gone along with the status quo in the South. (Looking at photos of its 50-member board, I could spot only three, possibly four, black faces.) Mrs. Tillie Cheyney of San Diego told me that when she was a young Red Cross caseworker in Miami in the 1940s ("Although I was then unmarried, I was giving sex information to married people," she laughed) a white man reported her because she took care of a black man who happened to be the first in line. "You call that nigger a *client*?" the white man had roared at her. Charges that the Red Cross is racist also stem from the World War II practice of labeling all donated blood either "black" or "white." In defense the Red Cross says that it was merely following the mandate of the military.

It was the military, too, who in other respects inadvertently contributed to the biggest black eye the Red Cross has ever suffered, one that since World War II and even World War I has brought the organization such an accumulation of ill will that even today, as one ex-GI put it, "Anyone who's been in the service hates the Red Cross's guts," and many have told me that they'd sooner drop dead than give a dime to the Red Cross. As in the case of some disaster victims, this animosity had its origin in the rumors of Red Cross sales—this time, of everything from coffee and doughnuts to cigarettes and sweaters and even blood.

Red Cross officials deny that such incidents were widespread or took place deliberately. A few of the thousands of Red Cross staffers overseas were known to have made a dishonest buck peddling Red Cross supplies, and some items were no doubt stolen and sold on the black market. Still others, during the cargo mix-ups common during the war, often wound up by mistake in post exchanges here and there. Some of the incidents, however, like much GI scuttlebutt, were entirely mythical. One persistent rumor tracked down by the Red Cross and discredited was that soldiers had to pay for blood plasma. This tale was traced to a GI who had lost heavily shooting craps. To pay his gambling debt, he wrote to his family for money, explaining he needed it to pay for "Red Cross blood."

The Red Cross acknowledges, however, that it did charge servicemen for food, tobacco, and hospitality at clubs in leave—but not combat—areas. The reason given is that it was ordered to do so by our War Department in order to conform to the practice of our British and other allies who, less affluent than we, were charging *their* military for similar items and services in their rear-area clubs. The charges, though extremely nominal—50 cents would buy a bed and breakfast, for example—were fiercely resented by our troops and represented another instance of the Red Cross kowtowing to local custom, if only by military fiat, at the sacrifice of its vaunted principle of giving freely.

Add to all this the traditional animosity of the soldier toward the civilian noncombatant, with the ubiquitous Red Cross worker the very personification of civilian "brass," and it is easy to understand why our returning GIs brought home with them hostile attitudes reflecting a skepticism toward the value of all Red Cross activities.

Even the Red Cross civilian blood program, which was initiated shortly after World War II (incidentally, by Basil O'Connor, while doing double duty as the head of both the Red Cross and the National Foundation), has been the subject of criticism. For one thing, this stems from the popular misconception that Red Cross blood is free to whoever may need it; technically, this is true and the Red

Cross makes much of the fact that since it does not pay for blood it does not charge for it. For this reason, hospital patients receiving Red Cross blood are often furious at finding a "processing fee" for it on their bills. Nor are they mollified when told that the fee, which is usually picked up by health insurance, is only to cover the cost of collecting, processing and distributing the blood, and is not for the blood itself.

Another criticism centers around the accusation that the Red Cross, despite the pleas of legislators, labor leaders, and medical authorities, dragged its heels for many years in expanding its blood program in order to help stop the flow of commercial blood from paid donors. This type of blood has been found ten times more likely to cause posttransfusion hepatitis (a liver disease that until recently killed as many as 4000 Americans a year) than blood from the usually more healthy volunteer donors. Moreover, critics say, the Red Cross assumed no leadership in correcting our woefully inefficient and fragmented blood collection and distribution system, which not long ago saw as much as 25 percent of donated blood—one precious pint out of every four—wasted, literally poured down the drain because it became outdated before it could be used; by contrast, wastage is as little as 2 or 3 percent in Britain, France, and Canada—in fact, in every other advanced industrial nation in the world. All, incidentally, have some sort of national blood program which makes blood available completely free to every citizen who needs it, and no one is allowed to make any profit on the blood, all of which is voluntarily donated.*

In this country, however, it was not until 1973 and only after threats and denunciations by the 14 million-member AFL-CIO, the agency's biggest source of blood, and the warning of a possible government takeover of the nation's blood program, that the Red Cross finally came out in favor of a Department of Health, Education, and Welfare-enunciated national blood policy having as its goal a safer, more efficient all-volunteer blood system, and joined with 46 other groups in the creation of an American Blood Commission aimed at implementing this policy.

Why did the Red Cross not choose to act earlier? Some attribute its lack of interest to its characteristic conservatism and bureaucratic timidity. Others, like Stanford University's Dr. J. Garrott Allen, generally regarded as the nation's leading expert on the use of blood, suggest that the inaction of Red Cross was to avoid stepping on the toes of such vested interests as the American Medical Association and its member doctors, many of whom operate or rely on commercial blood banks, and of pharmaceutical companies which, apart from using blood from paid donors, have many of their executives serving on Red Cross chapter boards. "For the life of me, I don't see how the AMA can in good conscience come out against the labeling of volunteer and paid donor blood," says Dr. Allen, who played a key role in stimulating the interest of the AFL-CIO and the Department of Health, Education, and Welfare in a national blood policy.

For its part, the Red Cross is now honest enough to admit that it did not act as

*In his remarkable book, *The Gift Relationship* (Pantheon, 1971), British social theorist Richard M. Titmuss argues that commercializing the blood transaction not only causes a breakdown in moral values but also results in increased rates of hepatitis and, in general, a less effective system of blood collection and distribution.

quickly as it should have. "There is a widespread feeling that the Red Cross has not done enough to expand its [blood] services to the nation," said a 1978 report of a top-level Red Cross Ad Hoc Group, headed by board member William M. Ellinghaus, after detailed interviews with professionals and volunteers, both within and outside the agency. "As a consequence of lost opportunities in the past, the nation's blood supply is fragmented with large and small units operating with different philosophies and different levels of quality and service."

In its zeal to make up for the lost opportunities, the Red Cross is now moving quickly—indeed, so quickly that it is now in open conflict with the American Association of Blood Banks (AABB) which charges that the Red Cross is trying to take over the nation's blood business. The AABB, whose some 2000 hospital and other nonprofit community blood banks use both volunteer and paid donor blood (there are also about 2000 independent blood banks that use only paid donors), is also apprehensive about recent plans for a Red Cross joint venture with Baxter Travenol Laboratories, through which the Red Cross hopes to cut its cost of producing plasma products by as much as 40 percent.

In this conflict, the Red Cross seems to be on the side of reason and the public interest. Whereas the Red Cross philosophy is that providing blood is a "community responsibility" and should be done on an entirely voluntary basis, the AABB and its allies—the commercial banks and fractionaters and the American Medical Association—hold to the view that patients (or their relatives and friends) should replace the blood they use or pay for it. The Red Cross answer to this, concurred in by Dr. Allen, is that replacement demands and the so-called "nonreplacement penalty" fees work unnecessary hardships on the poor when the fees are not already covered by insurance, and that the blood banks profiteer from the extra money for the blood not replaced, usually volunteer blood.

While the controversy rages, the Red Cross expansion of its blood services in recent years has had some measurable favorable effects. Today only about 10 percent of all the blood used in this country comes from paid donors, compared to roughly 40 percent in 1970; and the hope is that paid donor blood will be completely phased out by the early 1980s. Correspondingly, the incidence of transfusion-associated hepatitis deaths has dropped from 4000 to less than 1000 annually during the same period. And blood wastage, according to Dr. Allen, is down from 25 percent to around 10 percent. For all of this and the progress toward a long-overdue all-volunteer blood supply, the Red Cross deserves full credit.

In looking at the entire Red Cross record, however, there are frequent reminders that the organization has been at least as much concerned with its own survival as with meeting public needs. As already mentioned, tending the battlefield wounded was scarcely sufficient a challenge to an organization of any pretension; and so disaster relief, apart from serving a humanitarian purpose, also helped the Red Cross fill the peaceful lull before the Spanish-American War and between that short-lived, minor skirmish and World War I. With the end of World War I, the leaders of a greatly expanded Red Cross, confronted with a monumental decline of membership interest, cast about for a new activity "not only for the sake of whatever contributions could be made toward improving the conditions of American life, but *for the sake of the organization itself*" (author's italics), as Foster Rhea Dulles' official Red Cross history bluntly put it. The crisis was surmounted by the adoption of a new program for "the preservation and improvement of the public health."

The end of World War II, which saw not only demobilization, but disasters at an all-time low (strangely, during the war years, there was not a single major disaster in the United States), brought with it a new major crisis. The solution this time was the implementation of the Red Cross civilian blood program. Explaining the rationale behind the program, Dulles wrote:

> Apart from meeting a very real need, the national blood program also appeared the best possible thing for the Red Cross to undertake on its own account. Just as health activities had been promoted after the First World War to give the chapters something to do as well as to advance public health, so the new project was expected to provide an outlet for volunteer activity in the new period of peace which would bring together in one unified undertaking, the varied interests of the volunteer services.

To keep its volunteer and paid staff busy, the Red Cross also initiated its peacetime services to the military, which until 1972 remained its largest commitment and today is its second largest operation, ranking only behind the blood program and far ahead of its disaster relief activities; the agency also decided to give more emphasis to programs for the community at large.

For questions had long been raised as to whether the programs of the agency went far enough. In the early 1970s, community leaders affiliated with one local chapter of the United Way, which nationwide now accounts for over 80 percent of the contributions to the Red Cross, were reported as saying that Red Cross programs no longer related to people's current needs; they said that the Red Cross "stays in an ivory tower, changes nothing, reeks of tradition." Even the United Way's ranking national official, William Aramony, while stating he was in no position to be critical, suggested: "Members have seen lots of needs the Red Cross might fill. Want a litany? Venereal disease training. I'm not sure the Red Cross considers that its bag, but it's a public health problem. Care of older people. Nursing homes. We'd like to see the Red Cross move faster."

Red Cross employees themselves voiced similar criticisms, one young career man bitterly saying: "I believe in the organization but it's five percent of what it could be. It is conservative, afraid of risk. We tell people we're 'innovators, filling the needs of the community.' That's our 'tradition.' What about drugs? Drug abuse has been a serious, well-known national problem for eight years. Just this year [1972] we've established a task force to see what we *might* do! We're a decade late."

Appointed to head the task force to encourage change in the organization was a frustrated Red Cross official who complained it had once taken him four years to get approval for a small demonstration project to teach first aid to ghetto blacks. Established were guidelines for chapters aimed at fulfilling the newly stated aims of the Red Cross "to alleviate human suffering and to improve the quality of life through programs addressed to critical priority problems of the day." Chapters were encouraged to take an "active role" in community efforts to combat drug abuse, juvenile delinquency, and venereal disease and in programs for the elderly and the handicapped.

In 1978, six years later, I visited Red Cross headquarters to see what progress had been made in implementing these goals, which were not unlike those enunciated previously by the Red Cross from time to time. For example, the organization's 1966 annual report stated that the Red Cross, throughout its existence, has "constantly demonstrated its responsiveness to change by adapting its programs to meet new demands and by discontinuing programs when they have become outmoded." But during the course of my visit, Helen Bosserman, the national director of community volunteer services, while citing a home for runaway youngsters set up by the Birmingham, Alabama, chapter, admitted that only one percent of the 3100 chapters had any programs for juvenile delinquency or drug abuse—no more than existed six years earlier. She also said that less than 10 percent of the chapters had reported any participation in programs for the handicapped and no more than 20 percent in the various suggested programs for the elderly.

"Why is there such a disappointing response to the guidelines?" I asked. "The chapters are all autonomous and all we can do is strongly encourage activities," she answered sadly.

Complicating the difficulties of the Red Cross is its relationship with government. To preserve its public image as a voluntary organization, the Red Cross has long had an absolute phobia about accepting any government handouts. For example, when the great drought of 1930 compounded the suffering already wrought by the Great Depression, the Red Cross, in what has been called "one of the most curious and characteristic episodes" of that era, rejected a congressional proposal that would have given it $25 million "for the purpose of supplying food, medicine, medical aid, and other essentials to afford adequate relief" to the 2.5 million drought sufferers in the stricken areas. "All we pray for is that you let us alone and let us do the job," the Red Cross told Congress as the agency mounted an appeal to the public to contribute to a $10 million emergency fund. In 1932, however, the Red Cross accepted the assignment of distributing to the poor government-owned wheat and cotton valued at $73 million. In justifying this labor, the Red Cross said, "Commodity distribution can be handled without creating the precedent resulting from the appropriation of government funds to the Red Cross."

Although the Red Cross continues to perpetuate the myth that it relies only on donations, the fact is that over the years it has received literally hundreds of millions of dollars in federal funds. In 1975 and 1976 it received a total of almost $6 million in reimbursements for services rendered to Indochina refugees. In 1977 the Red Cross accepted $1.2 million of federal money for blood research plus more than $3 million in other government grants, including $246,000 from the Defense Civil Preparedness Agency. This does not take into account the value, estimated at as much as $10 million annually, of the services—transportation, communications, living quarters, shipping, and the like—that the Red Cross also receives from the Department of Defense to carry out its peacetime obligations to the military.

Of perennial concern to the Red Cross is the increasing intervention of the government in Red Cross's traditional relief, health, and welfare activities. A Red Cross report in 1946 warned that "clouds are appearing on the disaster relief horizon" because "government today is rendering a number of services to disaster sufferers that were rendered by Red Cross disaster relief 10, 15 or 20 years ago.'' Today, as a result of legislation passed in 1972, the federal government provides nearly all financial assistance for the rehabilitation of disaster victims and the role of the Red Cross is largely confined to providing emergency shelter, food, clothing, nursing, first aid, and other urgent necessities during the initial or rescue phase of the disaster. The government has also taken over many other activities that were once a Red Cross responsibility: military nursing, public health nursing, and the operation of army service clubs and recreation centers.

To Red Cross president George Elsey, it is inconceivable that government could ever entirely usurp the role of the Red Cross. ''I don't see how government could effectively do what we do in first aid, water safety, and other activities of that sort which call for literally hundreds of thousands of volunteers. These programs would be too costly for the government to run and, besides, there then wouldn't be the incentive for people to volunteer.''

What about disaster relief? he is asked. Why shouldn't government assume this entire function just as it does putting out fires or fighting crime?

''Because the government couldn't assume the entire function. Our present role handling the initial rescue mission, or the immediate response to the disaster, requires having trained volunteers in the region being able to act literally within minutes after a disaster strikes. The government doesn't have the manpower nor is it equipped to respond that quickly.''

Couldn't the armed forces?

''Again, there would be a problem of manpower and logistics. The armed forces aren't in Xenia, Ohio, for example. And it would have taken 12 hours, 36 hours, maybe even 72 hours to get the armed forces from the nearest camp into that area.

What about your services to the military? Elsey is asked. Why shouldn't they be performed by the military, particularly at times when the nation is not at war? In fact, in war or peace, why should private contributions be used to pay for things that should be as much an obligation of the Department of Defense as are the food, shelter, clothing, medical care, and other needs of the military?

''For one thing, our services to the military are spelled out in our charter,'' said Elsey. ''We are required to perform them. If we didn't, the military would be obliged to have offices in practically every county of the United States as well as in practically every part of the world in order to duplicate the communications network we have. And our feeling is that the link we provide between a serviceman, wherever he may be, and his family is just as vital and necessary in peace as well as in war.''

Elsey says that theoretically the government could ultimately take over many, if not all, of these and other activities performed by the Red Cross, but will not argue whether it should or it shouldn't. However, the possibility of such an occurrence was considered by Basil O'Connor in a speech entitled ''Can The Red Cross Survive?'' he gave at the organization's 1949 annual convention. In the speech, O'Connor said it was not only necessary to reevaluate the Red Cross's mission but also to ask the fundamental question as to whether an organization founded in ''the remote past of the nineteenth century still had any place at all in the vastly altered world of the mid-twentieth century.''

Nevertheless, more than a quarter of a century later and lambasted as the agency still is by critics, it would be hard to think of our society without a Red

Cross, with its many past accomplishments, its useful array of current activities, and its vast potential for the public good—with some reordering of its priorities, of course.

It is intriguing to consider, for example, what the Red Cross could accomplish if it phased out its *peacetime* services to the military—services that were not even specified in its original charter and are not performed by any other country's national Red Cross society. Eliminating this program, which I strongly feel should be a function of government, would make available around $50 million a year, to say nothing of nearly 1000 paid staffers and nearly 60,000 volunteers for other programs—for drug abuse, juvenile delinquency, the elderly and handicapped, and other community problems—that would benefit the nation as a whole, rather than a small uniformed segment of it, and so fulfill the promise and give real meaning to the slogan "America's Good Neighbor."

Chapter 14

Should Charity Support Social Welfare?

As television viewers of that 1938 film classic, *Boys Town*, may recall, shortly after Father Flanagan (Spencer Tracy) started his first home for underprivileged boys with $90 borrowed from a skeptical pawnbroker friend (Henry Hull), he found he was housing more boys than he could handle, and the wolf of bankruptcy was constantly at his door, waiting hungrily for the home's finances to cave in. In a touching Christmas Eve scene, Flanagan despondently confessed that he couldn't even afford a tree, let alone gifts, at which point the pawnbroker paid a surprise visit with presents for everyone. Even after a tough teen-age hoodlum named Whitey Marsh (Mickey Rooney) joined the juvenile community now known as Boys Town and, after causing all sorts of trouble, was elected its mayor, things did not get much better. In fact, in those early days the kindly Flanagan once got so far behind in his bills that Omaha merchants forced him to pay cash.

Certainly, 40 years ago, back in the days when Spencer Tracy and Mickey Rooney were running the place, it hardly seemed likely that Boys Town's biggest problem would ever be an embarrassment of riches. Nor that it would ever experience the continuing criticism it has in recent years. For few charitable institutions have enjoyed the esteem, good will, even popular affection of the internationally-renowned Boys Town, officially called Father Flanagan's Boys' Home. For decades, so great was the aura of righteous benevolence surrounding this legendary home for neglected, underprivileged, and homeless boys that to be critical of it was akin to blasphemy.

Father Edward J. Flanagan, who held the tenet that "there's no such thing in the world as a bad boy," started his unique "city of little men" in 1917 in an old mansion in the center of Omaha; in 1921 it moved to a farm ten miles outside the city and became an incorporated village governed by the boys themselves. At the time, this was a revolutionary idea and did much to change the public image of the institutionalized boy as a "bad boy" by treating him not as an inmate of an institution but rather as a citizen who, in spite of his faults, possessed dignity and rights.

For many years, Boys Town, even with its ties to the Roman Catholic Church—the Archbishop of Omaha always heads Boys Town's board of directors—faced financial problems similar to those of other institutions. Then in

1938 came that celebrated, saccharine MGM Spencer Tracy-Mickey Rooney movie which overnight brought Boys Town national attention and made it part of American folklore. Money poured into what was then a little-known local institution.

The money was used to finance a major building program, which included some $10 million worth of new dormitories, schools, a stadium and field house, industrial training shops, and administrative buildings. Completed in 1948, the year Father Flanagan died, they represented for all practical purposes the last big capital expenditures Boys Town was to make for decades—on a site that was to grow to 1700 acres.

Yet each spring and again before Christmas, Boys Town would send out as many as 33 million letters annually appealing for funds. Bearing idealized pictures of a snowy campus and a smiling youngster carrying a sleeping smaller boy on his back, with the legend, ''He ain't heavy, Father . . . he's m' brother,'' the letters, enclosing a sheet of Boys Town stamps and the offer of an ''Honorary Citizen of Boys Town'' certificate, would begin something like, ''There will be no joyous Christmas season this year for many homeless and forgotten boys to look forward to with eager anticipation as the more fortunate boys do,'' and ask recipients to send ''$1, $2, $5, or any amount you care to give.'' The contributions kept rolling in. But no one knew just how much came in or just what was done with the money, for Boys Town, as a church-affiliated organization, issued no annual reports and conducted its financial operations in almost total secrecy.

This secrecy was lifted quite by accident in the wake of the passage of the Tax Reform Act of 1969 which required nonprofit organizations and foundations, starting with the calendar year 1970, to file an annual Form 990 information return—a detailed report of income and expenditures. The law specifically exempted churches and their ''integrated auxiliaries,'' like Boys Town, from filing such returns. Boys Town, however, inadvertently filed a return.

In 1972 the *Sun Newspapers* of Omaha, a group of small weeklies, while digging into the affairs of Boys Town, came upon the return, which was used as the basis for an eight-page series of articles entitled, ''Boys Town: America's Wealthiest City?'' The articles, which were awarded a Pulitzer Prize, revealed that over the years Boys Town had amassed a total net worth of $209 million, primarily in cash and securities, this technically amounting to a net worth of $192,700 for each of the community's 993 residents. The *Sun* also pointed out that the institution's annual income of $8.1 million from investments alone was more than enough to take care of its operating expenses. In fact, investment income and the contributions in response to those appeals together added up to some $25 million a year—about four times as much as Boys Town needed to take care of its declining population of 665 boys. (Staff members and employees made up the balance of Boys Town's population.) Despite this, the institution's letters implied that it was in desperate financial straits.

Somewhat embarrassed, Boys Town put a moratorium on fund raising and announced plans to spend $30 million for the establishment of an institute for the study and treatment of hearing and speech disorders in children at nearby Creighton University and $40 million more for a national center for the study of youth development and juvenile problems. Early in 1973 Boys Town's board announced the hiring of the management consulting firm of Booz, Allen &

Hamilton to reexamine the institution's entire program and to recommend changes, a move the archdiocese had resisted for years. In October, 1973, Archbishop Daniel E. Sheehan named the Rev. Robert P. Hupp, a popular 58-year-old parish priest, to direct the home and implement the recommended changes. "We've got enough money to do things and we're going to do them because they're so long overdue," promised Father Hupp.

He cut Boys Town's population to fewer than 500 boys so that each could receive more counseling, changed the teaching program to better prepare the brighter boys for college (the previous emphasis had been almost entirely on vocational training), expanded the professional staff, and, to create a more homelike atmosphere, did away with such quaint practices as reading the boys' incoming mail, regulating their schedules by bells, feeding them in a giant mess hall, and denying them the use of telephones.

Because Boys Town's traditional institutional type of care has come under attack as outmoded in recent years, Hupp, in a radical departure from the past, sought to simulate today's more widely favored family style approach to child care by arranging for Boys Town's youngsters to live in groups of eight to ten in cottages under the supervision of married couples who function as surrogate parents. The couples, who are paid from $13,000 to $20,000 a year, are given a $44,000-a-year checking account to be spent on food, transportation, entertainment, even vacations, and other expenses of running their households. Currently, about 360 boys live in some 41 cottages on the campus, where the old large dormitories have been shut down, awaiting other uses; in addition, another 220 youngsters live off-campus in 31 similar Boys Town-directed "community homes" in 15 states.

Nonetheless, Boys Town still remains a subject of criticism. The National Information Bureau (NIB), which monitors and evaluates the nation's leading nonprofit organizations, questions the amount the institution spends on fund raising, which Boys Town resumed in 1973 and has brought in upwards of $7 million annually ever since then. Although fund raising expenses have dropped from 68.5 percent of regular contributions (30.2 percent of contributions plus legacies or bequests) in 1975 to 47.7 percent of contributions (18.2 percent of contributions plus legacies or bequests) in 1977, the NIB feels that this is still too high for its standards. "A general rule of thumb is about 30 percent of contributions, excluding bequests and endowment gifts," again says the NIB's Jane Pendergast, who also points out that Boys Town's net worth now stands in excess of $246 million. (However, Boys Town currently meets the standards of the Council of Better Business Bureaus.)

A new *Sun Newspapers* series of articles, published in late 1978, also took issue with other Boys Town practices. Among other things, the articles charged that even though the cottages alone, with a capacity of 410, could accommodate at least 50 more boys, Boys Town was turning away scores of boys each month, rejecting nine of every ten applicants for admission, because of an unwritten policy of accepting only "cream-puff boys," described as "kids who have little chance of failure." In response Hupp blamed the less-than-capacity enrollment on the inability to attract and keep suitable houseparents and said that over 40 percent of those who formally applied were accepted. (The *Sun* rejoindered that many boys were informally screened and turned down before they could submit formal applications.) The cost of care in an institution is also high, running to $30,000 a year for each boy in Boys Town, according to the latest *Sun* revelations. This figure includes $11,500 for residential care, $5500 for education (as much as the tuition in the nation's finest private schools), $1000 for supportive services, plus such indirect costs as utilities, maintenance, and other overhead expenses. To rear a child in a private home would cost only a fraction of that.

Although some child care authorities hail Boys Town's transformed family style of care as a step in the right direction, they still favor genuine foster homes over institutions. There are also some who are critical of the fact that Boys Town is still not designed to deal with—nor does it want—really delinquent boys—*bad* "bad boys," in contrast to the sanitized hoodlum type portrayed by Mickey Rooney. For these and other reasons, it is unlikely that the Boys Town population will ever again reach its one-time peak of over 900. A Boys Town guidance counselor told me he felt that the institution should take in "new types of boys," such as those with deep-seated emotional or drug problems. But Archbishop Sheehan himself sadly acknowledged, "Those problem kids won't fit into the type of institutional care that we can provide."

Boys Town furnishes an excellent example of how sentimentality rather than reality often governs charitable giving. Other examples may also be found among the many so-called "social welfare" organizations—a catchall category that includes private agencies serving children, youth, the handicapped, and the aged, special groups such as servicemen, veterans, and the poor, and the various agencies concerned with relief, recreation, community activities, character building, or physical fitness. The common denominator of all is the contribution each makes in its own way to the fabric of community life, a fact that philanthropy has long recognized through its support of these organizations.

But these agencies may be on the wane as evidenced, for example, by the declining number of people they serve. In addition to Boys Town, one could also cite the Boy Scouts which, during the past decade, has seen its youth membership drop from 4.4 million to 3.4 million. Since the early 1970s, membership in the Girl Scouts has declined from 3.2 million to 2.6 million, and that of the Camp Fire Girls has gone down from 620,000 to nearly 500,000. And to say that the Boys' Clubs of America has maintained a membership hovering at the 1 million mark for the past decade means that this organization, too, has lost ground in the face of rising population.

Among the five major philanthropic areas—religion, health, education, the arts, and social welfare—social welfare giving has been increasing at a slower rate than all the others, according to the American Association of Fund-Raising Counsel. One reason, of course, is the lessening need for private help as the government spreads its social welfare umbrella further and further year after year, as indicated by the figures given in Chapter 2.

By contrast, giving to social welfare was last estimated at only $4 billion a year, this figure representing no more than 10 percent of total U.S. giving. Moreover, virtually all of today's social welfare agencies and institutions receive at least some of their income from government; many receive well over half of their income from this source.

Should government assume the entire cost of all social welfare activities or should some, such as those in the recreational area—not among our most pressing social needs—be left wholly to private voluntary efforts? How valid and relevant are the activities of many of our private social welfare agencies which, even if they receive little or nothing from government, still indirectly derive a good deal of their support from taxpayer money (paid by you whether or not you contribute to the agencies) because of their tax-exempt status? Do the private agencies fulfill a role in catalyzing and challenging, if not assisting, government to bring about needed solutions to our nation's problems?

These are among the questions to keep in mind as we survey some of the other better-known charities in the youth and social welfare field.

Scout's Honor

A Scout tells the truth. He keeps his promises. Honesty is part of his code of conduct. People can depend on him.
—Scout Handbook, Boy Scouts of America

While Boy Scouts are told to tell the truth, their adult leaders sometimes do not. In the summer of 1974 America was scandalized to learn that overzealous staff officials of at least 15 local scout councils across the country had been padding their membership rolls in order to meet the ambitious quotas of a recruitment drive called Boypower '76, aimed at enrolling 2 million more boys into scouting by the time of the U.S. Bicentennial. In Chicago alone, there was evidence that as many as half of the city's 87,000 scouts listed on the roster did not exist. Moreover, to compound the fraud, the local scout council was receiving federal funds for the phantom scouts under a Model Cities program that paid the scout dues of ghetto youngsters, for the most part members of minority groups. Over a period of four years, the Chicago scout council alone had received $341,000 in such funds for the perhaps 40,000 fictitious poor kids on its padded roster.

The scandal brought to light problems that have been plaguing the Boy Scouts for the past decade or so. But first, a little bit of history. Scouting, as every tenderfoot knows, got its start in England around the turn of the century when Lt. Gen. (later Lord) Robert S. S. Baden-Powell, British hero of the Boer War, devised an outdoors program and code for boys based on his soldiering career as well as on his own childhood experiences of trekking and canoeing. In 1908 his ideas were embodied in a book called *Scouting for Boys*; it became the bible of a movement that quickly spread to other countries of the world and came to America in 1910.

For the next half century, enrollment climbed steadily and scouting, along with the flag and motherhood, became one of our most hallowed institutions, immortalized in Norman Rockwell's paintings of bright-eyed kids in khaki. The phrase "Boy Scout" evoked vignettes of white suburban striplings rubbing sticks together to make fire and helping old ladies across the street. Over 47 million red-blooded American boys embraced scouting on their way to manhood, and the scouts say that one of every two living American males has at one time or another been a scout or an adult volunteer, including some of our most celebrated citizens. Muhammad Ali, Walter Cronkite, and Jimmy Carter, reputedly the best-known Americans, were scouts. So were Presidents John F. Kennedy and Gerald Ford. (Richard Nixon claimed that he never became a scout because his family couldn't afford it.) Four members of our Supreme Court were scouts as were also 58 percent of the last Congress and 80 percent of America's astronauts. So were baseball's Reggie Jackson and Joe Morgan, football's O. J. Simpson, Nobel laureates Ralph Bunche and Ernest Lawrence, and the entertainment world's Irving Berlin, Johnny Carson, Bob Hope, Art Linkletter, and Henry Fonda, to name only a few.

Then, in the early 1970s, interest in scouting began to wane and membership dwindled year after year, dropping by 525,457 from 1973 to 1974, the year those scout councils were discovered to be padding their rolls. The top scout leadership had, of course, long been aware that the square knot of scouting was slipping fast.

In 1968 scout headquarters commissioned the research firm of Daniel Yankelovich to conduct a survey among scouts, nonscouts, parents, and scout personnel to answer the question, "Is Scouting in Tune with the Times?" The answer was inescapably, "No." For although most of those polled heartily approved of scouting, behind the ringing praise was also a significant number of negative views: "Not enough on the inner city," "camping and hiking aren't really important to my future," "scouting should teach more relevant stuff." Other criticisms held scouting to be "fun at first but not later," "too repetitious and boring," "too organized-restrictive," "discouraging initiative," "unresponsive to change," "overemphasizing the virtues of ruggedness and strength," and "too childish."

The feeling among the boys surveyed was that scouting pointed them not toward adulthood but toward a perennial childhood, that scouting leaders were treating them like children when what they wanted was to grow up prepared to cope with a real world.

Manifesting this discontent was scouting's high dropout rate. Six out of ten dropouts, the survey found, were at the Cub Scout level (for ages 8, 9, and 10). Too few of those who went on to become regular Boy Scouts (ages 11 through 17) elected to advance to the Explorer groups, geared for those up to 21 with special interests. Most dropped out by their sixteenth birthday to pursue jobs, careers, cars, or girls; the average life span of a scout was a mere 15 months.

There was criticism from other quarters, too. In 1968, Congress, which 52 years before had chartered the scouts to serve the youth of the nation, challenged the scouts to fulfill its mandate. "Which meant, after all the 'whereases' alluding to a glorious and vital past, that the BSA, Inc. was being admonished to get off its middle class rump and reach all boys," stated Bill Cardoso in *New Times* magazine. The head of the New York City Mission Society, which runs an alternative to scouting in the city's ghettos called the Cadet Corps, said that in order to make scouting work in the inner city one would have to take into account the fact that "the needs of children in the ghetto are different. Scouting doesn't start with the assumption that the number one concern is survival, and in the ghetto, that's what you have to start with."

In response to all this, scout executives came up with what they called the Improved Scouting Program, which was launched in 1972 with the publication of the first completely revised edition of the famous official *Boy Scout Handbook*, which, since first published 61 years before, had sold more than 26 million copies in seven previous editions. In deference to teen-agers and minorities who have long found the word "boy" demeaning, even the title was changed to *Scout Handbook,* this also allowing for the fact that the Explorer groups had gone coed the year before. For these reasons, the Boy Scouts of America adopted the new "communicative name" of "Scouting/USA" in 1977. Significantly, one of the four "scouts" (the new preferred catchall designation) shown on the cover of the new handbook is black, and black faces also populate its inside pages.

Missing from the new manual, however, are the earlier sections on such classical scouting standbys as signaling, map making, tracking, stalking, rowing, canoeing, tree identification, edible plants, and starting a fire with flint and steel. Although there is still page after page on camping and the outdoors, the hand-book has a new urban emphasis: It shows how to treat a rat bite as well as a snake bite, and it has a section on "City Hikes" which reminds scouts to carry "emergency change" for pay toilets and telephones. Other sections deal with such contemporary problems as drug abuse, smoking, air and water pollution, taxes, and the modern pressures that pull families apart. To the old list of merit badges that still includes "hog production" and "sheep ranching" (but now excludes "blacksmithing") have been added new ones in environmental science, consumerism, space exploration, oceanography, electronics, and computers.

To make it easier for scouts to advance up the ladder, they no longer have to earn merit badges in such mandatory areas as hiking, cooking, compass use, and Morse code; they can pick the merit badges they want to earn. They can now also advance by winning "skill awards" (one of the 12 awards offered is for "an understanding of drug abuse") which are easier to earn than merit badges. To deemphasize scouting's quasi-military character, the traditional ranks of Tender-foot, Second Class, First Class, and Eagle have been renamed "progress awards." Bright red berets or baseball-style caps are now alternatives to those wide-brimmed campaign hats, and the neckerchief is optional; girls in scouting can pick from a wardrobe of tunics, slacks, and shorts. (Yet the pages of *Boys' Life,* the official scout magazine, are still replete with ads for firearms, ammuni-tion, and such World War II relics as helmets, uniforms, and bayonets.)

In spite of all these changes, however, the Boypower '76 campaign, touchstone of the Improved Scouting Program, was far from a success. Only about half of the $65 million goal of the campaign was raised by the target year of 1976, and the campaign also failed to meet its goal of bringing 2 million more boys into scouting to raise total membership in the movement to 6.5 million in our bicentennial year. At the close of 1977, Scouting/USA served only 3.4 million young people, 1.5 million fewer than its peak enrollment of 4.9 million five years before and its smallest number in two decades. Moreover, there is no evidence that the campaign succeeded in its objective of boosting enrollment in ghetto areas and among the disadvantaged and minority groups. The scouts claim enrollment in these categories has increased about four times since the start of Boypower '76. But how seriously can one accept this estimate after the revela-tions already mentioned, particularly when total enrollment has been at a con-stant decline?

Yet, in spite of this decline, Scouting/USA still remains an awesome enter-prise, with about 4000 paid employees, nearly 1.3 million adult volunteers, and vast real estate holdings, valued at $233 million in the mid-1970s and including, according to varying estimates, from 140,000 to 288,000 acres of land and a $38 million office building complex at the organization's long-time national head-quarters in North Brunswick, New Jersey. (The complex, however, was sold when plans were made to move headquarters to Dallas in 1979.) Revenues of the national headquarters came to about $26 million in a recent year. Nearly two-thirds of this, or $16.6 million, came from registration, local council, and other fees, and another 18 percent from the profits on its $40 million business of selling uniforms, supplies, and other paraphernalia—the 6000 separate items range from official basket-weaving merit-badge kits to heart-shaped bracelets stamped with the scout emblem for den mothers—which are sold in some 2800 outlets throughout the country. A good deal of the expenses went for salaries to the 700 employees at the national office, including the $56,000-a-year chief scout execu-tive. (However, the local council executives do quite well, too: Nashville's chief scout executive and three members of his family were recently reported as drawing salaries totaling $68,000.)

The same year, the more than 400 local scout councils had a combined income of $125 million, of which about 45 percent came from the United Way, consider-ably below the federated drive's average contribution of 65.5 percent in 1960; in some areas, the United Way now provides as little as 20 or 25 percent of local council budgets.* This sizable drop in support, which reflects the growing disil-lusionment with scouting, has resulted in the councils' recently running at a deficit of $8.7 million. A recent appeal from the Greater New York Council said that it needed $2 million to maintain present programs and expand efforts in the poverty areas where scouting, the appeal said, "helps disadvantaged kids to overcome the glaring deficits in their lives; helps them build self-reliance and self-esteem; teaches them that courage is not a gun and that doing one's best for God and country can point the way out of the hopeless chaos in which they live."

Good sentiments, which even I believed when I was proud to be a scout—back in those days immortalized by Norman Rockwell. But perhaps no one believes such things anymore.

The Girl Scouts: "Beyond Campfires and Cookies"

The Girls Scouts, contrary to what many people think, have no connection with the Boy Scouts, although the two organizations have a certain historical tie. The first American Girl Scout troop was formed in 1912 in Savannah, Georgia, by Juliette Gordon Low on the pattern of England's Girl Guides; this group was established in 1910 by the father of the Boy Scout movement, Robert S. S. Baden-Powell, together with his sister Agnes, primarily because the old general, a Victorian in his ideas about women, felt that the sexes should be separated as far as scouting was concerned. (One of the first rules he decreed was that Girl Guides were not to talk to Boy Scouts in uniform.)

However, like the Boy Scouts, the girls in green have been undergoing an identity crisis and an intensive period of self-examination in an effort to cope

---

*Other sources of council income include sustaining members, foundations, special events and projects, bequests, and investment income. The local troops, packs, and posts generally have their own small dues and money-raising projects to support their special-unit activities.

with the fact that their membership, too, has been steadily declining in recent years—from a peak of 3.2 million in the early 1970s to a current 2.6 million. The girls are generally grouped into four age levels (Brownies, 6 through 8; Juniors, 9 through 11; Cadettes, 12 through 14; and Seniors, 14 through 17) and, like their some 557,000 adult volunteer leaders, come largely from white middle-class suburban backgrounds. Illustrious former scouts have included such all-American specimens of wholesome womanhood as Debbie Reynolds, Grace Kelly, Candice Bergen, Dinah Shore, Dorothy Hamill, and Tricia and Julie Nixon.

To change their image and broaden their appeal, the Girl Scouts have not only abandoned their dowdy old green uniform dresses (a source of great unhappiness among teen-agers, they have been replaced by "mix and match" components, such as tunics, pants, and jumpers) but have begun to give special emphasis to activities demonstrating "the movement's concern for its ethnic and social diversity and for career opportunities and challenges for women."

Programs reflecting its new goals have included projects aimed at developing Girl Scout leadership in Mexican-American and other Spanish-speaking communities and bringing scouting to children of migrant labor families. Others have been designed to educate the scouts in parenthood, train them to help the elderly poor, and offer activities aimed at taking the girls geographically and otherwise beyond the activities of their own troop or council. In recent years the girls have been given the chance to visit Europe or to explore careers in oceanography, archeology, forestry, communications, politics, and to work with handicapped and disadvantaged children. All this, of course, is to supplement the traditional service work of the girls which has included visiting shut-ins and old people and collecting gifts for distribution by various welfare agencies.

Symbolizing the Girl Scouts' goal of going "beyond campfires and cookies" and bringing poor, minority children into the organization was its election in the mid-1970s of Gloria Dean Scott, a North Carolina professor of education, as its first black national president (an unpaid three-year post). As if this were not enough, the organization, about the same time, named feminist leader and former scout Betty Friedan to its board of directors.

Not surprisingly, the changing character of the organization has involved it in a number of imbroglios. When the group's board, in 1977, endorsed the Equal Rights Amendment, marking the first time it had ever taken a stand on a political issue, one girl burned her uniform in protest. The question of whether or not to admit boys to the organization has also been a matter of considerable controversy; those favoring the idea claimed that it would encourage older girls, who had the highest dropout rate, to maintain their membership. However, the proposal was finally voted down in 1975, even though the Boy Scouts had voted the year before to admit girls aged 14 to 21 to their Explorer division. The same year, the Roman Catholic Archdiocese of Philadelphia, critical of a new Girl Scout merit program dealing with sex education, family planning, and abortion, severed its ties with the organization and asked 8000 Catholic scouts within its jurisdiction to switch to the Camp Fire Girls, which an archdiocese spokesman described as more "God-conscious."

Not that the Girl Scouts can by any means be considered a radical organization. But as one of its officials put it, "We're very much of today and want them [the girls] to have all the choices of today."

No one, however, can take issue with the Girl Scouts' finances. About half of the national headquarters' income of about $13 million comes from membership dues (generally $2) and most of the rest from the net profits on the sale of scouting uniforms and equipment. Of the total receipts, slightly more than half goes to provide various services to the organization's 350 local councils that assist them in establishing programs, training adult leaders and staff, developing membership, raising funds, operating the Girl Scout camps, and subsidizing the *American Girl* and other publications and audiovisual materials; the rest is spent to operate the national headquarters, including expenses for salaries and membership registration.

In addition, the local councils take in about $90 million annually—37 percent, on the average, from United Way contributions, another 37 percent from the sale of those famous Girl Scout cookies and other items, and most of the remainder from camping fees, bequests, and investment income. (Overhead and fund-raising costs seldom run more than 20 percent of income.) As for the local troops, the little money needed to run them comes from occasional contributions from the girls themselves, their parents, organizations and individuals of the community, special money-making projects conducted by the girls, and, of course, a small bite—10 to 15 cents—from the sale of those cookies, of which 84 million boxes are sold annually.

The Camp Fire Girls: Flame and Crossed Logs

Although founded two years before the Girl Scouts—in 1910 by an educator named Luther Halsey Gulick—the Camp Fire Girls is a much smaller organization, with a membership today of nearly 500,000. The organization, while not necessarily more "God-conscious" than the Girl Scouts, as the Philadelphia archdiocese had declared, is considered somewhat more conservative and middle-American, perhaps because its membership is concentrated in the smaller urban and rural areas of America's heartland. In fact, it moved its national headquarters from New York to Kansas City, Missouri, in 1977 in order to be closer to its local councils: Fifty-five percent of the membership is located within a 600-mile radius of the new headquarters. Some people also consider the Camp Fire Girls to place more emphasis on the individual and to be more "home-oriented" than the Girl Scouts. The Camp Fire name and insignia—a flame and crossed logs—is supposed to symbolize the home (hearth) and outdoors (campfire), and one of the reasons the organization was founded was "to perpetuate the spiritual ideals of the home."

Actually, however, apart from the fact that the Girl Scouts sell cookies and the Camp Fire Girls sell candy and have admitted high school boys to membership since 1971, and younger boys since 1975, there are only subtle differences between the two organizations as far as membership and activities are concerned. Camp Fire Girls are divided into four age groups—Blue Birds, Adventurers, Discovery Club, and Horizon Club—which correspond, in order of increasing age, roughly to those of the Girl Scouts. Both organizations place a good deal of emphasis on community service as well as on personal development. Like the Girl Scouts and other youth groups, the Camp Fire Girls have also been faced with the problem of steadily declining membership—and for much the same reasons.

To cope with this problem, the Camp Fire Girls, after a long period of soul-searching, debate, and planning, has also come up with a renewal program of its own. Dubbed "A New Day" and launched in 1975, the program mandated the 330-odd local councils to provide new services in response to community needs; the services—and, in effect, Camp Fire membership—were to be extended to youth of both sexes from birth to age 21 with, however, the primary target remaining girls from six through high school age and boys of high school age. Programs already in operation or being planned include day-care services for working mothers, juvenile justice programs for first offenders, community-based services for troubled children, drop-in centers for "hard to serve" areas, and specialized programs for handicapped children.

The purpose of all this was "to provide, through a program of informal education, opportunities for youth to realize their potential and to function effectively as caring, self-directed individuals responsible to themselves and to others; and, as an organization, to seek to improve those conditions in society which affect youth." Accordingly, in addition to carrying on their traditional group and camping programs, the 330 local councils were mandated to "design multiple program delivery systems as appropriate to meet the needs and interests of youth within their territories."

In judging whether to give to the Camp Fire Girls, one may therefore wish to study the programs and finances of the council in your community. Generally, fund-raising costs are low since most local councils, like those of the Girl Scouts, receive a good deal of support from the federated United Way campaigns, the rest coming from the sale of candy and other products, supporting memberships, and the proceeds of special events and other fund-raising activities. The national headquarters' income of about $2.8 million, of which 60 percent is from council assessments, with the rest largely from the sale of Camp Fire clothing, equipment, and other merchandise, and from contributions. This is used for services to the local units, program development, administrative overhead, and fund raising. The councils take in about $22 million annually, of which one-third comes from United Ways, another one-third from the sale of candy and other products, and the rest from membership dues, camping fees, the proceeds of special events, and contributions.

Boys' and Girls' Clubs of America

Geared predominantly to the needy, the Boys' Clubs of America, which provide recreational, cultural, educational, social, and other activities for boys from 7 through 17, was formed in 1906 when some 50 clubs joined together to form the national organization. Today there are about 1100 affiliated clubs, some dating back to the 1860s, serving about 1 million boys in 700 communities in 50 states, Puerto Rico, and the Virgin Islands. The ranks of "alumni" have included Joe DiMaggio, Danny Thomas, Irving Berlin, actor Ben Gazzara, governors, mayors, congressmen, and tens of thousands of lesser-known doctors, lawyers, scientists, clergymen, business leaders, and other sterling citizens. Grants and scholarships have helped subsidize college students and promising young talents in the performing and creative arts.

In Chicago, Marvin Gordon, a wealthy marketing man, proudly showed me around the Boys' Club (one of 17 in the Chicago area) he serves as a board member. "I want you to know that this very club sent me to summer camp when I was a poor nine-year-old welfare kid, and the experience meant very much to me," said Gordon. Started in 1952 in a converted old mansion, the club is now housed in an impressive $1.25 million building, with an Olympic-size swimming pool, a huge gym, and a warren of arts and crafts rooms in what has become an all-black neighborhood. If a youngster cannot afford the modest membership dues ($1 to $3, depending on age), he is allowed to "work out" the amount through a job at the club. Gordon's club serves 1500 boys on an annual operating budget of $150,000, this averaging out to $100 per boy.

Combined annual expenditures of all the clubs were last reported to be about $105 million, most of this coming from contributions by business, foundations, individuals, and the twenty or so civic, fraternal, veterans, and labor organizations with which the clubs maintain continuing relationships. Most are also supported by United Way or similar federated drives and, because their work is believed helpful in combating juvenile delinquency and solving the problems of ghettos, many of their programs also receive some government support. Although the caliber of the clubs may vary from place to place, the organization as a whole now meets the standards of both the National Information Bureau and the Council of Better Business Bureaus (as do also the Boy and Girl Scouts, Campfire Girls, and the Girls Clubs).

The Girls' Clubs of America, a completely separate and smaller organization, founded in 1945, provides similar after-school programs for 200,000 girls from 6 to 18 (68 percent of them from low-income urban families) in some 250 clubs in the United States and Canada. To keep pace with the changing times, the programs have moved away from recreation and the preparation of the girls for a once-predictable life among the domestic arts; they now include sessions on sex, drug abuse, teen-age pregnancy and other social problems, and career and job development workshops, as well as a variety of cultural and art activities. Since the girls pay no dues, the clubs are funded primarily through the United Way and other private contributions, including some from foundations.

However, it is the feeling of the Girls' Clubs' executive director, Edith B. Phelps, that there is a prevailing cultural bias toward men and boys when it comes to giving to organizations like hers. She points out that only $1 out of every $4 that corporate foundations donate to youth agencies goes to girls' organizations, which also receive only one-third the amount of regular foundation grants given to boys' organizations. For this reason, she is concentrating on seeking the sort of financial and personal support from women executives that upwardly mobile men have traditionally given boys' clubs.

She says: "We need women corporate managers and executives and stockholders to pressure American industry to give as many pro bono dollars to girls' organizations as they now give to boys' organizations—agencies serving girls can no longer operate efficiently with a stove, a sewing machine, and a loving heart.

Junior Achievement: Cradle of Teen-Age Tycoons

To encourage upward mobility among our teen-agers is the task of Junior Achievement, which traces its birth to Springfield, Massachusetts, in 1919. This admittedly capitalistic, if nonprofit, enterprise offers groups of high school boys and girls the opportunity to gain practical business experience by forming and managing miniature "corporations" of their own under the guidance of adult advisers enlisted from the ranks of business and industry. The teen-age tycoons, in groups of 15 to 25, select their own board of directors, work force, and sales staff, elect officers, decide on a product or service to produce, sell stock in their enterprise, set up production lines, actually sell their product or service, pay themselves salaries or commissions, keep company records, pay rent and taxes, disburse dividends, and work out the amount of their success or failure in dollars and cents. The junior businesses, which are phased out at the end of the academic year, have ranged from making leather belts, soda can lamps, and chess sets to running a student bank, putting out a newspaper, and operating an advertising agency. In South Bend, Indiana, a JA group created and produced a 15-week TV program for a network-affiliated station. (Said the group's adult adviser, "You don't find many TV-production companies where your vice-president for sales had to resign because he's failing algebra.") About 80 percent of the companies, which usually start with from $100 to $150 in working capital, realize a profit.

JA has grown from its original 300 youngsters to an organization now involving nearly 250,000 participants in more than 7500 junior enterprises in about 1000 communities. What one thinks of this largely business-supported "educational" movement aimed at giving our young people "an understanding of the American private enterprise system" would depend on how one feels about tax-deductible dollars being used to promote the doctrines of any special-interest group. But those who feel that what's good for business is good for America will no doubt applaud the objectives of Junior Achievement.

4-H: Head, Heart, Hands, and Health

Also tied in with a special-interest group and not even a charity in the conventional sense are the nation's 4-H Clubs, whose origins go back to the late nineteenth century; they are a sort of rural equivalent of the scouting groups, but with the added utilitarian purpose of training young farmers and, in general, strengthening the quality of life in our declining number of agricultural communities. (Between 1940 and 1977 the U.S. farm population dwindled from 30.5 million to 7.8 million.) The name of the clubs is derived from their fourfold purpose of improving head, heart, hands, and health. Since the 4-H program, which has a total membership of 5.5 million boys and girls in about 140,000 clubs, is predominantly financed and run by the government (through the Cooperative Extension Service of the Department of Agriculture), they may be of only marginal interest to the average contributor to charity. Nonetheless, the relatively few private citizens whose contributions supplement the government funds going to the clubs might well ask why the government should not pay for the entire cost of the program if it is seemingly so much in the national interest. On the other hand, since 4-H Club work does involve certain "character-building" activities, one could also well ask if any government money in effect should be used to control such aspects of youth training. In a recent year about $110 million in government funds—federal, state, and local—was appropriated for the 4-H program, compared to the $3.5 million raised by the nonprofit National 4-H Club Foundation, about half of this from private donations and most of the rest from such activities as the training of volunteer leaders and research and development programs to augment the work of the Cooperative Extension Service.

"Benevolent Octopus": The Ys

Serving the old as well as the young and the urban and rural are the Young Men's Christian Associations. From its early days as an overtly Protestant religious movement having as its purpose "the improvement of the spiritual and mental conditions of young men," the YMCA, which is sometimes called "the poor man's country club," has metamorphosed to the point where its name is now a misnomer. "Actually, we're no longer just a "Y'—more than half of our membership is now over 18," Robert Galloway, an official of the National Council of YMCAs, told me. "Nor is the 'M' in our title strictly true—at least a third of our members are now women and girls. Nor are we really 'Christian' any more, except in tradition and orientation. People of any religious faith can join or use our facilities.* And, of course, none of the local Ys are really an association in the dictionary definition of the word."

Soon after the Y's establishment here in 1851, bodily health was added to its goals of spiritual and mental development. During the late 1850s the Y began adding gyms to its facilities, and as the organization grew its chain of buildings also included facilities for group meetings, classes (the first were in language and music), and dormitory living. The turn of the century saw the Y organizing night schools and technical and vocational courses. During this period, the YMCA began admitting women and girls to membership, although the heavy influx of females did not start to take place until the 1950s and 1960s.

Despite its traditional "gym and swim" image or the popular conception of it as a place offering inexpensive lodgings (as little as $10 a night), the average Y today offers a bewildering welter of activities. At one Y or another, one can take courses in Oriental cooking, speed writing, belly dancing, art, ballet, karate, and the hustle as well as in accounting, law, and various trades. (YMCAs run eight degree-granting colleges and numerous vocational schools.) One can also get vocational guidance, psychological counseling, and tax assistance and participate in adult study or discussion groups on a wide variety of topics, from ecology to family relations, or in social activities such as dances, games, parties, and picnics.

*YMCA membership today roughly reflects the religious affiliations of our population: About 60 percent is Protestant, 28 percent Roman Catholic, 4 percent Jewish, and 8 percent affiliated with other or no religious groups. Although, ordinarily, local Ys are affiliated with the local interdenominational council of churches, and the National Council of YMCAs is a related agency of the National Council of Churches of Christ in the U.S.A., this is about the extent of the YMCA's affiliation with Protestantism; it has no organic ties to any church. Of course, prominent lay Christians do dominate Y boards, a fact that may have been responsible for the Y's long-time "cool" relationship with the Roman Catholic Church. However, this changed during the 1960s and the church now gives its adherents general approval to participate in and support Y activities.

Offering as it now does something for almost everyone, the YMCA has grown to be the largest philanthropic institution in the United States, spreading over our sociological landscape like a "benevolent octopus," as a writer once put it. Its 1835 local associations here (there are also 12,000 centers in 89 other countries) have 8.7 million members, own buildings and other assets worth $1 billion, have an annual operating budget (including national headquarters) of nearly $400 million, and, in a recent year, had 102 new building projects or major renovations in progress at an estimated cost of $109 million. The local YMCAs also operate over 600 resident camps and 800 summer day camps, serving 1.3 million people of all ages annually, and conduct outreach programs serving another 500,000.

Other YMCA statistics are equally staggering. In a recent year, attendance at Y gyms was 33,540,000 and at Y swimming pools, 43,954,000. A total of 926,754 was taught to swim. The Y's 42,853 rooms, which make it the nation's eighth largest hotel chain (ranking just behind Howard Johnson's, with 58,977 rooms), were occupied 10,950,000 nights. Y members participated in 566,152 organized activity groups which, together with the Ys themselves, were run by 187,816 volunteer leaders, 166,287 volunteers, and a full-time professional staff of 5839. Few people are aware that Y staffers invented basketball (in 1891) and volleyball (1895).

Understandably, the Y has followed the middle-class migration to the suburbs where it has located almost all of the 130 branches it has developed over the past ten years. (Unlike most other charitable organizations, it conducts no national fund drives; it has to go where its contributors and constituents are.) However, in keeping with its commitment to the solution of the urban crisis, it has not neglected inner city areas. Two of the largest YMCAs built in recent years—one in Stamford, Connecticut, and the other in Portland, Oregon—were located in inner city areas so that they could better serve the poor and minority groups there. (The nation's largest YMCA is in Chicago.) Branches in metropolitan areas often reflect their ethnic and neighborhood character. In the Miami area, for example, one branch in the "Little Havana" section opens meetings with the "Star Spangled Banner" followed by the Cuban national anthem; another branch, in a predominantly black neighborhood, emphasizes black heritage in its programs.

In most communities, the YMCA is the largest organization concerned with recreation, social, and other group activities. At the Stamford YMCA, a visitor shared a no-nonsense lunch of roast beef on white bread, potato chips, and coffee (cost, $2) with its director, Horace A. (Red) Smith, and several members of his staff.

Red recalled that when he first went into Y work in 1935, it would hire only members of certain Protestant denominations. "No Lutherans. No Catholics, of course. But that's now all changed."

"Do you still have Bible classes?" he was asked.

Smith said no, not nowadays. "Jesus taught by example and that's what we do." He led the talk away from theology by telling how Y leaders handled fights, arguments, and other disciplinary problems by sending the culprits away to "think things over."

Somebody asked about "scholarships" for poor kids.

"No one's barred from the YMCA because of lack of funds," said Red. "I feel very strongly about that. Not just kids but a 40-year-old man or an 80-year-old man. We do ask them to establish need. A kid who says he can't pay is asked to bring his parents in to talk to us. We try to get $25. (The regular membership is $45 for youths 16 to 18.) But we'll take even a token fee of a dollar. We've found that if you pay something, it means more.''

Smith went on to tell about a free boxing class that quickly folded, in contrast to a $2 class that kept most of its kids. ''Mom and Dad said, 'We paid for it and you'd better go!''' said Smith.

Don Collins, the Y's physical education director, mentioned that there were some scholarship kids who, ''believe it or not, had never before swum in a pool.''

At the equipment checkout counter, Don pushed a buzzer so that a gym-suited man could enter the door to the Stamford Y Athletic Club. SYAC members pay $325 a year, in contrast to the regular men's membership of $130, but enjoy such extras as a nap room, sun room, sauna, massage—and a special window to the coffee shop.

Smith showed off the coffee shop and grill, which serves off-the-street customers as well as in-the-building diners, and also caters parties, meetings, and other affairs. Like the parking garage, the grill is ''farmed out'' to private concessionaires for a percentage of the profits.

He said that the Stamford Y, like others, is ''locally autonomous, not legislated to by our National Council.'' However, it is certified by National which also gives consultations, programs, advice—for example, on how to build a handball court or swimming pool. For this, the Y pays National 10 percent of its adjusted gross, figured by formula, Smith said.

Of the total YMCA annual income of $431 million, a relatively small proportion—$96 million or about 22 percent—comes from contributions, most of this from the United Way. Another $37 million or so comes from government and foundation grants (to finance the social programs) and the bulk of the rest comes from membership dues, activities and camp fees, room charges, investment income, and so on. Fund raising, therefore, is only a minor factor in the expenditures of the local Ys. However, since the programs of the local Ys may vary in each community, would-be contributors should base their decision on an appraisal of their Y's activities and financial report.

The First Women's Libbers: The YWCAs

The Young Women's Christian Association, it should be said right off, is *not* the women's branch of the YMCA. It is a completely separate organization, although in some cities it does share building space and offers similar facilities and programs; some YWCA programs, however, are geared to what are thought of as women's interests: instruction in cooking, dressmaking, hatmaking, flower arrangement, typing and shorthand, for example. Assertiveness training for women has recently become one of the more popular courses. Men can take part in YWCA programs and activities but only as ''associates''; in contrast to the YMCA, people of the opposite sex cannot be voting members.

This is because the YWCA, in spite of its ''Christian'' roots (although like the YMCA, it is now open to people of all faiths), has from the beginning regarded itself as a women's movement, dedicated to improving the lot of women. The organization traces its origin to England when two groups merged in 1855. One was a London ladies' prayer union concerned with the welfare of women and girls coming to the city from rural areas as a result of the Industrial Revolution; the other was a home for nurses returning from the Crimean War. In 1866 the first American YWCA was started in Boston with 30 members.

Soon after, classes were offered in penmanship, bookkeeping, astronomy, and physiology. According to an official history, the YWCA was the first organization in the country to offer sewing machine lessons (in 1872). Stenography, china painting, domestic science, and cooking were soon added to the courses offered, as was also typing—after doctors conferred and decided that a woman's delicate constitution could probably withstand the strain of using the new machine. To equip women for the other physical strains of daily living, classes in calisthenics were organized in the late 1870s, and by 1895 swimming had also become an important part of the sports curriculum, these marking the beginnings of today's large health, physical education, and recreation program.

Today there are about 400 local accredited YWCAs as well as some 50 student associations with 2.8 million members and program participants, about 370,000 of them male associates. Collectively, they own buildings carried on the books at $275 million (estimated replacement cost, $650 million) and have operating budgets totaling $105 million a year. The fact that the YWCA and YMCA share buildings and facilities and even conduct joint programs in some localities has led to frequent recommendations that the two organizations merge. Among those pressing for the merger are the United Ways—on the rationale that dollars would be saved and service would be increased by the operation of one agency instead of two.

But the mere thought of merger is anathema, if not a fighting word, to national YWCA officials who have revoked the charters of the few local associations (for example, those in Ann Arbor, Newark, and Eugene, Oregon) that have merged. "To merge would dilute our voice and decrease our effectiveness as a woman's organization," a YWCA official told me. "In nearly every instance where there has been a merger, the women have been swallowed up and lost their leadership roles on the new boards. This is why we don't even allow men to be regular voting members."

"Besides," she went on, "in spite of their superficial resemblance, our organizations have different goals. We took the first national stand for women's rights back in 1911—long before women's lib—and this is still one of our primary concerns, whereas the YMCA"—she laughed—"is concerned more with physical fitness and a clean mind and a clean body. We're more politically oriented. The YW has taken a strong stand against racism. The YM hasn't. We've also given strong support to such causes as voter registration, integration, the Equal Rights Amendment, and gun control legislation. The YM hasn't."

The YWCA support of gun control legislation in 1973 embroiled it in a dispute with the National Rifle Association and other "sporting" groups that threatened a boycott of local United Way drives from which the women's organization derives about one-third of its financial support. (Another third comes from program and service fees and the rest comes from dues, contributions and bequests, investment income, and government and foundation grants.) In Tucson, Arizona, the United Way campaign chairman even found a bullet hole in the window of his office. No one knows how effective the boycott was but the United Way had what was up to then the best year in its history; and Jean Whittet, director of public policy for the national YWCA, later said that most local groups, despite the deluge of hate mail they had received, had weathered the storm very successfully, both financially and in enhancing the YWCA image across the country.

"We've always been more than an organization with a swimming pool and a residence," she added.

The YM-YWHAs

The first Young Men's Hebrew Association was established in Baltimore in 1854, just three years after the first YMCA; and the first Young Women's Hebrew Association came into being as an auxiliary of New York's 92nd Street YMHA. Unlike their Christian counterparts, the YMHA and YWHA, apart from being American inventions, are and have long been fully integrated joint enterprises. Today there are about 300 combined YM-YWHAs in the United States (outside of New York, they are generally called Jewish Community Centers) with 900,000 members and a total budget of $82 million; there are another 200 similar Jewish groups in about 15 foreign countries. In this country their principal source of support are the fund drives of the Federation of Jewish Philanthropies; for the rest of their income they depend on individual contributions and bequests, membership dues, program fees—in general, the same sources as the YMCAs and YWCAs.

In spite of their differing religious orientations, many of the programs of the Jewish and Christian groups are virtually indistinguishable. "You don't have to be Jewish to enjoy us," said an official of New York's 92nd Street YM-YWHA, which observed its centenary in 1974 and is perhaps the most celebrated of all the Jewish centers. In the Y's 26 floors of space in two buildings, its 9500 members, many of them Gentiles, indulge in the usual Y sports and educational and other activities (the actor Zero Mostel once taught an adult class in life painting there). The Y is also a world-renowned showcase for such "intimate" arts as the dance, poetry, and chamber music; and the performers in its auditorium have included such illustrious names as T. S. Eliot, Dylan Thomas, Martha Graham, Isaac Stern, Norman Mailer, and the Budapest and Guarneri Quartets.

The Changing Junior League:
Social but Socially-Conscious

The Junior League has come a long way since it was founded in 1901 by a group of New York City debutantes headed by Mary Harriman, an older sister of Averell Harriman, the diplomat and former New York governor. "I remember Mary proposing that we should get together and work in some way for city betterment," later recalled a member of the original group, which also included Eleanor Roosevelt. Since then the image has persisted of the Junior League as an elite organization of socially prominent and wealthy do-gooders who busy themselves in hospital and museum work. This impression is not entirely without foundation for most of the 120,000 young (18 to 35) women who today belong to some 230 Junior Leagues across the country are expensively dressed white

WASP suburban housewives born to the blue; and as a service to transient members the Association of Junior Leagues maintains a block of rooms at New York's posh Waldorf-Astoria.

However, during the past decade or so, many league rosters have also included the names of more and more working women (who now make up about 15 percent of the total membership) and other unpedigreed whites as well as blacks, and their influence has no doubt played a role in the leagues' increasing involvement in innovative social action projects. Even many of the leagues' older, more staid members, after first opposing this new direction, have come to the realization that the organization had to change with the times. "I was on the verge of resigning because I felt the league was risking irrelevancy," said one Cleveland Heights society matron. "When I was a provisional [the first phase of membership], they put me in a soda shop in a hospital as my volunteer work. What did I know or care about that?"

While continuing their traditional service projects, new league activities have included setting up halfway houses for alcoholics, homes for runaway children, drug centers, and counseling centers for juvenile delinquents. In Washington, D.C., 60 league members signed up for paralegal training to help women fight job and housing discrimination. In Iowa, league volunteers serve as presentence investigators and probation officers for the courts; in Rochester, New York, the league sponsors seminars on rape. And in New York City, the first of the leagues is involved in such projects as an early childhood development center, a newspaper for the elderly, a campaign urging victims to report rapes, and a program counseling pregnant prisoners and training them and other female prisoners in business skills prior to their release.

To support these and other projects, the leagues now raise about $6 million a year. In keeping with their new image, fancy dress balls and society horse shows have declined as major fund-raising projects. Instead, they have been replaced by federal and foundation grants and such events as a $30-a-plate buffet supper that the New York league recently cosponsored with Manhattan's black Urban League—an event symbolizing the new directions of both organizations and one that would have been unthinkable in 1901 or, for that matter, even twenty or ten years ago.

The Salvation Army: Billion-Dollar Church

One thing to keep in mind the next time you flip a coin into one of those Salvation Army kettles is that you are giving to a church—a distinct denomination with a ministry and specific doctrines.* Another is that you are giving to a very rich church, one with a total net worth of at least $1 billion, perhaps even twice that or more. This is not to denigrate the army's many good works which, in fact, are an integral part of its origin and its reason for being.

*The Salvation Army preaches that the teachings of the Bible, such as those dealing with the Creation and the Fall of Man, are fundamental, and that man's rebirth and salvation come through the sacrifice of Jesus Christ and man's ability through the power of God to grow in righteousness. However, the organization holds, according to an official statement, that "the sacraments observed by some Protestant denominations—baptism and the Lord's Supper—are not essential to the soul's salvation and it does not observe them." Nonetheless, the army, while regarding itself as "chiefly Protestant," says it does not stress this tie "because we serve all beliefs and no beliefs and have people of all faiths on our advisory boards."

The story begins in England with William Booth (1829—1912), who, after beginning life as an impoverished pawnbroker's apprentice, left the Methodist ministry in 1865 to preach in the slums of London's East End as an independent evangelist. Booth quickly discovered the futility of talking God to hungry, homeless men when their physical and social needs also required urgent attention. Since many of his prospective converts felt uncomfortable in regular churches, he, joined by other evangelists, set up Christian Mission Centers which, in 1878, reorganized along military lines (patterned after the British army), became the Salvation Army. The missions became "corps"; the members, "soldiers"; the ministers, "officers"; and Booth himself, "general." (In the same military mode, the army's bulletin is called the *War Cry*.)

In spite of the opposition to the army from both high and low—Queen Victoria had some qualms about the private army that the evangelistic "general" was raising in her kingdom, and the gin makers and brothel owners worried that the army might siphon off their best customers—followers, rallying to the cry, "Soup, soap, and salvation," multiplied, and the movement soon spread to other countries, coming to these shores in 1880.

Today, the army, with a claimed worldwide membership of about 2 million and 25,000 officers, operates some 15,450 corps (also known as community centers) in 82 countries. In the United States alone, there are about 3600 active officers, almost 400,000 members or soldiers (the equivalent of members of other congregations), and 15,400 "civilian," or nonarmy, employees, manning 1100 corps and 8100 outposts, service units, and other centers, such as dispensaries and clinics, hospitals and maternity homes (including 23 for unwed mothers), day nurseries, emergency lodges, homes for senior citizens, skid-row centers for alcoholics, employment services, boys' clubs, and "Evangeline" residences for young women.

To give an idea of the awesome scope of the Salvation Army's work, here are some of its U.S. statistics for a recent year: 8,107,756 meals served, 1,942,730 lodgings supplied to homeless or transient men and women, 3,968,261 patients visited in 16,030 hospitals and nursing homes, 133,535 persons placed in jobs, 1450 missing persons located, 48,387 armed forces inductees aided, 3,833,409 persons given family welfare services, 2,612,298 persons given Christmas or Thanksgiving aid (usually food, clothing, and toys), 4249 unwed mothers counseled or sheltered (the army also provides pregnancy testing and family planning), 94,528 prison inmates visited, 116,621 persons helped at centers for alcoholics, 29,750 children enrolled in camps, and 125,703 boys and girls enrolled in youth clubs.

At the army's four officer-training schools in this country, enrolled in any given year are from 350 to 400 cadets. Officer candidates must be between 18 and 30 (at times this is extended to 40 or even 45) and must have a high school diploma or its equivalent and at least six months of satisfactory service as a "soldier" to be eligible for the two-year intensive training course. The course, though touching on the liberal arts, is devoted mostly to such tools of the theological trade as Bible studies, public speaking, the preparation of sermons, music, church discipline, pastoral counseling, and bookkeeping. Upon graduation, all are ordained ministers with the rank of lieutenant, authorized to perform marriage and funeral services and other ministerial duties. Officers are not allowed to marry outside the ranks, and marriage only between officers is encouraged. A wife shares her husband's rank. Since more single women than men become officers—the recent ratio is about two to one—many women officers are destined to become spinsters. Other traditional taboos include lipstick (although unobtrusive makeup is tolerated), liquor, tobacco, playing cards, and swearing; until recently, officers weren't even allowed to watch movies. Not that officers can really afford to indulge in such vices. Starting "allowances" are $50.25 a week for a single lieutenant and $81.50 for a married couple, with additional allowances for any children. Out of this, officers must pay most of the cost of their uniforms. However, they do receive free housing accommodations.

New officers are first assigned as pastors or administrators of local church "units"—the corps—or to one of the army's social institutions and are then promoted on the basis of seniority and merit. Above lieutenant, the successively higher ranks are captain, major, brigadier, colonel, commissioner, and, finally, the top and sole international rank of general. Soldiers work at regular jobs but may wear uniforms when participating in army functions or volunteer work, such as performing in bands or singing groups or manning the army's Christmas kettles.

The familiar Christmas kettle was first used in San Francisco in 1891 when an enterprising Salvation Army captain, faced with the problem of providing 1000 free Christmas dinners, commandeered a soup kettle and a bell from a ship chandler's shop and started the cry, "Keep the pot boiling." The response was so generous that the entire movement quickly took over the idea. (Salvationists have found that when women are on kettle duty, donations come three-to-one from men; when men man the kettles, donations come three-to-one from women.)

Just how much the Salvation Army raises or spends is difficult to estimate because of its complicated organizational structure and byzantine bookkeeping. Fund raising is conducted primarily by the 1100 corps community centers, which give 10 percent of their income to their divisional offices. Each of the 39 divisions, which also do some fund raising on their own, in turn gives 10 percent of its income to its territorial office. The four U.S. territories (Eastern, Central, Southern, and Western), which may also receive large gifts such as legacies, in turn furnish funds on a formula basis to support the national headquarters, based in New York, which does no fund raising at all.

Confounding matters is that the army, like most religious organizations, is not required to report its financial figures or to disclose them publicly. To satisfy the needs of local United Ways or other federated funding campaigns, the 39 divisions and some of the 1100 corps may produce some sort of financial reports, which may or may not be audited; these are often available to the public. The four territories also prepare financial statements, which are generally not available to the public. But no over-all consolidated statement is available, at least for public eyes, covering all the nationwide activities.

I secured a copy of a recent report of the Greater New York division, which embraces 29 corps units, and found that not all of the army's services fall into the category of sheer charity: A good chunk—nearly half—of the division's stated $18.1 million income came from the charges by its residences, hospitals, senior citizens' homes, narcotics addicts' centers, and other institutions (32.6 percent) and from the government (16 percent). The division got another 9 percent of its revenues from investment income and nearly 5 percent from thrift shop sales and contributions from officers and soldiers. Contributing the remainder—about one-third—of the revenues was the public at large, either directly or through federated drives and through legacies and bequests.

One wonders, however, how seriously one could take these figures, as well as those on the expense side of the ledger, for they were not prepared in accordance with generally accepted accounting principles and they were based on corps reports, many of which were admittedly unaudited. All administrative overhead costs were also allocated to program expenses instead of to supporting services, contrary to customary practice, and there was no separate breakdown for fund-raising expenses.

Similar obfuscations and distortions were found in the territorial and national headquarters reports which the army's national treasurer-business administrator, Lt. Col. Wesley Sheppard, graciously made available to me. For example, with the transfer of funds from divisions to territories and even within these entities, it was often impossible to ascertain if certain stated figures duplicated others. Different categories of terms used in the various reports also made comparisons difficult.

Nonetheless, certain conclusions could be formed that would give at least some idea of the army's impressive wealth. The net worth of the Eastern territory alone, which has 11 divisions, appeared to be about $293 million, and the net worth of all of the four territories and national headquarters was shown on the organization's books to total $712 million. However, even this latter figure did not reflect the army's real net worth, as even Lt. Col. Sheppard conceded. For one thing, the army's portfolio of marketable securities was listed at cost or donated value—$217 million—rather than at market value, which was much higher.

More significantly, the army's real estate holdings were also listed at cost or at their appraised value when donated and, on this basis, were carried at a mere half a billion dollars—$492 million, to be exact. But with the army having acquired many of its properties at least 40 to 50 years ago, it is quite obvious that they would now be worth many times their original value. The army's national head-quarters, for example, an imposing 11-story structure in New York erected in 1932, is carried on the books at its depression-years cost of only $168,155, although experts say that the property could today easily fetch a sum in the high six figures or even more. An extremely conservative estimate would place the current market price of the army's total real estate holdings at perhaps three or four times their stated value; this alone would bring the army's net worth to anywhere from $1.5 million to $2 billion. And taking into account the market value of the army's securities could bring the total net worth to well over $2 billion.*

Of course, this may not be a great sum of money, considering the army's vast facilities and the services it provides at a current annual cost, according to Lt. Col. Sheppard, estimated to be in excess of $275 million. Again, it should be stressed how cooperative he was in providing the information that he did and how much he regretted that he could not furnish more precise figures, saying that they

*This figure, it should be stressed, may not include other assets owned by the divisions and corps.

would be difficult, if not impossible, to gather in an organization as complex as his. One wonders, however, if such an answer would satisfy the prestigious business and community leaders who serve on the army's advisory boards or whether they would accept the army's accounting practices for their own enterprises, many of them far more complex and gargantuan (Avon, AT&T, New York Telephone, Manufacturers Hanover, Equitable Life, Reader's Digest, J. Walter Thompson, Exxon, Touche Ross, to name only a few).

None of what has just been said is to denigrate the army's superb and dedicated services of which remarkably few complaints are ever heard. I am full of admiration for the army and its good works. But contributors solicited in the public marketplace have every right to know just how their money is being spent, particularly in the case of religious organizations when it is not clear just how much is going to support social services and how much is going to support religious activities—and a church. Doing this may be difficult for the army because its two principal functions of service and salvation are so closely related; it could, however, at least try.

Santas, Service, and Salvation: Volunteers of America

Despite its secular-sounding name, the Volunteers of America (VOA), whose bell-ringing Santas are familiar figures in most major cities during the Christmas season, is a religious organization quite similar to the Salvation Army. It is even patterned along the same quasi-military lines: Its officers wear uniforms and bear titles from general down to captain. All this is not surprising since the VOA is actually an American offshoot of the Salvation Army. The perhaps apocryphal story goes that Ballington Booth, commander of the Salvation Army in the United States around the turn of the century, asked his father, Salvation Army founder Gen. William Booth, if he, too, could be a general. The father is said to have retorted, "There can be only *one* general in the Salvation Army." Whereupon the younger Booth quit and formed the Volunteers in 1896. The official VOA history, however, says that the son was fired from his post when he set about "Americanizing" the army—among other things, he replaced the British crown with the American eagle on the army crest—and, moreover, refused to send any of the funds he had raised to the mother church in England. Whichever story is true, the fledgling organization set up shop in a rented three-room New York flat furnished with packing cases for desks and grocery boxes for files and concentrated its early efforts on ministering to the needs of Bowery bums.

Today the organization, headquartered in New York in a handsome red brick building, has some 30,000 members, about 600 of them officers, and operates nearly 800 "program centers" in 80 cities across the country, which offer much the same array of services as the Salvation Army, but on a smaller scale, to 3 million Americans of all races, creeds, and ages. Maintained at many of the centers are such facilities as preadoption nurseries, day-care centers, vocational guidance clinics, women's residences (where a room and two meals are available for as little as $48 a week) and missions providing free lodging and spiritual solace. The Volunteers, however, don't push religion quite as much as the Salvation Army. "We believe in feeding people before we preach to them, and we don't force anyone to attend religious services," said Gen. John F.

McMahon, the VOA commander-in-chief since 1958 and, incidentally, the first person outside the Booth family to head the organization. VOA officers are also allowed to marry anyone; they can even be members of other churches. (However, in order to join the VOA, Jews and Catholics are required to have a letter from a rabbi or priest.)

Among other activities, the VOA also runs 24 nonprofit housing complexes for low-income families and the elderly, 16 nursing homes, 54 group homes for children with family or behavioral problems, 40 halfway houses for alcoholics, and 56 centers preparing prisoners for reentry into society. Its other activities— summer camps for children, clubs for the aged, sheltered workshops, emergency and disaster relief services, and the collection and distribution of clothing, furniture, and other discards—also pretty well parallel those of the Salvation Army.

But financial data on the Volunteers are as vague and incomplete. Furnished me was only an unaudited consolidated statement that showed income and expenses to total about $40 million. However, expenses did not include any allocations for fund raising, overhead, or the strictly "church" aspects of the VOA operations. Income indicated fees for services and housing to make up about 60 percent of the receipts, with only about 5 percent coming from public contributions—part of this presumably from collections by those sidewalk Santas. Incidentally, they are paid and are not even Volunteers. Many are former alcoholics who, before being sent out to solicit, are given a list of such dos and don'ts as "Keep your breath clean—avoid eating garlic or onions" and "Don't promise children that they'll get gifts they ask for, but send them away hopeful and happy." All Santas are also warned they will be blacklisted if they are ever found drinking on duty.

Goodwill Industries: "Not Charity, But A Chance"

Like the Volunteers of America and the Salvation Army, Goodwill Industries, a network of 159 autonomous affiliates in the United States (and about 20 more in foreign countries), collects and sells used clothing, furniture, and other household items. Like the other organizations, Goodwill has also had certain religious overtones: A young Boston minister, Dr. Edgar J. Helms, brought it into being in 1910 as the National Cooperative Industrial Relief Association (its present name was adopted in 1946) and in its early years it was run to a large extent by the Methodist Church and considered itself in part a religious organization; however, it no longer has any religious ties.

Where Goodwill differs from other organizations that collect household discards—and what makes it unique—is that the donated items form the basis for a program that trains and gives employment to the handicapped in keeping with Dr. Helms's conception of a plan of "not charity, but chance." The plan was and remains ingeniously simple. Clothing and household goods are collected from homes and other places. Handicapped (including disadvantaged) men and women are given the opportunity to acquire job skills and learn trades by repairing and cleaning the various articles. (For this reason, Goodwill will take some items—such as broken-down furniture, automatic washers and dryers, dish washers, hot water tanks, television sets, even automobiles—that many other agencies won't touch.) Resale of the restored articles in Goodwill's more than 800 store outlets provides the money to give the handicapped workers an income and helps pay for the professional rehabilitation and vocational services needed to prepare them for work in private industry. Goodwill services include psychological counseling, physical therapy, medical treatment, nursing care, and placement in jobs. In some communities, Goodwill facilities include day nurseries, summer camps, and housing for the aged and handicapped; a 292-unit apartment complex in Houston, Texas, offers 24-hour attendant service, low light switches, shopping service, and in-house entertainment.

In a recent year, Goodwill rehabilitation facilities and workshops employed some 30,000 persons, provided rehabilitation services for about 45,000, and placed 10,000 in private jobs. Of the affiliates' combined income of $150 million, around 70 percent comes from the workshop and rehabilitation-related activities, another 7 percent from contributions, and most of the rest from government grants and rehabilitation fees. As we've suggested in the case of other organizations which collect and spend their money locally, you should check the operations and finances of your local affiliate before deciding whether or not to give your support.

The USO's New Look

To many ex-servicemen, the USO (United Service Organization) may be a virtually forgotten relic that, during those nostalgic war years, brought them such morale boosters as Bob Hope and other camp shows and whose club facilities provided camaraderie, female friendships, dances, table tennis, books, movies, snacks, and other comforts. But with over 2 million still in uniform, the USO survives, if on a less grandiose scale, operating some 45 regular centers in the United States and 18 overseas. With today's volunteer army, however, the USO has shifted with the times and has expanded its services to include drug and alcohol abuse education, job referrals, housing assistance, and classes in child care and home economics for young wives. In these efforts it still has the cooperation of the agencies which originally joined forces in 1941 to set up the USO: the YMCA, the YWCA, the National Jewish Welfare Board (the national body of the YM-YWHAs and other Jewish community centers), the National Catholic Community Service, the Salvation Army, and Travelers Aid.

Even today, the operating budget of the USOs runs to about $8.5 million, roughly half of which comes from USO-provided services and sales. Most of the rest had been contributed through United Way drives, but that support has gradually decreased—from $4 million in 1973 to $1.8 million in 1977. Since the USO receives no U.S. government funds, it must therefore turn to the public for additional donations to keep out of the red. While the cause is worthy, there remains the question, also asked in connection with the Red Cross, as to why public donations should be solicited at all to subsidize any aspect of military life and activities.

"Helping" the Veteran

Next to children and animals, veterans are the most effective means of tugging at the heartstrings and loosening the pursestrings of the unwary. In fact, to refuse to respond to appeals of veterans, especially handicapped ones, is considered downright unpatriotic. You feel like a rat, even a turncoat, if you don't give something for that proferred poppy, or don't mail an offering to that organization which is doing so much, you are told, for our heroic countrymen in khaki who did so much for us in wartime. Yet the veterans' organizations have traditionally been associated with some of the sleaziest fund-raising practices in the world of charity, and virtually all of these organizations are condemned by such monitoring agencies as the National Information Bureau and Council of Better Business Bureaus.

Largest and best known of the veterans' organizations that depend on the public for support is the Disabled American Veterans (DAV). Founded in 1920, the DAV was chartered by an act of Congress in 1932 "to aid and assist worthy wartime disabled veterans, their widows, their orphans and their dependents." Headquartered in Cold Spring, Kentucky (a Cincinnati suburb), the DAV recently boasted a membership of about 510,000 veterans in some 2200 local chapters plus a women's auxiliary of 55,000 relatives of service-connected disabled veterans.

Of its total annual income of $29 million in 1977, only a fraction—about $4.8 million—came from membership dues ($10 a year or lifetime dues of from $50 to $100, depending on age). For the major portion of its revenues, the DAV relied for many years on the proceeds from its mailing of unsolicited merchandise, notably its famous "Idento-Tags." These key-chain miniature facsimiles of auto license plates bearing the owner's name and address were mailed to virtually every car owner in the country—as many as 40 million went out in a single year. The idea, of course, was that if a car owner lost his keys bearing the DAV tag, the finder would drop them into a mailbox and the DAV, upon receiving them, would promptly forward them postpaid to the owner. The DAV says that it returned as many as 50,000 sets of lost keys during the course of a year. (But no one knows how many less-than-honest finders relished this ready means of locating the key-owner's car and even home.)

So successful have been the DAV's fund-raising techniques, which have included the mailing of personalized name-and-address stickers (about 25 million sets a year) and the operation of so-called "thrift" shops (more about which in Chapter 18), that contributions to the organization increased at a phenomenal rate, rising from $8 million to $29 million in the last decade.

Yet the DAV has consistently spent so large a proportion of its revenues to bring in its contributions that it has long been the subject of scrutiny and criticism. In 1953, for example, auditors for a New York State legislative committee found that, of the $21,480,000 collected by the DAV during the preceding three years, at least 79 percent had been gobbled up by fund-raising and administrative costs. Although fund-raising costs of an organization are supposed to go down over the years as it builds its donor lists, this did not apparently happen in the case of the DAV. For in 1966 it was still spending 79 cents out of every dollar it received in response to its Idento-Tag mailings, which, because of continuing criticism, were discontinued in 1975.* Since then, the DAV's fund-raising costs have dropped somewhat but they still remain appallingly high. In 1977 these costs amounted to 34 percent of mail contributions, and overhead expenses

*For the long, unsavory history of the DAV's involvement with the Idento-Tag, see Chapter 17.

accounted for another 6 percent for a total of 40 percent—still far above the average of most charitable organizations.

What does the DAV do with the rest of its money? Some of it goes for publishing and mailing a monthly magazine for members (cost: about $826,000 in 1977), for lobbying for more veterans benefits, and for throwing an annual national convention at which resolutions are adopted promoting the cause of the disabled veteran but which, at one time or another in the past, have also favored the fingerprinting of everyone in the United States, the picketing of movies considered pro-communist, and the opposing of amnesty and the seating of Red China in the United Nations. Some DAV money also goes to provide college scholarships for veterans' dependents, emergency relief for needy veterans, assistance to disaster-struck veterans and their families, and to support Boy Scout troops of the handicapped. The DAV hierarchy also extends its helping hand to itself: Five of the organization's officials make more than $49,000 a year, and the top man's salary is nearly $63,000.

Well below half—43 percent—of the DAV's expenditures goes for its congressionally chartered purpose of counseling and assisting veterans to obtain the government benefits to which they are entitled under law. Contrary to popular belief, disabled veterans do not receive these benefits automatically; a claim must be filed for them in every case. Accordingly, stationed in all Veterans Administration offices and many VA hospitals across the country are 260 DAV salaried representatives, most of them disabled Vietnam veterans, whose job it is to counsel veterans and their dependents on just what benefits they are entitled to and to help them file claims for such things as disability compensation, hospitalization, medical treatment, educational and vocational training, insurance, and social security.

All of this may seem worthwhile. But ten other veterans' organizations plus the American National Red Cross are also chartered by Congress, and 14 more private national organizations are authorized by the VA to provide exactly the same service and, like the DAV, they are even given free space and office facilities in VA installations for this purpose. (Also recognized by the VA for this purpose, but not given free space, are 46 state organizations.) Of course, not all of these organizations have representatives in all VA offices. But in the VA's New York office, for example, I saw separate cubicles manned by representatives of the American Legion, the Blinded Veterans, the Paralyzed Veterans, the Catholic War Veterans, the Jewish War Veterans, and the Veterans of Foreign Wars, as well as the DAV—all, incidentally, dispensing not only advice but also membership applications. The strange thing, however, is that an army of VA counselors, paid by taxpayer money, is also on hand in VA offices to provide exactly the same advice and help. For that matter, almost any veteran can easily get such assistance by phoning the VA's toll-free counseling service.

The point should also be made that the cost of private counseling services is not cheap. If only a third of every tax-deductible dollar donated to the DAV is being spent on its counseling services, this means that to pay the salary of a DAV counselor earning, say, $15,000 a year, DAV supporters are actually contributing $45,000—which is certainly far more than the Veterans Administration pays its counselors. Moreover, it is rather ludicrous that private organizations should solicit funds from the public to provide services that are already being provided by the government.

And apart from the fact that they are redundant and duplicate each other, one also wonders about the value of these private counseling services. Take the celebrated case of Leroy Bailey who, as an 18-year-old GI, lost his sight and most of his face to a rocket in Vietnam in the spring of 1968. After three years at a veterans hospital outside Chicago, Bailey was told nothing could be done for him. He still had no face and could receive nourishment only by squirting liquid foods down his throat. Turning to the DAV for help, he was advised to see a private plastic surgeon and was assured that the VA would pick up the bills. With this assurance, Bailey underwent the first of what was to be a long series of operations. When the VA refused to pay the bills, the still faceless and blind veteran once more turned to the DAV for help. "The counselor gave us a lot of forms to sign and said he would file an appeal for us and keep us informed," Mrs. Grace Bailey, Leroy's sister-in-law, told me. "That was the last we ever heard from him." In desperation, a friend of the Baileys told *Chicago Daily News* columnist Mike Royko about the case, and Royko wrote a column about the runaround Bailey was getting. The column caused a national furor and led the White House to order the VA to give the veteran its immediate attention. Since then, the VA has been picking up all of Bailey's medical bills and has trained him and supplied him with equipment to enable him to embark on a career as a furniture maker. But the DAV had nothing whatever to do with this.

Like the DAV, AMVETS (American Veterans of World War II, Korea, and Vietnam), with 150,000 members in 30 state groups and 1100 local groups, is also chartered by Congress to help veterans but it, too, devotes much less than half of its expenditures directly for this purpose. Through its fund-raising arm, AMVETS National Service Foundation (NSF), it took in a total of $1.5 million in 1977, virtually all from contributions. Against this income, it reported 47.7 percent for fund-raising expenses plus another 3.3 percent for overhead (a total of 51 percent), seemingly high enough. But they were even higher. For the organization charged off to "program expenses" its so-called Americanism program which, among other things, offers through mail solicitations such items as U.S. flags "to heal the wounds of war and promote the unity of patriotism in this time of peace." Properly allocating these expenses to fund-raising would boost NSF's fund-raising and overhead costs to 66 percent, leaving only 34 percent for direct services to veterans. But evidently, the organization finds that there's no business like mail business. In addition to the flags, it uses in its mail solicitations such items as personalized name labels, book plates, and greeting cards. Several years ago, AMVETS estimated its mailing list to be worth $2 million, and one of its officers was quoted as saying: "You hit 50 percent in the mail business and you're doing pretty good. It's the darndest business anybody's ever seen."

One could go down the list of veterans' organizations and come up with pretty much the same findings; so let's just look at another different sort of organization in this field. Help Hospitalized Veterans (HHV), based in San Diego, is actually nothing more than a business masquerading as a charity. This is not to deny its high-minded purpose—to send to patients in VA and military hospitals, paint-by-number, wood sculpture, stitchery, and other arts and crafts kits, all bought with contributions solicited by mail. The operation is frankly called a "nonprofit buying service" by its creator, Roger Chapin, a fast-talking 45-year-old entrepreneur who in the late 1960s gave up his job of promoting franchises for Heavenly Donuts to turn his talents to fund raising.

Since then, he founded the now-defunct Vietnam Gift Pac, which airlifted 600,000 gift packages, with a retail value of $5 million, to GIs in Vietnam. Another of his brainstorms, Welcome P.O.W.s, set up with a great publicity fanfare for the purpose of giving every homecoming prisoner of war a free vacation, a new car, a color TV, and other gifts, died aborning when the National League of Families of American Prisoners and Missing in Southeast Asia, opposed the scheme on the ground that it was "not in the best interests of the returning P.O.W.s and their families and could serve to undermine the interests of men who are still 'missing.'"

Meanwhile, Help Hospitalized Veterans, organized in 1971, remains a flourishing enterprise. Since its founding, it has shipped about 2.5 million kits with an estimated value of $10 million to some 275 hospitals, and the contributions HHV receives annually have risen from $500,000 to $2 million. Chapin says that he draws $33,600 a year plus expenses from the operation to supplement his earnings from a direct mail insurance business he runs on the side. Apart from these revelations, he is rather closemouthed about HHV's finances. When I finally caught up with him in his San Diego headquarters, which looks something like Macy's warehouse, he said that the reason he persistently refuses to let anyone see his annual reports is because of the fear that people might "misinterpret" them. (At this writing, I have yet to receive any of the reports Chapin has been promising to send me over the years.)

It is easy to understand why: The reports HHV has had to file with the Internal Revenue Service and New York State (in order to solicit there) clearly indicate that 45 percent of the money Chapin takes in goes for fund raising and overhead; the rest is used to pay for the arts and crafts kits which Chapin buys wholesale for 40 to 50 percent of their stated retail value. The clever mail solicitations, which are prepared by the ubiquitous fund-raising firm of Richard Viguerie, do not, of course, say all this. Instead, they leave the impression that a $6 donation will pay for one $6 kit, a $12 donation will pay for two $6 kits, and so on. However, buried in the appeal letters is a brief disclaimer to the effect that part of the contribution is also used to pay for the costs of warehousing and shipping the kits and the mailing—just how much is not spelled out.

"Don't you think it would be fair to let the people you solicit know that only about half of their contribution is going to purchase the kits?" I asked Chapin.

Chapin looked at me as if I'd suggested something obscene.

"If we did that," he said, "no one would send us any money."

What need there is for his operation in the first place is another matter. In his fund-raising appeals, Chapin has stated that "because of severe budgetary limitations, our VA and military hospitals are only able to meet a fraction of the need for arts and crafts materials in occupational therapy departments and wards." He also showed me a sheaf of letters from grateful hospital directors attesting to the need for the kits. However, the VA itself, when questioned, replied that "arts and crafts are used for rehabilitation purposes as medically prescribed activities" and that "the VA has been most generous in providing the needed material for these activities and has not curtailed them for budgetary reasons."

The VA added, however, "Some veterans may like to do some crafts on their own during weekends for which these packages might have some, but limited, use''; but it also said, ''If the money could be made available to the different hospitals for outings and entertainment, it might prove more beneficial for the patients.''

Meanwhile, we have the little-known story of George I. Silberberg, a retired New York consulting engineer who, since 1947, has presided over ''Hobbies For All Ages,'' an organization that distributes, free of charge, hobby and crafts materials to hospitals, schools, and prisons throughout the world. With only volunteer help, Silberberg has disbursed materials worth some $25 million—from art books and crayons to postage stamps and cowhides. The materials are donated by individuals and corporations as is also Silberberg's time and managerial skills. The cost of the entire operation for one recent year was only $11,464.52.

Chapter 15

Orphans and Other
Aspects of Foreign Aid

"The eyes of Remedios can't see beyond the next scrap of food."

So read the headline in an advertisement that showed a forlorn little Indian boy, with inexpressibly sad eyes, peering pathetically from the magazine page. "It's a hungry world that Remedios Guanzon has seen during the short five years of his life," the advertisement of the Foster Parents Plan (FPP) went on to say. "His father is dead, his mother is blind. Remedios sometimes can earn a few pennies begging—his older brother has become a proficient scavenger. Remedios and his family find it hard to see beyond today's paralyzing hunger toward a better tomorrow."

For only $16 a month, readers were then told, they could "adopt" someone like Remedios and provide their foster child with food, clothing, medical care, even a chance for an education. In return, they would get a photo and précis of "their" child, periodic letters from the child, and progress reports compiled by FPP's social workers in the field.

"17 Million Men, Women and Children Are Threatened with Starvation . . ." read another appeal that came to me by mail from West Africa Emergency Relief. Sent on a letterhead marked URGENT, it pleaded, "They Need Your Help *Now* If They Are To Survive."

A CARE appeal, on behalf of other of the world's unfortunates, promised that a $5 contribution would give 1000 malnourished children a glass of fortified milk, that $10 would provide space for a child in a school classroom, that $25 would give a group of needy farmers the expert training to help them grow more food, and so on.

How valid are such appeals? How worthwhile is the work of the agencies responsible for them? How efficiently do they operate? Is most of the money contributed actually used for the purpose described in those heart-rending appeals or is it put to some other use or simply frittered away? Indeed, is there any need at all for these private agencies?

Such questions are pertinent in the light of what we have already learned about such foreign-aid agencies as the Pallottine Fathers and the David Livingstone Missionary Foundation. Several years ago, the government's financial watchdog, the General Accounting Office (GAO), took a close look at five overseas children's charities, including the three leading "adopt-an-orphan" agencies:

252

Foster Parents Plan, Christian Children's Fund, and Save the Children Federation. After an intensive investigation, the GAO concluded that, while the agencies were generally "using their resources for worthwhile purposes and in the public interest," many aspects of their operations left much to be desired.

Their appeals, for example, were often misleading, according to the GAO. The Foster Parents Plan's Remedios was found to be not a five-year-old boy, as described in the ad, but rather a 12-year-old girl. Morever, she was not starving: During the seven years since her picture had been taken and been used in ads, she was being supported by regular donations by an Ohio couple.

In what may have been the most prolonged death scene since Camille, another forlorn little Indian girl called Margaret was described by the Christian Children's Fund (CCF) as "dying of malnutrition" in ads that ran in national magazines over a period of four years. And her name was not really Margaret. Christian Children's Fund and Save the Children Federation (SCF) admitted that they endowed the children in their ads with fictitious names and, in SCF's wont, with fictitious case histories: Copy writers were usually given about ten case histories of children in a given area to concoct their composite of a "typical" child.

None of the agencies, the GAO also found, had any established procedures for measuring the effectiveness of its programs, and some had only slipshod supervision over how their money was being spent. GAO investigators discovered, for example, that CCF had been sending monthly subsidies to a school in Greece to support 172 children it sponsored there, even though the school had closed a year before without CCF's knowledge. CCF also conceded that its contributors' money had been going to support 118 children at a Hong Kong school for nearly six months after the children were no longer enrolled at the school; the school, which contended that it had neglected to report this because of a "clerical oversight," was simply using the money for other purposes. CCF said it did not even know of this diversion of funds until it was turned up in the GAO reports. Of the 21 CCF-funded projects in Hong Kong, only 11 had been inspected by the agency. In the Philippines, only 46 of 78 projects were inspected; in Mexico, 44 of 147; and in Kenya, 6 of 68. In Kenya, only 25 percent of the special gifts CCF urged sponsors to give their children as birthday and Christmas presents ever reached their designated beneficiaries. The GAO study showed that one child was handed only $4 of the $35 gift money sent him.

In spite of the impression given in the ads that contributions would go to help the tattered tykes most in need, this was not quite true. In Colombia, the GAO reported a CCF project director as saying that the neediest children were not selected "because they were undernourished and, as a result, cannot study effectively." The Foster Parents Plan, also said the GAO, "will not accept [children of] the most needy families because they are less likely to achieve the goal of becoming self-sufficient." In many cases, however, children were not even screened to evaluate their need for assistance. In Mexico, 20 children had been sponsored for as long as 27 months before CCF social workers learned that they were not sufficiently needy. In Colombia, at least 10 children in one project were found to have *two* sponsors—one from CCF and one from SCF—with neither foster parent aware of the other.

As for how much of your monthly contribution actually goes to help the child, we'll get into that a little later.

America's concern for the have-nots of the world goes back to colonial times and was first manifested by the activities of our religious missionary societies which, of course, combined proselytizing with their good works. In the early days of our Republic, private secular agencies came into being to lend a hand to refugees and other disaster victims in Santo Domingo (1793) and to the victims of a Venezuelan earthquake (1812). In the wake of other natural or man-made disasters, Americans were invariably ready to help with money, goods, or services. During the 1820s they gave aid to the Greeks during their war of independence, and in the 1840s they sent more than $1 million dollars to the Irish during their famous famine. Later recipients of American generosity included the Russians, the Indians, the Chinese, the Cubans, and, of course, the proverbial starving Armenians. These relief operations were largely private, for the U.S. government did not really become deeply involved in foreign aid until World War II.

Today the government is responsible for the great bulk of this aid with its principal instrument the State Department's Agency for International Development (AID) through funds authorized and appropriated by Congress. In addition to AID's programs, the United States has been rendering economic assistance to developing countries since 1954 under Public Law 840, popularly called Food for Peace, which provides for the donation or sale (through long-term low-interest loans) of food and other agricultural commodities. However, there are also at least 460 private and voluntary organizations, both religious and secular, concerned with one aspect or another of foreign aid, their combined efforts now accounting for an estimated $2.6 billion a year, or 6.5 percent of all U.S. giving. Of these organizations, 94 are registered with AID's Advisory Committee on Voluntary Foreign Aid, which was set up to replace the President's War Relief Control Board in response to a 1946 directive by President Truman "to tie together the Governmental and private programs in the field of foreign relief. . . ." In the latest year for which figures are available, these 94 organizations took in an estimated $868 million—$548 million from private contributions, which included supplies and equipment, and the remaining $320 million from the government in the form of donated Food for Peace and excess government property, reimbursement for overseas shipping costs, and contracts and grants. (The Food for Peace donations accounted for the greater part—$237 million—of the $320 million total.)

Collectively, the major private dispensers of overseas aid are religious or church-affiliated organizations. Since many of these agencies have been dealt with in earlier chapters, what now follows is a look at a few of the larger or better-known secular foreign-aid charities, grouped according to their primary concerns—children, medicine and health, disaster relief, and food aid and development—although many agencies are involved in a combination of these activities.

One general caveat! One shouldn't regard the fact that an agency is registered with AID's Advisory Committee as a Good Housekeeping seal of approval. Technically, under the Foreign Assistance Act, agencies have to register with the committee to be eligible to participate in the U.S. government's Food for Peace and excess property programs as well as to be reimbursed for any overseas freight costs. But actually, only 24 of the 94 agencies registered receive any of these benefits and only six distribute Food for Peace commodities, with just two—CARE and Catholic Relief Services—accounting for 97 percent of the total distributed by all six agencies!*

Why then do the other agencies bother to register? Most of those once surveyed frankly admitted that they registered only for prestige reasons and to facilitate fund raising; their ads and mail appeals, by referring to the fact that they are registered, capitalize on the committee's assurance—mandated by its charter—of trustworthiness. As a committee report pointed out: "The most direct significance of voluntary agency registration to the American public is in the implied assurance of credibility, efficiency, and effectiveness of the agency, and the confidence it imparts to an individual that his contribution will be properly applied to the purpose he favors." To meet registration standards, an agency must show that it is controlled by a responsible board, must submit periodic audited financial statements, and "obtain, spend and distribute its resources ethically, without unreasonable cost for promotion, publicity, fund raising and administration." Committee guidelines specify that "remedial action" will be taken when fund-raising costs reach 20 percent of public cash and in-kind contributions.

All these strictures sound very good. However, several years ago, an official of the committee admitted to me that it did not bother to monitor and audit the activities of many of its registered agencies, and that the financial reports it "reviewed" were often incomplete, unaudited, or otherwise insufficient for meaningful analyses. The five children's charities investigated by the GAO, as mentioned earlier, were all registered agencies. Furthermore, although the committee claims that it has recently tightened up its registration requirements and monitoring procedures, the Council of Better Business Bureaus and the National Information Bureau still disapprove of, have reservations about, or haven't been able to obtain adequate information about one or another of a dozen of the agencies registered with the committee. (The figure would probably be much higher, but not all of the committee's agencies are monitored by the CBBB and NIB.) Small wonder that James A. Duff, associate director of the GAO's international division, told a Senate Labor Subcommittee on Children and Youth some years ago that "the registration program may be more misleading than beneficial [by] unwittingly permitting the public to be misled."

More on Those Children's Charities

Children are the special concern of many foreign-aid agencies, and since there is no word that can so readily tug at the heartstrings and loosen the purse strings of Americans as *children* or, better yet, *orphan,* probably no field of charity is so subject to abuse. Until recently, Korea alone had as many as 440 orphanages with 65,000 children—most abandoned by their parents, wise to the fact that some foreign agency would take care of their children. Devoted to the support of

*The other four: American Jewish Joint Distribution Committee, Church World Service, Lutheran World Relief, and Seventh-Day Adventist World Service.

these orphanages have been no less than 85 foreign relief groups, most of them American, that in one year contributed to them $28 million—more than ten times the budget of the Korean health ministry. To be sure, many of the orphanages are authentic, scrupulously run, and their existence has meant the difference between life and death for their charges. Some, on the other hand, have been tainted by scandal. A veteran missionary in Korea, writing in *Christian Century*, disclosed that some orphanage directors were the possessors of huge bank accounts. Korean racketeers soliciting funds in this country often use the names of legitimate orphanages, but give a different post office box number where money should be sent. One bogus appeal was accompanied by a testimonial from a Roman Catholic priest who, however, knew nothing about the orphanage his name was connected with.

What precautions should you take if you are asked to contribute to the support of an orphanage or a child overseas? For one thing, don't send your donation directly aboard; your money should go to an address in this country. If the organization claims to have a religious affiliation, check it out with the pertinent church here or with your clergyman. Even if you get a positive reading on an organization, ask such questions as: How much of the money actually gets to the child or children for whom it is intended? How much goes for overhead, fund-raising, and other nonprogram costs?

The danger of being taken in by prestigious names may be seen in the sad story of the scandal-ridden Pearl S. Buck Foundation, which was founded in 1964 by the world-famous author to support the unwanted offspring of American servicemen and Asian women. The foundation, headquartered in Philadelphia, began its work in Korea and then extended its operations to Okinawa, Thailand, the Philippines, and Taiwan. Although Miss Buck consigned a major portion of her royalties to the foundation, it also had to rely on outside donations; donors had no reason to question the foundation's operations because of the prestige of the Buck name as well as that of the many prominent Americans on the foundation's board of governors—Art Buchwald, Joan Crawford, R. Sargent Shriver, Sophie Tucker, and Mrs. Elliott Roosevelt, to mention only a few.

Unfortunately, however, Miss Buck entrusted the running of the foundation to a 32-year-old former Arthur Murray dancing instructor, Theodore Harris (aka "Red" Hair), on whom she lavished her fortune and affecton for the last ten years of her life. Named the foundation's president in 1964, Harris lost no time in using his post and foundation money to indulge his sybaritic tastes. Within seven months, he had obligated the foundation for nearly half a million dollars to acquire, among other things, an elegant $146,000 townhouse (complete with a full-time cook and houseboy) and a chauffeur-driven Cadillac. This was later followed by purchases of thousands of dollars worth of new clothing, a sapphire stickpin with 56 small diamonds, a Daimler automobile (one of three Harris owned by now), an expensive camera, and a second swimming pool for a foundation facility outside Philadelphia that housed only 17 American children. Meanwhile, the foundation was doing little to help its children in Korea who were ostensibly being supported by the $15-a-month gifts solicited from Americans; at one dormitory, a small boy drowned because there was no money to erect a fence around a pond on the property.

In 1969 Pennsylvania revoked the foundation's license to solicit funds after a local magazine published an article charging Harris with financial mismanagement and certain improprieties, which included making sexual advances toward Korean boys brought to this country by the foundation. He was also charged with placing former dancing teacher colleagues in key positions with the foundation. Harris, while protesting he was innocent of all charges, resigned shortly after. Miss Buck, on whom Harris apparently had a strange Svengali-like hold, called the allegations ''a bunch of downright lies,'' then assumed the duties of president of the foundation, remaining its head until her death in 1973.

Although the foundation regained its license in 1970, it remains a relatively small operation with an annual income of only about $1.3 million; however, it now meets the standards of the National Information Bureau and the Council of Better Business Bureaus. Of the $21 monthly contributions currently asked of donors for the support of a child, about 22 percent, or $4.70, is used for fundraising and administrative costs; the remaining $16.30 goes for the care of about 5000 Amerasian children in Korea, Okinawa, the Philippines, Thailand, and Taiwan.

The largest of the ''adopt-an-orphan'' agencies are Christian Children's Fund, Save the Children Federation, and Foster Parents Plan, in decreasing order of size. CCF, headquartered in Richmond, Virginia, and with current annual revenues of about $30 million (compared to $10 million a decade ago), started out in 1938 as China's Children Fund in response to the needs of the young victims of the Sino-Japanese War; today it has about 165,000 children covered by programs in some 20 countries, including the United States (about 3 percent of the children are American Indians). SCF, with headquarters in Westport, Connecticut, and with an income of around $12 million, was established during the Great Depression in 1932 to aid the children of Appalachia; today about 60 percent of its 25,000 sponsored children are in the United States (for the most part, on Indian reservations but also in Appalachia, urban ghettos, and southern black and Chicano neighborhoods), with the rest in some 20 countries of Europe (mostly Greece), Latin America, Asia, Africa, and the Middle East. FFP, based in Warwick, Rhode Island, and with an income of nearly $8 million, originated in 1937 during the Spanish Civil War and expanded its operations two years later to care for the war-orphaned and abandoned youngsters in all of Europe; today its 33,000 sponsored children are in 17 countries, primarily in Latin America, Africa, and the Far East.

All three children's charities claim to have tightened up their supervisory procedures and toned down their advertising appeals since the GAO investigation. Remedios has been retired by FPP, CCF's Margaret is no longer dying of malnutrition, and magazine readers are no longer tormented with guilt feelings by being exposed to such SCF messages as, ''You Can Help Save Maria Almanzar [or Maria Pastora, Rina Begum, etc.] for $15 a Month. Or You Can Turn the Page.''* Not that their appeals still aren't somewhat misleading or perhaps too easily misread. Over the years—in fact, even before the GAO investigation—the agencies, with orphaned and homeless children comprising a declining portion of their caseloads, have been shifting their emphasis to providing assistance for the child's entire family and, particularly in the case of SCF, for the community as a

*SCF currently asks for $16 monthly, CCF for $15, and FFP for $19.

whole. However, the agencies' appeals, while sometimes alluding to this, continue to feature the theme that help is being sought for a specific child; in fact, recent FPP and CCF coupon ads—one of the latter's is headlined, "SALLY STRUTHERS TALKS ABOUT HER CHILD"—in what seems to be a new gimmick, offer to send a photo and case history of a specific child *on approval*—so you can "meet" the child. If you like what you see, "you will then have 10 days to make a decision to share your love with a child," says an FPP ad which then promises that, as a foster parent, you will receive regular letters from the child, an annual progress report and new photo and, among other things, the privilege of mailing letters and special money gifts.

What the appeals also neglect to say, however, is that the sponsor's monthly contributions do not entirely support the child or family; they therefore generally have to be supplemented by funds from other sources, perhaps even other sponsors, which means that you may be sharing "your" child with other "parents." Nor is it made clear to sponsors that, varying with the agency, only from four-fifths to two-thirds of the money sent in actually goes to the child or family, either directly or through the community. Fund-raising and administrative expenses, plus the cost of those photographs, progress reports, and the translations involved in correspondence with the child, and the personnel to handle all of this, eat up the rest.

All in all, person-to-person giving of this sort is a relatively expensive form of charity, and is therefore not used by many foreign-relief agencies. On the other hand, there can be no denying its appeal and the fact that it draws contributions from people who might otherwise not give at all. There can be no question, too, that the agencies perform a useful service in rendering at least some help to people in need, although just how well they do this is difficult to gauge. But generally, the agencies sincerely try to do a good job, are open and aboveboard to the extent they will send their financial reports to anyone, and all three now meet the standards of the Council of Better Business Bureaus and the National Information Bureau.

UNICEF

No roundup of foreign children's relief agencies can fail to include UNICEF (United Nations Children's Fund), whose "Trick or Treat" Halloween solicitations and greeting card sales are among the most familiar of all fund-raising gimmicks. Few Americans, however, may be aware that their contributions (and those of citizens of other countries) to the United Nations agency, created in 1946, account for only 30 percent of the organization's $140 million annual income; the rest comes from some 132 governments. In this country, private contributions are channeled through the United States Committee for UNICEF, which has counterparts in 29 other countries.

About 38 percent of the $10 million income of the U.S. committee comes from the net proceeds of the sales of the greeting cards and also calendars and other sundries (the purchases of which, incidentally, are not tax deductible). This country buys about 29 million of the 100 million cards sold annually throughout the world. The first UNICEF greeting card came into being in 1949 and was the handiwork of a seven-year-old Czechoslovak schoolgirl, whose painting of children dancing around a Maypole was her way of expressing thanks for food she and her playmates had received after the war. Since then, many world-famous artists, ranging from Georgia O'Keefe and Salvador Dali to Raoul Dufy and Oscar Kokoschka, have donated their designs; over the years, cards with "Peace on Earth" themes have been among the top sellers.

The "Trick or Treat" campaign, which accounts for about 28 percent of tne U.S. committee's income, originated in 1950 when a youth group in the Brides-burg Presbyterian Church in Pennsylvania went out on Halloween and collected $17 for UNICEF. The idea spread like wildfire and today over 3.5 million children in some 1300 communities ring doorbells on October 31 and collect about $3 million a year. To spearhead the campaign, comedian Danny Kaye hops around the country every fall in a chartered plane which he pilots himself; he made the *Guinness Book of World Records* when he visited 65 cities in five days, logging 17,000 miles, during one campaign.

Actually, because of the expense of producing and distributing the greeting cards, only slightly more than one-fourth of the gross proceeds of their sale goes toward helping children in need, and only two-thirds or so of UNICEF's overall revenues go for this purpose. While this may seem to leave too much—one-third of revenues—for administration, fund raising, and public information, the U.S. committee justifies this on the basis that one of its major functions is building public knowledge and generating support for the work of UNICEF.

That this may require heroic efforts stems from the fact that the work of UNICEF—which may range from providing food, medicine, and shelter for children to helping their countries equip and staff schools, establish health and nutrition centers, grow food, and dig wells—is not without controversy. Opponents of the United Nations grumble about the fact that UNICEF money goes to countries under Communist control such as Vietnam, Laos, and Cambodia; they also see something sinister in the fact that the first UNICEF chairman was a Polish Communist and that "Communists" like Picasso have designed UNICEF cards advocating peace.

In response to such charges, UNICEF says that its mandate is to aid needy children regardless of their race, nationality, religion, or politics and points out that countries receiving UNICEF assistance must abide by strict rules governing its use; it also cites the fact that the organization has been endorsed by five U.S. presidents, the U.S. Department of State, and three major religious groups—the National Council of Churches of Christ, the American Jewish Committee, and the Roman Catholic Church. In 1965, UNICEF was awarded the Nobel Peace Prize as the organization "which has worked most or best for brotherhood amongst the nations." The citation also declared, "The aim of UNICEF is to spread a table, decked with all good things that nature provides, for all the children of the world."

More serious is the charge by some that UNICEF practices what they call "Band-Aid foreign aid." The charge, of course, may be applied to most foreign-relief agencies and is one we'll comment on later in this chapter.

Medical Relief

Of the countless foreign-relief agencies specializing in medical aid, perhaps the largest and best known is the People-to-People Health Foundation, whose principal activity is Project Hope. Founded in 1958 by Dr. William B. Walsh, a former Navy physician, the charity's chief claim to fame for many years was the operation of the S.S. *Hope,* a 15,000-ton hospital ship that Dr. Walsh, with President Eisenhower's blessing, resurrected from the Navy's mothball fleet and converted into the world's first peacetime floating medical center. Embarking on her maiden voyage in 1960, the S.S. *Hope* steamed around the world to Indonesia, South Vietnam, Peru, Ecuador, Guinea, Colombia, Ceylon, Tunisia, the West Indies, Nicaragua, and Brazil, stopping at each place for nine or ten months at a time to serve as a temporary medical school and treatment center. Over the years, the 108-bed hospital ship's dedicated staff of modestly salaried professionals and volunteers treated nearly 200,000 people, performed some 19,000 operations, immunized about 3 million people, and trained more than 7000 foreign physicians, dentists, nurses, and allied health personnel. Then in 1974 Project Hope announced that it was giving up the ship primarily because of mounting operating costs, which had spiraled from $2.5 million to $6 million a year.

Since then the organization has concentrated on less costly land-based projects, most recently in Egypt, Tunisia, Guatemala, Brazil, Peru, Colombia, the Caribbean, even the United States (in Texas). Today, it has an annual income of about $8.5 million, nearly one-third of which comes from U.S. government grants, and has fund-raising and overhead expenses amounting to about 20 percent of the contributions, bequests, and other support it receives from private sources.

Another former Navy physician, the legendary late Dr. Thomas A. Dooley, together with Dr. Peter D. Comanduras, founded MEDICO—short for Medical International Cooperation Organization—in 1958 to act as "physicians to the world." Formed under the aegis of the International Rescue Committee, which is primarily a refugee organization, MEDICO was merged into CARE (more about which later) in 1962, a year after Dooley was struck down by cancer at the age of 34. MEDICO's so-called long-term staff is made up of some 60 physicians, nurses, technicians, and therapists who volunteer for two-year overseas stints, during which they receive relatively modest salaries ($11,000 to $19,000 a year), full maintenance, transportation, and the usual fringe benefits. They are assigned to teams which in recent years have operated out of hospitals and clinics in Afghanistan, Belize, the Dominican Republic, Honduras, Indonesia, Jordan, Nicaragua, Tunisia, and Vietnam. These teams are supplemented by about 110 physician specialists a year who take "working vacations" by volunteering, entirely at their own expense (paying even their own travel and living costs), to serve for one month at a MEDICO outpost, practicing and teaching their specialties. For, in keeping with the organization's "treat and teach" philosophy, on its annual budget of nearly $2 million, MEDICO not only provides medical care, treating some 500,000 patients a year, but it also trains local medical staffs to do the healing in the future.

Actually, Dooley never had any connection with the Thomas A. Dooley Foundation, which in fact did not come into being until August, 1961, eight months after his death, as a competing organization to MEDICO. It was formed by members of Dooley's family and some of his supporters who had sharp differences with Comanduras almost from the moment he and Dooley had been brought together by Harold Oram, a New York fund raiser, to form MEDICO. Comanduras favored expanding MEDICO into an organization much larger than the one Dooley had envisaged, even if it meant accepting government help or merging it into an organization, such as CARE, with far greater resources than the International Rescue Committee. On the other hand, Dooley, who was something of a maverick, did not want to be beholden to the government or any other funding group that might restrict MEDICO's independence. With messianic fervor, he also saw medical aid as a tool for fighting communism. For these and personal reasons, no love was lost between the two men. "Publicly, they were buddies, but privately they hated each other," says Dr. Vern Chaney, founder-president of the foundation formed to perpetuate Dooley's name and ideas. (Comanduras, now a member of MEDICO's advisory board, will to this day not speak of Dooley.)

Over the years, the Dooley Foundation, headquartered in San Francisco, has remained a relatively small organization, with a current annual income of about $800,000, and the Dooley name has probably been a greater hindrance than help in the furtherance of its self-described objectives "to provide technical and material assistance to the developing countries of Asia in the fields of curative medicine, public health and community development on a self-help basis." Because of the persistent association of Dooley with hard-line anticommunism, the foundation was forced to discontinue operations in Vietnam, Laos, and Cambodia several years ago; it is currently operating only in Nepal. Its last reported fund-raising expenses were about 36 percent of cash contributions, and 24 percent of cash contributions plus bequests and "donated drugs, supplies and services."

Medical missionary work seems to attract zealots—Dooley in Asia and Albert Schweitzer in Africa are probably the two foremost modern examples. Another was Jim Turpin, a young California physician who turned to medicine after receiving a college degree in theology and who in 1961 decided to launch his own medical mission. Turpin had gotten his first taste of what it was like to help the underprivileged by working as a weekend volunteer at a clinic in Tijuana, Mexico, just across the border from Coronado, California, where he had a lucrative general practice. Hearing of the even more desperate needs of the people in Hong Kong, he moved his family there in 1962 and, with the help of some friends, set up a clinic in the Walled City area, which is generally regarded as the world's greatest slum. This clinic was soon followed by two more treatment centers, one a floating clinic on a converted Chinese junk to bring aid to Hong Kong's floating population of 200,000, many of them too superstitious to set foot on land. Casting about for a name for his organization, Turpin was at first stumped. He was partial to such words as *hope* and *care* but they were already taken. Thumbing through the dictionary, the word *concern* caught his eye, and his wife, Mollie, who later went on to become a physician herself, suggested using the word *project* with it, à la Project Hope. And so Project Concern was born.

Turpin left Project Concern in 1974 to return to private practice because his dedication to the organization had exacted too great a personal toll. However, his legacy continues as Project Concern now treats 500,000 people a year and conducts public health education, preventive medicine, and paramedic training programs in 20 health-care facilities in Hong Kong, Mexico, Bolivia, Guatemala, Bali, and two rural areas of the United States—the Navajo reservations of New Mexico and Arizona. The organization was also active in Vietnam up to 1975.

About 70 percent of Project Concern's total income of about $3.5 million a year comes from the organization's annual "Walk for Mankind"—walk-a-thons held in some 100 communities. Since about 40 percent of the "Walk" proceeds are returned to other local sponsoring groups, Project Concern realizes only 60 percent of the total, and its overall fund-raising expenses come to nearly 37 percent of contributions, with administrative expenses accounting for an additional 12 percent—for a total of 49 percent.

And so, one should be aware that only about half of a contribution of $50 for paying the "salary of a native village medical assistant and basic medical care for an entire village for one month" or of $1 for providing "seven days of treatment for removal of parasitic intestinal worms" actually goes for these purposes.

In spite of their good intentions and the useful services they provide, the days of the big medical relief agencies may be numbered as more and more governments, in recent years, have been assuming the responsibility for the health care of their citizens. Even the Dooley Foundation's Dr. Chaney concedes this to be likely, citing the changing attitudes toward Americans in general and proselytizing missionaries in particular. "People are getting tired of do-gooders passing out pills and chanting hymns," he says. "Besides, the developing countries no longer want therapeutic medicine; they feel that it is better to fight TB, for example, by immunizing people against it than by treating it. And to do this, one has to get into the smaller rural areas and villages and place increasing emphasis on country-wide health-delivery systems, which the governments are better equipped to do than we. Only if we can help in this regard will we continue to have a role."

Disaster Relief

When a severe earthquake struck Guatemala in February, 1976, leaving an estimated 22,000 dead, 74,000 injured, and more than a million homeless, literally dozens of private relief organizations rushed to the scene to distribute food, clothing, and other supplies and to take care of the health and housing needs of the devastated people. The same thing happened when a hurricane hit Honduras in 1974, killing as many as 10,000 people and leaving 300,000 homeless. Scarcely a year goes by when floods, famines, droughts, typhoons, and other natural or man-made disasters do not take place somewhere. Inevitably, they are quickly followed by public appeals to finance emergency relief efforts for the victims and, later, to carry on the critical task of reconstruction and rehabilitation in the disaster area.

For example, within weeks of the first news reports in 1973 of the great drought, the worst in a century, in West Africa's Sahelian zone, a region on the southern edge of the Sahara Desert covering six countries (Mauretania, Mali, Chad, Upper Volta, Niger, and Senegal) with a total population of about 22 million, my mailbox was cluttered with heart-rending appeals from many small, little-known organizations with such names as Project Relief, RAINS (Relief for Africans in Need in the Sahel), Catholic Medical Mission Board, World Mercy Fund, and West Africa Emergency Relief, the last-mentioned warning me, as stated earlier, that 17 million of the drought-stricken Africans were threatened with starvation. The Catholic Medical Mission Board estimated, somewhat more conservatively, that 6 million faced starvation *"in the next month."* (A Carnegie Endowment for International Peace report, issued a year later, said that perhaps 100,000 to 250,000 lives were lost, but no one will ever know for sure just how many.*)

Should one respond to appeals of this sort and, if so, is there any way of making sure that one's contribution helps the people it is intended for? One is inclined to be cynical about giving at all after reading that relief food in Chad, for example, was diverted to feed the military, and that in Mali and Niger some of the donated grain would up with merchants who sold it at enormous profits to their starving countrymen. Or that in Ethiopia, another drought-stricken area, the government, while appealing for 200,000 tons of free, imported relief grain, had access to large supplies of local grain and, moreover, had a foreign-exchange reserve of more than $300 million that could be used to buy grain. Everywhere, because of the lack of roads, piles of donated foodstuffs were often left at the docks, an easy prey for thieves, rats, and locusts. An official of RAINS, a program of the Interreligious Foundation for Community Organization, was frank enough to say that the Sahel situation was "a crisis of such dimensions that only massive emergency aid from the U.S. government can effect a change."

To this the Agency for International Development, whose functions include coordinating disaster relief, says:

> Often, in such instances, a voluntary agency is the only organization on the scene able to cope with the most critical phase of disaster recovery. The agency's staff is familiar with local customs and culture, as well as with the resources which can be mobilized. Indeed, voluntary organizations are sometimes the first to report a disaster to the outside world, and are the first to launch public appeals to finance relief efforts. These agencies usually continue their services to the stricken area after major governmental and intergovernmental efforts are discontinued, and thereby sustain the critical task of reconstruction and rehabilitation.
>
> In some politically sensitive situations, outside governmental assistance is inadvisable or unacceptable and in such cases voluntary agencies, often in cooperation with indigenous voluntary groups, are able to perform an invaluable function which governments cannot.

One, however, must be wary of the fly-by-nights, many claiming religious affiliations, in this field; some are so small that they are not monitored by the CBBB or NIB. (The latter, moreover, does not monitor religious groups unless they solicit the general public.) But if you decide to give and want to make sure

---

*Exact death counts were difficult because many of the victims were nomads in remote areas which had virtually no contact with the world outside.

that you're giving to a reliable, efficient agency of some standing, ask for its latest financial report. If it won't send you one, you're better off to channel your giving through such known quantities as the Red Cross, Salvation Army, Church World Service, Catholic Relief Services, or CARE, all of which play key roles in all major disasters.

Food Aid and Development

Although food aid programs are usually associated with the feeding of disaster victims, starving children, or refugees, they are also an increasingly important factor in self-help and development activities in line with new concepts that the long-term solution to the problems of impoverished countries lies in getting them to help themselves.

Under so-called food-for-work programs, made possible by Food for Peace, workers are paid in part by food and commodities for their labors in land clearing and irrigation projects, the building of small dams, schools, housing, and roads, the installation of village potable water systems, the development of inland fisheries, and the construction of cattle dips. In this way, food-for-work programs provide employment, help to alleviate the immediate need for food, often help to increase local agricultural production, and, hopefully, put dependent communities and countries on the road to self-sufficiency.

Church World Service was the first multipurpose agency to come up with the idea of using Food for Peace commodities as wages on development projects through a tree-planting program in Algeria in 1961. Since then its food-for-work programs have involved as many as 390,000 persons in India in community development projects; in Brazil, it has sponsored 1800 local committees in food-for-work programs employing half a million people. However, today Catholic Relief Services is even a bigger factor in such programs, and CARE gives more food-for-work assistance than any other private agency.

The World of CARE

So identified in the public mind is CARE—an acronym for Cooperative for American Relief Everywhere—with its renowned CARE package that most people are not aware that the agency has long been involved in a myriad of other foreign-aid activities; in fact, as many will also be surprised to learn, distribution of the CARE packages was discontinued back in 1967. But the package is the reason this remarkable agency came into being.

CARE was formed in November, 1945, just six months after V-E day, by 22 American religious, relief, labor, civic, and service groups as a cooperative emergency relief organization to get food packages to the people of war-devastated Europe. The original CARE package was the so-called U.S. army "ten-in-one" ration, which was designed to feed ten soldiers for one day or one soldier for ten days; indeed, CARE was actually set up for the specific purpose of distributing the huge amounts of these rations the army was left with after the war. For $10 (later $15) a donor could arrange for a gift package to be sent to a designated individual or organization, with delivery guaranteed within 120 days.

In the beginning, CARE serviced only Europe—the first packages arrived in Le Havre, France, on May 11, 1946, six months after CARE was born. (Nonpolitical from the start, CARE, in response to the request of a donor, delivered its first package in Bavaria to the wife of Martin Bormann, one of Hitler's closest aides.) In 1948, however, at the request of General MacArthur, CARE expanded its operations to Japan, Korea, and Okinawa and then to other countries that were in need, not necessarily as a result of the war.

CARE was never intended to fill more than a temporary need—the distribution of those surplus army rations. However, like other charitable organizations, it did not relish the idea of quietly fading away once its mission had been accomplished. And so as stocks of the ten-in-one rations dwindled, CARE began to diversify its operations. Going beyond its original mandate, it started to create food parcels of its own, including a kosher package for Europe's Jewish families, and one made up of baby foods. Responding to the need for items other than food, CARE also began assembling packages containing such items as clothing, household linens, knitting wool, school supplies, and medicines—even iron lungs and midwife kits. Over the years, more than 100 million packages of various kinds were shipped, and the term "CARE package" became part of our everyday vocabulary, used to describe any parcel of supplies.

All this was not without some resistance on the part of several of CARE's "parent" organizations, which saw their famous offspring's broadening of its operations as competition to their own established activities. Indeed, as early as 1947, Church World Service and the American Jewish Joint Distribution Committee, after failing to get CARE to fold its tents, went so far as to resign from the cooperative. CARE faced another threat to its existence as Europe made its dramatic recovery in the late 1940s, and contributions began to drop to the point where they could not support the worldwide network that had been established for the distribution of the relief packages. For self-preservation as well as humanitarian reasons, the organization, in the early 1950s, shifted its emphasis from relief to development and self-help, beginning by sending coal to the Netherlands, plows to Greece, Pakistan, and India, and seeds to a multitude of countries. What really kept CARE from going under, however, was the birth, in 1954, of the Food for Peace program, that happy creation of the postwar era when a surplus of American generosity coincided with healthy surpluses of grain. Over the years, CARE has gradually become the program's largest distributor, sending abroad in a recent year about $109 million of the commodities.

Today, operating in 35 developing countries of Asia, Africa, Latin America, and the Middle East, CARE's major emphasis is on mass feeding and nutrition programs for school and preschool age children, and on self-help projects in which the agency, local communities, and host governments work together on building such facilities as schools, roads, pure water, and irrigation systems, nutrition centers, clinics, housing, and community centers. As already mentioned, through MEDICO it maintains medical treatment and training teams in 9 countries, augmented by volunteer specialists on one-month tours of duty. Finally, the agency is a ubiquitous presence at most disasters, meeting not only emergency needs, but also helping in any necessary reconstruction.

To operate its programs, CARE, headquartered in a former New York brewery, has a domestic staff of 311, and employs 172 Americans (plus some Canadians) and 2000 foreign nationals in its overseas locations. The organization's operations and finances have been deservedly free from criticism. Unlike most other charities it doesn't even sell or rent its mailing lists. In 1977 it received a total of $183.8 million, of which $109.2 million was in the form of Food for Peace commodities and $37.3 million in government reimbursements for overseas shipping costs. Of the balance, $17.3 million represented cash donations by the public (another $2.1 million were contributions-in-kind), and the rest was largely the proceeds of United States and foreign government contracts. Fundraising costs amounted to $4.7 million and administrative costs to another $2.6 million. Measured against cash donations, these came to 27 and 15 percent, respectively. Although these may seem high, they should be measured—because of the special nature of the CARE operation—against the commodities distributed and other program services provided. On this basis, fund-raising and administrative costs collectively represent only 4 percent of the value of CARE's services, and the organization is quite justified in its claim that each dollar donated makes possible more than $10 in overseas aid.

Is There A Valid Need for Private Foreign Aid?

Public opinion polls indicate that Americans favor the concept of foreign aid. One recent survey showed 52 percent of us to favor such aid while 38 percent opposed it. (The rest had no opinion.) However, support for foreign aid rises to 79 percent versus 13 percent opposed when our citizens believe the aid actually reaches the people for whom it is intended. Americans also believe that the aid should come from private rather than government sources. A poll taken for the Overseas Development Council, a private organization interested in the problems of developing countries, disclosed that 43 percent of Americans favor cutting the U.S. foreign-aid budget and 57 percent believe foreign-assistance projects should be financed by voluntary contributions, not taxes.*

Private agencies have certain advantages over governmental or intergovernmental agencies as dispensers of aid. As John D. Lange, Jr., a U.S. Treasury international expert, sums them up:

Unlike UN agency or official bilateral agency staff generally, the field staff of

*These beliefs apparently are shared by our elected representatives. Belying the persistent myth that Uncle Sam is a generous giver to the world's needy, the United States now ranks twelfth among the 17 richest non-Communist countries in the proportion of national income it devotes to helping less-fortunate countries, contributing less than one-fourth of 1 percent of its gross national product (GNP) for this purpose, or considerably less than what the American people spend for alcoholic beverages or pet food or cosmetics or toilet articles. (Only Austria, Italy, Finland, Switzerland, and Japan contributed a smaller percentage; Sweden, the Netherlands, Norway, France, and Denmark had the highest.) Moreover, the United States has become increasingly stingy with its foreign aid over the years. During the Marshall Plan era following World War II, the United States gave 3 percent of its GNP to help other countries get back on their feet; in 1960 this country gave one-half of 1 percent. This means the United States is giving today one-twelfth as much as it gave three decades ago to relieve hunger and suffering in other countries. By contrast, individual Americans and foundations have been digging deeper into their own pocket books year after year, their donations increasing by over 60 percent during one recent ten-year period.

private agencies live in the remote rural areas of less developed countries with the victims of underdevelopment and share their problems and aspirations. They tend to know more about what is culturally possible and whom to support and encourage in a rural community because they know their religious and social mores and motives. But because they are foreigners, they are less subject to the political and social pressures of the society in which they live, and are thus best able to encourage social action in their communities.

Small and decentralized as private agencies usually are, they find it easier to experiment and innovate, as Lange also points out, and many are flexible enough to act quickly in funding projects and other matters.

The private foreign-aid agencies, however, do have their faults, some stemming from the fact that, like other charitable organizations, they are, after all, private and as such are virtually free from any regulation or public accountability, notwithstanding even the registration requirements of AID's advisory committee. Moreover, as we've already seen, their faraway operations are difficult to supervise and evaluate. Their selection of countries in which to operate, many have observed, is sometimes whimsical, and so are some of the projects in which they choose to become involved. Some of the missionary or other church-sponsored agencies are primarily interested in attracting potential converts—to such an extent that the Indian and Nigerian governments, among others, have banned proselytizing. Although theoretically apolitical, some agencies do use aid as a tool to effect political and social change in the direction of their own beliefs.

It is also no secret that the United States has long been sending food overseas not only for humanitarian reasons but also—at least equally as much—for political purposes, especially to dissuade countries from turning to communism. The Food for Peace program has come under fire in recent years for this reason; this in turn has led to the charge that the private agencies using Food for Peace commodities have to some extent compromised their independence.

Whether true or not, there can be no question that many of the private agencies are independent to the point where they often fail to keep each other or government agencies informed as to what they are doing, and that a lack of coordination has always been a problem endemic to the foreign-aid field. Even Kenya, which has been an enthusiastic host to almost any foreign-aid agency wishing to operate within its borders, has recently begun to question the desirability of having as many small organizations there as it now does. A GAO report, assessing the 1976 Guatemalan earthquake relief efforts, singled out the lack of communications and coordination among the various donor agencies, with the consequence that "tons of unsorted, unsuitable, or outdated clothing, food, medicines, and other commodities were received . . . clogging an overloaded logistics system and diverting manpower from more important tasks."

All this is not to denigrate the efforts and sincere intentions of many of the private agencies. Certainly, with all their shortcomings, their work makes survival and even a better life possible for tens of millions of the world's unfortunates. For this reason, generous people should continue to give to the more efficient and dedicated of these agencies. But it would be delusion to believe that their largely uncoordinated Band-Aid piecemeal practices will ever be even remotely equipped to deal with the needs of a world in which an estimated 800 million people still suffer from malnutrition, 85 out of every 100 have no regular access to health services, one out of every five children dies before the age of five, the great majority of people (95 out of every 100, in some countries) cannot read or write, and uncontrolled population growth is inhibiting the economic, social, and political development of most members of the brotherhood of nations.

In the long run, only concerted international government action can deal with the extraordinarily complex and interrelated problems of this magnitude in which hunger, poverty, low living standards, disease, illiteracy, lack of transportation and roads, outmoded customs, and other factors together form a vicious cycle, one that even U.S. aid alone—more than $26 billion in Food for Peace donations and loans since 1954—has come nowhere near breaking. Indeed, some observers, like Benedict Nightingale, argue that such bilateral government aid and the presence of the private foreign-aid agencies have postponed a more permanent solution and make international government action unlikely, just as in the nineteenth century, the existence of private domestic charities here served as a palliative, lulling people into believing that government involvement in our social problems on the home front was unnecessary.

Abroad as well as at home, the needs of charity have become too big and too important to be left to the charitable organizations.

Chapter 16

The Quality and Equality of Life

Beethoven's Fifth Symphony boomed out over the radio. Abruptly the music stopped. An announcer cut in:

"We stopped the music to start you thinking that the music *could* stop. Some day a live concert by the New York Philharmonic may be a thing of the past because we are fighting a crippling deficit. If great music is important to you, please help. . . ."

From the New York Public Library came this appeal: "As you know, the Library has had to cut its services drastically. Some branches are open only two days a week. Hundreds of dedicated librarians have been laid off. Tens of thousands of precious books are literally crumbling to dust in the research libraries because we cannot afford to preserve them. To keep the Library going, we are asking you to help out with a tax-deductible contribution of as much as you can afford."

"If *ars gratia artis* means art for art's sake, what does *ars gratia pecunae* mean?" began this letter from New York's Museum of Modern Art. It continued: "Art for money's sake? Well yes, but we don't really mean it. It's just our way of suggesting that your membership in MoMA is not only an enriching, stimulating encounter with great art, but it's also a terrific value. . . ."

And, finally, this letter from my wife's alma mater with this arresting opener: "I refuse to believe that with a fine career like yours you can't spare five bucks. No, I don't want you to buy me drinks. And I don't want you to take me to lunch. And I certainly don't want you to buy me a carton of cigarettes. What I would like, however, is your five-dollar check made out to New York University. I don't have to tell you that the School of Education needs it. . . ."

One does not ordinarily think of colleges, museums, libraries, or symphony orchestras in connection with charity. Certainly, they are far removed from the institutions or organizations our *Webster*'s has described as engaged in the "free assistance of the poor, the suffering, or the distressed" by providing them with what are generally regarded as the necessaries of life, as described in the preceding chapters. But with all the talk in recent years about the *quality* of life, also worthy of consideration are such forms of philanthropy as education, the arts, and humanities, as well as those concerned with the conservation of our rights, resources, and heritage. That these activities also serve the common good is

269

suggested by the fact that the government allows tax deductions for contributions to support most (if not all, as we shall see) of them. Yet these contributions represent only a relatively small portion—about 9 percent—of the philanthropic pie, although they inspire much the same questions raised in connection with giving in other areas: To what extent should these activities be supported by government and to what extent by philanthropy? Which are most important in terms of the nation's needs? What does it say of our sense of values when we compare the roughly $300 million our government (federal, state, and local) spends on the arts in a given year with the $130 *billion* or so spent for education or, for that matter, the $1 billion it costs to build a single aircraft carrier or Navy destroyer? What should one make of the fact that nonprofit citizens' groups are needed to fight for the rights guaranteed to all of us under the Constitution or to conserve the resources our government should be more concerned about than it now is?

The Plight of Education

Of the $131.1 billion spent on education in the United States in 1977, only $4.6 billion, or about 3.5 percent, came from private contributions, these representing 13.2 percent of total U.S. giving.* Of these private gifts, about 40 percent went to elementary and secondary schools, the remainder going to colleges and universities. Contributions from individuals accounted for 50 percent of the gifts; grants from foundations and business for another 21 percent and 17 percent, respectively; churches contributed 5 percent, the rest coming from miscellaneous and unidentified sources.

Gifts to education have nearly doubled in the past decade; those to colleges alone reached a new high in 1977, according to the Council for Financial Aid to Education.** Nonetheless, as at least half a dozen major studies have indicated, many of the nation's private (or, as they are now also called, "independent") schools, particularly colleges and universities, have deep financial problems which, if anything, are likely to worsen in the years to come—and for a very simple reason: Income doesn't match outgo.

Accounting in part for this situation are rising costs and the cumulative drain of inflation over the years—coupled with shrinking, or at least relatively stable, endowments, the result of the generally lackluster bond market and static stock market of the late 1970s. A survey of 67 colleges and universities by the fund-raising counseling firm of Brakeley, John Price Jones showed their contributions in 1976–1977 to total $800 million—$200 million less than they needed to meet the rising costs of energy, faculty, and other operating expenses.

*In 1978, as mentioned in Chapter 1, private contributions to education amounted to $5.5 billion, this accounting for about 14 percent of total U.S. giving.

**Harvard University received $64.9 million during the 1976–1977 academic year, allowing it to maintain its usual position at the top; it was followed by its perennial runners up: the University of California System, with $56.2 million, and Stanford, with $56.1 million. Rounding out the top ten were: University of Southern California, $37.1 million; University of Minnesota, $33.9 million; University of Chicago, $33.1 million; Columbia, $32.6 million; University of Pennsylvania, $31.0 million; Massachusetts Institute of Technology, $29.4 million; and Yale, $28.6 million. Of these, the only public institutions are the University of California System and the University of Minnesota.

Moreover, the schools have not been able to rely on private giving to the extent they once did. The proportion of their total revenues from philanthropy has declined from 29 percent in 1929 to 6 percent today; contributions from alumni account for only about one-fourth of this and appear to have been pushed to their upper limit. Although the total number of alumni who respond to their colleges' annual campaigns appears to be large—an estimated 4 million in a typical year—they represent only about 14 percent of all alumni.*

In desperation, hard-pressed schools have even begun tapping overseas sources for funds, although the foreign gifts almost always come with strings attached. In recent years, the Japanese government gave over $10 million to ten American universities to further Japanese studies, the Shah of Iran bestowed a donation of $1 million on the University of Southern California for a new chair in petroleum engineering, and the Krupp Foundation of Western Germany gave Harvard $2 million to support a European studies program. In 1977 Columbia had some qualms about accepting a $1.5 million gift from South Korea because of the adverse publicity Harvard had received after accepting a $1 million donation from the same country two years earlier, critics contending that the Harvard gift had actually been arranged by the Korean Central Intelligence Agency in an effort to improve Korea's image in the United States.

The New York State Department of Education recently estimated that as many as 80 of the state's 120 private colleges will soon face the threat of folding— unless they receive more public funds in the form of tuition assistance and grants. In the past two decades, 201 institutions of higher education across the country have collapsed—all but 36 of them private institutions—and Peter Pouncey, the ex-dean of Columbia College, issued the dire prediction that all 1500 of our private universities would disappear within the next 15 years unless they received new and bigger subsidies.

This doomsday vision may be vastly overstated, but it is a fact that many of the nation's 128 predominantly Negro colleges are facing near disaster. The schools, which have an enrollment of some 130,000 students, depend on private funds for roughly three-fourths of their income. Yet, of the $2.7 billion in gifts that went to higher education in 1977, only $15 million went to the United Negro College Fund (UNCF), which conducts a joint fund-raising campaign for 41 of the largest Negro colleges. The funds raised represent only 5 percent of the operating budgets of UNCF's member colleges. The colleges cannot afford to charge their students much—tuition, room, and board average only $2600 a year—because half of them come from families earning less than $5000 a year; only 2 percent come from families with incomes over $20,000. Teacher salaries are also well below those at other schools, full professors commanding an average of about $15,000 a year. The schools have no well-heeled alumni constituency to speak of. And to compound their difficulties, a recently ordered desegregation of universities in six Southern states seems likely to drive the best black teachers and students to the more prosperous, traditionally white colleges that were once virtually closed to blacks.

*President Charles Eliot of Harvard is generally credited with being one of the first college officials to formally solicit alumni. In his inaugural address in 1869, he formally admonished alumni of ''the debt which they owe, not to the college but to the benefactors whom they cannot thank, save in heaven.''

Probably the factor most responsible for the difficulties of private colleges, black and white, is the growing competition from state universities and other public colleges which, supported as they are largely by taxes, can attract students with tuition and fees that are generally substantially lower than those of private schools.* (Recently, they averaged $741 a year at public colleges and $3403 in private ones.) Today, private colleges and universities, though comprising about half of the some 3000 of our institutions of higher education, enroll less than one-fourth of all students; as recently as 1950, they enrolled about half, and at the beginning of the century as many as 60 percent.

The endless arguments in the raging debate on public versus private colleges are so familiar that there is no point in restating them here at length. The advocates of the private schools argue that they bring a needed element of diversity to our educational system, are more inclined to innovate and experiment, and often achieve an exceptional quality lacking in our public schools. Their independence, it is also argued, helps them to nurture academic freedom and, of no little consequence, their very being saves taxpayers billions of dollars a year—$5 billion according to one estimate—by educating students who would otherwise be in public colleges and universities.

In actual practice, however, there is now often little distinction between many of the two types of schools in terms of quality. Nor do our public institutions of higher learning necessarily operate more efficiently and economically. For example, in the mid-1970s it cost $17,400 per year to produce a dentist at a public institution in New York State, compared to the $8000 this cost at New York University, a private school.

There is therefore general agreement that all our colleges and universities, public and private, be regarded as resources to be cultivated and supported. Meanwhile, abhorrent as it may be to some to see private funds solicited for what, ideally, should be entirely a public responsibility, as it is in most other civilized countries, one must agree with the statement by Raymond C. Johnson, a former president of the Council for Financial Aid to Education, to the effect that for many colleges voluntary contributions have meant the difference between excellence and mediocrity—and for some the difference between surviving and closing their doors.

Supporting the Arts: How Much to Pay the Piper?

The arts and humanities in America are booming as never before. During the past decade, dance audiences have zoomed from 8 million to 15 million, as dance companies increased in number from 37 to 157. With 110 symphony orchestras now located in virtually every population center of 50,000 or more, some 29 million now attend concerts every year, compared to 20 million in the mid-1960s when there were only 58 professional symphony orchestras. As opera companies have expanded from 27 to at least 80 (a dozen of them with annual budgets of over $1 million), not counting the 1100 opera-producing organizations of all

*Public universities depend on tuition and fees for only 13 percent of their operating revenues, 64 percent of which comes from federal, state, and local public sources, according to a recent study. On the other hand, private universities receive 36 percent of their revenues from tuition and fees, and only 17 percent from public sources.

sorts and sizes, opera attendance now exceeds 10 million annually, double the number of a decade ago; this does not include the millions more who "attend" the live radio broadcasts and telecasts from the stages of the Metropolitan Opera and other companies. Museum attendance is up to 50 million annually (300 million or more, according to some estimates), and is marked by such phenomena as people waiting in line for twelve hours or more to see the celebrated touring "Treasures of Tutankhamun" exhibition, which alone attracted some 7 million viewers. Attendance also keeps rising at science museums, historical exhibits, zoos, and botanical gardens.

If our cultural institutions were hamburger chains or department stores, they would be prospering. But for them, success only breeds expense—and increasing deficits. For museums and libraries, rising attendance means more attendants and other personnel, more overtime, more maintenance, not counting the usual added costs that go with our continuing inflationary spiral, which has now caused earned income to account for less than 65 percent of the budget of most nonprofit cultural groups. And so, ironically, in the face of their growing popularity, many of these institutions have been forced to cut their staffs, services, and hours of admission. The widening gap between operating costs and ticket receipts has created even more serious problems for the performing arts groups. Ticket receipts at New York's Metropolitan Opera have never covered much more than half of its annual operating costs—in recent years, about $35 million. And so even playing to 95 percent capacity and with a house scaled up to $50 a ticket, the company loses $30,000 every time it rings up the curtain. Part of the annual deficit, which has run as high as $13 million in recent years, is made up by other company earnings, for example, from recordings and broadcasts; most of it, however, is made up largely by contributions from individuals and foundations.

This is in keeping with the old American tradition of giving to the arts. From our earliest years, it was philanthropy, rather than government support, that established our symphony orchestras and opera companies, founded our museums, art galleries, and libraries and, in general, made the arts an integral part of our national life. It was a private citizen, John Jacob Astor, back in 1839, who donated the $400,000 that gave New York its first library, the seed of today's famous New York Public Library, just as Andrew Carnegie later helped establish other of the nation's libraries. Henry L. Higginson of Boston set the pattern for the founding of the nation's symphony orchestras when in 1881 he provided $1 million to serve as the principal "to hire an orchestra of sixty men and a conductor, paying them all by the year."

Today, about $2.5 billion is given annually to support the arts and humanities, this accounting for 6.3 percent of total private giving. Of the $2.5 billion, 75 percent comes from individuals, 15 percent from foundations, and the remaining 10 percent from corporate contributions. However, the day of the big individual giver is almost gone, although from time to time one reads stories like that of the spinster who, after living a Spartan existence in a basement apartment, left $1.5 million to the New York Public Library, or of this or that obscure millionaire leaving a comparable bundle to a museum or symphony. Perhaps the most notable example in recent years was hi-fi equipment manufacturer Avery Fisher's donation of at least $8 million to New York's Philharmonic Hall. But of the contributions made to symphony orchestras, for example, over 85 percent are in amounts of less than $100.

Government support of the arts has been slow to come in this country, although it has long been a tradition in Europe. Michelangelo's artistic achievements may never have flowered without the largesse of Lorenzo de' Medici and other wealthy patrons, who were often indistinguishable from government. Haydn produced most of his enormous musical output during his 29 years of service with the Esterházy family. Mozart had his King Joseph II of Bohemia and Hungary, whom he served as court composer and chamber musician, as well as an array of other benefactors. True, much of the art created under such sponsorship was mainly for the delectation of a small private circle of connoisseurs, and the artists and composers themselves were often regarded as little more than hired hands, expected to produce specific works to order for specific occasions. (Medici artists, a *Harper's* magazine article once noted, often wisely thought to include a Medici or two devoutly praying in the corner of a painting.) But perhaps because of this precedent of noble patronage, most European countries continued to subsidize the arts even after their kings and princes had passed into limbo, and so the custom of government support still prevails abroad today.

In this country, however, except for the WPA (Works Progress Administration) program of the depression years, which was designed more as a job-relief measure than as a subsidy of the arts, our government did not really become involved in the sponsorship of the arts—for art's sake—until 1965. In that year, President Johnson, translating into reality a concept that had originated in the Kennedy administration, signed a bill that established two new federal agencies, the National Endowment for the Arts and the National Endowment for the Humanities. Launched with a paltry budget totaling $5 million, the agencies have since grown into bureaucracies with a combined annual appropriation of $230 million.* Large as this sum may seem, it works out to only about one dollar for each of our men, women, and children, far less than the per capita outlay for the arts in most European countries: The corresponding figure in West Germany, for example, is about $2.40.

However, the comparison is not entirely fair. The U.S. outlay does not include the money our government also in effect gives by allowing tax-deductible gifts to the arts, a practice not permitted in most other countries. Nor does it include the state funds appropriated for the arts through our 50 state arts councils, which received a total of $62 million in 1977, compared to $4 million in 1965, nor the money from our municipalities, which render much-needed financial assistance to their local orchestras, opera companies, and other performing groups and cultural institutions. Museums, for example, depend on government support for about 40 percent of their income, much of this from state and local sources, and libraries are now dependent on local government funds for virtually all of their support.

Yet even this support has been insufficient to keep pace with what has become our newest growth industry. Our nation's 31 major symphony orchestras—those with annual budgets above $1 million—continued to pile up huge deficits totaling

---

*This is divided almost equally between the two agencies. Arts is concerned primarily with providing funds for the performing arts, such as theatrical, musical, and dance organizations, as well as for painters, sculptors, and other artists; Humanities makes grants to museums (for example, for the Tutankhamun exhibition), libraries, public television stations ("The Adams Chronicles"), universities, and fellowship programs. A budget of $296 million was requested for the two agencies for 1979.

$6 million in 1977 after expenses of $121 million—in spite of government grants and private contributions. In recent years, the Dallas, Denver, and San Diego symphonies were forced to suspend operations temporarily, and others have been in a state of perpetual crisis. After eight years of operating losses, the Metropolitan Opera finally managed to get into the black in 1977 and 1978. But this was only because it somehow boosted its private contributions (which came to $12.5 million in the latter year). Nonetheless, executive director Anthony Bliss glumly looks at steadily rising costs of production, materials, and labor. "Our labor costs go up 7 percent a year and the cost of new productions is rising steadily," he said. "A production that cost us $250,000 last year [1977], we estimate, will cost $400,000 by 1980."

Responsible for the precarious position of the performing arts, in particular, is the fact that they are so heavily "labor-intensive." As much as 70 percent or even more of the budgets of major orchestras, opera companies, and dance and theater groups may go for wages; this is in marked contrast to, say, the meat packing and oil refining industries or other conventional businesses where labor costs are as low as 10 percent. Moreover, the performing arts do not lend themselves easily to improvements in efficiency or productivity. Although a philistine businessman is once said to have suggested eliminating his local orchestra's second violin section ("If they're not good enough to be first violins, we don't need them"), it is quite obvious that the number of musicians in an orchestra or the number of actors in a play cannot be reduced regardless of economic pressures.

Raising ticket prices will not solve the problem either because, as arts consultant Alvin Reiss points out, "the size of the audience would undoubtedly decline in the face of prohibitive prices."

What is the solution? Opera star Beverly Sills, pointing to a money crisis in the arts, suggests that the federal government increase its annual appropriation for the arts to $1 billion, or about four times its present level.

But even though the *idea* of government subsidies for the arts is now generally acceptable, even respectable, there is still the question of how far it should go. Some—artists as well as legislators—and not necessarily those who equate government-subsidized art with creeping socialism, fear that such art would be subject to political control, much as it is in Communist countries. Yet our WPA program, which subsidized writers, painters, sculptors, musicians, and other performing artists, remained remarkably free of political influence. Significantly, the program nurtured the talents of such as Orson Welles, Saul Bellow, Jackson Pollock, and Mark Rothko, to mention only a few. From a pragmatic point of view, it may also be pointed out that the approximately $10 million the program used to support painters and sculptors alone during the depression was later returned to the government many times over in the form of the taxes eventually generated by the work of these artists.

Then we come to the question of priorities. Quite obviously, the government cannot provide for *everything* unless taxes are raised to astronomical levels. Should more money be spent on the arts when as many as 20 or 30 million Americans are living in poverty and such basic needs as health, housing, education, and child care are still not completely filled? To this, people like Hollywood's Garson Kanin respond: "The funds expended on a single moon shot might have provided enough to prime a coast-to-coast renaissance that could have fed the hungry spirit of our country with the magical nourishment of the arts.''

But *which* arts? Another debate raging on the funding of the arts today centers on what one might call elitism versus populism. The elitists argue that if any more money is to go to the arts it should go to such established cultural institutions as museums, ballet, symphony orchestras, and the opera—institutions with a relatively small following—although the effect of this aid would do no more than ensure that the top price of a ticket to, say, the Metropolitan Opera, would be kept at $50 instead of $60 or $75.

At the other extreme, there are those typified by the congressman who, during deliberations on a proposal to increase arts funding, inquired if there was "any allowance for Buck Owens, Merle Haggard, or the Grand Ole Opry''—in other words, forms of entertainment that appeal to a far broader and less affluent segment of the population. "What it really boils down to,'' said Tom Bethell in a *Harper's* article arguing against federal funding of the arts, "is an appeal to tax the mobs listening to country-and-western, or rock, or soul, because *we*, the wonderful ones, have something more elevated on our minds that *deserves* your subsidy.''

Certainly, something may be said for both sides, difficult though it may be to say if Bach is better than rock. Yet there can be no doubt that funding has generally favored the elitists. In New Jersey, in the mid-1970s, 88 percent of state and federal arts money went to the New Jersey Symphony; and in Missouri, around the same time, two orchestras—the St. Louis Symphony and the Kansas City Philharmonic—customarily received 75 to 80 percent of the state arts appropriation, while the eminently worthy but less politically powerful St. Louis Community Music School, which served youngsters in the inner city, applied to the state arts council for modest grants on three separate occasions and never even received an acknowledgment. (In the years since, much has been done to correct such imbalances.)

A recent Harris survey, while concluding that "the arts must emerge from the cloistered chambers of elitism,'' also reported sometimes paradoxical tastes, preferences, and views in grassroots America. In music, for instance, the survey found 90 percent of the young to be committed to rock, pop, and jazz, and their parents to prefer popular songs, country and western, and folk music. All in all, only 40 percent of those polled chose classical as their favorite music. Yet 75 percent disagreed with the statement "symphony concerts are just for highbrows,'' and nine out of ten regarded it as important "to the quality of life in the community to have facilities like museums, theaters, and concert halls.'' Moreover, a substantial majority—nearly two out of three—indicated they would be willing to dig into their pockets and pay anywhere from $5 to $50 additional in annual taxes to maintain and operate such facilities. Projecting these figures onto the taxpaying population would yield a potential $1.7 billion annually for cultural purposes, a sum nearly eight times the current federal appropriations—more than enough to support all of the nation's some 1820 art and history museums, zoos, botanical gardens, and aquariums, 100 or so of the nation's symphony orchestras, and many of our opera companies and theater and dance groups!

With this enormous potential in mind, Rep. Frederick Richmond of New

York, an arts activist, has in recent years been proposing a bill that would require the inclusion on IRS tax return forms of a check-off box whereby taxpayers could indicate whatever *voluntary* contribution they might wish to make to the arts. This contribution would be added to the amount of tax due. The funds raised this way would supplement and not affect the amounts appropriated annually by Congress for the National Endowments, but would go directly into endowment projects and not be used for any administrative purposes.

The idea is a fascinating one, but its optional provisions still perpetuate the stepchild status of the arts and continue to enable government to shirk its responsibility for subsidizing them when subsidies for everything else—from agriculture to shipping—are accepted as commonplace. It may be, too, that the proposal tends to draw a line between the arts and education when one may be viewed as an extension of the other. "We have no problem with supporting departments of English in colleges and universities, yet we are still debating support for museums and symphonies," says Arthur M. Doty, president of the Alcoa Foundation. He rhetorically asks: "Why is it more important for youngsters to understand the works of the modern poets than it is to understand the French Impressionists? Will it give them more pleasure? Will it make them more civilized? Is it more important for them to know the political philosophers than to know Bach, Beethoven, and Brahms?"

"To understand what is happening to the arts today, you have to go back generations ago to the time when education was going through a similar crisis," says Amyas Ames, chairman of Lincoln Center. "Everyone wanted universal education, and government funds at all levels were provided to meet the needs. The same thing happened with medical research. Now the time of the arts has come."

The New York Times' Harold C. Schonberg agrees: "The time will come when government at all levels—state, city, and federal—will actively subsidize the arts. The cost is really minuscule in relation to total budgets, and the aid is imperative."

But until that time comes, philanthropy will have to continue to play a vital role in the survival of the arts.

The Struggle for Equality and Justice

As long as prejudice exists, there will always be organizations to look after the interests of our various minority groups—Negro, Indian, Puerto Rican, Chicano, and Jewish, among others. For some groups, considerable progress has been made in combating prejudice. For example, although there is still anti-Semitism and some industries still hire only a few token Jews (almost none of them in high executive positions), Jews have long been accepted in the mainstream of our society; in fact, being Jewish has almost become a status symbol in certain circles. For most minorities, however, discrimination and the tensions it breeds constitute perhaps our most serious major social problem, one that philanthropy has dealt with only marginally.

The largest and oldest of all the antidiscrimination groups is the National Association for the Advancement of Colored People (NAACP) which, with pointed symbolism, was founded in 1909, the centennial of Abraham Lincoln's year of birth, with the goal of helping the Negro to realize the full citizenship rights that were expected to accrue to him with the end of slavery. Formed as the direct result of the lynching of two Negroes the year before in Springfield, Illinois, most of the NAACP's early efforts were directed against lynching—and with considerable success. In 1911, for example, there were 71 lynchings in the United States; 63 of the victims were Negroes. By the 1950s, thanks to the efforts of the NAACP, several years would go by without a lynching. In other areas, too, the association could be credited with some impressive achievements. As early as 1915, it had sufficient size and clout to organize a partly successful boycott of the movie, *The Birth of a Nation,* which portrayed the Negroes of the Reconstruction era in a distorted light. It played a major role in the landmark 1954 Supreme Court Brown decision, which ended the separate and equal doctrine of the land by banning segregated schools,* as well as in the passage of the 1957 Civil Rights Act and subsequent civil rights laws, which, among other things, strengthened the right of the Negro to vote.

The winning of court decisions and the enactment of laws, however, is one thing; getting them enforced is another. Accordingly, the association has also been endlessly engaged in the campaign against segregation in public transportation facilities, restaurants, theaters, libraries, hotels, and other public places. It has also been active in the efforts to integrate housing, particularly in the North, and to secure equal employment opportunities for Negroes; currently, it is also involved in such activities as the establishment of day-care centers, voter registration, assistance to ex-felons, securing military justice for black servicemen, and housing construction.

All in all, probably no other single organization has contributed more to improving the lot of the Negro. That progress can be made by working within the system is indicated by the fact that complaints about exclusion from public accommodations have almost disappeared, that more than 44 percent of black families earn $10,000 or more a year, and that more than 45 percent of black high school graduates now go on to college. Yet, with blacks still at least twice as likely to be unemployed as whites, with one-third of all black families with incomes below the poverty level (under $6200 for a nonfarm family of four), compared with 9 percent of white families, and with blacks on the average earning 60 percent of what whites do, the NAACP has in recent years been criticized for not being aggressive enough.

Although the organization still remains the most influential civil rights group in the United States, some feel that its influence is waning. Whether true or not, its paid membership of 420,000 in its 1700 local chapters is well below its peak membership of 460,000 in 1975. Since then, the organization has also been plagued with financial difficulties and, because of the conflicting views of its membership about how militant it should be, it has also been racked with dissension.

*In *Brown* v. *Board of Education of Topeka,* the court set aside a Kansas statute permitting cities of more than 15,000 population to maintain separate schools for Negroes and whites, ruling that segregation in public schools is "inherently unequal." Earlier court decisions had ruled only on whether facilities for Negroes and whites were equal, not on whether the separation of races itself was unconstitutional.

The possible beginning of a new era for the organization came when that grand old civil rights war horse, Roy Wilkins, reluctantly stepped down in 1977 at age 75 after 22 years as its executive director and was succeeded by 52-year-old Benjamin Hooks, an attorney, a former Baptist minister, and a Federal Communications Commissioner. In his first major move to revitalize the organization, the NAACP's new head chastised a conference of local chapter officials for the group's small membership in a nation with a black population of about 25 million, and set a goal of 2 million new members. In 1978 Hooks also announced that the NAACP would lead a major lobbying effort on affirmative action programs and would monitor the programs of educational institutions, businesses, and other organizations. Recently, the NAACP found itself embroiled in a major controversy, one that disturbed some of its more conservative supporters, by opposing President Carter's national energy plan and arguing for more energy expansion to stimulate the economy and create new jobs. "Our first priority must be the attainment of economic parity for black Americans," said Hooks. "We are tired of eating the crumbs off the table of democracy. We are tired of being America's stepchildren." Shortly after assuming his new post, he also said, "We have no apologies for coming to the white community for help because we feel that what we do benefits the whole nation." But the task confronting Hooks is a monumental one in the face of a still sometimes demoralized NAACP membership and meager funds.

Membership dues account for about half of the $2.5 million annual income of the NAACP's national headquarters. (A combined financial statement for the headquarters and affiliates is not available.) The dues and any contributions to the NAACP are not tax deductible because of the organization's lobbying activities. However, contributions are deductible to the NAACP Special Contribution Fund, which uses its income of $2.8 million to fund such programs as voter registration, housing, and veterans and military affairs; also deductible are contributions to the completely separate NAACP Legal Defense and Educational Fund, with an income of about $4 million, which provides legal aid in court cases involving civil rights and furnishes scholarships to black college students.

Like the NAACP, the National Urban League is thought by many people to be a bourgeois "Uncle Tom" organization where middle-class blacks and liberal whites get together and salve their guilt. Vernon E. Jordan, who at age 36 succeeded the late Whitney Young, Jr., as the league's executive director in 1971, is often criticized by more militant blacks who find his camaraderie with whites distasteful. He is a frequent caller at the White House, maintains amiable relations with scores of governors and municipal officials, and fraternizes with board chairmen, serving as he does as a director of a dozen blue-chip corporations and foundations, ranging from Celanese and Xerox to the John Hay Whitney and Rockefeller Foundations.

Jordan, who is now regarded as the nation's most powerful black leader, has no apologies for all this. "I don't believe one can do much about changing attitudes and behaviour unless he has access to the people who have some impact on the national conscience," he once told *Black Enterprise* magazine. "In the process of gaining access, we have not compromised the Urban League's basic principles, nor have we compromised our institutional or my personal integrity."

That this is so was indicated when he made front-page headlines across the nation in 1977 by using the Urban League's annual conference as a platform from which to assail the Carter administration for not working more aggressively to improve the lot of the blacks and the poor. His stand took some courage inasmuch as the Urban League is heavily dependent on federal funds to carry out its programs.

Founded in 1910, a year after the NAACP, its original purpose was to help black people who were migrating from the South to the North. Today, says Jordan, the league's basic objectives are the "economic and political empowerment" of black people in every section of the country. Since jobs are basic to the fulfillment of these objectives, the league's major activities include recruiting and motivating dropouts to complete their education, conducting manpower training programs, and, in general, preparing Negroes for jobs and placing them in trades, business, and industry. To this end, the league maintains a computerized "skills bank" for matching jobs and job-seekers.

It can readily be seen how the league's ties with white industry and labor leaders (half of the trustees in the league's 110 affiliates are white) are essential to the success of such programs, many of which are funded by government grants. And for the balance of the financial support it needs, it does not hurt the league to have on its national board and fund-raising committee the top executives of companies like Xerox, IBM, Westinghouse Broadcasting, and Time, Inc. Of the league's national headquarters' income of about $13.5 million, nearly 30 percent comes from corporations, foundations, and individual contributions, about 65 percent from government grants and contracts, and the balance from the dues of affiliates, special events, legacies and bequests, and a variety of miscellaneous sources. Cost of fund-raising figures against contributions comes to about 6 percent. Although no combined statement for the affiliates is available, their income was recently estimated at about $51 million—$34.5 million from government grants and most of the rest, $11.5 million, from the United Way and other federated drives.

Space limitations do not permit more than a mention of the other leading, if much smaller and less influential, groups supporting the cause of Negro rights: the Southern Christian Leadership Conference, founded by the late Dr. Martin Luther King; the Rev. Jesse Jackson's Operation PUSH; and the Congress of Racial Equality (CORE). The latter, which at one time was regarded as equal in status to the NAACP and the National Urban League, has recently been beset with difficulties from within and without. Its fund-raising practices have been under investigation by North Carolina, New Jersey, Massachusetts, and Alaska; the latter has barred CORE from soliciting its citizens. In late 1978 a dissident faction of CORE filed a suit charging that the group's chairman, Roy Innis, had unlawfully diverted funds solicited from the public, had conducted organization meetings in secret, and had failed to hold elections since 1968.

There are no national organizations of any consequence to speak for the nation's second largest minority group—the estimated 12 million (19 million, according to some estimates) Spanish-speaking Americans, largely of Mexican, Puerto Rican, and Cuban origin. And because our 800,000 American Indians are supposedly under the protective wing of the government's Bureau of Indian Affairs, the 47 or so voluntary agencies working for the rights and welfare of the so-called forgotten Americans, perhaps our most neglected minority group, are relatively small. One of the oldest and largest, the Association on American Indian Affairs, operates on an annual budget of around $675,000. The Southwest Indian Foundation, as we have already pointed out, is concerned largely with its own interests.

Women, as everyone has been made aware for at least a decade, may also be considered a minority group—if not numerically so. However, it would be somewhat beyond the scope of this book to cover the various women's groups, for many are membership organizations that do not rely heavily on outside public support.

Worthy of mention, however, is one group—the League of Women Voters, founded in 1920, the year women were given the right to vote under the Nineteenth Amendment, in order to educate women in the intelligent use of their newly won suffrage. Over the years its stated purpose has been broadened "to encourage informed and active participation of all citizens in government and politics." Nonpartisan from the start, the league does not support or oppose political parties or candidates for office, although it does, in many localities, provide biographical material and other factual information on candidates and the issues. As many may recall, the league was the sponsor of the widely acclaimed presidential and vice-presidential television debates of 1976. Through its 1340 local chapters and 50 state leagues, the organization's 135,000 membership (which now includes men) is kept informed—via bulletins and public meetings—on questions dealing with the machinery of government and with American institutions. Working on such issues as public schools, housing, health services, and tax reform, many local leagues have spearheaded improvements in the structure and efficiency of town and city government. Typical national concerns of the league and its members have included environmental quality, foreign policy, the United Nations, civil rights, employment, and housing—here, too, with the aim of improving our entire political, economic, and social structure. Because these idealistic efforts are construed as lobbying, contributions to the league, which amounted to about $35 million in a recent year, are not tax deductible. However, contributions made specifically to the league's Education Fund, whose activities are solely of a research and education nature, are deductible.

Also founded in 1920, the American Civil Liberties Union is staunchly devoted to upholding free speech, free assembly, and other constitutional rights, and provides legal counsel to those it believes have been deprived of these rights. In a recent year, the ACLU's national headquarters, 50 state and regional affiliates, and some 400 local chapters were involved, either as counsel or through friend-of-court briefs, in about 6000 cases. One resulted in an award of $12 million in damages for 1200 persons who had been illegally arrested during an antiwar demonstration. Others ranged over such matters as wiretapping without a warrant, the confidentiality of bank records and tax returns, and the use of marijuana by adults in their homes.

In carrying out its mandate of being "wholly without political partisanship," the ACLU at times finds itself defending such disparate ideological bedfellows as revolutionaries and atheists on one hand and white supremacists and John Birchers on the other, contending that they have the same constitutional rights as other citizens. Among the more celebrated cases in which it has been involved in recent years have been the conspiracy trials of Dr. Benjamin Spock and Father Daniel Berrigan. Defending the rights of those with unpopular or even dangerous views has made the ACLU itself an object of considerable controversy both from within and without. When, in 1977, it began a legal battle to allow a Chicago-based Nazi organization to hold a parade in Skokie, a heavily Jewish suburb of the city, about 30,000 ACLU members resigned or did not renew their member-ships, which now number 185,000, compared to a high of 270,000 in 1974. Thousands of other members also quit because of the ACLU's court action opposing Bakke's admission to medical school.*

In addition to its court actions, the ACLU lobbies for and against laws affect-ing civil liberties—this to such a degree that dues and contributions to the organization are not tax deductible. (However, contributions to an ACLU Foun-dation are.) Although a combined financial statement for the national headquar-ters and its affiliates is not available, the ACLU is believed to raise around $8 million a year. All in all, there is much to be admired about the organization, taking on as it does causes that few organizations would want to take on—and that few in fact do.

Illustrating the difficulty of drawing a distinct line between lobbying and working for the public good—at least for tax-exemption purposes—are the rela-tively new "public interest" groups, of which perhaps the best known is the conglomerate of consumer endeavors of Ralph Nader. It is difficult not to admire Ralph Nader for his selfless dedication to the cause of consumerism. Certainly he has made an invaluable contribution to U.S. society through his more than a dozen organizations—the Center for Study of Responsive Law, Health Research Group, Public Citizen Litigation Group, Corporate Accountability Research Group, Congress Watch, Aviation Consumer Action Project, among others with equally high-sounding names operating under the umbrella organization called Public Citizen.

However, it is difficult to understand why Nader is so secretive about the finances of his consumer groups, particularly in view of the fact that he has built a large part of his reputation by criticizing American business and government for *their* secrecy. "Information is the currency of democracy," once wrote Nader, who was also influential in the passage of the Freedom of Information Act.

When I asked the Nader command post to send me financial data and answer some questions about its operations, I was told it did not have the staff to respond; others have met with similar rebuffs. However, it was possible to learn from other sources that Public Citizen, a tax-exempt body, now has an estimated income of about $1 million a year, largely from public donations averaging about $15 per person. Why Nader refuses to confide this information to his contributors

---

*The ACLU lost both cases. In 1978, the Supreme Court, by refusing to hear arguments by Skokie officials, let stand a court order allowing the Nazi demonstration. (The Nazi group, however, changed its plans to demonstrate in Skokie and decided instead to hold two summer rallies in a Chicago park.) The same year the Supreme Court, in a Solomonlike decision, paved the entrance of Bakke into medical school by first holding that he had been discriminated against because he was white, and then holding that affirmative action programs for minority groups were constitutional so long as race was regarded as only one of many factors to be considered.

and, in general, chooses to shroud his operations in secrecy, is something that should trouble us all deeply.

On the other hand, John Gardner's nonprofit lobbying group, Common Cause, to which contributions are *not* tax deductible, is not reticent about its finances. The group, which is classified under the Internal Revenue code as a 501(c) (4) tax-exempt organization (meaning that its income is exempt from taxes), had a recent income of $6 million, of which 36 percent came from contributions and the remainder from dues from the 250,000 Common Cause members, who are polled annually for their views on issues in which the organization is active. The overall, if amorphous, purpose of the organization is to encourage greater government responsiveness to the public's needs. Current activities are focused largely on two areas: government revitalization, which embraces such programs as civil service reform, strengthening lobbying disclosure, and extending public campaign financing to congressional elections; and energy reform which, among other things, supports stronger public accountability by federal and state energy regulatory agencies, the exploration of a broader range of energy sources, and research on developing conservation and environmental measures—a subject to which we now turn.

Safeguarding Our Environment

Philanthropy is concerned with safeguarding not only our civil and other rights but also our environment—an endeavor with a connotation that has changed considerably over the years. Not long ago it meant preserving our wilderness areas and other scenic resources as well as their resident wildlife, largely for the pleasure of explorers, hikers, hunters, bird watchers, nature lovers, and other outdoors types. This was made clear when the 1916 Act of Congress creating the National Park Service stated that its purpose was "to conserve the scenery and the natural historic objects and the wildlife therein and to provide for the enjoyment of the same in such manner and by such means as will leave them unimpaired for the enjoyment of future generations." The American Forestry Association and Wilderness Society have long sponsored hiking and horseback riding trips through the forests primeval. Ecologists, concerned as they are with such things as the balance of nature, have their own special reason for protecting the environment. And others have mixed motives. Ducks Unlimited, while no doubt sincerely dedicated to the preservation of duck and other waterfowl breeding areas, also sees the value of maintaining a continuing supply of the birds for its hunter constituents, just as the National Wildlife Federation is in providing a plenitude of all feathered and furred denizens of the wild as targets for its broader-based membership. Not surprisingly, the latter organization owes its birth in 1937 to the initiative and benevolence of the sporting arms industry.

In recent years, however, the meaning of environment has been broadened to include everything in both primeval and urban areas. With the growth of technology and the spread of its by-products—chemicals in the air, water, and food—pollution, along with environment, has today become a popular catchword as more and more people have been aroused about its dangers to public health and well-being. Generally accepted, for example, are estimates indicating that between 75 and 90 percent of all cancer in humans is of environmental origin.

Unless the degradation of the environment is halted, many warn, not only our country's—but man's—very survival will be at stake.

To deal with this threat, some of the old-line conservation organizations have been expanding their goals in recent years. The National Audubon Society, for example, has traditionally been concerned primarily with the protection of bird life, particularly any species in danger of extinction; in fact, the society was actually formed in 1905 for the specific purpose of saving an endangered species, the egret, from plume hunters in Florida. "It is still our purpose to save an endangered species," said a recent Audubon board chairman Gene Setzer, "only now the endangered species is man himself." Accordingly, the society, in further recognition of the interdependence of birds, plants, soil, water, and animals (including man), has been involved in battles against the misuse of pesticides and in stopping such construction projects as a jetport in the Florida Everglades and the hotly debated Storm King Hudson River pumped-storage power plant proposed by Con Edison, the New York utility. Probably the biggest and best known of all the conservation groups, the National Audubon Society has a membership of nearly 400,000 in 400 chapters across the country, and an annual budget of around $10 million.

The venerable Sierra Club, founded in 1892, continues to work for its original purpose of keeping the wilderness unspoiled; its current agenda also includes such traditional objectives as saving the redwoods and finishing out the national park system. But a list of priorities drawn up in the late 1960s put at the top a new item, "environmental survival," this encompassing air and water pollution, pesticides, and even urban planning and population control. About a decade ago, the club lost its tax-deductible status when the Internal Revenue Service ruled that its successful efforts to stop the damming of the Grand Canyon constituted lobbying.

Although this meant that contributions to the club were no longer tax deductible, the favorable publicity attracted by the club caused its income to increase from about $1.8 million in 1966 to $7.2 million in 1977. However, so that tax-deductible contributions could still be received to support Sierra's non-legislative activities, the club promptly reactivated a dormant subsidiary—its Sierra Club Foundation—created in 1960 to support the club's "educational, legal, scientific, and literary projects." In 1971 Sierra also formed the Sierra Club Legal Defense Fund "to engage in litigation in protection of the environment," representing primarily the club but also other organizations. Both the foundation and the fund, with incomes of about $1.3 million and $700,000, respectively, can receive tax-deductible contributions because they meticulously avoid lobbying.

To avoid tax troubles, some of the newer and probably most militant and effective of the growing number of environmental and conservation groups—there are at least 150 national organizations and thousands of local groups—have chosen to concentrate their battles in the courts. Their rationale is that judges are more receptive to change than legislators or bureaucrats and that, although more environmental laws and regulations are needed, there are now a great many on the books that are not being enforced.

For example, as the Natural Resources Defense Council (NRDC), one of the leading new organizations of this type, points out: "Under the Clean Air Act and the Federal Water Pollution Control Act, the Environmental Protection Agency (EPA)* has statutory authority to control carcinogens [cancer-producing agents] found in the air and water. It has a performance record which leaves much to be desired. EPA issued standards for highly carcinogenic asbestos only after being sued, and in some areas, notably New York City, it has been slow to carry out its legal obligation to reduce air pollution to within federally-established limits. Perhaps EPA's greatest failure is its refusal to take immediate action against selected waterborne toxic substances, as it is required to do under the Water Act. . . . NRDC and the Environmental Defense Fund finally brought the agency to court and negotiated a favorable settlement.''

The Environmental Defense Fund (EDF), another leading group in this field, organized in 1967, scored its first major victory by winning a lawsuit that brought about the banning of the pesticide DDT in the United States. The group, a nationwide coalition of volunteer scientists, lawyers, and economists—many of them the top people in their fields—available to work on or testify in EDF's cases, first came to my attention through a mail appeal signed by actor Paul Newman, one of EDF's 43,000 members (Robert Redford is a trustee). ''Shouldn't we leave what EDF is doing up to the government?'' rhetorically asked Newman. His answer: ''EDF has shown that its action through the courts and administrative proceedings is one of the most effective ways to get government agencies to respond to the needs of the people.''

At any one time, EDF may therefore be investigating or fighting as many as 80 different legal actions across the country, often in conjunction with other groups. Together with the Wilderness Society and Friends of the Earth, it mounted a complex legal attack on the Alaska pipeline that resulted in Congress' including new environmental safeguards when it rewrote the laws to allow the building of the pipeline, causing a serious and costly delay for the companies involved. It also led the less successful battle to ban the Concorde, the SST plane developed by Britain and France. Among other things, it has also been involved in court actions opposing PCBs (polychlorinated biphenyls, the dangerous chemicals used extensively in household and industrial products), carcinogens, pesticides, dam and levee projects, and countless other cases involving water and land resources, wildlife, transportation, and energy.

''I don't think the time will ever come when groups like ours aren't needed,'' said EDF staff attorney Bob Rauch, a young, tall, genial Harvard Law graduate, informally attired in a striped shirt and slacks, who has spent his entire professional life in the environmental field. (He started on Earth Day as a college undergraduate.) ''Government should be doing the job we do but the people there just don't seem to have the desire we do.''

Certainly, EDF has an influence quite out of proportion to its modest salaried staff which, numbering less than five dozen, works out of offices in four cities across the country: Washington, New York, Berkeley, and Denver. Or to its

---

*The U.S. Environmental Protection Agency was established in 1970 to bring together in a single agency the major federal environmental control programs. With a staff of more than 12,000 and an annual budget of $5.3 billion, the agency is mandated by Congress to control and abate pollution in the areas of air, water, solid wastes, pesticides, noise, and radiation. The agency's authority to carry out these missions also lies in laws that have been passed in each of these areas.

budget of about $1.8 million*—no larger than the revenues of a successful corner gas station. Indeed, it is quite likely that the revenues of *all* the more than 150 national organizations in the environmental field do not exceed by much the $125 million or so taken in annually by the American Cancer Society.

All in all, philanthropy's contribution to the environmental and conservation organizations is relatively small considering the leverage they exert and the magnitude and importance of the problems with which they deal—problems that should concern our government far more than they now do.

Animal's Lib

"We're the only cat house in the city that doesn't make money," laughs Gloria Shelton, founder of Chicago's Animal Protective Association, whose bylaws forbid the killing of any cat or dog, no matter how sick or old, it takes in for adoption. Cutting down the pet population, preferably through birth control, rather than through an altering operation, is the APA's other major goal.

On the other hand, because the supply of available animals by far exceeds the demand, euthanasia is an unavoidable fact of life at most shelters. For example, Orphans of the Storm in Deerfield, Illinois, receives 1300 lost and abandoned cats and dogs a month from surrounding pounds, but limited cage space and slow adoption rates (an average of only 10 percent) require that most of the animals eventually be put to sleep.

Across the country, there are perhaps thousands of so-called "humane" organizations dedicated to the prevention of cruelty to animals and other aspects of animal welfare. Many, in fact, feel that animals are as much discriminated against as women, blacks, gays, and other minority groups. The 41,000-member Humane Society of the United States (HSUS), for example, includes the following among its major goals: "To reduce the overbreeding of cats and dogs; to eliminate inhumane conditions in animal shelters and pounds and in pet shops; to eliminate cruelty in hunting and trapping; to expose and eliminate brutalities committed on animals used in biomedical research and testing; to eliminate abuse of animals in entertainment; to correct inhumane conditions for animals in zoos and other exhibits; to stop cruelty to animals that are mass produced for food; to give advice and information to humane groups." The century-old American Humane Association (AHA), a federation of some 1500 humane organizations, has similar goals, although it is also becoming increasingly concerned with the prevention of cruelty to children.**

Since an estimated 13 to 15 million unwanted cats and dogs are destroyed annually, people in the humane field are particularly sensitive about the euthanasia issue. Speaking at a National Conference on the Ecology of the Surplus Dog and Cat Problem some years ago, HSUS president John A. Hoyt

---

*About 60 percent comes from membership dues ($15 a year) and most of the rest from contributions or grants from individuals, foundations, or such allied groups as the National Audubon Society.

**Broadening its concerns even more, the AHA recently embarked on a fledgling program to train dogs to become "ears" for the deaf. The dogs are trained to respond to certain sounds—doorbells, burglar and smoke alarms, running water, a baby's cry, or a teakettle whistle—and to alert their masters by nudging them and running to the source of the sound. The $1800 cost of training each dog comes from donations; no charge is made to the recipients.

declared: ''We are tired of being called murderers; we are tired of having our facilities described as Auschwitzes and Buchenwalds; we are tired of having to defend this destruction in the name of humaneness.'' But the only alternative he could suggest was the neutering of pets to prevent them from breeding indiscriminately, this by no means a startling new idea.

Since virtually all of the humane organizations are local, singling out any for special mention would not be of general interest. However, animal lovers may apply to any local group the same guidelines already suggested for evaluating a national organization: Take a close look at the group's facilities and philosophy (its stand on euthanasia, for example) as well as its finances and management. Even so, one cannot be too careful. Even so prestigious a group as New York's American Society for the Prevention of Cruelty to Animals (ASPCA), the nation's pioneer humane society—it was founded in 1866—has been the subject of occasional criticism. In the mid-1970s, some of the society's own members, charged it in a lawsuit with ''extreme indifference and neglect'' of animals and gross mismanagement resulting in a waste of public funds. (About 20 percent of the society's $6.5 million annual revenues come from a city contract to pick up, care for, and dispose of stray animals; the rest comes from dog license fees, membership dues, contributions, endowments, legacies, and fees for the treatment of sick animals.) Among other things, the lawsuit—brought by actress Gretchen Wyler—accused the society's then $40,000-a-year head of availing himself of such perquisites as a chauffer-driven car, private club memberships, and nonitemized restaurant bills, haircuts, and manicures. (The case was settled out of court, with the society agreeing to certain stipulations.)

In addition to the HSUS and AHA, two of the more active national organizations are Cleveland Amory's Fund for Animals, founded by the well-known author in 1967 for the purpose of promoting the humane treatment of all animals, wild and domestic (one of its crusades is against the use of steel-jaw traps), and the Friends of Animals, organized in 1957, which, with its legislative arm, the Committee for Humane Legislation, has a somewhat similar purpose. The Friends, however, also champions spaying as a means of coping with the pet overpopulation problem, and has a program that processes 500,000 spays a year for lower-income pet owners. Both Fund and Friends are relatively small; the lastest available figures show the Fund to have a budget of around $1 million a year, and Friends one in the neighborhood of $1.3 million.

Perhaps the most questionable national group in the humane field—a field with many questionable groups—is the Sacramento-based Animal Protection Institute (API), founded in 1968 with the stated objective: ''To eliminate or alleviate fear, pain, and suffering among all animals, primarily through public humane education.'' Back in 1974 the National Information Bureau reported that the contract between API and its paid staff head, Belton P. Mouras, called for him to be paid a commission based upon funds raised. Mouras responded by saying that he did not regard the percentage as a commission, but rather as a bonus on his then $33,000-a-year (more recently, $48,000) salary. The National Information Bureau also took a dim view of the fact that API advertising was handled by a Mouras agency. In early 1976 the California attorney general filed a civil suit charging that API had misappropriated more than $100,000 in donations and was spending 90 percent of its revenues of nearly $900,000 on salaries, administration, and fund-raising appeals. The suit further charged that, contrary to the content of the appeals, API was providing no substantive direct services for animal protection. In the recent settlement of the suit, Mouras was ordered to resign from the API board and to account for $17,000 in unauthorized spending.

Of the few remaining national organizations in this field, most are identified with the protection of specific species of wildlife. Probably the best known is the International Fund for Animal Welfare, based in New Brunswick, Canada, which spends about half of the $800,000 it takes in annually (80 percent from U.S. contributors) inspiring and organizing protests against the annual commercial seal hunts off the northeast coast of Labrador. Depicted in a typical emotionally charged fund ad is a winsome photo of a newborn dewy-eyed baby harp seal, with the accompanying message describing how this "trusting, gentle, and almost immobile" creature is cruelly clubbed to death so that his pelt can be used to trim boots and hats and to make coin purses and other trinkets and toys, including even stuffed toy seal dolls. "I do not think baby seals should die to make trinkets," says Brian Davies, the fund's bearded founder and executive director.

The subject is fraught with controversy even though the total economic value of the seal hunt to Canada's Atlantic region is estimated at only $3.5 million annually. Davies was spat at, pelted by snowballs and jostled by fishermen when he once led a pack of 40 newsmen to the seal country to witness what his fund's ads refer to as a "barbaric, commercial slaughter." On the other hand, defenders of the hunt like Walter Carter, the provincial Minister of Fisheries, denounce "the so-called conservationists who like to spread the word that we are a bunch of ruthless, insensitive barbarians." He and other partisans, citing published scientific studies that clubbing brings a quick painless death with no psychological distress, go so far as to say that the seal-killing techniques are far more humane than any slaughterhouse methods, and see killing a seal pup as no different from killing a calf or hog or, for that matter, hooking a fish. "If a seal pup had a face like a pig, it wouldn't matter," says Carter.

As for the perhaps even more serious charge that harp seals are an "endangered species," neither side of the controversy has been able to come up with any sure statistics as to whether the size of the herd in Canadian waters is actually decreasing or increasing. Some experts believe the latter to be the case and feel that the seals are not threatened with extinction; there is, however, general agreement that they were being overhunted in the early 1970s.

Then there are organizations dedicated to saving the dolphin and the whale. There is also an Animal Horse Protection Association, concerned with seeing to it that the nation's some 65,000 wild horses (there were 2 million at the turn of the century) do not go the way of the buffalo. And WHOA! (Wild Horse Organized Assistance) is another group with a similar goal. There is even a Committee for the Preservation of the Tule Elk (a rare species found in east-central California). Seemingly, no cause is too exotic to be beyond the pale of philanthropy.

Chapter 17

Fake, Hoax, and Charity

In front of a Queens, New York, shopping center, Emily Levine, a winsome, young, Junior Leaguish-looking brunette is sitting at a card table, making red paper rosettes. Hanging from the table is a placard with the words, "National Alopecia Foundation," and on the table itself is a blue canister bearing the same legend. As the shoppers scurry by, Emily sings out, "Hi, I'm collecting money for the National Alopecia Foundation. Could you please help us out?"

Now and then a shopper comes to the table, wordlessly drops a few coins into the canister, accepts a rosette from Emily, and moves on. To the few who, before deciding whether or not to contribute, bother to ask what alopecia is, Emily delivers the following patter: "The horrible thing is that nobody knows too much about it. It's an old disease but it's only recently been isolated as a syndrome and given a name. And a lot of people are suffering from it. At first, we thought it struck only the elderly. Well, we now see many victims in their early twenties, and find that even babies are being born with alopecia."

What are its symptoms? some people ask.

"The most dramatic one is the sudden and often total loss of hair," says Emily. "With this comes symptoms of anxiety, depression, and antisocial behavior. So alopecia is also treated as a mental disorder, and mental hospitals are filled with people suffering from it. We need money for research and also to set up clinics and educate the public because a lot of people who have alopecia don't know where to get treatment for what has become quite a social stigma."

Alopecia, as some of you may have already guessed, is nothing more than the medical term for baldness, but the foundation itself was a phony. It was concocted by the enterprising news team of the National Broadcasting Company's New York TV outlet to show how people would respond to a solicitation for an unknown charity. (Emily Levine, the solicitress, was an actress hired for the occasion.)

That the generosity of Americans is equaled by their gullibility is indicated by similar eleemosynary experiments conducted from time to time. Reporters for a Philadelphia newspaper once discovered that people were quite happy to contribute to such improbable "charities" as a "Heroin Fund for Addicts," an "American Communist Refugee Fund," and a "National Society for Twinkletoed Children," the canister for the latter showing a pair of human feet with the toes pointed outward. A group of New York University psychology students also had no trouble at all in filling containers bearing the label, "Help Buy Rustproof Switchblades for Juvenile Delinquents," and other waggish researchers and reporters have solicited successfully on behalf of such causes as a "National Growth Foundation for African Pygmies" and a "Fund for the Widow of the Unknown Soldier."

If Americans can give so impulsively, yet casually, to such make-believe causes, one can imagine the extent to which they are taken in by what may be called *genuine* phonies. In one year alone, the New York attorney general received complaints about no less than 1600 phony philanthropies. One of them was headed by a convicted felon who, posing as a rabbi, raised $75,000 for a nonexistent synagogue and school in Israel before he was arrested. In Westchester County, New York, a so-called "blind shop" sold $2000 worth of concert tickets in its behalf before authorities discovered the shop to be nothing more than a store that sold venetian blinds.

In addition to such out-and-out fakes, there are charities which, though legitimate enough, are also questionable in that most, if not all, of the money contributed to them never gets beyond the pockets of their promoters and functionaries. In effect, there may therefore be little difference between these charities and the fraudulent ones; in both cases, the contributor is duped about—or at least is not made fully aware of—what's being done with his donation.

Several years ago in Washington, D.C., for example, a United Police Fund was launched "to aid the widows and orphans of slain policemen." In less than a year the fund, with the aid of a tear-jerking solicitation letter signed by Congressman Sam Devine of Ohio, raised a total of $140,121. Of this, the "widows and orphans" received $18,000; the rest went for "expenses, fees, and a salaried employee."

The widows and orphans were lucky. For not one penny of the $218,000 reportedly raised on a New York telethon for the Foundation for Research and Education in Sickle Cell Disease ever went to that organization; in fact, the telethon promoters claimed that their expenses had exceeded donations by $78,000, although the Sickle Cell Foundation charged that it was never provided with complete and accurate records.

A Philadelphia charity was set up to solicit funds to train paraplegics for gainful employment, help them find jobs, and get them wheelchairs. One year the group collected $70,000; of this, only $181 was spent on paraplegics, much of the sum going to buy shirts for a wheelchair bowling team. The rest of the $70,000 went for "expenses," including fund-raising costs and salaries.

Obviously, there is no sure way of knowing for exactly how much the public is taken every year through such flimflammery, although anywhere from $500 million to $1.5 billion a year is estimated to wind up with charity's charlatans. Whatever the exact figure, there is general agreement that too much is lost. A Council of Better Business Bureaus' survey once ranked charity rackets among the top four of the nation's swindles.*

The New York attorney general's office says that the best way to open a person's wallet is to say *children* or *animals*. The California counterpart of this office is inclined to give the edge to animals, noting that cat charities in particular, preying primarily on sympathetic old people, are very much in vogue these

---

*Why organized crime has overlooked the charity rackets is mystifying. But who knows? Back in 1969 a Suffolk County, New York, grand jury found that some of the men who ran a "charity" for crippled and retarded children had ties with the Mafia.

days. "It's easier to raise money for a home for crippled cats than for crippled children," said a lawyer in the California attorney general's office. The lawyer furthermore noted that the fund raisers often imply they run a shelter that turns out to exist only in the imagination.

People are also most vulnerable to fakers at certain times of the year. In a Yuletide press release headed, "'Tis the Season to be Wary," Fern Jellison, general manager of the Los Angeles City Social Service Department, perhaps the nation's most vigorous municipal monitor of charities, once warned, "Yes, you *can* cheat an honest man, and charity racketeers take advantage of the Christmas spirit. If you don't give with your head as well as your heart, you may be squandering money that legitimate charities need." She suggested, "A good general rule to follow in Christmas giving is to make your donations to reputable local philanthropic organizations."

Philanthropy's fakers are infinite in their variety: They range from simulated Santas, counterfeit clerics, and pseudopolicemen to oily telephone pitchmen, mail order mendicants, high-powered promoters, and beggars and panhandlers.

On the lowest rung of the eleemosynary ladder are the beggars and panhandlers, ubiquitous social phenomena that have persisted in all ages and cultures. The appeal of the beggar is usually through the display of some gross disease, deformity, or infirmity, real or pretended, and there is scarcely a main thoroughfare in our land where some blind, crippled, or senescent soul soliciting funds cannot be found. In some cases, to avoid a brush with the local laws, there is the pretense of peddling some useless trifle—customarily displayed are shoelaces or a few weatherworn pencils—which the giver is not expected to take when he drops a coin into the beggar's cup.

The panhandler generally offers a contrived tale of woe, culminating in a request for some coins for "coffee" or "carfare," although everyone knows that their handouts are invariably put to more potent use—many panhandlers are alcoholics. Entire families of beggars and panhandlers may take to the road. One family of eight, traveling in two claptrap cars from city to city, told hard-luck stories that enabled them to reap $5500 in donations in Los Angeles alone.

All in all, however, Sweet Charity makes it difficult for many a soft-hearted samaritan, particularly those with deep-seated religious impulses, to resist the approach of an outstretched hand or a proferred tin cup which on a busy street corner can net $25 to $100 a day, in some cases enough to pay for luxury vacations, apartment houses, and fancy clothes. But, if one paused before giving, one would realize that facilities for feeding and sheltering the indigent and providing services and even work for the disabled exist in virtually every American community. And that giving to phony or dubious causes diverts funds from those who legitimately need them.

Street solicitors come in all manner of guises and garbs. There are, for example, phony nuns who rent their habits by the day and solicit alms in subways, bars, restaurants, office buildings, railroad stations, and other public places. Usually they keep all the funds they collect, but in Brooklyn a ring was once uncovered; it was headed by a "bishop" who received a portion of the collections, which amounted to from $75 to $100 a day per "nun."

A Wall Street friend swears that the following story is true. He says he was once seated in a bar near his office with a group of cronies when a nun approached them for a handout. A besotted securities analyst, depressed by the action of the day's market, looked up at her and said: "Get out of here, you bitch!" The nun, momentarily nonplussed, shouted back, "Don't you talk to me like that, you c———r," and fled. An official of the New York archdiocese, however, told me of a better, or at least more genteel, way of spotting a phony nun. "Have her show you her diocesan permit to solicit," he said, pointing out that only eight of the some 100 communities of nuns in the New York area have permission to solicit alms.

Many organized charity frauds try to hide under the vestments of religious endeavor, and are often successful at it because public officials find it difficult to prosecute cleric-disguised swindlers, particularly members of so-called religious organizations which, because of the doctrine of church-state separation, are virtually free from government scrutiny.

Some summers ago, however, the Better Business Bureau of Bergen, Passaic, and Rockland Counties in northern New Jersey became suspicious of a so-called United Missions Corps, which was dispatching "volunteers" in that area to solicit money "to feed hungry children." "United claimed it was a religious organization, so the local officials took a hands-off attitude toward it; but we were concerned," said a BBB staff member. "The volunteers were actually paid workers, and the orphanages and other organizations reputed to be beneficiaries were getting only token fees."

The BBB therefore took the information it had to a local newspaper, *The Record,* which dug into the matter further and reported its findings in a front-page story. The volunteers, the newspaper disclosed, were being paid a salary of $75 a week plus 50 percent of their daily take over $50; one volunteer interviewed reported collections of $400 a day.

The founder of United, *The Record* also learned, was a Lewis T. Lewis who, state records showed, had in 1970 been convicted of carnal abuse, for which he received a suspended sentence, a $1000 fine, and five years' probation. Although none of United's officers was ordained—in spite of the fact that they used the honorific, "Reverend"—one officer stoutly maintained that the corps was a religious organization. When asked about the group's religious affiliation, one member said, "Our religion is the love of children."

"If they call themselves a religious organization, it's difficult to prove otherwise," wearily said an official of the Internal Revenue Service, with which United was registered as a tax-exempt organization.

In a class by themselves are the sharpies who masquerade as solicitors for well-known organizations. A Brooklyn man soliciting funds for the Police Athletic League while dressed in a police uniform was tripped up by a pair of *brown* shoes which he had made the mistake of wearing; the sartorial mismatch was spotted by an intended victim. A Cleveland character with an "S" on his collar asked for contributions to be deposited in a large iron pot next to him. Many people, of course, mistakenly assumed that he represented the Salvation Army. But since he had not *said* he did, he could not be arrested. New Yorkers were recently victimized by boys posing as members of the Boys' Club and soliciting money door to door. Isolated instances of the same dodge have also turned up in other cities: a 15-year-old Kansas City lad financed his bowling by conning coins from neighborhood residents after telling them it was to be used for a Boys' Club tickets for them. Of the more than $40,000 raised by the team and their solicitors, only 20 cents out of every dollar went to the organizations, which included a Jewish center, a YMCA, a volunteer fire company, a fraternal lodge, a veterans' organization, and a hospital guild. The problem here is that the organizations had agreed to the deal, apparently on the theory that even their small share represented money they otherwise wouldn't have gotten. But we don't go along with this, for our feeling is that the donor has the right to know if the greater part of his dollar isn't going to charity.''

The Boiler-Room Caper: Dialing for Dollars

Many such fly-by-night promoters use telephone solicitors in what has come to be known as a ''boiler-room'' operation, a hoary fund-raising technique that has flourished for decades. A boiler room is a room with a battery of telephones, usually in low-rent quarters (hence, the term ''boiler room,'' although the hot air emanating from the room may also have contributed to the origin of the term). At the phones sit smooth-talking solicitors who, using telephone and business directories or other ''sucker lists,'' call great numbers of people and, in the name of some local sponsoring organization, try to sell them tickets to an entertainment or perhaps space in a program or yearbook—all for the sake of Sweet Charity, of course. The solicitors may be practiced professionals (known to the trade as ''phonemen'') or part-time workers such as students. They deliver their sales spiels from carefully prepared scripts that bristle with vivid descriptions of the plight of the worthies to be helped—most often, crippled, handicapped, orphaned, or underprivileged children. (U.P.C., the cynical shorthand trade term for underprivileged children, appears as a come-on in ads for phonemen in industry papers like *Amusement Business*.). Once the desired sales quota has been met or the entire city or community has been canvassed—a matter that may take anywhere from a few days to a few months—the boiler-room operator leaves town and sets up shop elsewhere.

Now, ostensibly there is nothing wrong with all this. In many cases, there actually *is* a local sponsoring organization, such as the Jaycees or Lions or a local policemen's or firemen's association, although the organization may also be entirely mythical. In many cases, too, after signing a contract with the organization, the promoter is careful to comply with the law by procuring, wherever necessary, the required licenses to solicit. For receiving a certain sum of money with virtually no time or effort on its part, the organization is quite happy to permit the use of its name in the solicitation. The problem, however, is that, unbeknownst to the unwitting contributor, most of the funds raised sticks to the fingers of the promoter, much of it for ''costs,'' with only a mere pittance—as little as 10 or 15 percent—going to the cause.

On the way to their windfalls, many a boiler-room operator and his crew are also not above indulging in a little hanky-panky. The telephone pitchmen, for example, in their zeal for sales, may pass themselves off as clergymen or—depending on the cause and callee—as police officials, politicians, or other noteworthy local figures.

To learn more about boiler rooms first hand, I decided to get a job in one. But project. (Note: The Boys' Clubs do not allow boys to solicit door

In Washington, D.C., some years ago, the good names of the Gir
of First Lady Pat Nixon were used in an elaborate rip-off. As Maxii
reported the details in her Washington *Post* column, two attrac
dressed women hatched the fanciful, though plausible, tale that Mrs.
planning a tea at the White House to honor 100 outstanding Girl Sco
from all over the country. Armed with this tale, the women, passing t
off as Washington socialities, invited manufacturers in New York'
district to help outfit the worthy teen-agers with dresses, furs, jeans
handbags, luggage, watches, and other sundries. Each manufacturer wa
that the event would receive maximum nationwide news coverage.

What also made the chosen companies most happy to cooperate was
once they were not being asked to donate their goods, merely to supply
cost. The bills, however, were to go to Washington hostess Barbara
whose name, unbeknownst to her, was given as "chairwoman" of the ev
save the bother and cost of shipping, the two women were even obliging e
to offer to take with them the items they had selected, an offer that, ir
instances, was gratefully accepted. The cumulative value of the mercha
they walked away with was later estimated at from $30,000 to $40,000. Nee
to say, the women were never heard from again.

The hoax came to light when several manufacturers, fretting that their bi
Mrs. Howar had gone unpaid for months, checked with the Girl Scouts wh
turn alerted the FBI. The FBI found that the culprits, in addition to drop
Mrs. Howar's name everywhere, had even stolen and used her personal
stationery to give the scheme an added semblance of authenticity.

Police, Better Business Bureau, and city and state agency files are also full
tales of unscrupulous promoters who, after worming their way into the go
graces of well-known organizations, get permission to conduct fund-raisi
campaigns for them and then walk away with as much as 80 or 90 percent of tl
proceeds.

"A charity that employs an outside professional fund-raising organizatio
without checking on its background is a lamb waiting to be fleeced," sai
Herbert J. Wallenstein, New York State's assistant attorney general in charge ol
charity frauds. A beefy, gray-haired man in a red, white, and blue short-sleeved
shirt, he proceeded to give me some case histories from his files.

"Recently, we got a court order against an outfit called Kayem Programs
which ran a campaign to raise money for the Police Athletic League. This it did,
turning over about $10,000 to PAL but keeping over $110,000 for itself. Kayem
also conducted campaigns, ostensibly to benefit the Sickle Cell Foundation, the
NAACP, and the United Negro College Fund. However, these organizations got
only $200 of the $61,000 raised on their behalf. All in all, Kayem kept more than
90 percent of the nearly $200,000 it collected over a two-year period.

"A favorite device of the gyp," Wallenstein went on, "is selling tickets to
something like a ball, a dinner, or a show. When a local group lets an 'outsider'
handle the ticket sales for them, you should be suspicious.

"Take Holari Productions, an upstate fund-raising firm run by a husband-
and-wife team named Reiter. We caught up with them after they were hired by
eight organizations in Rockland County to put on benefit shows and also sell the

how? Surprisingly, the opportunity came sooner than I expected when my phone rang one March evening and the following conversation ensued.

"Hello, Mr. Bakal?" began the friendly voice on the phone, "I'm calling for the New York City Jaycees circus. How are you tonight?"

I said I was fine.

"Mr. Bakal, we're calling to ask you a favor," the voice continued. "The Jaycees are holding their first annual circus at Belmont Park Race Track in August. This year we have a special family ticket that will admit two adults and three children for only seven dollars. If you are unable to attend, your ticket would send seven less fortunate children to the circus as your special guests. May I drop a ticket in the mail to you?"

What else did the Jaycees do with the money? I asked.

"Oh, they use it to help children with muscular dystrophy and multiple sclerosis. And to take poor orphan children Christmas shopping. Things like that."

Could he send me something in writing that would further describe the circus as well as the use to which the proceeds of the ticket sales were to be put? He said he would.

I continued to keep him on the line and asked if he was a Jaycee. The Jaycees, of course, are made up of young men between the ages of 21 and 36 dedicated to providing leadership training for its members through active participation in local community betterment programs.

"No, sir," he said very politely. "I'm just a high school student helping out in my spare time."

Are you being paid? I asked.

"Yes, I am," he replied, again politely. "I receive a minimum hourly wage."

We chatted for a few more minutes in friendly fashion. He told me he was 17 years old, and worked four hours every day from 5 to 9 in the evening. Could the place use any more young people like him? I asked, thinking of my then teen-age daughter Stephanie. He said he didn't know, but he gave me the address, phone number, and name of the "manager" of the office. The wheels in my head had already started turning.

A few days later, a form letter on the letterhead of the New York City Jaycees arrived. It stated that the George Matthews Great London Circus would give ten performances during a five-day period at Belmont Park Race Track. The letter described the circus as incorporating "all of the finest traditional acts from all four corners of the earth, such as elephants, lions, tigers, clowns, high wire, etc., under the magic of a 240-foot-long tent" and said further that my contribution would make it possible for "deserving children to share an experience that they would otherwise never have."

Above and beyond this, the letter continued, the proceeds from the show would, among other things, be used for the following: "Jaycees 'Summer Camp' for underpriviliged (sic) children" and "Jaycees 'Fund for Worthy Causes' such as Muscular Distrophy (sic) and Multiple Sclorsis (sic)."

Intrigued by all this, I ordered a family ticket. I also had my daughter phone the "Show Office" at the number listed and ask for King Peterson from whom, the letter said, further information was available.

Could he use any more telephone salesmen? she asked Peterson. He said sure and asked her to come down and see him. An hour later, she phoned to say she had been hired and would start work immediately. My plan was to pick her up at work on the pretext that I didn't want her traveling home alone that late in the evening. Changing from a business suit into an old sweater and jeans, which I sensed would be more de rigueur in the ambience I anticipated, I arrived half an hour early, which gave me the opportunity to look around.

The boiler room was on the top floor of a dingy, five-story building on West 39th Street at the fringes of New York's garment center, sandwiched between a coffee shop and a woman's apparel store. The room, 15 feet by 40 feet, was bare of the customary office accoutrements and quite obviously intended only for short-term occupancy. Three of its sides were partitioned into some 30 makeshift plywood cubicles, each containing a pushbutton telephone on a board that spanned the width of the cubicle. Crouched over the phones, speaking intently, were the solicitors, most of them young people in their teens or early twenties, In one of the cubicles, I spotted Stephanie who, uncharacteristically, for once did not look at all happy talking on the phone. Because of the chatter from all the cubicles, a moderate hubbub filled the room.

Seated at a five-foot-long folding table at the far end of the room was the boiler-room manager, King Peterson, a genial, gray-haired man, perhaps in his forties, wearing tinted sports-type glasses, a brown safari jacket, red corduroy trousers, and brown boots. Assisting him in overseeing the crew was his wife Vickie, a shapely woman of about thirty in a blue turtleneck and trousers, her dirty blond hair in a long crew cut.

Periodically, Vickie would make the rounds of the cubicles to pick up the sets of slips containing the names and addresses of people who had bought tickets, and hand the slips to Peterson. He would then take the top slip and place it together with the circus tickets in an envelope to be mailed to the purchaser; the duplicate slips, I later learned, were kept in a file for follow-up mailings to those who were slow in responding with their donations.

While watching and waiting, I also had a chance to engage Peterson in some casual conversation. Did he have any trouble getting help? I asked at one point.

"Christ, I can use all the help I can get," he said. "But most of the people who come in aren't worth a damn. I've got a call out to some employment agencies and I've already spent $485 for classified ads in *The New York Times* and *Daily News*."

He said he was looking for two kinds of temporary workers to handle the phones: students or other young people to work four hours every evening and all day Saturday for $1.75 an hour, phoning residences, and more mature individuals to call businesses and professional people at their offices during the day for a commission of 20 percent of sales.

I wondered out loud if I could do the latter and Peterson asked me to come in the next morning to give it a try. He asked me nothing about my previous job experience; in fact, he didn't even ask my name.

On the way home that evening, Stephanie filled me in on her experiences. Upon her arrival, she was assigned to an empty cubicle, given a 5-minute perfunctory orientation and handed her "sucker list"—a page ripped from the Manhattan telephone directory—together with a sheaf of mimeographed sheets containing the script of her pitch (termed the "presentation") as well as detailed instructions on how to deal with special situations or answer any ticklish questions.

For example, for those curious enough to ask how much of the proceeds the Jaycees would actually get, a "response sheet" suggested: "WE HAVE NO WAY OF KNOWING UNTIL SALES ARE FINAL AND COSTS ARE KNOWN AND TOTALED." Costs, the even more curious were to be told, included phones, printing, postage, rental, tables, chairs, envelopes, and the circus performance itself.

Since time on the phones meant money, Stephanie was also instructed not to waste much time speaking to those who, early in the conversation, pleaded "financial hardship or a personal or family tragedy." She was asked to mark off each name on the directory page after the call was completed, and to skip all business and government numbers.

In two hours, she managed the tedious task of calling 61 numbers, 35 of which responded. (The others were either no-answers or discontinued numbers.) From those who responded she secured a total of eleven pledges for $77 worth of family tickets. King and Vickie were delighted, she said. Beginners were expected to make only two sales an hour even though about three sales an hour were needed for the operation to break even. She had averaged five and one-half. Those who turned her down said they were sick, had no money, were out of work, had a death in the family, contributed to other organizations, were going to be out of town, or said they were simply not interested. "I don't think this is the way money should be collected for charity or diseases," one person snapped, although all had listened to her pitch politely.

During a 15-minute break, she helped herself to a cup of coffee (charge, 15 cents) and talked to some of her fellow solicitors. Most had gotten their part-time jobs through their high school referral service. One, however, had learned of the job through her local precinct police station!

On my first morning on the day shift, only about half of the cubicles were occupied, and the solicitors, all of them men, ranging from people in their twenties and thirties, seemingly between regular jobs, to elderly retirees on social security, welcoming the opportunity for extra cash as well as company. My neighbor, a thin, elderly gabby former salesman who said he averaged $30 to $40 a day in commissions, obviously relished the chance the job gave him to chat with others.

When Peterson briefed me, he stressed that, when making my pitch, I should say that I was calling *for* the Jaycees rather than say I was *with* the Jaycees; the semantic subtlety, he told me, would be lost on the average person and yet not leave the soliciting firm open to a charge of misrepresentation. I asked Peterson if I had to use my right name. "Nah," he said, "use any name you want. We don't care."

Otherwise, the routine and approach of the day shift differed somewhat from that used in the evening. All of us worked from a pile of index cards—each with the name, address, and telephone number of a business firm. All this information was copied from a special crisscross directory which lists telephone numbers by street addresses, and rents from the telephone company for $197 for a six-month period. (Teen-agers were paid 1.5 cents for each card they copied.) Our sales script specified that we start off by getting the *first* name of the owner or manager of the business being solicited—as a means of establishing a note of rapport, perhaps even leading the recipient of the pitch to believe that he knew you. This was the suggested gambit:

"HELLO, THIS IS *CHARLIE BROWN* (my pseudonym). SAY, WHAT'S THE NAME OF THE MANAGER THERE AGAIN, I FORGOT? (Pause). NO, I MEAN HIS FIRST NAME? GOOD, IS HE IN NOW?"

This information obtained, the pitch continued:

"HELLO, (say his first name), THIS IS (say your first name). I'M CALLING FOR THE NEW YORK CITY JAYCEES. (His first name), I CALLED TO ASK YOU A FAVOR. (Pause). WE'RE HOLDING OUR FIRST ANNUAL CIR-CUS. CAN WE COUNT ON YOU, (first name), TO SPONSOR A BOOK OF THE KIDS' TICKETS TO THE CIRCUS? (He'll ask you how much they are.) WELL, THE TICKETS ARE A DOLLAR APIECE IN BOOKS OF 50, 25, AND 15. CAN WE SEND YOU THE FULL BOOK? (If the respondent pleaded business was bad, the solicitor was told to be sympathetic and offer a "small, personal book" of ten tickets for only ten dollars.)

On calls to doctors, the following special approach was suggested:

"HI, THIS IS———. IS THE DOCTOR IN? IS HE BUSY WITH A PA-TIENT? LISTEN, WOULD YOU DO ME A FAVOR? HAVE THE DOCTOR CALL ME WHENEVER HE HAS A MINUTE. WHAT IS THIS REGARD-ING? OH, IT'S JUST A LITTLE PERSONAL MATTER."

Once a contribution was pledged, no chance was taken that the pledgee change his mind: A runner, or messenger, was dispatched to pick up the businessman's contribution. Our runner was an attractive, young black girl in a yellow halter top and green tight-fitting slacks.

Apparently, I learned quickly enough to become the boiler room's star sales-man. During my first morning at work, I racked up seven sales totaling $160 in just two and one-half hours. One $15 sale was to a lawyer who, like many others, listened to my sales spiel without even bothering to ask me any questions.

"You've just made yourself $32," exulted Peterson, cautioning me, however, that sales were not to be regarded as final until the runner had picked up the money. (In some cases, the would-be donor later changed his mind or could not be found at the address listed.)

"Is that good?" I asked Peterson.

"You're above the national average," he said.

"What do you mean, national average?"

Peterson momentarily stopped his customary routine of endlessly inserting tickets and bills into envelopes to explain that the George Matthews Great Lon-don Circus had a total of 800 to 900 "salesmen" like me selling tickets in some 25 cities across the country, with the average solicitor scoring four pledges totaling $60 an hour. My seven sales, against only thirteen turn-downs (plus eleven no-answers), had worked out to an average of about $70 an hour. "Our people in D.C. are now doing $100 an hour, which is tops," said Peterson. "Maybe that's because they're calling in the name of a police organization there. It's pretty hard to turn down the cops."

Over the next few weeks, I reported for work at the boiler room every other day or so, putting in two or three hours on the phone each time. To avoid any sudden appearance of affluence I kept my faded old jeans and some worn, shabby slacks and sport shirts at my regular Madison Avenue office, and changed into these before proceeding to my undercover job. During this period, I established a close enough rapport with Peterson for him to tell me more about the business—I even intimated that I might be interested in working up into a job such as his—as well as about himself.

I learned that Peterson was a relative newcomer to circus sales, having previously been a salesman of "laser beams and things like that." In fact, he had been in the boiler-room business for only some six months following his completion of a two-week training program at circus headquarters in Martinez, California, just outside San Francisco. In the "Help Wanted" columns of the *San Francisco Chronicle,* I was later to learn, the George Matthews organization periodically advertises for "sales promotional directors" to "hire, handle, and organize telephone sales crews" and to manage "sales offices" at a salary of $800 monthly plus commissions after a stipend of $100 per week while training. An occasional George Matthews ad also calls for an "enthusiastic booking agent" to sell the circus to sponsoring organizations, with promised annual earnings of from $15,000 to $50,000 in salary and commissions.

From the Better Business Bureau of San Francisco, as well as from others around the country, I learned more about the George Matthews Circus. Under the corporate aegis of International Productions, it is owned by one Sid Kellner whose reputation is such that he chose to bestow on his circus the given names of his two sons rather than his own. The chosen name was presumably dictated by the ubiquitous presence in BBB files of the circus under its previous name, the James Brothers Circus, a whimsical designation that once inspired a *Chronicle* reporter to characterize it as "the biggest holdup since Frank and Jesse harried the Union Pacific in old Missouri." The reporter was speaking only of the quality of the show. "A greater array of unemployables would be hard to cull from the whole spectrum of show business," he wrote, noting, for example, that the show's pachyderms performed "probably the most elementary elephant stunts in circus history."

But the term "holdup" would no doubt also apply to other aspects of the circus' operations. A BBB bulletin headed, "Beware James Brothers Circus Promotion," quoted this commentary on a Jaycees-sponsored circus in Sacramento: "What this claque of do-gooders and profit-takers, the Jaycees and the James Brothers, did to Thursday's circus at Cal Expo would make P.T. Barnum and Elmer Gantry look like Patience and Prudence." The bulletin went on to report that 20,000 tickets had been sold or distributed for a circus tent that would seat only 3000, and pointed out that similar situations involving the James Brothers had also been reported in other cities.

Other more serious complaints, I also learned, centered around the high percentage of the monies collected that was retained by the circus people. In a typical basic contract the George Matthews Circus signs with a sponsoring organization, the circus first skims off half of the gross proceeds of the telephone sales to pay the solicitors, collectors, and printing costs and to pay itself a handsome personal commission. From the remaining half of the proceeds are paid the telephone bills, the cost of the circus acts ($2500 to $3500 a day), the rental of facilities for the circus, and miscellaneous other expenses. Whatever is left is divided equally between the promoter and the organization, usually against a guarantee of, say, $1000 or $2000 to the latter.

How little the organization actually gets is indicated by the experience of a circus sponsored by the St. Louis Jaycees some years ago. Of the $44,000 grossed in ticket sales, the Jaycees received only $5800, or 13 percent, of the proceeds. In San Francisco, a circus for the Police Athletic League grossed nearly $54,000, of which PAL received $6300—less than 12 percent. And in the same city, a chapter of the International Footprinters Association (dedicated to providing scholarships to deserving young men interested in law enforcement) received only $76 of the $7000 collected in advance ticket sales! (A random sampling of circus promotions, taken from Better Business Bureau reports from 13 cities around the country, showed the sponsoring organizations' share of gross receipts to range from 11 to 25 percent, with an average of 18 percent.)

Such experiences are commonplace in hundreds, perhaps even thousands, of communities across the land. For, in addition to the Matthews circus, there are other touring tent shows: Miller-Johnson, the Hoxie Brothers, and the well-known Clyde Beatty, to mention the names of only a few of the dozen or so that roam the country every year. Many, if not all, owe their survival to the boiler-room business. Some have operations much like Matthews'; others rely on outside independent entrepreneurs—"telephone promoters," as they are referred to in the trade. Of the $980,000 the Hoxie circus grossed on a recent 32-week tour, $205,000 went to professional telephone promoters, and $195,000 went to the sponsoring charitable organizations.

From his headquarters in Central City, Pennsylvania, Mearl Johnson, ranked by *Amusement Business,* the boiler-room bible, as one of the nation's top telephone promoters, arranges for the appearances of circuses around the country; in two seasons in the Washington metropolitan area alone, Johnson's solicitors sold well over $150,000 worth of circus tickets. Like other telephone promoters, Johnson, a handsome, bearded man in his late forties, also books and sells tickets for rodeos, magic shows, country-western shows, variety shows, and other fun fund-raising crowd catchers; an ox roast, of all things, is an annual featured event in the Detroit area, which was the scene of no fewer than 26 telephone solicitation campaigns during a recent year. In the Cleveland area, there are now more than a dozen such operations annually, with as many as four going on at the same time.

So big has the boiler-room industry grown in recent years that it now even has its own trade association, euphemistically titled the International Telephone Sales Promotion Association. At its initial meeting in Nashville in 1973, some forty delegates (dozens more who could not attend sent messages of encouragement) elected Mearl Johnson president and mapped out a campaign to burnish the boiler-room image and fight antisolicitation laws. According to an account of the meeting in *Amusement Business,* the view was expressed that "phone promoters have placidly accepted the stigma of their trade and that, unless some organized voice is created, the business appears doomed to be legislated out of existence."

Not that the boiler-room boys really have too much to fear. The few laws that exist are flaunted, ironically, most of all by those enforcers of the law, the police, who, through their benevolent associations, fraternal orders, athletic leagues, and other do-good groups have probably lent their names to more boiler-room operations than even the Jaycees, encouraging activities that are at best deceptive and at worst criminal. In a brilliant feat of investigative reporting, *Connecticut* magazine, in April, 1975, revealed that police in at least 25 of the state's 92 local police departments had formed liaisons with high-pressure professional solicitors and, moreover, had failed to register as required by Connecticut's Charitable Solicitations Law. Nor had they bothered to file any of the required records showing how much money was raised (in some cases, by calling potential donors as many as eight times a day) and how it was spent. More seriously, some police groups had even gone so far as to work with felonious firms. One firm, among other offenses, had been found guilty of having its phonemen impersonate police officers during the course of their solicitations, and the firm's head had been convicted on 15 counts of fraud during a previous fund drive.

In Louisville, Kentucky, one of many other places that could also be cited, not one of the four police organizations that sponsored phone-room solicitations during a recent year bothered to obtain the required city permit, according to a series of articles in the *Louisville Courier-Journal*. The newspaper also reported that most of the city's charity groups also ignored a local ordinance forbidding solicitations costing more than 15 percent of the money raised, and that the city's law enforcement director admitted he wasn't doing very much to enforce the ordinance. If he took any action against the phone-room operators, he lamely explained, then he might be expected to take action against civic theater groups and other nonprofit ticket sellers not meant to be covered by the ordinance.

If the telephone promoters had any complaint, it was not so much about the ordinance itself as about the extent of the competition fostered by its nonenforcement. "This is a well-worked town," said the local manager of the phone room selling tickets for a George Matthews circus sponsored by the city's retired firefighters. "We're going to lose money. There are just too many solicitations going on here."

The same was not quite the case in New York where boiler rooms, although they do exist, are a relative rarity, the consequence of tough laws that are enforced. While putting in time at my boiler room, I gleaned additional details of the economics of the boiler-room business. In addition to the solicitor's commission of 20 percent, the runner, I also learned, got 6 percent (elsewhere, as much as 10 percent). Although he did not tell me outright what he made, I gathered that King Peterson took 10 percent of the take, which is about standard in the industry for boiler-room managers. All this alone, therefore, amounted to 36 cents out of every donor dollar. Postage was, of course, a variable, but Vickie once indicated to me that this came to roughly $1000 a month. "It runs to this," she complained, "because only half of the people who order tickets send us checks right away and we have to mail the others reminders."

She said she sent out four of these reminders at intervals of eight to ten days and then made one final follow-up call before giving up.

At one point, Peterson also complained to me about the cost of the phones. "Boy!" I said, "they must cost you a fortune."

"You're not kidding," he said. "With each phone going full blast, the bill for *each* phone can run to $230 a month. With 30 phones, our total phone bill can come to nearly $7000 a month.''

"What would all your expenses amount to?" I then asked.

After doing some figuring on a scrap of paper, he said they ran to "about $10,000 a month.''

"You must have to sell an awful lot of tickets to come out ahead," I then suggested.

"But we're not," he said. "In fact, we're losing our shirts. The trouble in New York is that most people don't even know who the Jaycees are. And some of the people we call, like the blacks and Puerto Ricans, don't even know what a circus is. We're also too far from Belmont Park Race Track—many people from here don't want to go to the outskirts of the city. We should be operating out of Long Island or Queens.''

"How many tickets have we sold so far?" I then asked.

Peterson avoided giving me a direct answer. However, on another occasion, he let slip the fact that the operation had sold $20,000 worth of tickets during the month it had been in New York.

"I have to sell a lot more before our circus gets here," he added. The circus had started out from Santa Ana, California, on its tour of 98 cities on March 25—just a week before—and would spend one or two days in most cities while crossing the country.

He also continued to complain about the difficulty of getting help, particularly for his day shift. "The only ones who answered my ads in the *Times* and *News* were three professional phonemen, one with his own 10,000 cards of contacts. But they all wanted 30 or 40 percent commissions, which is more than we pay.''

I suggested that he try an ad in a paper like the *Village Voice,* and he gratefully accepted my offer to write one for him. I said that in order to help it pull, I would put in something like "long hair acceptable.''

Other problems continued to plague the boiler room. A man once called to ask the names of the orphanages to which tickets were being distributed. Peterson promptly got on the phone to Jim Durkan, the Jaycees vice-president and "coordinator" of the benefit, and said, "For Chrissakes, Jim, you forgot to give me the names of the orphanages. I must have the list right away." When the list arrived by messenger, Peterson read off the names of the dozen or so orphanages on it to the man who had called. A few hours later, the man called again and said he had checked with the orphanages; none apparently knew anything about getting free circus tickets. "That goddam Jim!" Peterson exploded. "He forgot to tell them.''

Strangely enough, though, apart from an occasional call like this, no one, as I soon learned, was inquisitive enough to check with city officials or the local Better Business Bureau regarding the legitimacy of the solicitation. Not a soul. Except me.

And in doing so, I was inadvertently responsible for the closing of the boiler room. One day, curiosity prompted me to call the appropriate city agency—the Public Solicitations Section of the Welfare Commission—and confide in a contact there about what I was doing. I asked if a license had been issued for the solicitation and, as a favor, I also asked that if there were no license any action be postponed for a few days in order to give me more time to complete my investigation. My contact agreed and said he would look into the matter.

Reporting for work at the boiler room the following day, I found it closed. "What happened?" I asked, after managing to reach Peterson on the phone.

"The police shut us down," he said. "Those stupid Jaycees didn't know enough to get a license. Those stupid sonsofbitches."

I called my contact at the city agency who told me that a license had indeed not been issued for the solicitation. "Ordinarily, none is required by the city if you're just sending out mail or making telephone calls," he said. "But if the organization is also making direct personal contact with the person solicited by, like you said, sending out runners, then it must apply for a permit."

"But you agreed not to shut them down," I said.

"*I* didn't shut them down. But I felt I at least had to call the state attorney general's office and tell Wallenstein what was going on. I hope you don't think I asked him to do anything. All I said was that I had an inquiry."

I got on the phone to Herb Wallenstein, the assistant attorney general in charge of charity frauds.

"Yes," he said, "we had them all down here yesterday afternoon—the Jaycees, the boiler-room people, their attorneys, and someone from the city licensing agency. I was here until almost eight o'clock with those people. It was my position that the circus guys were professional fund raisers and, according to state law, had to be registered with our Charity Registration Bureau. The Jaycees are a registered charity but they can't use an unregistered professional fund raiser. But that was no problem; the circus could get a bond and register. The big issue was the contract between the Jaycees and the circus. It was my position that there weren't sufficient monies going to the charity. The percentage charged off to fund-raising expenses was too high."

"What would a proper percentage be?"

"I can't tell you that because, as Lord Coke said in the sixteenth century, each case stands on its own bottom. But we get a little uptight in situations where the fund-raising expenses get above the 35 to 40 percent mark. There's no statutory rule on this. [For solicitations by *mail* including unordered items in New York State, fund-raising costs may not exceed 50 percent of the amount collected.] This is a position we've taken based on our own experience."

"So how was the situation left?"

"They agreed to shut down the operation and submit a new contract to us. Nobody is happy about the situation. The circus sees $15,000 or $20,000 going out the window because we shut them down. The Jaycees are unhappy about losing part of this money. But we have to take the view that the public's side has to be considered, too. And the public was getting screwed, because it was under the impression that its funds were going to charity whereas, when you look at this situation, only something like 10 to 15 percent was going to charity."

I then phoned the New York City Better Business Bureau which, after calling the Jaycees, confirmed the fact that they were to receive only about 50 percent of the *net* receipts from the sale of tickets to the circus.

Feeling now somewhat like Judas, I phoned Peterson almost daily on the pretext of asking when I could go back to work and then paid him a visit two weeks later. He was alone in the boiler room. "I still don't know anything," he said morosely. "The hangup is getting the authorization from the state. First from the state, then the city."

"Couldn't you sell tickets to the circus anyway strictly as a business venture?" I asked. "At a $1 a ticket, a lot of people would probably buy them."

"No, we've already tried this," he said. "And our experience has been that we can't sell enough unless there's a charity tie-in."

A few more weeks went by and I decided to check with Wallenstein.

"Oh, yes," he said, "the circus people did send some sort of proposed new contract back to the Jaycees. But we found it quite abhorrent and, as far as we're concerned, the whole matter seems to have died. If they're soliciting now, it's not for charity."

When I called the boiler room a month later, I learned that its phone had been disconnected.

What would now happen to the circus tickets already sold? It was now about a month before the circus was due to come to town.

In my other guise as a ticket holder, I phoned Jim Durkan of the Jaycees, reaching him at his office at the New York Life Insurance Company.

"Is the circus still going to be held?" I asked.

There was a long pause. Then hesitantly, "Yes, but for only one or two performances instead of ten. The date is August 10. And we might have to get another place for it. You'll be notified by mail of the new site."

"What happened?"

"What happened is that we sold only enough tickets for a one-day stay and Belmont wouldn't give us the place for just one day. Why are you calling me about this?"

"Well, I called the sales office but it was closed down. Then I found your name on some literature it had sent to me. By the way, while I have you on the phone, could you tell me what's done with the proceeds of the ticket sales?"

"Why do you ask that question?" He suddenly seemed to be on his guard.

"Well, the circus is for charity, isn't it?"

With the hearty assurance of the insurance salesman, he briskly rattled off the laundry list of good-works activities with which the Jaycees are involved, concluding with the statement, "So, actually, all the monies that come from the circus will be helping us carry on our work throughout the year."

"But aren't there expenses involved in putting on the circus? What percentage of the proceeds goes to the Jaycees?"

"Say, yours is more than just a regular inquiry." Now he was really getting suspicious and asked me just who I was and where I was from. I told him I was only a ticket holder and repeated my last question.

Quite reluctantly, he answered, "We're going to have 50 percent of the profits." He didn't say *net* profits. Then to brush me off, he said, "I have to go now. You'll be notified where the circus will be."

A week before the circus I still hadn't been notified. I called Durkan again.

"Weren't you notified?" he said with what could have been genuine surprise. "The circus people were supposed to have sent out a notice to everybody. I'll be sure to see that you get one. We're also distributing tickets to orphanages throughout the city. There'll be thousands of children there. We'll have seats for

4000 people. Then he gave me the address of the new circus site—a Manhattan parking lot on West 42nd Street at 11th Avenue, near the Hudson River.

I had the feeling that I wasn't the only one not notified of the new site, and so I went out to Belmont the day of the circus. I saw car after car pull up to the race track gates and then drive away, many filled with disappointed children. Some people were simply told that the circus had been canceled; others were redirected to its new location in Manhattan, about an hour away.

Meanwhile, I had a friend look in at the parking lot. He reported that, in contrast to the customary overbooked situations elsewhere, fewer than 200 people had shown up to watch the circus—well, a circus of sorts with half a dozen lethargic lions, a couple of unenthusiastic elephants, and some tired tight-rope walkers among the featured acts. In fairness, though, he also reported that many of the youngsters in the audience seemed to enjoy themselves and gave the acts the same slack-jawed uncritical attention they accord a television rerun.

But where was the huge crowd one might have expected on the basis of the $20,000 worth of tickets that had supposedly been sold? What had happened to the thousands of tickets that ostensibly had been distributed to orphanages as well as to underprivileged children elsewhere? I called a random number of the orphanages that had been on the list I had seen in the boiler room. None had received any tickets or had even heard of the circus.

I then phoned Durkan and asked him why so few people had shown up to see the circus.

"What do you mean?" he said, "We had 1000 people there."

"But you said there would be thousands."

"I don't know why the others didn't show. But think of all the kids who did and had the chance to see a circus for free."

For free? I made a quick mental calculation. Assuming that $20,000 worth of tickets had been sold and there were as many as 1000 people in the audience, as Durkan would have me believe, this still worked out to roughly $20 a head.

I next asked Durkan how the Jaycees had come out on the deal financially. He refused to say, apparently unmindful of the public-service pamphlet put out by his own New York Life Insurance Company that warns readers of the sharpies who conduct boiler-room drives and advises: "Check carefully before giving. Get the facts about the organization that is soliciting funds. If you get a telephone plea for funds, tell the caller you want all data sent to you in written form."

"You know," said Durkan, somewhat testily, "no one has ever asked me questions like this before."

Maybe that's the trouble.

The Mail Mountebanks

Far more numerous than the telephone promoters are the fraudulent schemers who, with the helping hand of Uncle Sam, use the mails to mulct the public of untold more millions. In most cases, the stated cause, although varied, is again noble, with children, diseased or defenseless, the subject of most appeals. The end result is invariably the same: Most or all of the donated money is squandered on fancy salaries or is used to pay the extravagant expenses of the promoters who send out the mailings.

In looking at these mail miscreants, let us first move back several decades, for no account of philanthropic flimflammery would be complete without some mention of the legendary exploits of one such promoter, Abraham L. Koolish and his covey of relatives and associates, whom E. J. Kahn, in his book *Fraud*, once characterized as "close to being the nonpareils of tainted fund-raising." Certainly no one before or since Koolish in the charity field has practiced chicanery on so heroic a scale nor reaped such robust gains, enough to give him a net worth of $4,382,348 in 1952. That year, incidentally, Koolish, a son-in-law, and some cronies, one a former associate of racketeer Frank Costello, bought the controlling interest in RKO Pictures Corp. from Howard Hughes. When the *Wall Street Journal* exposed the men's backgrounds in several front-page stories, Koolish and his colleagues withdrew.

Koolish began his career peddling punchboards* in the depression year of 1930, and then branched out a decade later selling insurance through the mail. Both of these activities, as well as a number of others, involved Koolish in frequent brushes with various federal authorities, one brush culminating, in 1948, with his indictment for the fraudulent use of the mails. The indictment was later dismissed on the ground that it was faultily drawn (one person named in it had not actively been involved), although the federal grand jury investigation of the insurance operation revealed that it had netted Koolish and his cohorts $1.5 million over a six-year period.

This sum, however, turned out to be mere chicken feed. Koolish, by now a veritable Merlin of the mails, casting about for a less constricting means of earning an easy dollar, finally settled on charity—where, unlike business, few people asked questions. In the course of his operations here, he was a pioneer, forging, as Ralph Lee Smith has noted, "an entirely new set of tools for charity swindling."

His first tool involved the mailing of unordered merchandise—a first in the charity field. For this purpose, he formed the Idento-O-Tag Company in 1941 to manufacture those personalized miniature facsimiles of auto license plates for car owners' key rings. Then he worked out a deal with the Disabled American Veterans whereby the veterans' organization, in return for the use of its name, would receive a small percentage of the proceeds from mass mailings to car owners across the nation. Since Koolish would mail out as many as 30 million tags a year, the project proved tremendously profitable for him, particularly since another of his firms, Gayton Associates, handled the mailings. How profitable it indeed was came to light some years later when the DAV, persuaded by Koolish that, in order to have the golden eggs, it should own the goose, in 1945 purchased the entire Ident-O-Tag operation from him for $1,365,000, a sum that seems excessive for what involved little more than a nonpatentable novelty item. But along with the sale went the services of Koolish as a "consultant" at $1000 a month for a seven-year period, during which he apparently taught the DAV enough for them to get more than their money's worth.

For when a New York State legislative committee looked into the affairs of the

---

*Small boards with many holes, each filled with a rolled-up printed slip; one paid a small sum to punch out a hole containing a slip that would hopefully entitle the gambler to a prize. The boards were a favorite gambling device of that era.

DAV in 1953, the committee found, as mentioned earlier, that at least 79 percent of the $21,480,000 raised by the organization during the preceding three years had been gobbled up by fund-raising and administrative costs. Yet the mailing pieces for the Ident-O-Tag solicitations could quite correctly claim: "No professional promoters or outside interests benefit from your donation and no royalties or commissions are paid anyone." Which technically was true, for Koolish was now on the DAV payroll at that monthly salary.

Meanwhile, Koolish had also been busy with other mercenary matters. Back in 1948, his Gayton Associates had worked out a nifty arrangement with the National Kids' Day Foundation, set up to promote the *idea* of a National Kids' Day as a vehicle for aiding needy children, an enterprise that enlisted the unwitting cooperation of local Kiwanis Clubs across the country. However, anyone giving a quick, careless glance at the fund-raising flier, which had Bing Crosby crooning "Here's a grand way to help kids" (the singer later denied that he had given the promoters permission to use his name) and was accompanied by a personalized ball-point pen or personalized name stickers, could be forgiven for believing that his donation was going directly to a needy child. Of course, not a dime did. Nor, for that matter, did much ever get to the foundation itself. For of the $3,978,000 collected from 1948 to 1953, 82 percent went to pay for fund-raising. Much of this money wound up with Koolish, who had a deal on which he couldn't lose. For his Gayton Associates received 63 cents for each of the 2 million or so mailings of pens it sent out. In addition, another Koolish firm, Wesco, had a cost-plus contract, ultimately worth $154,000, for each piece of incoming mail it opened for the foundation. One might say Koolish had it both coming and going.

The story was much the same for the many other charities, some of them well-known reputable groups of long standing, others ephemeral fly-by-nights, with which Koolish hooked up, among them the National Association for Asthmatic Children (to which John Wayne had been induced to lend his name), Meals for Millions, Gold Star Wives and War Orphans, Boys Town of the Desert, the National Haven for the Blind, and the Handicapped War Veterans, some of which caused Koolish some trouble—but not enough to inhibit his activities.

The biggest Koolish killing, however, and the one that eventually led to his downfall, came through his involvement with the Minneapolis-based Sister Elizabeth Kenny Foundation, named for the Australian nurse who developed a helpful technique for the treatment of polio patients. From 1952 to 1959, a period when polio was perhaps the most popular charitable cause in America, Koolish-controlled firms flooded the mails with about 140 million fund appeal letters, enough to reach every U.S. family three times. The mailings produced $19.5 million in contributions, of which the Kenny Foundation received only about $8 million; the remaining $11.5 million went to the Koolish companies that conducted the campaigns. However, the Minneapolis Better Business Bureau found the foundation to be extremely reticent about disclosing the actual cost of the mail campaigns. Curious about just how the money had been spent, Walter J. Mondale, who was then Minnesota's attorney general, began looking into the matter. Digging into the foundation's books, he discovered that the bulk of the mail costs diverted to the Koolish interests had been charged off to such euphemistic activities as "therapist training operations," "medical and education training programs," "public education and information services," "grants for medical research," and the like.

To fatten his take, Koolish had also brazenly charged the foundation $20 per 1000 for a mailing list of nearly 10 million names, many from the foundation's own files, and others plucked from telephone directories and as such worth no more than 2 cents per 1000. On the side, Koolish was also turning a neat profit renting out the valuable Kenny mailing list of proven contributors to other charities, including those in which he was also involved.

What made all this possible was the connivance of two of the foundation's key officials, Marvin L. Kline, its executive director, and Fred Fadell, who headed its public relations and fund-raising operations. Both had sufficient clout to ease off the foundation board any directors inquisitive enough to ask too many questions; equally important, Kline, a former Minneapolis mayor, and Fadell could also take it upon themselves to give those lucrative mailing contracts to Koolish without asking for competitive bids. In return, the two shared in the spoils, receiving from Koolish not only an array of gifts ranging from television sets to an electric organ but also, during a seven-year period, kickbacks amounting to $359,000 which Koolish entered on his books as costs of preparing mailing materials. This lagniappe was in addition to the handsome rewards Kline and Fadell reaped from the foundation itself. Though relatively small as charities go, the foundation was somehow able to provide Fadell with a car and office space for his publicity firm, from which he could also conduct nonfoundation business, and a budget of $261,891 in 1959 for those efforts expended on foundation business. The same year, Kline, without asking anyone's permission, had illegally raised his annual salary from $25,000 to $48,000; it was this disclosure that led to his departure from the foundation and his conviction on a charge of grand larceny in 1961.

In 1963, Kline, along with Fadell, Koolish, his son, David, and two others connected with the Koolish campaigns, were all found guilty of mail fraud and conspiracy. Koolish, then 71, his son, and Kline were each sentenced to 10 years in prison; the two Koolishes were also each fined $17,000 and assessed court costs of $16,000—both paltry sums in comparison with the millions they had gulled from the public; Fadell was sentenced to a year and a day. Later that year, the Kenny Foundation agreed to a $251,000 settlement of a $3 million civil suit against Kline, Fadell, and the foundation's former auditor; in 1966, the foundation, renamed the American Rehabilitation Foundation, accepted a $1 million settlement from the two men who had started it all, Koolish and his son.

Yet, big as he was, Koolish was only one of a number of promoters, large and small, who were to make a fortune out of charity as it grew even bigger in the years to come.

Scarcely a decade after Koolish was sent to jail, his nemesis, Walter J. Mondale, by now a U.S. senator, was looking into similar suspect dealings as the chairman of a Senate Subcommittee on Children and Youth. One of the organizations that came under the scrutiny of his investigators in early 1974 was the Asthmatic Children's Foundation, headquartered in Miami Beach. Over an 11-year period, it had collected $9.9 million in mail contributions for the stated purpose of aiding the approximately 3 million youngsters in the nation afflicted with asthma. However, of this sum, only $1.4 million went for research and the treatment of children. And not many children at that: The foundation's two "residential treatment centers," one in Miami Beach and the other in Ossining, New York, housed only 50 patients.

Most of the rest of the money—86 cents on the dollar—was spent on fund-raising or administrative costs; no less than three-fourths of it—a total of $7.4 million, or more than five times as much as that spent on asthma—went to the Chicago-based fund-raising firm of V. H. Giesler & Co. for writing, printing, and sending out the mail solicitations.

No skullduggery could be proven as in the case of Koolish, although the foundation officials admitted that they had allowed the Giesler firm to charge them whatever it wished without going through the bother of competitive bidding, submitting accounting records, or even signing a written contract. The foundation was also careful not to solicit in cities and states with limits on the percentage of the monies collected that could be used for fund raising; the hearings brought out, however, that the foundation had resorted to the neat stratagem of absorbing certain expenses on mailings to New York one year in order to circumvent that state's law, which sets a 50 percent limit on the cost of fund-raising mail campaigns that include unordered items.

At the hearings, Dr. M. Murray Peshkin, the 81-year-old founder and president of the foundation, while conceding that his organization's fund-raising costs were high, defended them by turning to the Bible.

"It says in the Bible that if you save one life you save the world," he told the subcommittee. "And you don't care what it costs."

When Mondale, in order to document the organization's high fund-raising costs, started to list its total contributions and costs year by year beginning with 1963, Israel Friedman, the group's $25,000-a-year executive vice-president, interrupted immediately.

"Remember, this [1963] was a time when we were just getting started. All of these mailings went to what we called prospective contributors. When you send mail to prospective contributors, the returns are comparatively small and the cost is high. Once people are contributors, then the percentage of return is much higher and the cost drops."

At which the senator continued his year-by-year tally which revealed that whereas fund-raising costs were 76 percent of contributions in 1963, they had somehow risen to 80 percent by 1970, and in 1972 and 1973 were, respectively, 75 and 71 percent.

"According to your own records," Mondale summed up, "in your best year, only 26 cents out of a dollar actually got to the children, and in most years 15 cents, and in a couple of years only a dime out of a dollar got to those children.

"How do you explain this to your contributors?" he then asked Friedman.

Friedman, reading from a foundation mailing enclosure—a name sticker—quoted this statement: "A portion of your contribution to the Asthmatic Children's Foundation covers the cost of these labels and materials sent to you."

"What do you suppose would happen if you said instead, 85 percent of the money you contribute would go for purposes other than children?" asked Mondale. "How much money would come in?"

"I agree there would be some reticence," said Friedman.

As for fund-raiser Giesler, all he would say is that it costs money to make money. For whom, however, he did not indicate.

Should a limit be placed on the amount of money spent to raise money for a charity? I posed the question to Patrick J. Gorman, a Washington, D.C., promoter and fund raiser who was responsible for the campaign of the United Police Fund mentioned earlier in this chapter.

"Frankly, I think it's very difficult," said Gorman, a husky, blond, genial man of perhaps forty. "That's because of the start-up nature of the business, and fund raising *is* a business. The start-up costs in any business, you know, are much higher than the costs in an established business."

Over one 18-month period, Gorman raised $4.5 million by mail in behalf of an assortment of fledgling enterprises, which also included Friends of the FBI, Americans United for Life (antiabortion), Save Our Symbol, New Spirit of '76, and other flag-waving conservative causes. The fact that very little of this money ever reached most of his clients involved Gorman in a certain amount of notoriety and on occasion attracted the attention of such ordinarily lackadaisical government observers as the Postal Inspection Service and the Internal Revenue Service.

To hear Gorman tell it, he didn't get much of the money either. However, whatever he did get—he would admit to only $450,000 over the period—was apparently enough to maintain him and his staff in style in a smartly appointed suite of modern offices with a reception room featuring one wall covered with bark squares and another wall adorned with gold-framed prints.

A graduate of Fordham University, where he majored in "English and the communication arts," Gorman set up shop in 1967 as a "direct marketing consultant," as he is described on his letterhead. Earlier, one of his first forays into fund raising was in connection with Barry Goldwater's presidential bid in 1963. This was followed by a stint as promotion manager on William Buckley's *National Review* ("We also had a consulting service there for conservative-type causes, where I really learned a lot about fund raising") and a job with the Richard A. Viguerie Company, also in the Washington, D.C., area and probably the nation's leading fund raiser for conservative causes.

Gorman is not without a certain roguish Irish charm. Our paths first crossed as the result of an article I once did for *Reader's Digest*; in my draft I mentioned the "tear-jerking" solicitation letter from his shop that had helped to raise about $140,000 for the United Police Fund. When the article was checked with him prior to publication, he objected to my use of the term, "tear-jerking."

What would you call the letter? he was asked.

"Well, it was sort of emotional," he said.

The characterization was therefore changed to "emotional," which Gorman also later objected to as a "smear" word. He then challenged my statement that only $18,000 of the monies raised had gone to the fund's widows and orphans.

"Is the figure wrong?" the magazine's researcher asked him.

"No, but look at it this way," he said, "they got $18,000 they wouldn't have gotten otherwise. But to state that without saying just how the rest of the money was spent is misleading."

Now, in Gorman's office, I asked him just how the rest of the money was spent.

"I don't really feel the need to show you my ledger cards," he said. "But the costs incurred were for printing, postage, mailing costs, salaries, and fees."

Apart from his fees, which run from $1500 to $3000 a month, Gorman also makes a good deal of money on the expenses of a campaign. Like other agencies, he takes the customary 17.65 percent markup on all production and printing costs, a 15 percent commission on all advertising, and a 20 percent commission on mailing lists he rents from brokers. Unlike other fund raisers, however, Gorman also has his own mailing lists, reportedly containing over a million conservative names, which he rents out to clients as well as to others at $25 to $30 per thousand names. In the first four months of his campaign for the Friends of the FBI, he billed the project nearly $50,000 for the use of his mailing lists.*

Of the first $380,000 collected for Friends of the FBI, formed to counter criticism of the G-men and so "keep up the fight to preserve law and order and justice in our country," at least $256,000 went to Gorman and his two outside partners in the venture: Lee Edwards, a public relations man specializing in conservative causes, and Luis Kutner, a Chicago lawyer whose so-called Commission for International Due Process of Law, it was planned, would shelter the FBI project under its tax-exempt umbrella. Gorman's share was $138,000 for fees and expenses, which included the use of his mailing lists.

The Friends soon became involved in no end of difficulties. Although the group claimed to be friendly with the FBI, the feeling wasn't mutual and the FBI disclaimed any connection with it; the Internal Revenue Service questioned its claimed tax-exempt status; the postal inspectors investigated charges of misrepresentation; and the partners had a falling out—Kutner, according to an article in the *Washington Post,* accused the others of endangering the organization's tax-exempt status by failing to keep proper records and to account for income and expenditures; in addition, Kutner said that Gorman's submission of charges for the use of his mailing lists could be looked upon "as an unconscionable dilution of contributors' funds. . . ." As criticism mounted, the group's honorary chairman, Efrem Zimbalist, Jr., star of the television series, *The FBI,* also disassociated himself from the project, accusing the partners of "fraud and misrepresentation."

Gorman's efforts on behalf of the short-lived Underground Bible Fund, a project of the National Captive Nations Committee, led to the continuing interest of Rep. Lionel Van Deerlin of California in legislation—at this writing, not enacted—that would require all organizations soliciting contributions through the mails to clearly disclose how the contributions are to be used and give a detailed breakdown of fund-raising costs. Gorman's solicitation, addressed to "Dear Fellow Christian," presented the plight of our Scriptureless "persecuted Christian brethren" in the godless countries under Communist rule and promised that each $2 donation would enable the Fund to publish and somehow deliver five special Bibles to the faithful behind the Iron Curtain.

---

*One incongruous name on them, according to an item in *Playboy,* was that of Rev. Daniel Berrigan who was residing at the Federal Prison at Danbury, Connecticut, when he received the Friends of the FBI solicitation.

.Van Deerlin challenged the fund's arithmetic, contending that with fund-raising costs the price per Bible would come to over $3, not 40 cents. His contention was based on the fact that contributions to the fund amounted to $11,529 which, after deducting the $11,450 cost of the mailing, left only $79—obviously not enough to produce the 3750 Bibles the fund said it would print.

Van Deerlin, quite logically, arrived at his per Bible cost—$3.25 to be exact—by dividing the total number of Bibles to be printed into the total dona-tions of $11,529. Gorman, however, does not figure the way the rest of us do: He arrived at his per Bible cost by dividing the number of copies to be printed into the $79 left over for this purpose.

Yet Gorman berated Van Deerlin for issuing a press statement that give this as an example of how Gorman was misleading the public.

"Why?" I asked. "Was what Van Deerlin said incorrect?"

"Not exactly," said Gorman. "But still his statement was unfair. It should be obvious to him, just as well as everybody else, that there were fund-raising costs involved. It was implicit."

"Why was it implicit?" I asked. "Your fund-raising material clearly stated that the donor's $2 would pay for five Bibles. That's pretty explicit to me."

For once, Gorman had no response.

"Where would you draw the line between the ethical and unethical charity, the good and the bad?" I then asked.

"Well, frankly, I think all charity is good," he said. "Of course, if one is proven to be fraudulent or has costs that are not meeting a reasonable level—now don't ask me what that is—I would draw the line."

"Then do you feel that any laws, like the one Van Deerlin proposes, should be passed to regulate fund raising?"

"No, I happen to be against too many laws. I'm against Big Government; I tend to be in the libertarian area. And my opinion is that there are already enough laws on the books to take care of all the things that can go wrong in the fund-raising business."

Not quite.

At the moment, as already mentioned, there are no federal laws regulating charities, and the few state and local charity laws are generally ineffectual, unenforceable, or unenforced—as we shall see at greater length in Chapter 26.

In addition to keeping an eye on fund-raising costs, some law enforcement officials have also been cracking down on a variety of organizations which, although giving the appearance of being charities, actually are not.

At the 1974 Mondale hearings, for example, there was some fascinating tes-timony about several Fagin-type operations that recruited underaged children, usually from ghetto areas, to peddle overpriced candy from door to door in the affluent suburbs with the promise of earning up to $20 a week and the hope of winning scholarships and trips to Disneyland and summer camps.

Now, it would take an extremely hard heart indeed to let the modest price of a box of candy stand in the way of a tattered tyke at the door and the golden opportunities described in his sales pitch. Especially when the young peddler proudly introduces himself as a representative of such worthy-sounding organizations as the National Youth Clubs of America or Youth Incentives. The former, in its promotional materials, used an emblem showing an adult and child silhouetted against the American flag, and a message that, in addition to describing the aforementioned advantages the club afforded its young people, also mentioned the opportunity given them to "develop their character through public contact."

What few people realized, however, and what the Senate Subcommittee on Children and Youth learned, was that such organizations were nothing more than profit-making ventures cloaking themselves in the mantle of implied charitable endeavors, and, of course, that the juvenile candy-pushers were simply innocent dupes, often working in violation of the state labor laws. For each $1.50 box of candy sold, the children kept 25 cents; the crew manager pocketed another 25 cents; the balance was turned over to the distributor and the national organization. Since the cost of the candy was only about 40 cents, this left them with a neat profit.

The "clubs" of the National Youth Clubs were as illusory as its scholarships and other enticements. Actually, the organization was nothing more than a franchise operation, its licensees in 32 states paying $5000 down initially and promising to buy $20,000 worth of candy products through the national office in Lake Zurich, Illinois. Morrie Friedman, executive director of National Youth Clubs, estimated it used 25,000 to 30,000 children, starting them at the age of eight or nine, and grossed about $3.2 million in sales a year.

"Would not the name, 'National Youth Clubs,' lead the public to believe that you were running a charitable enterprise rather than a business," Mondale asked the 29-year-old candy tycoon.

"Probably," Friedman blandly admitted.

Evidence presented indicated that the children were not only exploited but abused. Donald T. Mulack, the Illinois assistant attorney general concerned with charities, furnished the subcommittee with this example:

> In January of this year, four children, ages eight, ten, eleven and twelve years, were taken from a lower economic neighborhood after school and transported far away by a crew manager to sell candy in the low-freezing temperature. After two hours of selling, the children were cold and sought to enter the car to warm themselves, but were refused by the crew manager because they had not sold enough candy. When the children attempted to enter the auto, the crew manager physically grabbed the 11-year-old girl by the leg and pushed her into the snowy wet street. The children were then informed they were fired and were abandoned in a strange neighborhood without money for transportation to return home.

On other occasions, said Mulack, if the crew manager felt that the children had not made their expected sales quotas, he would assess them 50 cents apiece for his gas. "Which meant that a kid who had worked all night to make a dollar could go home with possibly 50 cents remaining in his pocket."

Youth Incentives was an essentially similar but smaller operation, grossing between $750,000 and $1 million a year before its demise, shortly before the hearings. Which seems a shame considering its proclaimed purpose. In a prepared statement read to the subcommittee, Gerald Winters, the organization's creator said that he had founded Youth Incentives to help ghetto children earn money, provide them with work experience, expose them to a different environment, build their character, and keep them out of trouble.

Apparently, Winters, who at one point angrily broke off his testimony by pleading the Fifth Amendment, was perfectly qualified to provide the proper guidance to youth along these lines. He admitted to Mondale that he had been found guilty innumerable times for peddling without a license and had also been arrested, though later acquitted, on an array of other charges ranging from contributing to the delinquency of minors to murder.

Friedman, too, in spite of his tender years, had managed to build a police record that included a plea of guilty to grand larceny in Florida, an injunction calling for him to make restitution and pay fines totaling $50,000 in connection with a charge of theft by fraud in Wisconsin, an indictment for mail fraud in Illinois, and a bankruptcy petition by a Friedman company, United Boys Group, also in Illinois, stating that Friedman had diverted $50,000 in company funds to his own personal use.

Toiletries and a host of household products are also often sold, usually by mail or telephone, by similar entrepreneurs who, using such magic words as *blind, handicapped,* or *retarded,* lead you to believe that the proceeds of your purchases are going to a charitable organization for the benefit of the afflicted. At times a token number of these unfortunates is even employed—at minimal wages—to package or solicit sales for the products, generally at exorbitant prices; in most cases, none of the supposed objects of charity are involved in the operation at all.

Until the New York attorney general caught up with them and nailed them for fraud, two Westchester County men, operating under the name, "Toiletries Packed by the Blind," and using a crew of telephone sales people, all of them sighted, sold 80,000 bottles of shampoo, cologne, and other toiletries. They charged $1.99 for a bottle of shampoo that could be bought in any store for 75 cents. When one of their colleagues, who was later apprehended, emerged from jail, he was soon caught again in a similar fraud, this time for the benefit of the mentally handicapped. Two New York hustlers, in another pitch for the mentally handicapped, went so far as to use the name of Mrs. Rose Kennedy, the mother of a retarded daughter.

This is not to say that all such ventures are downright fraudulent. Torch, an operation that sells such things as light bulbs by telephone in some 16 cities, will admit to being a profit-making organization. But one might not readily discover this unless one asked the right questions. Here is the way a conversation went when my phone rang one day and I suddenly found myself on the receiving end of a call from a Torch solicitor:

"Hello, this is Mike Rye," said the caller. "I'm a handicapped person and I work for Torch Products. We sell special light bulbs. They cost $1.99 each with a five-year guarantee."

At this point, the average sympathetic householder, hearing that magic word, *handicapped,* and succumbing to that almost instinctive charitable impulse to help the less fortunate, might agree to buy a bulb or two, even though their price seemed much higher than that of similar bulbs in the store. After all, the difference was going to charity, wasn't it? But I pressed on.

"How much would such bulbs cost in the store?" I asked.

"Fifty cents, but without a guarantee. If the bulbs you get from us burn out we replace them."

"Are you a charity?"

"No, we're a profit-making organization. But we employ handicapped people."

"What sort of handicapped people?"

"Well, I have arthritis. Others have polio or are crippled; some have only one arm. We all share in the profits of the business. . . ."

Maybe so. But New Jersey public hearings on Torch's operations revealed that its employees earn only a bare minimum wage and are fired quickly if they don't meet a certain sales quota. At the hearings, it also developed that Torch gives a rather broad definition to that word *handicapped,* including employees who might be suffering from nothing more than, say, an iron deficiency. As for the special bulbs themselves, the technical-minded may want to know, the reason they last longer than other bulbs is because they emit a lower level of light than ordinary bulbs of equivalent wattage.

Some precautions one can take to avoid being fooled by the frauds just described are given in Chapter 26. Whether or not they will help everyone is another matter.

For as long as there are gullible people there will always be people with guile. In an article for *True Story,* of all places, Lester David told of the enterprising young man who mailed out enormous amounts of inexpensive trinkets, receiving in return more than $100,000 from charitable-minded buyers. When some claimed they had been misled, the promoter was brought to trial on charges of mail fraud and found guilty. However, his conviction was reversed by an appeals court. The reason: In his promotional literature, the young man had clearly stated that the trinkets were being sold for his own personal benefit.

The classic story, however, is of the legendary genius who placed the following advertisement in the personals column of the *Los Angeles Times:*

LAST DAY TO SEND IN YOUR DOLLAR!— BOX 124

That's all the ad said.

What do you think happened? Surprisingly, or perhaps not so surprisingly, thousands of people fell all over themselves to send in their dollars.

PART IV

THE TECHNIQUES

Chapter 18

Getting People to Give: The Art of Fund Raising

A smiling young Girl Scout came to my door the other evening and sold me a box of cookies. In my mailbox that morning was an Indian-style key chain (untouched by Indian hands) accompanied by an appeal for funds from the Southwest Indian Foundation. As Pan Am's Flight 101 from London neared New York's Kennedy Airport the same day, passengers were given, along with their customs forms, little envelopes bearing the following message in seven languages: "You can't spend your unused foreign money in the U.S.A., but you can mail it to UNICEF."

In New York's Central Park Zoo that evening, a combination dinner-dance and auction, which offered such goodies as trips to Spain and Jamaica and $1500 cases of wine, raised funds to decorate the home of the zoo's new baby gorilla, Patty Cake. In the same park that afternoon, I was one of 5000 riders (among them Rita Gam, Tammy Grimes, and sportscaster-baseball player Jim Bouton) pedaling for palsy in the "Bike-A-Thon," an annual benefit for United Cerebral Palsy.

Infinite in their variety are the ways our charities have of prying open the public's pockets. And they are often ingenious, too.

In Atlanta, for example, some restaurants charge a dollar a pack for cigarettes—with the extra profit going to the American Cancer Society and the Georgia Heart Association. To fight the big C, the inventive Georgians also pioneered the charity pie-throwing contest: As mentioned earlier, contributors bid for the opportunity to throw pies at their local politicians, television and radio personalities, and members of the Atlanta Flames and Falcons.

In Evergreen Park, Illinois, Mayor Anthony Vacco kicked off the local March of Dimes campaign to fight birth defects by allowing himself to be "fined" $10,000 and incarcerated, wearing striped prison garb and a ball and chain, in a specially constructed jail set up in the lobby of the village hall. During the mayor's six-hour jail sentence, contributors to the campaign could specify whether their donation was to "Bail Him Out" or "Keep Him In." (The vote was $1884 for bail and $851 for jail.) Vacco agreed to go along with the idea, which also had the teen-age jail attendants dressed as Keystone cops, because one of his children suffered from a crippling disease. "People won't respond, even to worthwhile efforts to raise money, unless you've got a gimmick," he said.

Back in the days when the March of Dimes was primarily concerned with polio, a group of Alaska prostitutes contributed part of their proceeds to the campaign, varying the organization's slogan, to read, "We Lay So Others Will Walk."* The collection, needless to say, was not officially sanctioned by the March of Dimes which, however, has had few peers in the concoction of imaginative fund-raising events; in addition to "Jail and Bail," another of its creations is "Spook Insurance," described in the organization's campaign guide as "an insurance policy sold for $1.00 or more guaranteeing that a teen will clean up any minor mischief that a Halloween spook may cause." During the streaking vogue of the mid-1970s, five male students of Hagerstown Junior College in Maryland impulsively stripped and pranced through the college coffee shop, collecting $40 for the March of Dimes.

Here are some other novel fund-raising wrinkles used by various causes:

A Greenport, Long Island, church took over a former porno drive-in theater to help raise funds for the construction of a retirement village. Boy Scout troops in Jackson, Wyoming, hold an annual litter cleanup in the National Elk Refuge and in the process, gather antlers shed by elk; the antlers are eventually sold at auction to dealers who supply makers of chessmen, buttons, buckles, and furniture. The fact that the antlers when powdered are a cherished ingredient in Oriental aphrodisiacs has driven up their price to the point where the scouts, in one recent year, realized nearly $20,000 for about 4000 pounds of the elk discards. A Girl Scout troop in Belle Center, Ohio, captured and sold enough fireflies over a three-year period to help send seven of its members and three chaperones to Europe. A chemical company paid up to a penny apiece for the fireflies, whose luminescent tails are used in cancer research and other scientific studies.

Such novelties, however, have not replaced the traditional fund-raising techniques, which range from advertising, mail appeals, and door-to-door solicitations to the familiar so-called special events. Let us look at some of the more frequently used of these techniques.

Advertising Appeals

Who is one of the biggest advertisers in America? Ranking right up there with the purveyors of soaps, cigarettes, foods, and cars is the Red Cross, which used some $54 million of time and space in one recent year. However, unlike commercial advertisers, the Red Cross gets its time and space *free*. Even so relatively unknown a nonprofit organization as the American Social Health Association managed to promote some $15 million worth of advertising some years ago to wage its long-time war against VD. One catchy jingle aimed at television audiences went, "VD is for everybody, not just for the few/Anyone can share VD with someone as nice as you." Used to dramatize the message were pictures of such middle-class types as a librarian, a businessman, a young girl, a jogger, a farmer, a secretary, and a model. Space ads in magazines, newspapers, and on billboards combined the same kinds of models with this hard-hitting copy: "In

*More recently, the good citizens of the wild and wooly city of Darwin, Australia, put their special stamp on a comparable project to raise money for spastic children: A party was held at which topless waitresses served beer, the audience was shown Danish-made porno films, and five prostitutes were offered as raffle prizes.

the suburbs VD is more prevalent than chickenpox.'' Or, under a picture of a businessman at his desk: ''Pillars of society who are falling at Christmas parties or out-of-town conventions are bringing VD home to their wives.''

Such national public service campaigns are run largely by the Advertising Council, the industry's 37-year-old do-good, nonprofit arm which now places about $600 million worth of advertising annually for causes ranging from the prevention of forest fires to the promotion of the sale of Savings Bonds. Of the 300 requests for advertising support the council receives every year, about half are turned down for failure to meet certain criteria*; and only 25 to 30 evolve into major national public campaigns announced in the council's bimonthly *Public Service Advertising Bulletin,* which is distributed to some 20,000 media outlets—daily and weekly newspapers, TV and radio stations and networks, consumer and business magazines, and outdoor and transit advertising operators.

After the request for support has been approved by the council, a volunteer advertising agency, nominated by the American Association of Advertising Agencies, is assigned to produce the advertising; the only expense to the charity are the out-of-pocket costs for materials—artwork, engravings, printing, paper, TV film, and slides—which, however, can run from $75,000 to $150,000 for a typical campaign. The agency admen devote their time and talent to what is often a taxing assignment. A member of the Wells Rich Greene team on the Kidney Foundation account confessed: ''We joke about it at the agency; we say the kidney-disease account is a pisser. But kidney disease is not *glamorous.* And it's not even like heart disease, you know, beautiful, THE HEART. And it's not even like cancer which is—you know. . . . Kidney disease is—you know, you think of *urinating.*''

However, even after a campaign has been produced, there is no sure-fire guarantee that it will get free time or space because more and more charities have been competing for this over the years. Although *Newsweek* publishes over $1.5 million worth of public service advertising a year, it can sandwich not more than half a dozen charities or so into an average issue; a recent issue contained messages from the Red Cross, the Easter Seal Society, the United Way, Project Hope, and the U.S.O. ''We generally are inclined to favor the bigger organizations or the ones we know something about like the Cancer Society or Smokey the Bear,'' said Mary McNamara, *Newsweek*'s assistant advertising manager.**

In spite of the simon-pure motives and general effectiveness of public service messages—the Red Cross claimed that one year it received over $15 million in contributions as a result of its emergency flood relief campaign—they have not gone without criticism. In his column for *Advertising Age* several years ago, Harry McMahan charged that the ''public disservice'' TV commercials, as he called them, cluttered up the airwaves. ''In spite of (or because of) the Advertis-

---

*Among them: that the project be noncommercial, nonpartisan politically, nonsectarian, national in scope and of public importance to Americans generally, and that the organization meet the standards of such accrediting agencies as the National Information Bureau and Council of Better Business Bureaus as to fund-raising methods, accountability, management, program and purpose. (See Chapter 26).

**In addition, *Newsweek,* like many other publications, has a special ''public interest'' rate—generally half of its regular advertising rate—for religious and other nonprofit organizations that, for one reason or another, do not meet the standards of the Advertising Council and/or the National Information Bureau.

ing Council, there is insufficient control of all the Disaster Lobby commercials force-fed into the airlanes,'' McMahan lashed out. ''Everyone's afraid: refuse the commercial and you're against God, mother, safety belts and good health.''

Street and Door-to-Door Collections

Although still prevalent, street collections have been on the wane in recent years, for one thing, because of the increasingly tighter controls on this type of solicitation—in many localities, only approved charities and their solicitors are issued authorizations to solicit the public directly—and, for another, because more and more volunteer solicitors, usually women, have been taking jobs to augment the family income. Also on the way out are the so-called ''tag day'' collections whereby persistent street solicitors, armed with coin canisters, pin poppies or other symbols on passersby who contribute; in fact, this mild form of blackmail, intended to shame nongivers into giving, is now even banned in some cities.

Door-to-door collections have also been diminishing, again largely because many one-time doorbell ringers have taken to gainful employment. High-rise apartment buildings in suburban communities and the fear of crime also present increasing problems. The American Cancer Society, though continuing to use the door-to-door approach, suggests that its solicitors in urban areas place the collection envelopes from their campaign kits into their neighbors' mailboxes. However, the Mental Health Association has given up its door-to-door collections in many suburban areas, substituting mass mail drives. Even the March of Dimes' famous door-to-door drive, known as the ''Mother's March,'' though still accounting for about 13 percent of its contributions, has also been abandoned in some communities, or has had to recruit men (wearing ''I'm a Mother'' stickers) to act as mothers or to escort mothers into high crime areas.

Silent Salesmen

The Leukemia Society, the March of Dimes, and other charities employ what are called ''silent salesmen''—coin-collecting devices of various sorts strategically placed in stores, restaurants, and other public places. Such coin collectors, says a March of Dimes campaign guide, are ''a direct invitation to the public to give their dimes and dollars right there on the spot.'' They are also an invitation to thievery and pilferage. Many of the coins, I've been told, wind up in the pockets of the after-hours cleaning people. Not unusual is also the experience of the Lexington, Massachusetts, Texaco dealer who reported that, while he was busy at the pumps, somebody walked in and stole his adding machine and leukemia-fund can. Obviously, many other things can also happen to the coins before they are actually deposited in the charity coffers; for example, they can stick to the fingers of volunteer counters. To thwart this, some local banks offer to tally the coins as a public service.

''Something'' for the Money: Special Events

Then there are those activities, so dear to the hearts of fund raisers, known as special events—defined in an American Cancer Society *Special Events Manual* as "out-of-the-ordinary activities designed to amuse, titillate, gratify, interest and reward the individual who wants a 'something' for his money." The 62-page manual offers detailed suggestions for sponsoring and conducting activities ranging from cake sales and car washes to bazaars, fashion shows, and house tours, as well as luncheons, dinners, dances, balls, bridge and theater parties, auctions, airplane flights, telethons, walk-a-thons, bike-a-thons, and other "thons"—the possibilities are literally endless. Virtually every sizable charitable organization puts out a similar manual. That of Planned Parenthood, entitled *The Fun in Fund Raising,* recommends to its volunteers a variety of wine tasting events and a phantom dinner party ("the recipients of the invitation send in their check for $5 for the privilege of staying home and enjoying themselves"). United Cerebral Palsy's manual, coincidentally called *Fun in Fund Raising,* suggests a "come-as-your-favorite-song ball" and the showing of old-time movies. Leibert and Sheldon's *Handbook of Special Events for Nonprofit Organizations* offers detailed instructions for conducting over 100 different special events.

Although an enjoyable and comparatively painless way of raising funds, special events are not always the big moneymakers they are reputed to be. Very often, after expenses, only a small fraction of the money given for the "something" the donor gets in return (the theater ticket, the dinner, cake, etc.) actually goes to the beneficiaries of the cause. (However, most of the costs of a special event are not considered fund-raising expenses; therefore, only the net receipts of the event are included in most campaign reports.) And so, special events are expected only to provide additional revenues to supplement the funds raised in an organization's big annual drive—provide "the icing on the conventional Crusade cake," as the American Cancer Society puts it. However, in addition to bringing in at least some money, the special event has another purpose: It attracts volunteers to the organization and, no less important, serves as a vehicle for generating publicity about it. As one experienced fund raiser put it, "the event gives us an opportunity to really explain our purpose, why we exist."

Here is a rundown of the more common events of this sort, together with other fund-raising techniques that have proven successful:

Selling Services and Things

Although charities can pick up a few dollars by having volunteers donate their time and labor for such services as car washing, lawn cutting, and window washing, much more money can be raised by selling things.

Kiwanis International nets $750,000 a year from the sale of peanuts; and about 37 percent of the income of the local Girl Scout Councils comes from its famous cookie sales, which now gross over $100 million annually.* Bakers licensed by the national organization compete each year by sending quotes and cookie samples to the some 350 local councils across the nation. The samples, which are carefully taste-tested by local cookie committees, must adhere to standard for-

---

*Not all of this goes to the Girl Scouts, of course. Of the $1.25 typically charged for a box of cookies, the supplier gets around 40 percent or 50 cents. Of the remaining profit of 75 cents, from 10 to 15 cents goes to the vendor's troop and the rest to the local council for operating expenses and camp facilities. Actually, a small portion of the 37 percent comes from the sale of candy, nuts, and other such items.

mulas for the three basic Girl Scout cookies—chocolate mints (the national favorite), shortbread, and sandwich cookies—which have proved popular and which may not be sold through regular retail channels.

All manner of other things are also sold in the name of charity. In fact, an entire industry has sprung up to supply premiums for fund-raising purposes— items such as cakes, candies, candles, calendars, and place mats—at markups running to about 40 percent. From "national fund-raising advisor" Jan Wintters of Nashua, New Hampshire, for example, are available some 90 "great fund raisers," such as trays and coasters, animal candle kits, pen/key chains, peek-a-boo mailaway note paper, recipe cards, memo boards, and greeting cards. Charity solicitors can take orders for these from a sample collection case and have 60 days in which to pay for the merchandise sold. Abigail Martin, based in Bridgeport, Connecticut, promises that "your group or organization can earn $221 to $3210 in one weekend!" by selling her candle creations, which are adorned with everything from frolicking children to Currier & Ives scenes. Subsidiary Merchandising of Natick, Massachusetts, specializes in the sale of tulip and other spring-flowering bulbs.

Tom Wat Inc., another Bridgeport merchandiser, which claims it supplies more than 10,000 school, church, and scout groups, says that it differs from most of its competitors in offering a constantly changing showcase of items. Using the Tom Wat Kit, a favorite of young fund raisers, which features some 20 items ranging in price from $1 to $3 and in variety from candles and lint removers to iron-on transfers saying "Beer Drinkers' Hall of Fame," a 25-member Cub Scout Pack in Springs, Long Island, took in $2000 one recent Christmas; of this, the boys kept 35 percent and the rest went to Tom Wat. W. Thomas Watson, the firm's president, says he takes a paternal interest in each campaign, checking first to make sure the money will not be "frittered away or misused," an occurrence, he says, that would mar the Tom Wat image. "However, it does happen from time to time," he acknowledged sadly. "I can recall one case where the cubmaster ran away with a den mother on the proceeds of the project."

Even Tiffany, the celebrated Fifth Avenue jeweler, has gotten into the act. A recent ad in *The New York Times* offered "TRY JESUS" sterling silver pins— made to be distributed by churches for a donation of $10—in lots of 100 at a wholesale discount of 70 percent.

Some charities produce premiums of their own, a favorite being cookbooks. The Planned Parenthood group of Santa Cruz, California, put together a zucchini cookbook as a fund-raising device, and the Friends of the Kennedy Center for the Performing Arts in Washington, D.C., offers for sale a celebrity cookbook. UNICEF is famous for its Christmas and other greeting cards.

Other charities secure sale items free or at cost from people or manufacturers (who, of course, receive tax deductions for their donations) and sell them in a variety of ways—at thrift shops, rummage sales, boutiques, and bazaars. In what was believed to be the largest event of its kind, more than 290,000 books— ranging from first editions to James Bond thrillers—were put up for sale in a Wilmette, Illinois, shopping center, the proceeds going to the Brandeis University Library.

The biggest event on the Los Angeles charity circuit is the annual Colleagues Glamour Clothes Sales, the proceeds of which—about $125,000 in recent years—go to support the Big Sister League home for girls and unwed mothers and day-care center. Shoppers come from as far away as Arizona and New Mexico for the event, some waiting in line as early as 3 A.M., to buy such items as linen dinner napkins with 50-cent price tags and new or practically new couture clothes, priced for as little as $50, donated by actresses and name designers, as well as by such stores as Saks and I. Magnin.

Not infrequently, articles are also sold on consignment, with, say, two-thirds of the sale proceeds going to the consignor and the remainder to the charity.

Second-hand Chic

Because of the way they have mushroomed in the past decade or so, special mention is due charity-run thrift shops. New York City alone has about 60 such shops, at many of which one can also find not-very-worn and, on occasion, even new designer clothes and custom-made furniture. At the Kips Bay Boys Club shop, a bargain hunter was recently able to buy a black velvet Cardin cocktail suit for $15 and a floor-length Adolfo dress with jacket, valued at $700, for $75. Countless budget-conscious New Yorkers have furnished their apartments, entirely or in part, at Aunt Sally's—their affectionate name for the Salvation Army's three-story block-long emporium in midtown Manhattan, the largest of its 147 stores in the Greater New York area—where they can pick up everything from $5 lamps, $20 tables, and $200 down-cushioned brocade sofas to bric-a-brac, glassware, crockery, cooking utensils, appliances, and books for 10 cents apiece, regardless of title. In Washington, D.C., six thrift shops—operated by the American Rescue Workers, AMVETS, Goodwill Industries, Value Village, Salvation Army, and Volunteers of America—are so large that they rival Sears in the quantity of clothing they have for sale, and, in addition, there are dozens of similar smaller shops in the city.

Although the nation's thrift shops were once a standby of the poor, inflation has brought about a recent broadening of their clientele; today, many middle-class or even fairly affluent people find it cheap and chic to shop at them. The manager of a Nashville Salvation Army store commented: "When you look at our parking lot, you now see Cadillacs as well as old beat-up jalopies." This situation, however, has produced a strange paradox: The thrift shops' well-heeled customers have become increasingly reluctant to part with their own used goods—the shops' stock-in-trade. Eugene Mills of the Volunteers of America says that many former donors are staging garage sales instead of giving their things away.

Some "charity" thrift shops, however, are so in name only. For example, several years ago, Kansas City residents who thought they were donating their household goods and clothing to the Disabled American Veterans later learned that their donations were actually going to a private company that paid the DAV the flat sum of $15,000 a year for the use of its name, regardless of how much merchandise it picked up or sold. The company refused to reveal the amount of its revenues, which were apparently sufficient to support the rental of three stores and the salaries of 18 sales persons, three truck drivers, and 30 to 70 parttime telephone solicitors who falsely identified themselves as being with the DAV. However, in 1974, a similar operation in Nashville, Tennessee, grossed more than $275,000, of which only $6000, or 2 percent of the gross, went to the DAV, according to an investigation by the Nashville *Banner*. When *Banner* reporter Larry Brinton asked the national DAV adjutant, Denvel Adams, for further information about this arrangement, Adams, after declaring vigorously that he had "nothing to hide," finally exploded: "You bastards, goddammit, I've already told you I'm not going to tell you anything." Nonetheless, when the *Banner*'s investigation disclosed that the DAV held similar contracts with 36 stores of a California-based company operating in 21 states, the DAV executive committee terminated the contract and the thrift-shop fronts were no longer permitted to use the DAV name.

This is not to say that the DAV does not have any thrift shops that it operates on its own. But very little of the revenues of these shops gets to the veterans either. Columnist Mike Royko, in the now-defunct Chicago *Daily News*, revealed that the city's 12 DAV thrift shops took in more than $1 million during a typical year, but netted only $78,000, or only 7 percent of their gross. That return might possibly be acceptable for a private, profit-making business. But the DAV does not pay for its stock of merchandise—it is donated to the veterans' group.

Where did the rest of the money go? According to the annual report the DAV was required to file with the state, the manager of the thrift operation was paid more than $43,000 in salary and bonuses. The shop's other employees were paid $454,320, this not including $128,201 in payments made to solicitors. A total of $105,933 went for rent, and the rest of the shops' income was eaten up by the expenses found in most retail operations. By comparison, the Salvation Army's 14 Red Shield Stores—no-frill, pipe-rack outlets in the same poor sections of town—made $280,000 in profits on gross sales of $1,154,311 the same year.

Why the difference? Royko tried to get the answers from the top local DAV officials, but they refused to talk to him. A year later, however, when the state attorney general, according to Royko, started poking around and putting pressure on the DAV to get out of the thrift store business or face being taken to court, the DAV said it would turn over the operation of the stores to another organization, the Paralyzed Veterans of America. Under the slick arrangement worked out, the DAV in exchange was to get a cut of the stores' revenues—$70,000 a year for the next 10 years.

Auctions: Live and Televised

America's love for bargains has also made the auction a perennial, fund-raising favorite. Most auction items are donated. But to raise money for itself not long ago, New York's Museum of Natural History auctioned off some 70 pieces of its own memorabilia that had been gathering dust in its basement; among the items sold were a whale's glass eye ($530), a huge Victorian telephone booth ($100), and the gun case of explorer and taxidermist Carl Akeley ($425). In response to a request for a donation for an auction benefiting the Civil Liberties Union, novelist Kurt Vonnegut, Jr., came up with a unique contribution: He promised to name a character in his next book after the highest bidder. Bidders at an auction of Sidwell Friends School in the Washington, D.C., area bought the chance to be a clown in a circus ($160), to do a walk-on part in a movie ($350), and to conduct the National Symphony ($425). Items offered at a "Fun Auction" for Manhattan's Industrial Home for the Blind included a facelift, Doris Day's sunglasses, and an initialed handkerchief of Clark Gable's.

Ever since San Francisco's public television station, KQED, auctioned off Kim Novak's lavender bedsheet in 1955, televised auctions have become a fund-raising staple for the nation's hard-pressed public-TV stations in many cities. In fact, ever since the Ford Foundation began to cut back on its support of public broadcasting in the early 1970s, many stations have come to depend on these auctions to help keep them solvent, now raising about $16 million a year by this means. In the mid-1970s, New York's WNET/Channel 13 raised over $1.1 million in a nine-day marathon auction that one TV critic described as "an upper-middle-class version of *Let's Make A Deal*." While 500 celebrities acted as auctioneers, the station's viewers phoned in bids on donated goods and services, ranging from basketball star Julius Irving's autographed sneakers ($201), Catfish Hunter's baseball cap ($125), and Paul Newman's hat ($1000) to a one-hour violin lesson with Isaac Stern ($510), a night at the opera with Tony Randall ($1000), and a Victorian-style *Upstairs/Downstairs* dinner for eight served by a butler and maid ($4200). Other of the 7000 offerings, obtained by some 3500 volunteers, included: a year's supply of lox and bagels, a 45-volume record of the impeachment proceedings against former President Nixon signed by the 38 members of the House Judiciary Committee (fittingly, auctioned off by committee chairman Peter Rodino himself), Joe Namath's T-shirt, Bette Midler's corset, Bob Hope's cigarette lighter, Neil Simon's baby grand piano, a lunch with Truman Capote, Warren Beatty's working script for *Shampoo,* a replica— via Bloomingdale's—of Joanne Woodward's bedroom, and works by such artists as Warhol, Dali, and Picasso. After deducting expenses,* the station netted slightly more than $500,000, which the Ford Foundation promised to match.

Televised auctions have also been used by other than TV stations. In the late 1970s, seven of Brooklyn's cultural institutions, including the Brooklyn Academy of Music, staged a five-hour auction over two television stations, with the usual wild array of items: a dinner date with Miss Universe, a wedding ceremony at the Cloisters, and eight gallons of the winning bidder's fantasy flavor of ice cream whipped up especially for him by Baskin-Robbins.

Art Shows

In recent years, art shows and exhibits have also become increasingly popular as fund-raising vehicles, and the art gallery opening is probably the most painless benefit. "Since it is usually preceded or followed by dinner at an attractive home, and calls for less dressing up and only a brief appearance at the gallery, it is especially popular with men," New York *Post* society editor Eugenia Sheppard once noted. Where the artwork is not donated, the sponsoring agency receives a portion of the proceeds, usually 10 to 20 percent of the proceeds of the sale. Actually, this commission is generally added to the price the artist sets for each work and is included in its final selling price. The public may also be

---

*The major expense was the one-time-only cost of $250,000 for renovating the giant former movie studio—as long as a football field—used for the auction and warehousing the auctioned goods. The other expenses were chiefly for the rental of a mobile television unit, the employment of a 23-man union production crew, security guards and full-time auction staff, and promotional costs.

charged an admission fee, particularly if the works exhibited are not for sale.

At New York's posh Hammer Galleries, I attended a champagne preview of Fleur Cowles Meyer's bright-hued fantasies of flowers, birds, and beasts for the benefit of the Society for Rehabilitation of the Facially Disfigured, whose main activity is the support of an Institute of Reconstructive Surgery. Certainly, few of the "beautiful people" who attended the opening seemed in need of such surgery. As the Montebello Brut '64 was poured, I recognized such familiar New York faces as Paulette Goddard, Beverly Sills, Arlene Dahl, Andy Warhol, and Arlene Francis. On my way out, I asked an animated, pretty young lady at the reception desk if any rehabilitated, facially disfigured beneficiaries of the society were present. "Yes," she answered pleasantly, "I am one."

Fashion Shows

Fashion shows are usually held in connection with a luncheon. "As long as women have an active interest in clothes and are curious about what's going on in the fashion world, these events will continue to flourish and endure," says Leibert and Sheldon's *Handbook of Special Events for Nonprofit Organizations*. Perhaps the *grande dame* of all charity fashion shows anywhere and an institution of half a century's standing in Chicago is the Presbyterian-St. Luke's Fashion Show, a two-hour extravaganza that packs the Medinah Temple's 4000-seat auditorium year after year. The grand finale of one show, which used 158 models, featured the appearance of two white horses pulling an English court carriage. Over the years, the show has raised well over $2 million for the medical center bearing its name. In the perennial search for something different, Saks Fifth Avenue which, like other stores, finds the shows good for business, recently staged a fashion bash called "Couples," a $35-per-person affair in celebration of some of Manhattan's so-called "fun couples," who served as models for the event. "Some of the couples were married to each other, and others were married, but not to each other, and still others were unmarried people who hadn't even laid eyes on their partners before," reported *The New York Times*, "but they pranced out on the runway arm-in-arm for the benefit of the American Cancer Society's New York City Division, which raised $14,000 from the affair."

Other People's Houses

Together with 200 other people, virtually all of them women, I waited in a line that stretched for one block to get into Mrs. Mary Lasker's fabled townhouse on New York's fashionable Beekman Place. The Lasker house, which was recently sold to the Shah of Iran's twin sister, was one of five outstanding homes on the annual spring house tour sponsored by the New York chapter of the Arthritis Foundation, which has been using this type of event to help finance its activities since 1954.

Inside the Lasker home, the visitors, some of whom had come from as far away as Chicago and Washington—a contingent of 100 signed in from Pennsylvania—were bedazzled by a wall-to-wall treasure trove of paintings rarely found outside a museum. Even the elevator was adorned with a pair of

Chagalls. But what impressed visitors the most was finding a Picasso and a Miró in one of the bathrooms.

Because most people are curious about how the rich and the famous live, the house tour, an institution that makes nosiness respectable, flourishes each spring as surely as the crabgrass. Casting a patina of politeness over snooping around other people's houses is the fact that this universal urge is being satisfied in the name of charity. For the small fee one is asked to contribute—$20 in the case of the New York Arthritis Foundation tour—goes to benefit one cause or another. In New York City, from April to June, one can choose from at least two dozen different house tours, each featuring five or six different homes or apartments; in the city's suburbs, there are perhaps three dozen more tours—of gardens as well as homes. In Charleston, South Carolina, some 75 houses and gardens are opened to the public with the blooming of the azaleas. In Washington, D.C., no less than 47 such events were listed in the newspapers during one recent year.

To woo the curious, many charities prepare enticing brochures describing the special attractions of the homes on their tours. The Manhattan League for the Industrial Blind, whose tours vie in popularity with those of the Arthritis Foundation, one year offered, along with the homes of playwright Lillian Hellman and milliner Mr. John, the Park Avenue digs of a beautiful, young former French countess with a midnight-blue and silver bedroom inspired by the boudoir of the late Jean Harlow, plus a millionaire haberdasher's townhouse with a living room where—the brochure said—"You mustn't miss the French music box on the coffee table whose figurine waves a fan and puffs smoke as the music plays, 'Smoke Gets in Your Eyes!'"

Financially, the house tour is one of the most profitable of all special events. The Arthritis Foundation tour took in about $17,000, virtually all of which was profit. "Our only major expense was for printing and postage which, with the insurance we have to take out on each house, came to $1000 or so," Patricia Hartung, the tour coordinator, told me. "And, oh yes, this also included the cost of the Pinkerton guards we now station at each house." Volunteers, serving nominally as "hostesses," are also stationed strategically throughout the house or apartment to keep an eye on things, as well as to prohibit smoking and answer questions.

With people increasingly nervous about allowing strangers into their homes in these crime-conscious days, there are some who feel that the house tour may have had its heyday. "Year after year, it becomes harder and harder to get places to show," said Mrs. Hartung. "This year I had to make 130 telephone calls to find the ten homes on our two tours, and I was lucky; I heard that another tour organizer had to make 50 calls for each home she finally managed to get. There are some really fantastic apartments I could have gotten, but many were in co-op buildings, which, concerned as they are with security, simply wouldn't allow it. Yet we don't like to lower our standards. At one time, we had only society people or people like Mary Martin, Averell Harriman, and the Duke and Duchess of Windsor. We still get some marvelous people, but we now also have to fill in with the homes of decorators and fashion designers, who are always agreeable because they have something to gain by being included on a tour. Still, there's a lot of rivalry to get the good homes."

Some people are reluctant to lend their homes, Mrs. Hartung said, because they worry about the damage a horde of snoopers will do to their rugs and floors. Before entering one home on the Arthritis Foundation tour, all of us had to take off our shoes and don paper slippers. Rainy days are a particular horror to tour organizers. "On those days, I feel like jumping off the George Washington bridge," said Mrs. Hartung.

The few home owners who choose to remain on their premises during the tours are also often repelled by the antics of the visitors, some, incidentally, accompanied by their decorators. Said Bronnie Kupris, who with her artist husband Val lives in a funky Federal house in New York's Chelsea district: "Here we have an enormous art collection, beautiful antiques, 14-foot bookcases, and things like an altarpiece for a headboard, and what do people do? They want to see what's in our medicine cabinet, in our refrigerator, in our closets. They check to see if there's dust on our shelves. And the stupid, dumb questions they ask! Like, 'How do you reach the books on the top shelves of the bookcase?' One out of every two or three people asks that. Isn't it reasonable to assume that we have a ladder?"

The Kuprises don't lend their home anymore.

Movie and Theater Benefits

"The awarding of film premieres takes place on a cruel, dog-eat-dog battlefield on which every combatant, the charities as well as the film companies, is out for himself."

These harsh words were uttered by Robert Massie, author of the 1967 best seller, *Nicholas and Alexandra,* which was made into a movie several years after its publication. Since the film had hemophilia as one of its central themes, it would seem logical that the customary charity premieres of the new film would be for the benefit of the National Hemophilia Foundation. But to his dismay, author Massie learned that the all-important New York premiere had instead been given to Project Hope, an ultrasocial charity then known largely for its support of a wandering hospital ship. Enraged, Massie asked Columbia Pictures, which had made the film, for an explanation. "Columbia does not want to give it to hemophilia," a company spokesman said, "because they do not regard it as useful from a promotional point of view to link the film with hemophilia." Sam Spiegel, the film's producer, put it more crassly. "Charity premieres are for publicity," he said. "I don't care what charity the money goes to." In London, Massie also learned, the premiere had been given to the British Spastics Society (concerned with cerebral palsy) because, as Columbia also explained, "the Spastics can deliver the Queen." In other words, here, too, it was felt that hemophilia, small in size and influence, could not attract the glittering names and the publicity that Columbia considered essential. In his frustration, Massie decided to help the Hemophilia Foundation sponsor a *third* "premiere" of the film, but that's another story, which you can read about in Massie's absorbing book, *Journey* (Alfred A. Knopf, 1975).

Of course, such contretemps may not accompany all film premieres, but it does serve to indicate the importance of them in the world of charity. The Massie-arranged premiere, which was combined with a dinner, grossed $68,000, of which half was clear profit. In Los Angeles, a world-wide premiere showing of *The Sound of Music* which, like most events of this type was also combined with an associated function—in this case, a champagne reception—grossed $65,000 and netted $53,000 for the American Cancer Society. In the same city, *Superman* recently made $150,000 for the American Diabetes Association, and annual movie premieres have raised more than $3 million for Cedars-Sinai Medical Center since 1958.

Basically, the financial details of such an event are quite simple: The charity buys up all or a certain number of the seats in the movie house at their regular price and resells them at prices high enough to provide a substantial profit and yet low enough to attract ticket buyers (who may, of course, take a tax deduction for the difference between the price they pay and the regular price).

Much the same procedure is followed for other theatrical events. For plays, benefits are arranged for any performances in addition to the premiere, often through special theater party agents. Their advance sales of shows, usually arranged months prior to their opening, can account for as much as 25 percent of a show's gross. Ronnie Lee, whose Theater Party Associates is the giant of the field, told *The New York Times* how his firm works: "We deal with over 2000 organizations, mainly in the metropolitan area. Some of our steady customers include the Red Cross, the Salvation Army, the Hudson Guild, and Congregation Rodeph Sholom. The way we service our organizations is both simple and complex: When a Broadway producer takes an option on a show, we receive the information. We learn the approximate date when the show will open. It might be in six months. It might be earlier or later. Usually, we are sent a script of an upcoming play, and we read it. If it's a musical, we are invited to an audition. In fact, producers set up auditions *just* for theater party agents. We are all there. If we like a script or an audition, we then go to work."

Since tickets are usually sold simply on the say-so of the agents (who are paid 10 percent of the full box-office price), their success depends on how consistently good their recommendations are. "Of course, Neil Simon sells himself and a big-name star will do the same," said Lee. "But it's with the unknown quantities that things get tricky. Look, charities and religious organizations are appealing to a broad segment of the population. They must be careful of what they support in a theater party. We may all have gone to see *Hair* or *The Boys in the Band,* but they weren't party material. Most of our organizations tend to support 'safe' shows."

The charity ladies who arrange film premieres have to make similar judgments. "You can't possibly have a benefit with something that's erotic or brutal," said Pat Hartung who, as head of the Arthritis Foundation's women's division, is also concerned with film benefits. "For example, you can't expect 80-year-old ladies to look at the kind of brutality you find in *Papillon*. They want a Claudette Colbert-type of movie. And so in these days of X- and R-rated movies, it's become harder and harder to tie in with film premieres." (Yet, the producers of *Papillon* managed to sell it as a benefit for the Will Rogers TB hospital.)

In a class by themselves are concerts, from Bach to rock, which are often the biggest money-makers of all theatrical benefits—and possibly also among the oldest.* To kick off a $6.5 million drive for itself in 1976, Carnegie Hall raised $2.5 million at a $1000-a-seat gala that featured such musical superstars as Vladimir Horowitz, Leonard Bernstein, Dietrich Fischer-Dieskau, Mstislav Rostropovich, Isaac Stern, Martina Arroyo, and members of the New York Philharmonic. At Carnegie Hall several years earlier, Frank Sinatra performed at a benefit that netted $150,000 for Variety Clubs International, which supports children's charities. And his magic name, along with those of Robert Merrill and Walter Cronkite, raised more than $800,000 in a 1977 Carnegie Hall benefit (chaired by Jacqueline Onassis) for Lenox Hill Hospital and the Institute of Sports Medicine. Former Beatle George Harrison, Bob Dylan, and their friends have raised millions of dollars for Bangladesh and UNICEF through benefit performances at Madison Square Garden; and Mick and Bianca Jagger once raised $400,000 at a single concert there for the earthquake victims of Nicaragua.

Fun and Games

Sports events—golf, tennis, football, basketball, polo, horse shows—are another popular way of raising money. One of the more successful golfing events is San Diego's Tournament of Fun, which has been an annual event for the American Cancer Society since 1961. With rare exceptions, each invited player, professional as well as amateur, pays a $300 entry fee. Additional income is derived from donations by nonplayers and the sale of cocktail-buffet tickets. The prizes, which include cars and color TVs, are usually donated by manufacturers and wholesalers. To justify the "Tournament of Fun" name, special features include teeing off from a mattress, shooting an approach shot over a clothesline, and trying to hit an outhouse from a distance of 250 yards. The event now grosses about $120,000, netting $90,000 after expenses. At other events, professionals are hired to play, and the income comes largely from admissions fees, with the charity receiving a certain percentage of the gate, or whatever is left after expenses. The famous Westchester Golf Classic, for example, which is billed by its sponsors as "the world's most charitable sports event," generates $300,000 a year for several of the county's hospitals.

As fund-raising events, star-studded tennis tournaments, like the sport itself, have also recently skyrocketed in popularity. The largest, the City of Hope Invitational Tournament in Los Angeles, features cinema celebrities. In the East, another major court event, the Robert F. Kennedy Pro-Celebrity Tennis Tournament, held annually at Forest Hills to benefit the program for disadvantaged supported by a memorial foundation named for the late senator, pairs such celebrated hackers as Walter Cronkite, Art Buchwald, Merv Griffin, George Plimpton, Janet Leigh, and, of course, members of the Kennedy clan, with such leading pros as Arthur Ashe, Stan Smith, and Pancho Segura. Tickets can be charged through American Express, Diners Club, and other credit cards. A new company called Limelite Internationale specializes in staging celebrity pro-am tennis tournaments, guaranteeing the presence of at least 20 tennis-playing

---

*Back in the mid-1700s, Handel not only gave London's Foundling Hospital an organ for its chapel, but also raised £728 for it with a special performance of his *Messiah*. At about the same time, David Garrick, the legendary English actor, also gave performances of Shakespeare for the benefit of Middlesex Hospital.

celebrities, and promising earnings of anywhere from $10,000 to $80,000 to participating charities.

In recent years, backgammon has also become one of the most popular fund-raising pastimes, joining such other long-time indoor standbys as mah jongg and bridge. Every year, about $125,000 of the proceeds of games run by the American Contract Bridge League go to a different designated charity.

Backyard and street carnivals are popular warm-weather events with the kiddies. Those put on by the Muscular Dystrophy Association alone involve some 150,000 youngsters across the nation and now raise more than $1.5 million a year for the association.

Gambling: Leaving Charity to Chance

Capitalizing on man's age-old urge to bet—the nation's biggest industry, according to some experts—virtually every form of gambling is also used to raise money for charity.

The practice in this country dates from colonial times, when lotteries helped build such universities as Harvard, Yale, Princeton, Brown, Dartmouth, and Columbia, as well as our early churches, bridges, canals, and roads; lotteries even helped finance the American Revolution, and had such staunch advocates as Washington, Franklin, and Jefferson.

Nowadays, one form of gambling or another is used by many of our most respected institutions—not only schools, churches, and synagogues but also hospitals, fraternal orders, civic clubs, veterans' groups, and volunteer firemen. "Bingo Tonight" signs in front of churches, Elks Lodges, American Legion halls, and meeting places of other organizations are familiar features of the American landscape. "Las Vegas Nights" or "Monte Carlo Nights"—evenings of blackjack, poker, craps, roulette, and other wheel games—are popular fund-raising adjuncts of charity balls, church bazaars, dinner dances, and similar social functions. My mail in recent years has included raffle books from schools and synagogues and sweepstakes offerings of brand new Plymouth Dusters and Chevrolet Impalas and a plethora of other prizes from the Pallottine Fathers and the Salesian Missions.

As an indication of the auto industry's deference to the Deity, a *Sports Illustrated* ad once featured a nice-looking woman, a book of raffles at the ready, seated at a curbside card table next to a Volkswagen topped by a sign reading: "St. Mary's Bazaar. Take a Chance on a Luxurious Car! Only 25¢." The copy, which began, "Dear Reverend, Father or Rabbi," suggested that Volkswagens, rather than Cadillacs or Continentals, were the best cars to raffle off for that church or synagogue fund-raising drive.

Sacrilegious as it may seem, religious groups are perhaps the principal proponents of gambling as a fund-raising device. In some of New York City's houses of worship, illegal casino-style gambling—the so-called "Las Vegas Nights (or Nites)"—is said to pull in an estimated $50 million a year. A typical scene is at Queens' Rego Park Jewish Center, where every Saturday and Sunday night finds more than 400 people crowded around 21 poker tables, 12 blackjack tables, 2 craps tables, and a Big Six wheel, with many patrons waiting to get game seats.

Some houses of worship seem to have only tenuous religious ties. In nearby Forest Hills, a six-nights-a-week casino operation called Congregation Kol Israel fills all 12,000 square feet of a newly acquired former supermarket with gaming tables, except for a tiny 30-by-50-foot area designated as a chapel which, however, was not used for religious services—at least when visited by one reporter. When asked about this, a staff member of the building said. "The rabbi has been falling down on that. We'll have to get on him."

Such operations are illegal because New York State law, under current regulations, restricts religious and other charitable organizations, wishing to raise money through games of chance, to only one gambling session a month, requires them to use scrip instead of money, and places a limit on how much can be bet and how much can be won. Poker is also not on the list of games the law permits.

Although the police, district attorneys, and city and state officials have known about these illegal activities for years, there has been only an occasional crackdown, religion being the sacred cow that it is. To say nothing of charity.

For similar reasons, in Pennsylvania, where all forms of gambling except horse racing and lotteries have been outlawed for over a century, the threat of stiff penalties (up to five years in jail or a $10,000 fine) hasn't stopped an odd assortment of lawbreakers—ranging from clergymen to war veterans and volunteer firemen—from turning the state into a bingo player's paradise. St. Elizabeth's Church in Philadelphia, for example, offers cash prizes large enough (up to $4000 a night) to lure busloads of tourists from nearby New Jersey and Delaware—two of the 39 states where bingo is legal—which have ceilings on prizes (up to $1000 nightly).

To publicize the games, which generate estimated annual gross revenues of $130 million (of a nationwide total of $2 billion), signs are posted along Pennsylvania's highways; in Philadelphia, the Roman Catholic High School Alumni even advertise their bingo games in the Yellow Pages. But here, too, enforcement authorities look the other way because, as one police official put it, "public sympathy is with the charitable organizations" that run most of the games or, as is often the case, serve only as ostensible sponsors, lending the use of their names to professional operators for a flat fee or a small percentage of the take.

Police everywhere, however, are increasingly concerned about the questionable reputation of many of the game operators, some of them professional gamblers with links to organized crime. In East Chicago, Indiana, not long ago, the Northwest Indiana Crime Commission discovered two veterans' clubs operating as gambling fronts with ties to a Chicago crime syndicate overlord. In 1974, Steve Cirillo, a reputed member of the Joe Gallo gang, was fatally shot at a dice table in the social hall of an Orthodox Jewish synagogue in Brooklyn. A week later, the police arrested ten alleged promoters of a "Las Vegas Night" at another Brooklyn synagogue. Four of the ten were found to possess previous arrest records, as well as Neapolitan names not normally associated with habitués of a Jewish house of worship.

"I don't think that the rabbis knew that criminal elements were running the games," Chief Inspector William Fitzpatrick of the New York City Police Department's public morals division told me. "Some of the outsiders may have gotten in by approaching members of the congregation, none of whom ever bothered to look into the backgrounds of the professionals." Since then, more than two dozen synagogues in New York City and the rest of the state reported they had been approached by questionable characters with possible Mafia ties seeking to take over their "Las Vegas Nights." All of the synagogues said they had rebuffed the approaches. Nonetheless, Pasquale (Paddy Mac) Macchiarole, a mobster who was found murdered in the trunk of his car in 1978, was revealed to be a silent partner in the 35 "Las Vegas Nights" operating in Queens alone.

Why are these and other forms of illegal gambling—for charitable purposes or otherwise—allowed to continue to the point where they now account for 90 percent of the $500 billion Americans bet every year, according to John Scarne, the celebrated gaming expert? One reason is the recent rapid spread of *legal* gambling: Today, 44 states permit some form of wagering, and 14 of them run lotteries. "The state lotteries begin to blur people's ethical and moral values," says Jonathan L. Goldstein, former U.S. attorney in New Jersey. "They make gambling respectable and thus create new clienteles for organized crime to prey upon." From the state lottery, he says, it's a short step to illegal gambling, which enriches organized crime. Studies have also shown illegal gambling to be most prevalent in states with legal gambling because of the reluctance of people in those states to abide by the legal limitations on their winnings, and because they see a sizable chunk of their legal winnings eaten up by taxes.

Moreover, Americans, like other people, have generally been ambivalent in their attitudes toward gambling. Many may practice it in private, yet condemn it in public, or say that it may be right under some circumstances but not others. "Many people who think it is wrong to bet on races unhesitatingly buy tickets on lodge raffles," a *Redbook* article once pointed out. "Yet, a churchgoer who has no objection to using gambling games at a parish bazaar might be horrified if he saw his pastor shooting craps."

Surprisingly, there is no specific biblical injunction against gambling. However, the rabbis of the Second Temple classed gambling as a form of thievery and barred gamblers from the witness stand. A long list of Catholic bishops also sermonized aganist gambling, at least up to the Middle Ages. In practice, though, while Protestant opinion has condemned gambling, many Catholic and Jewish leaders have tolerated it. In fact, Catholic churches used lotteries and other games of chance here in America as far back as the early 1800s; and bingo, because it first flourished in parish halls and meeting rooms of such lay Catholic groups as the Knights of Columbus, probably in the 1920s, was once identified as a "Catholic" game.

But even within each of these religious groups there are sharp differences of opinion. Among the Protestants, the Baptists regard all kinds of gambling as sinful; and other denominations, while not regarding church games as sinful, feel them to be an "unscriptural" method of financing religious work. The New York Board of Rabbis, back in the 1950s, opposed bingo on the ground that the game lowered the synagogue's "high standards of morality and dignity"; and in 1977 it passed a resolution opposing all forms of synagogue gambling. "The excuse that a synagogue needs these funds to survive is as shameful as the activity," said the board. "It cannot be that four thousand years of history should depend on dice, cards or a roulette wheel." In 1977, the Rabbinical Council of America, which represents 1000 Orthodox rabbis, also condemned all forms of gambling in synagogues.

Even within the Catholic Church, there is far from unanimity from diocese to diocese and parish to parish. "No Catholic theologian would say that gambling per se is bad, whether it is done at the race track or in a bingo parlor," a New York chancery official told me. "It would be wrong only if it were to harm the person by, say, leading to other abuses, or by affecting people close to him. A lot would also depend on why it's done and what's done with the money." However, other archdioceses and dioceses, particularly in the Midwest, South, and Southwest, flatly forbid gambling of any kind whatever, even where it is condoned by civil law.

In spite of such strictures, many churches and synagogues still do as they choose on the rationalization that the money gambling brings in is necessary for their programs, if not survival. "I find 'Las Vegas Nights' distasteful, and so does my rabbi," said the president of one Brooklyn synagogue, adding that the from $750 to $2000 the synagogue cleared from each of the eight games it ran annaully paid for its Hebrew school and youth programs. At the parish hall of a Brooklyn Roman Catholic Church, the president of the church's athletic club spoke in a similar vein: "We're trying to make a few bucks and hope the law looks the other way. We have 400 boys, 8 to 17 years old, and it costs us $12,000 a year to put on our basketball and baseball programs."

"In many parishes," says James Gollin in *Worldly Goods,* "the fifteen or twenty thousand dollars a year the pastor can count on from bingo is the margin that makes the difference between a struggling but solvent parochial school and one that must either cut back or else close its doors." Although the revenue from this and other forms of gambling may amount to no more than 10 or 12 percent of a parish's income, one high New York chancery official was quoted as saying: "If they ever outlaw games of chance in this archdiocese, we're dead."

Yet gambling is a horrendously inefficient way to raise money for charity. When professional operators run the games of chance, very little, if any, of the proceeds may filter down to the charity since there is really no way of knowing if an operator may be "skimming" money by underreporting receipts and overstating expenses in illegal games conducted on essentially a cash basis. In Alexandria, Virginia, in late 1978, nearly $66,000 of the $282,000 grossed in bingo games run in the names of the local YMCA and volunteer fire department and a church were siphoned off and disappeared. The Crime Commission of Philadelphia told me of one local bingo game which produced profits of an estimated $3 million during the course of a year; the charity received only 3 percent, or $135,000, of this.

Even when honestly conducted, gambling is still a relatively inefficient method of raising money. Some revealing figures come from the New York State Bureau of Bingo Regulation, which reported that of the $205 million legally wagered by the state's bingo players one recent year, only $55 million or one-quarter of the gross wound up with the sponsoring organizations. (The rest was paid out in prizes or went for taxes and license fees.*)

There can be no question, though, that gambling for charity does not require the time, effort, and manpower involved in such fund-raising techniques as

---

*Nor do states do much better with their gambling enterprises. In most states, an average of about 40 cents of every lottery dollar taken in is left for the state general fund or specific programs. The remaining 60 cents goes for prizes (45 cents) and administration and overhead (15 cents). On the other hand, states generally spend only 5 cents to collect each tax dollar.

door-to-door collecting, bazaars, balls, walk-a-thons, and cake sales or—to cite
the unique homey specialty of St. Joseph's Catholic Church, in Meppen,
Illinois—the sale of snapping turtle soup, an annual event that calls on the
collective efforts of all the church's 300 parishioners.

Nor can one deny that gambling fills a social and entertainment purpose for
many people, even those who do not find it fun. "I don't really enjoy it," said a
Queens, New York, widow on her way to her weekly bingo game, "but it gives
me something to do." That is still another reason why law enforcement officials
think twice before daring to close down a game. "You'll never realize how
vicious an indignant old lady can be when you shut off her weekly bingo game,"
a Gary, Indiana, police captain, said.

When the pastor of a Roman Catholic Church in West New York, New Jersey,
had the temerity not long ago to end his church's bingo games, bazaars, and other
"carnivals," and suggested tithing to make up the lost revenues, his parishioners
were up in arms. After the intervention of the vicar general of the archdiocese,
the bingo games were allowed to continue.

Yet the pastor's action can be understood for, in spite of gambling's popularity, there is something that rankles about leaving charity to chance. Those inclined to this view like to quote the advice Horace Greeley, the nineteenth-
century editor and presidential aspirant, once gave to a member of a church that
was foundering for support. The worried parishioner explained that fund-raising
festivals, suppers, parties, socials, and such other "unscriptural" methods (a
category into which some present-day clerics would place bingo) had all proved
unavailing, and asked what else could be done. Said Greeley, "Why not try
religion?"

Sore Feet for a Cause: Walk-a-thons and other "Thons"

Which brings us to the walk-a-thon, an event which enables Americans of all
ages to combine their passions for exercise and helping a cause. In this event, as
everyone knows, participants are pledged a certain amount of money for each
mile they walk over a predetermined route, usually about 20 miles. The pledges
are secured from friends, relatives, neighbors, local merchants, and other
sponsors—the more the better—and are usually from 10 to 20 cents per mile and
up; some sponsors have been known to pledge as much as $500. To prevent
cheating, walkers have to pass through a series of check points to have their
mileage verified and entered on their walk cards. At the end of the walk-a-thon,
each walker collects from his sponsors the donations pledged.

There is scarcely a city or hamlet that does not have at least one walk-a-thon
during the course of a year. The March of Dimes alone staged over 1100 in 1978,
more than anyone else, and they collectively accounted for over $17 million or
28 percent of the organization's public contributions. The largest, involving
some 40,000 walkers, was the 25-mile hike in, of all places, Baltimore, which
raised a whopping $700,000! In Dallas, where the event brought in nearly
$125,000, a 15-year-old high school track team member completed the 20-mile
course in two hours. But surpassing this remarkable achievement was that of a
27-year-old man who took six hours—but with just one leg and on crutches.

Claiming to be the first users of these fund-raising walks in this country (they are said to have originated in England) is Project Concern, the international medical relief organization, which depends on the 300 walks (called "Walks for Mankind") it conducts annually for the major part of its income. In what is believed to be a record, one Kansas City Project Concern walker is said to have picked up $12,000 in pledges after a 36-mile hike. Other big users of the walks include Cerebral Palsy (which puts out a 26-page guide for conducting them), Muscular Dystrophy, Diabetes, and, outside the health field, the United Jewish Appeal-Federation of Jewish Philanthropies, which entered the field in 1977 by staging walk-a-thons, with an estimated one-half million participants in 185 communities across the nation.

With the encouragement of the Bicycle Institute of America, the industry's trade association and public relations arm, which is happy to send any organization monographs bearing such titles as *The Bike-a-thon as a Fund-Raising Activity,* cycling for a cause has also come into its own in recent years. In Massachusetts, a Hike-Bike for the Retarded (participants can either walk or bike) brought in over $140,000 one year for the local chapter of the National Association for Retarded Citizens. Other charities using bike-a-thons include the American Cancer Society, the March of Dimes, the American Heart Association, UNICEF, and Cerebral Palsy.

The spectacular success of the walk-a-thon and bike-a-thons has spawned no end of other types of "thons." Aside from the familiar telethons (which are the subject of a later chapter) and radiothons, there are also swim-a-thons, dance-a-thons, and, as a variant of the latter, even belly-thons, one such 30-hour event in New York featuring 34 belly dancers undulating for the benefit of the Muscular Dystrophy Association. There are also snowmobile, basketball, hockey, and, presumably, other sports marathons. In Stamford, Connecticut, 27 teen-agers raised $2200 for crippled Vietnamese children by staging a rock-a-thon; each participant was pledged a specific sum of money for each hour he or she kept moving in a rocking chair, the winners rocking for 14 hours. For the American Cancer Society, six Paducah, Kentucky, teen-agers raised $450 and claimed the world record for continuous handclapping; and in Kansas City's St. Andrew's Episcopal Church, 100 parishioners, in teams of two, read the Bible for 100 straight hours, probably a world record for continuous Bible reading. The National Multiple Sclerosis Society raises about $3.5 million a year through a read-a-thon in which schoolchildren read as many books as they can within a given time span and persuade sponsors to agree in advance to donate an amount of money for each book read. (The champion reader may be an Oregon first-grader who read 361 books in six weeks!) In Schaumberg, Illinois, a Florida couple locked lips for 14 hours to win a national kiss-a-thon, with the proceeds going to St. Jude's Children's Hospital. For the cause of cancer research, the Ohio Cosmetologists' Association holds a yearly "hair-a-thon"; for 24 hours straight, association members offer a $2 shampoo and set to all comers, raising over $6000 in a typical year. The Christian Rural Overseas Project, a nationwide church-oriented program to alleviate world hunger, conducts marathon fasts, with sponsors paying a fixed amount for every hour participating teen-agers go without food; the fasts usually run about 30 hours.

And now that sex is becoming more than a household word, who knows what we can expect next?

Chapter 19

They've Got You on a List

"It seems I can hardly come home without being confronted by a letter asking me to contribute to some organization or another," a Michigan resident complained to the Detroit *News'* "Problem Solver." A Parker, Indiana, woman, the wife of a retired factory worker on a small pension, voiced a similar complaint to me. "Each year we get a tie, usually one that is not usable in my husband's wardrobe, from some charity for the blind," she said. "I have on numerous occasions returned them as refused but we still keep on getting them, as well as articles from other charities. Are we on some kind of sucker list?"

Edwin L. Dale, Jr., of *The New York Times* once devoted an entire column to the fact that over the course of a year he found his mailbox cluttered with no less than 389 separate appeals from 138 different causes. (Heard from most frequently: the International Rescue Committee, Thomas E. Dooley Foundation, American Kidney Fund, and Common Cause.) Other statistical-minded bemused citizens have kept similar tallies. The annual intake of a Scarsdale, New York, couple weighed 13 pounds and included 359 letters from 104 sources, plus such items as plastic American Indian dolls, thermometers, gummed name-and-address labels, greeting cards, pennies, and miniature auto license tags. In what may perhaps be a record, one 72-year-old Albuquerque retiree reported receiving 439 letters from 95 charities in a 12-month period.

I myself kept count one year and found that my wife and I received a total of 224 pieces of mail, many with sundry souvenirs, from 109 different organizations. Topping our list of correspondents were Friends of Animals and UNICEF, each with eight letters, three from Friends of Animals arriving on a *single* day! The runners-up were Christian Appalachian Project (of which more anon), WNET/Channel 13 (New York's public television station), Ralph Nader-Public Citizen, Alumni Federation of New York University (my wife's alma mater), Southern Poverty Law Center, and St. Labre Indian School.

Probably no other form of fund raising is as annoying to people as the mail appeal which, according to an A.C. Neilsen study, now accounts for well over half of all the monies raised by U.S. charities every year; in fact, some of our best-known charities—notable examples are the American Lung Association with its Christmas Seals, the National Easter Seal Society for Crippled Children and Adults, and Boys Town—depend heavily on mail appeals for the major part of their income, 90 percent of it in the case of the ALA. Some people resent the appeals on the ground that they are an invasion of privacy and clutter up their mailboxes. Others are appalled by their wastefulness and cost, which may often be more than what a charity spends to carry out its purported objectives—a fact not generally disclosed on its mail appeals.

Some irate mail recipients have been annoyed to the point of action, and these are not necessarily people with hearts of stone. Take, for example, John Ruedi, a 47-year-old Coronado, California, golf pro who gives over $1000 a year to 40 different charities because, as he says, "I feel sorry for them." But after accumulating nine pounds of solicitations and unordered merchandise (including eight combs and 17 sets of greeting cards) during one ten-month period, he decided enough was enough, and sent the bundle to his congressman. Similarly, W. G. Flangas, a 47-year-old Las Vegas mining engineer, who gives between $1000 and $1300 annually, bundled up a 20-pound pile of solicitations received in one year, including 21 separate appeals from the St. Labre Indian School, and dispatched it to the White House with the request that something be done. "I wasn't trying to be a big, nasty bastard," said Flangas. "I was just getting concerned about these organizations spending all this money on things it wasn't intended for."

Ironically, Uncle Sam is as responsible as anyone for the increasing avalanche of charity mail. Most charities have long enjoyed a special nonprofit rate, currently 3.1 cents per letter, compared with the 8.4 cents third-class rate now paid for advertising and other so-called "junk mail," and the 15 cents charged for first-class mail. To make up for the lower postal rate of nonprofit organizations, Congress now provides the Postal Service with $600 million of taxpayers' money annually. Moreover, our friendly mailmen, in delivering the appeals, are unwittingly replacing the legions of fund-raising door-to-door volunteers who once were the mainstays of many organizations. "It's unfortunate because mail tends to be a more expensive way of raising funds, but the old ways just don't work anymore," says Helen O'Rourke of the Council of Better Business Bureaus. "However, because of the competition, organizations have to reach larger and larger audiences to raise funds, and with direct mail they can reach huge numbers of people."

Fund raising by mail has also burgeoned in recent years with the development of sophisticated computer technology, which has made it possible to sift and group, economically and quickly, the names of potential and actual donors on the basis of their interests, backgrounds, incomes, and giving habits, even categorize them according to the size and frequency of their contributions. Some computers can alphabetize and classify a list of 100,000 names in 10 minutes; others can be programmed to prune lists in order to eliminate duplicate mailings or to remove the names of "nixies"—people who have moved or died and who can make up 10 to 35 percent of the names on a poorly maintained list. With the skillful selection and use of mailing lists a key ingredient in the success of fund-raising campaigns, even the priests who run today's religious charities speak learnedly of "cold" lists (containing names new to the charity) and "donor" or "house" lists (previous contributors), and know how to eliminate wasted effort and money by limiting their solicitations to recent previous contributors or to new prospects who are most apt to respond because of the magazines or books they read, the organizations to which they belong, the things they buy (preferably by mail), the credit cards they use, and, what is perhaps most important, the causes to which they contribute. They know, too, that it may cost, say, 55 cents to get one new contributor but only 5 cents to bring back a previous one.

So, although a charity will concentrate on building and maintaining its own lists, it will also have to use outside lists in order to seek new donors to replace those lost by attrition for one reason or another.* The Epilepsy Foundation of America uses more than 100 outside lists a year. Charities get these lists either by trading their own with other charities or by buying or renting them from brokers, publications, or other specialized sources. Literally thousands of lists are in existence—Standard Rate and Data Service's catalog alone contains about 5000—and there are said to be at least 1 billion names on lists, counting repetitions, of course. It has been estimated that the average consumer is on 200 mailing lists. The rental charge usually runs from $25 to $50 per 1000 names each time the list is used.

Some typical offerings culled from advertisements and announcements in recent issues of *Fund Raising Management:* 105,000 contributors to health and welfare causes at $25/M (or 1000); 96,661 nonsectarian donors of $2.00 to $4.99 to mission appeals for emergency relief at $25/M (or donors of $5 or more at $30/M); 136,006 contributors to conservative political causes at $30/M; 8798 conservative businessmen at $50/M; 73,776 contributors to local animal shelters and societies (average donation: $5) at $25/M; 56,617 donors to Jewish appeals at $25/M. The Los Angeles Lung Association offered 400,000 of its donors ("primarily middle and upper income people over 40 . . . all gave within 3 years") at $30/M; and the Coolidge Company, a New York list broker, offered, quantity unspecified, lists of conservative donors ($50/M), good government givers ($40/M), contributors to appeals for racial equality, human rights, and peace ($40/M), foreign-relief contributors ($50/M), and just "nice people who donate" ($40/M).

Once you've gotten on even a single list, it is amazing how quickly your name can spread—almost in geometric progression—to others. To see for myself just how names proliferate, I decided to conduct a test. Endowing myself with a previously nonexistent middle initial, I mailed a $2.50 check, signed Carl O. Bakal, to the Christian Appalachian Project one November. About six months later, a solicitation addressed to Carl O. Bakal came to me from the American Kidney Fund. The following month, another mail appeal (this one containing two ball-point pens), also addressed to Carl O. Bakal, arrived from Missionhurst. During the course of a year, Carl O. Bakal had also been blessed with appeals from the Dakota Indian Foundation and the Epilepsy Foundation, the latter's including a shiny penny.

Over the next two years I, in my new identity, received thirteen more appeals from seven different charities: Missionhurst (which next sent me a pair of combs) plus the Southwest Indian Foundation ("Thunderbird" key chain), Salesian Missions (sweepstakes tickets giving me a chance to win a new Chevrolet Impala or $3500), St. Labre Indian School (North Cheyenne letter holder), Pallottine Fathers (greeting cards), Korean Relief (Christmas cards), the North Shore Animal League ("I Love You" cat and dog animal stamps), and the Bangladesh

*Depending on the type of organization, attritions can range from 5 percent (extremely strong alumni groups or prestige cultural or community organizations) to 20 percent ("sympathy causes"), according to San Francisco's Institute for Fund Raising.

Emergency Mission, the only organization that failed to send a gift. My $2.50 donation to the Christian Appalachian Project had spawned a total of 17 appeals, most of them with gifts, from ten charities in three years.

Meanwhile, CAP, presumably now regarding me as a hot prospect, continued to bombard me during the same period with no less than 16 appeals, many containing such gift items as name-and-address stickers, Christmas cards, greeting cards, chive seeds, a key chain, and, ironically, "Thank You" note paper— all of which I am sure, must have cost much more than the $2.50 I had originally given; in addition, I continued to receive similar CAP appeals addressed to plain Carl Bakal. To none of these did I respond. In its persistence, therefore, CAP showed itself to be a paragon of patience and profligacy. For most charities drop deadheads after five or six fruitless follow-up appeals, if that many.

Obviously, mailing just anything to a list is not enough; equally important to the success of a campaign is the message. Campaign letters, once said Francis Pray, a former vice-president of the Council for Financial Aid to Education, should be "love letters," seeking "to marshal winning words to convince the recipient of our regard for him and our need and desire for his regard for us and his support for our enterprises." Jerald Huntsinger, a Richmond, Virginia, consultant, and one of the best letter writers in the business, urges the utmost simplicity in writing and the use of a chatty, write-as-you-talk style. "Poor spellers make good letter writers because they usually don't try to use big words!" is one of the things he likes to say at the endless conferences at which he speaks. Another thing Huntsinger, a former minister, tells his audiences: "In each letter tell the story of a real flesh and blood person who is receiving help from your program. For example, instead of quoting figures about starvation in Central Africa, tell the story of one father who is watching his family starve. Instead of explaining in great medical detail the principle causes of lung cancer, tell about one single person with lung cancer, the fears, the expense." All this, Huntsinger feels, means long letters; and his experience has shown that four-page letters usually outpull one-page letters.

Advises veteran fund raiser Harold J. Seymour in his *Designs for Fund-Raising:* "Vary the format with underlined words and indented paragraphs. Stress the note of urgency with some reasonable or plausible deadline. And whatever else you do, finish the letter with a last paragraph that asks for something specific, preferably in terms of program. (Will you send that kid to camp for a week?)" A CARE appeal on behalf of the world's hungry illustrates this: "$2 sends enough CARE seeds for them to grow fresh nutritious vegetables to help feed more than 85 starving people a week. A $10 donation supplies enough seeds, insecticides, fertilizers and tools to produce food for 445 hungry people. . . ."

Fund-raising experts also know that it is often helpful to salt the letter with various personal touches—for example, by using a computerized automatic typewriter to fill in the recipient's name in the salutation and, occasionally, even in the body of the letter. "Dear Mr. Bakal," evangelist Billy James Hargis once wrote me in an appeal for funds for his American Christian College, his letter continuing, "To me, you're a special person and frankly, a very valuable friend. Your support of American Christian College shows me that you're an American who really cares about our youth, our country, our heritage." (By an amusing coincidence, the letter was typed a month after Hargis denounced me in his *Christian Crusade Weekly* as "no friend of mine" and as someone who would "undermine the people's confidence in those who would save the country" because of a *Reader's Digest* article of mine that questioned his charitable activities.)

The design and size of the letter and outer and reply envelopes, the nature and number of enclosures, the quality and color of paper and even of the ink used, the character of the graphics used and type faces—these are among the dozens of factors that can contribute to the psychological impact of the mail "package" and, hence, influence the return. For the envelopes, experts favor warm-colored stock over white, which is usually associated with junk mail, as is also the standard #10 business envelope, especially with address labels. Experts suggest the use of window envelopes, which are typically used for invoices and are, therefore, most likely to get opened. Two-color printing (but with inks other than black) is also usually thought to be best; three-color printing is felt to look too expensive, and one-color printing too cheap. Business reply postage has also been found to induce a greater response. "Asking the responder to supply a stamp," says San Francisco's Institute for Fund Raising, "doesn't really save money, because it loses donors who don't have a stamp handy."

Even the timing of the mailing is important, with the best delivery days being Tuesday, Wednesday, Thursday, and Saturday; Monday is bad because of the heavy accumulation of mail generally delivered on that day. Of the months, apart from the consideration that some mailings must be timed to tie in with a charity's concentrated publicity activities, November is most likely to induce a favorable return. December, on the other hand, coinciding as it does with the Christmas shopping period, when people are short of cash, in a month when many charities ease up on their mailings. The poorest months of the year are those from May through August, a period when people are away on vacation.

Some charities, like Boys Town (which, incidentally, is one of the few that will not trade or rent its lists), the Pallottine Fathers, St. Labre Indian School, the Disabled American Veterans (DAV), and the larger health agencies, conduct their own mail appeals from start to finish.

At DAV national headquarters in Cold Spring, Kentucky, where nearly 1000 people have been employed at peak periods to produce some 40 million pieces of mail a year, high-speed computers maintain and update the organization's mailing lists, produce mailing labels, and log the complete donation histories of every DAV contributor. The equipment there even includes optical scanners, which "read" the data on the coded cash-return envelopes and transfer this, with the aid of keypunch operators, onto punched cards or magnetic tape.

Other charitable organizations use such outside specialists as Creative Mailing Consultants of America (CMCA) and Patrick Gorman, whom we met in earlier pages. A recent issue of *Fund Raising Management* listed no less than 40 firms offering "creative" mailing services of various kinds, and these firms represent only a fraction of those available. American Fund Raising Services, Inc., of Waltham, Massachusetts, with branch offices in Chicago, New York, and Washington, D.C., is known in the trade as a "one-stop shop," offering as it does a supermarket of services. For a flat fee, it plans an entire campaign, drafts the appeal letters, provides the lists of prospective givers, sends out the mail (60 million pieces a year on behalf of all its clients), and even handles the returns. In the Washington, D.C., area, CMCA, also a one-stop shop, has 4 high-speed machines that together can affix address labels at a rate in excess of 1 million per day.

Raymond La Placa, president of CMCA, which numbers among its past and present clients such illustrious eleemosynary enterprises as the Southwest Indian Foundation, the Christian Appalachian Project, St. John's Missions, and the American Kidney Fund, told me that the average cost of a simple mass mailing is about 10 cents, offering this budget breakdown: "The outer envelope will cost $8.50 per thousand; the return envelope, $7; the letter, $10; art and copy, $5; mailing list, $25; assembly and mailing services, $12; miscellaneous data processing, $5; and postage, $31. All of which adds up to $103.50 per 1000, or 10.35 cents per unit. Of course, with elaborate enclosures and a premium, the unit cost could easily double or even triple."

One of the biggest of the mail fund raisers is Richard A. Viguerie, of Falls Church, Virginia. Staffed by 300 employees, his firm grosses $22 million a year, preparing and dispatching some 100 million pieces of mail for such "cause" clients as the David Livingstone Missionary Foundation, the Korean Cultural and Freedom Foundation, Help Hospitalized Veterans, the National Rifle Association, Citizens for Decency Through Law, and this or that emergency drive for the starving in Sahelian Africa or Asia, as well as for various right-wing political candidates.

In the process, Viguerie has on several occasions come to the attention of the law. In late 1975, for example, the New York state attorney general, Louis J. Lefkowitz, took steps to ban Viguerie from all fund-raising activities in the state on the ground that his contracts with his clients, which permitted him to retain up to 75 percent of the funds raised, were "unconscionable and constitute a fraud upon the contributing public."* A state audit showed that of the $1.5 million Viguerie raised that year for the Korean Cultural and Freedom Foundation (KCFF), less than 7 percent had actually been used for the purposes specified in the solicitations of the foundation, which was later discovered to have ties to the Rev. Sun Myung Moon; the majority of the funds—nearly 61 percent, $920,302—went to Viguerie for fees and expenses. Since in that same year, Viguerie advanced tens of thousands of dollars in fund-raising services to the presidential campaign of then Alabama Governor George C. Wallace, it is conceivable that a good deal of the funds contributed to the KCFF could have been put to use in the Wallace campaign. Whether true or not, one questionable practice uncovered in the audit of the KCFF's books was the undocumented transfer of large sums of money to South Korea. In 1977 the KCFF was banned from soliciting in New York State.

Such abuses should not, of course, damn all fund raising by mail. Nonetheless, many of the things associated with this solicitation technique, even when used by respected organizations, still remain major sources of irritation: the trading or renting of donor names, duplicate mailings, unordered merchandise, the overemotional and often exaggerated nature of many appeals, and the secrecy usually surrounding their inherently expensive costs—often out of all proportion

---

*In 1978 the case was settled when Viguerie, without admitting any legal violations, agreed to limit his fund-raising fees for New York charities to no more than 35 percent.

to the funds that remain to carry out the proposed work of the charity involved.

In response, the users of mail appeals have no end of answers. For example, they explain duplicate mailings as "simply an unfortunate outgrowth of the costly computer age," to quote a note one charity included in a mailing to prospects. "The technical way names are put on and taken off, and the cost of manpower and computer time, has made it financially and physically impossible for us to cross-check all of the lists for duplicate names." The note went on to say that to cross-check the many lists used would cost 15 cents to 35 cents for each name.

Some charities insist that they can raise more money by mail, and others contend that some donors, particularly those who contribute to certain less-popular causes, prefer to contribute by mail. "For us, direct mail works best," says the Epilepsy Foundation of America (EFA). "It may be because we know more about it or it may be because epilepsy favors the anonymous contribution." The EFA, which until recently used a shiny penny in its solicitations, and others also defend their use of premiums on the ground that they bring in a greater return. The Disabled American Veterans (DAV) has conducted test mailings, with and without an enclosure of 100 address labels. "If the 50,000 letters with the 100 stickers in them produce more net dollars, there isn't any question which we are going to mail," says DAV assistant national adjutant Thomas G. Dehne. Father Ralph Beiting of the Christian Appalachian Project also says he is person-ally disturbed about his organization's use of premiums. "It burns my soul that we use them," he ruefully says. "I know that they boost the cost of our mailings. Without them, we could cut the cost of our mailings in half. But every test we've ever conducted shows that they bring in twice as much money as mailing without them. A foolish gift is apparently the best way to get to the guilt feelings of people."

While conceding that people who receive too many solicitations have a genuine complaint, Richard J. Crohn, a New York fund-raising consultant, plain-tively asks, "But how is the American Cancer Society to know that the American Lung Association just sent a letter to one out of xxx,000,000 Americans?" Then Crohn, quite irrelevantly citing the multiplicity of commercials for breakfast cereals and other products, says, "The point simply is that charitable organiza-tions, in common with American business, *have* to use the means of communica-tion and advertising which reach the public." And to those who regard the use of names on lists as an invasion of privacy—the American Civil Liberties Union even regards the practice as a violation of the First Amendment of the Constitution—the list users wave the banner of free enterprise, one Ohio list broker referring to the mailing list as "an important cog in the gears of the economy."

Does all this mean that nothing can be done apart from implementing the frequently made suggestion that legislation be enacted requiring all charities soliciting money through the mail to provide in the solicitation itself information about the use to which the money is to be put, including the proportion of it that has been budgeted for fund raising? Rather than subject themselves to such legislation, and possibly ceilings on their fund-raising costs, Jerald Huntsinger has proposed that all charities voluntarily make a complete disclosure of all costs. "If your costs are high," he told a fund-raising conference several years ago, "explain the facts, and respect the intelligence of the public to decide whether or not the nature of your work justifies high costs."

He also urged the wider use of "merge and purge" programs to eliminate duplicate mailings—a procedure that can in fact often more than pay for itself in savings in postage and printing, as some charities, such as CARE, are beginning to learn. Huntsinger, among others, has suggested that donors be notified if their names are to be traded or rented so that they have the privilege of saying no, and has also recommended that the charity business maintain a master list of names of people who do not wish to receive charity appeals.

Meanwhile, if you are the harassed recipient of charity and other mail appeals, you already have some measure of relief available to you. The Direct Mail/ Marketing Association (6 East 43rd Street, New York, New York 10017), an industry group of some 2700 companies and organizations that use or control mailing lists, have name-removal forms. If you fill in and return this form, DMMA members will be notified that you want your name taken off their lists. Since all charities do not belong to the DMMA, you may also want to write directly to any offending charities and tell them you want no more of their mail. All this will probably reduce your mail substantially.

If not, there are still more drastic steps you can take to get your name off mailing lists. As New York City list broker Ed Burnet once told the *Wall Street Journal:* "You have to move and leave no forwarding address. Then you have to be very careful. You can't buy a car, you can't have a phone in your name, you can't own a house, you can't join a club, you can't join a church, you can't open a charge account. . . . You just have to fade away."

And, of course, you have to stop giving to charity.

Chapter 20

Behind the Scenes
of a Telethon

If you had the opportunity, what media would you choose to tell the cerebral palsy story to your community with the greatest impact?

Undoubtedly, you would say . . . "television of course!" This is the basic concept of a United Cerebral Palsy Telethon. The telethon brings your cerebral palsy story into virtually every home in your community rich with the drama . . . the excitement . . . of a Broadway opening night . . . the peer of a special documentary . . . the dignity of a humanitarian cause.

> — Promotional Brochure, United
> Cerebral Palsy Associations

What a telethon is—and anyone who tells you different is a fool—is a twenty-or-twenty-two-hour-long commercial.

> — Myles Harmon, free-lance telethon producer
> of Easter Seal and other telethons

No one paid much attention to the two casually dressed young men who walked into a cable-television office in Gainesville, Fla., last week. They smiled at a young volunteer manning a telephone for the Jerry Lewis muscular dystrophy telethon, laid a brown paper bag in front of her, and said pleasantly, "Here, this is for you." Then they left. Local Muscular Dystrophy Chairman Ron Bauldree opened the bag and found ten bundles of mostly $20 and $100 bills. Attached was a note: "$10,000 for M.D. collected by the Gainesville Marijuana Dealers Association, Right on!"

> — News item, *Time*, September 17, 1973.

> *Look at us, we're walking!*
> *Look at us, we're talking!*
> *We who've never walked or talked before.*
> *Look at us, we're laughing!*
> *We're smiling and we're laughing.*
> *Thank you from our hearts forever more.*

As Jane Pickens, one of the three famous Pickens Sisters of yesteryear, sings these lilting lyrics, sixteen adorable, crippled children, aged four to twelve, some wearing braces, hobble on crutches in a circle around the stage. It is a few minutes after noon on a Sunday in February and the annual Cerebral Palsy Telethon, now in its fifteenth hour, has reached what could be called an emotional peak.

It is a moment Louis Clapes, town clerk of Stamford and Cerebral Palsy's Telethon cochairman for Lower Fairfield County, Connecticut, had been looking forward to. A stubble of graying beard on his face, he has been up all night, helping direct the volunteers manning the phones at Stamford's telethon headquarters at the Pitney Bowes Training Center on Washington Boulevard.

"When those kids start marching around," Clapes had said, "and *our* kids come on, the phones will start ringing off the hook!" (Actually, to cut down on bedlam, the phones flash rather than ring.) He is referring to Kathleen Walsh and Caroline Johnson, both four years old, Fairfield County's cute "celebrity girl" participants in the parade of the palsied. .

"Look, there are our kids now!" he yells excitedly. And all of the 25 phones set up on a horseshoe-shaped table in the room do indeed flash as Kathleen's and Caroline's faces come into view on the color TV. They and the other cerebral palsy poster children, fixed smiles on their faces, continue to circle the stage as the marching song is repeated three times and finally concludes:

> And some day they'll be walking,
> Some day they'll be talking.
> Imagine walking to the candy store.
> But the fight has just begun.
> Get behind us everyone.
> Your dollars make our dreams come true!
> Thanks to you, thanks to you.

"Now, before we meet some of the stars of this telethon," says its emcee, Dennis James, the famed, ebullient game-show host, "let me first say one thing here for those who might be joining us for the first time. When we first brought out youngsters like these many years ago, people said, 'How *dare* you exploit those youngsters?' Let me tell you something. It's *no* exploitation. You talk to the therapists of these boys and girls who look forward to this every year to *prove* to you the kind of progress they have made. It's no exploitation. We don't parade them as a bunch of little freaks. We parade them as beautiful human beings who are able to demonstrate to you what progress has been made over one year because *you* were kind enough to make a contribution. If we didn't have them on the stage, a lot of them would be tremendously disappointed. Now let's meet these stars in person."

First he introduces Kathleen Walsh, a blond little cherub of a girl with pink ribbons in her hair. "Kathleen, can you sing?" he asks. "Any song you want." She hesitates shyly as he coaxes her. "If you sing, I'll bet you right away, somebody is going to pick up the telephone." She sings a few snatches of a nursery rhyme. "Now, let me see you walk," he says, telling the audience, "She couldn't walk at all last year." Kathleen takes a few steps to a tremendous round of applause. "Now is that exploitation?" Dennis asks. "Did you see her face, that tremendous sense of accomplishment? That's what this telethon is all about.''

"All right, Hope Lewis, it's your turn now," says Dennis to a little four-year old black girl with plaited hair and glasses whom he also asks to walk. Then he talks to Eddie Mack, a white boy who, Dennis says, no longer needs to wear the braces he wore last year. "If you sent us even a dollar, you take credit for Eddie Mack. Go ahead, Eddie, show 'em! No braces, no crutches!" One by one, the other children from the New York metropolitan area also get their turn in the spotlight. Finally he turns to the other Connecticut girl, Caroline Johnson. "If I asked you to throw both crutches away, would you try to walk without the crutches?" he asks. "If you fall, are you going to cry? No? Then throw the crutches away and come to me. Throw them as far as you can throw them. That's it, get out of here, you old crutches! Now come to me." Caroline goes to him as the studio audience applauds.

"Now, you people at home will have to walk to your telephones," says Dennis. "Because that's what this is all about. That's what this is all about. . . .''

Later, Dennis James, with twenty-odd years of telethons behind him, is to tell me: "You know, it takes a greater effort to get a nonhandicapped person to move from his chair to the phone than it does to have a youngster with cerebral palsy walk with his crutches over the same distance." It is a favorite phrase of one of America's most persuasive pleaders for the physically afflicted. But that people go to the phone at all is a tribute to certain highly sophisticated techniques of telethon orchestration, as well as to the persuasive powers of him and other pleaders.

The telethon is as much a part of American folklore as, say, the dance marathon, roller derby, six-day bicycle race, flag pole sitter, and other extravaganzas of endurance and entertainment. All probably share the same hypnotic source of appeal. Will that master of ceremonies (dancer, skater, etc.) be able to remain on his feet after all those, oh so selfless, sleepless hours? In that race against time, will a record be broken—that is, when the telethon has run its course, will the final figures on the tote board exceed those of last year? And for any self-respecting telethon not to exceed its previous year's total is unthinkable. Then, there is the attraction of all those big names from the worlds of entertainment and sports, even politics, who appear not only as performers or public figures, but as *people*, human beings, humanitarians, friends of the afflicted.

Norman Kimball, who doubles as United Cerebral Palsy of New York's public relations director and telethon coordinator, sees the telethon as an outgrowth of the radio marathon, which Kate Smith initiated in the early 1940s to sell U.S. War Bonds.

The forerunner of the telethon we know today was a 1949 telecast which saw Milton Berle on the air 16 consecutive hours for what was then called the Damon Runyon Memorial Cancer Fund, an effort Berle later described as "probably the longest sustained vaudeville performance on record." The event, shown on 12 TV stations across the country, pulled in more than $1 million dollars in pledges. Two years later, United Cerebral Palsy of New York produced the first in the series of telethons that is today known as "The Holiday Star Telethon for Cerebral Palsy." Jerry Lewis, teamed with his old sidekick Dean Martin, made his telethon debut on Berle's historic 1949 telethon and did an occasional local telethon for muscular dystrophy in the years that followed. However, his annual Labor Day series did not get under way until 1966, although it now seems that it has been with us forever.

Although the prophets of doom will have you believe that telethons have had their heyday, it is difficult to avoid one if you watch TV with any regularity. The Cerebral Palsy telethon, the nation's oldest, is now shown just before New Year's simultaneously on nearly 80 TV stations across the country.* Jerry Lewis' annual Labor Day weekend Muscular Dystrophy appeal, the nation's biggest, is telecast over a coast-to-coast network of more than 200 TV stations. And rounding out the Big Three is the Easter Seal spectacular for the miscellaneous crippled, which originated in 1972 and is now shown around Easter, of course, on some 114 stations.

But there are literally hundreds of others put on annually, nationally or locally, for an astonishing variety of causes: to improve the lot of the arthritic and mentally retarded, raise funds for Israel, further the cause of highway safety (with Sammy Davis, Jr., an auto accident victim, as host), and help flood victims and Cuban refugees.

Not every cause lends itself to a telethon appeal. It is more than coincidence that the three most successful telethon perennials in the health field are for the benefit of people, principally children, with *visible* handicaps. Although more than half of those served by the National Easter Seal Society for Crippled Children and Adults are adults, and a large proportion of the children served have only speech or hearing difficulties, the society nonetheless features only kids on crutches, never adults, on its telethons: How in the world would you show a *deaf* child with the same sort of dramatic impact?

"Television is a visual medium, and only a visual problem can be effectively dramatized in a visual medium," says United Cerebral Palsy's Norman Kimball, who has masterminded the telethons not only for his agency but also on occasion for other causes.

"In the late 1950s I did a telethon for Mental Health of New York," Kimball recalls. "It was an excellent show but it just didn't move the community. The mental health handicap is not visual for the most part, and I was not even allowed to show patients who had been helped. That sort of positive approach would at least have enabled me to do something. In other words, if you bleed before a community, literally bleed, you will not find people running forward in great numbers to give you a Band-Aid. People are basically deniers—they do not want to see negative things.

"A prognosis of positive help is of tremendous importance. If I tell you,

*Until the first nationwide network telethon by the United Cerebral Palsy Associations was held on December 30–31, 1978, the various UCP local affiliates conducted their own regional telethons, which were shown on from 35 to 40 stations at different times, usually in January or February. The telethon described in this chapter was put on by United Cerebral Palsy of Greater New York and shown on 12 stations from Maine to Chicago and as far south as Atlanta. Since it was a multiple telethon, it was fairly typical of the nationwide telethons, although differing in one respect from recent Cerebral Palsy telethons, which several years ago discontinued the use of the song, "Look at Us, We're Walking," at the request of many organizations representing the handicapped.

'Look, this kid has cerebral palsy and nothing can be done for him,' what will your reaction be? You'll shake your head and say that's too bad. If I can't help him, what's the sense of giving him my money? That's why our children are shown in a positive way, in an *active* way. They move, they walk, they talk. If I have a kid who last year couldn't talk, and this year we have little Debbie on again and Debbie is able to say three words, that to me is something that should be shown and should be *heard*. For during the past year she has been given speech therapy to the extent that she is now able to form three words in her uncontrolled mouth. So while it may be a little insensitive to see the child struggle to say, 'Mamma,' at least she is saying it. That's what I mean by a positive sense.

"Now, Jerry Lewis doesn't believe in showing his children the way we show ours. That's his shtick. He's been very critical of us without mentioning cerebral palsy."

True. Several days later, Jerry Lewis, resplendent in a blue blazer and canary-yellow shirt, tells me: "I'm not going to criticize the other shows. Everybody has their own way of doing it, and if that is doing an effective job of helping those kids and if the psychiatrists say—as I've heard it said—that it doesn't affect the child to be seen on TV, it seems to me that they have the option of doing it that way. It's been our feeling all along that that's not the way to do it."

Easter Seal telethon producer Myles Harmon, however, minces no words. A good-looking, bushy-haired man of 35, he says, "That march of the crippled kids? I couldn't do that. It really turns my stomach."

Yes, some people do cringe at the sight of those crippled kids marching across the TV screen. But still one wonders what difference there really is after all between showing them in motion and displaying them seated solemnly in wheelchairs, as they are on the other shows, with Jerry Lewis emotionally proclaiming, with considerable license, "In the next 20 hours, 80 of my kids will die, I repeat, 80 of my kids will die." (Actually, nobody knows just how many people die of muscular dystrophy.)

Is it any less exploitation to have Jack Lemmon appear on the muscular dystrophy show and read, in a tear-choked voice, the first-person account of a 42-year-old father of three facing the reality of dying of amyotropic lateral sclerosis, while family album snapshot pictures accompany such poignant phrases as, "I don't want to die. I want to stay with my wife and children"? Or of actually *showing* in a wheelchair the helpless figure of former world heavyweight champion Ezzard Charles, unable to speak, unable to move, and in the throes of dying of the same disease?

And if it is exploitation, by whatever standards of judgment one can muster, what difference does it make as long as the money comes in? For after scenes like these, it is pretty hard to resist the inevitable pitch for pledges.

No one who watches a Jerry Lewis or a Dennis James for long can fail to be convinced of their sincerity and deeply felt dedication to their cause. Nonetheless, critics like Richard Carter, author of *The Gentle Legions*, while conceding the telethon to be a useful promotional tool, refer to it as an "interminable orgy of uncertain entertainment and bathos, with its processions of the afflicted and its other carefully planned vulgarities."

Possibly for this and other reasons, the fund-raising fraternity has always had some reservations about the telethon. None of the really big charities, like the Red Cross, Cancer, or Heart, have ever used it extensively, at least in recent years, and the March of Dimes has long abandoned its use, too. "First of all, it's a costly operation," says one former March of Dimes official. "Secondly, it involves a great deal of staff and volunteer time. Three, there's a lot of attrition. From my experience with telethons usually only 40 to 60 percent of pledges are honored." However, the Cerebral Palsy people claim an average of 93 percent and Muscular Dystrophy, on a recent telethon, a return of 109 percent! (Accounting for the latter are people deciding to give more than they had pledged, and also money coming in from people who did not phone in a pledge.)

Rumors are also rife about all sorts of shenanigans and hanky-panky: the hefty fees and expense accounts given to big-name entertainers; the killings made by flashy, fraudulent promoters; the highly imaginative bookkeeping that leaves little of the proceeds for the cause. In the early 1970s, a New York telethon for the Sickle Cell Foundation received pledges of $800,000, not one penny of which went to the cause. For, despite the pledges, only $217,870 in donations trickled in, according to the telethon's promoters who, as already mentioned, furthermore claimed that their expenses had exceeded donations by $78,000. When the foundation charged that it was never provided with complete and accurate records, the resultant wrangle became the subject of an investigation by the state attorney general's office. During the 1978 telethon for muscular dystrophy, Jerry Lewis responded to letters raising that frequently-asked question as to whether he has ever received any money (as much as $500,000, according to some rumors) for organizing and hosting the telethon. "I receive nothing from the telethon," he said. "Every dime is accounted for . . ." This is the same answer he has given to me privately and I am inclined to believe it; however, I have never been able to obtain a detailed breakdown of the telethon's expenditures.

A spokesman for the Democratic National Committee, planning a June telethon, approached Jerry Lewis and asked, "What's your secret?" He was really asking how Lewis has managed to raise all that money for muscular dystrophy.

Lewis said: "The secret is twenty-three years of *concern* and an obsession that all children ought to be given the same rights. Do you think you can put something like that together by June? Do you think you can write a check and in the corner where it asks for its description, you can write in there *Concern?*"

"Are you being facetious, Mr. Lewis?" asked the Democrat.

"You can bet your ass I am," said Lewis.

"What would your services cost?" the Democrat then asked.

Lewis hung up on him.

Jerry Lewis has other definite ideas about what makes for a successful telethon. "It's the aesthetics. What do I mean by that? My people can give you figures, statistics, all sorts of things, and then run them through the computers to give you the information you want. But when it all boils down, it comes down to a very simple premise: The people either believe you or they don't. They trust you or they don't. And so it comes right down to two factors: They *know* I can't have my kids dying like this. And I *tell* them. It's *that* simple."

What else goes into the making of a successful telethon? Norman Kimball ticks off some of the key essentials: "First, of course, is a top personality who knows the cause and is known to the television audience. I've already mentioned that the cause, particularly in the health field, must deal with a problem that can be effectively dramatized in visual terms. The cause must also concern a sizable segment of the community. You need a constituency both as a source of financial support and as a source of volunteers. Literally thousands of volunteers must be enlisted from the community to fill the myriad jobs involved in running a telethon—telephone answerers, verifiers, bookkeepers, messengers, food and commissary workers, transportation people, and experts in the fields of finance and accounting, publicity, and entertainment."

A budget must, of course, be prepared. "Ours usually runs about 10 percent of what we expect to net," says Kimball. "Our budget this year is about $255,500. This means that we expect to take in about $2.5 million, compared to the $2.1 million we took in last year. Most of our budget—about $160,000—is to pay for preempted time station charges and other TV production costs. Another big chunk, $47,000, is to pay for the musicians and stage hands. The stars and other talent on the show of course donate their services, but we pay their expenses if they have to come in from out of town. About $12,000 is budgeted for hotels, studio rent, and telephone installation charges. A certain percentage of our receipts also goes to Theatre Authority, the organization of entertainment unions and theatrical guilds that clears the telethon and other benefits on which the performers can appear.

"The selection of performers is important. There certainly is enough talent to go around but when you try to put on a show that has a certain amount of class, style, and drawing power, it's tough. We are lucky to have Paul Anka and Steve and Eydie with us every year. Our policy is to pick the ten most popular shows and try to get one or more of the personalities who are on these popular programs. Buddy Howe, chairman of the board of Creative Management Associates, one of the largest talent agencies in the country, volunteers his services as chairman of our talent committee and as our executive producer. Buddy is responsible for the enlistment of the talent, the slotting of the talent, and the presentation of the talent."

In the conference room of Creative Management Associates, the volunteer talent committee is discussing plans for the telethon scheduled to take place three weeks hence. Buddy Howe opens the meeting with a request for a list of entertainment "availabilities." For his own agency, he reports commitments from Vikki Carr, Alan King, Helen O'Connell, Robert Goulet, and other luminaries.

Dick Fox and Tom Illius of William Morris, one of the three other talent agencies represented, reel off twelve names ranging from Carol Channing and Julius La Rosa to Barbara McNair and Bobby Vinton. "However, Phyllis Diller is still a question mark," says Fox. Queens Booking comes through with Aretha Franklin, Gladys Knight and the Pips, and Sammy Davis, Jr., and International Famous with nine other illustrious names from stage, screen, television, and the night-club circuit.

Norman Kimball reports that, as an additional special attraction, personalities appearing in Las Vegas on January 21 have agreed to tape a segment with talent host Paul Anka at Caesar's Palace, for integration into the overall telethon; and

Buddy Howe says that once again a one-hour live segment would emanate from Hollywood featuring Steve Lawrence and Eydie Gorme, national UCP honorary chairmen. For Chicago, one of twelve cities to carry the telethon, announced is the availability of Shari Lewis and columnist Irv Kupcinet as emcees and the talents of Theodore Bikel, Chuck Connors, and Tommy Esposito, the Chicago Black Hawks goalie.

Slotting or scheduling the performers is also extremely important. "You use your prime performers on prime time to attract the largest possible audience, and that's on Saturday night," Norman Kimball tells me. Advance gifts or pre-telethon pledges are another important secret of every successful telethon. Cerebral palsy solicits this "pretel-money," as it is called, through mass mailings and phone calls starting six weeks before the telethon. The mailings and phone calls go to previous telethon contributors and other likely prospects—individuals and organizations. Although the average gift is $8 or $10, they can range anywhere from $25 to as much as $5000 or even more.

"No telethon can make it on just on-the-air pledges, which are generally much smaller," Kimball continues. "Besides, the phone pledges are variables you have absolutely no control over. But I can take our pretel money, which this year amounts to $500,000, or about 20 percent of the total we hope to get, and feed it into the tote board at regular intervals or, at certain times, to boost our total for dramatic impact—prime the pump, so to speak—particularly when our phone response is not as effective as we want it to be."

Backstage at the Ed Sullivan Theater of New York's Broadway, home base of the Cerebral Palsy Telethon. It's 9:30 Saturday night, half an hour before air time. All is pandemonium. People wearing "Transportation" badges are dashing in and out of the stage door to pick up and deliver the celebrity panelists and stars who will appear on the show.

The characteristically sunny Dennis James is glum. "This is the worst telethon I've ever been on," he tells Jerry Ball, Cerebral Palsy's national campaign director.

"Why?" I ask.

"Telethons are supposed to bring in money," he explains. "This telethon has to by necessity concentrate on entertainment. And when you concentrate on entertainment, you lose money. When you should be pitching to get people to send in money, you're playing Sammy Davis, Jr. Everybody is sitting there and enjoying Sammy Davis, Jr. And people don't phone in when they're entertained. We're doing 75 percent entertainment tonight. That leaves only 25 percent for pitches. I think we should try to make it more like 60–40."

Dennis is also unhappy because the basketball game preceding the telethon is running overtime. "Boy, that lost 30 minutes is going to cost us $50,000," he says. "That's like losing the whole borough of Queens."

The celebrity panelists take their places at the ten phones on stage. Among them are the bosomy Sylvia Miles, Greta Thyssen, and Monique Van Vooren, all in décolleté, all familiar fixtures on other telethons, too.

Finally, the countdown and a drum roll. The telethon is under way. Dennis introduces talent host Paul Anka who sings a couple of numbers and then in turn introduces a parade of acts—Carol Channing and Sonny and Cher on tape. Piped in from Hollywood is the start of the one-hour segment, presided over by Steve Lawrence and Eydie Gorme, the husband-and-wife singing team, and featuring a glittering array of other acts.

Interspersed is an occasional pitch by Dennis who exhorts: "Last year, we went off the air with two-million-one and I say that with a little concerted effort, man oh man, we can now go to two-million-five." Also shown at the rate of one an hour are the series of taped cerebral palsy demonstrations, or "demos"—public education spots, prepared especially for the telethon, showing the types of programs and services which the viewing audience is being asked to support. The phone numbers for the viewers to call are frequently flashed on the TV screen, and soon the periodic totals of the phoned-in pledges are announced and appear on the tote board.

By 1:30 A.M., the tote board shows a total of $140,000. Dennis exultantly announces: "Our monies are more now than they were last year at the same time and I hope this is a trend. We all get worried. We're all afraid the total might drop down, and our only goal is to get it at least above where it was last year. In 23 years of telethons, in every year but one it was more than it was the year before."

In the wings, Normal Kimball is relieved, too, as he studies some cards in his hand. "These cards tell me how our telethons did at 15-minute intervals for each of the last three years. If I see that in the first two or three hours, we're running 15 percent ahead of the previous year, as we're doing now, I know that this will probably hold for the balance of the telethon."

Across the street at the Americana Hotel, a huge meeting room, the size of a basketball court, has been converted into a telephone answering room. There, at fourteen rows of long tables that stretch across the width of the room, volunteers man some 255 telephones, each with a flashing light to signal calls from viewers with pledges. On a dais at the front of the room overseeing the operation sits Phyllis Barchas, head of New York Cerebral Palsy's women's division and a key figure in the telethon operation.

"I know what percentage of phones are in use by looking at the room," she explains. "I know that each row accounts for a certain percentage of the total room. That multiplied by the number of rows gives me an overall percentage of what's going on. If the front half of the room is lit up, I know it's 50 percent of the phones. If it goes up to three-quarters of the room, I know it's 75 percent. If it goes all the way, I know it's 100 percent."

"When do you get 100 percent?" I ask.

"Usually on Sunday when the children start coming in. When the children parade to that marching song, the 100 percent may be kicked off even in the middle of the march. There may also be a particular child with whom the audience is empathic. If a star comes over to the child, and the child does something particularly sweet—say, puts her arm around the star or kisses her or cries—the audience will respond to that. If we see that happen and see how people respond to it, we know what to do to kick off such a response again.

"If there's a long entertainment bit on, there's usually not much of a response. If it's a pitch they're doing, this may kick off a great response immediately. That's why we always try to follow a long entertainment bit with a pitch. Of course, a lot depends on what the entertainer is doing. When Paul Anka does a straight ballad or song, there may not be much of a response. On the other hand, when he does a particular number that's heart-rending, like "Thank God for Little Girls," a song he wrote for his own daughters, you get people calling in the middle of it. Naturally, if a top name performer is on, I, of course, don't suggest that Norman cut his act. But if it's a second-rate performer or a bad act that's dragging, I do. I might say, 'Can't you do something to cut it and have Dennis make a pitch or maybe supe some phone numbers over the act.' For after all, our main business is to get the phones working and make money. I'm in constant communication with Norman, maybe five or six times an hour, and on Sunday afternoon even more often."

Just then the voice of Norman is on the tie-line phone. "We're going to put the Cooper tape on within the next five or ten minutes," he says. "Watch for it and call me right back. I'm anxious to know what sort of response you get."

On the TV sets spotted throughout the phone room, a film clip is soon introduced. It shows Dr. Irving S. Cooper of the St. Barnabas Hospital for Chronic Diseases demonstrating a new electric brain pacemaker. He explains how the pacemaker, implanted under the scalp to stimulate certain portions of the brain, can control the tremors that occur with cerebral palsy. Several patients, one a little girl, are shown being treated with the pacemaker. The effect is startling, showing as it does, the tremendous improvement made possible.

Phyllis watches with growing excitement. When the demonstration started, only 20 percent of the phones were lit up. Now, more and more phones flash and by the time the nine-minute film reaches its midway point, every phone in the room is lit up—a five-fold increase in response. She rushes to call Norman. "You won't believe this but we have a 100 percent response—every phone is in use right now."

She asks me if I would like to answer one of the phones. In rapid succession I receive pledges of $2, $5, and $10, taking down each caller's name, address, and phone number on a special IBM multiple form. The forms are collected periodically by the supervisors assigned to each table. "One copy of the form is fed into those IBM tabulator machines down at the end of the room," Phyllis explains. "Another copy is immediately mailed out, with a return envelope, so that the callers receive them in the Monday mail to remind them of their pledges. Two weeks later we do a follow-up mailing to the people the computers tell us haven't sent in their pledges. And then if we still haven't heard, we do a telephone follow-up.

"Another reason we take down people's phone numbers is because every pledge of $25 or more must be verified before it can be fed into the machine. Most people phone in pledges of between $2 and $5, although there are some $10 pledges, too. But the larger pledges, particularly those of $100 or more are relatively rare, apart from those arranged as advance gifts. That's why when we receive a pledge of $25 or more, we first look in the phone book to see if the number exists. If it does—often it doesn't or is the number of a bar—we call the number and thank the person who answers for his pledge in an effort to determine whether or not he really did make it."

Occasionally, Phyllis tells me, a verified pledge of $5000 or even $10,000 does come in cold over the phone. But she as well as other telethon veterans also have their share of favorite stories of pranksters who, in whiskey-flavored voices, phone in outlandish pledges in the names of slumbering friends and neighbors or on the condition that the emcee or star take off his clothes or sing a certain song.

On my phone, one caller, who sounds much too young to be up after midnight, asks me if her $2 pledge could be announced on the telethon. Following the directive on my printed instruction sheet, I answer: "We will try to announce your pledge if time permits—keep listening." The sheet also counsels: "It is not possible to connect you with (Star) because all the lines are tied up." Also: "If any gifts of $100 or over depend upon talking to (Star) say, 'We will have (Star) call you back if possible.' INFORM SUPERVISOR."

"With only ten lines to the phones on the celebrity panel and over 250 phones, the chance of someone reaching a celebrity is pretty slim—about 25 to one when all the phones are in use—except in the middle of the night or during a big entertainment segment," says Phyllis. "Still, you'd be surprised at the number of people who insist on speaking to some celebrity."

I look around at my telephone-answering colleagues. Virtually all of them— perhaps nine out of ten—are women. A surprising number are teen-agers or young people in their early twenties, informally clad in sweaters and jeans. "We're the ones who give, the ones who really care," a 16-year-old high school junior tells me. Although some are first-timers, most have made the telethon an annual ritual, coming from Brooklyn, Queens, as far away as Long Island, usually with a group of friends. Although volunteers are asked to serve only a four-hour shift, many choose to work around the clock for the entire 20-hour course of the telethon, almost as if they relish this test of their endurance and dedication.

One such volunteer, Sheila Goldfisher, a willowy N.Y.U. accounting student, says she got involved nine years before because of her mother, who is president of the Mayfair League, a cerebral palsy chapter in Brooklyn. Others become involved because of friends or relatives with cerebral palsy. One young man, a hospital receiving clerk, is an admitted telethon freak. "I *like* to volunteer," he says, "but I do only telethons. I also do Muscular Dystrophy and Highway Safety."

Offering me a danish and coffee in a makeshift cafeteria at the end of the room is Sandy Levin, a svelte thirtyish blond who runs a travel agency. She tells me she is treasurer of Pals for Palsy, another Brooklyn chapter, whose 140 women members were assigned the commissary duties at New York telethon headquarters many years ago. To fuel the army of 5000 telephone answerers, donations processors, and other volunteers in the Greater New York Area takes 20,000 sandwiches, 16,000 pieces of cake, 10,000 cups of coffee, 400 quarts of milk, and 4000 bagels. In addition, 10,000 pieces of hard candy are dispersed to soothe the throats of those on the telephones. These figures, however, do not take into account the 5000 additional volunteers located at the centers in the other eleven cities where the telethon is also being shown.

Back at the Stamford phone room, one of four in Connecticut. It is 2 A.M., Sunday morning. A light flashes on the phone in front of Lou Clapes. "Hello," he says. "Lou Clapes speaking. Why, it's you, Julie. How are you?"

It's somebody he knows. Part of the kick in calling is to talk to a local celebrity, which town clerk Clapes is. Another celebrity phone answerer is young, dark, handsome State Senator Bill Strada, who sits in an anteroom near a table piled with donated pastries and soft drinks. He's talking to long-time telethon volunteer Joe Mallozzi, in charge of the members of Local 478, International Union of Operating Engineers, who are manning the phones. (The union is made up of operators of such heavy equipment as cranes and steam shovels.)

"The union's been helping out on the telethon for about ten years," says Mallozzi who, in a two-piece, open-throated, wine-colored velour suit, doesn't look much like a steam shovel operator. "If we catch a contractor in a violation [of the union rules], we make him pay the fine as a donation to Cerebral Palsy."

Why is the union so active in Cerebral Palsy? "Ten years ago," says Mallozzi, "our business manager saw the center at Bridgeport and was so impressed by what it was doing for the kids that we've been in it ever since."

Why is Clapes in it? He looks wide-eyed that anyone should ask. "Once you see one of those little kids and see what can be done for them, how much can be done for them, with a little money, then you're hooked!"

Sitting at his post, Bill Fraterolla, a volunteer from Local 478, is checking the pledges of $25 or more. He has just called one number and been told by a sleepy man that no, he had *not* just pledged $50 to Cerebral Palsy. Bill decides to defer any further checking until 10:30 Sunday morning.

Sunday morning at the Ed Sullivan Theater. Norman Kimball, who took a three-hour break during the middle of the night to have a shower, catch a nap, and change clothes, is back looking refreshed. The character of the show has also changed.

"Saturday night the show is heavy on entertainment, which makes up 70 percent of the time, with the rest of the time devoted to taped demonstrations and low key pitches," says Norman. "The purpose of the entertainment is to attract an audience with the hope of bringing them back on Sunday, when the entertainment is cut down to 25 percent and the emphasis is on heavy pitching as well as community participation. We also show more live involvement. We bring the kids in, have people come in with collection presentations, and have civic, business, and labor leaders make appeals and appear with our celebrity panel. Our eleven other participating stations do the same with their local people."

In keeping with the spiritual nature of the Sabbath, a traditional Sunday morning feature in each city is a religious segment. At the New York studio, against a huge backdrop of a stained glass window, the Angelic Choir of the First Baptist Church of Nutley, New Jersey, renders a couple of spirituals, and a black-robed lady minister, a cerebral palsy victim, delivers a prayer and a sort of sermon keyed to the cause. Two rows of crippled kids, seated in little chairs, make up the mock congregation.

Dennis James accepts the annual presentation of a "mile of pennies," or $855 worth, from a representative of an American Legion Post in Queens. "God bless you guys for keeping that interest up," says Dennis. Throughout the telethon, similar divine blessings are frequently bestowed on other contributors as well as performers.

Then Dennis, who first came to fame as an innovative wrestling announcer (he would, for example, crack celery stalks to simulate the crunch of breaking bones), introduces old-time wrestler Antonino Rocca, resurrected from the

Golden Age of TV, who goes to the mat in a demonstration with a 27-year-old cerebral palsy victim.

Now it is time for the kids, Jane Pickens, and some heavy pitching. "Now when you see this, when you listen to Jane, do me one favor," says Dennis, with the same sincerity he used to muster for the dancing cigarettes and other subjects of his countless TV commercials. "If you're a parent, think of your own child in one of these situations . . . or if you're a young lady *expecting* a child, just realize how beautiful it is to know a lot of things have already been done to prevent your child having cerebral palsy. . . . So, while you're listening to Jane and while you're looking at these youngsters, honest to God try to put it into perspective and think of it in terms of your own family and not that we're on television. We're *live* here. This is not film, it's not tape, it's not a piece of glass. It's a live beautiful woman with a lot of live beautiful children.''

Jane, tall, patrician, and titian-haired, who, I was told, has a cerebral palsied child of her own, starts "working" the seven kids in braces and wheelchairs lined up in front of the studio audience facing the tote board, which shows a total of $320,000 at 11:20 A.M. "That gives us 40 minutes until 12 o'clock to go to half a million dollars," says Dennis. "Can we do it, audience?" There is a chorus of yeahs.

Jane goes down the line of kids, talking to each in turn. "Now, what about you, Shana?" she says to a four-year-old black girl in pigtails and ribbons. "What do you like to do?" She reads from a label attached to the child's clothing: "Shana is a bright, friendly child who likes to converse with adults," and asks, "What do you like to talk about? Anything?" The child answers, "Yes," "What do you want to do when you grow up?" No answer. "You'd like to get married, I suppose. Have—you—got—a—beau, somebody you like a lot?" "Yeah, my brother," Shana says. "Well it's so nice to have you, Shana. We'll see you a little later when we say [and she sings], *Look at us, we're walking. Look at us, we're talking.*"

Now Dennis takes over. After introducing gravel-voiced sportscaster Howard Cosell, who in turn introduces football star O.J. Simpson, Dennis brings out a beautiful, tousle-haired four-year-old boy and places him in Simpson's arms. "Now here's a boy who can walk only with the use of his crutches and braces, and I want to tell you that you can make it possible to *unlock* those braces," Dennis tells the audience. Reading from the boy's label, Dennis says, "Jimmy plays imaginatively with friends, likes working with magnets and electricity, and makes a good ghost or monster. If you wind him up, he becomes a wonderful robot." He asks Jimmy to walk like a robot. As Jimmy does, Dennis says, "That's a good robot," and the studio audience bursts into applause.

As O.J. Simpson goes to man one of the celebrity phones, another four-year-old, in a Buster Brown haircut, without crutches, stumbles across the stage. "A year ago, this little boy couldn't walk, he couldn't even stand alone." Dennis proclaims. "Now he took four or five steps *without* crutches. Next year, we'll have him run all around the darn stage." Seeing the boy's father start to cry, Dennis says, "May I ask what brought tears to your eyes?"

"I can't explain it," says the father.

At noon, Dennis, after asking for a drum roll and fanfare, announces a total of $505,883, and the march of the crippled kids is about to begin.

In the wings just offstage, Norman, one eye on the stage action, is constantly
on the phone. Most of the time he is in contact with the phone room, which he
refers to as "the constant pulse of the community." He is also in frequent touch
with Accounting, where the IBM computers are located. "This is where I get the
actual dollar numbers that I put on the tote board," he says.

At 1:48 P.M. the figure on the tote board is nearly $922,000. On the TV
monitor, Tony Bennett is singing "The Good Things Were All Mine" on a replay
of the Las Vegas tape. Norman, his ear to the phone, asks Dennis to make a pitch
at the conclusion of this number. "We need $78,000 more before two o'clock,"
Dennis announces. "The power is in your hands. Let's see if we can't get this
telethon to a million dollars before two o'clock."

Dennis then reads off a string of pledges: $100 ("from a Brooklyn man in
honor of a young couple with cerebral palsy who just became engaged"), $5000,
$200, $100, $2000, mentioning the names of the contributors. Obviously, most,
if not all, of these are pretel pledges. By two o'clock, the tote board hits the
$1 million dollar mark.

To reach this mark, Norman has fed $20,000 of pretel money into the tote
board, the balance of the $78,000 boost coming from the phone pledges, accord-
ing to Accounting figures. "Every time I make a feed of my own, I'll make
a deduction on these cards in my hand, and I'll tell Accounting on the other side
how much money I'm putting in so that they can add this to their total," he
explains. "I started using the advance money sometime Sunday morning and by
noon today I had used up about one-fifth of the half a million dollars I started
with. This means that from noon on I was hung up with four-fifths of the advance
money, roughly $400,000. Now you can't feed this into the tote board at one fell
swoop. You have to divide it into a number of pieces so that the feeds look
reasonable, like they're part of the response of the community. So what I do is
take the hours from 12 noon to six and divide the remainder of my advance gifts
by six. I then know that every hour I have to slowly feed in an average of
$65,000 or $70,000 of the money."

He interrupts to call Accounting to ask for the latest totals in the machines and
for estimates as to the backlog of pledges that haven't yet been tabulated. As the
afternoon wears on, Norman's calls to Accounting become more and more frequent because more than half of the 20-hour telethon's total intake comes in just
in its last four hours.

With his ear on the voice of Accounting and on the pulse of the community,
his eye on the stage action, and his hand on the pretel pledges, Norman is much
like a symphony conductor manipulating the musicians under his control. In fact,
says Norman, "To me a telethon is a very complicated instrument because
everything is in play."

With about an hour and a half left to go, the tote board figures stand at just
over $2 million. "Where do you think we'll be when we go off the air, based on
what's coming in now?" Dennis calls to Norman in the wings. "If we hit two
million five, what a telethon that would be! What do you say, Norman? Two
million four? Well, I say we can do two million five. I *know* you people."

Norman, of course, should know. As the telethon goes off the air, the figure on the tote board reads $2,424,624, a figure making the event the most successful in the Greater New York telethon's history.*

"If you saw nothing else this year," says Dennis in his closing words, "remember that wonderful tape of Dr. Cooper and the brain pacemaker that is getting people out of wheelchairs and having them walk."

And as the parents of the crippled kids wheel them off the set and out the stage door, one of the kids, a smile on her face, can be heard softly singing something that sounds like *Look at us, we're walking. . . .*

---

*With the revenues from the telethons conducted in 27 other cities added to the funds received in the 12 cities associated with the New York telethon, the UCP's total telethon take that year was about $6 million. The most recent UCP telethon, shown on 77 stations, raised over $11 million. The most recent Easter Seal telethon (114 stations) raised $12 million, and the Jerry Lewis Muscular Dystrophy telethon (213 stations), about $28 million.

Chapter 21

The Charity Ball Game

Charity ball, charity ball.
Noblesse oblige! We give our all.
We are dancing for disease, we are waltzing
    for bad health.
The afflicted and addicted need our gold and
    our wealth.
We are dancing for disease 'cause we're conscious
    of our rank.
So we like to take the night off,
It's an income tax write-off,
The retarded have us to thank.
There's hepatitis at the Hilton, the Regency
    has TB,
We put down the Biltmore for heartburn,
    Howard Johnson has the VD.
There's rheumatism at the Plaza, they're doing
    the St. Vitus dance.
We're richer than Croesus
We loathe all diseases
The hemorrhoids, tomorrow's transplants
Plagues, pests, seizures and fits,
Infections, strokes, petit mals,
Champagne and welfare bits
If you've got the bladder, we've got the
    gall.
Scratch, itch, fevers and pains never got
    under our skin,
Heart disease and cardiacs, this year are
    very "in."
We are dancing for disease, we are waltzing
    for a cause.
It's enthralling when we're balling,
But we give our menopause.
We are dancing for disease, and the drinks
    are really swell.
But the waltzing is turning,

My stomach is churning.
Excuse me, I don't feel well.
> — *Charity Ball,* from the album
> *Gracious!? Dining at The Crystal*
> *Palace,* recorded at the Crystal
> Palace Restaurant, Aspen, Colorado*

"Mr. Pugh wants to be seated with the Iranians, and the oil people want to sit near the ambassador. So does Arlene Dahl. The *whole world* wants to sit near the ambassador. What are we going to do? They can't *all* sit in Zahedi's lap."

In a little reception room just off the banquet office of New York's Waldorf-Astoria Hotel on a May morning, several years before the downfall of the Shah's régime, the very social Mrs. H. Donald Sills, a stylish woman in her fifties, with fluffy, reddish-blond hair, is laboring over the seating arrangements for the Million Dollar Imperial Persian Gala, a charity ball to be held five days hence in the Waldorf's grand ballroom. Mrs. Sills, perennial chairman of this annual event, which every year had a different foreign theme, is talking to Mrs. Florence Lazere Molomut, the secretary and wife of the director of the Waldemar Medical Research Foundation, a small, private Long Island cancer research institute, the beneficiary of this series of balls.

Spread out in front of them is a seating diagram for the ball. On the table between the two women is a small cardboard box full of alphabetized pink and green cards, each representing a person or company that has purchased the tickets to the ball. So far, 825 tickets, priced at $100 each, have been sold, but Ruth Sills is confident that the number will eventually reach 1000, the usual attendance at these balls. She points with pride to the fact that 180 of the expected guests will be what she calls "my people," meaning the people who unfailingly attend any event she chairs.

As any harried hostess knows, working out the seating for even a small dinner party at just one table can be difficult enough. Imagine the problems, then, involved in trying to seat an entire ballroomful of people at some eighty tables!

To illustrate the pitfalls, Ruth Sills recalls the time she once placed deadly enemies, two men involved in an unpleasant legal battle, directly across from each other at a narrow table. "Now, how was I supposed to know this?" she asks, smiling sheepishly. "Florence and I know most of the people who attend our balls. But how can you possibly keep track of *every* feud, know at any given moment who is not on speaking terms with whom?"

Marital breakups and extramarital intrigues present another problem. "Sometimes, you don't know if a man is coming with his wife or girl friend," she says. "And if you know both of them, that's a sticky wicket, too." Mrs. Sills finally hit on a Solomonlike solution to this problem. In *Sweet Bitter Charity,* a how-to guide she wrote on society fund raising, she tersely advises: "Have place cards made out for both the wife and the girl friend. Then wait nervously near the entrance to the ballroom and as soon as you can see them (the couple) enter, sprint for the table and place the proper card there."

*Copyright © 1973 by Fiddleback Music Publishing Co., Inc.

"Everybody wants a ringside table," Mrs. Sills also says. "Or Mrs. So-and-So wants to sit with Mrs. So-and-So. Or *doesn't* want to sit with Mrs. So-and-So. Then with all the dignitaries we have, there's also the protocol problem to further complicate things." In addition to the entire Iranian diplomatic corps, acceptances have already been received from the ambassadors of Turkey, Uruguay, Morocco, and Japan, as well as from a sprinkling of senators, "honorables," princes, princesses, counts, barons, and other celebrities.

"Now, Hoveyda [Iran's representative to the United Nations] has to be seated," Mrs. Sills, sipping a Scotch, tells Mrs. Molomut. "And I'm told protocolwise he's as important as Zahedi [then Iran's ambassador to the United States]."

"Hoveyda's also an honorary chairman," says Mrs. Molomut, a matronly, brisk lady with blondish-gray streaked hair.

"But he's not *the* honorary chairman," snaps Mrs. Sills.

Both diplomats are assigned to separate ringside tables.

"Do you think Robert Keith Gray would rather sit with Chuck Carey or with the ambassador?" asks Mrs. Sills, after shuffling through the file cards. Charles T. Carey, a prominent hotel chain executive, is chairman of the Gala's Washington committee. Gray, a former high official in the Eisenhower administration and thus entitled to the honorific "Honorable" in front of his name, is now a Washington public relations man.

Gus Ober, the society press agent who is handling the publicity for the ball and who, too, knows all the right people, joins them. A chubby, cherubic man in a black blazer and maroon slacks, Ober speaks in a well-modulated, cultivated voice. "Florence," says Ruth Sills, "Gus has just brought this list of people who want to be near Carey and the other nice people." Ober also wants to know the names of the celebrities who will be present.

Over a lunch of shrimp salad, the threesome go over the mountain of minutiae still to be resolved. "Now what about Mrs. Cafritz's table? Do you have checks from all those people?" Mrs. Sills asks. "Sapounakis I consider very important, and von Waveren, too. Do you all agree?"

The phone rings. It is Mohsen M. Goodarzi, Iran's consul general in New York and one of the event's seven honorary chairmen.

"What *about* the belly dancer?" Ruth Sills asks him. She listens for awhile. Goodarzi has had second thoughts about having a belly dancer entertain at the Persian bazaar to be set up just outside the ballroom.

"Yes, we've canceled her at your request," she reassures him. "If I tell you there isn't going to be a belly dancer, there isn't.' '

The seating, I'm told, will take nine hours to complete. "We'll probably make fifteen thousand changes," Mrs. Sills tells me with a sigh as I leave in the early afternoon. "Right now, all I know is that I have no more important tables. And I still have to seat people who've bought four tables for the past nine years. And also all the important oil companies. This year, I'll probably have to move a lot of people from the front to the back."

Contradicting the uncharitable cries of the Cassandras who periodically prophesy the demise of the charity ball, this predominantly American phenomenon still flourishes, perhaps now more than ever before. Indeed, in virtually every city and town of any size in the United States, the charity ball in fact is a tried and true method, as someone once put it, for the upper and upward-reaching classes to gather under the guise of good works. The social calendar published every September by *The New York Times* alone lists some 200 major charity balls every year—an average of one every night from September through June when the prestigious Belmont Ball winds up the New York social season. The calendar, as Russell Edwards, for many years the newspaper's society editor, is careful to point out, for reasons of space probably reflects only about half of the fund-raising events that take place locally—not only balls, but also dinners, luncheons, buffets-dansants, fashion shows, art exhibits, and other diversions that provide a painless way of separating man from his money in the name of Sweet Charity. "On some nights," says Edwards, "you could attend as many as four or five charity events."

Edwards used to go to 15 or 20 balls annually during his forty-odd years of writing and editing society news, but he attended only about four or five in the years preceding his recent retirement. "You got sated after awhile. I generally went to the Diamond Ball, which benefits the Institute for International Education and is perhaps our most prestigious ball. It has the greatest list of patrons— all achievers and doers who run America—that I know of, and there's also a tremendous guest list. I also went to the Million Dollar Gala and every other year to the April in Paris Ball, which aids the American French Foundation." However, he regards these two as somewhat less social than the Diamond, in the sense that their guest lists do not ring with as many names of Old New York, such as Vanderbilts, Astors, and Whitneys.

Other New York balls he considers important or noteworthy for one reason or another include the New York Infirmary Debutante Cotillion and Christmas Ball, its rival International Debutante Ball for the Soldiers', Sailors' and Airmen's Club (which in 1973 saw the debut of Mary Jean Eisenhower, granddaughter of the late president), the Ball of Roses for the benefit of Roosevelt Hospital, Cerebral Palsy's annual "Night in Las Vegas," the J.O.B. (Just One Break) Feather Ball for the handicapped, the Boys' Club Ball, and the Metropolitan Opera Ball.

Elsewhere, cities like Stamford and San Diego may have five or six major charity balls and perhaps a dozen lesser ones a year. Kansas City boasts no less than 14 major functions of this type. Some of these hinterlands affairs may exceed, by any yardstick, anything held in the New York area. In Texas, where everything is bigger than life anyway, the famed two-decades-old Crystal Ball of Dallas, which benefits a different charity every year, raises about $200,000 annually for such causes as the Society for Abandoned & Neglected Children and the Kidney Foundation of Texas. In the 1972 version, the 1300 guests (another 1700 persons were on the waiting list) included not only such celebrated locals as former President and Mrs. Lyndon B. Johnson and the Honorable and Mrs. John B. Connally, in fact, *everybody* from Texas, but also such peripatetic out-of-towners as Madame Herve Alphand (the wife of the former French ambassador), Baron Alexis de Rede, king of the Paris party givers, philanthropist Mary Lasker, advertising lady Mary Lawrence, and Princess Diane von Furstenburg, who wore a simple little number that was topless save for a pair of three-inch-wide suspenders. All cavorted in a Cecil Beaton re-creation of London's Crystal

Palace. But even this event was overshadowed by Houston's less-heralded Gourmet Gala, which one year raised $500,000 for the Texas Heart Institute.

Probably the biggest ball moneymaker of all time anywhere was the Mandarin Ball, held in Palm Beach in May, 1973, which raised $2 million for St. Mary's Hospital, the achievement meriting a front-page story in *The New York Times*. Since only about 800 persons paid $150 apiece to attend the party, it can readily be seen that ticket sales accounted for only a small proportion of the total take; most of the rest came from additional donations, one of which was for $250,000, with many of the others in five figures. Cattiest remark of the evening, according to *The New York Times*: "Matron (dripping with jewels) staring at another woman wearing a mousy fox stole—'Oh, my! Such a vulgar display of poverty.'" The social secretary of one *grande dame* also said: "People naturally support the hospital better than other charities because they know they'll eventually need it."

In the desire to be different, the Jewish Women's Club in Atlanta once held its annual ball in a bank, and a New York professional fund raiser staged a benefit New Year's Eve ball in Grand Central Station. As an example of *radical chic*, the Phoenix House Foundation for drug rehabilitation once held its annual revels in New York's proletarian Roseland Ballroom, attracting the best in pop and top society (Andy Warhol, Alice Cooper, the William Buckley, Jrs., Mary Rockefeller Strawbridge). Recalling the first of these events, a Phoenix House representative told *Town & Country:* "We made it a real *party,* not a stuffy ball or dinner dance. Very down to earth. Spontaneous, you know. Everyone sat on the floor and ate out of paper boxes."

But, inside or outside New York, most charity balls tend to be conventional affairs. To illustrate the spread of the charity ball syndrome, *Town & Country* in 1973 compiled this city-by-city sampling of some of the more noteworthy non-New York balls:*

Atlanta: Piedmont Ball ($90,000, Piedmont Hospital)
Chicago: Tiffany Ball ($170,000, Chicago Boys Club)
Cleveland: Orchestra Ball ($75,000, Cleveland Orchestra)
Dallas: Crystal Charity Ball ($200,000, Kidney Foundation of Texas and Society for Abandoned & Neglected Children)
Fort Worth: Jewel Ball ($125,000, Fort Worth Children's Hospital)
Houston: Gourmet Gala Ball ($300,000, Houston Grand Opera, March of Dimes)
Los Angeles: The Thalians ($245,000, Thalians Community Mental Health Center)
Nashville: Swan Ball ($220,000, Tennessee Botanical Gardens and Fine Arts Center)
Philadelphia: Academy of Music Anniversary Concert and Ball ($330,000, Academy of Music)

Charity balls have been an important part of the American social scene for more than a century. The big mystery is why. They have been termed crashing bores, even by many of the people who attend them regularly. These devotees could of course simply mail a check to the charity in question and skip the ball,

---

*The parenthetic material indicates the most recently reported gross receipts and beneficiaries.

but very few choose to do that. In fact, back in the late sixties, there were several attempts at the ''no-ball ball''—where people paid money and stayed home—but this fad soon fizzled out.

Why then have charity balls persisted, if not flourished, particularly during the years since the close of World War II? There are probably a variety of reasons. First, there is the matter of taxes which, back in the forties and early fifties, saw up to 90 percent of the gains of the rich go to the government. Those were the days, too, when the *entire* amount of a ticket to a benefit could be deducted as a charitable contribution. Today, of course, taxes are not as high as they used to be, and only the amount in excess of the cost of the function is deductible; but it is still a fact that people have no guilt about spending their money to help others when even a percentage of that money is tax deductible.

With the chronic help shortage and, in turn, the decline in private parties, charity balls also provide an ideal substitute for the formerly traditional home entertainment or even an evening on the town. One woman at the Palazzo Ball, a Westchester County, New York, benefit evening for Channel 13, said: ''Three or four couples will decide to get together at the ball instead of at home or in town. It works, too—the setting here is beautiful, the food is excellent, we can eat and talk together and dance all night, and the cost is deductible.''

Not to be overlooked, too, is the fact that benefits, apart from raising a lot of money for more or less worthy causes, also enrich a big sector of the business community: hotels, orchestras, food suppliers, wine and liquor merchants, florists, printers, decorators, dressmakers, jewelers, hairdressers, limousine services, social secretaries, promoters, publicists, and fund raisers.

Charity benefits are second only to conventions as a source of revenue to hotels. New York's $175-a-ticket April in Paris Ball, a giant extravaganza held, incidentally, not in April but in October, to aid various French and American charities, blossomed from the brain of the Waldorf's then banquet manager, Claude Philippe who, one day in 1950, noticed a blank date on his ballroom calendar, and decided to create an event to fill the vacuum. Indeed, even the Million Dollar Gala was born under similar circumstances, the panjandrums of the New York Hilton, the original site of the series, dreaming up and persuading the Waldemar Foundation to sponsor this event to fill *its* grand ballroom.

Finally, and perhaps most important, as even Ruth Sills will reluctantly concede, there is the social-climbing aspect of charity balls. Let it be said at once that some ball devotees are genuinely concerned with helping the cause. Others may even find balls fun, or at least an excuse to doll up in their latest finery and be seen and envied by friends and acquaintances—even strangers.

Needless to say, there is a certain amount of *quid pro quo,* particularly among ball chairmen and committee members. As Mrs. Valerie Straith of Detroit put it, ''You go to someone's ball because you expect that person to go to yours.'' Ego is involved, too. For those already rich and socially prominent, publicity provides one way of remaining in the social swim, which explains why some New York and Palm Beach socialites pay press agents princely sums, reportedly up to $50,000 a year, to try to get their names and pictures into Suzy's and Eugenia Sheppard's columns. Commenting on the charity ball efforts of the so-called prominent, one public relations girl said, ''Who says they're prominent? By running charity balls, they get their names in the papers; without that, they don't exist.''

For .those who've come into money recently or are well-heeled, upward-striving newcomers to a city, attending a charity ball and, better still, serving on one of its committees, thereby meriting invitations to the pre-ball parties, are as good a means as any of taking those first steps up the social ladder and, in the process, turning from a social nobody into a social Somebody.

Listen to this exchange from William Wright's book, *Ball,* a hilarious, bitchy, biography of New York's April in Paris Ball, between Mr. and Mrs. Lester Kronick, a prosperous upward-climbing couple, as they are having breakfast in their East 70th Street townhouse.

> She was going through her mail—a bill from Georg Jensen, a notice of a sale from Bergdorf's, a postcard from friends on a South American cruise. ''Here's a letter from Claude Philippe,'' she said to her husband (a man of about sixty who struck it rich in the construction business). ''He wants me to be on the committee for the April in Paris Ball this year. Isn't that exciting?''
>
> ''What'll it·cost me?'' Lester Kronick grumbled.
>
> ''Oh, I don't know,'' she answered. ''I think committee members are supposed to take a table—what would that be? About $1,800. But it should be fun.''
>
> ''Why fun?'' He looked up from his newspaper. ''I thought it was a crowded free-for-all last year. There wasn't enough food. And who is that Brownie McLean who runs the thing. Is she anybody to know?''
>
> ''Oh, Lester, Brownie's adorable. You liked her. You said so.''
>
> ''Does that have to cost me $1,800?''
>
> ''It's probably the biggest ball and one of the most important—and it's all that Palm Beach crowd—Mary Sanford, Estée Lauder, the Algur Meadowses. And if we're thinking about buying a place in Palm Beach, we should get to know them. It would be very good for my prestige to have my name on an invitation like that.''
>
> ''What makes you think so?'' he said. ''April in Paris is not that good any more. The crowd looked like Seventh Avenue to me. Why don't you get on the New York Infirmary Ball committee? That's got some of the best names in New York.''
>
> ''You know damn well I've tried, but I haven't been asked. There's a lot of nobodies with the April in Paris. But there's a lot of good people, too. And Brownie sees to it that you meet the ones you want.''
>
> ''Maybe we could try taking a table if you want it so much, but if we do it's got to be on the dance floor. I'm not going to let that Philippe put us behind a pillar the way he did the Strandhams last year. But find out first who else will be on the committee, you know. . . .''

And so on. Nowhere in the Kronick's colloquy was there any mention of the names of the beneficiaries of the ball, to say nothing of the worthiness of these charities.

As with most major balls, preparations for the Million Dollar Imperial Persian Gala began almost a year before the actual event. With salutes to Spain, Italy, Mexico, the Netherlands, and Japan already behind her, Ruth Sills's first chore was picking a new theme built around a country that was suitably exotic, promotable, and politically palatable, that is, not too controversial. ''We would never do Israel, just as we would never do Egypt or Saudi Arabia,'' she says. And so she settled on oil-rich Iran which, under the Shah's régime, had somehow managed to remain in the good graces of both Israel and the Arab world. (It has since been at odds with Israel.)

A hotel had to be booked, and the Waldorf on Park Avenue is Mrs. Sills's favorite. "The people there do a fantastic job of working with you, and the chef is fabulous." The only other New York hotels with ballrooms big enough to accommodate the crowd of 1000 or more expected at the Gala were the Hilton and the Americana, both located on the West Side. But the sort of people Mrs. Sills likes to attract would rather be found dead than venture to New York's West Side except to attend the theater. Three other hotels she considers acceptable are the Pierre, the St. Regis, and the Plaza, but their ballrooms can hold only 500 or 600 people at the most.

Although her ball is essentially a one-woman operation, Mrs. Sills spent most of the long, hot summer before the event cajoling some 350 of her society friends to head or serve on the Gala's various committees. To accomplish this, she talked tirelessly on one of her two phones, wrote letters, and lunched with prospects at posh places like La Côte Basque or Le Madrigal.

For the sixth consecutive year, she induced her good royal friends, the Prince Paolo and Princess Marcella Borghese, who maintain residences in Italy and Switzerland, to serve as the Ball's international chairmen. As honorary chairmen, in addition to the three Iranian diplomats mentioned, she coralled New York's governor and mayor. Mrs. Sills had the title of general chairman, but there were also two other categories of chairmen: cochairman (Mrs. Woolworth Donahue) and honorary national chairman (Barbara Hutton). The Washington committee, headed by Charles T. Carey, boasted 16 ambassadors, nine senators, and such people as Perle Mesta. The men's committee listed such names as Yehudi Menuhin, Hugh O'Brian, and John Gavin.

Many of these names were, of course, nothing more than window dressing. In fact, with the exception of the Borgheses, whose name appears on a line of cosmetics, few were eventually to materialize at the ball itself. Yet, like many of the names on other charity ball committees, they served to enhance the prestige of the ball. "If the right people are on your committees, you could give a party every night in the week and get prominent people to come," says New York society publicist Marianne Strong. Other people with no prestige at all were listed on committees simply because they could be counted on to buy or sell a certain number of tickets. Naturally, the greater the number of committee members, the larger the number of likely ticket buyers.

Mrs. Sills also sweet-talked some 50 of her friends into becoming "patrons" of the ball, an honor that called for them to do nothing more than contribute $200 apiece to a fund to pay for the preliminary expenses—telephone calls, postage, clerical assistance, etc.—that arise before the ticket money starts to come in. It takes about $10,000 of such patron money for a major ball like the Gala to get going.

Most committee members are, of course, workers. Some sell raffle books, others badger their friends, their husband's friends, or other contacts for prizes for the raffles and gift bags; still others solicit ads for the ball's souvenir journal which, incidentally, is responsible for the ball's largest single source of income. To hand out these assignments, Mrs. Sills takes a busload of 60 to 70 committee members, principally the new ones, to Waldemar's every February. "This is so they can see the lab and the work the scientists are doing," she says. "We have cocktails and dinner out there and then I tell them what has to be done and hand out worksheets on which they check off what they want to do. Apart from this, I don't have any more committee meetings."

Otherwise, Mrs. Sills, with the aid of Mrs. Molomut, handles all the other details of the ball herself. Charged by some with running a "paper" ball with paper committees, she nonetheless says, "I don't believe in all those committee meetings. It's not like the balls in the smaller towns. There you can spend hours at meetings with your volunteers trying to decide whether to have cookies or crackers or what kind of canapés to have. I find that with the more sophisticated groups, such as ours, it is better to present them with a fait accompli: We are having this, we are doing this, we are charging so much." Mrs. Sills also hired a Meyer Davis orchestra, arranged for decorator Chuck Lawrence to give the Waldorf ballroom the ambience of a Persian tent, and held a series of meetings with banquet manager Steve Kozik and chef Arno Schmidt to plan the Persian-inspired menu.

All major balls are preceded by a series of private parties to drum up and maintain the interest of prospective ball attendees and committee members as well as the society press. "You can have an entire social season in New York on the April in Paris Ball and the Million Dollar Gala alone," says society press agent Gus Ober, who handled the publicity for both.

"For our event, there are at least five large parties running from October to just before the Gala itself in May," says Ruth Sills. "First, there is the party the Iranian consul general gives here for the ambassador. This gives a lot of our committee members a chance to meet the ambassador. This is followed by a party the ambassador gives for our Washington committee.

"Then I give a party in my home for the consul general and, after the Borgheses arrive, someone will give a party for Marcella and someone else will give one for me. Then, the day after the ball, I'll give a small cocktail thing for Marcella and the whole group of people coming with her from Italy and Switzerland on a charter flight. Before the ball, our journal committee chairman will also give a party for his committee and a group of business and labor leaders. Then, the junior committee will be having a party of its own, too."

While this progression of events was taking place, the Persian Gala was not Ruth Sills's sole charity concern. A veritable philanthropic pooh-bah, she was simultaneously also organizing a November ball and an Easter Sunday luncheon-fashion show and cocktail dansant for the New York Heart Association and, as a member of the New York State board of the Easter Seal Society, was involved in that organization's forthcoming telethon. Still, this was a relatively slow year for her. "I now do only three parties a year," she says. "I used to do as many as six." Although she has lost track of the exact number, she estimates she has run at least 100 fund-raising gigs of every conceivable sort, from art auctions and balls to house tours and theater parties, for causes ranging from Korean orphans to the Community Service Society.

On a Saturday two months before the Gala, Mrs. Sills is sitting propped up in her apricot-draped queen-sized bed on the second floor of her duplex apartment addressing *by hand* the invitations to the ball. She has been up since 6 A.M., her customary awakening hour, to begin this labor. She could, of course, have had a professional secretary attend to this chore but that would have cost money, and Mrs. Sills takes pride in seeing that the highest possible percentage of proceeds goes to the charity functions she runs. "Besides," she explains, "my people are more likely to respond to something that is in my handwriting."

Hour after hour she works and before the weekend is over she will have spent 20 hours in addressing 3000 envelopes, enclosing a little personal note with many; meanwhile, Mrs. Molomut will have addressed another 2000. "We know that we can figure on a one-to-five ratio of acceptances," says Mrs. Sills. "That is, to get the attendance of the 1000 or so we want, we have to send out 5000 invitations."

Two weeks later. Just behind Ruth Sills is the annual Easter Seal Society telethon for which she had helped to solicit advance pledges. "I was also there practically the whole weekend to help out and answer phones," she laughs. "I was there Saturday night, went home to get two hours of sleep, and then went back again. It was a very exhausting thing." Yet she says this as though she relished the experience. A week away is the luncheon-fashion show for the New York Heart Association. "I tried to get out of this event, but there wasn't anyone else who could do it, particularly the fashion show." However, this is now firmly under control, with only the rehearsal and the seating arrangements to be taken care of. Meanwhile, she is also involved in the endless details of the Gala, which is only six weeks away.

"There isn't a day when there aren't decisions to make," she tells me in her book-lined study, where her two phones are always ringing. "I work with the decorator; I work with our PR person; I work with our coordinator, Mrs. Molomut, down at the office; I work with the consul general here in New York; I work with the ambassador in Washington." She pauses for a breath. "I have to see that the ads for the journal are coming in, that the raffle books are being sold."

The phone rings. It is the president of a big oil company. After hanging up, she tells me: "He's taking a table and he's taking an ad. Being the head of a big oil company, he wanted to know if everyone listed from Washington on our invitation was coming so that he could arrange to invite some of those people to sit at his table. I also told him of others who were coming. I know that the ambassador of Iran has invited the Ted Kennedys as his *personal* guests. So I know they're probably going to be there. [They weren't.]

"Every morning I call the office at Waldemar to see what reservations have come in, what contributions have come in, how the journal ads and the raffles are going. We have two raffles—a $10 raffle and a deluxe $100 raffle. This week we have a test-tasting of the entire dinner at the Waldorf. We're going to have it for lunch so that we can see if it works out in reality as we planned it. The chef will be there, also the banquet manager, the coordinator, the PR—and me.

"The menu we've planned is really something. We start with caviar, the very best, 200 pounds of it donated by the Romanoff caviar company. Then comes a poached cold bass in dill aspic and a Persian curried melon soup. The main course is also typically Persian—boneless chicken breasts with a pomegranate sauce and walnuts, served with rice pilaff. We'll have Persian bread. The dessert is what we call Omar Khayyam's delight, which is ice cream and cake with a fruit sauce.''

At the tasting, it is felt that the portions of bass are too large. The salad dressing is also pronounced too heavy. Otherwise, there are no changes. ''This year was unusual,'' says Mrs. Sills. ''At some previous Galas, we sometimes had to make many changes. We didn't like the way something tasted or the way it looked. At the Olé, for example—the salute to Spain—the dessert was awful. It was a kind of flan that tasted and looked like an instant Jello pudding. Now, when people are paying a hundred dollars a ticket, you can't give them a dessert like that, even though it is a traditional Spanish dish. It has to be much more spectacular.'' A near-gaffe at her Japanese Gala centered not so much on the character of the dessert as on the name given it on the preliminary menu. An exotic cherry mousse dessert, it was listed as ''Tokyo Bombe.'' Mrs. Sills, horrified, renamed it ''Cherries Flambé on Mt. Fuji Snow.''

Friends marvel at her stamina and at the time and dedication she devotes to her charitable causes from which, incidentally, she accepts not a nickel for her services or expenses. What she lays out for lunches, cocktail parties, taxi rides, telephone calls, and other incidentals involved in her commitment to her charity functions is said to cost her somewhere around $10,000 a year. (By contrast, other charity ball chairladies, ostensibly volunteers, are said to pocket as much as $50,000 a year, mainly through padded expense accounts; and professionals in the charity benefit field charge fees that run as high as $10,000 per function, receiving perhaps an equal amount for expenses.)

What makes a woman like Mrs. Sills, who was born to the blue and educated in the best private schools, work as hard as she does for charity? With her husband a wealthy New York corporation lawyer and her only child grown and married, she has the means and the time to pursue a carefree life of ease.

The initial impetus no doubt stems from the fact that both her parents died while they were relatively young, her father of cancer at the age of 41. Although she does not spell out the details, she herself also admits to a history of malignancies so serious that she was expected to die in 1950. When she miraculously recovered, she vowed to devote her life to helping others. She tried hospital volunteer work for a while, but found it terribly depressing. ''I'd been through too much myself,'' she says, ''and what I saw was much too close to me.'' Moreover, it did not provide her with an outlet for her formidable organizational talents and boundless energies, and left her with too much time on her hands.

''I can't stand playing bridge and I hate to shop,'' she says. ''Going to the hairdresser and those gossipy luncheons are also a waste of time. And attending a movie or a play in the afternoon puts me in a complete mental fog.'' Schooled in all the social amenities, blessed with a gregarious nature and a huge circle of well-heeled friends and acquaintances—and a lover of parties—she soon decided that she could best indulge in good works by organizing charity balls and other functions. Her special interest in Waldemar was kindled when friends told her that the institute was working on that Holy Grail of cancer research—an "anti-cancer" virus that was supposed to be very effective.

The evening of the Gala. While Mrs. Sills is in a Waldorf Towers suite at the customary private pre-ball cocktail party for the diplomats, committee chairmen, and other V.I.P.s, the other guests are arriving and milling around in the reception areas adjacent to the ballroom. The men, tuxedoed and tanned, few of them under 45 or 50, exude the self-assurance that usually comes with a big bankroll. Most have the jaded, bored look of those who have attended more charity balls than they care to remember. The women, only slightly younger, also sport sybaritic tans and are carefully coiffed, bejeweled and begowned in an assortment of chiffons, beads, and feathers.

They drink from three well-stocked bars, and feast from an elaborate Persian buffet that includes such exotica as quail eggs, sea urchins, baby octopus, lamb and fish kebob, and roast peacock. In the main mirrored reception hall, they eye such boutique offerings as a $12,000 Piaget lady's gold and diamond watch and, where the Persian bazaar has been set up, wedding mirrors, ivory miniatures, necklaces, and other native handicrafts. But the main preoccupation of most of the ball-goers, particularly the women, as they parade around, seems to be looking at each other, and solemnly, carefully scrutinizing one another's clothes. None seem to be having as much fun as a plainly dressed lady dwarf, said to be a Waldemar researcher, who is dashing madly about carrying a closely guarded chart showing the location of the V.I.P. tables.

In a large room off the main foyer, in progress is a Persian rug auction, part of the proceeds of which are to go to the Waldemar Foundation. The auctioneer begins by reminding his audience of 40 to 50 persons that rugs provide "the strongest means for the investment of money." Then, after unfurling a 6-foot by 9-foot example of "the primitive weaver's art" (with a bird of paradise) that he says will sell for $100,000 in three years, he starts the bidding at that price. The audience is silent. Gradually he lowers the price to $80,000, to $60,000, to $30,000. Behind me, a lady nudges her husband, "Maybe it *is* a good investment," but he does not respond. At $24,000 there are still no takers and the rug is removed. Rug after rug is shown at somewhat lower offering prices, until finally one 4-foot by 10-foot forty-year-old Sarouk is offered at $500. But this, too, goes begging. "What's five hundred?" the auctioneer pleads. "You can blow that in three days at the Waldorf."

By the time dinner is announced at nine o'clock (over a loudspeaker), only two prayer rugs, the size of bath mats, have been sold, one for $450, the other for $250. "It's a disgrace!" says the auctioneer. Crestfallen, he turns to his two assistants and in a choked voice tells them: "Take away my beautiful rugs." He sounds as if he is about to cry.

The grand ballroom, festooned with green streamers, with a large red silk chandelier suspended over several prop Iranian columns, does indeed look like a Persian tent. Ten thousand roses, the national flower of Iran, flown in from Holland, also bloom in a garden area in the center of the ballroom and adorn the centerpieces on each table. From the stage, mammoth portraits of the Shah and Empress of Iran stare out at the assemblage.

At Table 26, one of the two reserved by Ruth Sills for 50 of her friends (another 130 of her friends are at other tables), my wife and I are seated between a lady decorator and a middle-aged engineer and his wife. Opposite us is a retired textile consultant who, asking for the native bread, wisecracks, "Please pass the Persian matzoh," as the first course, the caviar, is served.

The chitchat covers children, college, and terrace gardening. Most of our tablemates, it seems, have penthouse terrace gardens. What do you know about the Waldemar Foundation? I ask. Most of our neighbors never heard of it or have only a vague idea as to just what Waldemar does.*

After a welcoming speech by Mrs. Sills, another by Dr. Norman Malomut, who says that Waldemar's anticancer M-P virus is showing encouraging results with a breakthrough expected within a year, and a special five-minute film featuring the Empress, the other dinner courses alternate with intervals of dancing, while Ruth Sills circulates among her friends to make sure everybody is having a good time. People move around the dance floor to tunes like "Stardust" and occasionally to a snappy samba or a polite rock beat. Ambassador Zahedi, tall, dark, and handsome as a movie star, is engaged in earnest conversation with some oil company officials.

About 11 o'clock, the drawings for the deluxe $100 raffle are held. The prizes, the kind that are for people who have everything, include a Persian rug from the Empress of Iran, a luxury vacation for two in Iran, ten pounds of caviar, a 56-carat carved emerald, a month of summer school in Switzerland for two youngsters, and a chinchilla wrap. The latter is won by a man of Medicare age, who is described as the oldest bachelor in town. By the time the drawing ends, close to midnight, people start to leave in droves. There is a scramble for the roses on the tables. On the way out, each departing woman is handed her $100 souvenir gift bag—an attractive Iranian cloth carry-all containing, among other things, several sample products from the Princess Marcella Borghese line, including a linen and leather shoulder bag, two Muriel ladies' cigars, one *Nature Window* basic growing kit with red cabbage and cantaloupe seeds, a Golden Science workbook entitled *How Plants Grow,* three-one-hundredths of an ounce of Matchabelli cologne, a worry bead necklace, a small enamel miniature painting of birds, and an Iranian silk necktie.

As the ballroom empties out, one jaded jet-setter says that the Gala has been fairly typical—no livelier and no duller than other charity balls he has attended. To Ruth Sills, however, the ball has been both a personal and a financial success. Looking intensely weary, she accepts the congratulations of the straggling well-wishers to whom she says that the event has taken in close to $250,000 for Waldemar.

A few days later, she tells me that the proceeds from ticket sales to the 923 attendees amounted to roughly $80,000. Another $45,000 has come in from the sale of merchandise and donations (including a $20,000 gift from the empress),

---

*Actually, even in cancer circles, Waldemar is little known. No nationally known scientists have been affiliated with it for any length of time, and the institution has had no important findings to its credit since its founding in 1947. Even its findings regarding its chief claim to fame—its anticancer virus—have yet to be verified.

$20,000 from the raffle tickets, and $97,000 from ads in the souvenir journal—all making a grand total of $242,000. Against this, there have been expenses of $60,000 (for the cost of the dinner, music, decorations, printing, postage, and other items), leaving $182,000 for Waldemar.

The expenses of $60,000 are only 25 percent of the ball's proceeds—a highly respectable showing and somewhat below average for functions of this sort. An April in Paris Ball once showed expenses of 32 percent, and a tabulation by the New York State attorney general's office showed expenses of some 15 charity balls to range from 18 percent to 80 percent. Although that office has no hard and fast rules as to how much of a charity function's proceeds should go for expenses, it becomes unhappy and may take action when expenses go beyond 50 percent. Some years ago, it found that one group had actually managed to roll up expenses in excess of 100 percent the year of its first—and, it goes without saying, last—charity ball. The attorney general also dissolved another charity which had spent $40,500, or 85 percent, of the $47,000 it had raised for its ball.

The $182,000 netted by the Million Dollar Gala, however, added to that raised by the previous galas in the series, had so far brought Waldemar a total of $700,000. This figure was still short of the million-dollar goal implicit in the Gala's name, and so the Galas are expected to go on and on, probably even after the goal is reached, certainly as long as Ruth Sills can draw a breath of life. Already, she is making plans for the next Gala and is bubbling over with enthusiasm for a movie premiere-supper dance she is planning for Heart.

And after all, why not? There were people at the Iranian Gala who had even had fun. What if all that many knew about Waldemar was that it was a tax-deductible cause? Some people had even had their names and pictures in a big, splashy story in *The New York Times,* which said that the event "should settle once and for all the question of whether the big charity party is alive and kicking."

Postscript three months later: Ruth Sills has been in the hospital three times since the Gala, twice because of some new growths she had developed. "Dr. Molomut of Waldemar thought it was time for me to take his anticancer virus," she says. But she had hesitated. "Who knows if the virus might not trigger something else?" she asks. "Much more has to be done with it before we can make any cure claims."

One year later: Ruth Sills has put on another Gala, and then abruptly ended her association with Waldemar. "Frankly, I didn't see they were getting anywhere with the virus," she says. "I began to think that it wasn't all that much."

Since then: Ruth Sills's last Gala has turned out to be Waldemar's final one as well. In 1977—the foundation, unable to meet its financial obligations, according to Waldemar's president, sold its two-story $1.5 million building and 10-acre site in Woodbury, Long Island, and moved to smaller quarters in nearby Westbury. Dr. Molomut was no longer there, and the staff, I was told, had shrunk from a peak of 50 to only five. Whenever I phoned Waldemar in its new home, the only people who responded were a receptionist or a handyman—when the phone was answered at all. The annual reports, repeatedly promised, have never come. And we all know what's happened to the Shah.

PART V

PLANNING, PLEDGES, AND PRESSURES

Chapter 22

Putting It All Together:
The Fund-raising Campaign

Scott, blond and blue-eyed, is bright and active. He can recite ABC's, count and say the "Pledge of Allegiance." Plays cowboys and Indians (the Indians always lose). Says he uses crutches "because I'm paralyzed." When he grows up, Scott wants to be a policeman, school principal, pilot, artist, fireman or Superman.

—March of Dimes publicity handout

Why did the tomato blush? Because it saw the salad dressing.
What is a chicken after it's five days old? Six days old.
Why did the window squeak? Because it had a pain.
Five-year-old Scott Hafen of Las Vegas, Nevada, the National Foundation-March of Dimes national poster child of the year, was at center stage in Kansas City telling some of his favorite jokes to members of the city's press corps. That day, his schedule also called for appearances at a fund-raising breakfast and luncheon and a visit to a school for handicapped children. Scott himself had been born with spina bifida (open spine), which had left him paralyzed from the waist down, but he could now get around with braces and crutches. As the publicity handout mentioned, he had also been born with myelomeningocele (protrusion of the spinal cord) and hydrocephalus (water on the brain), but both of these conditions had been corrected by surgery. Blond, blue-eyed, and winsome, he was an ideal choice for this tour across the country to promote the March of Dimes' annual January appeal for funds for the prevention and treatment of birth defects.

Obviously, both Scott and his mother, who accompanied him on the tour, had been well prepared for their public appearances, which were carefully scripted in a four-page single-spaced "backgrounder." Also used as a publicity handout, the backgrounder contained vital statistics on all the Hafen family members, and listed not only Scott's favorite jokes but also his favorite foods, pastimes, talents, toys, songs, girl friends, and television programs; it even furnished ready-made quotes for mother and son to use in response to questions.

Now Scott was getting off another of his scripted corny riddles. "What did one elevator say to another?" he asked.

"How about a lift?" guessed an interviewer.

Scott grimaced and shook his blond little head. "No, that's not the answer," he said; and he fell silent a monent to let his mother, a March of Dimes volunteer for eleven years, talk about him.

"No hope was the prognosis for Scott when he was born," she said. "The doctors didn't think he would live. If he did, they said he would be a vegetable."

"Oh, Mommy, I'm not a vegetable," Scott piped up.

"No, you're not a vegetable," the mother said, hugging him.

"What about Scott's future?" someone asked.

"The years ahead won't be easy for Scott and he must adjust to his place in life," she answered. "But we realize how much we do have to be thankful for, how many things could have gone wrong and didn't. We're grateful and we'll try to give Scott the support and solidarity of a strong family unit he'll need as time goes by.

"I must say I also don't want pity in any way whatsoever. I want to give hope to other parents with birth defect children. I don't look at Scott as an invalid. He can do anything any other child can do. Maybe not as fast, but he can do it."

"All right, now what about the answer to that elevator riddle?" Scott was finally asked.

"Something's come up," he giggled as he scampered off on his braces and crutches.

Their remarks were word for word from the backgrounder, which also eased the job of the reporters in that they could easily have written their stories without even attending the press conference. "The selling of the kid!" sighed one as he left the room.

Kansas City was the twenty-second stop on the poster child's five-week, 25-city, 15,000-mile coast-to-coast tour. The week before, mother and son had gone through much the same routine in Chicago, where Scott, among other things, had been photographed with Pizza Pete and John Cardinal Cody. And now his next stop would be Washington for that most prestigious of all publicity coups—a White House meeting with the First Lady of the Land. The ceremony would appear on the major TV networks, and some 600 newspapers would also run photos and stories of the event, further serving to remind a large segment of the public of the fact that some 250,000 children are stricken each year in the United States with birth defects and of what the March of Dimes is doing about this.

"What is a chicken after it's five days old?" a UPI story had young Scott asking the First Lady. When she indicated she didn't know, he responded, "Six days old." (The room reportedly rocked with laughter.)

A traditional ornament, if not necessity, of most health-agency campaigns is a national poster child (never a poster *adult*). Cerebral Palsy, Muscular Dystrophy, Cystic Fibrosis, Epilepsy, and the Easter Seal Campaign—all these and others have one. The tradition started in 1942 when a 4-year-old named Gerry King, appearing for the March of Dimes, became the charity world's first poster child. The National Association for Retarded Citizens scored another philanthropic "first" several years ago by coming up with poster *twins*—five-year-old Down's syndrome brothers. Selected for their charm, cuteness, and photogenic appeal, the national poster children, like Scott Hafen, are programmed like a computer, invariably photographed with the president or First Lady, and paraded around the country to open up the hearts and, hopefully, the pocket books of the nation.

For publicity purposes, a concomitant of every campaign is also a covey of celebrities, one of whom is usually designated its "national chairman"—a post that requires the celebrity to endure endless press conferences, dinners, and other public appearances. Indeed, no entertainment or sports figure can be said to have arrived unless his or her name has been associated with one cause or another, preferably a disease. When actor Tony Randall is asked why he became involved with the Myasthenia Gravis Foundation, to which he has been dedicated for the last 10 years as its national campaign chairman, he often replies with a deadpan, "My agent told me I needed a disease." To many people, the frenetic Jerry Lewis is "Mr. Muscular Dystrophy," just as Danny Kaye is the personification of UNICEF; and opera star Beverly Sills, the mother of a retarded epileptic son and a congenitally deaf daughter, has been identified as the volunteer leader of the March of Dimes' Mothers March for many years. Others whose names have long been linked to various specific causes include Paul Newman (Environmental Defense Fund), Dustin Hoffman (Civil Liberties Union), and Perry Como (North Shore Animal League). Most often, however, the celebrity serves during the course of just one annual campaign, although his commitment to the cause may extend beyond his period of service. The American Cancer Society usually has *two* campaign chairmen; in a recent year, columnist Ann Landers was "National Crusade Chairman," and actor John Wayne (later to die of cancer) served as "Honorary Crusade Chairman."

A charity can also reap publicity mileage, and the money that goes with it, by the familiar device of inducing a well-known figure to accept an award at a gala luncheon or dinner, which may command as much as $150 or even more per plate. A popular honoree is comedian Bob Hope who was the recipient in one year of both United Cerebral Palsy's "Humanitarian Award" and the Salvation Army's annual Citation of Merit.

Celebrities and kids are only the facade of the highly organized fund drive, one utilizing all of the techniques described in earlier chapters and involving planning and logistics comparable to those in a complex, large-scale military maneuver. The analogy is particularly apt in the case of the American Cancer Society, which incessantly issues pronunciamentos of the "war" on cancer, and uses such designations as "captains" and "colonels" to refer to the more than 2 million volunteers it recruits annually to participate in just its fund-raising "Crusade," the blueprint for which reads much like a battle plan, with duties and lines of responsibility and communication carefully spelled out. The society's basic 62-page *Crusade Guidebook,* part of a ten-pound package of promotional materials and paraphernalia that goes to each of its 58 divisions and nearly 3000 local units, contains organizational charts that would be the envy of the Pentagon— plus detailed timetables delineating who does what when in the pursuit of such targets of the campaign as Residential, Trades & Industry, and so on. (Hefty guidebooks are also available dealing with each of these campaign elements.)

Although the Crusade is conducted predominantly in April, preparations for it begin the previous September, by which time each local Cancer Society has already named its unit Crusade Committee and selected its Crusade chairman and vice-chairman. By the end of September, also enlisted are the chairmen for each subcommittee assigned to a specific phase of the solicitation, such as the already-mentioned Residential and Trades & Industry, plus Independent Business, Clubs and Organizations, Special Gifts, Memorial Gifts, Special Events, and Publicity.

Then begins the recruitment of the volunteers needed for each subcommittee; this is done according to a certain formula that is more or less standard in the philanthropic field. "In setting Crusade assignments," suggests the *Crusade Chairman's Handbook,* "solicitatons' chairmen will find the '5 and 10 rule' the best guide: Only five individual contacts should be assigned to a Special Gifts Crusader, while the Residential and Independent Business solicitor should be assigned no more than ten homes or businesses. In other words—the larger the prospective gift, the more time the Crusader should spend telling the ACS story." Another traditional Crusade requirement is a team captain for every ten Crusaders and, if the size of the community warrants it, a district chairman for every ten captains; and beyond this, even a section chairman (called "colonel" in some units) to supervise ten district chairmen.

Recruiting and then training the vast array of manpower (womanpower, too, of course) needed is not without its difficulties and may take until January or February, sometimes even shortly before April, to complete, particularly for the low-echelon workers. Meanwhile, each committee meets frequently, perfecting its plans, checking its recruitment progress, compiling prospect lists, and assigning teams of Crusaders to the prospects.

Let us look in at the Residential Crusade in Kansas City, Missouri. Its vice-chairman, after having served three or four years in lesser posts, is Mrs. Pat Stevens, a vivacious former school teacher in her thirties, going for her Ph.D. in education at the University of Missouri. She is the mother of two children and the wife of an insurance agent who miraculously survived surgery for a cancer malignancy five years before. Hence, her interest in the Crusade. Serving under her and her chairman are eleven section colonels (one for each of the sections into which the Crusade has divided the Kansas City area) who, through the descending ranks of the hierarchy, are responsible for about half of the 10,000 volunteers involved in the Crusade.

"The colonels were selected by the first of November," says Mrs. Stevens. "Then the chairman and I got the colonels together at a coffee. We explained to them the goals of the Crusade, both from a money-raising and from an educational point of view, and told them how important it was for their Crusaders to *both* let people know how to protect themselves against cancer and to explain why more funds are needed to carry on the work of the society. Then we gave each of the colonels a kit, which had a time schedule for everything that had to be done by them and the workers at each level below them.

"According to the schedule, the colonels were to find their district chairmen by the first of December, and the district chairmen in turn were to find their neighborhood captains by the first of February. And then it was up to the captains to find their workers—the Crusaders—by the first of March, ideally. Actually, things rarely go according to schedule. However, on March 19, there were still some Crusaders, and even some captains, to be appointed. Many people said they couldn't serve because they were too busy or because they were already involved in X, Y, and Z. But we also hear some pretty strange excuses from time to time. Back in January one woman, who was asked to be a worker, said she couldn't do it because she was planning to attend a funeral on April 22!''

Volunteers are those who have worked for the Crusade before or those who agree to work because a friend or neighbor asks them to. But since they were still short of people, Mrs. Stevens suggested trying to fill out the roster by using what is called TR or telephone recruiting—that is, telephone operators, some of them volunteers, but most of them paid, to call lists of people who usually had no previous experience with the Crusade but, in response to a flat request by telephone, might agree to help.

In Wellesley, Massachusetts, an affluent suburb of Boston, Independent Business chairman Gus Williams, a friendly, forceful, conservatively dressed banker in his fifties, had his recruiting problems. ''What happens is that I would call up a guy and ask him if he'd be willing to be a captain,'' said Williams. ''Usually he'd say, 'No, I'd like to but I really don't have the time.' But then you ask him if he'd be a solicitor and he'd usually say yes. After you'd repeated this process with a number of people, you could call up a guy and say, 'Look, I'd like you to be a captain. I've already lined up all your solicitors for you, so you won't have to worry about that.' When you put it to a guy that way, how could he turn you down?''

In any event, by the end of March all is in readiness—or as ready as it will be. All the committees, subcommittees, and teams hold their pre-Crusade meetings, firm up their assignments, and distribute the Crusade materials, long since arrived from national headquarters—volunteers' handbooks, identification cards and badges, collection envelopes, ''Sorry, I missed you'' envelopes, solicitation kits and report forms, perforated sheets of ''thank you'' receipts, plastic sword pins for contributors, roster forms, prospect cards, red cardboard presentation swords (''May be used to knight Cancer Crusaders as they start solicitation activities, or as a prize for outstanding teams or committees''), posters, window stickers, banners, flags, cancer and leukemia leaflets and fact sheets, even cancer prayers for distribution to churches and synagogues.

In March, the unit publicity committees, which previously had been concerned primarily with routine stories and announcements on the appointment of chairmen and committee members and the need for volunteers, begin to move into higher gear. Armed by national headquarters with a *Crusade Press Kit* containing proposed fill-in news and feature stories, fact sheets, fillers, editorials, cartoons, mats, photos, logos of the Crusade ''Sword of Hope,'' and sample ads, the committee members make the rounds of local newspapers and other publications, as well as of the radio and TV stations in their area, with the suggestion that the materials be used just prior to or during April, which is usually proclaimed Cancer Control Month by mayors as well as governors and the president. The units are also asked to work with local religious groups for the promotion of a Cancer Sabbath and Cancer Sunday in April as occasions for offering the special cancer prayers (usually a week before the residential solicitation).

Also available to the committees is a *Crusade Press Guide,* full of proven publicity ideas and suggestions for placing stories and pictures which, like the prepared materials, are aimed at telling of the society's efforts in research, education, service, and rehabilitation—and of how these activities are helping people in the community. "Run stories about cured cancer patients and how they were saved through early detection, about services to cancer patients by the society, such as visiting nurses, Reach to Recovery, International Association of Laryngectomees, etc.", advises the guide. "In each story the theme of hope for the victims of cancer should be stressed again and again." (Although people must be frightened about the horrors of a disease, the health agencies also well know that, unless they hold out some hope, people will understandably think it pointless to contribute.)

Reinforcing the local efforts during this period are the national stories, telecasts, radio and TV spots, film showings, and celebrity appearances arranged by the American Cancer Society's masterful public relations operation. Much of this publicity, too, radiates a pervasive air of optimism, even intimating that a cure for cancer might be just around the corner—all again on the not unreasonable assumption that donations will be higher if people are exposed to good news about cancer shortly before the Crusader comes knocking at the door. Much of the good news emanates from the famous, brilliantly conceived science writers' seminar that ACS stages every year in late March, always at some plush resort in Florida, California, or Arizona.

The seminar, whose origins go back more than twenty years, is a unique institution, much envied by the other health agencies. In a preseminar memo addressed to reporters invited to attend one seminar, Alan C. Davis, ACS vice-president/science editor, characterized it as a "meeting where scientists doing the most advanced and newsworthy work in cancer and related areas come to talk specifically to journalists about their latest findings." Mentioning reports to be presented on the virus-cancer story ("concentrating on two intriguing angles"), immunotherapy, and on "important advances" in radiotherapy, chemotherapy, and other areas by the leaders in their fields, including three Nobel laureates, Davis went on to say, "The convergence of basic science and clinical application continues, and new evidence of the intimate relationship between progress against cancer and progress in fundamental science will be presented."

With the promise of such exciting revelations, most important newspapers, wire services, magazines, and radio and TV stations send representatives to the seminar. Since their organizations are paying their expenses, the journalists in attendance are under no obligation to file stories, but because they have to justify their trips to their editors and may want to bask in the sun again next year, many do file even daily dispatches—a recent seminar generated some 300 stories. And since editors, in their never-ending quest for circulation, find the spectacular to be more salable than the mundane, the stories are for the most part optimistic, conveying the feeling, at least through their headlines, that something is actually, or is on the verge of, happening. Here are some typical seminar-inspired headlines: "Tide in Cancer Battle Turning" (*Chicago Today*, April 19, 1974); "U.S. Aide Cites Great Progress in Cancer Fight" (*The New York Times*, March 22, 1975); "New Cause for Hope in Fighting Cancer" (*U.S. News & World Report*, May 24, 1976); "New Findings on Lung Cancer Show Early Promise" (*The New York Times*, March 27, 1976); and "New Tactics in Battle Against Cancer; Medical Science is Gaining on One of Mankind's Most Dreaded Diseases" (*U.S. News & World Report*, April 18, 1977).

As can be seen, the headlines do not vary much from year to year and, in fact, are virtually identical to those of twenty years ago. On the cover of *Life* magazine of May 5, 1958, for example, was this blurb: "Fresh Hope on Cancer—Twelve Pages on the Newest Methods to Save You from Malignancies." Inside the magazine, the article bore the title: "Cancer on Brink of Breakthrough." On the cover of *Collier's* of June 8, 1956, was this blurb: "Four Medical Triumphs Just Ahead." Inside, the article talked of the possibility of important breakthroughs occurring in the next five or ten years in the conquest of cancer, as well as in heart disease, mental illness, and the viruses.

This is not to say, of course, that such headlines and accompanying stories may not literally be true—at least, at the time—although what is being reported may not always be *news*. As Alan Davis himself frankly admitted, "People usually have reported their findings before the seminar even if only at a very small meeting of some sort."

There is no doubt that the seminars are of considerable value in giving reporters first-hand exposure to leading cancer researchers, many of whom they may have known before by name only. Yet a growing number of sophisticated science writers are beginning to feel that the news to which they are exposed, even if legitimate, may be overblown and sanguine. Writing in *The New York Times* of April 19, 1977, Harry Schwartz, the medical specialist on the newspaper's editorial board, said: "The society itself published a self-examination noting that a fair number of ideas propounded at [its] seminar five years ago have run into blind alleys. The disillusionment could also be measured by the fact that some of the nation's most important newspapers chose to skip [this year's] meeting after years of eager attendance."

Kickoff! With the spring surfeit of cancer news comes the kickoff to signal the opening of the Crusade. At kickoff breakfasts, kickoff luncheons, kickoff dinners, and other kickoff events across the nation from mid-March to mid-April— their dates are staggered so that the national chairman and other celebrities can appear at as many as possible—the leading volunteers are offered varied programs blending entertainment and inspiration aimed at both amusing them and building their morale. There is a national kickoff, usually coinciding with the White House proclamation and photograph, then the state division kickoffs, and, finally, the unit kickoffs, all of which, of course, provide publicity vehicles to prepare the public for the Crusade.

Kicking off the Illinois campaign one year, national cochairwoman Mrs. Birch Bayh, wife of the U.S. senator from Indiana, delivered the message that she was to repeat at endless press conferences and other meetings during the course of the year: "Cancer does not have to be a death sentence." As proof she told her rapt audience about her own active life since she'd had a cancerous breast removed three years before.*

The kickoff luncheon of the Kansas City unit marked the beginning of the four-day house-to-house appeal for funds in that area. Pat Stevens, in addition to her supervisory duties, solicited the 15 homes on her block in the pleasant, upper-middle-class Country Club district; she found people a little less inclined to give than in the past, but attributed this partly to inflation and partly to the greater number of fund drives. Yet, after the contributions were passed up the chain of command, from the solicitors to the colonels, the Residential Crusade—in terms of monies collected—was one of the best on record, accounting

---

*Mrs. Bayh, known to friends as Marvelous Marvella, died in April 1979.

for $39,000 of the total campaign money turned in by the end of May. Because of the laxity of some of the Crusaders and captains, small sums continued to trickle in until August 31, when the society closes the books for its fiscal year.

In Wellesley, Massachusetts, Gus Williams, the chairman for Independent Business (which goes after firms with less than 25 employees and also professionals, such as physicians, dentists, and lawyers), said that, of the third to half of the 200 small businesses solicited, almost all gave. "It was hard to say no because most of the solicitors were also businessmen who knew the people they were calling on," said Williams. "And so when one of our solicitors would walk into, say, a store, and ask for some money for cancer, the owner would say, 'Sure,' and take five dollars out of the cash register. What we generally got was pretty much five- and ten-dollar stuff, although once in a while we'd get a one-hundred-dollar donation."

In the average community, the Residential Crusade is the backbone of the fund-raising campaign, accounting for at least 25 percent of all Crusade contributions and, together with the Independent Business collections, generally brings in about one-third of the total Crusade income. Another third comes from corporations, foundations, and special gifts, all of which, involving as they do potentially large contributions, call for a somewhat select breed of Crusader.

In selecting Special Gift and Corporation Crusaders, a Cancer Society manual advises Crusade chairmen, "make certain that each has rapport with his prospects or that he has special contacts with them." On this point, a veteran fund raiser once said, "The important thing is to match the solicitor to the prospect, like matching a couple of pearls. If the big banker attends a meeting with an assistant teller who is just out of college and the teller asks him for a contribution, he'll give five dollars. But if the teller keeps his damned mouth shut and leaves the old boy to the important lawyer who plays golf with him every week, we'll get a hundred dollars, not five."

The Cancer Society also suggests that the best solicitors of special gifts ($50, $100, $1000, or more) are board members, industrial executives, past contributors of special gifts, cured cancer patients, persons having a special contact with the prospect, local bankers, generous memorial contributors, wealthy retired persons, attorneys, and community leaders. Although mail is commonly used to solicit gifts, the society urges Crusaders to make contacts face to face, rather than by letter or telephone, presumably taking to heart the classic advice of the legendary fund raiser, James R. Reynolds: "No cow will let down her milk in response to a letter or a telephone call. You have got to sit down beside her and go to work."

Most of the remaining one-third or so of Crusade income is gathered from the Combined Federal Campaign, special events, and memorial gifts. Special events, although now the fastest-growing source of Crusade income, still provide only a relatively small proportion—around 10 percent—of it. Among the more noteworthy of the special events is the National Walter Hagan Golf Championship, held annually in December; the culmination of local tournaments throughout the country, it raises about $1.2 million a year for the society.

Unlike most other Crusade contributions, memorial gifts—those given to honor the memory of loved ones, business colleagues, and others—are also solicited throughout the year, and now account for as much as 25 percent of Crusade income. Virtually every charity has a similar memorial campaign, which

the areas of the country with large concentrations of Lehigh alumni. Detailed calendars were prepared for meetings and other activities, elaborate promotional pieces were printed for use in conjunction with the solicitations, and publicity was issued periodically reporting on the progress of the campaign.

Quietly working behind the scenes, directing every detail of the operation, was Marts & Lundy, a New York firm of professional fund raisers. The firm itself did not solicit any givers, its name did not appear on any of the campaign literature, and most givers, in fact, were unaware of its existence. Its job was to provide the know-how that is essential nowadays for raising large sums of money.

Such firms are a little-known yet important part of the charity establishment. Sooner or later, nearly every college, school, hospital, or other nonprofit organization needing new capital to put up or renovate buildings, furnish or expand its facilities, or buy equipment calls in one of these firms to direct its campaign, or at least counsel it in its fund-raising efforts. The American Association of Fund-Raising Counsel (AAFRC) estimates that its 32 member firms, which collectively have a hand in perhaps 90 percent of the nation's capital fund drives, help their clients raise at least $2 billion a year.

They get high praise from their clients. "Without these professionals, you flub around and can't get organized," said the headmaster of Hotchkiss School in Lakeville, Connecticut, after it had raised over $6 million in the 1960s with the help of Marts & Lundy. "It's less expensive to hire a fund-raising company than to increase your own staff," said an official of Brown University, which had a successful $15 million campaign, also directed by Marts & Lundy.

All of the large, reputable fund-raising firms—other big names in the field include Brakeley, John Price Jones; Will, Folsom and Smith; Ketchum; Tamblyn & Brown; and Oram Associates—work for a flat fee, agreed to in advance, rather than for a percentage of the funds raised; the latter practice, the AAFRC feels, leads to high pressure, hit-and-run solicitation tactics that alienate potential donors. ("It doesn't sit well with someone asked to give a large sum, like $100,000, if he knows that a certain percentage of his contribution, say 10 percent, is going into the pockets of the fund raiser," one college development officer told me.) AAFRC members are also forbidden to guarantee the results of a fund drive.

The fee can range from $1500 to $7000 a month, the exact amount depending on the manpower and time allocated to the project, rather than on the size of the campaign. For this reason, the cost of using a professional fund raiser may be prohibitive if the amount of money to be raised is relatively small; most of the leading firms won't bother with campaigns for less than $250,000 or $350,000, and some will work only on fund drives of $1 million or more. In addition, the client also pays the cost of out-of-pocket expenses, such as printing, postage, travel, clerical help, telephones, and others incidental to the campaign. All in all, however, according to AAFRC studies, the total fees and costs of well-managed capital fund drives rarely exceed 6 or 7 percent of the money raised (3 or 4 percent for the large-dollar drives), with the fund-raising firm's fee alone usually working out to somewhere between 1 and 2 percent. By contrast, as we have already seen, the cost of the mail appeals conducted by the professional direct mail specialists can be as much as 50 percent or more of the total raised, with most of this winding up with the mail entrepreneurs.

How fund raisers typically operate can perhaps best be seen by looking at the way in which the Lehigh campaign was masterminded by Marts & Lundy. Since its founding in 1926 by two fund-raising pioneers, Arnaud C. Marts and George E. Lundy, the firm has organized, directed, and counseled campaigns that have raised over $2.6 billion for a blue-ribbon roster of some 3600 clients—colleges and universities, private secondary schools, hospitals, medical centers, churches, seminaries, and organizations such as the YMCA and YWCA. Today the firm, with a full-time staff of 35 people, including campaign directors, staff writers, and survey makers (called "surveyors"), is ensconced in handsome, dignified wood-paneled offices on New York's Fifth Avenue.

Campaign director on the Lehigh account is Marts & Lundy senior vice-president Tozier Brown, who joined the firm in 1950 after a career as a corporate lawyer. "Actually, the two professions have a great deal in common since fund raising, like law, is essentially a counseling business," he said. "But what attracted me to fund raising is the greater opportunity it gave me to work with people." Affable, conservatively dressed, bespectacled, with iron-gray hair, Brown radiates confidence and enthusiasm.

Every successful campaign, according to Brown, must have four essential ingredients. "First of all, there must be an urgent cause and by that I mean an underlying rationale for the campaign. A strong case must be made explaining why the funds are needed and just what they will accomplish. Without such a case, none of the other essentials can be effective. Second, you need very strong leadership, made up of the kind of people who not only have stature but who are also hard working and dedicated and can surround themselves with peers who are equally hard working and dedicated. Third, you need a very large group of volunteer workers because in our kind of fund raising the only way to raise sizable amounts of money is face to face, not by writing letters or making phone calls. And finally, it goes without saying that you need enough potential givers—what we call a constituency—to make it possible to reach the campaign goal."

Because of its experience in thousands of campaigns, said Brown, Marts & Lundy has a fairly good idea of how realistic a campaign goal may be. The firm knows, for example, how much money a church of 600 members and a $50,000 annual budget could probably raise for a new building ($250,000 to $300,000); or how much a college with 20,000 alumni, situated in a city of 50,000 people, could raise for a new library ($700,000 to $800,000). It knows, too, the amount that a hospital with a constituency of 2000 could expect to raise for a nurses' home ($250,000 to $300,000).

Nonetheless, he said, before undertaking any new campaign, Marts & Lundy insists on making a preliminary survey of the institution's needs, constituency, and potential leadership in order to assess the campaign's chances of success. Confidential in-depth interviews are conducted with from 50 to 75 key people to whom the prospective client would be looking for support, both as contributors and volunteer fund raisers. The firm charges a flat fee of $4500 for such a survey, which usually requires about five or six weeks for the interviews and an additional equal period for the study and analysis of them. "If we find that a large proportion of the key people won't support the campaign, we suggest that it be abandoned or postponed," said Brown.

However, once the decision is made to go ahead, Marts & Lundy assigns to the campaign a full-time resident director—and, if needed, also one or more associate directors—who move into the institution for a period that may range anywhere from six months to two years. In the case of the Lehigh campaign, Brown also assumed the functions of the resident director. At Lehigh, Brown worked closely not only with the school's vice-president for development but also with its trustees, officers, and staff members to forge an effective campaign organization and program.

Specific tactics may differ from campaign to campaign, but some principles have stood the test of time. One is the assumption that most of the money in the average drive will come from relatively few wealthy donors. More specifically, experience has shown that about 90 percent of the money collected in a campaign comes from no more than 10 percent—perhaps as few as 5 percent—of the donors. Countless fund drives have also confirmed the old but reliable "rule of thirds," which holds that about one-third of a campaign's contributions will come from the ten largest gifts, roughly another one-third from the next 100 largest gifts, and the last one-third from all the rest.

Accordingly, in aiming for its goal of $30 million to be raised during the first phase of its $66.8 million campaign, Lehigh's gift table—a chart of the size and number of anticipated gifts—projected $11 million to come from ten gifts—one for $3.5 million, one for $2 million, three for $1 million, and five for $500,000. Proceeding down the table, also projected were ten $250,000 gifts, 20 $100,000 gifts, 50 $50,000 gifts, and so on, incrementally, down to 400 $1200 gifts for a total of 1655 such large gifts, these accounting for $28,380,000, or virtually all of the $30 million goal.

To get gifts of such magnitude, one principle of strategy calls for potential donors of large sums to be appointed to key leadership posts in the campaign, not only because of the need for their contributions but also to give credence to the maxim that giving, like most other things, begins at home: The campaign leaders and other volunteers are expected to be givers if they will be asking others to give—hopefully, at least as much as they do.

The key volunteer leader is, of course, the drive's chairman. Named as head of Lehigh's national campaign committee was Harold S. Mohler '48, the multimillionaire board chairman of the Hershey Food Corporation and president of the university's board of trustees. He and the 15 other well-heeled national committee members were charged with soliciting potential givers deemed capable of giving "leadership gifts" of $50,000 or more. Other prominent alumni were named to "special gifts" committees in each of the 40 campaign areas to concentrate on prospects for contributions from $1200 up to $25,000.

Tozier Brown was heavily involved in the selection of these committees, in scheduling and organizing their meetings, in training the volunteers on how to make productive solicitation calls, in working up the all-important lists of potential donors, and in deciding how and by whom they were to be contacted. Successful fund raising requires that whenever possible prospects be solicited by at least their peers—socially, professionally, or by the projected size of their gift. Consequently, a businessman tabbed as able to give $5000, for example, is called on, ideally, by a friendly businessman-volunteer who himself has given $5000 or more.

For these reasons, before an alumnus is approached for a contribution, it is considered important to find out how much money he might be able and willing to give. At Lehigh, as elsewhere, this is the function of so-called screening committees. Tozier Brown explained how they work. "In Philadelphia, for example, we invited to an evening at the Racquet Club about 30 people whose interest in the university had been demonstrated over a long period of time and who would likely know a lot of their classmates and other alumni—close to 1500—in the area. Then working from lists of these persons, arranged by class, everyone present was asked to indicate: (1) which ones were special prospects, that is, could probably give at least $1200; (2) just what amounts these prospects would probably consider giving; and (3) which people would be effective leaders or workers in the campaign. In rating people, taken into consideration might be the fact that this or that fellow drove a fancy Cadillac, had nine kids and an ex-wife to support, lived in a certain section of town—that sort of thing. If a person was rating a fellow lawyer, he would probably also have a pretty good idea of what he was making. Of course, since no one of the committee members knows all of the people in the area, we might have only two or three evaluations for a particular person. But they often turn out to be surprisingly similar."*

Ratings and other personal data in hand, the volunteers and workers now begin calling on prospects, usually after first sending them promotional brochures and other materials, prepared under the supervision of Brown, as is also a solicitor's guide book, which stresses the importance of seeing prospects in person. "The best way to raise money is to look somebody in the eye and ask him for it," once said Melvin Brewer, the long-time chairman of Marts & Lundy.

"Since we do our homework rather well, what with the screening process and a look at the prospect's previous giving, we find that we don't often miss the mark by asking for too much or too little—in many cases we are right on the nose," said Tozier Brown.

However, fund-raising pros don't necessarily look on the prospect's dollar rating as a fixed star, and use some time-tested methods to indicate they have guessed right. Said one fund raiser, "I tell my clients that if a prospect doesn't grab his desk so hard his knuckles turn white, they haven't asked for enough." Others apply what they call the flinch test. As veteran fund raiser Harold Seymour explained it: "The man says he will give $500. And does he say it without flinching? Then follow up with the soft suggestion: 'For three years?'"

One of the classic fund-raising stories tells of the time Dr. William H. Welch of Johns Hopkins went to see the financier J. Pierpont Morgan for money for the Eye, Nose and Throat Clinic at the famous medical center. As fund-raising consultant Paul Franklin recounted the story in *Fund Raising Management:*

> He sent in his card and Mr. Morgan saw him. After talking awhile, not about financial needs but about medicine in general and the Clinic, Mr. Morgan expressed interest and said he would give him $10,000.
>
> Dr. Welch just nodded pleasantly in thanks and went on talking. After a bit, Mr. Morgan said he would give him $25,000. Dr. Welch nodded thanks again and

---

*Of the 1459 persons rated in the Philadelphia area, four were tabbed as $25,000 gift prospects, 54 as likely givers in the $5000 to $10,000 range, and 240 as potential $1200 givers; 193 were also singled out as possible campaign workers.

continued his talk and Mr. Morgan showed increased interest and said he would give $50,000.

Welch continued talking, whereupon Mr. Morgan rose and said, "I will give you $100,000 but, Dr. Welch, I cannot afford to have you stay any longer!"

The story illustrates another well-known fund-raising maxim. Austin V. McClain, a former Marts & Lundy president, once expressed it this way: "Do not ask for money. Do ask for a better laboratory, a better dormitory, better equipment. . . . Talk about the 'something' not about money." Putting this into practice, the training sessions developed by Tozier Brown instructed solicitors to first talk about Lehigh and the broad objectives of its campaign and then to determine and discuss the prospect's primary field of interest, after which the prospect would be told that he could help with, say, the new chemistry complex being planned. "At this point," said Brown, "you're hoping that the prospect will ask, 'Well, what can I do?' If he asks that question, then the solicitor should say, 'Could you see your way clear to providing an office somewhere in the building?' If this is done right, the prospect will soon ask, 'Well, how much?' And then the solicitor mentions the figure, which he, of course, had in mind from the very beginning. The donor is also told that he can even have a plaque with his or a relative's name on the door."

To stimulate giving by tying donations to such memorials (discussed in detail in Chapter 3), Lehigh put out a catalog of "named gift opportunities," ranging from rooms ($5000 and up), laboratories ($10,000 to $150,000), and locker rooms ($25,000) to auditoriums ($75,000 to $500,000), scholarship funds ($50,000), and faculty chairs ($100,000). For $1 million, one could have a name attached to an entire classroom building; lesser amounts would give donors a plaque on a microscope or other piece of equipment.

However, even with such blandishments and all the arts of persuasion, it was impossible to convince everyone. A favorite reason for refusing to give was the fact that the prospect's child had been turned down by the school's admissions office. "You'd be amazed at how much of this there is," said Brown. "The loyal alumnus thinks that the institution owes his child an education, regardless of whether the child could get through the place." Other prospects, Brown also pointed out, professed disgust with modern student mores, as exemplified by coed dorms, or cited campus unrest as their ostensible reasons for refusing to give.

Alumni, of course, were looked to for the backbone of gift support.* How-

---

*That alumni may be worth their weight in gold—an average of 14 percent of all graduates give to their alma maters—is indicated by the trouble some educational institutions take to track down their "lost" or "unlocated" alumni. Some schools even avail themselves of the services of the Tracers Company of America, a New York-based outfit that specializes in tracking down errant husbands and wives, deadbeats, heirs, and other missing persons. The firm's founder and head, Daniel M. Eisenberg, claims that he has brought back about 200,000 alumni into the fold of their alma maters. He also estimates that there are more than 12 million missing alumni with a giving potential of $50 million, and says that his searches more than pay for themselves in terms of funds eventually raised. "For Marquette University, we found about 2200 alumni," he says. "It cost about $6000, but their immediate return was about $35,000." His biggest search, he also says, was for Columbia University. "I think we found about 11,000 alumni for them. This roughly cost them about $33,000, and their returns were close to $150,000."

ever, parents of students and friends were also solicited and corporations and foundations, in particular, were tapped for many of the larger gifts hoped for.

At the Leadership Conference kicking off the campaign in April, 1972, Hal Mohler announced that nearly $3 million in advance commitments had already been received, and by February, 1974, total commitments had reached slightly less than $22 million, according to a newsletter sent periodically to alumni, friends, and other givers and prospects. Of this total, $8 million had been contributed by various foundations; and more than $3 million had come from major corporations, among them the Aluminum Company of America, Bell Laboratories, Bethlehem Steel, General Motors, IBM, RCA, Western Electric, Westinghouse, and U.S. Steel.

Periodic meetings were also held to discuss the progress of the campaign and to plan new strategies. At a meeting of the national campaign committee in the New York offices of Marts & Lundy in April, 1974, Lehigh president W. Deming Lewis reported briefly on three calls he had recently made, one on a corporation, another on a foundation, and a third on an individual. None had made up their minds yet, said Lewis, but the chances were good that they would give something. Lewis was followed by three Marts & Lundy staffers, who brought the committee up to date on the status of the area campaigns and projected the amounts that would eventually be raised in each area. Finally, each committee member stood up in turn and reported on his progress with the prospects for which he was personally responsible. Said Ed Gott, a former board chairman at U.S. Steel, who had been working with the foundations headquartered in Pittsburgh, "I was again in touch with the Sarah Mellon Scaife people, and they said they would welcome a further proposal from us next year. They are already fully committed for this calendar year."

Several weeks later in Bethlehem, Tozier Brown was conferring behind closed doors with Lehigh's vice-president for development, Paul Franz, Jr., and two members of his staff. "Don't interrupt unless it's someone with $100,000," Franz good-naturedly yelled to his secretary. A tall, youthful man in a blue suit and tie, Franz has been working for the university since his graduation from Lehigh in 1944.

The major item on the agenda was a forthcoming trip to Detroit by Hal Mohler and Deming Lewis to see Lee Iacocca, then president of the Ford Motor Company and long one of America's highest-paid businessmen. (In 1976 his income was $970,000.) Though a Lehigh alumnus, Iacocca had been only a sparse contributor to his alma mater in spite of the fact that he had been an object of continuing cultivation for many years.

"As you may recall," began Brown, "when Hal visited Iacocca last fall, we suggested that he invite Lee to become a member of the board of trustees, with the thought that this would involve him more closely in Lehigh's affairs. Hal reported that Lee was concerned about the time this would take, even though it would have meant just four board meetings a year. Hal and Deming should again stress, as Hal did last fall, that three out of the four meetings are in Bethlehem, which is not far from Allentown, where Lee's family lives. I also feel that one of the biggest points that must also be stressed is that we need his leadership. It would be extremely important to our constituency—alumni, business, and foundations—to have him as a board member."

"Now let's talk about the proposal to the Ford Motor Company itself," said Franz. The proposal was for a $150,000 contribution for the 120-seat auditorium in the new chemistry classroom building.

"I've been over a draft of the proposal and I have the feeling that maybe we didn't emphasize enough the reasons why Ford should make the contribution," said Brown.

"I think that's probably bothering me, too," said Bob Holcombe, the director of development under Franz.

"I know what's wrong," said Brown. "The proposal has a great statement on the overall campaign and a great statement on the need for the chemistry building. But Ford has already told us that their main interest in Lehigh is as a source of trained engineers. So engineering has to be the crux of the proposal. But we somehow have to combine engineering with chemistry."

"Why not?" ventured Franz. "Chemistry has a great bearing on the training of engineers. Every damned engineer has to have some chemistry."

"Well, then let's go back and try it again," said Brown. "The way I now see it would be to first talk about engineering as the main thrust of the proposal and then move into chemistry as an integral part of engineering education. Then we talk about the chemistry building fund."

"Right," said Franz.

"So mainly we're going to have Hal and Deming talk about the link between engineering and chemistry," said Brown. "Then we have them give the proposal to Iacocca and say, 'Lee, won't you turn this over to your experts?' From this they go on to say, 'But what we're trying to do is build a bridge between Ford Motor and Lehigh University. And, of course, Lee, part of this bridge is to have you on the board of trustees.' "

"Beautiful!" said Franz.

The schedule called for the $30 million initial goal of the Lehigh campaign to be reached by the end of 1975. Actually, the goal was exceeded by $1.3 million, with the phonothon, used as the campaign went into its home stretch, contributing about $100,000 of the total raised. During the final year of the campaign, a mail appeal to those who had not yet contributed also brought in nearly $100,000 in pledges of from $300 to $3000, payable over a three-year tax period.* The $31.3 million total also included the largest gift ever received by Lehigh—a $5,250,000 donation from the Fairchild Foundation. The Ford Motor Company also came through as expected: It gave a $100,000 contribution, and Lee Iacocca, who finally did join the board of trustees, personally gave another $50,000 in memory of his father. The 26-member board of trustees, including the newly installed Lee Iacocca, set a good example, by collectively contributing over $2 million. All in all, 6802 gifts were received from alumni, friends,

---

*Pledges, which were also used for some of the larger gifts, can, of course, go bad, usually because of death; but in a large capital campaign like Lehigh's, this "shrinkage" seldom amounts to more than 1 or 2 percent of the total raised. Actually, most pledges are legally enforceable because spending is planned "in consideration of the promise of others." But, as a practical matter, few institutions sue to collect on pledges, for one thing, because of the adverse publicity that would result. However, in a recent celebrated case, a Nassau County, New York, surrogate court ruled that a casual promise for a $5 million gift to the Metropolitan Museum of Art by the late Joan Whitney Payson must be honored by her estate, even though the former owner of the New York Mets baseball team had put nothing in writing.

foundations, and corporations. In the Philadelphia area, giving even exceeded the findings of the screening committee: Some 478 alumni, parents, and friends pledged $780,000. The total cost of the campaign was $820,000, or 2.6 percent of the amount raised.

With the commitments received, Lehigh has since been able to construct its new chemistry building, athletic and convocation center, and Sherman Fairchild Laboratory for solid state studies, renovate other of its laboratories, gymnasiums and campus buildings, and provide for professorships, fellowships, and scholarships. And enjoy a restful hiatus before it prepared, with the help of Marts & Lundy, for phase two of its $66.8 million campaign, which moves into high gear in the early 1980s.

In a new twist in fund raising, several years ago Hamline University, a small, staid liberal arts school in St. Paul, Minnesota, reversed the usual procedure of asking old grads for contributions: Hamline *gave* money to its alumni—$80,000 altogether.

There was a catch, of course. The 104 alumni who received varying amounts of money—in parcels of $100 to $1000—did not get to keep it. Instead, they were asked to invest it in money-making projects and in a year's time return it and any profits to the college. In this way, Hamline hoped to double or triple its investment—which would have been quite an achievement since the school's $14 million endowment was growing only at the rate of 6 percent a year.

As reports from the alumni began to trickle in, Hamline found that it was financing, among other things, a fledgling earthworm farm, a sailboat trip down the 2000-mile length of the Mississippi (the sailor was asking Hamline alumni and others to sponsor him for so much a mile), a hybrid gladiola greenhouse, an inventor working on a new kind of collapsible table, and an assortment of people who said they were buying gold coins, Indian artifacts, commodity futures, and stocks.

The beauty of this arrangement was that the alumni would not only be helping Hamline but helping themselves. For any money the alumni returned to the school was tax deductible even though Hamline's ''gift'' to them was not considered taxable income.

But the noble experiment turned out to be a disaster. As Dean Trampe, the school's director of alumni and community relations, ruefully said: ''We couldn't have launched it at a less propitious time—just before the declining stock market and recession of the mid-1970s. An alumna of ours in Wyoming lost not only all our money but also her cattle ranch. Our inventor got into patent difficulties. Even the earthworm farm went down the tube—the earthworms died. One of the few projects that made money was the boat trip, which brought us about $5000 or $6000. On other projects we broke even. So far, we've gotten back most of our $80,000, and we may get the rest of it eventually. Some people are still holding onto the stocks they bought with the hope that they'll go up again.''

There's a rosy side to the story, however. ''The publicity we got on the experiment was priceless,'' said Trampe. ''We had stories in everything from the *Wall Street Journal* to *The New York Times*. As a result, we got contributions from alumni we hadn't heard from in years, and these contributions are still coming in.''

Chapter 24

Why Jewish Fund Raising
Is So Successful

A man and his son were on their way to a Jewish fund-raising dinner. Since the son had never before been to such a dinner, the father was briefing him on what to expect there.

"Now, at some point during the dinner, they're going to call your name," said the father. "When they call your name stand up and say you'll give one hundred dollars."

"What do you mean, they call my name?" said the son.

"They call everybody's name."

"I'll give the hundred dollars anyway, but I don't want them to call my name."

"You have to let them call your name."

"Why?"

"Because if you say you'll give a hundred dollars, the Katz boy will also give a hundred dollars."

One reason Jewish philanthropy is so spectacularly successful is because of its guileful, strong-arm techniques of fund raising, some of them unique to Jewish giving. Indeed, the world of philanthropy is indebted to the Jews for many of its most innovative fund-raising techniques. As already mentioned, it was the Jews who, just before the turn of the century, first successfully solicited a single donation on behalf of a multiplicity of charities—an innovation that was the forerunner of the present-day United Way. It was also a Jewish banker, Jacob Schiff, who personalized Benjamin Franklin's concept of the "matching gift" when he agreed to put up half the money for a particular cause on the condition that the rest of the community contribute the remainder.

Another technique, pioneered by Jewish fund raisers but now also widely used by others, is the organization of a campaign into various business, trade, and occupational sectors. The army of volunteers used in the annual combined campaign of New York's United Jewish Appeal and Federation of Jewish Philanthropies is typically organized into 118 distinct fund-raising committees, each manned by members of a specific trade group or profession who are charged with wringing as much money as they can out of their peers in Advertising, Alcoholic Beverages, Amusements, Brushes and Bristles, Carbonated Beverages, Corsets and Brassieres, Hardware, Insurance (General), Insurance (Life), Jewelry, Ladies Underwear, Law, Meats, Medicine, Mens and Boys Shirts, Pest Control, Real Estate, and so on down through virtually every category of human endeavor. (Of course, there are also other committees concerned with such targets as Women and Special Gifts.)

However, sui generis as a means of raising money is the arm-twisting techniques of "card calling" or, euphemistically, public pledging, invented in the 1930s, and still a uniquely Jewish phenomenon. With this technique, the names of the guests invited to a fund-raising function are read off one by one from a stack of index cards, each card bearing not only the name of the invitee but also a notation of his previous pledges to the organization. Upon hearing his name called, the person stands up and publicly announces his new pledge. Naturally, it behooves him to pledge an amount that makes him stand tall in the eyes of his peers, friends, neighbors, and other members of the assemblage.

During a recent two-month period in the New York metropolitan area, there were no fewer than 231 United Jewish Appeal-Federation fund-raising affairs of this sort, usually dinners or luncheons, but some of them breakfasts and cocktail parties—held in hotels, synagogues, community centers, even private homes. At most card-calling affairs, such as those thrown for a trade or professional group, guests can give whatever they wish. Other functions, however, are carefully graded according to the financial status of the guests, who are drawn from a broad cross-section of the community. The bigger the function, in terms of its fund-raising potential, the more prestigious the hotel in which it is held, and the more illustrious its featured speaker who, for the really top functions, is usually a figure of national or even international importance. At some events, a floor is even set for minimum contributions.

I was invited to attend one such event where every guest (with the exception of me) was expected to pledge at least $10,000. It was a UJA-Federation black-tie "Special Gifts" dinner in the New York Hilton's Grand Ballroom in honor of investment banker William Rosenwald, whose fortune derives from Sears Roebuck & Co., the "family store" headed by his father, Julius Rosenwald (1862-1932), one of philanthropy's most celebrated figures. Fund-raising functions frequently pay tribute to a leading public, philanthropic, or industry figure, this serving a sentimental as well as a practical purpose; it is de rigueur for the guest of honor's friends, suppliers, customers, accountants, bankers, business associates, and sometimes even competitors to attend and stand up and be counted as donors to his favorite cause. Previous fund-raising dinners of that year's campaign had already drawn impressive amounts: More than $750,000 was raised among 100 guests at a Lawyers Division dinner; $1 million at a dinner of the Wall Street-Investment Banking Division attended by 550 guests; $1,175,000 from the 240 clothing industry leaders at a dinner of their group; and $1.5 million from the 450 guests at a Grocers Division dinner. But the dinner honoring William Rosenwald promised to surpass them all.

While sipping a cocktail and munching some chopped liver from the mountainous buffet (kosher, of course) that preceded the actual dinner, the Federation's PR man, Robert Smith (sic), let me in on some secrets of card calling: "First, let me tell you that there's no deception, nothing underhanded about this kind of function. In general, the people here know what they're here for. When they accept the invitation, they know that they're expected to make a contribution and—in the case of this function—one of at least $10,000. Of course, we would like them to pledge much more than this. That's why there's a special art to card calling. Sometimes the names are called in alphabetical order, but usually it's more effective to call some of the biggest givers first and then proceed in descending order before calling on a few other big givers. Of course, we make it our business to learn in advance just how much many of the people at a function plan to give, and our experience has shown that calling on the big givers first tends to get the smaller givers to raise the pledges they originally had in mind.

"So does calling a series of names on the basis of their personal or business relationships. Let's say, for example, that some of your friends or business competitors are prepared to pledge about $50,000, and we would like to get you to pledge a similar amount, too. We would first call their names, and then immediately after we would call yours. After hearing them announce their $50,000 pledges, it might be difficult for you not to do the same, even though you might have had only something like $20,000 or $30,000 in mind. After all, you want people to think you are at least as well off as your peers. That's what we mean by peer pressure."

By now, the nearly 400 guests, who had paid a relatively modest $25 for a ticket, were seated in the Venetian-style white and gold Grand Ballroom, which was festooned with huge photos showing the institutions and activities supported by the Federation here and the UJA abroad. The ceremonies opened with "The Star Spangled Banner" and the stirring strains of "Hatikvah" ("Hope"), the Israeli anthem, followed by a benediction by Rabbi Fabian Schonfeld of a Kew Gardens temple and one of the few men in the room wearing a yarmulke. Dinner chairman Lawrence Buttenweiser, president of the local Federation, announced the progress of the national fund-raising campaign. After three months, he said, "we have already received 1274 special gifts of $10,000 and over, bringing our total gifts so far to more than $86 million. All in all, we have raised almost $150 million—a noble achievement which brings us more than halfway toward our $280 million goal." Going on to describe the goods and services the campaign funds would provide, Buttenweiser, a member of a prominent banking family, concluded: "We cannot and must not fail Jews in need in Israel and overseas and we cannot and must not fail Jews in need here at home. This issue is truly Jewish survival. For our children . . . and for our children's children . . . and for ourselves."

After dinner and coffee and an emotional address by Major General Aharon Yariv, special assistant to Israel's prime minister (who also greeted the assemblage by telephone from Israel), came the main business of the dinner—the calling of the "roll of honor," another euphemism for card calling. The first to assume this chore was Herbert Tenzer, an attorney and cochairman of the local campaign. Traditionally, both the card caller and the guest of honor must set the pace with generous gifts. Therefore Tenzer, upon stepping up to the microphone, started the ball rolling by pledging $65,000 on behalf of his law firm.

"Now," Tenzer said, "as I call this roll of honor, I'm going to start with our guest of honor, Bill Rosenwald. Bill?"

Rosenwald is as celebrated a figure in philanthropy as was his father before him; the dinner was honoring not only Rosenwald's seventieth birthday but also his four decades as UJA's principal volunteer. During this period, he is said to have had a personal hand in the raising of a quarter of a billion dollars, this, of course, in addition to the tens of millions he himself has given to Jewish causes, perhaps more than any other living person.

Rosenwald, from the center of the dais, now announced that he and various members of his family were pledging a total of $2,003,000. The audience burst into waves of applause as he named the contribution of each and especially his own, which was for $1 million.

"I now have the privilege of calling on our good friend Joe Mazer of Hudson Pulp and Paper," said Tenzer. "Joe?"

"On behalf of my wife and children, I pledge $100,000," said Mazer.

Two pledges, also obviously arranged in advance, were then announced for $250,000 and $300,000. These were followed by lesser, though still considerable, pledges for $40,000, $23,500, $30,000, and $59,000. It was time to boost the pledges again. Tenzer, picking through his pile of cards, called out a name and a pledge of $112,500 was announced for the Simplicity Pattern Co. In an assemblage of this sort, it didn't hurt to have the name of one's company mentioned. When Tenzer called out the name of "one of my favorite accountants," a partner of Touche, Ross & Co. pledged $425,000 for the firm.

Occasionally, Tenzer, while exhorting the guests to give all they could possibly afford, said he would understand if some would have to limit their contributions because of a bad business year. This remonstration, of course, served only to boost contributions. Who would want to admit that they had had a bad year? Many, in fact, announced their pledges in a most casual and cheerful manner, as if giving away huge sums of money meant nothing at all to them. Some announced they were contributing an extra amount of $20,000 or so "in honor of Bill Rosenwald," while many, like Rosenwald, prefaced their pledges by enumerating all the members of their family on whose behalf their contributions were being made.

As he read from the cards strategically arranged in front of him, there were few surprises for Tenzer. Most of the pledges were now in the low or middle five-figure range: $30,000, $41,000, $50,000, and so on. No matter what the amount, it was followed by a round of applause and a hearty "Thank you" from Tenzer. When the amounts had dribbled down to the $20,000 and $15,000 level, industrialist Meshulam Riklis, head of the Rapid-American conglomerate, rose from his position on the dais and announced a pledge for $5 million—yes, $5 million—almost as casually as if he were placing a $10 bet in Las Vegas. His announcement was greeted by a standing ovation, although many in the audience knew that Riklis was going to pledge such an amount. (In fact, Riklis had already pledged this amount—that is, the same $5 million—at a previous dinner; indeed, announcing one's campaign pledge at several functions is a common and acceptable practice.)

At this point, the other campaign cochairman, Alan Tishman, the real estate man, took over the card calling chores.

"Meshulam Riklis' donation is a hard one to follow," he began. "So I'll do it myself with confidence, perseverance, and realism." The audience laughed appreciatively and applauded as Tishman continued: "To Federation, $85,000, and another $85,000 for UJA, for a total of $170,000."

After the customary applause, he went on: "Now maybe Larry Tisch can help out with more."

"For my brother-in-law and myself, $2 million," said Larry Tisch, the balding board chairman of the Loews Corporation, who was then also president of UJA of Greater New York.

The cards of many big givers had been left for Tishman to call and so now there came another wave of pledges for amounts like $400,000, $300,000, $450,000, $250,000. Again, money seemed to have lost all sense of reality, and the atmosphere in the room was much like that at an auction or in a gambling house. One of my tablemates told me that in the fever pitch of excitement he had impulsively increased his pledge from $45,000 to $100,000.

"Whatever you choose to make as your announcement," Tishman reminded the audience, "I would appreciate your filling in the pledge card that is in front of you on the table."

More pledges: $285,000, $175,000, $150,000, $125,000, $275,000. Finally the pledges again dwindled down to the relatively small sums of $80,000, $63,000, $75,000, $50,000, $36,000, $30,000, $22,000. There were perhaps no more than half a dozen pledges for $10,000.

"Is there anyone in the room we've overlooked?" asked Tishman, after his pile of cards had been exhausted. A few guests meekly announced $10,000 pledges.

"Thank you, Herb and Alan for a splendid calling of the cards," said Lawrence Buttenwieser, resuming his place at the podium. "And thank you, ladies and gentlemen, for such a generous response to that call."

Generous indeed! My pocket calculator tallied a total of $19,600,000 in less than an hour—more than many a good-sized national charity may take in during the course of a year.

To learn more about card calling, I went to see its inventor, Joseph Willen, a vigorous, ebullient man in his eighties, who joined the New York Federation of Jewish Philanthropies in 1919 and, for many years after his retirement as its executive vice-president in 1967, used to put in a daily stint as its executive consultant. During his nearly 60 years in Jewish fund raising, Willen, who also devised the technique of organizing a campaign into various business and other specialized sectors, estimates he has been responsible for the raising of more than one billion dollars. Although he does not regard himself as particularly religious in a formal sense, he considers it mildly ironic that both of his children married Gentiles, as did ten of his mother-in-law's eleven grandchildren. "The lone grandchild who married a Jew is the only one who's gotten a divorce," he noted wryly with a twinkle in his eye.

The first attempt at card calling, Willen recalled, took place in the early 1930s at a dinner chaired by the late Lawrence Marx, president of the Cohn Hall Marx Company, a textile firm. "The big problem was to make it socially acceptable to the prestige families, to convince them that it was all right to announce their gifts publicly. After all, Marx was only a cloak-and-suiter, and our feeling was that if the new device was to be effective, the card calling should be done by someone with more status, like an important banker. So we went to Felix Warburg, a partner in Kuhn, Loeb & Co. and a member of one of the 'Our Crowd' families, and said, 'If you do it, it has social status.' And Felix Warburg did it.''

He hit on the idea for card calling, Willen said, through his readings of Thorsten Veblen, the economist and social scientist. ''I was greatly impressed by his theory of conspicuous consumption. Conspicuous consumption is, of course, the mark of wealth. Now, it seemed strange to me that for a person to show off his wealth by conspicuous spending—for example, by buying art collections or fancy homes and cars for himself—was considered good form, whereas conspicuous giving was considered bad form. Not all forms of giving, mind you. The Rockefellers and the Mellons have given away conspicuously; in fact, almost everything they've given to bears their names in blazing lights. Why then couldn't more modest givers also give conspicuously, simply by announcing their gifts in public? What I therefore did was simply transfer the idea of conspicuous consumption to card calling. It was really nothing new. Harvard is an example of card calling all over the place. Why should putting up a building at Harvard with your name on it—what I like to think of as card calling in concrete—be any more respectable than announcing your gift in public?''

In a waggish moment, Willen once offered a college president a novel suggestion for raising money. ''I told him,'' recalled Willen, ''that the big givers could have their names on buildings, gyms, laboratories, libraries—things like that. But what about the little givers of, say, $1000? For them I foresaw a sort of posterity in the john. Every time a student would flush a toilet, a phonograph record would say, 'This flush was made possible by so-and-so.' You know, after I proposed the idea, I was terrified by the thought that the college president would use it.''

How, I wondered, did such public giving square with the Talmudic principle that twice blessed is he who gives in secret? Or with the views of old Maimonides, who ranked anonymous giving among the highest of his eight degrees of charity?

''In spite of Maimonides,'' said Willen, ''anonymous giving, with few exceptions, is poor giving. Less than one percent of the contributions we receive are anonymous. Most anonymous giving is simply a reflection of a man's desire not to give. You must remember, too, that Maimonides ranked highest what was seldom achievable by human beings. That's why he had eight degrees of charity.''

''But you can't deny that card calling is a form of pressure.'' I said.

''If you give, it's an honor; if you don't, it's a form of pressure,'' said Willen. ''I'm reminded of the time Karl Marx was asked the question, 'Since revolution in your judgment is inevitable, why do you bother to organize it?' Marx answered, 'It's always good to nudge the inevitable,' And that's what we do. All we do is nudge the inevitable—the generous impulses that most people tend to keep under control.''

Yet, even people who go along with card calling have ambivalent feelings about it; many will concede that it is a form of social blackmail. ''I don't particularly like it, and no one particularly likes it,'' merchant Andrew Goodman once told an interviewer from *The New York Times*. Goodman, president of New York's fashionable Bergdorf Goodman, is regarded as one of the foremost practitioners of this art of persuasion. "It's awful, but it's the most effective way of raising money," investment banker Gustave L. Levy, another master of this technique, told the same interviewer.

Effective it certainly is. A survey of Jewish givers found 80 percent to feel that people give more if asked to announce their contributions at a fund-raising meeting. Why? Almost half of those polled felt people are shamed into giving more, and one-third said people give more to seek favorable publicity. "You feel like a big shot when you give a big amount," said one person. "Most people give because of pressure socially," said another.

True, no one need attend a function involving card calling if he objects to the practice. There are rare exceptions, of course, like a doctor friend of mine who, without quite knowing what he was in for, inadvertently found himself at such a function back in the days when he was a poor intern making only $20 a week. He therefore blanched when he found people popping up all around him announcing pledges for such then astronomical sums as $200, $300, even $500. The young doctor, with scarcely a dime in the bank, was suddenly considering how best to slip away when his name was suddenly called. Hesitating for a moment, he thought quickly before blurting out, "I pledge one week's salary."

Boon or blackmail, card calling is a way of life in most Jewish communities. So are other forms of social pressure. "The universal objective is to make it impossible for a man not to give," one fund raiser is quoted as saying in Roger Kahn's *The Passionate People*. "You appeal to whatever you think is best: fear, vanity, sympathy. You want results."

In some cities, the Jewish federations publish a book at the end of each campaign. The book lists the names of all contributors together with the amounts they have contributed; in some cities, like Cleveland, it is mailed free to every affiliated member of the Jewish community. "If one is an accountant, a lawyer, or in some other business that depends on referrals, he'd better be listed in the book and look good in it, too, if he wants his business to do well," said one fund raiser. In many Jewish communities, applicants for country club memberships are often evaluated on the basis of their charitable contributions.

A kind of card calling, on an intimate level, is described by James Yaffe in *The American Jews*. It involved Max Fisher of Detroit, one of the nation's biggest givers to Jewish causes. Fisher, a former UJA national campaign chairman, had just been appointed chairman for Detroit's Allied Jewish Appeal, and a Gentile friend of his, who was the new campaign chairman for the nonsectarian Community Chest (now the United Way), came to him for advice. "How do you Jews manage to raise so much money?" asked the friend. Fisher invited him to sit in on the first meeting of the board for the new Jewish campaign:

> A dozen men attended this meeting, all of them wealthy and prominent. Mr. Fisher opened the proceedings by telling them that they themselves, in the past, had always made inadequate contributions to the campaign. How could they expect other Jews to be generous if they didn't lead the way? "I'm naming no names," he said, "but I'm going to start the ball rolling with a pledge of thirty thousand dollars." He then asked the man on his right for his pledge. In a tentative voice this man pledged $3,000. The man said, "Isn't that enough, Max?" Mr. Fisher shook his head wearily. The man said, "How much do you think I should give?" Mr.

Fisher said, "In view of your circumstances, Sam, I think you could afford thirty-five thousand." Sam gulped a little, but he came across with his pledge. When Mr. Fisher continued around the room to the other board members, none of them wasted his time with inadequate pledges. By the end of the meeting the board itself had pledged half of the campaign goal.

Afterward Mr. Fisher went up to his gentile friend and said quietly, "That's how we do it."

Jewish fund raisers, while conceding that the pressures they exert may be rough, justify their strong-arm techniques in any number of ways. They point to the huge sums of money they have raised, much more than they would have through conventional fund-raising techniques. They talk of Israel, and of the long list of hospitals, homes, and other agencies the funds raised have helped to support. "Sure, we've used pressure," readily admits the federation's Robert Smith, "but there's so few of us around that we've got to use pressure in order to raise money. On the other hand, nobody else has done what Jewish philanthropy has done. We've sustained a nation. And we've built a network of institutions the likes of which no other philanthropic organization ever has."

Chapter 25

Sweet Charity Gone Sour:
The Not-So-United Way

On a sunny October day not long ago, a flag was being raised to the top of the flagpole in front of the Old Town Hall of Stamford, Connecticut, a suburban sanctuary of 110,000 souls some 35 miles northeast of New York City. The flag displayed the United Way's symbol—a rainbow of red and orange growing out of a huge helping hand (outstretched palm, as construed by cynics) supporting a stylized tiny human figure with arms upstretched in hopeful supplication*—and the flag-raising was to kick off Stamford's annual six-week fund-raising drive on behalf of a grab bag of local and national charities.

That evening, at the traditional kickoff dinner, the city's captains of commerce and industry, labor chiefs, and other civic leaders were shoulder to shoulder at the head banquet table.

"The main thrust of the campaign this year," declared campaign chairman Francis W. Heintz, "is to emphasize the services provided to the community by the 29 member agencies of the United Way.

"Money is crucial to the provision of services," said Heintz, president of Machlett Laboratories, a manufacturer of electrical parts, "but not enough people are aware of what is really available in Stamford."

Stamford's 29 member agencies—and beneficiaries of the campaign—include local affiliates of such well-known national groups as the Red Cross, Boy Scouts, Girl Scouts, Boys' Clubs of America, YMCA, YWCA, Mental Health Association, USO, Salvation Army, and the Urban League as well as such purely local groups at the Domus Foundation (for wayward boys), what was then known as the West Main Street Community Center (a neighborhood center for the black community), the Stamford-Darien Homemaker Service, St. Joseph's and Stamford Hospitals, and the Jewish Center.

Twice during the evening, the 300 people seated in the big ballroom heard warnings that if United Way didn't do a good job of collecting and disbursing charity money, somebody else might take over. In giving the invocation, the Rev. Gabe Campbell, pastor of the First Congregational Church, suggested that the job of helping people might revert to the churches, the dispensers of most charity up to the mid-1800s. Campbell, a youthful, exuberant man in his forties

---

*The open hand, the rainbow, and the guy being held up by the United Way is the way one fundraiser describes the symbol.

who preaches far-out sermons and is partial to such things as yoga and medita-
tion, is known in Stamford as an advocate of social action and as an outspoken
critic of the United Way, which he regards as a capitalistic tool of the middle
class. (Asked later in private why, in view of this, he was asked to give the
invocation, he said airily, "Oh, I'm kind of the invocation-giver for the business
guys around town!")

In the main speech, William Aramony, the $100,000-a-year national chief
executive of United Way of America, who had flown up from Alexandria,
Virginia, for the occasion, talked energetically of the vital role of the voluntary
sector in our changing times, exhorting, "Unless we take an active role in the
lives of our communities, our communities will fail." A short, stubby man in his
forties who spoke in staccato sentences, he suggested that an alternative to the
kind of charity the United Way was dispensing would be government-run charity. His implication was that government-run charity would be vastly less
desirable.

Earlier, the mayor, who also doubled as chairman of the campaign's public
employees division, paid tribute to the some 1500 volunteers involved in the
campaign. "The money value of their services would add up to over a million
dollars," he said. "And none of us would be here tonight if we weren't convinced that this year's campaign would be the most successful even in
Stamford."

That fall, like every fall, some 2300 communities across the land conducted
similar campaigns with similar high hopes. In some communities, however, the
campaigns may bear such names as United Fund, United Givers, United Appeal,
United Torch, United Crusade, Crusade of Mercy, and Community Chest—
vestiges of their early origins. Whatever their names (the old ones are gradually
being replaced), the campaigns, all of them autonomous, operate today under the
aegis of a national organization known since 1970 as the United Way of America
and have a combined volunteer strength of 20 million. That the hopes of the
campaigns are generally realized is indicated by the fact that they now collectively raise from some 40 million contributors more than $1 billion a year (an
estimated $1.3 billion in 1978, compared to $465 million in 1959) for 37,000*
charities, making the United Way the nation's largest charitable fund raiser—
termed by some "the IBM of the charity business"—and a goal has been set of
tripling its annual intake to $3 billion by 1985.

Does the United Way deserve its preeminence and support? Is the money
collected being raised efficiently and spent wisely to meet community needs,
fulfilling the promise of many local campaigns that a gift to the United Way is
"one gift for all"? Is one to believe those familiar fall TV commercials which
have National Football League stars telling their millions of fans every year
how well their United Way contributions are being spent and that "Thanks to
you, it's working . . . the United Way"? Is the United Way the only way—the
American way?

It would seem almost sacrilegious to ask such questions, for the United Way
has long been perhaps the most sacred of charity's sacred cows, revered by many

*A good part of the 37,000 is made up of the hundreds and thousands of local chapters of the Red
Cross, Boy Scouts, YMCA, and other big national agencies.

almost as a religion for its purported goal aimed at bringing some order into the chaotic world of charity. In many communities, the United Way enjoys a status just below motherhood. But in recent years particularly, there is the growing suspicion that this sacred cow may be giving sour milk. More and more, one hears criticism of the United Way's purpose and performance, relevancy, and methods from those both inside and outside the charity field. One also hears demands for reform, sometimes backed up by lawsuits—a new element in the usually placid world of Sweet Charity. In fact, the stage is now being set for a showdown that may drastically alter the future course of the United Way and some of our most esteemed charitable organizations, as well as change the methods by which millions of Americans give to charity. We'll go into the details of this showdown later. Suffice it to say for now that the battle centers around accusations that the United Way is guilty of racism, elitism, sexism, even coercion, and other unfair competition practices that have enabled it to gain a ruthless domination of the charity marketplace.

How could an organization believed to be doing so much good for decades for so many seemingly worthy agencies have come under such heavy fire in just the past few years? Certainly, no one can quarrel with the basic United Way idea of a single large campaign instead of a multitude of small ones. In principle, the "united" or one-gift-for-all concept (putting "all our begs in one askit," it was waggishly termed) seems a sensible approach to solving one of philanthropy's most perplexing problems: the multiplicity of campaigns and the wasteful duplication of costs and efforts they entail. (United Way officials claim—not quite correctly, as we shall see—that their fund-raising and administrative costs average only about 11 percent of all the monies raised, or far below the 20 percent average of the major health agencies). Moreover, at least in theory, the average citizen, dunned monthly via a payroll deduction, is promised liberation from the nuisance of a barrage of charity appeals; to fend off those that come to his home, available to him now is the convenient rejoinder, "I gave at the office." He is also relieved of the burden of choosing which charities are worthy of his support: The United Way decides for him where and in what proportion his money should go.

United, or federated, giving is also a boon to business which, in fact, has played a crucial role in the success of these drives. For although the concept, as we've mentioned earlier, goes back to the 1800s and flowered into World War I's "war chests" which in turn grew into the famous postwar "Community Chests"—the term was coined in 1919 in Rochester, New York—the present-day United movement did not really catch on until 1949 when the auto industry clutched the concept to its bosom. At that time, Detroit's citizens were being besieged—at home, on the street, and at work—by at least 50 pleas for money every year; and some of the city's employers were receiving as many as three requests a week for in-plant solicitations, corporate gifts, or both. The problem was most acute in the auto industry, the area's biggest employer. The Ford Motor Company, for example, calculated that every charity solicitation in its plant meant a $40,000 loss in time and production, apart from the cost of contributions. In self-defense, the industry, under the leadership of Henry Ford II, created a single all-encompassing annual campaign known as the Torch Drive to raise money for the local Community Chest and for various specified national and state charitable organizations. The drive was a spectacular success and, soon after, the rubber industry brought the idea to Akron, and the steel industry established it in Pittsburgh. With few exceptions, the initiators and chief supporters of the United Way drives have since been local industrialists and businessmen.

More than one-third of the 27 members of the Stamford United Way board in a recent year were senior representatives of such major corporations as Xerox, Olin, Continental Oil, and General Electric Credit. Sitting on the 63-member board of San Francisco's United Bay Area Crusade one year were 26 top officials of such enterprises as Bank of America, Standard Oil, Kaiser Industries, Transamerica, and Southern Pacific. Of the Minneapolis United Way's 57 board members, a majority are from business. At the national level, the names of 23 of the 34 members of the board of the United Way of America read like a Who's Who of Industry, representing as they do the board chairmen or presidents of such Fortune 500 companies as AT&T, Exxon, Monsanto, Prudential Insurance, Honeywell, Bank of America, Johnson & Johnson, Bethlehem Steel, General Motors, IBM, and Sears Roebuck.

In addition to their desire to avoid a gaggle of competing and costly appeals, businessmen have many other reasons—some practical and some altruistic—for supporting the United Way (or, for that matter, any charity drive). They feel it helps maintain their cities' reputation for business involvement in community affairs. They find it a safe, noncontroversial way to make business contacts and build prestige. Active sponsorship of a campaign also enables a company to burnish its public image and thereby help divert attention from other company actions that may be contrary to the public interest. Exxon, for example, whose board chairman sits simultaneously at the head of the United Way of America board, basks in the good will it receives through its support of public television's *Great Performances,* while it also overcharges buyers of its natural gas liquids by $316 million—according to a suit filed by the federal government against the company in late 1978. Other examples are rife of companies turning out shoddy, overpriced products or polluting our air and waters while making a token appearance in the charity arena.

Business also supports charity to help perpetuate the belief that private voluntary efforts can solve community problems and hence stave off continued government inroads into the private sector. "The alternative would be total government services," the November/December 1974 issue of *Society* quoted a United Way of America senior official as freely admitting. "The tax burden would come back, and corporations would end up getting stuck with a bigger piece of the tab," he said. With present voluntary efforts costing far less, it is the view of Roldo Bartimole, a Cleveland muckraking journalist, that "United Way is a well thought-out scheme to avoid corporate taxes. It is a tax dodge, pure and simple."

The "United Way-business nexus," as Robert O. Bothwell, head of the National Committee for Responsive Philanthropy, has put it, is today reflected in the fact that more than 20 cents of every corporate philanthropic dollar goes to local United Ways; these corporate contributions, together with those given individually by corporate employees, also account for about 75 cents of every dollar the United Ways take in. Without this support, there can be no question that the United Way would practically disappear. Yet, it is the very dependence of the United Way on business that underlies the charges levied at the fundraising organization—those mentioned earlier plus these charges: that it is run by conservative boards, with conflicts of interest, who are insensitive or unwilling to adapt to changing community needs; that its budgeting process for allocating funds to its agencies is a charade; that it uses high-pressure tactics to solicit contributions, often with false or misleading claims. Ironically, the basis for many of these charges stem from what is also the United Way's greatest source of strength—the fact that most of the money it collects comes from payroll deductions.

Under the United Way's "Fair Share" giving guidelines, employees with incomes under $1000 a month are generally expected to contribute the equivalent of an hour's pay per month (or six-tenths of 1 percent of their gross earnings), while those above this income level are asked to pledge proportionately more, up to as much as 1.5 or 2 percent. Employees who give their Fair Share are honored with simulated gold or plastic lapel pins or other regalia, and companies are awarded plaques or certificates commemorating their level of achievement in securing maximum employee participation, ideally 100 percent. Naturally, it behooves a company to make as good a showing as possible so that it stands high in the eyes of its corporate colleagues and the community. The 100 percent goal, however, is rarely achieved.

Nonetheless, the zealous pursuit of this goal has led to a common complaint of employees: that they are often pressured to give. Sometimes, as a Chicago executive put it, the pressure rests on an implicit threat: "Cough up or you're going to find a long gap between pay increases." However, just as often the threat is quite explicit. A Detroit auto executive once said: "If you don't pledge your 'Fair Share,' you keep getting reminders until you do, and it can be traumatic getting pitches from successively higher executives each time. You're expected to be a team player, and the implication is pretty clear that if you're not, the rewards—promotions, plum transfers, and merit raises—might just as easily go to someone else who is." A memo from a Pacific Telephone and Telegraph executive to his subordinates went like this:

> We have tried not to push you too hard where UBAC [United Bay Area Crusade] is concerned but, frankly, our results look terrible. We are among the lowest of the low for Fair Share givers. I have bent over backwards seeing that you be given maximum salary treatment. Next year is another year. Will you please sit down and reconsider your pledge?

The arm twisting often starts at the job interview. One Pennsylvania factory worker complained, "When I first applied for my job, the personnel man handed me a form to sign for the United Fund appeal. He said most people did, so I signed. Could I say no?" Ohio Bell Telephone has gone so far as to use computers to get print-outs of its employees who later cancel or reduce their original contribution pledges. The print-outs are sent to the employees' supervisors and union leaders for "review," admitted the Ohio Bell vice-president and general manager who, however, denied that any pressure was intended.

United Way officials themselves invariably deny that they condone any pressure tactics—and it may well be that these tactics are not universal. However, 75 percent of the calls solicited from viewers of a recent television talk show were to ask for advice on how to deal with company pressures to sign United Way pledge forms. Moreover, a United Way annual report once euphemistically referred to the shakedown of new employees as the "new hire program," and set the expansion of these programs as a priority for developing financial support. Pressure tactics are no doubt also encouraged by a United Way "Solicitor's Guide," which instructs solicitors to "see each prospect in private" and to "use pledge cards to avoid cash contributions and single payments." The National Organization for Women's Des Moines chapter reported that Northwestern Bell Telephone employees are called one at a time down to "a little room" where they are met by their supervisor and union steward and told how much to give. The same procedure was reported to prevail in many of the city's other firms: A tire company employee who told his supervisor he did not intend to give to the United Way was sent to his department head to explain why. When he still refused to make a gift, he was sent to see the personnel director. In many cities, some firms, in order to obtain the coveted 100 percent plaque, even turn in the names of noncontributing employees as pledgees, paying the contributions on their behalf.

The pressure, it is also charged, falls hardest on lower-income employees, those who can barely support their own needs, let alone donate any portion of their income to charity and who, in addition, have the greatest job vulnerability. (In many areas, the United Way's suggested "Fair Share" guide for giving applies to workers earning as little as $6,200 a year—a figure equal to the poverty level for a family of four; yet, workers in this income bracket are asked to give $31 a year.) "My supervisor came around today and told me how much I am expected to pledge for the coming year," a Chicago citizen complained to columnist Mike Royko. "I felt like telling him to go to hell because I'm having enough trouble making ends meet and supporting my family. But I can't because he can make me or break me in my job. I had to go along." In Cleveland, one young YMCA employee, under severe financial strain due to his wife's lengthy hospitalization, pledged $12 to his company's drive. His employer demanded $18. When the employee stated he was unable to increase his contribution, he was summarily fired.

Yet, also in Cleveland and at about the same time, it was reported that Horace A. Shepard, the millionaire board chairman of TRW, contributed not a penny of his $212,000-a-year salary to his own company's drive—after telling fellow business elites at a United Way dinner that some stronger methods were needed to get employees to pick up a bigger slice of the United Way tab. "You control their paychecks and jobs, and you can certainly help spread the load," bluntly said Shepard, a member of the United Way goals committee. Although Cleveland Trust, the city's largest bank, carefully recorded its employees' pledges so that they could be checked by management, the bank's $190,000-a-year president, M. Brock Weir, when asked about his personal contribution, said it was "a private matter." When E. Mandell de Windt, while doubling as the $344,000-a-year chairman of the Eaton Corp. and Cleveland's United Way drive, was asked to reveal his personal gift, he was equally closemouthed. Cleveland's Roldo Bartimole chronicled so many similar revelations showing the gifts of wealthy businessmen to be often either nonexistent or proportionately far less than they demanded of their lowest-paid employees that the local United Way finally stopped publishing its annual list of $300-and-over givers.

In Cleveland and elsewhere, corporate treasury contributions, which nation-wide account for about 26 percent (down from a one-time 40 percent) of all United Way collections, in contrast to the nearly 50 percent or so that come from company payroll deductions and other employee contributions,* are also often shrouded in secrecy. "It isn't anybody's goddam business to know how much individual corporations give, and you can quote me on this," San Francisco's United Way then campaign director told the authors of the aforementioned *Society* article.

It is easy to understand why. In one recent year, the San Francisco-based Bankamerica Corporation gave only $250,000, or one-seventh of 1 percent, of its net profits of $164 million to the United Bay Area Crusade—this in contrast to the 5 percent tax-deductible maximum permitted by law. In Des Moines, Firestone Tire and Rubber, after exhorting all of its employees to give their "Fair Share" to meet the company's quota, saw fit to make a corporate contribution of only $20,000, or *one-eightieth* of 1 percent of its net profits, coincidentally, also $164 million. If Firestone subscribed to the same Fair Share standards it set for its own employees, the company should have given $2,460,000, or 1.5 percent of its net profits.

The fact that United Way boards and key committees are dominated by business leaders leads to the criticism of how United Way dollars are spent. The United Way, this charge goes, operates as a sort of Robin Hood in reverse, using the contributions of largely lower-income people, many of them members of minority groups, to support, year after year, established, traditional, safe, uncontroversial agencies that serve a largely white middle-class clientele—agencies that are crowd-pleasers instead of boat-rockers, in the words of one critic. Today the local affiliates of just 15 or so large national charities (such as the Red Cross, YMCA, YWCA, Salvation Army, Boy Scouts, and Girl Scouts) receive about half of all the monies the United Way raises—or as much as they did a decade ago. The Red Cross alone receives nearly 15 percent of the total, more than any other single agency.

On the other hand, small, struggling agencies, particularly those representing black and other minority groups, receive only a tiny fraction of the United Way allocations—only 2 percent according to the leader of one group. The United Way, on the other hand, claims that 13 percent of its dollars are allocated to "predominantly minority-oriented" agencies, basing its estimate on a survey of 37, or 1.6 percent of its 2300 affiliates, and says that $335 million goes into the black community every year through agencies the United Way funds. The fact remains, however, that only $45 million of United Way funding is channeled through *black-run* agencies, as *Forbes* recently pointed out. A black leader in Kansas City bitterly complained that United Way money is going for "things like lily white Boy and Girl Scouts, but not to homes for Negro orphans." In Pittsburgh, blacks mentioned the substantial money going to the scouts, even

---

*Of the remainder, 11 percent comes from government employees, 5 percent from education system employees, 2 percent from nonprofit organization employees, and 6 percent from professional people.

though there were few black scouts in the city. A Tucson citizen voiced a smiliar
complaint in terms of the poor: ''What poor kid can really afford the uniform and
other costs of being a scout?'' Stating that the top ten of the city's 37 United Way
agencies had been the same for the past two decades, she also made the point that
the allocations discriminate against women: ''Two agencies have no female
counterparts—the Marshall Home for Old Men, and Big Brothers. The Boy
Scouts get more than the Girl Scouts, the YMCA more than the YWCA, and the
Boys' Club more than the Girls' Club.'' Sexism is an issue also raised by the
National Organization for Women (NOW), which points out that in Des Moines,
for example, the United Way allocates nearly twice as much per Boy Scout as it
does for each Girl Scout and Campfire Girl. United Way promotional material,
says NOW, also reflects sexist attitudes, one pamphlet used in Des Moines
specifying that the allocation to the Boy Scouts is for ''character building and
citizenship training,'' while that for the Girl Scouts is to prepare ''girls for home
and community responsibilities.''

Action-oriented groups, which feel that charity should also be concerned with
social change and justice, have their difficulties, too. In the San Francisco area,
the Alameda County Welfare Rights Organization was given United Way funding to carry out its mission of helping to organize poor people to press for a
guaranteed income in lieu of welfare. However, when the organization began
making waves, its monthly allocation of $2600 was suddenly terminated. Simi-
larly, in St. Louis, the Legal Aid Society, which provides free legal services to
the poor, was booted out of the United Appeal for allegedly helping black
militants. In Philadelphia and Atlanta, the society was threatened with the loss of
support when the police, charging that the legal group was antipolice, reduced
their contributions to the United Way. The acquiescence of the United Way to
pressure tactics was also seen in Cleveland where teachers' unions cautioned the
organization that it would have fund-raising problems unless it got Legal Aid to
stop its activities on behalf of school desegregation. In Gary, Indiana, a local
affiliate of Planned Parenthood, as a result of Catholic pressures, actually lost its
United Way funding after announcing plans for an abortion clinic, even though
the board of the family planning group specified that the clinic would be supported by patient fees and not by United Way money. The United Way's defense
clearly revealed its consensus ethic: ''The United Way must represent a composite set of values that is acceptable to virtually all citizens of the area.'' In the
Sacramento, California, area, a United Way director equated these values with
dollars: ''You've got to remember you're trying to raise money from the middle
class. If you want to get that money, you've got to hang in there with the middle
class.''

William Aramony, the top salaried official of the United Way of America
(which receives 1 percent of the monies raised by the local United Ways),
justifies its support of the traditional safe agencies in similar terms: ''When we
raise money, our antennae have to be very sensitive because we have to know
just how people are likely to respond. We've got to get the bucks of the broad
spectrum of the public.'' An Atlanta United Way official was more specific.
''Are you going to drop the Boy Scouts with all those former scouts walking the
streets?'' he asked. ''You'd start losing the middle-class support on which you
depend, and then you'd really start screwing things up.'' Other officials

elsewhere also frankly acknowledge that any drastic shift away from the support of the traditional agencies, whose board members—usually white, male, conservative, and upper middle or upper class—often serve simultaneously on United Way boards, might make it more difficult to muster support for the local drives.

The Rev. Arthur B. Smith, white pastor of the all-white First Presbyterian Church of the predominantly black community of East St. Louis, Illinois, says that he was eased out of the local United Fund, which he had served faithfully for ten years—as president and campaign chairman, as well as in various other posts—when he began pushing for greater black involvement in the fund. "Yet, East St. Louis, with a population 80 percent black, has never had more than one black on its United Fund board," says Smith, who also lost a good percentage of his "flock" when he marched for civil rights in the 1960s and tried to encourage blacks to join his church. "I was written off because I wanted more blacks on the board of the fund and support for more black agencies. Of the fund's 20 agencies, only one or two are black. Even the Urban League hasn't been able to get in. One of the problems, I was told, is that blacks can't raise much money on their own. And if a radical black group like ACTION,* whose followers do things like chain themselves to church pillars, got in, even our whites, I was also led to believe, would really raise Cain and their contributions would probably drop off."

To meet such criticism, some United Ways have taken steps since the late 1960s to revamp their structures and reassess their priorities. About a decade ago, Detroit's United Community Services (UCS), for example, which distributes most of the money collected by the city's Torch Drive, the nation's largest, replaced its self-perpetuating board with an assembly, including representatives of the young, the old, and the needy, and rated 47 different kinds of services by priorities "to gear in to the desires and aspirations" of those needing the services—rather than according to what UCS itself wanted. In the mid-1970s, the San Diego United Way set up a $300,000 Demonstration and Development fund to bankroll such groups as an Institute of Chicano Urban Affairs and Operation Samahan, the latter a service for the city's Filipino-American community. In Indianapolis, a city that is 17 percent black, the local 40-member United Way board now includes six blacks. At least one United Way has even funded a gay-rights group.

Other United Ways have instituted similar programs or announced plans to increase their allocations to agencies serving the poor and minority groups. Some of these actions have been sincere and well-intentioned; others have been merely public relations gestures. But whether or not anything is done, no one is left completely satisfied. After the announcement of Detroit's new priorities system, there were some pledge cancellations and vocal protests, one housewife commenting wryly, "If you give money to welfare mothers, there won't be any left for anyone else, because no one's going to give." "Suburbanites claim we tend to favor the inner city, while inner city residents claim we favor the suburbs," said Richard Huegli, executive director of the city's United Community Services. "Middle-class girls have needs, too," complained the executive director of a suburban Girl Scout unit.

However, the roster of member agencies at most United Ways has remained

*Not to be confused with the federal government volunteer agency of the same name.

relatively static in the years since 1968—years that witnessed a rising public sensitivity to the problems of drugs, ethnic minorities, the aged, and so on. During the past decade, the Sacramento, California, United Way, for example, added to its roster such agencies as Suicide Prevention, Aquarian Effort, Meals à la Car, and Concilio—certainly all responses to changing contemporary community needs. A number of agencies, such as the Catholic Ladies Society, Fairhaven Home (for unwed mothers), Guide Dogs for the Blind, and Visiting Nurses, were dropped for one reason or another.

But, according to James Mills, executive director of the local Community Services Council, itself a United Way member, ''The basic package of agencies hasn't changed significantly,'' The big, traditional agencies, Mills said, continued, over the decade, to command the lion's share of the allocation. In 1968, he pointed out, the Red Cross, Boy and Girl Scouts, Family Service Agency, Salvation Army, and YMCA and YWCA got about 40 percent of the total allocated. A decade later, these same groups got about 42 percent of the pie.

In a letter in *The New York Times* of April 14, 1978, John Hanley, national chairman of the United Way of America, boasted that ''over a recent nine-year period, United Way admitted over 1,000 new organizations.'' However, considering the fact that there are 2300 local United Ways, this means that, on the average, only one new organization is admitted each year to every 20 United Ways. And, reflecting the congenitally conservative nature of the United Way boards, proportionate allocations to member agencies also vary slightly from year to year, having changed an average of only one-tenth of 1 percent for 54 principal agencies during a recent three-year period.

Part of the reason lies in the United Way allocations process which, though aimed at ''supporting the most urgent needs of our community''—to quote the directive of a typical local—actually seems to have little to do with that goal. Allocations, for the most part, are usually based on past appropriations, which are supplemented by percentages of any increase in campaign revenues. In the allocations process, a select board committee, made up largely of the United Way's principal officers, first decides how to cut the pie, with so much to go to child-care services, so much to family services, so much to youth and character-building services, and so on. Within the boundaries of these figures, budget panels, composed of sterling citizens, usually ''Fair Share'' givers, generally drawn from the middle-class, managerial ranks of the community, review the requests for funding from member agencies in a specific field of service. (Low-income budget panelists are eschewed because they are felt to lack the background, training, or other credentials needed to judge the requests.) The panels, recruited in the summer or early fall, do most of their work in the winter and spring months following the fund-raising campaign, and the recommendations they make for each agency wend their way up the United Way chain of command for final board approval. (The panel recommendations, however, are seldom turned down.)

To get a better idea of the process, I was allowed to sit in on a couple of budget hearings in Stamford—a rare privilege since all budget meetings and, for that matter, all United Way committee or board meetings are usually closed to the press and public, even to United Way contributors. (Apparently, United Way business is a private affair even though it concerns the community.) The hearings usually take place in May, about two weeks after the budget panels have made the customary on-site visits (called "visitations") to the agencies they have been assigned to review. One of the hearings I attended was for the city's YMCA, the other for a black community center.

First, the YMCA hearing.

In the United Way conference room, the seven members of Panel III (one of four panels) and two United Way officials sat ranged around three sides of a big table, poring over Xerox copies of the 14 detailed budget forms that the YMCA people had been asked to fill out the month before. Horace A. (Red) Smith, the Y's wiry, athletic executive vice-president, and Charles M.D. Reed, of the Y board, walked in, looked wryly at the chairs waiting for them at the deserted side of the table, and sat down.

Preliminary pleasantries involved the Y's new $4 million nine-story concrete building on Washington Boulevard in downtown Stamford. It is a far cry from the 26-foot by 17-foot rented room on Atlantic Street, which was the city's first Y home in 1868.

"Getting settled down?" asked Walter Cortese, a slight, dark, serious-faced broker with Merrill Lynch, Pierce, Fenner & Smith.

"We've had some aggravations," answered Red ruefully. "Water has a way of coming in when it's not supposed to. Then when they come to fix the leaks, it's not raining."

Right off the bat, Andy Moore of Machlett Laboratories, the round, voluble panel chairman, asked why Form 4 was missing. (This form covers the program services offered by an agency.)

Red, with a Huck Finn smile and a duck of the head, said: "I blew this one. I interpreted it wrong . . . after doing it for eighty-eight years!" (Smith, on the verge of retirement, has had Y service spanning some 43 years, 24 with the Stamford Y.) He added that he would send over the completed form soon.

Next, Moore turned to Form 5 (Budget Recapitulation). He mentioned deficits.

Red said, "Till we get the monster running, we'll show deficits!"

"That will come from capital?" asked Moore.

"Yes," said Red. He added: "The fire didn't help us in projecting . . ." (For a year before the move to the new building, the Y operated out of a fire-damaged building.)

Someone asked if the new Y served the inner city. Red said, "We always have and we always will. That's one reason for the new location."

"What about people who can't afford . . .?" asked Gary Ostroke, a tall, young United Way planning associate.

"I'll answer that the same way I always do," interrupted Red. "No one will be denied because of inability to pay, whether they're two years old or eighty years old."

Also discussed were the Y's investment income, staff size, purchases, and other expenditures. After two hours, the panel members had gone through the 14 forms, and had no more questions. Red and Reed gathered up their papers and left the room.

After the door closed behind them, Homer Schoen, budget division chairman said, "They're real charm-boys!" Everybody agreed. Schoen went on: "But we shouldn't let that—and the fact that the Y is traditionally okay—keep us from looking carefully at the request."

Panel chairman Moore grumbled: "That budget was hastily put together. Lots of pieces missing." He added, "But the staff can get the missing information."

"We shouldn't have to hunt around," someone said. "They did the same thing last year, when they also had to fill in the missing pieces."

Talk turned to the deficit—the amount the Y was asking for this year. "I think it will come to $65,000 or even $75,000," said Moore. "But the deficit is normal, even at the higher figure. Stamford will get three or four times more service from this new Y."

Joan Vandervliet, a big, toothy woman, compared this year's budget with the previous year's. "It's an awful big jump from 59 [thousand] to 75," she said.

Schoen insisted on playing the devil's advocate: "I'm not entirely satisfied with what we have here." Still fretting about the missing Form 4, he grumbled, "They should have been able to give us the documentation of their services. They're good guys. But I don't know if we should trust them."

But panel chairman Moore was decisive. "We will get the form," he said. "I see no reason to believe we won't." Then he made a motion that the panel recommend approval of the Y budget to the executive budget committee, from which recommendations go to the United Way board. The motion carried.

In September a couple of the panel members went to tell Red how he had fared. Although Red had actually asked for $65,000, the board had voted to give him $75,000. It said it didn't think some of the expense figures on the forms he had filled out were high enough.

Now, the hearing of the West Main Street Community Center* which is located in a predominantly black part of Stamford.

Seated at one end of the conference table was Ed White, the center's bulky, bearded, black executive director for the past five and one-half years. He was flanked by the center's bookkeeper, Ray James, and finance chairman, Eugene Davis. All three were nervous and apprehensive. For they knew that there would be considerable resistance to their request for at least $150,000, more than twice as much as the $74,000 they had been allotted by the United Way for the current year.

The higher figure, Ed firmly believed, was what it would take to run the new West Main building, foundations for which were then being laid. To build its new center in the black heart of Stamford, West Main had managed to collect $2 million in pledges, largely from local industry, in a capital fund drive begun four years before. However, it was no secret that the United Way had long been at odds with West Main about not only the cost of the expanded programs being planned by the center, but also about the nature of the programs themselves. "Just because they're having a new building, they think they're entitled to go in all new directions," a panel IV member had earlier confided to me. "And they really weren't planned or thought out well, taking into account the needs of the community." The United Way was also concerned about the center's deficit for the two previous years.

*Since renamed the Yerwood Center, after one of its founders.

In his opening statement, White, wearing a blue-checked sport jacket over a white turtleneck, said the new building would be ready for occupancy by the end of the year, and asked the panel to consider the fact that his agency was the only Stamford facility "run by the black community to serve the needs of the black community."

"What puzzles me," said Jack Wycker, looking at the famous Form 4, "is that last year you had $5700 from membership dues, but that you're now only projecting $5500 from dues, while at the same time indicating that you're going to have an increase in members."

"We've recently become rather hard-nosed on membership fees," said White. "But we have to face the fact that most of our users do not have the ability to pay very much, if anything at all. And I'm not sure that we can tell them that they can't come in unless they have a membership."

"For five years you received grants from certain government agencies—in '72, $64,000, in '73, $52,000, and so on," said another panelist. "Has that been terminated?"

"Yes," said White.

"And there's no chance of getting more federal funds?"

White turned to his bookkeeper. "This year the only program we might be funded for was a day-care program, but at the time the application had to be filed we didn't have a facility for it," said Ray James.

Talk turned to the reason for the $13,000 deficit of last year. White explained that the surplus to pay it off had evaporated with rising fuel costs and the need to buy tables and chairs—the latter expenditure occupying some 15 minutes of discussion time.

"You have a substantial increase in your staff compensation costs—from 63,000 to 147,000 [dollars]," said budget committee chairman Homer Schoen. "How many of the new people you're hiring are really needed to run this new facility?"

"Everybody that's listed," said White, patiently explaining their duties.

"Well, if you plan to have an administrative assistant, a program director, a community organizer, and a recreational director, what do you consider your function?" asked Schoen. "Where do you fit into this picture?"

"To see that all the pieces fall into place," said White, who also then spent several minutes to justify his salary increase (to $18,400), after taking a voluntary cut the year before.

When the hearing ended, he said, "I'll be glad to answer any other questions you may have. And I'll get back to you with the exact figures on the cost of the tables and chairs."

All in all, I felt, the West Main people had had a rougher time of it than their counterparts at the YMCA budget hearing.

"To put it vividly and bluntly, things are in quite a mess there," agreed even Manny Randle, a black United Way staffer, in the closed-doors discussion later. "The big question is: Can they handle the rapid expansion they want, or should it be more gradual?" Some panelists said they even doubted if the new building would be open by the end of the year.

At the end of October, seven weeks after the Y learned it had been voted $75,000, Ed White said that the United Way had made only a partial decision on its budget request. "Contrary to custom, they said they weren't going to give us just any set amount, but would give us money as we develop and grow, the amount depending on our growth. What we have to do is ask for money from time to time—as we need it."

Vast as their collective revenues of over $1 billion a year may seem, the practical reality facing United Ways everywhere from Stamford to San Diego is that the monies they take in and disburse are enough to meet only a small portion—an average of about 25 percent—of the budgets of their member agencies. Consequently, nearly all of the agencies have to supplement their United Way allocations by raising money on their own—a practice that seems to contravene the basic United Way concept of a "single campaign annually" to reduce the number of appeals.

Thus, the Girl Scouts and Campfire Girls, for example, depend on the sale of cookies, candies, nuts, and other products for anywhere from one-fourth to one-third of their funds, and the Boy Scouts local councils, which get only 45 percent of their income from United Ways, must conduct special fund drives for the rest. In a typical community like Cleveland, the Ys raise more than twice what the local United Way gives it, Catholic Charities four times as much, and Jewish Federation five times as much. Even the Red Cross, which receives more than 80 percent of its public support from the United Way, has its own special annual campaign in order to get the remaining funds needed to support all of its programs. Going to the other extreme, hospitals receive only a minuscule portion of their operating budgets from United Way contributions, which they do not even really need. "You might say we need the hospitals more than they need us," said one United Way official. "For if we failed to list them among our beneficiary agencies, we'd lose the support of hospital board members, who are usually powers in the community. And we'd also lose the support of people who place a high priority on giving to health causes, just as other people like to know that part of their United Way contribution is going to causes like the scouts and Red Cross."*

The United Ways also fall far short of their utopian idea of encompassing *all* charities, contrary to the false implication of their familiar slogan, "One Gift for All." In some parts of the country—in San Francisco, Los Angeles, and Boston, for example—this boast has been modified with statements to the effect that the United Way represents "90 percent of the voluntary service organizations in the community," but this claim is equally false. In actual fact, United Way member agencies represent only a small fraction of the voluntary agencies in a community—in Stamford, 29 out of 180; in San Diego, 80 of some 500; in the San Francisco Bay Area, only 196—about 14.5 percent—of 1349; and nationwide, the 37,000 agencies for which United Ways claim to provide funding represent only 17 percent of the country's voluntary social-welfare agencies. And

---

*Technically, United Way participating agencies may only raise money on their own for capital funds or to continue certain "traditional" methods of fund raising with which they have long been identified—the Girl Scout cookie sales and the Salvation Army kettle collections, for example. But if the United Way stuck too rigidly to its rules, it would lose some of its best-known agencies—those with proven appeal and crucial to the success of its drives. And so, in practice, many of the member agencies are allowed to conduct their own campaigns as long as they do not take place at the same time as the United Way drives, and, of course, are not in-plant corporate and employee solicitations.

the more than $1 billion a year the United Ways receive accounts for less than 4 percent of total annual U.S. giving to charity.

Marring the federated concept is the fact that many of the large national health charities—the American Cancer Society, American Heart Association, American Lung Association, National Foundation-March of Dimes, among others—have from the outset preferred to remain outside the United Way umbrella, fearing the loss of their identity and arguing, often quite justifiably, that they could raise more money on their own. The American Cancer Society has bluntly stated, "Almost everyone will give more if he gives four times than if he gives once for four causes." Favoring this claim is the obviously greater emotional effectiveness of the health appeals. "Whoever heard of anyone dying of United Way?" said a spokesman for one of the major health agencies. "You die of a specific disease." The American Cancer Society says that most major medical advances have been the result of the "specific disease" approach, rather than the "whole man" one advocated by the United Way, whose local budget committees, according to the health agencies, are not qualified to pass judgment on the monies needed for national research programs. Nonetheless, back in the 1950s, many health-agency local chapters, bowing to community pressures, joined up with the early federated drives to the dismay of their national offices. However, any that do so now face almost certain expulsion by their parent bodies, although a few health agencies permit the early joiners to remain with the United Way under a so-called "grandfather" clause.

To capitalize on the potential of payroll deductions, however, during the past decade a number of the leading health charities have organized combined appeals of their own. As yet, they have not spread beyond more than a dozen communities (among them, San Diego, San Francisco, Omaha, Baltimore, and Hartford) where they are usually called CHAD (for Combined Health Agencies Drive). The ten or so participating agencies in each CHAD may vary somewhat from place to place, but usually include the local chapters of the American Cancer Society, the American Heart Association, the Mental Health Association, the Muscular Dystrophy Association, in addition to Multiple Sclerosis, Cystic Fibrosis, Arthritis, and the Easter Seal Society. The CHADs, however, do not replace the house-to-house or mail campaigns of their member agencies, each of which can also continue to have its own fund-raising special events; the combined drives were set up for the sole purpose of soliciting contributions from commerce and industry and their employees, none of which have ever been important sources of revenues to health agencies.

How can the CHAD concept be justified in view of the long-standing opposition of many of the health agencies to combined drives? For one thing, a large portion of CHAD monies collected goes to the agencies for research, which United Way generally does not fund. The agencies can also spend their research money any way they wish, and CHAD does not limit the funds agencies receive to predetermined budgets, as United Way does its member agencies. Important to the autonomy of the health agencies is also the fact that CHAD donors can designate the agency or agencies to which they wish their gifts to go. Although United Way donors in many areas are told they can do this, too, in practice no member agency generally gets any more than what it would anyway, for designated gifts are usually first applied against its preestablished allocation. (Few people are also aware that agencies are usually asked to refund to the United Way the amount of any check made out to them, rather than to the United Way; all contributions thus usually end up in the same pot.) Many United Ways discourage designations by keeping silent about this option, wherever it is available, and by failing to provide any spaces on their pledge forms for givers to earmark their donations for a specific charity or charities.

The United Way and CHAD are by no means the only examples of combined multiagency appeals. In the some 535 cities with federal employees and military personnel, there is a Combined Federal Campaign, which raises about $85 million a year; the funds are apportioned, according to an agreed-upon formula, among the United Way, designated national health agencies, international service agencies, and the Red Cross (where not included in local United Ways). Some cities also have comparable combined campaigns for municipal employees or such specialized groups as teachers. As we already know, each of the three leading religious groups—Catholic, Protestant, and Jewish—conducts annual federated drives in many cities for the hospitals, schools, and other institutions they sponsor. In a growing number of communities—39 in 23 states, according to the latest available figures—United Arts Funds raise money jointly for the museums, symphonies, nonprofit theater groups, and other cultural ornaments of their areas. For more than a quarter of a century, the nation's perennially financially pressed black colleges have conducted a joint appeal through the United Negro College Fund.

More recently, other black groups, disenchanted with the ways of the United Way, have begun to organize comparable federated drives of their own. So far, the National Black United Fund (NBUF) movement, as it is officially called, is relatively small, with only 16 affiliates which raise about $600,000 annually. Walter Bremond, NBUF executive director, says that his organization, formed in 1971, "grew out of the realization that we as a people had a responsibility to assist in our own development, that we could not forever go to the larger white community and ask for support of programs we believe important to our survival without doing something ourselves."

Operating in Southern California for the past two decades is also Associated In-Group Donors (AID), a group that collects money from employee groups through payroll deductions, and then doles it out to donor-designated charities, including United Way member agencies. For many years the United Way happily took this AID money on behalf of its member agencies, and it even conducted amiable side-by-side joint campaigns with CHAD groups in some cities. Then, in 1976, the United Way did an about-face and, presumably to lose no time in realizing its just-promulgated "Program for the Future" fund-raising goal of $3 billion annually by 1985, decided to do away with, or at least curb, other campaigns competing for the payroll-deduction dollar; obviously, it could only further the goal of tripling its fund-raising capacity at the expense of the other campaigns,

Elements of this strategy were spelled out in an internal memorandum by the American Heart Association (AHA) detailing a July 8–9, 1976, meeting between its three key executives and four United Way of America (UWA) top officials, including its head, William Aramony. The memo, which has neither been retracted by the AHA nor denied by the UWA, referrred to what the UWA euphemistically called "problem solving . . . in order to clear impediments from the path" of the "Program for the Future." More specifically, as examples of problem solving, Aramony was quoted as citing the "reduction-elimination of competitive federation campaigns," such as AID in Los Angeles and the CHADs in the various cities in which they operated. The memo also reported that the UWA's new program was to involve a "new inclusiveness" aimed at embracing such old health holdouts as Heart and Cancer—this hopefully to the detriment of the CHADs. In Aramony's words: "We won't sit back and let Combined Health Agency Drives happen; we anticipate cooperation or confrontation; Heart and Cancer, if cooperative, will solve the CHAD problem." Another aim of the UWA program, according to the AHA memo, was for the United Way to win authorization as the *single* source of payroll deductions from corporations. First targeted for "special attention" were 91 Los Angeles firms, with a total of 477,000 employees, that were to be wooed away from AID and converted to United Way support. "Of these, 24 'critical' firms have been contacted initially and 95 percent have agreed to the conversion," said the memo, which confidently predicted that all 91 would convert.

Whether or not the memo is precisely accurate, it was not long before all of the tactics described were put into effect. In some parts of the country, efforts were made to persuade Heart and Cancer chapters to break away from the CHADs and to throw in their lot with the United Way, with the threat they really had no other alternative if they wanted to have any future in corporate gift and payroll deduction fund raising. In Sacramento, California, the Cancer Society was warned that if it didn't join it would "not be raising any dollars within three years in the business community." Some Heart and Cancer chapters—in Dallas, Los Angeles, Minneapolis, Honolulu, and Cleveland—actually did sign special "sweetheart" contracts with local United Ways, the contracts promising the health agencies a guaranteed income, regardless of the success of the local United Way campaigns.

The Charity War, as some observers called it, moved to the courts as the other federated fund-raising organizations struck back. When AID saw its fund raising drop from $18 million in 1976 to $8.5 million the following year, it filed a law suit against the United Way of America and its Los Angeles affiliate, accusing them of trying to eliminate AID by having "conspired and attempted to monopolize . . . charitable fund-raising in the Greater Los Angeles area." AID also claimed that the United Way had begun an aggressive campaign to steal away its employee donor groups and—incredibly—had refused to allow United Way member agencies to accept $1 million earmarked for them by AID. The Salvation Army even had to return $72,000 already given to it. Introduced as evidence was that damning AHA memo, as well as a United Way letter to agencies such as the Salvation Army and Boy Scouts, warning them not to accept AID funds. Under the terms of a court-ordered settlement in March, 1978, AID was guaranteed the right to fund United Way charities; and the United Way, the apparent loser, was forced to accept the $1 million, but was barred from interfering with AID.

Just what bearing this judgment will have on similar cases is not yet clear, for in July, 1978, a California court rejected a charge by San Francisco's CHAD accusing four local United Ways of unfair competition practices. Meanwhile, still awaiting settlement in the federal courts, at this writing, is a three-year-old lawsuit by the National Black United Fund against the U.S. Civil Service Commission for not allowing it to participate in the United Way-dominated Combined Federal Campaign. In late 1978, the 16 national health charities (including the American Cancer Society and American Heart Association) already participating in the federal campaign also sued the Civil Service Commission, but for quite a different reason—to force the commission to revise the formula whereby the proceeds of the campaign are divided; at present, the United·Way receives the bulk—an average of 70 to 75 percent—of the campaign's receipts, even though most of the designated gifts are for the health charities.

In still another suit, believed to be the first of its kind in the country and one that could have a nationwide impact, the United Black Community Fund of St. Louis recently sued the Chrysler Corporation for $550,000 in punitive damages. The fund alleged in the class action suit that some 900 workers at Chrysler's St. Louis truck plant had designated the UBCF to receive their payroll deductions, but the company refused to permit it because of its commitment to the United Way.

Although the term *antitrust* has not been used in connection with any of these suits because the term has generally been interpreted to apply only to trade or commerce, their antitrust implications are still intriguing. "If even one such suit wins anywhere in the country, that could change the whole ball game," says Patrick Maguire, the bright, young executive director of the San Francisco-based Concerned Citizens for Charity, a new, feisty, nonprofit, Naderesque advocacy group that is one of the nation's most vocal opponents of the United Way. Maguire's organization was one of eight groups, including AID, the National United Black Fund, the National Council for Responsible Philanthropy, and the various CHADs, that recently found themselves on a United Way of America confidential "enemies" list. The criticisms of the groups, the UWA said, "strike at the United Way Agency system."

The system, it is now clear, has not worked out as well as originally envisioned for the many reasons already given. In addition, many people—as much as 40 to 50 percent of the population, according to some polls—have not taken to the idea of payroll deductions for charity, at least the United Way way. "What is the point of having voluntary private agencies handling social problems instead of the government," asked one disgruntled factory worker, "if your employer is going to be as demanding as the tax collector in making you pay for it?"

Nor have the efforts of business made the United Way what could be called a growth industry, in spite of its historic increase in dollar intake. From 1960 through 1976, United Way giving increased at an average rate of only 5.7 percent annually, and for the last seven years of that period, this increase was outpaced by the rate of inflation, this resulting in an actual loss of nearly $65 million in purchasing power for the donations received.

United Way's constantly proclaimed low fund-raising costs are actually considerably higher than many have been led to believe. Although claimed fund-raising and overhead costs may technically come to only about 11 percent of donations—or about half those of most of the big national health agencies—this is because they do not include the outlay of money and materials by United Way member agencies and corporate sponsors who not only supply an army of volunteers but bear such ancillary campaign costs as payroll deduction, accounting, posters, flyers, and so on. Many companies also often pick up the tab for other campaign materials as well as for training volunteers, luncheons, dinners, rallies, and other pump-priming apparati—not a penny of which is ever figured in the United Way's stated fund-raising costs. And one wonders if even these costs are really as low as they are claimed to be. For example, in 1977, United Way of Los Angeles claimed its fund-raising and other "functional" expenses to come to only 12 percent of every dollar it raised, which would lead one to believe that the remaining 88 percent of the contributions would go to the purpose for which they were raised—allocations to the United Way's member agencies. However, securing a copy of the United Way's CT-2 form (from the California attorney general), I found that of the $34.6 million in contributions received that year, only $25.8 million, or 75 percent of every dollar, had been allocated to the member agencies.

One also wonders how well the community's needs are being served when, for example, about 27 percent of the more than $1 billion raised annually by the United Way across the country is allocated for recreational services. Do United Way donors really know this is the way their money is being spent?

Is there a better way than the United Way? Can that original dream of one all-encompassing united or federated drive ever be realized? To some extent it can, and this is how.

Donors should have a much greater say—indeed, complete freedom—in deciding just where their dollars should go. This, of course, is hardly a new concept, but it is one, perhaps, whose time has come. "The idea of letting donors choose just how their dollars are spent has a popular pluralistic ring to it," said John McIlquham in an editorial in the May, 1978, *Fund Raising Management.* "The unique enterprise of American philanthropy has its roots in that kind of donor participation. . . ." Certainly, it is an idea with which the United Way can scarcely disagree in view of its continuing public pronouncements and advocacy of the virtues of a pluralistic society.

Donor choices could be made within the framework of federated giving by offering employees, as sociologist David Horton Smith of Boston College, among others, has suggested, "a plurality of *types* of charitable contributions to make, not just the usual health, welfare, and recreational package that is represented by the United Way. This plurality of choices should not simply be a ruse, breaking the United Way campaign into component service areas for health, welfare, recreation, and so on. The pluralism should instead be a real one, offering real choices of where charitable contributions should go. . . ." The concept, of course, would allow federated groups representing health, the arts, minorities, environment causes, and others to compete for payroll deductions at work places with the United Way, each group soliciting for its own constituency. Provision would also be made for contributions to individual charities.

Some companies are already demonstrating the feasibility of this type of pluralistic fund raising. For example, at the Redondo Beach, California, operation of TRW, a major aerospace company, employees are encouraged to contribute through payroll deductions to any of their favorite charities. More than 400 have so far benefited from this arrangement. The Reliable Life Insurance Company even offers a matching gifts program whereby employees can contribute to almost any IRS-recognized charity. In some places, however, laws may have to be enacted to overturn the practice of allowing only one federated group to participate in a company's or organization's fund-raising drive.

Noting that it was never possible to make the United Way's idea of ''one gift for all'' a reality, the Concerned Citizens for Charity's Patrick Maguire says, ''Today, what *is* possible is 'one campaign for all.' '' Unless the United Way opens its mind to this idea to the extent it now opens its symbolic helping hand, and brings an end to the Charity War, disenchanted donors may stop giving not only to the United Way but to all charity.

PART VI

YOU AND CHARITY

Chapter 26

The Art of Giving Wisely

How difficult it is to be wisely charitable—to do good without multiplying the source of evil. To give alms is nothing unless you give thought also.
—John Ruskin

For what he has he gives. . . . Yet gives he not till judgement guide his bounty.
—Shakespeare

During a recent five-month period, my friend Harry Cantor, the Bay Shore, Long Island, businessman we met in an earlier chapter, found in his mailbox 93 requests for money from 54 different charities. Many of the solicitations were accompanied by such "gift" items as key chains, cookie cutters, gummed name-and-address stickers, greeting cards, ball-point pens, and miniature auto license tags. In addition, several times a week he answered his telephone or his doorbell to find someone—a neighbor or even a stranger—soliciting money for some supposedly worthy cause.

"In January it was the March of Dimes and the cerebral palsy people, and in February the heart and kidney campaigns," recalls Cantor. "Then, in March, the Red Cross, in April Easter Seals and cancer, and, in May, arthritis and multiple sclerosis, with a lot of other diseases and causes in between. I'd like to give to all, but obviously I can't. How do I decide?"

Irving Caesar, the lyricist best known for his "Tea for Two" and "No, No, Nannette," faces a similar dilemma. In his office on New York's Times Square, Caesar, a spry octogenarian whose clothes and speech exude a Broadway flavor, estimated he gets at least 2000 requests for money each year. "I don't want to seem stingy or unsympathetic," he says, "but I find that I can't possibly contribute to everything. I have to draw the line somewhere. But what can I possibly do to weed out the worthy causes from the unworthy causes?"

The quandary of Cantor and Caesar is shared by millions of other Americans who, bombarded by appeals from an increasing and bewildering number of organizations, are faced with the problem of deciding which ones are most deserving of their charity dollars.

Even the rich and super-rich have found that while giving money away is easy, doing it well is difficult. Julius Rosenwald, the Chicago merchant prince, who gave away $60 million during his lifetime, once observed that it is "nearly always easier to make one million dollars honestly than to dispose of it wisely.'' John D. Rockefeller I, who used to receive 50,000 letters a year imploring him for money, said he nearly had a nervous breakdown before he learned how to give money away wisely.

''It was Rockefeller who once told me that you can't give to everything and everybody—you have to learn to say 'no,'" said D. Paul Reed, who for 32 years was executive director of the National Information Bureau. Under the leadership of Reed, one of America's grand old men of philanthropy, the bureau assumed a pioneering role in helping maintain and strengthen philanthropic standards, exposing charity racketeers, and questioning unethical practices of some of the giants of the field.

Giving, Reed suggested to me shortly before his death in 1973, should be approached from two points of view. First, set up a budget for donations, much as you would for food, housing, clothing, and so on. A good time to do this is at the beginning of the year while you are listing tax deductions for charitable contributions you have taken during the previous year. At this time you can decide which charities you really want to support and to what extent.

In your budget, Reed also said, you should set aside a small amount for what he called ''public relations'' or ''goodwill'' giving—in answer to appeals from friends and neighbors with whom you want to maintain harmonious relations. This may call for an occasional contribution of a dollar or two, even though you may be dubious about the specific charity involved. Of course, if you have really serious doubts about the charity or a sizable contribution is requested, you have a problem.

The big question is how to decide which charities are worthy of your largesse—whether they be your own pets, your neighbors' or friends' favorites, or those of strangers knocking at your gates. Unfortunately, it isn't always easy to tell on the basis of certain surface criteria.

Reputation alone, for example, is no surefire guide to wise giving. Many well-known and highly regarded organizations are efficiently run and dedicated to a real social need. Others, however, although equally sincere in purpose, are badly run or directed toward an outmoded or not particularly urgent need; by and large, as we've already seen in these pages, many seem to be mostly concerned with their own self-perpetuation and growth.

It is also often too easy to be swayed by an emotional fund-raising appeal showing, say, a photo of a pitiful overseas orphan. But such appeals may make us tend to overlook the charity's efficiency and quality. As we've also seen, in at least several of the agencies that raise money for the support of children overseas, as little as two-thirds of the money received may actually go for the support of the children; fund-raising and administrative expenses, including the cost of photographs and translations involved in correspondence with the children take the rest. Older people are particularly susceptible to emotional appeals, says Helen O'Rourke, the attractive, knowledgeable and long-time director of the Philanthropic Advisory Service of the Council of Better Business Bureaus, the umbrella group for the nation's Better Business Bureaus. ''They see their own children or grandchildren in the appeals and so they respond,'' she says.

Nor can one always judge the quality of an organization by the big names on its appeals or letterhead. With such names now a dime a dozen, they may no longer mean much. Though many prominent board members do actually serve with genuine responsibility, dedication, and devotion, many others allow themselves to be listed indiscriminately only for publicity or egotistical reasons—or as a well-meaning favor to the people running the charity. Many may even be unaware of the true nature of the enterprise to which they are lending their names.

Generally, however, one does not have much protection against unscrupulous or inefficient charities. Thirty-five states and the District of Columbia and several dozen cities do have laws regulating charities but most of these are ineffectual, unenforceable, or unenforced. "Most states are woefully understaffed for the purpose of regulating charitable solicitations," said a report made for the Filer Commission. About half the state laws place a limit on the amount of money that charities can spend on fund raising. In Florida, for example, the limit is 25 percent of the funds raised; in Pennsylvania and North Carolina, the limit is 35 percent; and in New York and New Jersey, it is 50 percent (much too high in the opinion of many experts) but it applies only to mail solicitations that include unordered merchandise. The other states have no percentage limitations and require only that the charities file some sort of annual report. Some of the local laws are even more ludicrous in their laxity. New York City requires a permit only for solicitations involving a person-to-person contact, such as door-to-door or street solicitations. An official of a large eastern city once complained that any group could get a permit to collect money "for snowblind Eskimos and report that 99 percent of the money raised was used for administrative costs. There would be nothing we could do."

Nor are there any meaningful federal regulations. Contrary to what many believe, the Internal Revenue Service (IRS) does not certify an organization's legitimacy by granting it tax-exempt status. All this means is that the organization has a stated benevolent or educational purpose and is operated on a nonprofit basis. The IRS only requires that organizations granted such status (but not churches and certain other religious groups) file annual financial reports (on Form 990). These, however, are rarely audited; if they are, the IRS is concerned only with the accuracy of the reported figures, not with the efficiency of any expenditures, even though most may go for fund raising, exorbitant salaries, or expense-paid trips to Hawaii.*

The U.S. Postal Service, the only other federal agency concerned with charities, steps in only when it learns of those which may be violating the mail-fraud statutes. But it has only 400 local inspectors to handle the nearly 6000 cases of *all* kinds it is called upon to investigate annually; and so, in spite of the tremendous number of fraudulent charities operating, only 122 were under investigation and 15 were indicted during 1978.

What, then, can you do to size up a charity and judge whether you are giving wisely?

One way of judging is by its fund-raising methods. Here are some time-tested

*At this writing, there are reports of a major revision of the Form 990, indicating that it will call for a breakdown of expenditures into three functional categories: "program services," "fund-raising," and "management and general" (or administrative overhead).

rules formulated by experts like Melvin Van de Workeen, a mild-mannered former math teacher and minister, who succeeded D. Paul Reed as head of the National Information Bureau:

Never give to an organization in response to a telephone call from a stranger—particularly if he claims to be a minister, priest, rabbi, judge, policeman, or fireman, since these are some of the occupational identities assumed by "boiler-room" operators. "Always ask the caller to write instead, enclosing detailed information about his organization," says Van do Workeen. "Any legitimate organization will be willing to send you this information, although few solicit by phone because of the high cost of this type of fund raising."

Have street and door-to-door solicitors show you a complete set of credentials, including the I.D. card from the organization they claim to be representing and the permit required by many municipalities. Be suspicious of any person who approaches you without these items or is unwilling to give or send you written information about his organization.

Don't put money in canisters or those slotted devices displayed in public unless you are satisfied that the organization is worthy of your gift. Even so, this is a dubious collection method for there is no sure way of knowing that your contribution will get to the organization.

Say "no" to any organization that mails you an *unordered* item of merchandise, such as name-and-address stickers, key rings, medallions, neckties, greeting cards, or similar "gifts," along with a request for money. (In fact, don't even acknowledge or return the gift—by law, you are not required to—for it will only be mailed to someone else.)

"We reject this fund-raising approach for two reasons," says Van de Workeen. "For one thing, it is a blatant appeal to your sense of guilt, which you are apt to feel if you don't send money. Secondly, this approach is exorbitantly expensive, often costing more than 90 cents of every dollar contributed." In contrast, the fund-raising and administrative costs of most of the health-agency members of the National Health Council range between 20 and 30 percent of contributions.

Whatever its solicitation methods or reputation, another test is the willingness of the charity to make available a budget and a complete, independently audited (by a certified public accountant) annual financial report to anyone requesting them. Most reputable organizations will provide this information. If it does not or will not answer any reasonable questions regarding its programs and operations, be suspicious of it. In the course of researching this book, I wrote to 100 leading charities asking for copies of their annual reports and for other materials. Thirty-three failed to respond either to my letter or to my follow-up request; they included the National Federation of the Blind, Christian Appalachian Project, Southwest Indian Foundation, American Kidney Fund, Korean Relief, and the Pallottine Fathers. Not surprisingly, all of them, as I later learned from other sources (and as I've already pointed out in my descriptions of many of these organizations), have one characteristic in common: extremely high fund-raising costs.

Not that this would necessarily have been apparent in these organizations' annual reports. For although most leading charities now use uniform accounting procedures, many annual reports often mask fund-raising costs under such euphemisms as education, public information, administration, and program services. Nonetheless, in evaluating a charity, give some weight to the fund-raising and other overhead costs as best as you are able to determine them.

As we've already pointed out, one popular rule of thumb is that in a well-run charity fund-raising costs should not exceed 25 percent of total income; more tolerant experts and a few of the applicable state laws, however, accept 35 percent or even as much as 50 percent, particularly for new organizations and unpopular causes. Other experts prefer to measure costs against public *contributions* (instead of income), and still others favor a ratio including only certain contributions and excluding, for example, legacies and donations through federated fund drives. Whatever the preferred yardstick, however, there is no general agreement on a reasonable or acceptable percentage that would apply to all charities because of the many variables involved in fund-raising and other costs.

It may therefore be meaningless to say that the best-managed charities have costs as low as 10 or 15 percent, or that in the case of campaigns for universities and hospitals, costs may be 4 or 5 percent or less.

An unfortunate consequence of the customary fetish for focusing on costs, or even financial accountability, is that it leads one away from considering what should be the most important question in judging whether or not to contribute to an organization: Is it actually serving any useful purpose? Certainly, there are many organizations with low fund-raising costs, but with completely ineffectual programs that may accomplish very little and, moreover, may duplicate the work of other organizations or government agencies. We have given some guidelines for evaluating these qualitative aspects of health charities in Chapter 9; their performance can also possibly be checked with your doctor, medical specialists, and your local hospital and university medical school, as well as the people the charity has been set up to serve. For charities in other fields, you may solicit the opinions of comparable authorities. Your church, for example, may be able to give you information about the religious or quasi-religious charities that appeal to you for funds. Throughout this book, I have also attempted to evaluate the performance of some of the nation's better-known charities.

What other criteria can be used in evaluating a charity?

Look into how and by whom it is managed and controlled. A good sign is an active, responsible governing board, no voting member of which receives any compensation from the organization, directly or indirectly. The reason is obvious: Paid staffers on the board may be faced with situations that present opportunities for conflicts of interest in matters of hiring and firing, determining salaries, and awarding contracts for services. An almost certain sign of weakness is a one-man board of directors or a board that never changes in composition; another is a board that meets infrequently or with a relatively small number of its members present. In judging whether or not an organization meets its standards, the National Information Bureau (NIB) takes into account the frequency of its board meetings and the attendance at them; the NIB also favors a limitation on the number of years members may serve so that boards can receive an infusion of new blood periodically. Another guide is the stature and reputation of board members, although it has already been mentioned how the presence of big names can sometimes be deceptive.

In order to screen the 2000 requests for money he receives every year, Irving Caesar drafted a form letter which he sends to each of his supplicants.

"I am flattered to have so many organizations, many of them undoubtedly dedicated to noble and humane ministrations, consider me one who not only loves his fellow man, but is financially in a position to help,'' the letter begins. Then, pleading a limited budget, the letter continues: ''Henceforth, tickets for banquets, dances, raffles, and merchandise of every description, calendars, crucifixes, mezzuzas, pencils, pens, seals, socks, ties, tokens, etcetera, will be disregarded unless specifically ordered by us through the mails. Solicitations via telephone will not be recognized and it is hoped that the minimum reception accorded such calls will not be considered as rudeness.''

The letter goes on to say that solicitations will be considered only from those organizations supplying certain information answering questions asked on an attached form: When was the organization formed? Is it registered with state authorities? Is a professional fund raiser helping with the drive and, if so, what percentage of the receipts is he going to get? What are the salaries of the organization's highest-paid employees? What percentage of all contributions are directly spent on the organization's stated objectives? Does the organization receive any government subsidies? How often have the organization's board members or sponsors, as listed on the letterhead, met during the course of the past few years, and how many have attended each meeting?

Asking these questions, however, hasn't done the conscientious Caesar any good. Since 1959, he acknowledges with some chagrin, he has yet to get a single reply.

You may not have the patience, time, or know-how to investigate even a single charity, let alone go to all the trouble Caesar does. Even so, there are still several ways you can learn more about any charities to which you are thinking of contributing or which you may have doubts about.

The Council of Better Business Bureaus (CBBB) maintains files on about 7000 national charitable, educational, religious, fraternal, and other organizations that solicit public support, and publishes a rating list (revised quarterly and costing $1) of the 360 or so most active ones, indicating those that do and those that do not meet its standards.* (Nearly half do not.) Free for the asking are detailed reports (three at any one time) on any charities regularly followed by the CBBB. Send your request with a stamped, self-addressed, business-size envelope (plus $1 if you want the rating list) to your local BBB office or to the Philanthropic Advisory Division, Council of Better Business Bureaus, 1150 17th Street, N.W., Washington, D.C. 20036.

The nonprofit National Information Bureau, 419 Park Avenue South, New York, New York 10016, publishes a rating list (revised monthly) of some 365 national charities (but not religious, fraternal, or political groups), indicating whether or not the organizations meet the NIB's eight basic standards,** which in certain respects are slightly more stringent than the CBBB's. For example, whereas the CBBB gives positive ratings to the Epilepsy Foundation of America,

*The standards cover methods of fund raising, publicity, and advertising; auditing procedures; disclosure of finances; activities and accomplishments; compliance with federal, state, and local laws; and the nature of the organization's management and governing body.

**To meet NIB standards, organizations must have an ''active and responsible board, clear statement of purpose, a program consistent with that purpose, reasonable expenses, ethical promotion and fund-raising, and a detailed annual budget approved by the board.'' The organization must also furnish an annual audit of revenue and expenses, preferably in an annual report.

the National Easter Seal Society, and the Muscular Dystrophy Association, none of these groups meet all of the NIB's standards; also meeting the CBBB's standards are such groups as the American Kidney Fund, American Lung Association, Arthritis Foundation, Girls Clubs of America, Junior Achievement, and United Cerebral Palsy, all of which the NIB has reservations about—that is, it has questions about these charities that make it unable to conclude whether or not they meet NIB standards. (Both the NIB and CBBB, however, agree in their disfavor of the following groups: American Brotherhood for the Blind, AMVETS National Service Foundation, Christian Appalachian Project, Cousteau Society, David Livingstone Missionary Foundation, Disabled American Veterans, Guiding Eyes for the Blind, Help Hospitalized Veterans, Korean Relief, Paralyzed Veterans of America, Salesian Missions, Seeing Eye, Southern Poverty Law Center, Southwest Indian Foundation, and World Changers).

For a free copy of the NIB rating list (called "Wise Giving Guide") and in-depth individual reports (usually three to eight pages in length) on any three charities on the list, write to the National Information Bureau, 419 Park Avenue South, New York, New York 10016. Postcard requests are preferred. A modest contribution to the NIB entitles you to write or phone for an unlimited number of reports at any time.

For information on *local* charities, including chapters of any national charities operating in your area, check with your local Better Business Bureau, United Way, department of welfare, police department, or state attorney general's office. Some states and cities (New York City, Dallas, and Los Angeles, among others) also have special governmental or private agencies (often called "Contributers Information Bureaus"), and are able to advise if any charities are the subject of complaints or are in violation of any laws.

If you are not sure that a charity is a nonprofit, tax-exempt organization (if not, your contribution won't be tax deductible), check with the local office of the Internal Revenue Service. (For other tax considerations in giving, see the following chapter.) The IRS can also make available to you the Form 990s, or financial reports, filed by most charities, but not by church or church-affiliated groups. These, however, may be two or three years old—even older by the time they become available—and so they will not give any information you may want about an organization's current status. (Besides, if you have to resort to the IRS to get information about an organization, have nothing to do with it.)

On the theory that something is better than nothing, you may finally decide to give money for that starving orphan, needy Navajo, or handicapped person anyway, even after you learn that only a small portion of your contribution will reach these people. For if you do not give, you may be troubled by the thought that the people in need may get no help at all.

In making your decision, however, remember: Money unwisely given may perpetuate an unworthy charity or even an outright racket. Money wisely given will not only reach those who need it most, but will also discourage incompetent or unethical charities or encourage them to mend their ways.

But, as the NIB, among others, points out, wise giving is more than avoiding unworthy organizations or contributing to the safe, traditional standbys. It means weighing one organization against another so that there is the best return for every contributed dollar. "Donating $25 to help prevent unwanted pregnancies, for example, may return tens of thousands of dollars to the community in reduced expenditures for schools, social welfare, and so on,'' says Dr. John H. Tanton, a Petoskey, Michigan, eye specialist. "Supporting a home for unwed mothers, on the other hand, will have far less impact on the community in the long run, even though it may produce more immediate results.''

Rather than give to the same old organizations year after year or sit back and screen the new ones that solicit, you can derive more personal satisfaction by seeking out some of your own causes to support. ''You might, perhaps, give to some worthwhile community project, or to an outstanding student who needs financial help, or help purchase a piece of historic land that should be preserved,'' suggests Dr. Tanton. Unhappy with the impersonal, lackadaisical ways of the organizations they contributed to, six Midwestern couples set up a charitable corporation to give anonymously to their small town's needy schoolchildren. If you have at least $5000 to give, you may even consider setting up a trust fund—possibly bearing your name—or contributing to a community foundation, a type of giving mechanism described in Chapter 4.

Finally, if you cannot always give a money gift, consider giving of yourself—your time, thought, skills, or energy. For there are many worthwhile needs that money alone cannot buy. ''How poor is a man who has nothing but money to give,'' someone once observed. ''The simplest act of service has no cash equivalent. It is the rent we pay for our room on earth.''

Chapter 27

The Basics of Taxwise Giving

At the charity ball described in Chapter 21, a Persian rug auction was one of the side attractions. "Ladies and gentlemen, the purchase price of these rugs is completely tax deductible," the auctioneer said as part of his sales pitch. "Every dollar you spend you can take off your income tax because these rugs were flown in from Iran to be sold for charity."

He was wrong. So are the people who think that the cost of the tickets they buy for, say, a theater party is completely tax deductible. Why this is not so we shall learn later in this chapter. We shall also learn that there are ways to contribute to charity that can reduce the cost of a donation considerably—sometimes to very little.

The fact is that the tax deduction is much misunderstood, and few people know how to take full advantage of it in planning and making their charitable contributions. A 1973 survey by the University of Michigan's Survey Research Center for the Commission on Private Philanthropy and Public Needs found that, although givers are generally aware that the deduction benefits them, "even at high income levels the degree of tax sophistication is quite low." Another surprising finding of the survey was that very few people even know how much a deductible charitable contribution reduces their taxes; in fact, in only 12 of the nearly 2000 interviews conducted did people even mention taxes as reasons for changing their patterns of giving. In its other findings, too, the survey found people to be appallingly ignorant of the tax savings possible in connection with charitable giving. For example:

The great bulk of giving is in cash, although many taxpayers could get extra tax benefits by donating appreciated property, such as securities or real estate.

In the small number of cases where the total amount given exceeds the deductibility limit (generally, 50 percent of adjusted gross income), only a few givers carry their contributions over to another year or change the timing of their contributions to reduce their tax payments.

Many people give to nondeductible organizations, thus losing out on tax savings.

All in all, the tax sophistication of even the wealthy seldom goes beyond a general awareness of the advantages of itemizing deductions over using the standard deduction on tax returns.

Tax law is complicated, and regulations are constantly changing. For this reason, it may be well to consult a knowledgeable accountant or tax attorney if you make even moderate contributions to charity. Meanwhile, here are some general guidelines to taxwise giving. As you will see, what you save in taxes will depend not only on how much you give and to whom, but also on the form of your gift and how and when you give it. First, however, let us look at the actual cost of making a contribution at various income levels.

What a Charitable Contribution Really Costs

The key point is that only part of any deductible charitable contribution comes out of your own pocket; the government, in effect, pays the rest by reducing your tax.

The following table shows the out-of-pocket cost of a $100 deductible contribution at various levels of taxable income. The costs would be somewhat different if the taxable income consisted only of "personal service" (formerly "earned") income or included capital gains. The table also does not apply to people who use the standard deduction, now known as the "zero bracket amount."

For corporations with a taxable income of up to $25,000, the after-tax cost of a $100 contribution under the current rules is $83; with a taxable income of up to $50,000, the cost is $80; up to $75,000, it is $70; up to $100,000, it is $60; and over $100,000, it is $54.

The cost of a contribution is even lower when state and local income taxes are also taken into account. These, of course, vary widely.

	A $100 Contribution Costs	
If Taxable Income Is	Married taxpayers filing jointly	Single taxpayers
$ 6,000	$84	$82
8,000	82	81
10,000	82	79
15,000	79	70
20,000	76	66
25,000	68	61
30,000	63	56
40,000	57	51
50,000	51	45
60,000	46	37
70,000	46	37
80,000	46	37
90,000	41	32
100,000	41	32
110,000	36	30*
125,000	36	30
150,000	36	30
200,000	32	30
over 215,400	30	30

*Applies when taxable income is over $108,300.

To Whom Can You Give?

You may deduct only charitable contributions made to certain qualified organizations. (Contributions given directly to needy or worthy individuals are nondeductible.) A case in point: On Long Island not long ago, youngsters representing a Helping Hand Rescue Mission were selling candy door-to-door, alleging that all the proceeds would go to develop a children's camp. The local Better Business Bureau, however, warned cautious callers, "Helping Hands seems to be greasing its own palm," and pointed out that the Mission was not listed as a nonprofit organization and that contributions to it were not tax deductible.

This does not mean that contributions would necessarily have been deductible if the Mission had been a nonprofit organization. There are 20 categories of nonprofit organizations that are exempt from payment of federal income tax under various provisions of the Internal Revenue Code. However, most of those also eligible to *receive* tax deductible contributions fall under Internal Revenue Code Section 501(c) (3), which covers organizations "operated exclusively for charitable, religious, educational, scientific, or literary purposes, or for the prevention of cruelty to children or animals." Such organizations include orphanages and old-age homes, hospitals and schools, libraries, museums and symphony orchestras, churches and synagogues, boys' and girls' clubs, and such organizations as the Red Cross, the Salvation Army, Goodwill Industries, the Ys, the American Cancer Society, American Heart Association, and CARE—in fact, virtually all dealt with in this book. You can also deduct gifts to some organizations that fall under other sections of the Internal Revenue Code, such as volunteer fire companies, veterans' organizations, and certain fraternal lodges or civic associations using the contributions exclusively for charitable purposes. *Not* generally tax deductible are contributions to chambers of commerce, nonprofit business leagues, social clubs, labor unions, and foreign charities (except certain Canadian ones); however, contributions to some of these may be deducted as a business expense.

Any organization should be able and willing to tell you if contributions to it are tax deductible. If in doubt, check with your local Internal Revenue Service (IRS) office or consult the IRS's *Cumulative List of Organizations* (Publication 78), which contains the names of all organizations to which contributions are deductible. Although this annual publication is updated with quarterly supplements, it may be a good idea to get an opinion from the IRS, too, for organizations have a way of suddenly losing their tax-exempt status for a variety of reasons.

For example, an organization may lose its tax-exempt status if it devotes a *substantial* part of its activities to "attempting to influence" legislation or to participating in political campaigns. In a celebrated case of this sort, the IRS, in 1966, withdrew the tax exemption of the Sierra Club when the conservation group paid for a series of full-page newspaper ads arguing for the defeat of legislation authorizing the construction of two power dams on the Colorado River. Similarly, a court decision once ruled against Billy James Hargis' right-wing Christian Echoes National Ministry for attempting to mold public opinion on various legislative and political issues through its newsletters, pamphlets, and other materials.

In 1971 the IRS revoked the tax exemption of Bob Jones University of Greenville, South Carolina, for quite another reason: the fundamentalist religious institution's policy of refusing admission to black students. (In 1979, however, a U.S. district court overturned the ruling, the court stating that the school's policy, which forbade interracial dating and marriage, was an integral part of its religious practice.) And in 1975, the IRS ruled that it would no longer permit tax deductions for contributions to the Bach Mai Hospital Emergency Relief Fund, an organization based in Cambridge, Massachusetts, that was collecting money to finance the rebuilding and resupplying of the hospital, which is located near Hanoi. The reason given was that "there is no indication that the Government of the Democratic Republic of Vietnam has yielded or will yield any of its sovereign power so as to enable the fund to exercise any effective control" over the uses of its aid. (Several weeks later, the IRS said it was reconsidering its ruling, and decreed that contributions to Bach Mai would be regarded as deductible until further notice.)

How Much Are You Allowed to Contribute?

Generally, contributions to most qualified charities are deductible up to 50 percent of your adjusted gross income.* However, there may be a 30 percent ceiling for certain types of property or particular situations, as noted later. Whatever the ceiling, gifts in excess of it may be carried over and deducted until used up during the next five years, each subject to the annual ceiling. In this way, the tax savings on an extremely large gift in one year can be used in part to reduce taxes in the following years. A corporation is allowed to receive deductions for charitable contributions up to 5 percent of its pretax net income, with the same carryover privileges.

What You Can Give: Securities and Real Estate

Exactly *what* you give away will affect the amount of your tax deduction. Instead of giving away cash, you can increase your tax benefits considerably by making your contribution in the form of securities or real estate which has appreciated in value and which you have held for more than twelve months. You benefit in two ways: You aren't taxed on the appreciation and you get a deduction for the full present value of the property (but subject to a 30 percent deductibility ceiling of adjusted gross income—with a five year carryover—rather than the 50 percent ceiling applicable to cash gifts). For these reasons, direct donation of the property is preferable to the sale and donation of its after-tax proceeds.

To illustrate the ramifications of all this, here is a hypothetical case history of a donor in the 50 percent tax bracket prepared for me by New York attorney Conrad Teitell. The donor, whom I'll call Clifford, was considering whether to give a $10,000 cash donation or long-term appreciated securities worth that much. Either way the charity would have been just as happy since it would have wound up with the same $10,000. But the type of gift would have made quite a difference to Clifford. By giving cash, he would save $5000 in taxes and would therefore cut the out-of-pocket cost of his donation to $5000. But he also has

---

*A 20 percent limitation applies to most private nonoperating foundations and to certain other organizations. An organization should be able to tell you which limitation applies to it.

$10,000 worth of stock that he had bought years ago for $6000, and which he plans to sell. Under the current capital gains rules, a sale of the stock would result in an $800 capital gains tax (20 percent of his $4000 profit). By giving the stock to charity, he avoids the $800 tax and has an additional $5000 in tax savings generated by the $10,000 charitable deduction—bringing the out-of-pocket cost of his gift down to $4200. Still another alternative was to donate land with a current market value of $10,000 that he'd bought years before for $1000. If Clifford sold the land, his tax on the profit would come to $1800 (20 percent of $9000), netting him $8200. However, by giving the property to the charity (which could sell it), he would avoid that $1800 tax and also get the $5000 tax saving for his charitable deduction, or a total saving of $6800, bringing the net cost of his $10,000 gift down to $3200.

What about appreciated property that's been held short-term—twelve months or less? If donated, there is also no tax on the appreciation, but the charitable deduction is limited to the property's cost basis. However, the gift is now deductible up to 50 percent of adjusted gross income—with a five year carry-over for any excess. In this case, it would probably be preferable to sell the stock, pay the tax on the transaction, and contribute what's left to charity. To show why, let's say you're a married person with a taxable income of $22,000 and own stock which has increased in value from $1000 to $1400 in the eleven months since you've bought it. If you contributed the stock to a charity, you would receive a tax deduction of $1000. On the other hand, if you sold the stock and were in the 24 percent tax bracket, you would have to pay a tax of $96 (24 percent of $400) on your short-term gain, leaving you with a net of $1304 ($1400 minus $96) to contribute to the charity. This would give you a bigger tax deduction—$1304 instead of $1000—although the charity would get less—the $1304 in cash instead of the $1400 in stock.

The same rule applies if your stock, whether held short-term or long-term, has decreased in value since you bought it. If you donate the stock, you forfeit your tax loss. Instead, sell the stock, claim the tax loss, and then donate the proceeds.

Suppose you don't want to part with stock that has appreciated in value? In this case, contribute your stock and then repurchase it at the current market price. This way, there is no tax on your profit, and any future gain or loss can be measured against your new purchase price.

However, if you do give securities, you have to be sure that they're bona fide. In 1974, the *Wall Street Journal,* in a series of front-page articles, revealed that several hundred well-intentioned but misled celebrities, ranging from Barbra Streisand and Jack Benny to former Secretary of Defense Thomas S. Gates and Walter J. Wriston, chairman of New York's First National City Bank (now Citibank), had for over a decade given shares in Home-Stake Production Co., a now-bankrupt Tulsa oil-drilling tax-shelter concern, to their favorite charities. The beneficiaries of their largesse included the American Cancer Society, the American Red Cross, the Salvation Army, the Boy Scouts, the Jewish Federation Council of Greater Los Angeles, the Lincoln Center for the Performing Arts, the Library of Congress, Harvard University, and literally hundreds of other agencies, universities, hospitals, and institutions.

"The donors originally paid a total of about $26 million for the shares they gave away," said the *Wall Street Journal,* "and they generally claimed that the securities were still worth at least that much when they made the gifts and took tax deductions for them.'' But after Security Exchange Commission allegations that the value of the drilling shares was vastly inflated, if not virtually zero, and that the donors were victims of a classic Ponzi-type swindle, the Internal Revenue Service challenged the tax deductions of the donors—an action that could cost them millions of dollars in back taxes.

Giving Paintings and Other Works of Art

Giving paintings, antiques, and other objects of art presents some peculiar problems. You can deduct the full market value of, say, a painting and not have to pay a capital gains tax on its appreciation if you are giving it to a publicly supported art museum or other organization using the gift for the charity's tax-exempt purpose; another valid donee would be a college that plans to put the painting in its art collection or display it in its library for study by art students. In this case, the 30 percent ceiling on deductible contributions applies with the usual five-year carryover, subject to the annual limits.

If the use of the painting is unrelated to the charity's tax-exempt purpose—for instance, if the college sells the painting to raise money—then all you can deduct is its cost plus 60 percent of its appreciation. Here the ceiling on deductibility is 50 percent. If the painting, whether given for related or unrelated use, has been held for twelve months or less, your deduction is limited to its cost basis, again with the 50 percent deductibility ceiling.

The sticky thing about donating works of art is their valuation. If you are claiming a good-sized deduction, it should be supported by one or more expert appraisals, and even these may be questioned, for the IRS, using its own staff and an advisory panel of art experts, gives special scrutiny to deductions for charitable contributions of art objects. Hofstra University was once blessed with an unsigned painting of a nude, "Susanna," which the donor claimed was by Tintoretto and was worth $150,000. The IRS experts, however, questioned the painting's authenticity and contended it was worth only $2000. Whereupon the donor brought in his experts who insisted that the painting was by Tintoretto and offered evidence to the effect that his works had been fetching prices of more than $100,000. The Tax Court, which never feels comfortable in such Solomon-like situations, refused to rule on the authenticity of the work in question, but finally placed its value for tax purposes at $10,000.

The reason the IRS is so wary is because of the significant number of cases it has found of taxpayers conspiring with so-called experts to arrange for the purchase, overappraisal, and donation of the most dubious articles. Another recent case before the Tax Court involved two Michigan men who donated to a college a huge wooden object, described by the *Wall Street Journal* as a "conglomeration of furniture parts and carved wooden fragments weighing a ton and a half and measuring ten feet by ten feet by three feet." Although the object had been purchased from a "dealer" several months before for $3000, the men claimed a $100,000 deduction for it. The IRS brought in a dealer in old furniture who testified that anyone who could get even $200 or $300 for the monstrosity would be a "financial genius." The best the taxpayers' expert could do was to say that if the object were disassembled, its parts might bring $25,000. The Tax

Court finally decided that the object, at least for tax purposes, was worth no more than its original purchase price—$3000. (During the past decade, the IRS has reviewed deductions for more than $250 million of donated art and recommended adjustments—in the government's favor—of some $75 million.)

What if you donate a masterpiece you yourself have painted? The IRS says that the deduction for any self-created work of art is limited to the cost of the materials that go into it.

Giving Other Personal Property

If you contribute used clothing, old furniture, books, or other personal property to your church or to an organization like the Salvation Army or Goodwill Industries, you can deduct the fair market value of these items—that is, the price you know or feel buyers of such items would be willing to pay for them.* In most cases, this will be considerably less than the property's original cost when new. For items on which you are claiming a sizable deduction, it would be helpful to have on hand something to support your claim, such as appraisals, canceled checks, or the receipts from your purchases. Some recognized charities which receive contributions of used personal property will, upon request, give donors a written receipt and valuation of the donated property. Not that the IRS necessarily accepts such valuations. In one case, an individual gave various charities used clothing that had originally cost $1300 and some draperies that had been purchased for $200, and claimed a deduction of $895. The IRS, however, estimated their value at $297 and the Tax Court allowed $500.

Special Deductions for Volunteers

Volunteers with qualified groups often overlook the deductions to which they are entitled. You cannot, of course, deduct the value of the services you give to the organizations with which you are involved. But if you work with the Scouts, for example, you can deduct the cost of transportation to and from the scene of your volunteer activity. (A Nashville couple, however, were denied the $117 charitable deduction they claimed for transporting their kids and, on occasion, other kids, to Girl Scout and Cub Scout meetings; the Tax Court ruled that the expense mainly benefited the individual children, rather than the Scouts as a group.) If you use your car, you can either deduct your expenses for gas and oil (but not for repairs or maintenance) or figure your deduction at a flat 7 cents a mile plus any parking fees and tolls. (This means that if you and your spouse travel, say, 5000 miles a year getting to and from meetings or participating in activities of your church or local PTA or Red Cross group, you are entitled to a deduction of at least $350 for this alone.) In neither case, however, are the costs of depreciation and insurance deductible.

*Fair market value, as defined by the IRS, is "the price at which property would change hands between a willing buyer and willing seller, neither being under any compulsion to buy or sell, and both having reasonable knowledge of the relevant facts." For detailed information on how to determine fair market value, see IRS Publication 561, *Valuation of Donated Property*, available free by sending a postcard to or phoning your local Internal Revenue office.

As an example of the transportation costs that are permitted, the IRS has even allowed some members of the National Ski Patrol System, a nonprofit ski safety organization, to deduct the plane expenses needed to get them to their skiing posts.

If you have to travel away from home on behalf of a qualified charitable organization, you may deduct not only any unreimbursed transportation expenses but also a reasonable amount for meals and lodging (for yourself only, not for an accompanying spouse or family members). In the case of religious conventions, however, these deductions may be taken only by duly elected and unpaid delegates to the convention, not by other members of the church or synagogue. You may also deduct the cost and upkeep of uniforms (such as those used in hospitals) not suited for general use, but which you are required to wear in your volunteer activity.

Certain other out-of-pocket expenses are also deductible. If you're working with, say, a youth organization made up of underprivileged boys, you can, of course, deduct any money spent on them for such things as candy or admission to sports events. However, although the Tax Court recently ruled that a New York City couple could deduct the money they had paid for baby-sitters so that they would be free to do volunteer work, the IRS continues to disallow such deductions.

Timing Your Contributions

Ordinarily, contributions are deductible only if actually paid during the taxable year. However, a check is considered paid on the date it is mailed, not the date it is received. The gift to a charity of a properly endorsed stock certificate is also considered made on the date of mailing or other delivery. On the other hand, if you deliver a stock certificate for transfer into the name of the charity, your gift is not completed until the date the stock is actually transferred on the books of the issuing corporation. Donations via credit cards are deductible in the year the charge is made, not when you pay the bill.

Pledges and promissory notes are not considered deductible until payment is actually made. (Exception: If the board of directors of an *accrual-basis* corporation authorizes a charitable contribution in its taxable year, it can receive a deduction for that year if payment is made on or before the fifteenth day of the third month of the following year.) *Medical World News* reported the case of a physician who on the spur of the moment one New Year's eve telephoned a religious charity to inform it that he wanted to make it a gift of some real estate. He then immediately typed out a "To Whom It May Concern" letter to this effect and had it notarized. The Tax Court later denied his subsequent claim for a deduction, stating that the essential elements for deduction are "donative intent, effective delivery, and acceptance."

The proper timing of contributions can help cut taxes. For example, let's assume you expect to fall into a 50 percent federal and state tax bracket this year and into a 35 percent tax bracket next year. A $100 donation this year will actually cost you only $50, thereby saving you $50, whereas the tax saving shrinks to $35 if you make your donation after December 31. You may also want to consider the possible advantage of spreading a large contribution over several years so that it can be deducted from your highest income bracket in each of those years.

Giving After You're Gone, Or Deferred Giving

While you may want to commit yourself to a contribution now, you may not want it to be turned over to the charity until your death. If so, it is possible to have your cake and eat it: Give your money away—and enjoy it, too! This can be done through one of the techniques which philanthropoids, in their tactful way, delicately refer to collectively as "deferred giving," a phrase that must rank along with that other worthy frequently used eleemosynary euphemism, "development," for fund raising. (The Salvation Army, which goes after deferred gifts in a big way, even has a brigadier in charge of "deferred gift development.")

A deferred gift can take many forms. The oldest and most common is the bequest, which accounts for 6 to 7 percent of total giving and is an important source of income to museums, colleges and universities, and other institutions. Unlike the contributions you may give during your lifetime and receive deductions for, there is no restriction on the amount of money or property you can bequeath to a qualified charity (except in a few states). Another advantage of the bequest is that it is free from federal estate taxes, which can rise to as much as 70 percent. The bequest is also revocable or amendable by a codicil to your will at any time during your life, although it, of course, becomes irrevocable at death. The chief disadvantage of the bequest is that it does not give you any tax benefits while you are still able to enjoy them.

Special exceptions to this rule apply in the case of personal residences or farms. You can arrange to transfer the title to such properties to a charity, the actual transfer to take place after your death. Meanwhile, you can continue to enjoy the use of them and immediately receive a tax deduction for their fair market value less their estimated value during the period you use them—a value arrived at by actuarial tables. However, once you make such an arrangement, the gift is irrevocable.

There are also ways of making a gift and retaining an income from it during your lifetime. The three main ways are through the charitable remainder annuity trust, the charitable remainder unitrust, and the pooled income fund. Don't be intimidated by the names of these awesome-sounding tax-savings gimmicks. (They may also be identified in the fund-raising solicitations of the Salvation Army, the Boy Scouts, schools, hospitals, and an array of other charities by such key words as "gift annuity" and "life income contract.") For they are not nearly as complicated as their names would indicate. Nor, as many people suppose, are they forms of giving for only the extremely well-heeled.

Here is the basic procedure for getting a deduction through a charitable remainder annuity trust. You first decide how much money, securities, or whatever you want to leave to your favorite charity. Then you set up a trust (you'll need a lawyer for this), and transfer your property to it with the proviso that the assets of the trust pass on to the charity at your death. The trust is also required to pay you a fixed dollar amount (but equal to at least 5 percent of the initial value of the property placed in trust) annually for life or a set period of years (up to 20). The unitrust differs only in that you receive a fixed *percentage* (but not less than 5 percent) annually of the value of the trust's assets, as determined every year.

In either case, you receive an immediate charitable deduction based not only on the amount initially given to the trust (there is no capital gains tax on any appreciated securities transferred to it), but also on your age and the return you are to receive—all of this computed from IRS actuarial tables. (The older the beneficiary, the higher the charitable deduction, which is also higher for males than females because of the shorter life expectancy of the former.) How is your income from the trust taxed? Depending on the trust's makeup and changing fortunes, all or part of your returns may be variously treated as ordinary income, capital gains, tax-exempt income, or tax-free distribution of principal. The trust can also be set up to provide income to a wife, child, or other beneficiary either during your lifetime or after your death.

Here is another example given by attorney Conrad Teitell:

> Mr. Reed transfers $100,000 to an annuity trust. He elects to receive $5000 annually for life. If the trust income in any year is insufficient to make the annual tax payment, the deficit is paid to him from capital gains or principal. If the income is greater than $5000 in any year, the excess is reinvested in the trust.

Getting involved in a pooled income fund (a relatively new tax term for life income plans) is probably even simpler. Here you transfer your money or securities to one of the many colleges, hospitals, or other public charities that has set up one of these funds. Some funds accept as little as $1000 to $5000, although others have much higher minimums. The fund agrees to pool (hence, the name) and invest your contribution along with those of other donors and to pay you (or a beneficiary) a proportionate share of its income for life. (To boost income, a fund may sell a donor's low-income growth stocks and buy an equivalent amount of high-yield securities.) On your death, the fund withdraws and has free use of your share of the capital. Meanwhile, you get an immediate tax deduction for the value of your gift.

To see the practical consequences of this type of trust, let us look at a hypothetical case history from an article by tax attorney Dorothea Garber Cracas in *Medical Economics;* the case history is of a Dr. Allen, age 53, married and with a net taxble income of $43,000:*

> He puts $20,000 into his college's pooled income fund, which has been paying 5 percent annually. The valuation of his gift—which will be the amount of his tax deduction—is determined by Treasury's tables and depends on the fund's past rate of earnings and the age of the person or persons receiving the life income. According to the Treasury's tables, Allen's charitable deduction would be $8,242—giving him a tax saving of $3,580 on his annual return. That means Allen, in effect, has only parted with $16,420 ($20,000 less $3,580 in tax reduction), but his share in the fund is still worth the full $20,000. And since the fund earns 5 per cent, he'll receive an income of $1,000 each year on a $16,420 out-of-pocket investment. His effective yield thus would be about 6.1 per cent.

But these are not necessarily all the benefits Dr. Allen would reap. If, as *Medical Economics* points out, his $20,000 gift had been made up of stock now

---

*The figures in the original article have been updated to conform with the present (1979) income tax rates.

worth $9000 more than what he had paid for it, he would also have saved—under the present (1979) income tax rates—a capital gains tax of $1764, in effect reducing the out-of-pocket cost of his gift to $14,656. Under most circumstances, his estate would also reap significant tax savings.

One drawback of the pooled income fund is that its payouts are taxed entirely as ordinary income, unlike the annuity trust and unitrust. Moreover, the fund's payouts are not fixed or guaranteed, since they are determined by the fund's earnings. So, before contributing to a fund, be sure to look into its performance record, portfolio makeup, past earnings, and management know-how. In the case of the pooled fund, as well as the other types of trusts, be sure, too, that you may not need at some future date the capital you are giving away. For once your gift is made, it is irrevocable, unlike the simple bequest. Before making a decision, consult your advisors to see what may be best for your special situation.

Space does not permit a discussion of every ramification of deferred giving, so let us look just briefly at gifts of life insurance, which are finding increasing favor among donors. This type of giving, of course, would interest you only if your beneficiaries no longer need the insurance policy's protection. A fund-raising brochure, "Leaving a Living Estate," put out by the Boy Scout Trust Fund, sums up the advantages: "The donor is entitled to a charitable deduction equivalent to the cash surrender value of the policy. He will also be entitled to a yearly deduction in the amount of the premium if he continues to pay it. [Otherwise, suggests Conrad Teitell, the donee may opt to continue to pay the premium itself, and so eventually receive the full face amount of the policy; or elect to receive a paid-up policy in a reduced face amount with no further premiums payable; or surrender the policy for its cash value.] Some donors take out policies specifically for their favorite charities, paying the premiums until death or such time as the policy is paid up. There are no estate taxes on the proceeds of such policies at the death of the donor."

A word of precaution, however, if you want to receive the estate benefits as well as the regular charitable deduction: When making the charity the owner as well as the beneficiary of the policy, you must keep one so-called "incident of ownership" in it. The incident of ownership can be something as simple and meaningless as the right to retain, jointly with the charity, the right to change the policy's beneficiary to another charity (clearly, something you or the favored charity will never do), or the right to change the mode of premium payment. But in keeping such a right, and with it the obligation of keeping up any future premium payments, the policy will be part of your estate at death. And because the policy increases the size of your estate, this will result in a larger marital deduction for the surviving spouse (who is allowed to deduct up to the greater of $250,000 or one-half of the adjusted gross estate).

To give you some idea of what this means, let's take a person with an estate of $500,000 and a life insurance policy with a cash value of $100,000. By giving the policy to a charity outright, his federal estate taxes would amount to $23,800. On the other hand, by retaining an incident of ownership in the policy, his estate taxes would be only $7800, making for a savings of $16,000.

How Do Your Deductions Compare with Others?

Now that you've gotten some idea as to the kind of deductions you can take, how do the deductions you actually take compare with those of others? Here is a table based on the latest available IRS data, which show the average deductions for contributions taxpayers in various income brackets took on their 1976 tax returns. (AGI is adjusted gross income in thousands of dollars.)

AGI	$5-6	$6-7	$7-8	$8-9	$9-10	$10-15	$15-20	$20-25	$25-30	$30-50	$50-100	$100-up
Contrib.	$428	$392	$453	$393	$441	$414	$472	$542	$646	$939	$2015	$9901

Simply staying near the average will not necessarily protect you from an audit. But if your deductions are substantially higher, the chances of your return being audited are proportionately greater. This does not mean that your deduction will be disallowed. But it does mean that you may be asked to substantiate every dollar you have claimed as a deduction.

Making and Keeping Records of Your Contributions

Here are some precautions to observe and some pitfalls to avoid:

You should keep records, receipts, canceled checks, and other evidence to substantiate your donations. Try, whenever possible, to get receipts for cash contributions.

If you give property other than money, you must attach to your return a description of the kind of property (for example, used clothing, paintings, securities), its cost (except for securities), and your basis for determining its value at the time of the contribution. If you are claiming a deduction of more than $200 for any one gift, you must also attach to your return a statement explaining any conditions attached to the gift and how you acquired it (for example, by purchase, gift, bequest, etc.), and showing the cost or other basis relating to its acquisition by you. Your statement should also include a signed copy of any appraisal.

A canceled check made out to a charity does not mean that you are automatically entitled to a deduction, at least for all that you claim. One reason is because of a neat trick I've known some people to use: They collect funds, usually in cash, in their office or neighborhood for a charity, keep the funds, and then write out a personal check to the charity for the total amount, which they claim as their deduction.

Still another reason for not accepting a check at face value brings us to those tickets you may buy for charity balls, theater parties, sporting events, or other benefits. When a person pays $50 for tickets to an event of this sort, he in many cases deducts the entire $50 on his tax return. Actually, if tickets to the event would normally cost $15, his proper deduction would be $35, even though the tickets may have printed on them, "Contribution—$50." Some charities, however, do indicate on the ticket the amount being allocated as a gift, although this is not legally required. But you should have this information in the event you are questioned.

You should also take the same precaution when you buy something at a charity auction or bazaar: You can charge off as a deduction only the amount in excess of the fair market value of the merchandise or property.

Proposals for Tax Reform

The charitable contributions deduction has been a continuing fixture of our federal income tax law since 1917: It was made part of the law not only to create an incentive for giving but also—perhaps what is even more important—to preserve our system of voluntarism and keep it free from government control—indeed, to lessen the possibility of government usurping the traditional functions of the voluntary sector.

In the past few decades, however, the charitable deduction and several related provisions of the tax law have come increasingly under attack as part of a growing general objection to the use of tax incentives to implement various elements of public policy. Many of the tax critics not only hold the deduction to be a "loophole" that greatly favors the high-income over the low-income taxpayer, but encourages taxpayers to donate money rightfully belonging to the public treasury. In effect, they contend, those "private" dollars given to charity are not so private after all, but are really nothing more than government subsidies for certain activities which are determined outside the normal appropriations process. On this interpretation, they argue that no taxpayer should have the privilege of making a charitable gift, tax free.

Advocates of the opposite view hold that funds from private donors are more accessible than they might be through the process of periodic government—and bureaucratic—appropriations, and that, if anything, the law should be liberalized, perhaps by allowing all taxpayers, whether or not they take the standard deduction, to deduct their charitable contributions, in order to encourage programs it is felt properly belong in the voluntary private sector.

All of this leads once again to the fundamental questions of the basic purpose of charity and to what extent it should be regulated and perhaps even taken over by the government.

PART VII

THE FUTURE OF CHARITY

Chapter 28

Farewell to Alms?

Something happened recently that reminded me of a rich woman's exclamation once in New York. "Socialism! But wouldn't it do away with charity? And what would we do without charities? I love my work for the poor more than anything else."

—Lincoln Steffens

Why should there be any necessity for alms giving in a civilized society?

—Henry Ford I

At a conference held about a decade ago to ponder the future of philanthropy, Richard C. Cornuelle, a consultant to business on social problems, recalled the time he had attended a previous conference on the same subject. "Somewhere along the way, the chairman asked one of the participants, an economist, what he thought the future of private philanthropy was. He was quiet for a while; he seemed to be disarmed by the question. Then at last he said: 'Perhaps private philanthropy can finance dog cemeteries and bird sanctuaries and pay for mountain-climbing expeditions.'"

Cornuelle then commented: "I think his point was that private philanthropy had no future, that government's social responsibility would become very nearly total, but that government might leave little scraps of unfinished business in the road, and that these absurd little oversights would become private philanthropy's agenda."

Is this likely to happen? Would it be a good idea? Many think so. When England experienced its wave of major Socialist legislation in the late 1940s, the general feeling there was that charity had had its day, and some even rejoiced at what they felt to be the total rout of Lady Bountiful. Harold Laski, the noted British political scientist and father of the welfare state, declared it was better to tackle social problems "without the intervention of gracious ladies, or benevolent busybodies, or stockbrokers to whom a hospital is a hobby, or snobs who see in charity a ladder to acquaintaince for which they have been yearning."

In this country, however, many view such a prospect with horror, if not disbelief. But it is hard to ignore the fact that as certain minimal levels of health, education, and welfare have come to be recognized as rights of citizenship, if not actually necessary to the nation's well-being, government has gradually usurped these former traditional functions of charity.

In 1929, as we've already pointed out, government spending in the categories of health, education, and welfare amounted to 3.9 percent of the gross national product; by 1960, such expenditures had jumped to 10.6 percent; and by 1976, they had almost doubled to 20.6 percent, amounting to $331 billion, this constituting 73.1 percent of all public and private spending for "social welfare" purposes.

Philanthropy's ever-diminishing role in our nation's affairs can perhaps be seen most dramatically in the category of health. Whereas in 1929, philanthropic and federal government expenditures were approximately equal, by the late-1970s, federal spending was nearly nine times greater, and spending at all levels of government (federal, state, and local) was about 12 times greater. In the late-1970s, charity contributed to little more than 1 percent of all hospital operating costs and to only 2 percent of all medical research expenditures. And whereas almost all our colleges and universities were privately supported a century ago, today only about half are.

If health and other social needs are worthy of the considerable government support they now receive, it is not unreasonable to ask why they should not be supported *entirely* by government. If muscular dystrophy, for example, is important enough to be the beneficiary of tax-exempt philanthropic dollars, why should the fight against it be left to the voluntary and capricious collection device of the telethon? Why should it have to depend on the charismatic character of a comedian, even one so social-minded and noble in spirit as Jerry Lewis? As we've also already asked: What if other of our national endeavors, such as space technology or military defense, were dependent on similar voluntary efforts? Are our social and medical problems any less complex or important than a journey to the moon?

While I applaud the intentions of the annual do-good campaigns launched by newspapers across the country around Christmastime to solicit contributions for the poor, the sick, the aged, and the infirm, what repels me about these campaigns is that they perpetuate the notion that any members of our society should have to depend on anything so chancy as charity for the necessities of life.

Typical of the cases singled out in *The New York Times* "Neediest Cases Fund" appeal is that of Mrs. P. who, partially paralyzed in an auto accident eleven years before, is shown sitting in a wheelchair, looking sadly out of her window. Described as suffering from cardiac and kidney disorders, she is said to be in despair about her three teen-age children, two of whom need medical treatment for injuries stemming from the same accident, and also special training because they are mentally retarded. Mr. P.'s wages as a doorman, $163 a week, have precluded such attention, to say nothing of the winter coats needed by the children. Also featured in the appeal is frail Miss V., 86 years old, living alone in a housing-project apartment, but ineligible for Medicaid, and with no one to care for her when illness prevents her getting around.

Actually, the money raised through the Neediest Cases Fund is turned over to eight of New York's private social-service agencies to provide assistance needed by these and other of the city's million citizens whose income falls below the federally established poverty line. But why should such people have to depend on private handouts in the first place when other countries not as rich as ours provide entirely for their aged, their ailing, and their poor through an array of government and welfare programs? A commentary on what was then known as *The New York Times* "Hundred Neediest Cases" (the former name of the present fund) once noted that in England, for example, only ten of the hundred would have had to depend on private help; ninety would automatically have been entitled to the help they needed under one government program or another.

"Europeans, from the time of Bismarck in the mid-nineteenth century, have accepted the ultimate responsibility of the State for the well-being of its people," says George C. McGhee, a member of a Committee for Economic Development subcommittee on poverty and the welfare system, who proposes a new way of looking at welfare, which to most Americans is a dirty word. Pointing out that about three-fourths of all welfare recipients comprise the aged, the infirm, and dependent children, he says: "As we seek to improve it [welfare], why can't we view it with pride as we would our local United Givers Fund or any other community undertaking that enlists our social zeal? Why don't we think in terms of the indispensable role welfare plays in helping the elderly couple around the corner who have lost their pension through no fault of their own or the mother whose husband has died and who has children to support? Why do we always have to look at it in terms of cheaters? Why can't we take deep satisfaction in being citizens of a country that is compassionately concerned for its people?"

But if our government were eventually to assume full responsibility for the well-being, or at least the basic needs, of our people, what role would private philanthropy play in our national life? Should American society continue to encourage the formation and support of private organizations as a major means of satisfying our public needs? What would be the appropriate relationship between government and the so-called private sector in marshaling our national resources to meet public needs? Since private nonprofit organizations and institutions receive tax benefits, and so in effect withhold revenues that would otherwise go into the public purse, do the accomplishments of these organizations and institutions justify these tax benefits?

The answers depend to some extent on the kind of society we want. They also depend on how private philanthropy reassesses its functions in terms of the changing needs of society.

In justifying the existence and continued maintenance of private, voluntary philanthropy, all good philanthropoids, citing the division of our society into three sectors—the government sector, the business sector, and the independent nonprofit sector—are wont to utter the standard incantations regarding the virtues of pluralism. The voluntary agencies in this triad, it is argued, make for innovation because, being more flexible and independent than government bodies, they can act in ways which government bodies traditionally find difficult.

This argument was crystallized in these words by Kingman Brewster, while he was president of Yale:

> If all support for university teaching and research were to come from the government—if there were no sources of unprogrammed, non-political funds to bolster the controversial; to encourage the heterodox; to question the inherited assumptions—then progress would be stultified by conformity to the design of some one man or one group or one generation.

Amply documented in preceding chapters have been the many pioneering achievements philanthropy can deservedly take credit for not only in education but also in the arts, libraries, health care and medical research, civil rights and liberties, conservation, women's rights, family planning, urban affairs, special care of the blind, and other areas of our national life. As pointed out, the federal government did not adequately support research for cancer and diabetes, or the care of kidney patients, until voluntary agencies aroused public opinion in support of the legislation and funding needed to cope with such diseases.

All this may be true, say philanthropy's detractors, but times have changed and philanthropy is not nearly as creative as it once was, and the government has now developed a pioneering thrust of its own. Other critics, while recognizing philanthropy's past contributions, charge that it now fails to meet or barely meets the needs of many of the constituencies within our society.

With all this said, philanthropy still has some valid functions now and in the foreseeable future.

One, a stopgap function, is to perform the services which, while an acknowledged responsibility of government, are as yet being done imperfectly by government. Many activities of the health and social welfare agencies fall into this category.

Another is to continue to play an educational role and, where necessary, arouse public support to catalyze government to assume responsibility for services and research activities it *should* undertake. Again, this is a function of many of the health and social welfare agencies. A related function is to work for the enactment or implementation of laws that assure all of our citizens of their constitutional guarantees—a province of organizations like the NAACP, the National Urban League, and the American Civil Liberties Union. And, no less important, to goad government to enforce laws already enacted to safeguard our nation's natural resources and, in the process, our citizens' health—matters that presently are apparently of greater concern to our private voluntary environment agencies than they are to government.

In spite of Red Cross arguments to the contrary, government should assume primary responsibility for disaster relief, and perhaps also for an adequate, safe national blood supply since the voluntary efforts of a greatly divided private sector seem unlikely to make the national blood policy spelled out by the Department of Health, Education, and Welfare in 1973 an imminent reality. Nor should the Red Cross be relied upon to provide services for the military. Nor should voluntary contributions be allowed for providing services that veterans ought to receive as a matter of course from government.

Philanthropy, however, should continue to support certain activities in which government will never—and should never—become involved. Into this category fall the animal charities and the various recreational and character-building organizations, such as the Scouts and the "Ys." Support of these on other than a voluntary basis invokes memories of the government-controlled Hitler *Jugends* and Communist *Komsomols*.

In a somewhat in-between or gray area are such activities as the arts (including music, dance, theater, and so on), which are generally considered to enrich the quality of life rather than satisfy basic needs (although such a distinction is debatable). The arts, of course, could never be completely supported by government, but certainly they should receive much more support than they now do.

It may be that in some utopian future, government will take care of everything except perhaps such activities as "mountain climbing expeditions, bird sanctuaries and dog cemeteries." But until then, philanthropy, whatever its functions, should be more closely regulated than it is now in order to eliminate or reduce the wasteful, inefficient, and occasionally fraudulent practices which affect each of us as taxpayers—whether or not we contribute to charity.

As we've already seen, there is now no federal regulation of charitable solicitations, let alone other aspects of the operations of charities; instead, there is only a jumble of state and local regulations that vary greatly and, for the most part, are ineffectual, unenforceable, or unenforced. (In Washington, one of the 35 states with regulations, charities are the responsibility of the Department of Motor Vehicles!)

Over the years, model uniform state laws have been drawn up and proposed, but to no avail. For at least the past decade, unsuccessful attempts have also been made annually to pass federal "truth in giving" proposals of one sort or another that would require charities to disclose fund-raising costs and other financial data on their solicitations; some proposals have even placed a ceiling on fund-raising costs and called for a description of the charities' purposes and programs. While he was in the Senate, Vice-President Walter Mondale repeatedly introduced legislation that would have put a 50 percent limit on fund-raising costs and would have imposed some rather stringent disclosure and reporting requirements on charities. This legislation, too, as well as similar proposals by other lawmakers, failed to get anywhere.

The Commission on Private Philanthropy and Public Needs (the Filer Commission) of the mid-1970s also addressed itself to the question of federal regulations as well as to the other questions posed earlier in this chapter and in Chapter 1. But after laboring for three years at a cost of nearly $3 million, the much-heralded elephantine commission gave birth to a mouse. Its 240-page report clearly revealed that its main concern was preserving philanthropy's status quo for the benefit of the well-heeled taxpayer and other members of the Establishment. The commission, among its host of recommendations, rejected any limits on fund-raising costs, and timidly suggested federal regulations requiring only that solicitation literature say that financial data would be made available to curious donors *upon request*. Moreover, the commission recommended that religious organizations continue to be exempt from any reporting or disclosure requirements! (In response to complaints, the commission funded a so-called Donee Group, made up of social-change organizations and minority and women's groups, which dissented from most of the commission's recommendations.)*

Obviously, half-way, half-hearted measures of this sort would have little, if any, effect. To regulate our only unregulated major industry—indeed, a shocking dereliction!—what is needed is a newly created, independent, nonpolitical federal agency, comparable to the Securities and Exchange Commission (SEC),

*In 1976, these organizations formed the National Committee for Responsive Philanthropy as the successor to the temporary Donee Group.

which would oversee charities and take action against abuses. To free what might be called the Charities Regulatory Commission (CRC) from political pressures, its board members, perhaps five in number, reflecting all elements of philanthropy from donors to donees, would be appointed by the president with the consent of the Senate for relatively long terms of, say, five to seven years.

Just as the SEC requires full disclosure to investors of material facts about securities offered and sold across state lines and through the mails, the CRC would require nonprofit organizations to furnish comparable information to those solicited for funds. Detailed reports, following specified accounting and financial guidelines, would have to be filed periodically with the CRC. These reports would provide certain basic information about an organization, including its purposes, programs, priorities, plans; receipts and expenditures; names, addresses, and salaries or expenses of its officers, directors, or trustees; possible conflicts of interest; financial arrangements with fund raisers; past difficulties with the law; and perhaps some evaluation of the organization's performance—all in the form of a statement. The CRC would examine and audit the statement and could refuse registration, and hence the right to solicit, if the statement appears to be misleading, inaccurate, or incomplete.

A condensation of the data in the statement would be a required part of each printed solicitation, whether a mailing piece or an advertisement, and this condensed data would also be carried by door-to-door and street solicitors. This is not as impractical as one might think: The city of Los Angeles requires the use of such data, which take up no more space than a postcard. Radio and TV solicitations would, of course, present a problem, but they could include an announcement to the effect that the organization's condensed or full statement would be readily available to anyone by mail or could be inspected at CRC regional offices. Announcements regarding the availability of the full statement would also be required on the printed solicitations.

What about a limit on fund-raising costs? I am not greatly concerned about the need for this, with the full disclosure and registration requirements suggested. If the costs seem too high, I leave it to the intelligence of the public to determine whether or not the special nature of the particular charity justifies them, given the interpretation of the costs presented in the organization's statement.

Contrary to the recommendations of the Filer Commission, there is also no reason why churches and church-affiliated organizations should be exempt from regulation, religion, accounting as it does for nearly half of all American giving and, incidentally, a goodly share of the abuses committed in the name of charity, as we have already amply demonstrated. To allow these organizations to be exempt is a national scandal. Certainly, when an organization, religious or otherwise, enters the general marketplace in seeking funds, it has an obligation to publicly account for the use of these funds. Nor would this in the slightest interfere with its "free exercise" of religion as guaranteed under the First Amendment, although many religious groups would like us to believe otherwise for reasons known only to God and their financial officers. Indeed, to effect a really true separation of church and state in the spirit of the First Amendment, one could argue that religious groups should not even be exempt from taxes—an exemption that, in effect, gives them a state subsidy.

As a further means of protecting contributors to charity from misrepresentations and outright fraud, the Federal Trade Commission could apply to charities "truth in advertising" guidelines comparable to those the commission already uses to prevent the dissemination of false and deceptive claims by manufacturers of drugs, curative devices, cosmetics, and other products. However, it is unlikely that the commission's mandate could be extended beyond the commercial area, which keeps it busy enough anyway.

In spite of its noble purposes, a sector of our economy that now has an estimated tax-free annual income of over $100 billion, owns one-ninth of all the property in the country, employs at least 4.6 million persons, or 5.2 percent of the U.S. work force, and uses the unpaid services of perhaps as many as 50 or 60 million volunteer workers, is much too big and important to be left free from close scrutiny and public accountability.

As long as it remains so, notes The Grantsmanship Center's Jack Shakely, "it will not be the few fraudulent promoters or the occasional rogue institution that will turn Americans against charitable solicitations.

"The lack of credibility, the loss of trust that could bring trouble to the nonprofit world, may come from within by those who may have unwittingly spent decades making promises they can't keep."

And it may come from without, as millions of Americans stop giving as indiscriminately and as blindly as the sympathetic but unknowing people who dropped coins into the cup of the blind beggar with whom we started our long journey across Charity U.S.A.

Acknowledgments

Much of this book, as I said in the Foreword, is the result of my own first-hand observations and personal research, interviews, conversations, correspondence, and other efforts. The preparation of this book has, from beginning to end, been essentially a one-man job, involving me in some 10,000 miles of travel back and forth across the country. However, as I could not always be where I wanted to be at a propitious time, I also used a number of local researchers for special assignments. These researchers (actually, top-notch newspaper and magazine writers in their own right) included Luise Putcamp, Jr., of Stamford, Connecticut; Patrick Shellenbarger of the Detroit *News*; Marya Argetsinger Smith of Chicago; Sara D. Stutz of San Diego, California; William D. Tammeus of the Kansas City *Star;* and Deena Mirow of the Cleveland *Plain Dealer*. Their contributions, which included a continuous flow of clippings from their areas, did much to give this book the national scope I wanted it to have.

I also owe a special debt of gratitude to Melvin C. Van de Workeen and Jane Pendergast of the National Information Bureau, and to Helen O'Rourke, Nancy de Marco, and Marilyn Kolb of the Council of Better Business Bureaus, for providing me with reports and other material from their voluminous files. Jane Pendergast was particularly helpful in checking the basic facts and figures of many of the organizations included in this book; however, the final responsibility for their accuracy is, of course, mine.

Otherwise, all of the organizations and persons mentioned in the book have had some role, directly or indirectly, in its creation, and I am especially grateful to those who supplied me with information, answered my questionnaires as well as all sorts of other questions, and granted me interviews. Since I interviewed or spoke to nearly one thousand people during the five years it took to complete this book, they are far too numerous to list individually, although I have acknowledged some in the text or Notes and Sources.

In addition, I would like to single out several persons for various acts of kindness not specifically credited (at least, adequately enough) in these pages. Among those who supplied me with information, gave generously of their time, knowledge, advice, and insights, or took the trouble to read and critique certain sections or chapters in manuscript form were: Julian Block, tax editor of the Research Institute of America; George W. Bonham, editor, *Change;* Arthur J. Grimes and Peter Meek, former officials of the National Health Council, and Joseph Bergen, presently of the National Health Council; John J. Schwartz and Fred Schnaue, respectively, president and director of public relations of the American Association of Fund-Raising Counsel; John McIlquam, managing editor, *Fund Raising Management;* Alvin H. Reiss, editor, *Arts Management;* Dr. W. Homer Turner and Karen Furey of the National Council on Philanthropy;

458

Eugene C. Struckhoff, president, Council on Foundations; Joan Lundberg and Hayden Smith of the Council for Financial Aid to Education; Tozier Brown of Marts & Lundy; Constant H. Jacquet, Jr., editor, *Yearbook of American and Canadian Churches;* tax attorney Dorothea Garber Cracas of the Newark law firm of Rosen, Gelman and Weiss; Eliot Frankel, producer with NBC News; Patrick Maguire, head of the Concerned Citizens for Charity; Eleazar Lipsky, attorney, writer, and expert on Jewish affairs; Morton Yarmon of the American Jewish Committee; S. Peter Goldberg of the Council on Jewish Federations and Welfare Funds; my friend Alden Todd, a distinguished editor and writer; Dr. J. Garrott Allen of the Stanford University Medical Center; writer Andrew Hamilton; Eveline Hunt of Paine Webber Mitchell Hutchins; Joanne Freeman of Blue Cross/Blue Shield of Greater New York's excellent reference library; and my friends and summer neighbors Harry and Doris Cantor, two of the most charitable people I know. Needless to say, none of those named or others mentioned in the book are responsible for any errors that may have somehow crept into it. Nor should they be held to account for any opinions or statements not directly attributed to them; in fact, many may hold views that differ greatly from mine.

A special word of thanks is due three people: my friend and attorney Herman V. Traub for his skillful handling of some of the legalities involved in the birth of this book; my agent Julian Bach for effecting the "marriage" between me and the publisher responsible for its birth; and my editor Roger Jellinek for the care and devotion he lavished on the book in his role of midwife.

For assisting in the delivery through the thankless task of transcribing some 200 hours of tape-recorded interviews and typing the various stages of the manuscript, I am beholden to the yeoman (yeowoman?) efforts of Polly Cluderay, Linda Wood, Catherine Auld, Henriette Gray, Marcia Stein (a remarkable blind person!), and LaVerne Owens. Grateful thanks are also due Ethel Meserole, my secretary, who helped tremendously with thousands of details.

And, finally, I would be especially remiss if I did not express my endless gratitude to my wife Shirley and my daughters Amy, Wendy, Emily, and Stephanie for the occasional chores with which they assisted me and, what is even more important, for enduring with patience and understanding all the agonies of pre- and postpartum blues accompanying the delivery of a three-pound book after a seemingly interminable gestation period of sixty months (a metaphor which, in one additional acknowledgment, I should credit to my friend Murray Teigh Bloom).

NOTES AND SOURCES

To make for easy, uninterrupted reading, I have tried to avoid cluttering the text of the book with too many footnotes and citations. Accordingly, for the benefit of those interested in such matters, what now follows is a chapter-by-chapter breakdown of notes, sources, acknowledgments, and occasional personal comment. A few guidelines: The citations are keyed to the page of the text to which they refer. Where something is not credited or annotated, it should be understood that the source is the organization or person referred to in the text. For example, financial or other data about an organization came from the organization itself unless indicated otherwise. If this information is not based on an audited financial statement by an independent public accountant employing uniform accounting standards, or is subject to question for any other reasons, this is also indicated. Similarly, any unattributed quotes or comments were made directly to me (or one of my researchers).

For the sake of brevity, I have also resorted to abbreviations wherever possible. For example, I have used the acronym AAFRC to refer to the American Association of Fund-Raising Counsel, and the term "Filer Commission" as shorthand for the Commission on Private Philanthropy and Public Needs.

You will find that some reference sources appear several times within the same chapter and, on occasion, in more than one chapter. When such is the case, I give the full title of the source and its publisher and date of publication only the first time it appears in a chapter.

As you will see, in order to supplement my first-hand observations, interviews, and research, I consulted literally hundreds of books, periodicals, and other reference sources; and I estimate my reading must have amounted to tens of millions of words. But I read principally for background, usually of a historical nature, or to corroborate my primary research, fill in certain details, and gain certain perspectives and viewpoints that would enable me to present a rounded, well-balanced picture of the many complicated and often controversial subjects with which a book such as this must inevitably deal.

The references cited may be useful to those wishing to pursue any of these subjects further. So may several bibliographies prepared for scholars and researchers. One is the annotated bibliography by Margaret M. Otto contained in the *Report of the Princeton Conference on the History of Philanthropy in the United States,* Russell Sage Foundation, New York, 1956. The Princeton Conference, incidentally, pointed out the dearth of really adequate research on the history and other aspects of philanthropy. Much more recent is the bibliography prepared in 1973 under the title *Motivations for Charitable Giving* by Astrida Butners and Norman Buntaine for The 501(c)(3) Group, Suite 600, One Dupont Circle, Washington, D.C. 20036, from whom this 69-page reference guide is available for a modest price. Actually, the title of this guide is somewhat misleading for the 394 books, articles, and research papers listed and annotated are coded in eleven topic categories, such as religion, history, psychology, tax deductions, and so on. I also found useful a seven-page bibliography prepared by the American Association of Fund-Raising Counsel, 500 Fifth Avenue, New York, New York 10036, which is also the source of the indispensable annual yearbook, *Giving USA,* many references to which will be found in the following notes.

Also frequently mentioned is the Filer Commission's *Giving in America: Toward A Stronger Voluntary Sector,* Washington, D.C., 1975; and the material from which that report was condensed, the six-volume *Research Papers Sponsored by the Commission on Private Philanthropy and Public Needs,* Department of the Treasury, Washington, D.C., 1977.

The quotation from de Tocqueville preceding Chapter 1 is from his *Democracy in America,* Alfred A. Knopf, New York, 1945.

CHAPTER 1

Page 4   The estimate of the Girl Scouts' share of cookie industry sales is from *Business Week,* February 7, 1970. In 1978, the Scouts estimated for me the share as being "between 5 and 10 percent.

Page 8   The Lecky quotes are from F. Emerson Andrews' *Philanthropic Giving.* Russell Sage Foundation, New York, 1950, p. 21.

Page 9   The figures on the number of Baptist churches are from Martin A. Larson and C. Stanley Lowell's *The Religious Empire,* Robert B. Luce, Washington/New York, 1976, p. 31.   The estimate of 6 million organizations is cited from the Filer Commission's *Giving in America: Toward A Stronger Voluntary Sector,* Washington, D.C., 1975, p. 11.   The U.S. giving figures on this and the following pages are from the AAFRC's *Giving USA 1979* and previous issues of this series of annual reports.   The Canadian per capita figure is from *Canadian Tax Reform and Private Philanthropy* by R.M. Bird and M.W. Bucovetsky, Canadian Tax Foundation, Toronto, 1976. However, this report, which is a slightly updated and expanded version of a paper prepared for the Filer Commission, also suggests that annual private giving in Canada may be one-third that in the United States. This means that current Canadian giving could be as high as $60 per capita.   The British per capita figure is based on *Charity Statistics 1977/78,* Charities Aid Foundation, Tonbridge, Kent, England, 1978, which roughly estimated that total private donations to British charity in 1977 amounted to £700 million (about $1 billion at the average of that year's fluctuating exchange levels).   The comparison of U.S. giving and the budgets of foreign nations is based on the data in the "Nations of the World" section of the *1979 World Almanac.*

Page 10   The figure of over $400 billion is based on the annual estimates of the American Association of Fund-Raising Counsel from 1954 to the present; the estimates of F. Emerson Andrews are in his *Philanthropic Giving, op. cit.* (p. 72) covering the years 1929 to 1949; and the estimates for the years from 1910 to 1965 are to be found in Arnaud C. Marts' *The Generosity of Americans,* Prentice-Hall, Englewood Cliffs, N.J., 1966, p. 7.   The examples of the meaning of $400 billion are adapted from the comparisons made periodically by *U.S. News & World Report,* most recently in its February 20, 1978, issue.   The figures on the sources and allocations of giving are from the AAFRC's *Giving USA 1979.*

Page 11   The effort made at measuring the nonprofit sector's financial strength is described in *Non-Profit Report,* September, 1973, which came up with a figure of "124 billion plus."   The figures on universities and colleges are from the Council for Financial Aid to Education.   The hospital figures are from the American Hospital Association.   The number of religious sanctuaries and the value of their assets, both regarded as conservative estimates, are from Martin A. Larson and C. Stanley Lowell's *The Religious Empire, op. cit.,* pp. 18 and 20.   The $600 billion value of tax-exempt real estate—said to be one-third of all U.S. property values—is from Ben Whitaker's *The Philanthropoids,* William Morrow, New York, 1974, p. 119. The U.S. Department of Commerce's expert on property values, John Coleman, said that the $600 billion figure would probably be higher today, although there are no national statistics on this subject. However, estimates for various states appear in *Taxable Property Values and Assessments/Sales Price Ratios,* Bureau of the Census, Washington, D.C., 1978. Another basic source on this subject is Alfred Balk's *The Free List: Property Without Taxes,* Russell Sage Foundation, New York, 1971.   The Schwartz comments and examples are from *Vital Issues,* Center for Information on America, Washington, Conn., June, 1972.

Page 12   The $80.6 billion estimate for the total income of our nation's philanthropic institutions is from a study, "The Scope of the Private Voluntary Charitable Sector," by Gabriel Rudney in *Research Papers Sponsored by the Commission on Private Philanthropy and Public Needs,* Department of the Treasury, Washington, D.C., 1977. The employment estimates for the charitable sector are from a study by T. Nicholaus Tideman in the same collection of research papers. Other studies in this collection that deal with the size and scope of the charitable sector are by Dale L. Hiestand and by Burton A. Weisbrod and Stephen H. Long.   The incomes of the industries mentioned are from the U.S. Department of Commerce's Bureau of Economic Analysis and are for the year 1977. Private industry's employment figures are from *Statistical Abstract of the United States: 1978,* U.S. Bureau of the Census, Washington, D.C., 1978.

462										NOTES AND SOURCES

Page 13	Sources for some of the figures on volunteers are given in the Notes to Chapter 6.	The Elliot Richardson quote is from the AAFRC's *Giving USA 1979*.	The findings and recommendations of the Peterson Commission appear in *Foundations, Private Giving and Public Policy*, University of Chicago Press, 1970.	John Gardner is quoted from *The New York Times*, December 3, 1978.

Page 14	Figures on the caseload of the Catholic Social Services office in Galesburg are from an article by Timothy D. Schellhardt in the *Wall Street Journal*, April 23, 1979.

Page 15	Stephen McCurley and William Schafer are quoted from "Why Charities Tighten Their Belts," *U.S. News & World Report*, February 26, 1979.	Joan Hanlon and the National Council of Jewish Women are cited from an article by Steven V. Roberts in *The New York Times*, August 6, 1978.	The Disabled American Veterans salary disclosures are from "For Many, There Are Big Profits in 'Nonprofits,' " *U.S. News & World Report*, November 6, 1978.	The follow-up *Changing Times* evaluation was in its November, 1976, issue.

Page 16	Mondale's comments are from the *Congressional Record*, February 19, 1974, p. S1851.

Page 17	Figures on government's increasing expenditures for health, education, and welfare are from *Social Security Bulletin*, January, 1976, and January, 1977.

CHAPTER 2

The material in this chapter was culled from many—literally dozens of—sources. Among them were: Arnaud C. Marts' *Philanthropy's Role in Civilization*, Harper, New York, 1953, and his *The Generosity of Americans*, Prentice-Hall, Englewood Cliffs, N.J., 1966; F. Emerson Andrews' *Philanthropic Giving*, Russell Sage Foundation, New York, 1950; Scott M. Cutlip's *Fund Raising in the United States: Its Role in America's Philanthropy*, Rutgers University Press, New Brunswick, N.J., 1965; Robert H. Bremner's *American Philanthropy*, University of Chicago Press, Chicago, 1960; Benedict Nightingale's *Charities*, Allen Lane, London, 1973; and Ben Whitaker's *The Philanthropoids* (largely about foundations but with interesting historical details), William Morrow, New York, 1974. Many of these have excellent, detailed bibliographies that pointed me to other sources. Two lengthy papers prepared in 1974 for the (Filer) Commission on Private Philanthropy and Public Needs also contained a wealth of historical detail: Robert H. Bremner's "Private Philanthropy and Public Needs: Historical Perspective" (although it duplicated to a large extent his *American Philanthropy, op. cit.);* and Fred P. Crawford's "Non-Economic Motivational Factors in Philanthropic Behavior." The *Encyclopaedia Britannica* and other standard encyclopedias contained many useful references to charity or philanthropy in its stages of evolution. And other sources, wherever pertinent, will be cited in the notes that follow.

Page 21	"Biblical Conceptions of Charity" in *Jewish Social Service Quarterly*, March 1936, pp. 334–336, contains a short discussion of the various meanings and forms charity took in biblical times. "Charity and Charitable Institutions" in the *Jewish Encyclopedia*, Vol. 3, 1906, pp. 667–676, sets forth the principle of charity in Jewish culture as embodied in Mosaic law.	Early Christian charity is also touched on in Amos G. Warner's *American Charities*, Thomas Y. Crowell, New York, 1894, pp. 6–7.

Page 23	The Protestant influence on charity is cited in Horace R. Cayton and Setsuko Nishi's *The Changing Scene—Churches and Social Welfare*, Vol. II, The National Council of Churches of Christ in the U.S.A., 1955, p. 51. This subject and the changing attitudes toward begging are also dealt with in Frances Fox Piven and Richard A. Cloward's *Regulating the Poor*, Vintage (Random House), New York, 1971, pp. 8–11, and Joe R. Feagin's *Subordinating the Poor*, Prentice-Hall, Englewood Cliffs, N.J., 1975, pp. 16–22.	The Mill Quote is from his *The Letters of John Stuart Mill*, ed. Hugh S. R. Elliot, Longmans, Green, London, 1910, Vol. I, p. 307.

Page 24	The G. M. Trevelyan comment is from his *English Social History: A Survey of Six Centuries, Chaucer to Queen Victoria*, Longmans, Green, London, 1942, p. 230.	Cotton Mather is cited in Bremner, *American Philanthropy, op. cit.*, pp. 12–15.	A detailed account of Franklin's philanthropic activities appears in "Ben Franklin: Early Pioneer in Fund Raising Techniques" by J. Alexander MacMurtrie in *Fund Raising Management*, May–June, 1971.

Page 25   There are excellent historical details about early charitable activites in the United States in *Subordinating the Poor, op. cit., Regulating the Poor, op. cit.,* and Roy Lubove's *The Professional Altruist,* Harvard University Press, Cambridge, Mass., 1965.   The quotation from de Tocqueville is from his *Democracy in America,* Alfred A. Knopf, New York, 1945.

Page 26   Carnegie's celebrated essay is contained in his *The Gospel of Wealth and Other Timely Essays,* Century, New York, 1900.

Page 27   The Rockefeller benefactions are cited in Allan Nevins' *Study in Power: John D. Rockefeller, Industrialist and Philanthropist,* Scribner's, New York, 1953; Myer Kutz's *Rockefeller Power,* Simon and Schuster, New York, 1974; and numerous other biographies.

Page 28   Accounts of the early settlement houses appear in Bremner, *op. cit.,* Cutlip, *op. cit.,* and Alfred de Grazia and Ted Gurr's *American Welfare,* New York University Press, New York, 1961.

Page 29   Hoover's disparate views about the feeding of livestock and farmers are touched on in Richard Carter's *The Gentle Legions,* Doubleday, New York, 1961, and *Regulating the Poor, op. cit.* The latter and *Subordinating the Poor, op. cit.,* also give a good picture of changing concepts about charity during the New Deal years.

Page 30   The figures on the shift in government giving are from the *Social Security Bulletin,* January, 1976, and January, 1977.

CHAPTER 3

Page 33   Andrews, who died in 1978 at the age of 76, told the story of the farm woman in his *Philanthropic Giving,* Russell Sage Foundation, New York, 1950, p. 52, as well as in other of his works.   The postal worker's story is told at greater length in *The New York Times,* October 22, 1977, and in Gerald Moore's article, "The Impoverished Philanthropist," in *Reader's Digest,* May, 1978.

Page 34   The acts of benevolence described are from newspaper stories. The one involving the marijuana dealers is from a UPI dispatch in *The New York Times,* November 29, 1973.   The overall giving figures are from *Giving USA 1979.* Those by income groups are from *Statistics of Income, Individual Income Tax Returns for 1976,* Table V, Internal Revenue Service.   The breakdown of givers by education, marital status, and other characteristics is from a University of Michigan Survey Research Center-Census Bureau survey for the Commission on Private Philanthropy and Public Needs; it is summarized in the Filer Commission's *Giving in America,* Washington, D.C., 1975, pp. 53–60.

Page 35   The United Way survey comparing giving by professions is cited from *Medical World News,* February 15, 1974.   The Rockefeller material is based in part on the references cited for Chapter 2; also *Time,* July 24, 1978, and September 2, 1974.

Page 36   The Mellon benefactions are described in *Time,* May 8 and June 5, 1978, and "The Cost of Putting Footprints in Sands of Time" by Tom Buckley in *The New York Times,* October 17, 1973. The Mellon family history is recounted in Burton Hersh's *The Mellon Family,* Morrow, New York, 1978, and David E. Koskoff's *The Mellons,* Crowell, New York, 1978.

Page 37   For more on Stewart Mott, see "GM Produces A Maverick" by Timothy Saasta in *The Grantsmanship Center News,* May–August, 1978, and "The View from Stewart Mott's Penthouse" by Irwin Ross in *Fortune,* March, 1974.

Page 38   Harry Golden has written entertainingly and informatively about Jewish giving in his *Travels Through Jewish America,* Doubleday, New York, 1973.   Many of the examples of big bequests are drawn from the AAFRC's *Giving USA* annual reports.

Page 39   The Yankelovich survey, entitled, "Save the Children Federation's Performance in the Charity Market," was prepared in November, 1971.

Page 40   The survey of Jewish giving, *Motivations for Charitable Giving: A Case Study of an*

Eastern Metropolitan Area (Essex County, N.J.), was done for the United Jewish Appeal by the National Opinion Center of the University of Chicago, 1961. Dichter is quoted from a speech at the National Biennial Conference of United Community Funds and Councils in Detroit, February 10, 1956; Benedict Nightingale's "Why Do We Give" in *Intellectual Digest*, December, 1973; and various other sources. Lewis is quoted from his article in *Fund Raising Management*, November–December, 1973.

Page 41 The United Jewish Appeal survey is the one referred to on p. 40. The Rockefellers' rationale for giving is also dealt with in an article by William Manchester in *The New York Times Magazine*, October 6, 1974. "Andy Mellon's fire escape" is quoted from Martin E. Carlson's *Why People Give*, Council Press for Stewardship and Benevolence, National Council of the Churches of Christ in the U.S.A., New York, 1968, an excellent work that applies data from the field of motivational research to the theories of giving in a Christian context. Another useful source of information was Fred P. Crawford's paper, "Non-Economic Motivational Factors in Philanthropic Behavior," prepared for the Commission on Private Philanthropy and Public Needs.

Page 42 The Mandeville, Spencer, and Anna Freud quotes are from Ben Whitaker's *The Philanthropoids*, William Morrow, New York, 1974. The Kellogg quote is from Ben Whitaker, *ibid.* The Boulding quote is from his "Notes on a Theory of Philanthropy" in *Philanthropy and Public Policy*, National Bureau of Economic Research, Washington, D.C., 1962, p. 57. The concepts of altruism and selfishness are explored in David Alderman and Leonard Berkowitz's "Empathy, Outcome and Altruism," proceedings of the 77th Annual Convention of the American Psychological Association, 1969, and in Berkowitz's "The Self, Selfishness, and Altruism" in *Altruism and Helping Behavior*, Jacqueline Macauley and Leonard Berkowitz, eds., Academic Press, New York, 1970.

Page 43 The citation of San Francisco's Institute for Fund Raising is from its manual, *Techniques of Fund Raising*, 1972.

Page 44 Ruth Malone is quoted from her article in *Trends*, December, 1970.

Page 45 George Kirstein is quoted from his *Better Giving*, Houghton Mifflin, Boston, 1975.

Page 46 The origin of Oxford's Pembroke College as well as of the names of the American colleges is based largely on Arnaud C. Marts' *Philanthropy's Role in Civilization*, Harper, New York, 1953, pp. 86–91. The C.W. Post and Temple Buell College stories are from Tom Buckley in *The New York Times, op. cit.*

Page 47 Some of the material on hospitals, libraries, and family memorials is from Marts, *op. cit.*, pp. 87–89. The names of the Harvard University buildings are from Whitaker, *op. cit.*, p. 39.

Page 48 Buckley is quoted in *The New York Times*, October 17, 1973. The New York City memorialization offers are from a story in *The New York Times*, March 27, 1974. The Omaha lottery story is from *The New York Times*, December 3, 1973. The 90 percent estimate for the names of foundations is from Whitaker, *op. cit.*, p. 48.

CHAPTER 4

Some of the historical material in this chapter is taken from one or another of the following books, which are recommended for further reading: Waldemar A. Nielsen's *The Big Foundations*, Columbia University Press, New York, 1972; Joseph C. Goulden's *The Money Givers*, Random House, New York, 1971; Ben Whitaker's *The Philanthropoids*, William Morrow, New York, 1974; and Merrimon Cuninggim's *Private Money and Public Service*, McGraw-Hill, New York, 1972. Also of possible interest to those wishing to delve more deeply into this subject are: Warren Weaver's *U.S. Philanthropic Foundations*, Harper & Row, New York, 1967; and F. Emerson Andrews' *Philanthropic Foundations*, Russell Sage Foundation, New York, 1956, and his *Foundations: 20 Viewpoints*, Russell Sage Foundation, New York, 1965, to cite only a few of Andrews' many works on this subject.

Page 49 The quotation from Nielsen is from his *The Big Foundations, ibid.*

Page 50 The statistics on foundations are from the AAFRC's *Giving USA*, the Foundation Center, and *The Foundation Directory*, 6th edition, The Foundation Center, New York, 1977.

Page 52 Details of the Robert Wood Johnson Foundation's precipitous rise to the forefront of the foundation field are in *American Medical News*, September 10, 1973. A lively account of the Ford Foundation's first two decades is Dwight MacDonald's *The Ford Foundation: The Men and the Millions*, Reynal, New York, 1956.

Page 55 The most publicized and stormiest of the Patman hearings were before the House Ways and Means Committee in 1969. The Rand ventures are described in detail in *The Money Givers, op. cit.*, pp. 156–158.

Page 56 The decline in foundation assets is reported in the *Wall Street Journal*, October 1, 1974, and *The New York Times*, November 6, 1977. The death and birth of foundations is summarized from an article by Fred M. Hechinger in *The New York Times*, January 15, 1975. This is also documented in testimony of John G. Simon in *Hearings Before the Subcommittee on Foundations, Committee on Finance, U.S. Senate*, October 1 and 2, 1973, pp. 174–175; and an October 25, 1974, memo of Caplin & Drysdale, Washington, D.C., on "Analysis of Foundation Center Data on Creation, Dissolution and Reclassification of Private Foundations." The Hagler quote is from "Why Charities Tighten Their Belts," *U.S. News & World Report*, February 26, 1979.

Page 57 Hunter is quoted from *Foundation News*, July–August, 1975. For background on the Haymarket, Vanguard, and similar activist foundations, I drew upon articles in *Newsweek*, February 27, 1978; the *Wall Street Journal*, December 11, 1975; *The New York Times*, March 4, 1977; and *The Grantsmanship Center News*, July–August, 1975.

Page 58 The figures on the growth of community foundations are from various editions of *The Foundation Directory, op. cit.*, and from unpublished data from the Council on Foundations. Valuable insights into these types of foundations came from conversations with the council's president, Eugene C. Struckhoff, perhaps the nation's leading authority on community foundations, and author of the definitive two-volume *Handbook for Community Foundations: Their Formation, Development, and Operation*, Council on Foundations, New York, 1977. Much of my section on community foundations was based on the Struckhoff work, which consists of a 175,000-word text and voluminous appendix material, as well as on Jack Shakely's "Community Foundations" in *The Grantsmanship Center News*, March–April, 1976.

Page 61 The Rockefeller quote is from his article, "Why I Believe in Philanthropy," in *Reader's Digest*, December, 1969. The Byrnes and Senger quotes are from *Business Week*, December 7, 1974.

CHAPTER 5

Page 62 AT&T's corporate good works were the subject of an article in the *Wall Street Journal*, April 16, 1975. The material on Alcoa and Dayton Hudson came directly from those companies. Dayton Hudson's philanthropic activities are also cited in *The New York Times*, July 23, 1978, and *Forbes*, December 25, 1978. A word of caution about giving/PTNI ratios: As Dayton Hudson pointed out to me, it is not always possible to determine this by measuring a corporation's giving for a particular year against its pretax income as shown in the annual report. For one thing, federally taxable income is not necessarily the same as reported pretax income. The difference is due to very technical factors, such as methods of treating depreciation. (Companies use straight-line depreciation for external reporting and accelerated depreciation, which reduces taxable income, for IRS reporting.) Moreover, many companies funnel their giving through foundations, and the years the gifts are made may not coincide with the years the companies report their taxable income. The figures on how much American business gives is from *Giving USA 1979*.

Page 63 The historic comparisons are based on previous *Giving USA*s, government statistics, and material from the Conference Board. The Filer Commission quote is from its 1975 report, *Giving in America*, Washington, D.C., 1975, p. 157. The quote by Andrews is from his *Foundation Watcher*, Franklin and Marshall College, Lancaster, Pa., 1973, p. 116. Friedman's views have been quoted widely and appear in many of this chapter's reference sources, including Marion R. Fremont-Smith's *Philanthropy and the Business Corporation*, Russell Sage Foundation, New York, 1972, pp. 83 and 88. The Friedman–Goldston debate is excerpted in *Fortune*, November, 1973, p. 56. Samuelson is quoted from "The Hazards of Corporate Responsibility" by Gilbert Burck in *Fortune*, June, 1973, p. 115. Ford is quoted in "The Business of Giving" by F. Emerson Andrews in *The Atlantic Monthly,* February, 1953. Books dealing with corporate social responsibility include: Neil H. Jacoby, *Corporate Power and Social Responsibility,* Macmillan, New York, 1973; and Neil W. Chamberlain, *The Limits of Corporate Responsibility,* Basic Books, New York, 1974. The Ermann study is summarized at length in *The Grantsmanship Center News,* January–February, 1978, p. 4.

Page 64 The executive surveyed by the Conference Board is quoted in *Giving in America, op. cit.,* p. 153. The Sears example of giving is from *Newsweek,* August 28, 1961. The early YMCAs are described in Fremont-Smith, *op. cit.,* p. 6; the *Wall Street Journal,* October 17, 1970; and in the article, "Rethinking Corporate Charity," by Norman Kurt Barnes in *Fortune,* October, 1974. Further details about the Red Cross Dividend and the early years of corporate giving also appear in Fremont-Smith, *op. cit.,* and Barnes, *ibid.,* which also contain the Lord Bowen quote. Even greater details may be found in F. Emerson Andrews' seminal work, *Corporation Giving,* Russell Sage Foundation, New York, 1952.

Page 65 My account of legislation and the A.P. Smith case is based on Fremont-Smith, *op. cit.;* Barnes, *ibid.;* and Andrews' *Foundation Watcher, op. cit.* The Evelyn Davis anecdote is from Barnes, *ibid.* The statistics on corporate giving are from a 1975 research study, "Corporate Giving: Rationale, Issues, and Opportunities," prepared by C. Lowell Harriss, professor of economics at Columbia University, for the (Filer) Commission on Private Philanthropy and Public Needs.

Page 66 The data on giving by industry groups is from the *Annual Survey of Corporate Contributions, 1976,* published in 1978 by the Conference Board. The Andrews quote is from Barnes' *Fortune* article, *op. cit.*

Page 67 The advantages of giving through foundations are from "The Company-Sponsored Foundations" by Rembrant Hiller, Jr., in *Foundations: 20 View Points,* Russell Sage Foundation, New York, 1965, pp. 85–86. The ranking of company-sponsored foundations in the footnote is from *The Foundation Directory,* 6th edition, The Foundation Center, New York, 1977.

Page 68 The examples of Ford Motor Company Fund contributions are from the Detroit *News,* October 14, 1973. The data on matching gifts programs are from the Council for Advancement and Support of Education, which also estimates that the 700 companies contributed a total of $15 million to 1200 colleges and other schools in 1976. The breakdown of the corporate contributions dollar by field of activity is based on 1977 figures from the Conference Board.

Page 69 The survey indicating that most corporate contributions go to the same recurring drives is referred to in *Foundation Watcher, op. cit.,* p. 122. Lavin is quoted in Bernard Taper's *The Arts in Boston,* Harvard University Press, Cambridge, Mass., 1970, p. 78. The Hacker and Galbraith statements are from Fremont-Smith, *op. cit.,* pp. 84–88. The Jack Shakely quote is from his article, "Exploring the Elusive World of Corporate Giving," in *The Grantsmanship Center News,* July–September, 1977, p. 59. The comments about DuPont are from James Phelan and Robert Pozen, *The Company State,* Grossman Publishers, New York, 1973.

Page 70 The $5 billion estimate for the value of executive time was by Austin V. McClain, then president of the New York fund-raising firm of Marts & Lundy, on July 26, 1963. The Conference Board survey was for a report, "Corporate Philanthropic Public Service Activities," completed in 1975 for the (Filer) Commission on Private Philanthropy and Public Needs. The Filer Commission's recommendation is from its *Giving in America,* p. 157. The 50,000 and 2 million figures are from the Conference Board and the $10 billion estimate is extrapolated from an estimate in "Philanthropy, the Business of the Not-So-Idle Rich" by Ann Crittenden in *The New York Times,* July 23, 1978. The Johnson quote is from *Giving in America,* p. 156.

CHAPTER 6

Page 71 The Clarence Day quotation at the head of the chapter is from "The New American Samaritans," *Time,* December 27, 1971. So is the *Time* comment in the opening paragraph. The NCVA survey and Census Bureau estimates are cited from the AAFRC's *Giving USA 1978,* which is also the source of the gloomy AAFRC forecast and volunteer strength figures.

Page 72 Much of the material about Arch Avary was gathered from Avary himself.

Page 73 Some of the material about Mother Waddles is from *Time, op. cit.,* and the Detroit *News,* December 5, 1971.

Page 75 Nixon is quoted from *People Helping People: U.S. Volunteers In Action,* Books by U.S. News & World Report, Washington, D.C., 1971.

Page 76 The figures on the rising number of college-student volunteers cover the decade between the mid-1960s and the mid-1970s (no more recent figures are available) and are from the National Student Volunteer Program, a part of ACTION.

Page 77 The figures for the University Year for Action program are for 1978. Many of the examples of elderly volunteers are from *U.S. News & World Report,* September 2, 1974, and January 17, 1977; and it is hoped that they are still alive and continuing their good works as you read this. The volunteer profile survey is from ACTION's *American Volunteer—1974,* a February, 1975, report based on the 1974 Census Bureau survey.

Page 78 Patricia L. Lucas is quoted from *The Volunteer Leader,* Winter, 1975. The *Lilith* article cited is "The Locked Cabinet" by Amy Stone, Winter 76/77. Also pertinent is this statement by Dr. David Hyatt, president of the National Conference of Christians and Jews, on November 21, 1978: "The male chauvinism of our churches and synagogues is perhaps even more entrenched than most of our other establishment institutions."

Page 79 Ellen Strauss is quoted from *The New York Times,* June 7, 1974.

Page 80 The George Romney quote and supporting and opposing views are from *U.S. News & World Report, op. cit.* The Dorothy Height quote is from *The New York Times, op. cit.* The Ellen Strauss comment is from *Sphere/The Betty Crocker Magazine,* September, 1973. The Jacqueline Levine quote is from *The Volunteer Leader, op. cit.*

Page 81 Margaret Mead is quoted from her column in *Redbook,* September, 1975. NOW's answer is from its pamphlet, *Volunteerism: What It's All About,* undated.

CHAPTER 7

Page 85 The story of the Miami man suing his church was reported in the Los Angeles *Times,* January 19, 1975. (The suit was dropped when a sympathetic stranger sent the Miami man a check together with a note reading, "I have never tried to make a deal with God like that, but for 36 years my wife and I have found that God will honor those who honor Him.") The AAFRC's figures are from its *Giving USA* annual reports; the Filer Commission's are from its 1975 report *Giving in America,* p. 58. The estimated giving to church-related institutions is from an *Interfaith Research Study* prepared for the Filer Commission in 1974.

Page 86 Church membership figures are from *Giving USA,* 1978. Giving by denominations is from unpublished data from the National Council of Churches of Christ in the U.S.A. The ACTS program is described in *Giving USA Bulletin #2,* July–August, 1976, also in *Newsweek,* November 24, 1975. The data on this and p. 87 are from the *Interfaith Research Study, op. cit.*

Page 88 Some of the incidents described here and p. 89 are drawn from *Newsweek,* October 22, 1973, and *Time,* October 29, 1973; others are from newspapers across the country.

Page 89 Actually, America's Jewish population now stands at 5,775,935, according to the 1978 *American Jewish Year Book,* The American Jewish Committee, New York, and The Jewish Publication Society of America, Philadelphia, 1977, p. 250. There were 3100 synagogues as of June, 1978, according to the American Jewish Committee. The statistics on synagogue income and expenditures and school enrollment on this and p. 90 are from the *Interfaith Research Study, op. cit.,* and the 1978 *American Jewish Year Book, op. cit.,* p. 202, which indicates that no more recent definitive data are available. However, the AAFRC, in unpublished data, estimated giving to synagogues at $1.3 billion in 1977.

Page 90 The city comparisons are based on population figures and campaign data furnished me by S. Peter Goldberg of the Council of Jewish Federations and Welfare Funds, one of the authors of the *Interfaith Research Study, ibid.,* and probably the nation's leading authority on the statistics of Jewish giving.

Page 93 The figures on the number of camps and community centers are from the National Jewish Welfare Board. The attacks on the "defense" agencies and other of the criticisms and quotes following are detailed in James Yaffe's *The American Jews,* Random House, New York, 1968, and Paperback Library, New York, 1969, pp. 235–242 (paperback edition). The figures on Jewish intermarriage are from a three-year study by the American Jewish Committee, as reported in a UPI dispatch of January 24, 1979. The figures on allocations to education are from the Council of Jewish Federations and Welfare Funds.

Page 94 The figures on the subdivisions and membership of the Roman Catholic Church are from the *1977 Official Catholic Directory,* P.J. Kenedy, New York. The estimates as to the church's annual U.S. income are so varied as to be virtually meaningless. In his 1972 book, *Vatican U.S.A.,* Nino Lo Bello ventured an estimate of $12 billion. Dr. Martin A. Larson came up with a similar total, $13 billion, in his *1965* book, *Church Wealth and Business Income,* but placed the total at $9.6 billion in his 1976 book, *The Religious Empire.* James Gollin, in his 1971 book, *Worldly Goods,* said he considered Larson's $13 billion estimate to be high by about 30 percent, "though no one can say for sure." The AAFRC, in unpublished data, placed the figure at $6 billion in 1977, but this, like the Filer Commission's estimate of $2.8 billion, does not include giving for good works by "church-related" institutions, whose annual receipts, as we've already seen, were estimated at $5.6 billion by the Filer Commission. The figures quoted on the church's income and expenditures are from the commission's *Interfaith Research Study.*

Page 95 The figures on Catholic schools are from the *1977 Official Catholic Directory, op. cit.*

Page 96 The figures on hospitals and nurses' training schools are from the *1977 Official Catholic Directory, ibid.* The National Conference on Catholic Charities survey is cited in the *Interfaith Research Study, op. cit.*

Page 98 Protestant membership and denominational data are from the 1978 *Yearbook of American and Canadian Churches,* National Council of the Churches of Christ in the U.S.A., Abingdon Press, Nashville and New York, 1978.

Page 100 The references to the Hartford "appeal" are from *The New York Times,* January 6, 1976, and *Time* and *Newsweek,* January 19, 1976. The "pocketbook revolt" of many Protestant churches is described in *Newsweek,* April 16, 1973.

Page 101 Church World Service is cited in *A.D.,* March, 1974. The basic source for the reference to the CWS shipment to Vietnam is *U.S. News & World Report,* September 4, 1978. Details about the McCracken–Stockwell controversy are from an interview with McCracken and articles in *The New York Times,* July 16, 1974, and *Time,* October 21, 1974.

CHAPTER 8

Page 103 Much of the material about the Pallottines is from stories in newspapers, notably the Baltimore *Sun* (which broke the beginnings of the scandal in 1976), the Washington *Post,* and *The New York Times.* The material about most of the other groups that comprise the bulk of this chapter is based largely on my first-hand observations and research.

Page 111 The details in the footnote about Hargis' degrees and Belin Memorial University are from Arnold Forster and Benjamin R. Epstein's *Danger on the Right,* Random House, New York, 1964, p. 78.

Page 112 Hargis' fall from grace, referred to in the footnote, is described in detail in *The New York Times,* February 13, 1976, and *Time,* February 16, 1976.

Page 113 The revocation of the Christian Crusade's tax-exempt status was reported in *The New York Times,* October 22, 1966.

Page 115 Fascinating accounts of Hargis, Asa Alonzo Allen, Oral Roberts, the Reverend Ike, Billy Graham, and other men of God appear in James Morris' *The Preachers,* St. Martin's Press, New York, 1973. The minister extolling the potency of prayer cloths is quoted from "Beware the Commercialized Faith Healers" by O.K. Armstrong in *Reader's Digest,* June, 1971. The Church of Compassion material is based largely on articles in the Los Angeles *Times* of September 1, 1974,

October 19, 1976, and May 21, 1977. I am also especially grateful for information from Russell Chandler, the author of one of these articles.

Page 116 The estimates of the Reverend Ike's following and finances are from "The Golden Gospel of Reverend Ike" by Clayton Riley in *The New York Times Magazine*, March 9, 1975. The chief sources for the material on the Moon church are the *Wall Street Journal*, September 20, 1974; *Time*, September 30, 1974, and November 10, 1975. More recently, *Time*, November 13, 1978, in a story on the church's alleged ties with the Korean government and Korean Central Intelligence Agency, quoted Moon as claiming 7000 "core" U.S. members and a treasury worth at least $20 million.

Page 117 The disenchanted former follower of Guru Maharaj Ji is quoted from Martin A. Larson and C. Stanley Lowell's *The Religious Empire*, Robert B. Luce, Washington–New York, 1976, p. 191. The Billy Graham revelations are based on stories in the New York *Post*, September 24, 1977, and *Time*, July 10, 1978.

CHAPTER 9

Page 119 The figures on giving to health causes are from the 1978 and 1979 issues of *Giving USA*. The statistics on health expenditures here and later in this chapter are from the *Social Security Bulletin*, July, 1978, February, 1975, among other issues. The declining role in philanthropy is documented by Blendon in his article, "The Changing Role of Private Philanthropy in Health Affairs," in the *New England Journal of Medicine*, May 1, 1975.

Page 120 The hospital construction data are from *Giving USA* and the annual reports of the American Hospital Association. The 100,000 estimate is from a Rockefeller Foundation-sponsored two-year study published in Robert H. Hamlin's *Voluntary Health and Welfare Agencies in the United States*, The Schoolmasters' Press, 1961. The study also indicated that another 100,000 fraternal, civic, and other organizations sponsored some health activities as part of their programs.

Page 121 The figures in the table and later in this chapter were furnished by the agencies themselves or are from their financial reports. The disease prevalence and mortality figures, used as the basis for the comparisons here and following, are from the U.S. Public Health Service or the agencies mentioned.

Page 122 The ranking of diseases by various factors is based on data from the National Center for Health Statistics, published in *The New York Times*, February 10, 1973. The costs to the economy of the illnesses mentioned were obtained from the concerned voluntary health agencies, which in turn receive these estimates—and they are only estimates—from government agencies. (Amusingly, the latter often base their estimates on figures from the voluntary agencies. From time to time, there are also private studies, such as "The Economic Cost of Illness, Fiscal 1975," done by the Public Services Laboratory, Georgetown University, Washington, D.C., in April, 1977. The cost of cancer in this study was estimated at $22 billion a year, and so it can readily be seen how quickly the figures arrived at become outdated. An HEW study, reported by the *Associated Press*, October 18, 1978, estimated the annual cost of alcoholism at $43 billion. Earlier cost estimates for many diseases may be found in *The Killers and Cripplers*, David McKay Company, New York, 1976.

Page 123 Among the sources for the material on polio was "Who Gets Your Charity Dollars?" by Jerome Ellison in the *Saturday Evening Post*, June 26, 1954.

Page 124 The Illinois study was directed by Malvern J. Gross, Jr., of Price Waterhouse & Co., and presented at the 1975 convention of the National Society of Fund Raisers. The New York State study was prepared in March, 1975, by Arthur Jack Grimes as a report for the Commission on Private Philanthropy and Public Needs.

Page 127 I am grateful to Leonora Wagner of the National Institutes of Health for the special breakdown she prepared for me on medical research expenditures.

Page 129 The Starr quote is from F. Emerson Andrews' *Philanthropic Giving*, Russell Sage Foundation, New York, 1950, p. 123.

Page 130 The Chatham County, Georgia, tally is mentioned in Marion K. Sanders' "Mutiny of the Bountiful" in *Harper's*, December, 1958. The Green and Vincent quotes, the formation of the

National Health Council, and the situation that led to the Gunn–Platt study are taken from the published study, *Voluntary Health Agencies: An Interpretative Study*, Ronald Press, New York, 1945.

Page 131   The 1960 Rockefeller Foundation-financed study was conducted by Robert H. Hamlin, *op. cit.*

CHAPTER 10

Page 133   Gunn and Platt's *Voluntary Health Agencies*, Ronald Press, New York, 1945, from which the opening quote is taken, was also a source for the material on the early histories of the health agencies covered in this chapter; so was Richard Carter's excellent *The Gentle Legions*, Doubleday, New York, 1961.

Page 134   A basic, definitive source of the early years of the American Lung Association was *National Tuberculosis Association 1904–1954*, National Tuberculosis Association, New York, 1957.

Page 136   In his *Medical Nemesis*, Pantheon, New York, 1976, Ivan Illich points out that the tuberculosis rate had declined to 48 just before the use of antibiotics had become routine after World War II. And even afterwards, he says, the continued decline was largely due to other factors: "Drug treatment has helped to reduce mortality from tuberculosis, tetanus, diptheria, and scarlet fever, but in the total decline of mortality from these diseases, chemotherapy played a minor and possibly insignificant role." Most epidemiologists, including the British Dr. Thomas McKeown, are in substantial agreement.

Page 137   The disease rankings and statistics are from the *Monthly Vital Statistics Report*, January, 1978, U.S. Public Health Service, also an *ALA Memo*, August 4, 1978, "Facts About Selected Respiratory Conditions in the U.S."

Page 139   Other basic sources for the historical material on the National Foundation-March of Dimes are David L. Sills's *The Volunteers*, Free Press, Glencoe, Ill., 1957, and Scott M. Cutlip's *Fund Raising in the United States*, Rutgers University Press, New Brunswick, N.J., 1965.

Page 143   The Fort Worth chapter's fund-raising expenses are cited from the *Wall Street Journal*, July 5, 1967.   Those of the chapters in Florida are cited from the Pensacola *News-Journal*, August 28, 1977.   The revelations about O'Connor's "unpaid volunteer" status are from *The New York Times*, February 12, 1965.

Page 144   Some of the material on the March of Dimes's battle with the right-to-lifers and the federal funding for genetic health services and education is drawn from "Embattled Genes," *The New Republic*, August 19, 1978.

Page 147   The incident involving the Louisiana Easter Seal chapter is from the Greater New Orleans Better Business Bureau *Bulletin*, Nobember 30, 1972.

Page 148   The Ben Hinson story is from the Atlanta *Journal*, April 9, 1974.

Page 149   The estimated appropriations for the disabled are from unpublished data from the Rehabilitation Services Administration and the Public Health Service's Health Services Administration, HEW.

Page 150   The heart disease prevalence and cost figures are from the American Heart Association's *Heart Facts 1978*.

Page 151   Some interesting insights into the Association's methods for screening grant applications can be found in Dr. William Welch's autobiographical *What Happened In Between*, Braziller, New York, 1972. Dr. Welch is a former president of the New York Heart Association.   For information about the work of Drs. Gibbon and Lillehei, I delved into David Hendin's *Life Givers*, William Morrow, New York, 1976.

Page 154   The cancer mortality and morbidity figures here and following are largely from the American Cancer Society's 1979 *Cancer Facts and Figures*.

Page 155   Some of the historical background on the society is based on Carter's *The Gentle Legions, op. cit.*, Scott Cutlip's *Fund Raising in the United States, op. cit.*, and John Gunther's biography of Albert Lasker, *Taken At The Flood*, Harper, New York, 1960.

Page 157   The James Watson quote is from "The Anti-Social Cell," *Harper's*, June, 1976, p. 59, and appeared in somewhat more sanitized form in many newspapers, including *The New York Times*, March 9, 1975.   The War Against Cancer and the battle of the cancer experts are described at length in Richard A. Rettig's *Cancer Crusade: The Story of the National Cancer Act of 1971*, Princeton University Press, Princeton, N.J., 1977, and June Goodfield's *The Siege of Cancer*, Random House, New York, 1975.

Page 158   The Goodfield quote is from her *The Siege of Cancer, ibid.*, p. 151.

Page 162   The Ochsner prediction is from the Staten Island (New York) *Advance*, February 6, 1975.   The concept that environmental factors account for up to 90 percent of all cancers has been advanced since the 1960s by responsible scientists here and abroad. It was endorsed by Dr. R. Lee Clark, a former president of the American Cancer Society, and Dr. Frank J. Rauscher, Jr., a former director of the National Cancer Institute and currently senior vice-president for research of the American Cancer Society, in an article in the Washington *Post*, May 12, 1977.   The Sidney Wolfe quote is from the Washington *Star*, June 8, 1975.   The comparative figures on government spending for cancer research and tobacco subsidies are from *Hospital Tribune*, April, 1978.

CHAPTER 11

Page 163   The *National Lampoon's* TF spoof was in its May, 1975, issue.

Page 164   The figure of 10,000 ALS cases is from the National ALS Foundation, and is based on an estimate of the National Institute for Neurological and Communicative Diseases and Stroke (NINCDS). However, the Amyotrophic Lateral Sclerosis Society of America estimates 30,000 cases. The mortality estimate is very rough—for one thing, because most patients actually die of resultant pneumonia, heart failure, or other causes. The estimated cost of care—$30,000 a year per patient—is based on nursing costs of $15,000 (not reimbursed by Medicare) and on loss of earnings of $15,000, according to the National ALS Foundation.   Unless stated otherwise, all other morbidity, mortality, and cost figures in this chapter are from the concerned health charities or government agencies, usually one of the National Institutes of Health or the U.S. Public Health Service. Government expenditures, unless specified otherwise, are from NIH data or from U.S. Budget figures.

Page 168   The study referred to involved the use of the Swank low-fat diet, which is described in *The Multiple Sclerosis Diet Book* by Roy L. Swank, M.D., Ph.D., and Mary Ellen Dullea, Doubleday, New York, 1977.

Page 171   The EFA's efforts to win approval of solium valproate are the subject of an article in *Medical World News*, March 6, 1978.

Page 175   How the diabetics enlisted Senator Schweiker in their cause is told interestingly in Donald Robinson's "The Men Who Spend Your Money To Keep You Healthy" in *Parade*, September 11, 1977. The article also lists the key congressmen and committees concerned with health matters and describes the process by which requests for funds for medical research are acted on.

Page 177   The past and projected costs of the ESRD Program are from *Health Care Week*, October 17, 1977.   The cost of dialysis is from *Health Care Week*, April 17, 1978, and *The New York Times*, April 28, 1978; that of a transplant is from *Medical World News*, April 17, 1978, and *Newsweek*, July 31, 1978.

Page 178   The flop of the donor program, as mentioned in the footnote, is reported in *American Medical News*, September 12, 1977.   For detailed information on how you can "will" as many as 25 parts of your body, see *U.S. News & World Report*, December 18, 1978.

Page 180   The figures on the decline in mental hospital populations are based on reports in *Hospital Tribune*, July–August, 1978, and *Time*, July 7, 1975.

Page 181   The $21 billion figure for the cost of mental illness is from the 1978 report of the President's Commission on Mental Health; the $32 billion cost of alcohol abuse ($44 billion, including fire and auto accident losses, the cost of crime, etc.) is from a UCLA School of Public Health survey published in the *New England Journal of Medicine*, March 9, 1978; the $10 billion–plus drug-abuse cost estimate is from a 1975 Report to the President from the Domestic Council Drug Abuse Task Force.   The number of North Dakota's psychiatrists is based on the listings in the

Directory of the American Psychiatric Association, Bowker, New York, 1977. The estimate that community health centers can serve only 40 percent of the population is by psychiatrist Dr. Ellen L. Bassuk and psychologist Samuel Gerson, both of Harvard, as cited in *Newsweek,* May 15, 1978. Since the inception of the community mental-health center program in 1963, more than $2 billion in federal money has been invested in these centers, which are expected to number 723 by late 1979, according to the Alcohol, Drug Abuse, and Mental Health Administration (ADAMHA).

Page 182   The statement by Schorr, a social worker, is from *The New York Times,* July 24, 1978. His skepticism is well taken, for most presidential commissions have been created only to give the impression that something is being done about a particular problem. This also seems to be the likely aftermath of the efforts of the recent President's Commission on Mental Health, even though it was created at the special behest of a presidential wife, Mrs. Carter. It is no secret, as Schorr points out, that it was well—if tacitly—understood that the commission was not to recommend spending large sums of money. Bearing this out, the commission, in its initial report on September 15, 1977, while urging an increase of about $40 million in federally funded *research* programs, pointedly omitted requesting that large amounts of new money be invested in treating mental-health problems in spite of its dramatic announcement that as many as 32 million Americans needed mental-health care. The following year the commission recommended an increase in appropriations of $500 million over three years—an increase of about $150 million a year. But this increase has yet to be reflected in the federal budget, which called for $887 million ADAMHA expenditures in fiscal 1978 and $952 million, or only $65 million more, in fiscal 1979, both figures also including expenditures for alcohol and drug-abuse programs.

Page 183   The figures on the institutionalized mentally retarded are from the latest available report, *Residents in Public Institutions for the Mentally Retarded,* U.S. Office of Human Development.

Page 185   The findings of the President's Committee on Mental Retardation are from *Medical World News,* February 7, 1979, and still apply today, according to the National Association for Retarded Citizens. The comparison of educational expenditures for the gifted and retarded is from "The Unfavored Gifted Few" by Gene I. Maeroff in *The New York Times Magazine,* August 21, 1977.

Page 188   The $9.4 billion disbursed to welfare families is from a Newhouse-syndicated feature in the Houston *Chronicle,* August 17, 1978, which in turn was based on an article in the Planned Parenthood journal, *Perspectives.*

Page 189   The VD cost figures are from a telephone interview with Dr. Paul J. Weisner, head of the Venereal Disease Control Division of the Center for Disease Control, U.S. Public Health Service.

CHAPTER 12

Page 192   Jernigan's activities at the Iowa commission are cited at length in these 1978 issues of the Des Moines *Register:* March 10 and 20; April 18, 19, and 30; May 14, 15, 27, and 31; June 21 and 22; and July 2. His key role in the National Eye Care Association (NECA) is cited largely in these 1977 issues of the *Register:* May 1 and 3; October 16; and November 22. The story of the NECA is also told in the Des Moines *Register,* November 29 and December 24, 1978. The NFB's justification of Jernigan occupies 25 pages in the May, 1978, issue of its house organ, *Braille Monitor.*

Page 193   For further details on sheltered workshops, see the two-part series on this subject by Jonathan Kwitny and Jerry Landauer in the *Wall Street Journal,* January 24–25, 1979.

Page 195   The $10 million lawsuits are reported in the Des Moines *Register,* November 14, 1977, and May 13, 1978; American Optometric Association *News,* November 1, 1977; and American Foundation for the Blind *Newsletter,* June, 1978.

Page 196   The allegations of guns and fortifications are cited from the following 1978 issues of the Des Moines *Register:* April 20 and 23; July 26, 27, and 29; and August 1 and 19. The allegations are also mentioned in Ken Bode's "Number-One Friend" in *The New Republic,* August 19, 1978.

Page 197   The statistics on the "legally blind" are from *Statistical Abstract of the United States,* U.S. Bureau of the Census, 1977, and from the American Foundation for the Blind.

Page 200 The references to Bernard Gerchen and Fedco are based on various Dun & Bradstreet reports made available to me, and on correspondence with the Better Business Bureau of St. Louis.

Page 201 The $450,000 purchase of a plastics company is cited from *The First Thirty Years: A History of the National Federation of the Blind*, p. 38. The Post Office investigation of Federated Industries and the NFB is described in Ben Pearse's "Don't Fall for the Mail Frauds" in the *Saturday Evening Post*, March 29, 1958.

Page 203 For further reading on the blind movement, see the American Foundation for the Blind-sponsored 559-page *The Unseen Minority: A Social History of Blindness in America* by Frances A. Koestler, David McKay, New York, 1976. The figure on government contracts with workshops for the blind is from National Industries for the Blind.

Page 209 The estimate for government expenditures to support, serve or otherwise help the blind is from unpublished data furnished me by George Magers, director, Division of Rehabilitation, Bureau for the Blind and Visually Handicapped, HEW.

CHAPTER 13

Page 210 The reduction of the disaster reserves to zero is reported in *The New York Times*, June 5, 1973.

Page 211 The Tex Ritter item is from *Time*, January 24, 1974.

Page 212 Much of the historical background in this chapter is from Charles Hurd's *The Compact History of The American Red Cross*, Hawthorn, New York, 1959. Some of the material about Clara Barton is also from Robert Bremner's *American Philanthropy*, University of Chicago Press, Chicago, 1960, pg. 94.

Page 213 The quote about the Barton–Boardman rivalry is from Hurd, *ibid*. The Rapid City incident and the NAS study following are cited from an article by August Gribbin in the *National Observer*, October 7, 1972.

Page 214 The Red Cross–Salvation Army pact described in the footnote is from *The New York Times*, August 9, 1975. The coal miner quote is from the *National Observer, op. cit.*

Page 215 The charges of racism are from Hurd, *op. cit.*, pp. 236–237. The wartime experiences described are based largely on Hurd, *op. cit.*, pp. 245–246; Richard Carter's *The Gentle Legions*, Doubleday, New York, 1961, pp. 47–56; and the *National Observer*.

Page 216 The figures on hepatitis and blood wastage are from *The New York Times*, July 11, 1973, and March 7, 1974; the *Wall Street Journal*, July 2, 1973; and countless articles in general circulation magazines and medical journals that also provided useful background on the blood problem. The latter included Stuart Baur's "Blood Farming" in *New York*, May 19, 1975; "Labeling the Risk" in *Medical World News*, October 6, 1972; and Dr. J. Garrott Allen's "What Price Blood?" in *Stanford MD*, Fall, 1976. Also informative was Dr. Donald R. Avoy's pamphlet, *Blood: The River of Life*, The American National Red Cross, 1976. The feelings of the AFL–CIO about the Red Cross are cited from Gribbin's article in the *National Observer, op. cit.*, as well as in another Gribbin article in the *National Observer*, January 29, 1972, and have been confirmed by several other knowledgeable people in the blood field to whom I spoke. The inauguration of the American Blood Commission and other recent developments in the blood field are described in *Lab World*, June, 1975, and many issues of *American Medical News* and other medical journals during the past few years. I am deeply indebted to Dr. J. Garrott Allen who was particularly generous with his time, advice, knowledge, and insights, and who made available to me much data and material, both published and unpublished, from his files, including several chapters in manuscript from his book tentatively titled, *National Blood Policy and Its Implementation*, scheduled for publication by the Harvard University Press, Cambridge, Mass., in 1979. I am also grateful for the time, information, and candid comments of Dr. Tibor J. Greenwalt and other officials of the Red Cross Blood Program.

Page 217 The Baxter Travenol joint venture, which has been approved by the Justice Department, is reported in detail in *Business Week*, September 11, 1978, and *Forbes*, December 11, 1978. The quote from Dulles is from his *The American Red Cross*, Harper, New York, 1950.

Page 218 The quote from Dulles is from his *The American Red Cross, ibid*. The William

Aramony quote and that of the young career man are from the August Gribbin article in the *National Observer*, October 7, 1972.

Page 219 The account of the conduct of the Red Cross during the great drought of 1930 is based largely on Bremner's *American Philanthropy, op. cit.*, p. 145, and Hurd, *op cit.*, pp. 205–208. The Red Cross's agreement to distribute government wheat and cotton is described in Hurd, *ibid.*, pp. 210–211. The 1946 Red Cross report is quoted from Hurd, *ibid.*, p. 259.

CHAPTER 14

Page 223 The story of the *Sun* group's enterprising investigation is told by Paul N. Williams, its then managing editor, in "Boys Town: An Exposé without Bad Guys" in the *Columbia Journalism Review*, January/February, 1975. The *Sun's* exposé broke on March 30, 1972. The new *Sun* revelations are from its issues of November 22 and 30, 1978, and I deeply appreciate the cooperation of the editors in rushing these to me. My section on Boys Town is also based on a visit there and conversations with many of its officials and staffers, including Father Hupp and Archbishop Sheehan.

Page 225 The declining rate of social welfare giving is documented from the annual issues of the AAFRC's *Giving USA*. Trends in giving for social welfare are discussed in Ellen Winston's paper, "Some Aspects of Private Philanthropy in Relation to Social Welfare," prepared for the Filer Commission in 1975.

Page 226. The padding of the scout membership rolls is reported in the Chicago *Tribune*, June 9 and 10, 1974. Some of the historical background on the scouts and their recent struggles against declining interest are from Chip McGrath's "The Gang in the Red Berets" in *The New York Times Magazine*, December 21, 1975.

Page 227 The challenge of Congress is from Bill Cardoso's article in *New Times*, July 26, 1974. The head of the New York City Mission Society is quoted from an article by Barry Newman in the *Wall Street Journal*, February 10, 1974, which also gives a detailed picture of the scout bureaucracy and financial operations as of 1974.

Page 229 The salaries in Nashville are reported in the Nashville *Banner*, July 1, 1975.

Page 230 The Catholic action against the Girl Scouts is reported in *The New York Times*, February 27, 1975.

Page 233 Edith Phelps is quoted from an article by Barbara Gamarekian in *The New York Times*, December 24, 1977.

Page 235 The religious affiliations of YMCA members are from *The 1970 YMCA Constituency Study*, National Board of YMCAs, December, 1970, the most recent such study available.

Page 236 The comparison of the Y with regular commercial hotel chains is based on statistics from the American Hotel & Motel Association.

Page 241 The statistics given are for the year 1977 and are from a special summary prepared annually by the Salvation Army. Another reference source was *The Salvation Army Year Book 1978*, Salvationist Publishing, London. Much of the other information in this section was based on interviews and conversations with Salvation Army officials and members.

Page 246 The figures given are from an article on the USO in *U.S. News & World Report*, May 22, 1978.

Page 247 The 1953 findings about the DAV are from a *report of the Joint Legislative Committee on Charitable and Philanthropic Agencies and Organizations* (also known as the Tompkins Committee), New York State Legislature, February 15, 1974.

Page 248 The salaries of DAV's officials are cited from *U.S. News & World Report*, November 6, 1978.

Page 249 The Mike Royko column about Leroy Bailey appeared in the Chicago *Daily News*, December 10, 1973. Another Royko column the following day reported that, as a result of the first column, "the VA bureaucrats suddenly found new energy, compassion and ability to make a decision." On December 17, 1973, the Chicago *Daily News* also reported that Bailey had been invited to visit the White House.   The AMVETS official is quoted from a *Washington Post News Service* story in the Hackensack (N.J.) *Record,* January 2, 1974.

Page 250   The VA is quoted on the need for HHV's arts and crafts kits in a letter to the National Information Bureau dated January 25, 1972.

CHAPTER 15

Page 252   The material on Foster Parents Plan, Christian Children's Fund, and Save the Children Federation here and later is based on a GAO report to a Senate Subcommittee on Children and Youth, October 10, 1974; statements of officials of these charities before the subcommittee the same day; and *Associated Press* dispatches of October 12, 1974.

Page 254   Much of the historical material is from Merle Curti's *American Philanthropy Abroad,* Rutgers University Press, New Brunswick, N.J., 1963; and *War on Hunger,* a report of the Agency for International Development, July, 1976.   The $2.6 billion estimate is by the American Association of Fund-Raising Counsel. The other figures are from the 1975 AID report (the latest available), *Voluntary Foreign Aid Programs.*

Page 255   The committee report is quoted from a statement by James A. Duff, associate director, U.S. General Accounting Office international division, before a Seante Labor Subcommittee on Children and Youth, October 10, 1974.   Duff is quoted from his Senate subcommittee statement, *ibid.*

Page 256   The estimates of 85 foreign relief groups in Korea and contributions of $28 million are from an *Associated Press* dispatch in the Kansas City *Star,* April 19, 1974.   Much of the other information about Korean orphans is from the article, "To Give or Not to Give," by the veteran missionary, W. Guy Henderson, in *Christian Century,* March 11, 1970.   The heartbreaking story of the Pearl Buck scandal is told interestingly and in great detail in Greg Walter's "The Dancing Master" in *Philadelphia Magazine,* July, 1969.

Page 261   The quote about the relationship between Dooley and Comanduras came to me from Chaney himself.   For information about the relationship and background about MEDICO and the Thomas A. Dooley Foundation, I am also indebted to my friends Terry Morris and Lawrence Elliott, both of them authors of books on Dooley.

Page 263   The diversion of food to the military in Africa and the wastage and profiteering there have been widely reported in *Newsweek,* June 4, 1973, and August 5, 1974; *Time,* April 21, 1975; as well as elsewhere.   The AID quote is from *War and Hunger, op. cit.*

Page 266   The survey of those favoring and opposing foreign aid is from the pamphlet *AID's Challenge in an Interdependent World,* Agency for International Development, January, 1977.   The Overseas Development Council poll is cited from *U.S. News & World Report,* December 17, 1973, p. 53.   Lange is quoted from his article, "Private Support for the Underprivileged World," in *The Conference Board Record,* March, 1976.   The latest ranking of the United States and other donor nations is from *Development Co-Operation,* a report of the Organisation for Economic Co-Operation and Development, November, 1978. The 1960 figures are from the World Bank, as reported in *U.S. News & World Report,* December 17, 1973.

Page 267   The criticisms of private foreign-aid agencies are based largely on a paper by the Overseas Development Council's John G. Sommer entitled "New Roles for Private Organizations in Overseas Development: South Asia and Africa Trip Notes, March–April, 1975."   The GAO report on Guatemala was submitted to Congress, August 26, 1976.   Estimates as to the number of people suffering from malnutrition or barely fending off starvation range up to 1.2 billion—almost 30 percent of the world's population.   The figure on Food for Peace loans and donations is from the 1978 *Statistical Abstract of the United States,* U.S. Bureau of the Census, Washington, D.C.

CHAPTER 16

Page 270   The estimate of 9 percent for education, arts, and the conservation of our rights, resources, and heritage is from the AAFRC's annual *Giving USAs,* which are also the sources of the figures on education.   The comparison of the $300 million spent on the arts is from Dick Netzer's

The Subsidized Muse: Public Support for the Arts in the United States, Cambridge University Press, New York, 1978.

Page 271 The estimates on alumni giving and on the proportion of total revenues from philanthropy are by Hayden Smith of the Council for Financial Aid to Education. The reference in the footnote to Harvard's Charles Eliot is from a paper, "Private Philanthropy and Higher Education," by Earl F. Cheit and Theodore E. Lobman, III, prepared for the Filer Commission. The New York State Department of Education estimate about the threat faced by private colleges is reported from *The New York Times,* January 15, 1975. Peter Pouncey's prediction is cited from I.D. Robbins' "Chaos Among the Colleges" in the *Wall Street Journal,* March 27, 1975. For similar dire predictions and an analysis of the financial problems in higher education, see "Private Colleges Cry 'Help!' " in *Time,* January 15, 1979.

Page 272 The figures in the footnote on the sources of income for private and public colleges and universities are from Hayden Smith of the Council for Financial Aid to Education, based on *Financial Statistics of Institutions of Higher Education for 1975,* National Center for Educational Statistics, HEW. The figures on turning out a dentist are from I.D. Robbins, *op. cit.* An interesting argument for tuition tax credits as a way of sustaining private schools is presented in Daniel Patrick Moynihan's "Government and the Ruin of Private Education," *Harper's,* April, 1978. Most of the statistics on the boom in the arts are from an article by Richard J. Cattani in the *Christian Science Monitor,* July 21, 1978, and *Giving USA 1978.*

Page 273 Some of the data about the Metropolitan Opera is from *The New York Times,* December 19, 1977, and November 30, 1978. The figures on giving to the arts are from *Giving USA 1979.* The reference to the spinster, Mary Agnes Miller, a poet and writer, is from *The New York Times,* October 26, 1973.

Page 274 The *Harper's* article cited is Tom Bethell's "The Cultural Tithe," August, 1977. The per capita outlay in West Germany is from *The New York Times,* January 6, 1971, which also gives the outlays in several other countries.

Page 275 The "labor-intensive" characteristic of the arts is cited from Beth Crouch's "Earning a Living in the Lively Arts" in the quarterly *Catalyst,* Fall, 1975. For more of Alvin Reiss's views on the economic problems of the arts, see his book *Culture & Company,* Twayne, New York, 1972. The problems are also discussed in detail in the Rockefeller Panel Report, *The Performing Arts,* McGraw-Hill, New York, 1965.

Page 276 The distribution of arts money in New Jersey and St. Louis is cited from an article by Charles Christopher Mark in *The New York Times,* November 3, 1974. The Harris survey of "Americans and the Arts," released in 1974, is available in booklet form from A.C.A. Publications, P.O. Box 4764, Tulsa, Oklahoma, 74104. The potential $1.7 billion annually for the arts is an estimate by Rep. Frederick Richmond from an article by Harold C. Schonberg in *The New York Times,* April 3, 1977.

Page 278 Some of the comparisons between the economic status of blacks and whites are from *The New York Times,* April 2, 1978, and "The American Underclass" in *Time,* August 29, 1977. The NAACP financial crisis is reported most recently in *The New York Times,* December 21, 1978, and January 7, 1979.

Page 279 Vernon Jordan is quoted from *Black Enterprise,* March, 1975.

Page 280 CORE's difficulties are reported in *The New York Times,* November 16 and 24, 1978; the New York *Post,* January 3, 1979; and an article by Harry Zehner in the *Saturday Review,* April 28, 1979. The Hispanics are discussed in a cover story in *Time,* October 16, 1978.

Page 282 The ACLU's drop in membership is cited from *The New York Times,* April 17, 1978, and from J. Anthony Lukas' article, "The A.C.L.U. Against Itself," in *The New York Times Magazine,* July 9, 1978.

Page 283 For the source of the estimates that between 75 to 90 percent of cancer is of environmental origin, see the notes to Chapter 10.

Page 284 For one of the many accounts of environmental court battles, see Warren Weaver, Jr.'s article in *The New York Times,* October 30, 1977.

Page 286   Gloria Shelton is quoted from Marya A. Smith's "The Doggie in the Window" in the *Chicago Guide,* December, 1974.

Page 287   John A. Hoyt is quoted from the Chicago *Daily News,* May 23, 1974.   The criticisms of New York's ASPCA are cited from the New York *Post,* January 16 and December 1, 1975.   The charges against the Animal Protection Institute are cited from NIB and CBBB reports, CBBB's *In-Sight,* March–April, 1976, and *U.S. News & World Report,* November 6, 1978.

CHAPTER 17

Page 289   The experiment of the Philadelphia newspaper is cited from Ralph Lee Smith's *The Bargain Hucksters,* Thomas Y. Crowell, New York, 1962, p. 114.

Page 290   The "Fund for the Widow of the Unknown Soldier" hoax is described in Andrews', *op. cit.,* p. 160.   The Philadelphia charity described is from an article on charities by Rose DeWolf in *The Nation,* August 27, 1973.   The CBBB survey is mentioned in a Sylvia Porter column on charity rackets, January 14, 1966. The possible Mafia link to charity is reported from *The New York Times,* June 22, 1969.

Page 291   The lawyer in the California attorney general's office is quoted from *Money,* September, 1973.

Page 292   The description of the activities of the United Missions Corps is based on a Lani Luciano article in *The Record* (Hackensack, N.J.), August 7, 1973, and reports of the Better Business Bureaus of Bergen, Passaic, and Rockland Counties and of Metropolitan New York.

Page 293   The Maxine Cheshire column on the Girl Scout hoax was published on March 6, 1973.   The Kayem campaign is further documented in *New York,* October 14, 1974.   The Holari fund-raising effort is also described in the State of New York Department of Law *Annual Report,* 1973, and in a news release of April 18, 1973, from the office of New York State Attorney General Louis J. Lefkowitz.

Page 299   The San Francisco *Chronicle's* characterization of the James Brothers Circus is quoted from an article by David Braaten in the newspaper's August 2, 1961, issue.   The commentary on the circus in Sacramento is from the Sacramento *Union,* April 19, 1969.   For the foregoing quotes and much of the other background material on Sid Kellner and his circus under its various names, I am indebted to Kay Wilson of the Better Business Bureau of San Francisco.

Page 300   The items on the circuses in St. Louis and San Francisco are based on newsletters of the Better Business Bureaus in those cities. Lynn Ludlow of the San Francisco *Examiner* also provided me with much useful information.   The Hoxie Brothers figures are from an article on that circus by John L. Moore in the *Wall Street Journal,* November 8, 1978.   Mearl Johnson's operations are described in an article by Rudy Maxa in the Washington *Post's Potomac Magazine,* November 4, 1973.

Page 301   The Louisville *Courier-Journal* articles were written by Larry Werner, and appeared on June 25 and December 9, 1973. The articles are copyrighted 1973 by the Louisville *Courier-Journal.*

Page 306   Much of the material on Koolish and his colleagues in this chapter is based on E. J. Kahn's *Fraud,* Harper & Row, New York, 1973; Ralph Lee Smith, *op. cit.;* and Scott Cutlip's Fund Raising in the United States, Rutgers University Press, New Brunswick, N.J., 1965.

Page 308   The material on the Asthmatic Children's Foundation is from the subcommittee's published report on the hearings (Part 1), February 5, 1974.

Page 311   The story of Gorman's Friends of the FBI promotion is also told in *The New York Times,* July 21, 1971; New York *Post,* July 28, 1971; and the Washington *Post,* May 21, 1972. A detailed account of his entire operations is in the Washington *Star,* June 4, 1972. Also helpful to me were various reports and memoranda on Gorman from the Council of Better Business Bureaus and the National Information Bureau.   A letter of August 19, 1971, from J. Edgar Hoover to the National Information Bureau stated: "The FBI has no connection or relationship of any kind with this group [Friends of the FBI] and we do not endorse it."   Some of the material on the Underground Bible Fund is from the Washington *Star, op. cit.*

Page 313 The material on the National Youth Clubs and Youth Incentives is from the published report of the hearings before the Senate Subcommittee on Children and Youth, Part 1, March 11 and 12, 1974.

Page 314 The account of Toiletries Packed for the Blind is based on news releases dated August 9, 1971, and January 7, 1974, from the office of New York State Attorney General Louis J. Lefkowitz, and on an article in *The New York Times*, September 13, 1972. The pitch using the name of Mrs. Rose Kennedy is cited from an item in *The New York Times*, May 10, 1972.

Page 315 The reference to the New Jersey hearings on Torch is from an article by Rose DeWolf in the Philadelphia *Sunday Bulletin/Discover*, February 16, 1975. Lester David's article is from the December, 1961, *True Story*. Many people have told me of the Los Angeles *Times* ad; the version here is from a Leo Rosten column in *Saturday Review/World*, March 13, 1973.

CHAPTER 18

Page 320 The account of the wild Australian fund-raising party is based on an article on Darwin in *Newsweek*, December 3, 1973.

Page 321 The Kidney Foundation quote is from "Tales of the Heartbreak Biz" by Ron Rosenbaum in *Esquire*, July, 1974. The Harry McMahan charge is from *Advertising Age*, August 20, 1973.

Page 323 The Leibert and Sheldon *Handbook* is published by Association Press, New York, 1972. The figure on the Kiwanis peanut sales is from an article on the Rev. Sun Myung Moon by Jonathan Kwitny in the *Wall Street Journal*, September 20, 1974. Some of the material on the Girl Scout cookie sales is from *Business Week*, February 7, 1970; the rest is from the Scouts' National Equipment Service, which estimated annual sales at 84 million boxes of cookies for a gross of over $100 million, this accounting for "between 5 and 10 percent" of the output of the U.S. cookie industry.

Page 324 The Tom Wat enterprise, Girl Scout cookie sales, and other merchandise offerings are described in "Free Enterprise Thrives Among Smallest of Small-Business Men" by Georgia Dullea in *The New York Times*, March 20, 1976. Leads to firms that provide fund-raising premiums are available from the National Premium Sales Executives, 1600 Rt. 22, Union, N.J. 07083.

Page 325 The revelations about the DAV thrift shops are based on reports in the Kansas City *Star*, July 27, 1974, and a series of articles in the Nashville *Banner* that appeared periodically from May 14 to June 14, 1975. The Mike Royko DAV columns are from the Chicago *Daily News*, April 23 and 24, 1974, and May 15, 1975.

Page 327 Televised auctions are described in *Newsweek*, June 23, 1975.

Page 328 The description of the "Couples" fashion bash is based on a report in *The New York Times*, March 11, 1976.

Page 329 Mrs. Patricia Hartung is quoted from an interview with the author.

Page 331 Ronnie Lee is quoted from *The New York Times*, December 2, 1973.

Page 333 The *Sports Illustrated* ad is quoted from James Gollin's *Worldly Goods*, Random House, New York, 1971, p. 61. The Rego Park Jewish Center and Congregation Kol Israel gambling operations are reported in the New York *Post*, March 23 and 24, 1978, and New York *Daily News*, March 23, 1978.

Page 334 Pennsylvania's bingo games are described in the *Wall Street Journal*, May 20, 1977. The East Chicago, Indiana, gambling fronts are cited from newsletters of the Northwest Indiana Crime Commission. The fatal shooting of Steve Cirillo is reported from *The New York Times*, August 5, 1974. Chief Inspector Fitzpatrick is quoted from a telephone interview by the author.

Page 335 The approach to more than two dozen synagogues by Mafia-linked characters is reported from *The New York Times*, January 25, 1977. The Macchiarole murder is reported from the New York *Post*, March 24, 1978. The estimate of gambling and the Scarne quote is from "Gambling Spree Across the Nation" in *U.S. News & World Report*, May 29, 1978. The Goldstein quote is from a Neal R. Peirce article in the Denver *Post*, June 13, 1977, which also cites the National Gambling Commission study on the relative prevalence of illegal and legal gambling. The *Redbook* article, "Should You Gamble for Charity" by Robert Gorman, was published in July, 1955. The New York Board of Rabbis' resolution is quoted from a full-page ad in *The Jewish Week–American Examiner*, May 15, 1977.

Page 336 The Alexandria, Virginia, bingo game incident is reported in the Washington *Post*, November 1 and 3, 1978. The bingo figures are from the 1977 Annual Survey of Bingo Operations, Bureau of Bingo Regulation, New York State. The breakdown of figures on state lotteries is from a cover story on gambling in *Time*, December 6, 1976.

Page 337 The West New York, N.J., Roman Catholic Church incident is reported in *Time*, January 6, 1961. Horace Greeley is quoted from *Redbook, op. cit.*

CHAPTER 19

Page 339 The Dale experience is from an article of his in *The New York Times*, February 22, 1974. The Nielsen study estimate is somewhat higher than that of the Direct Mail/Marketing Association which, in its 1979 *Fact Book on Direct Response Marketing*, estimated that one in every three dollars given to charity is raised through the mails.

Page 340 The Ruedi experience is from an article in *Money*, September, 1973; that of Flangas is from the Washington *Post*, September 3, 1974. The $600 million subsidy for the Postal Service is cited from *U.S. News & World Report*, November 6, 1978. Nearly half (46.5 percent) of the nation's 71 million households moved in a four-and-one-half-year span between April, 1970, and October, 1974, according to a joint release by the U.S. Department of Commerce's Bureau of the Census and the U.S. Department of Housing and Urban Development, reported in *Fund Raising Management*, March/April, 1977.

Page 342 The Francis Pray quote is from Harold J. Seymour's *Designs for Fund-Raising*, McGraw-Hill, New York, 1966, p. 85. The Huntsinger suggestions are from an article of his in *Fund Raising Management*, November/December, 1973, and from a conversation with him.

Page 343 Hargis' denunciation of me was in the *Christian Crusade Weekly* of January 27, 1974. For my revelations about Hargis, see Chapter 8.

Page 344 Viguerie's difficulties in New York are reported in the New York *Post*, March 15, 1977; the Council of Better Business Bureaus' *In-Sight*, January–February, 1977; *U.S. News & World Report*, November 6, 1978; and in the full-scale accounts of his varied activities in the *Wall Street Journal*, October 6, 1978; *Time*, August 7, 1978; and in Nick Kotz's "King Midas of 'The New Right'" in the *Atlantic Monthly*, November, 1978.

Page 345 The Crohn quote is from *Fund Raising Management*, May/June, 1974. The invasion of privacy issue is discussed in Georgia Dullea's "Mailing Lists: You're the Target" in *The New York Times*, May 11, 1977, and *FRM Weekly*, September 6, 1978.

Page 346 Ed Burnet is quoted from the *Wall Street Journal*, February 19, 1974.

CHAPTER 20

Page 349 The early history of telethons is recounted at length by Norman Kimball in *Fund Raising Management*, May/June, 1971.

Page 351 Carter is quoted from his *The Gentle Legions*, Doubleday, New York, 1961.

Page 352 The Jerry Lewis denial that he receives telethon money is reported from the Washington *Post*, September 6, 1978.

CHAPTER 21

Page 366 The selection of noteworthy non-New York balls is from *Town & Country*, October, 1973.

Page 375 The tabulation of the expenses of charity balls and their difficulties with the New York State attorney general are from "Charity Dances: A Big Business, With High Costs and Few

Controls,'' by Philip Dougherty, in *The New York Times,* June 26, 1966.   The financial difficulties of Waldemar and the plans to sell its property are described in *Newsday,* March 23, 1977.

CHAPTER 22

Page 386   Reynolds' classic advice is quoted from Harold J. Seymour's *Designs for Fund-Raising,* McGraw-Hill, New York, 1966, p. 77, a standard text by a pioneer fund raiser—one of the founders and a past president of the American Association of Fund-Raising Counsel.

CHAPTER 23

Page 392   Seymour is quoted from his *Designs for Fund-Raising* McGraw-Hill, New York, 1966.   The J. Pierpont Morgan story is from an article by Franklin in *Fund Raising Management,* September/October, 1971.

Page 393   Daniel M. Eisenberg's techniques for tracking down "lost" alumni are described in his article, "A Goldmine Can Be Unearthed by Finding 'Lost' Alumni," in *Fund Raising Management,* September/October, 1971.

Page 395   The suit for the Payson pledge is from a story in *The New York Times,* March 7, 1978.

Page 396   The account of Hamline's experience is based on stories in the *Wall Street Journal,* October 19, 1973, and *The New York Times,* May 5, 1974, and conversations and correspondence with the school's officials.

CHAPTER 24

Page 402   Andrew Goodman is quoted from Marylin Bender's "Hard Sell Pays Off in Charity Appeals" in *The New York Times,* May 5, 1974.

Page 403   The survey cited is *Motivations for Charitable Giving: A Case Study of an Eastern Metropolitan Area,* National Opinion Center of the University of Chicago, 1961.

CHAPTER 25

Page 405   The description of the United Way symbol in the footnote is from an article, "Is Charity Obsolete," by James Cook in *Forbes,* February 5, 1979.

Page 408   The alleged $316 million Exxon overcharge is cited from the Washington *Post,* November 2, 1978. On January 6, 1979, *The New York Times* reported that this suit had been folded into another which the federal government was filing against nine large oil companies, alleging overcharges to customers of nearly $1 billion. Named along with Exxon were Atlantic Richfield, Cities Service, Gulf, Mobil, Phillips Petroleum, Shell, Standard Oil (Indiana), and Texaco.   The United Way senior official is quoted from an article on San Francisco's United Fund by Chester W. Hartman and Lynn Thomas in *Society,* November/December, 1974. The Bartimole quote is from the same article.

Page 409   The quotes by the Chicago and Detroit executives are from *Money,* December, 1973, p. 108.   The Pacific Telephone and Telegraph memo is quoted from Hartman and Thomas, *op. cit.*   The Pennsylvania factory worker is quoted from Richard Carter's "The Race for Your Charity Dollars" in *Good Housekeeping,* November, 1959. The article is ancient, of course, but it serves to indicate how far back such complaints go.   Ohio Bell Telephone's use of computers is described in Roldo Bartimole's Cleveland newsletter, *Point of View,* June 28, 1975.   The television talk show is mentioned in Jack Shakely's "Exploring the Elusive World of Corporate Giving" in *The Grantsmanship Center News,* July–September, 1977.

Page 410   The "Solicitor's Guide" instructions and Northwestern Bell procedure are documented in an "Open Letter to the Board of Directors of the Greater Des Moines United Way and to Citizens of the City of Des Moines" by the Des Moines chapter of the National Organization for Women (NOW) on January 28, 1975.   The "Fair-Share" guide for giving example is from the "Guide to Fair Share Giving" of the United Way of Central Maryland. In 1977 a nonfarm family of four was considered in poverty if its income was below $6191, according to the *Wall Street Journal,*

August 10, 1978. In 1978 the poverty level was $6200, according to the U.S. Bureau of Labor Statistics. The complaint to Mike Royko is from his column in the Chicago *Daily News*, November 3, 1975. The experience of the Cleveland YMCA employee is from Hartman and Thomas, *op. cit.* Horace A. Shepard's giving record and remarks are cited from *Point of View*, November 17–22, 1969, and September 28–October 3, 1970. Weir's and De Windt's reticence about their giving is from *Point of View*, November 26, 1976, and June 28, 1975; the latter issue also cited the United Way's decision to stop publishing its annual list of $300-and-over givers.

Page 411 Bankamerica's giving figures are from Hartman and Thomas, *op. cit.;* Firestone's are from the "Open Letter" by the Des Moines chapter of NOW, *op. cit.* The $335 million and $45 million figures are from *Forbes, op. cit.*

Page 412 Planned Parenthood's experience in Gary, Indiana, is reported in "Cornering the Goodness Market" by Ron Chernow in *Saturday Review*, October 28, 1978. The Sacramento United Way director is quoted from the Sacramento *Bee*, September 7, 1978.

Page 413 The changes in Detroit are based on reports in *The New York Times*, November 3, 1969, an *Associated Press* dispatch of July 6, 1971, and interviews with citizens of that city. San Diego's new projects are cited from interviews with that city's United Way officials. The changes in Indianapolis are reported from Chernow, *op. cit.*

Page 414 The account of the Sacramento situation and the James Mills quote are from the Sacramento *Bee*, September 7, 1978. A similar comment about the Hanley letter is made by Robert Bothwell, executive director, National Committee for Responsive Philanthropy, in a provocative article in *Fund Raising Management*, July/August, 1978. The same issue contains an article defending the United Way by George A. Shea, the national organization's executive vice-president.

Page 419 The early clashes—in the 1950s—between the United Way and the large voluntary health agencies are documented in J.L. Pimsleur's "One Drive—Or Many?" in *The Nation*, January 25, 1958; Marion K. Sanders' "Mutiny of the Bountiful" in *Harper's*, December, 1958; Philip Benjamin's three-part series in *The New York Times*, June 15–17, 1959; Richard Carter's *The Gentle Legions*, Doubleday, New York, 1961; among many other sources of that era.

Page 420 The United Way's discouragement of designations is mentioned in Ed Arnone's "United Way: Looking Out for Number One?" in the *Grantsmanship Center News*, September–December, 1978, and is known by the author to be true, based on his conversations with many United Way contributors. The Walter Bremond quote is from the article, "The Black United Fund Movement," in the *Grantsmanship Center News*, August–October, 1976. The American Heart Association memo is excerpted in Arnone's article, *op. cit.*, and is contained almost in its entirety in *The Charity War Papers*, a 222-page compendium of articles, legal briefs, memorandums, speeches, news stories, and other documents—some cited in these notes—that review the issues and arguments pro and con surrounding the United Way. The latest edition of this compendium was produced in June, 1978, by the Concerned Citizens of Charity, San Francisco, California, a group that is critical of the United Way and has taken an activist role in challenging its methods, purposes, and monopoly of workplace solicitation. An outline of the UWA's Program for the Future, including verbatim portions of its text, is contained in *The Charity War Papers, ibid.*

Page 421 The AID–United Way lawsuit is reported in Arnone, *op. cit.*, and Chernow, *op cit.*, as is also the CHAD suit following.

Page 422 The suits against the U.S. Civil Service Commission and the Chrysler Corporation are cited from Bothwell, *op. cit., FRM Weekly*, August 23, 1978, and an article by Robert Lindsey in *The New York Times*, April 3, 1978, which gives an excellent summary of the issues involved in the United Way controversy. Another informative basic document for those interested in more details of the issues is David Horton Smith's "The Role of United Way in Philanthropy," one of the research papers prepared for the Filer Commission in August, 1975. The figures on the growth of the United Way from 1960 through 1976 are from the pamphlet, *The National Corporate Development Program*, United Way of America, 1977.

Page 423 David Horton Smith is quoted from his article in *Society*, January/February, 1978. The TRW and Reliable Life programs are cited from Bothwell, *op. cit.*

Page 424 Maguire is quoted from *The Charity War Papers, op. cit.*

CHAPTER 26

Page 427 The Rosenwald quote is from F. Emerson Andrews' *Philanthropic Giving,* Russell Sage Foundation, New York, 1950, p. 17. The comment on Rockefeller is from Ben Whitaker's *The Philanthropoids,* William Morrow, New York, 1974, p. 56.

Page 429 The information on state laws is based on the tabulations in the AAFRC's *Giving USA Bulletin #16,* December 1978. The Postal Service figures are from George Head, manager, Fraud Branch, U.S. Postal Inspection Service.

Page 434 The Tanton quotes are from his article, "How to Give Money Away and Really Enjoy It," in *Medical Economics,* November 21, 1971.

CHAPTER 27

Page 436 The table is based on the tax rates of the 1978 Revenue Act, which went into effect January 1, 1979.

Page 437 The Helping Hand Rescue Mission incident is from the Better Business Bureau of Metropolitan New York's *Report to Business,* Summer, 1975. The Internal Revenue Service's *Cumulative List of Organizations* (Publication 78) is also available from the Superintendent of Documents, Government Printing Office, Washington, D.C., 20402.

Page 438 The revocation of Bob Jones University's tax exemption is described in *Fund Raising Management,* November/December, 1974; the restoration of the exemption is from an item in the *Wall Street Journal,* February 14, 1979. The IRS ruling on the Bach Mai Fund is from *The New York Times,* July 24, 1975.

Page 439 The example of the married man with a $22,000 income is updated from a case in a Robert Metz article in *The New York Times,* November 30, 1970. Details of the Home-Stake scandal are from the *Wall Street Journal,* June 26 and November 22, 1974, and August 20, 1975.

Page 440 The Tintoretto case is from the insurance industry-syndicated newsletter *On Tax and Financial Planning,* June, 1976. The case involving the Michigan men and the wooden object is from the *Wall Street Journal,* November 7, 1973.

Page 442 The National Ski Patrol case is from the *Wall Street Journal,* November 8, 1978. The baby-sitter case is from the *Wall Street Journal,* April 5, 1978. The story of the physician's spur-of-the-moment donation is from *Medical World News,* September 28, 1973.

Page 444 The Dr. Allen case is from an article by attorney Dorothea Garber Cracas in *Medical Economics,* November 6, 1972; the figures in the article were graciously updated by Mrs. Cracas.

Page 446 For more details on recordkeeping and on just what and how much is deductible, when, and to whom, see IRS Publication 526, *Income Tax Deductions for Contributions,* available free from the IRS.

CHAPTER 28

Page 451 The Cornuelle quotes are from his address before the National Council on Philanthropy in Houston, Texas, November 10, 1969. The quotation from Laski is from Benedict Nightingale's *Charities,* Allen Lane, London, 1973, p. 68.

Page 452 The figures given for the changes in government spending on health, education, and welfare are from the Social Security Bulletin, January 1976 and January 1977. The sources for the health expenditure figures are in the notes to Chapter 9. The needy cases described are from *The New York Times,* December 8, 1974, and December 21, 1975.

Page 453 The commentary on *The New York Times* "Hundred Neediest Cases" is from the Filer Commission's *Giving in America,* p. 93. The statements by McGhee are from his editorial, "A New Look at Welfare," in *Saturday Review/World,* April 6, 1974. The quotation from Brewster is from a speech of his before the Chicago Economic Club, May 8, 1969.

Page 455 For the sources of the material on laws and regulations, see the notes to Chapter 26. A more detailed source is *Philanthropy Monthly's Survey of State Laws Regulating Charitable Solicitations,* which is updated periodically.

Page 457 The figures on the income and employment of charities are based on two papers prepared for the Filer Commission: "The Scope of the Private Voluntary Charitable Sector" by Gabriel Rudney and "Employment and Earnings in the Nonprofit Charitable Sector" by T. Nicholaus Tideman. The Jack Shakely quote is from his article, "Ethics of Charitable Solicitation," in *The Grantmanship Center News,* February–March 1975.

Index